THE LIFE OF ABRAHAM LINCOLN
TWO VOLUMES IN ONE BOOK

ABRAHAM LINCOLN
Photographed in 1859 by S. M. Fassett

THE LIFE OF
ABRAHAM LINCOLN,

BY

WILLIAM E. BARTON

Author of THE SOUL OF ABRAHAM LINCOLN,
THE PATERNITY OF ABRAHAM LINCOLN, Etc.

TWO VOLUMES IN ONE

ILLUSTRATED

BOOKS, INC.
BOSTON   NEW YORK

To

CALVIN COOLIDGE

Like Lincoln a Man of the People
and a Leader of the Nation
This Work is Dedicated
With His Permission

CONTENTS

BOOK I

CONTENTS—*Continued*

CONTENTS
BOOK II

CONTENTS—*Continued*

LIST OF ILLUSTRATIONS
BOOK I

LIST OF ILLUSTRATIONS—*Continued*

LIST OF ILLUSTRATIONS
BOOK II

INTRODUCTION

He who adds another to the already long list of biographies of Abraham Lincoln should be ready to give a reason for the faith that is within him. My reasons are three:

The first is that the biographies of Lincoln already in print have not discovered all the important facts of his life. Their authors have shown, in the main, commendable diligence, and I am greatly indebted to my predecessors; but I have been able to explore with greater thoroughness some fields hitherto inadequately covered and to penetrate some areas hitherto unknown. Commonplace men are easily classified as tall or short, white or black, good or bad; but genius has the saving grace of inconsistency. Every really great man is easy to caricature—by so narrow a margin is the sublime separated from the ridiculous. Every great man combines in his personality, and generally in unstable equilibrium, a group of contradictory qualities. The character of Abraham Lincoln is so complex, so capable of misjudgment, we need for its interpretation every scrap of authentic information that will enable us more nearly to understand the hiding of his power.

The second reason is that all of the extant biographies of Lincoln contain inaccuracies, some of them trivial, others important, and a few of them very grave. I am able to correct some of these errors and I hope that I am not adding any new ones.

The third reason is that it is now possible to write a life of Lincoln with a perspective of more than half a century. Contemporaries are valuable witnesses but notoriously incompetent judges.

I have come to this task with a conviction of duty and the joy of a rare privilege. I was born in Illinois in the first year of the Civil War. My earliest memories are a child's wondering impressions of the departure of the last volunteers in the spring of 1865—my father's youngest brother among them; the funeral of a soldier, an uncle of mine; the north-bound trains of freight-cars on the Illinois Central, loaded inside and out with bearded men in faded blue, shamelessly throwing kisses to every woman in sight, and none of those women resenting it; and, in some respects most vivid of all, the death and funeral of Abraham Lincoln.

I passed the years of my boyhood among men who had known Lincoln. The years of my early manhood I spent as teacher and circuit-riding preacher in the hills of Kentucky and Tennessee among people akin to Lincoln and living as the Lincolns lived. Subsequent years brought me unusual, if not unique, opportunities of travel and research regarding Lincoln, till I had traveled in his footsteps the whole of his life journey.

I could not say of this book that its story of the birth of Lincoln was written in the cabin where he was born and the story of his death in the room where he died, and everything between in similarly appropriate places; the actual writing has been done under conditions more favorable to methodical literary composition. But if such a statement were to be made of the notes on which this biography is based, it would be far within the truth; I am confident that no biographer of Lincoln can have covered the actual ground as I have covered it, or visited the scenes associated with Lincoln's life so frequently or methodically as I have been able to do.

But I am not thinking of this book as chiefly justified by the aggregate of miles its author has traveled or the number of people whom he has interviewed, nor by the thousands of letters he has written and received. I am thinking rather that not many men of my generation have had such opportunities as these for learning about Lincoln, and that mine is the only generation that can combine the judgment of a sixty years' perspective with a body of testimony gathered at first hand from people who knew Lincoln. Whatever biographies of Lincoln the future may produce, this combination of direct testimony and historic perspective is possible now, and will never be possible to the biographers of any later generation.

I can not adequately thank the hundreds of correspondents and friends who have assisted me, but I must mention my special obligations to the Honorable William H. Townsend, of Lexington, Reverend Louis A. Warren, of Morganfield, Honorable Joseph Polin, of Springfield, Honorable L. S. Pence, of Lebanon, Honorable Otis M. Mather, of Hodgenville, Honorable R. C. Ballard-Thruston, of Louisville, Mrs. Jouette Cannon Taylor and Miss Nina Visscher, of Frankfort, and the Misses Mary A. and Martha Stephenson, of Harrodsburg, all of Kentucky; Professor James A. Woodburn, of the University of Indiana, and Honorable Albert J. Beveridge, of Indianapolis; Professor L. E. Robinson, of Monmouth College, Mr. Oliver R. Barrett, of Chicago, Mrs. Jessie Palmer Weber and Miss Georgia L. Osborne, of Springfield, Miss Caroline McIlvaine, of Chicago, and Miss Bernice V. Lovely, of Colchester, Illinois; Mr. A. H. Griffith, of Fisk, Wisconsin; Doctor Herbert Putnam, Mr. A. P. C. Griffin, Doctor Charles Moore and Mr. William Adams Slade, of the Library of Congress. This is a most meager list compared with the number to whom I am indebted, but I can not mention all, and I must not omit these to whom my obligation is so great. I must mention, however, the libraries that have given me most valued aid. These are the State Historical Libraries of Massachusetts, Virginia, Kentucky, Indiana, Wisconsin and Kansas; the Newberry Library of Chicago and that of the Chicago Historical Society; the McLellan Collection in Brown University; the Draper Collection in the Library of the University of Wisconsin; and the Durrett Collection in the Library of the University of Chicago. I reserve for special mention the Library of Congress, especially the Manuscript Division and the remarkably efficient Department of Bibliography, for invaluable aid, most cheerfully given, and the Illinois State Historical Society, whose assistance has been as constant as its courtesy has been unfailing. From this last society I have had the special courtesy of the use of the diary of Senator O. H. Browning, a remarkable document and a new and intimate source of knowledge of Lincoln, soon to be published, but furnished to me in advance of publication because I could not wait for its printing.

For the backgrounds of Lincoln's life in Kentucky, Indiana and Illinois I have a basis of knowledge in my own experience more valuable to me than books.

Biography is more than narrative; it is also interpretation. It is possible to compile a list of dates and events in Lincoln's life, and then to trundle past them, one after another, a bronze St. Gaudens' statue of Lincoln, formed in the mold of the biographer's invention, the castors audibly creaking and the biographer visibly pushing, from Hodgenville to Gentryville, across the prairies to New Salem and Springfield, and finally into the front door of the White House. Neither Lincoln nor any other great man has escaped this kind of biography; and there must be readers who prefer the story to be told in that fashion. But the actual Lincoln was developed by his successive environments. So fully did he realize this that he said he had not controlled events but been controlled by them. This was one-half of the truth. We can not understand Lincoln apart from his environments; neither can we understand his environments without a knowledge of the growing personality of Lincoln. If the Lincoln of the earlier chapters of this work is a less heroic figure than the man who emerges at the close, that is, as I conceive, as Lincoln should be portrayed. From the beginning of his life to the very end, the character of Lincoln grew and developed.

This book is, therefore, a study of the progressive evolution of one of the world's greatest leaders. Of him it may reverently be said that he increased in wisdom and in stature and in favor with God and man.

Abraham Lincoln did not enjoy reading biographies, which he said were falsified by their authors in the interest of eulogy. Closing in disgust the biography of a noted character, he said that the Bible, after all, was about the only book that told the truth about people. While he was president, a publishing firm that had issued a Life of Lincoln bound a copy in full morocco, and sent it to the White House in a vain attempt to secure from him a letter of commendation. The volume is in existence, and bears on its fly-leaf the inscription of the publishers. On the title-page is another written inscription. Just below the author's name appears the president's characterization of the author, "the premium liar of history." It would be interesting to know in what terms President Lincoln would have characterized some of his more recent and vastly more extravagant biographers. As Cromwell rebuked the artist who in painting the portrait of the great Protector omitted the wart upon his cheek, Abraham Lincoln would have sternly admonished his biographers, "Paint me as I am!" This book attempts to tell the truth about Abraham Lincoln.

I am striving not to repeat in this work any considerable part of what I have said in *The Soul of Abraham Lincoln* and *The Paternity of Abraham Lincoln*. The former was completely sold out, and is now appearing in a new edition with a few corrections, mostly unimportant. I have little to add to, and nothing to subtract from, the conclusions announced in that book. The same I can say also as to the main part of *The Paternity of Abraham Lincoln*. The book as a whole is true. But in the latter part of it, I included some incomplete material on matters germane to, but not directly involved in, the main line of inquiry. I can not say that I regret having printed those pages; for I gave the material for just what it might prove to be worth; but the conclusions which I appeared to be approaching in that part of the book, and at which I earnestly hoped to arrive, have not been sustained by subsequent evidence. The true answer to the questions propounded in that part of the book is found in this present work. But the book, *The Paternity of Abraham Lincoln*, taken as a whole, is reliable, and, as I believe, a permanent contribution to knowledge. The essential conclusions of both these books are assumed in this present work; for the evidence on which these conclusions rest, I refer to these two books themselves.

As the first draft of this book was written in my vacations, certain portions are reminiscent of places where I have sojourned for periods of rest and service. Some of the earlier chapters were written in the Mission Inn, at Riverside, California, and others in the Coronado Beach Hotel, and still others on the shores of Puget Sound, in the library of my friend, Professor Clark P. Bissett, of the University of Washington. Some of the last work was done amid the happy surroundings of Lake Placid Club in the Adirondacks. In these and other places I received marked courtesies which it is a pleasure to remember.

This manuscript, which has been several years in writing, and has traveled with me in whole or in part on innumerable journeys wherein I have followed the life trail of Lincoln, and also from coast to coast, accomplishes its final revision in a remote and quiet place where for many years I have had my summer home. The little lake beneath the windows of my Wigwam gives it a rippling smile of farewell, and the pine trees that for many summers have seen it unpacked and wrought over and packed up again, murmur after it a fragrant Godspeed. And I am thankful in this quiet spot for the strength and opportunity that enable me thus to bring to a close the labor of many years.

WILLIAM E. BARTON

The Wigwam
on Sunset Lake,
Foxboro, Massachusetts.

BOOK I

THE LIFE OF ABRAHAM LINCOLN

CHAPTER I

THE BIRTH OF ABRAHAM LINCOLN

BIRTHPLACES of eminent men are not selected with reference to the convenience of tourists and historians. If there had been an American traveler in London in 1564, and he had cared to ride across the moors to bear congratulations to Mr. and Mrs. Shakespeare on the birth of their son, William, his guide-book, if he had possessed a guide-book, would have afforded him little assistance. Stratford-on-Avon was then a long, long way from London, and few people in that city had ever heard of the squalid village where the greatest creative genius that ever spoke the English tongue lay, as he later lived, undiscovered. Not many of the gentlefolk of Edinburgh or Glasgow, or even of the scholars in the universities of those two cities, could have directed a traveler to the "clay-biggin" at Ayr, where Robert Burns lay in a built-in bed. Even now the fast trains thunder through Ecclefechan, a name which feels like a Scotch thistle in the mouth of him who essays to pronounce it properly, and most of the passengers, en route for their boats at Liverpool, have no suspicion that they are passing the home where Thomas Carlyle, even in his infancy possessed of "that diabolical thing, a stomach," once lay kicking with colic. As for Bethlehem, only the angels knew the way thither; the Magi had to stop in Jerusalem and inquire.

Abraham Lincoln was born three miles south of the present

site of Hodgenville, in what is now Larue County, Kentucky, on Sunday morning, February 12, 1809. Hodgenville has a court-house and several taverns and stores and a garage and a railway station and a school and some churches and enough inhabitants to make up a small town; but there was no court-house or store or school or church or village there when Lincoln was born. The larger county of Hardin, of which the present Larue was then a part, had only one town, Elizabethtown, or, as it was then and still now is often abbreviated, Etown. Abraham Lincoln never saw Hodgenville, and he stumbled over the spelling of the name, when, after his nomination for the presidency, he tried to tell just where he was born. The Hodgen family was there in Lincoln's day, and they had a mill, but the Lincolns did not commonly patronize it, the Kirkpatrick mill being nearer, and they moved away from that locality before Abraham ever rode a horse to mill. Hodgenville is now a town with a place on the map, and has come to fame because of a man whom it never knew and who never knew of it until many years after the event which linked their names together.

Of all the presidents of the United States, only Theodore Roosevelt was born in a large city, and he escaped to the plains. Birth in a log cabin is not an absolute prerequisite to a presidential election, and several millions of Americans have been born in log cabins who have not lived in the White House; but all in all, a log cabin has proved as good a place as any in which to be born if a man intends to be president. William Henry Harrison, who was not born in a cabin, was the first presidential candidate to boast of having lived in one, but Andrew Jackson was elected twelve years before Harrison, and his birthplace was a cabin. Millard Fillmore was born in a log house, and rocked in a split-log sap-trough, thus reversing Samson's riddle, for out of the sweetness came the strong. James A. Garfield was born in a cabin, and this is by no means a complete list. Abraham Lincoln was born in a log cabin.

There is variety in log cabins. There are small cabins and

large cabins; cabins with open spaces between the logs, and cabins with split chinking daubed with clay or even smoothly covered with plaster; cabins with doors and windows and cabins with just openings—maybe a blanket or a bear-skin hung in the aperture; cabins with the earth for a floor and cabins with puncheon or even with a floor whose boards were sawn at the mill; cabins with stick-chimneys and cabins with stone fireplaces. The one-room cabin is the germ-cell of American architecture. The cell becomes two cells, two log structures set end to end with doors facing, and an open space between, the two fireplaces being usually, though not invariably, at the two ends, and the roof-timbers extended across the open space. Then a third cell may be added for a kitchen at the back, the three architectural units adjoining each other like three black squares of a checkerboard, with the open porch as the white square enclosed by the black on three sides. Other units may be piled upon the top of these three, or over the front two, and the open porch becomes a long cold hall, with a staircase rising out of it. By this time the structure has become a good example of Colonial architecture, and may, if one likes, be weatherboarded, and painted white, with a portico in front, the columns surmounted by Ionic capitols.

There are "round-log cabins" and "square-log cabins." In each case the shape of the house itself is the same; it is the logs that are left round or are squared by hewing. Primitive American cabins were all, or practically all, round-log cabins; those built of hewn logs were a sign of prosperity.

There was not much hewing of the logs that framed the cabin where Abraham Lincoln was born. The cabin was of one room, had a door in the side, and a stick-chimney at the left hand as one entered the door. There was an unglazed window, closed by a hinged door, but it is doubtful if that was there when Abraham was born. There probably was not a single nail in the entire structure. What chinking there was between the logs we may not now know, but in most cabins of this character there was no lack of ventilation.

One day, many years ago, when I was teaching in an old log schoolhouse in Kentucky, a boy kicked with his bare foot through a crack between the logs at a boy who was passing on the outside, and the boy outside caught his foot. The crack was not large enough for the boy outside to pull the inside boy out, nor yet for the inside boy to pull the outside boy in, and so I caught them in their misdemeanor. That was an unusually large crack, caused by a curve in one log and a large knot in its neighbor log. But often when I slept in cabins that would have been well populated even if I had not been there, and the doors were shut and there were no windows, I was not wholly sorry for the daubing that had fallen off and the chinking that had dropped out or perhaps had never been.

Fuel was abundant, and if the stick-chimney caught fire, the accident was practically certain to occur when the family was awake and the blaze could be extinguished with a gourdful of water, the hissing noise of whose falling drops upon the blazing logs below made rather a cheerful sound. Fires did not often occur at night, at least not late at night, for the fire was covered with ashes before the family went to bed.

Good housekeepers did not let their fires go out. A few years ago, a log cabin in Missouri was torn down, and a fire extinguished on a hearth where it was alleged to have burned for eighty years. It was even claimed that before the beginning of that eighty-year period, the fire had been transported in an iron pot by day hung from the axle of a wagon, to new camps night by night, all the way from Kentucky where, it was said, it had alternately blazed and smouldered as occasion required ever since it was brought in another iron pot through Cumberland Gap from old Virginia about 1790. We may discount such a story somewhat, and suspect that there may have been a few occasions in the century and more when it had been necessary to borrow fire from a neighbor; but those occasions had probably been infrequent.

There was doubtless a good fire in the cabin on February 12,

1809, when Abraham Lincoln was born. It was the season for good fires, and Thomas Lincoln, who had been in Elizabethtown at court during a part of the week preceding, returned home before Sunday. So there was fuel enough. There was probably enough of everything else, as judged by the standards of the time, but the equipment of the cabin was meager.

The bed where Nancy Lincoln lay with her baby beside her had one leg, driven in the earthen floor, with a side-rail running to the wall on one side, and a foot-rail running at right angles to the other wall. There may have been a bear-skin on the floor where little two-year-old Sarah sat and played. There was probably a rough table, made by Thomas Lincoln, and there may have been two or three stools and as many chairs.

The bed was probably not uncomfortable. There was almost certainly a feather-bed on top of the straw or husk mattress, and there were homespun blankets and coverlets. Thomas and Nancy Lincoln owned livestock and poultry, and there was presumably milk for Nancy and the baby, besides the simple luxury which may have been afforded by fresh eggs and fried chicken. There was enough to eat and there was shelter and rude comfort. People who have never slept in log cabins are likely either to idealize them or to exaggerate the hardship of living in them. Life in a log cabin lacks much of luxury, but it is not necessarily uncomfortable. I have never lived in a cabin, but I have spent many days and nights in them, and conditions had not greatly changed from those of Lincoln's childhood.

Considering the unsanitary conditions under which the greater part of the human race is born, it is remarkable that the generations continue to follow one another with unfailing regularity, and survive to produce succeeding generations. The Lincoln cabin was lacking in all modern conveniences and most modern comforts. Nancy did not miss them; she had never known them. It would have astonished her to know that the rough logs of the cabin where she lay would one day be enshrined in an imposing granite memorial; she never dreamt she dwelt in marble halls. But she smiled a wan smile when she was told that her new baby was a boy. Both she and Thomas wanted a son, and their first child had been a girl. They could not give her the name which was waiting for a boy, so they had done the next best thing and called her Sarah.

Who were present when Abraham Lincoln was born?

If you are to believe the stories that are told you in and about Hodgenville, and the people who tell them intend to be truthful, the grandmothers of the entire present population of Larue County must have been there, with a number from counties adjacent. If all the people who are believed to have been present had actually been there, they would have packed the cabin and the front yard.

Nancy Lincoln had two aunts, Polly Friend and Elizabeth Sparrow, living near by, and one of those aunts was her foster mother. She did not lack for the attention which women are able to give to each other at such times. And there were other women in the neighborhood who were ready to assist. We may discount, therefore, the narratives of most of the truthful people who assure us that their maternal relatives were among those present. Of one thing we may be certain: Abraham Lincoln had such care at the time of his birth as was deemed requisite in the backwoods. His mother was not neglected, and the baby was passed around among an adequate group of well-intending women who were present to welcome him.

Not in 1809, but soon afterward, there died in Elizabethtown, Doctor Daniel B. Potter. He left a widow, and a large number of accounts due him from people to whom he had rendered professional service. I have ridden many miles in the Kentucky mountains side by **side with a doctor,ₗwho kept his** forceps within reach so that he did not need to dismount for so simple a matter as the extraction of a tooth, and who was ready for an emergency caused by anything from child-birth to gun-shot wounds. Doctor Potter was one of those hard-riding physicians who wore his life out in his fights with death, and who wasted little time except the weary waits at each end of life—for both birth and death are tedious processes to hard-worked physicians. He left debts to the amount of $1,560.35¾. The court appointed a commission to collect the much larger sum that was due him from those who had been his patients, to pay his debts and give the remainder to his widow. The commissioners brought into court their final report, showing that they had been able to collect a total of $864.89½, leaving the estate still in debt $695.46¼. The commissioners reported the men who had paid, and among them was the name of Thomas Lincoln. At the time of the doctor's death, Thomas Lincoln owed him an unpaid balance of $1.46. It is a simple matter, but it shows that when Nancy needed a doctor, she had one, and that Thomas Lincoln paid the bill.

It is not likely that Thomas and Nancy depended on or called a physician when Abraham Lincoln was born. Physicians were too uncertain for dependence at such times. No tradition that I have been able to discover affirms that Doctor Potter or any other physician attended Nancy at the birth of Abraham. A local mid-wife was there; they called her "the granny-woman." Apparently, she did the few simple things that needed to be done, and Nancy's two aunts and the neighbor women assisted. In due time Thomas Lincoln stood awkwardly beside the bed of Nancy, and looked into the face of his son. Nancy also looked. The new-born babe is seldom an object of beauty save as affection gives prophetic vision of qualities that lie more than skin-deep. But Thomas and Nancy were both happy.

When I first visited Hodgenville and recorded the traditions that were then obtainable, I gathered, as it had come down from the women-folk who were present that day or who called during the days that followed, that Thomas Lincoln was kind to Nancy, and immensely proud of his boy. Maternal pride is not circumscribed by petty considerations of pulchritude. Abraham was a fine baby; we may be sure that all the women said so, and no one disputed the fact. Thomas Lincoln was a solid, rather thick-set man, and so was the father of Thomas Carlyle. The two fathers were somewhat alike, and both the sons were tall and angular. We have no recorded word of Nancy concerning her first impression of her son, but there has been preserved a discriminating comment of Janet Carlyle. She said of her baby what Nancy might have said of hers, that he was "a lang, sprawling, ill-put-together thing."*

There was no discussion about the baby's name. It had been waiting for him ever since Sarah was born. It was a good name, the name of Thomas Lincoln's own father. A few years later there was a lawsuit concerning some land that had once belonged to him, and the question hinged upon the genuineness of a signature alleged to have been that of the father of Thomas Lincoln. The name in that signature was incorrectly spelled, and followed the backwoods pronunciation. Thomas Lincoln, an uncle of the president's father, was summoned from his home near Lexington to Frankfort, where he was shown the signature in the Land Office. He was asked whether he was familiar with the handwriting of his brother, and answered that he was familiar with it.

"How did he spell his name?" was the next interrogatory.

The answer under oath is still of record:

"He spelled it ABRAHAM LINCOLN."

---

*Carlyle Till Marriage. David Alec Wilson, i, p. 23.

CHAPTER II

THE PARENTS OF ABRAHAM LINCOLN

Both of Abraham Lincoln's parents were born in Virginia, and both migrated into Kentucky in early childhood. When they met each other is not known. The story that they were first cousins is without foundation. It is likely that they were not acquainted before 1804 or 1805. The families from which they sprang were poor; it is not easy to say how poor without making them seem more so than they really were. They have been called "poor whites." They were poor and they were white, but they were not poor whites. They were of decent, average American stock. They were sober, honest, virtuous, religious and not quite illiterate. He was able "bunglingly to write his own name" and she is believed to have been able to read and write, though in the one document to which her name is signed, she made her mark. There was nothing in either of them that would lead us to expect so great a son; neither was there apparent any marked disqualification for such high honor. Of each of their families account will be given in succeeding chapters. We recite here the important facts as they relate to Thomas Lincoln, together with some account of Nancy Hanks; but the detailed story of her life belongs with the narrative of her family in a later chapter.

Thomas Lincoln, son of Abraham and Bathsheba Lincoln, was born on Linville Creek, in Rockingham County, Virginia, January 6, 1778. This date we accept from the record of his son, Abraham, and we depart here from the chronology of Lea and Hutchinson, in their handsome volume on *The Ancestry of Lin-*

9

coln, which since 1909 has furnished most biographers with their data. Of that book it is high praise to say that it is not always wrong. It will be cited in a few places in the present work, but for the most part it is to be rejected.*

The journey of the family of Abraham Lincoln, the grandfather, from Virginia to Kentucky, occurred in 1782, when Thomas was four years old. In the spring of 1786, the pioneer Abraham was killed by an Indian. He left a widow, three sons and two daughters.

From the time he was sixteen until he left Kentucky, we are able to account for Thomas Lincoln in the various official records of the two Kentucky counties of Washington and Hardin.†

In 1795 the name Thomas Lincoln appears on the tax lists of Washington County, Kentucky, as a minor above sixteen years of age, and also on May 16, 1796, as a white male above sixteen and under twenty-one. In 1799 he is listed for the first time as above twenty-one. If he was above sixteen in 1795, and above twenty-one in 1799, he must have been born between 1777 and 1779, which accords with the date given by his son, Abraham Lincoln the President.

There was fear of an Indian uprising in 1795, and Thomas Lincoln, then a boy of seventeen, served thirty days from June eighth to July seventh, as a private in Captain George Ewing's Company of Washington County Militia, under command of Brigadier General John Caldwell.

President Lincoln has told us that his father became "a wandering laboring boy" who grew up "literally without education," and that "before he was grown, he passed one year as a farm-hand with his uncle Isaac on Watauga." That year of

---

*That book furnished the material for the inscriptions upon the walls of the Memorial at Hodgenville, and those inscriptions are sadly inaccurate.

†I refer to my *Paternity of Abraham Lincoln,* for a list of important dates, arranged particularly to account for his movements in the period preceding the birth of Abraham. Other important dates are now given here, for the first time.

absence must have been 1798. There are authentic and indisputable Kentucky records bearing his name in every other calendar year from 1795 to 1816.

In 1800, Thomas Lincoln was taxed as a resident of Washington County, above twenty-one years. He owned a horse. On August 5, 1802, he was listed and taxed in Washington County, and still owned one horse. Cattle and hogs were not usually taxed in Washington County at this period, so we do not know whether he had any other property; probably one horse, owned before the boy became of age,* was his only taxable property. After 1802 his name disappears from the Washington County tax lists.

It has been affirmed by many writers that Mordecai, the eldest brother of Thomas Lincoln, inherited the whole of his father's property; and that under the old Virginia law of primogeniture, Thomas, and perhaps with him the middle brother Josiah, was wronged out of his part of his father's estate.

This is a serious charge against Mordecai, by some authors extended to include Josiah also, and it has no known foundation. Indubitably the English law of primogeniture, which was the law in Virginia, held in Kentucky. As Abraham Lincoln died intestate, and all his children were minors, the court appointed administrators to serve until the eldest boy was of age. But it does not follow that Mordecai, either alone or in conspiracy with Josiah, was otherwise than just to his younger brothers and sisters. We have good reason to believe that in this, as in all else, Mordecai was a just man and a faithful older brother; and we have reason also to respect his brother Josiah.

Mordecai, when he came of age, accepted his inheritance under the law, for he, only, had standing in court as the heir-at-law of his deceased father. But soon after Josiah came of age, we find Mordecai selling part of his father's land, and Josiah buying land for cash; and, in 1802, we find Mordecai selling more land,

---

*He probably owned a horse before he journeyed into East Tennessee to spend a year working on the farm of his uncle.

and Thomas buying a farm and paying for it in cash. What Mordecai did with the money he received from the two sales of land is not, of course, a matter of court record; and by the same token there is no record showing where either Josiah or Thomas obtained money with which to buy land. But the inference* is unmistakable. Mordecai acted as guardian of the interests of his minor brothers and sisters and dealt honorably with them.

Another event of importance occurred. On February 3, 1801, a license was issued for the marriage of Nancy Lincoln, the younger of the two sisters of Thomas, to William Brumfield, and the marriage was duly celebrated.†

William and Nancy Brumfield removed to Mill Creek in Hardin County, and there, in time, Bathsheba, the widowed mother of the Lincoln family, went to reside, and continued to live there with her youngest daughter until her death in 1836. This was probably the reason why Thomas Lincoln invested his patrimony in a farm on Mill Creek.‡

From January, 1803, until October, 1816, we have numerous records of Thomas Lincoln as resident of Hardin County. His name appears regularly on the tax lists (and he paid his taxes), on jury-lists, in several lawsuits (in which he uniformly was the winner of the suit), in payments for guarding prisoners (for he was for a time a "patrolman" or sort of deputy constable), in

---

*I am pleased to see that Miss Tarbell adopts this view in her last book, taking her information from my address before the Filson Club of Louisville, Kentucky, December 4, 1922, on *The Lincolns in Their Old Kentucky Home*. This was, as I suppose, the first time the theory was propounded, and it is so reasonable and just, I am confident it will be generally adopted henceforth. I acknowledge Miss Tarbell's courtesy in the generous credit she gives me in this and other matters.

†The date of the bond is February third, and the marriage return is dated January 13, 1801, and signed by Thomas Kyle. This minister was of the Disciples Church, and he signed his name with bold flourish to each of his many marriage returns. Whether he made a mistake in the date of this return, or whether, as was sometimes the case, the minister himself issued a license, we may not know. When I was a circuit-riding preacher in the Tennessee mountains I was permitted by the county court to issue licenses and accept bonds, but I have not discovered a similar practise in Kentucky. It is a minor discrepancy, and of no great importance.

‡Concerning this farm, see my *The Paternity of Abraham Lincoln*. All previous works had been in error concerning it.

auction sales of estates which required to be reported to the court, and in other records which have survived the ravages of time, and have been exhumed in the course of research for this work.*

These records, more than a hundred in number, are commonplace enough taken singly, but they afford us what is to all intents and purposes a documentary chronology of the life of Thomas Lincoln from the time he was sixteen years of age until he left Kentucky. He bought his Mill Creek farm in Hardin County from Doctor John Toms Slater, September 2, 1803, having already become a resident of Hardin County. So far as we know, he never lived on this farm. He did not sell it until October 27, 1814, but neither did he abandon it. He paid taxes upon it, and it is to be supposed that he rented it to tenants, perhaps to the Miltons to whom he later conveyed it. He probably worked this farm in 1804, living with his mother and sister, but by 1805 he was in Elizabethtown, working at his trade of carpenter.

Recent fiction, published as biography, tends to make Nancy

_____

*When I began work on this book hardly a single correct date had been discovered by Lincoln biographers concerning Thomas Lincoln, save only those of his two marriages and his appointment as road surveyor. The dates both of birth and death were uncertain, and not one of the tax lists or court records above referred to was known to exist. I am indebted to a number of friends for assistance in this matter. Honorable Joseph Polin, County Attorney of Washington County, assisted me in the discovery of the Washington County lists, and it was he who helped me also to exhume three additional lists of marriage returns by Jesse Head, each one of them containing about a year's marriages performed by him. Honorable L. S. Pence, of Lebanon, Kentucky, and Honorable George Holbert, of Elizabethtown, added important data. Mrs. Cannon, of the Kentucky Historical Society, while engaged in search for me, discovered valuable lists in a lot of papers that had not seen the light of day for many years, and were to have been burned, these adding material of very great value. But most important of all my assistants as regards Thomas Lincoln has been Reverend Louis A. Warren. When I first met him, he was pastor at Hodgenville, and later removed to Elizabethtown, and thence to Morganfield. He has become an investigator of unusual skill and persistence, and is soon to release the results of his extensive research which includes the copies of over two thousand public records. Much of this unpublished material he has generously permitted me to use. To Mr. Warren and his forthcoming volume, I make grateful reference. His work will be invaluable to all who wish to possess a complete documentary account of the Lincolns in their Kentucky environment.

Hanks a blonde. She was tall, dark and sallow. Her hair was dark brown, almost black. Her eyes were small and gray. She had a prominent forehead, a feature remarked by all the relatives who have given account of her, and it was regarded by them as an indication of unusual mental ability. She was above medium height, and weighed about one hundred and thirty pounds. She had a slight stoop, and her appearance suggested a tubercular tendency. Her face was thin, sharp and angular. Her disposition was cheerful, and she had an exuberant spirit which sometimes broke over restraint and expressed itself in care-free merriment; but this mood alternated with one of melancholy. All who knew her and whose reports have come down to us, remark the habitual sadness of her features in repose. She was gentle, capable and strong; amiable, friendly and kind. Nancy's mother could write, but that was not true either of the Hankses generally or of the Sparrows among whom Nancy spent her girlhood. She, however, received some education; we do not know how much, but her relations thought it remarkable, and considering her circumstances it may be so regarded.

When, in 1851, Thomas Lincoln died, Abraham Lincoln broke over his habitual reserve, and spoke somewhat freely to his partner, William H. Herndon, of his father and also of his mother:

Mr. Lincoln himself said to me in 1851, on receiving news of his father's death, that whatever might be said of his parents, and however unpromising the early surroundings of his mother may have been, she was highly intellectual by nature, had a strong memory, acute judgment, and was cool and heroic.*

He was not speaking of her direct influence upon him, but of qualities which he believed himself to have inherited from her, when he used the much quoted expression regarding his mother; but we have good reason to believe that had she lived she would have had a potent influence for good upon his youth and young

---

*Herndon's *Lincoln*, i, p. 13. All references to Herndon's *Lincoln* are to the first edition.

manhood. With still better reason would he have said, "God bless my mother; all that I am or hope to be I owe to her."

We are hardly to credit the story that Nancy was living in the home of her uncle, Joseph Hanks, in Elizabethtown, when she became engaged to marry Thomas Lincoln, for Joseph was himself unmarried at the time. In May, 1806, he bought a farm with livestock and household goods, on Rough Creek, in Grayson County, near his brother William. Yet the story appears to have a basis of truth. Joseph Hanks, who had gone back to Virginia after the death of his father, had returned to Kentucky, and was working with Thomas Lincoln near Elizabethtown. They were both carpenters. Joseph had two married sisters living in that county, and with one of them, Elizabeth Sparrow, Nancy was living. It is therefore probably true that Thomas Lincoln's association as a fellow-craftsman with Joseph led to his acquaintance with Nancy Hanks.

We do not know why the marriage occurred in Washington County. The early home of Thomas was there, and his brothers resided where he had grown up; but the wedding did not take place in either of their houses. The bride's home had never been in Washington, nor had any of her immediate family ever resided there. But it is not strange that the wedding should have occurred in that place.

At the time of her marriage, June 12, 1806, she was in Washington County, in the home of one of the Berrys. Thither Thomas Lincoln followed her, and, his own mother having removed to Hardin County, and the homes of his two brothers being perhaps less suited to a wedding than the home of the Berrys, they were married there.

Undue reliance has been placed upon an account of the behavior of "one of the Hanks girls" at a camp-meeting which J. B. Helm, fifty-nine years afterward, thought he remembered having attended, and a Minneapolis lawyer, a Methodist, supposing that none but Methodists held camp-meetings, has accepted this story as proof that Nancy Hanks was a Methodist,

2

and that, honoring his mother as he did, Abraham Lincoln must have been of the same denomination.* But old men do not recall incidents that have lain buried for fifty-nine years, and tell them exactly as they occurred; and Helm did not pretend to know which of the Hanks girls it was who cavorted at the camp-meeting. It was not Nancy. She was not there. And camp-meetings were not held in corn-plowing time.†

The Lincolns were Baptists, and so were the Hankses. Thomas Lincoln and Nancy Hanks were married by a neighbor, the Reverend Jesse Head, who was a Methodist. This minister is an important part of the story of Abraham Lincoln, but his denomination was not the same as theirs.

President Lincoln did not know in what county his parents were married. When he was nominated for the presidency in 1860, Samuel Haycraft, the county clerk of Hardin County, wrote to him asking if he were not the son of Thomas Lincoln and Sarah Bush, and Lincoln replied that Thomas Lincoln was his father, but by an earlier marriage. Haycraft found the record of the marriage of Thomas Lincoln and Sarah Bush, but could not discover any record of Thomas Lincoln's marriage to Nancy Hanks. Such other search as was made immediately afterward yielded no satisfactory results; but, in 1878, through the efforts of R. M. Thompson, who had heard the story from an old man, William Hardesty, a search was made among the records of Washington County, and the county clerk, W. F. Booker, discovered the marriage bond of Thomas Lincoln for his marriage to Nancy Hanks, together with the marriage return of Jesse Head, as deacon in the Methodist Episcopal Church. This was

*A Defence of Lincoln's Mother, by J. M. Martin. It is based on Helm's story in Herndon, i, pp. 14-15.

†Mr. Helm, whose memory was at fault in other matters and may have been in this, told Herndon that the young woman who rode with him to the camp-meeting, and who witnessed this performance with him, and identified the leading participants, said to him that this religiously demonstrative Hanks girl and the young man who shared this incident with her were to be married in the following week. This makes us certain that the girl can not have been Nancy Hanks. She and Thomas Lincoln were married June twelfth, too early in the season for camp-meetings.

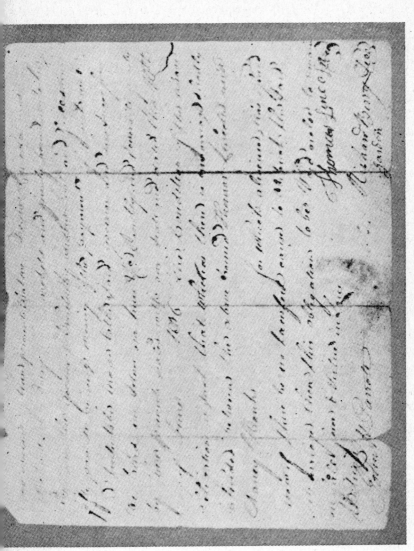

MARRIAGE BOND FOR MARRIAGE OF THOMAS LINCOLN AND NANCY HANKS
Photographed for this work

a most important discovery, and it started inquiry as to the personality of Jesse Head. This inquiry established the fact that Jesse Head spent his last years at Harrodsburg, but facts concerning him appeared to be meager. In 1882, Doctor Christopher Columbus Graham, who had owned the Harrodsburg Springs for several years prior to 1852, related his recollections of Jesse Head, whom he had known during a part of his residence in Harrodsburg. Doctor Graham was then ninety-eight years old, so it is not surprising that the old man forgot to tell that he had been present when Jesse Head married Doctor Graham himself to Theresa Sutton, October 8, 1820. Instead, he fancied that he had been present at the marriage of Thomas and Nancy Lincoln. The more he was interviewed, the more he remembered. His affidavit issued in his one-hundredth year elaborated considerably the original statement, and the final form of his story was that he had been present at the marriage of Abraham Lincoln himself.*

If Doctor Graham had actually been present at the marriage of Thomas and Nancy Lincoln, there was a period of several years in which he could have rendered a most valuable service by telling of the fact. He did not publish it then, nor until his story was practically valueless as evidence. At every point where he attempted to enlarge upon the information which the records gave, his statement was untrue. He probably never saw the Lincolns. Miss Tarbell has not assisted us in her wide-spread publication of Doctor Graham's story. He was an old man in his dotage, in the hands of men some of whom had their own reasons for wanting him to testify as he did. And it is this man's testimony that furnishes much of the information in the tablets upon the walls of the Lincoln memorial at Hodgenville!

It is discouraging to have these fabrications wide-spread by authors who intend to be truthful, and then accepted by a public that has all too little discrimination. Doctor Graham, in his gar-

*See his letter to Robert T. Lincoln in the Durrett Collection, University of Chicago.

rulous romancing, told that Jesse Head was an ardent abolitionist, Graham himself being a slave-holder and a southern sym-
pathizer; that Thomas Lincoln and both his wives were "chock-
full of the liberty-loving principles" which Head had derived
from Thomas Paine and others, and that thus Thomas Lincoln
became, and Abraham Lincoln was born, an abolitionist. He
further said that Jesse Head could have afforded slaves, but
did not own them. He might better have said that Jesse Head
could not afford slaves, but did own them. Both in Washington and Mercer Counties, Jesse Head was a slave-owner. And,
being editor of a newspaper, he had no scruples against advertising rewards for the arrest of runaway slaves, and their lodg-
ment in jail for return to their masters. He was a hard-hitting
Democrat of the old school, and he did not love Henry Clay, but
admired Andrew Jackson.*

On the question of slavery, Jesse Head was neither in advance
of nor behind his own generation. He was a good man, a worthy
and faithful pioneer preacher; but none of the things that Christopher Columbus Graham tells of him are true. Miss Tarbell's
friends were not satisfied with Doctor Graham's story, but added
a forged certificate of the marriage of Thomas and Nancy Lincoln, separate from the marriage return. She was imposed
upon by people whom she trusted.†

The Kentucky marriage law was the old Virginia law. It
required that before the clerk of the court issued a marriage
license, he should secure a bond from two responsible citizens,
to indemnify him against the possibility of issuing a license for a
marriage that might not legally be performed. The law did not
specify what citizens should sign the bond, but with practical
uniformity the first signer was the prospective bridegroom; and

---

*In the Appendix I give some account of this interesting man—Jesse
Head.

†This fraudulent certificate, published in entire good faith, appears in
Miss Tarbell's *Early Life of Lincoln*, p. 31. I note that the document itself
was sold in a New York book auction in 1921, and the catalogue called attention to the questionable nature of this certificate.

usually his surety was the bride's father, if she had a father, or some relative or friend who was known to represent her interests. This "guardian" was not appointed by the court, but was a friend who assumed a guardianship of the bride's interest for the purposes of the marriage license. Almost any bystander in a Kentucky court-house will sign a marriage bond; and in all the one hundred and fifty years during which they have been issued the Commonwealth has never once instituted suit.

Richard Berry signed Thomas Lincoln's bond as "guardian" of Nancy Hanks, she being then twenty-three years old, and sentimental writers have imagined that she must have been legally adopted by her "kind Uncle Richard Berry." Richard Berry, Sr., died in 1798; and the signer of the bond was Thomas Lincoln's friend, the second Richard Berry, whose wife, Polly Ewing, was a friend of Nancy.

The bond was issued June 10, 1806, and two days later, Thomas Lincoln and Nancy Hanks were married.

William Hardesty, born in 1798, and living less than a half-mile away, professed to have slipped over and attended the wedding; and so far forth his story is wholly probable. It was largely his recollection that led to the discovery of the marriage bond, and for it he deserves credit. But, unfortunately, like other old men who have interesting recollections, when he began to recall the part he remembered, he was able to remember also a number of events that never occurred, as, for instance, the birth of Abraham Lincoln in Washington County, and his having seen the little lad, Abraham, playing about the door of the house which he believed to have been that of Thomas Lincoln. But William Hardesty might easily have been at the wedding, just as he declared; and his evidence is much better than that of Doctor Graham, which is worthless.

The house where Thomas and Nancy are believed to have been married stood near an excellent spring, not far from Beech Fork of Salt River. A little settlement is near, sometimes called Beechland and sometimes Poortown. The latter name has not been satisfactorily accounted for; the inhabitants were not poorer than their neighbors; indeed, the community was rather prosperous than otherwise.

Weddings in the backwoods were joyous and boisterous affairs, with plenty to eat and more than enough to drink. In all probability there was a fiddle and a dance. But it was an orderly affair, as we may believe, for the Berrys and their neighbors were men and women of standing in the community, and the merriment is not likely to have exceeded proper bounds. Besides, Thomas and Nancy were religious people, and the time was one of religious activity in that locality.

It is not improbable that the widow, Bathsheba Lincoln, rode back from Mill Creek to attend the wedding of her youngest son. Mordecai and Josiah, with their wives, were doubtless there to see their brother married; Thomas's older sister, Mary, and her husband, Ralph Crume, may have been there. If Bathsheba was present, so also, in all likelihood, was her youngest daughter, Nancy Brumfield. There was no lack of Lincolns in attendance.

But who of the Hanks family was there when Nancy was married? None of them lived in Washington County. Nancy's welcome in the homes of that locality depended upon no known tie of kinship, nor yet of any friendly interest save that which she herself had earned or some member of the Sparrow family had won for her. It is not likely that her Aunt Elizabeth and her Uncle Thomas Sparrow, whom she called father and mother, were absent; and it is possible that her Aunt Polly Friend or even her Aunt Nancy Hall was there.

But I have not been able to stop with these probabilities. Only twenty miles away—I have measured the distance with a speedometer, an instrument of which she never heard, while riding in a vehicle that would have amazed her—lived another woman who was called her aunt.

I wonder if she was there.

I wonder if she could keep away.

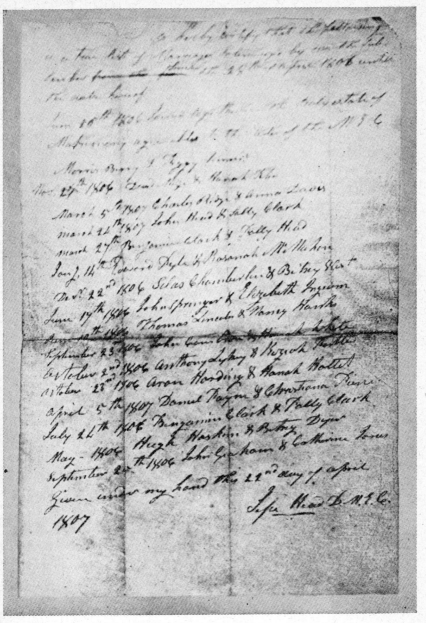

MARRIAGE RETURN OF REVEREND JESSE HEAD
Certifying the Marriage of Thomas Lincoln and Nancy Hanks
Photographed for this work

CHAPTER III

THE LINCOLNS

WHEN Abraham Lincoln wrote his autobiographical sketch for Jesse W. Fell, in December, 1859, he said concerning his ancestors of the name of Lincoln:

An effort to identify them with the New England family of the same name ended in nothing more definite than a similarity of Christian names in both families, such as Enoch, Levi, Mordecai, Solomon, Abraham, and the like.

Subsequent and more thorough investigation, however, made the identification complete. The Lincolns are of New England origin.*

Not only are the American Lincolns of New England extraction, but the family in colonial times was almost wholly restricted to Massachusetts. The adjutant general of the United States Army has searched the records of the War Department and finds not a single Revolutionary soldier of the name of Lincoln from Virginia or the states farther South. The United States records show soldiers of the name of Lincoln, Linkhorn and Linkon as follows: Maryland 1, Pennsylvania 4, New York 1, Rhode Island 1, New Hampshire 7, Connecticut 10 and Massachusetts 44.

---

*Waldo Lincoln's *History of the Lincoln Family,* Worcester, Massachusetts, 1923, will stand, I judge, as the authoritative record of the Lincolns in America. Marion Dexter Learned's *Abraham Lincoln, An American Migration,* Philadelphia, 1909, written to disprove the thesis of Louis P. Hennighausen that the Lincolns were of German origin, clearly makes that point and in addition gives a good account of the migrations of the Lincolns in America. Lea and Hutchinson, in their *Ancestry of Abraham Lincoln,* appear to have done good work in the English ancestry of the Lincoln family, but not to have established its connection with the family in America; and in their American line I have found them so often in error that I no longer trust them in any matter where documentary proof is not available.

These records, of course, are incomplete. A search of the records of particular states, including the enrollments of militia which may duplicate names, increases the preponderance of Massachusetts. Mr. Charles Z. Lincoln, in an address at Taunton, Massachusetts, July 12, 1906, said that he had made careful search among the state records, and had found one Revolutionary soldier named Lincoln from New York, one from Pennsylvania, and three from New Jersey—only six outside of New England, and only fourteen from New England States other than Massachusetts, while Massachusetts showed on her various muster rolls not less than 335 men named Lincoln.

It may be worth while to recall that Taunton long believed itself to have been the ancestral home of the forebears of Abraham Lincoln. At the time of the outbreak of the Revolution an important branch of the Lincoln family lived in that city. One of the sons, named Abraham, born November 9, 1761, is alleged to have had a violent altercation with a Tory, as a result of which he ran away from home and settled in Pennsylvania, married and was later killed by the Indians. The fact that the Taunton Lincolns were iron-founders, and that those in Pennsylvania were, some of them, of the same craft, lent color to this belief.* But this view has now generally been abandoned.

Concerning the spelling of the name and its alleged origin in other forms, as Linkhorn, and its supposed evolution into Lincoln,† little present comment is necessary.

Norman Hapgood, in his *Abraham Lincoln, the Man of the People,* a book written in an excellent spirit but with fine disregard of fact, says of Thomas Lincoln:

He was a Jackson Democrat who couldn't write his name until his first wife taught him to scrawl it, the farthest reach of edu-

---

*An extended and apparently conclusive article on this subject by James Minor Lincoln, of New York, was published in the *Taunton Herald-News* for February 10, 1909.

†See the chapter entitled "Was Abraham Lincoln a German?" in the author's *The Paternity of Abraham Lincoln.* Also *Abraham Lincoln, an American Migration,* by Marion Dexter Learned.

cation he ever acquired. His name was, under the circumstances, unstable; but in Indiana it showed a general drift toward Linkern, away from the favorite Kentucky form of Linckhorn, settling in its present spelling many years later in Illinois. (pp. 4-5.)

The name Lincoln, in common with all other names, was often misspelled in the backwoods. Pronunciations showed strange perversities, and spelling varied with the pronunciation. But Thomas Lincoln invariably signed his name Lincoln, and so did his father Abraham, and so did his grandfather John, and so did his great-grandfather Mordecai, and so did the original American ancestor of this branch of the Lincoln family, Samuel Lincoln, of Hingham, Massachusetts. Moreover, they were all able to write their names.

The misspelling "Linkhorn" and the other Kentucky variants are of no significance as concerns nationality or family lineage James M. Lincoln, of Wareham, Massachusetts, in a newspaper article published and copied in various papers in New England of the date of May 30, 1910, said that he had found in early Massachusetts documents the following variance in the spelling of the name Lincoln: Linkon, Linkhorn, Lincol, Linclon, Lincorn, Linkoln, Linkclon, Linkord, Linkhoom, Lincon, Linclin, Lancoln, Lincham, Lincolem, Linkhon, Linkton, Lincolan, Linchorney, Linckhorn, Lenks, Linchorn, Lincolin, Linkalon, Linklon, Linckin, Lincolon, Linculor, Linkhoren, Lincott, Linckhornew, Lincornew, Lynklyn, Linckomeal and Lincoln.

If they do such things in the green tree, what may be expected in the dry? If Massachusetts thus misspelled the name of one of her best colonial families, the name of one of her Revolutionary generals, of two governors and of many judges and members of her Legislature, there can be little wonder that on the frontier the name was occasionally misspelled. Those have disquieted themselves in vain who have striven to establish theories of their own based upon variant spellings of the name of the president's ancestors.

The name Lincoln is first a place-name, and then, by its application to residents in that place, a family name. It goes back to the days of Roman occupation of England, and shares with Cologne on the Rhine the honor of being one of the two names that preserve the Latin abbreviation for "colonia," or colony. "Lind-colonia" by successive abbreviations became Lincoln; the silent letter *l* is reminiscent of this derivation. The family of Lincoln presumably originated in the County of Lincoln, but that is too far remote for any accurate knowledge.

There is some reason to believe that the American Lincolns are descended from those of that name who, in the seventeenth century, lived in Hingham, England; and in the faith that this was true, a bust of Abraham Lincoln was dedicated in the old church in that English village as the World War was drawing to a close. The orator who represented the United States on that occasion was no other than the American ambassador to the court of St. James, the Honorable John W. Davis, and his speech, as printed in the English newspapers, was a good one. The question upon which the connection depends is: was Samuel Lincoln, who came to New England in 1637, sailing from Yarmouth April eighth, arriving in Boston, June twentieth, and after a brief residence with his employer Francis Lawes in Salem, making his home in Hingham, Massachusetts, the same Samuel who was baptized in Hingham, Old England, Sunday, August 24, 1622? If so, he would have been fifteen years of age when he reached New England, assuming that he was baptized within a few days after his birth. But Samuel Lincoln who came over with Francis Lawes in 1637 gave his age as eighteen, and when he died in 1690 his age was given as seventy-one. We can not very well believe that his baptism was postponed four years, for it was the custom of his father, Edward Lincoln, to appear at somewhat regular intervals at the old Hingham church with a baby for baptism, and he did so appear on March 28, 1619, with a son Daniel. This practically forbids our believing that Samuel was born to the same parents in that same year.

However, there is one possibility that must be reckoned with. Samuel Lincoln, being only fifteen, but apprenticed to an employer who wanted to take him to America and Samuel himself greatly desiring to go, may have marked his age up a matter of four years in fear lest his youth should cause his refusal, or in desire that he might earlier reach his majority in the freedom of the new world. I should like to accept this as the case; for there is considerable reason to believe that the Lincolns of Hingham in the new world came from Hingham in the old world.* It is but fair to state, however, that the hypothesis of misrepresentation of his own age by Samuel Lincoln does not solve the difficulty, which involves a longer genealogical discussion than is here practicable, and with no sure answer to the question.

Whatever uncertainty attaches to the English lineage, the first American ancestor of Abraham Lincoln, in the male line, was Samuel Lincoln. He was born in England, apprenticed as a weaver, and came to Salem, Massachusetts, June 20, 1637. He died in Hingham, Massachusetts, May 26, 1690, aged seventy-one. He married in America, before 1650, Martha, whose surname is unknown. She died April 10, 1693. Samuel and Martha Lincoln became the parents of eleven children, of whom eight survived them. Their fourth child, Mordecai, was born at Hingham, Massachusetts, June 14, 1657, and died November 8, 1727, aged seventy.

Mordecai Lincoln was an iron founder. He married Sarah Jones, daughter of Abraham Jones, of Hull. She died before February 17, 1701-2, on which date he took a second wife. It is probably through Sarah's father that the name Abraham became prominent in the Lincoln family.

The eldest son of Mordecai Lincoln and his wife Sarah Jones was Mordecai Lincoln, who was born in Hingham, Massa-

---

*Lea and Hutchinson, in their *Ancestry of Lincoln*, have accepted and made popular the theory of the rise of the Lincoln family in Hingham in England, and it is upon their authority that the bust was erected in 1919. Waldo Lincoln, in his new *History of the Lincoln Family*, is skeptical about it. I should be the more glad to believe that Lea and Hutchinson were right in this particular, because I have found them wrong in so many other matters.

chusetts, April 24, 1686, and removed before 1710 to Monmouth County, New Jersey. Like his father, he was an iron founder. He married before 1714, Hannah, daughter of Richard and Sarah (Bowne) Salter, of Freehold, New Jersey. He died May 12, 1736.

The eldest son of Mordecai and Hannah was John Lincoln, born May 3, 1716. He was a weaver, and lived in Caernarvon, Lancaster County, and subsequently in Berks County, Pennsylvania. He removed to Virginia about 1768. On July 5, 1743, he married Mrs. Rebecca (Flowers) Morris. Genealogists call him "Virginia John," probably to distinguish him from his nephew John, of Uniontown, Pennsylvania. His Virginia home was in the Shenandoah Valley, in that part of Augusta which is now Rockingham County, eight miles north of the present town of Harrisonburg. President Lincoln believed that his great-grandfather John was a Quaker. This belief was based upon a "vague tradition." In such investigation as I have been able to make, I do not find this tradition confirmed, or that there were any Lincolns who were Quakers, except as members of the Lincoln family now and then intermarried with Quakers, none of them in direct line of Abraham Lincoln. John Lincoln was about fifty-seven years of age when he removed to Virginia He and his wife Rebecca made deeds on August 7, 1773. The precise years of their deaths have but recently been discovered. John died in November, 1788, on Linville Creek, Virginia, and is there buried. His will was probated June 22, 1789. His widow, Rebecca, died July 20, 1806.

The eldest son of John and Rebecca Lincoln was Abraham Lincoln, the Kentucky pioneer, grandfather of the president. He was born in Berks County, Pennsylvania, May 13, 1744. As a young man he accompanied his father to Virginia, and from him, August 12, 1773, obtained a grant of two hundred acres of land on Linville Creek, in Augusta, now Rockingham County. He was a captain of Virginia Militia during the Revolution, but it is uncertain whether he saw active military service in that war.

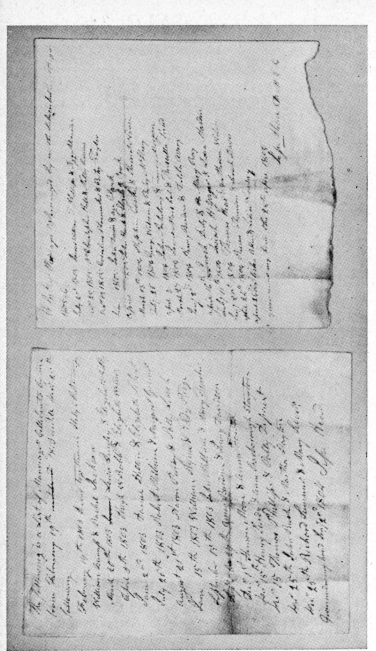

MARRIAGE RETURNS OF REVEREND JESSE HEAD

Immediately preceding and following that in which the Lincoln marriage is recorded
Discovered at Springfield, Kentucky, by the author and Honorable Joseph Polin

I find no record of the church membership of "Virginia John" Lincoln, or of his son Abraham; but Abraham's brother John was one of the most active official members in the Linville Baptist Church, some of whose services were held in the home of their brother, Jacob Lincoln.

The name of Abraham Lincoln's wife has been given in many books as Mary Shipley; and this name having been suggested to her great-grandson, Honorable J. L. Nall, he somewhat hesitatingly accepted it as that of his great-grandmother. He had a dim recollection of her, she having died in 1836, in the home of her daughter, his grandmother, Nancy Brumfield. Later it was discovered that Abraham Lincoln was licensed to marry, January 9, 1770, the name of the bride being omitted. Nicolay and Hay adopted Mr. Nall's view that the name of Abraham Lincoln's wife was Mary Shipley.*

Subsequently it was discovered that Abraham Lincoln had a wife living in 1780 and 1781, whose name was Bathsheba. One school of writers thereafter claimed Mary as the first wife, mother of all his children except Thomas; and a later school, finding this position untenable, advanced the theory that Bathsheba Herring was the first wife and Mary Shipley the second. Both were in error. There was no Mary Shipley Lincoln. The children of Abraham Lincoln had one mother; her name was Bathsheba, probably Bathsheba Herring.

In July, 1776, Daniel Boone's Survey Book entered a memorandum of one thousand acres of land in the name of "Lincoln." This can hardly have been Abraham Lincoln. It is more likely to have been Hannaniah Lincoln.

On March 4, 1780, there were issued to Abraham Lincoln three land warrants, Numbers 3333, 3334 and 3335, each acknowledging receipt of one hundred sixty pounds, and each calling for four hundred acres of land.†

---

*Abraham Lincoln: A History, i, p. 5.

†For information concerning the Virginia Lincolns supplementing my own investigations on the ground, I am indebted to Professor John W. Wayland and Honorable John T. Harris, both of Harrisonburg, Virginia.

The Entry Book of Jefferson County shows these two entries of 1780:

May 29, 1780. Abraham Linkhorn enters four hundred acres of land on Treasury Warrant lying on Floyd's Fork, lying about two miles above Teice's Fork, beginning at a sugar tree S. B. thence east three hundred poles thence north to include a small improvement.

June 7, 1780. Abraham Linkhorn enters eight hundred acres upon Treasury Warrant about six miles below Green River Lick including an improvement made by Jacob Gum and Owen Diver.

On October 12, 1784, an official survey was made of his eight hundred acres of land on Green River, in which survey he assisted, and for which he deposited his two Treasury Warrants 3333 and 3335. His patent was issued May 17, 1787, signed by Beverly Randolph, Lieutenant Governor of Virginia.*

A special interest attaches to the land patented under Treasury Warrant 3334. The original warrant is preserved, and is in the Durrett Collection in the University of Chicago, and there also is full record of the official survey. This was made May 7, 1785, and Abraham Lincoln, the president's grandfather, was present and assisted as a marker. This land is about fifteen miles from Louisville. It is located on Long Run of Floyd's Fork, and lies north and east of the little village of Boston. Most of the farm is situated in Jefferson County, but its eastern end is in Shelby.†

---

*This record is in the Land Office in Frankfort, from which I have certified copy.

†I am indebted to Mr. R. C. Ballard-Thruston, of the Filson Club of Louisville, for a painstaking search of documentary material which, with careful examination of the ground, enabled us to identify beyond question the Lincoln farm, and also the site of Hughes Station. The latter is on the patent of Morgan Hughes, surveyed on the same day as that of Abraham Lincoln, and adjoins it upon the north. Colonel R. C. Durrett located Hughes' Station at the mouth of Long Run, and in this was mistaken. We were accompanied on this expedition by Mr. Hardin Helm Herr, a nephew of Mrs. Abraham Lincoln. Mr. Ballard-Thruston and I have gone over the ground again, gathering up additional data which leaves no doubt of the correctness of our conclusions. On a subsequent visit we were accompanied by Reverend Louis A. Warren, and Mr. Thomas C. Fisher.

Abraham Lincoln's first journey into Kentucky appears to have been in the summer of 1780. He returned to Virginia, and later came again into Kentucky with his family. On December 11, 1780, he entered five hundred additional acres. For some reason the estate of Abraham Lincoln presented to the Nelson County court contained only a list of personal property. The administrators were men of probity, and the land-holdings must have been otherwise accounted for. For some reason, also, the lands that had belonged to Abraham Lincoln before his death were not accounted for in the earlier tax lists of Mordecai Lincoln. He paid taxes on the hundred-acre tract on Beech Fork in Washington County, but this was not an original Lincoln entry; it was purchased apparently by Bathsheba, the original entry having been made by Matthew Walton. This was all the land on which Mordecai paid taxes in his own name in 1792 and 1795. In 1796 he began paying taxes on five additional tracts of land:

400 acres on Floyd's Fork in Jefferson County, entered in the name of Abraham Lincoln.

1134¼ acres on Green River in Hardin County, entered in the name of John Reed.

800 acres on Green River, Lincoln County, entered in the name of Abraham Lincoln.

1000 acres on Kentucky River, Lincoln County, entered in the name of Abraham Bird.

1000 acres on Kentucky River, Lincoln County, entered in the name of Abraham Bird.

This makes a total of 4,334¼ acres.

In the 1799 list, the Jefferson County tract is not listed, though Mordecai did not deed that land to Benjamin Bridges till 1822. Doubtless the reason was that the land was already sold to Bridges under contract, as was the frequent custom, and that Bridges paid the taxes during the interval. The Jefferson County tax lists have been burned.

It should be noted that of the land listed by Mordecai in 1796, two thousand acres in Lincoln County, entered by Abraham

Bird, probably had not belonged to Abraham Lincoln. We are able to account for the four hundred acres on Floyd's Fork and the eight hundred on Green River, and the John Reed land is that about which the lawsuit occurred some years later.

The total land holdings of Captain Abraham Lincoln, therefore, would appear to have been 2,334¼ acres.*

The narrative of the death of the pioneer Lincoln was often rehearsed by his son Thomas in the presence of his own son Abraham, whose account of it is thus preserved for us by his associate:

The story of his death in the sight of his youngest son Thomas, then only six years old, is by no means a new one to the world. In fact, I have often heard the president describe the tragedy as he had inherited the story from his father. The dead pioneer had three sons, Mordecai, Josiah and Thomas, in the order named. When the father fell, Mordecai, having hastily sent Josiah to the neighboring fort after assistance, ran into the cabin, and pointing his rifle through a crack between the logs, prepared for defense. Presently an Indian came stealing up to the dead father's body. Beside the latter sat the little boy Thomas. Mordecai took deliberate aim at a silver crescent which hung suspended from the Indian's breast, and brought him to the ground. Josiah returned from the fort with the desired relief, and the savages were easily dispersed, leaving behind one dead and one wounded.†

It is of interest to inquire, where did this tragedy occur? Both Washington and Jefferson Counties claim the site of Captain Abraham Lincoln's death. Washington County advances as its proof the fact that the family are found living there very soon after the pioneer's death, and also that his estate was administered in Nelson County, from which Washington was subsequently formed. But the Nelson and Washington County records contain no evidence that Abraham ever owned land or lived in that coun-

---

*Mr. Warren thinks that Abraham Lincoln died possessed of 5,468 acres, including the Abraham Bird land. His conclusions are usually correct, but I have not found so large a total. In any event, the five thousand pounds of depreciated Virginia currency proved adequate for the purchase of a vast amount of Kentucky land, which was then almost incredibly cheap.

†Herndon's *Lincoln*, 1st ed., i: pp. 9, 10.

ty. On the other hand, it is certain that he owned land on Long Run, with an improvement, which was almost certainly a cabin. There is not known to have been any fort near enough to the land subsequently owned by the Lincolns in Washington County to have met the requirements of the situation.

I have been shown two additional alleged sites of the death of the pioneer Lincoln, one in Hardin County, which may be dismissed without comment, and the other in the heart of the city of Louisville. The latter calls for a moment's attention, because it appears to rest on good authority. It comes direct from Honorable J. L. Nall, of Carthage, Missouri, grandson of Nancy Lincoln and William Brumfield, and was first published over his signature in 1881. The account which he gave was specific and detailed, and claimed to have been derived from what he had heard from his mother through her grandmother, the widow of the pioneer Abraham Lincoln. But Mr. Nall was incorrect in this and in very much besides. Captain Abraham Lincoln was not killed within the corporate limits of Louisville.

Among the papers of Colonel Durrett is a sketch of Hughes' Station made by George Rogers Clark, and bearing this note in pencil in Durrett's handwriting:

Bland W. Ballard states that the station was erected by Morgan Hughes in 1780; that it stood on Long Run in Jefferson County not far from the Baptist meeting-house; that it consisted of eight cabins and four block-houses at the four corners, and that it was a weak fort, poorly built. In 1786 a man was killed here by an Indian while he was coming to the Station from his land near by on Long Run where he had been putting in a crop. His family resided in the station, and soon after his death the widow and children moved into Nelson County.

Colonel Durrett added to this note a penciled query whether this man killed might have been the president's grandfather, but subsequently erased it, thinking that that event could not have occurred at so late a date as 1786, since the death of Lincoln seemed to have been fixed two years earlier.

Major Bland W. Ballard relating his narration before the name of Lincoln had become noted or seemed significant, and thinking it unimportant even to learn the name of the man killed, or to record it if he knew, as he probably did, tells the story of the death of this unnamed man almost exactly as we know from other sources the story of the death of Captain Lincoln. It occurred in the spring, when he was putting in his crop; it was near the fort; his family removed to Nelson County, in which was included the present county of Washington. It is no wonder Colonel Durrett raised the question whether it was not the president's grandfather whose death is thus described. But Colonel Durrett believed that the death of Abraham Lincoln occurred in 1784, and Major Ballard was explicit in his affirmation that this murder occurred in 1786. If we knew that the date 1786 was not impossible, we should have no doubt that this description by Major Ballard, together with the testimony of President Lincoln, fixed the place and also gave the date of the tragedy.

The survey of the Long Run tract of May 7, 1785, showed that Abraham Lincoln was certainly alive a full year later than the Lincoln family tradition affirmed. These facts, and a careful survey of the several alleged sites of the tragedy, had convinced me that the real date of the murder of Abraham Lincoln, the pioneer, was 1786, when Reverend Louis A. Warren discovered a further confirmation in a suit of Mordecai, as heir-at-law of his father, in which Mordecai made oath that his father, Abraham Lincoln, died intestate, in May, 1786. The day of the month is not stated.

One other interesting and highly important document may be cited here completing the proof of the location of the home of the pioneer Abraham Lincoln, and the place of his residence at the time of his death. It is a subscription list, dated September 18, 1786, signed by Bland W. Ballard, Morgan Hughes and the other neighbors in the vicinity of Long Run, to arm and equip an expedition against the Indians, the expedition to be commanded by

George Rogers Clark. Most of the subscriptions are in kind, horses, cows, blankets and provisions. Half-way down the list is a gun, appraised at eight pounds, the gift of "the Widow Lincoln"! This document is in the Library of the University of Chicago, and it adds the last essential argument to the proof already cited. We now know where the Lincolns made their first home on the western side of the mountains, and where the tragedy occurred which President Lincoln was accustomed to say impressed him more than any tale he heard during his boyhood. "The Widow Lincoln" did not remove to Washington County, where she had relatives, until she had harvested the pathetic crop which her husband was sowing when he was killed; she was still living on Long Run in September, 1786.

Further investigations in the Hughes' Station neighborhood have resulted in a practical establishment of the site of the Lincoln home upon this Long Run farm, and also of the spring which supplied the water for the family. Unexpectedly, I have discovered also a considerable body of local tradition, which the records of the Long Run Church tend to confirm, as to the probable situation of the grave of the pioneer, Captain Abraham Lincoln.

That he was buried upon his own farm appears almost certain, and that the land now within the enclosure of the Long Run Baptist Church, located on that farm, was the community burying-ground from the beginning of the settlement, appears equally evident. The church was organized in 1797, but the place was used for worship at a date still earlier. The tradition, which is unusually clear and consistent, is to the effect that several of the oldest graves, five at least, were covered by the brick church edifice, on its enlargement in 1860, and that one of these was the grave of Captain Lincoln. It is rather more than probable that the brick building still in use as a place of regular worship by the Long Run Church covers the mortal remains of Captain Abraham Lincoln.

The discovery that Bathsheba Herring was the wife of Abraham Lincoln the pioneer, June 17, 1780, when they signed a deed

to their Virginia land, and September 8, 1781, when she relinquished her dower-rights, was first published by John T. Harris,
Jr., of Harrisonburg, Virginia, in an Open Letter to the *Century Magazine,* for March, 1887, (pp. 810-811).   The fact that
Abraham's wife was then Bathsheba was accepted by Professor
Learned and also by Lea and Hutchinson as affording indubitable evidence that the pioneer Abraham Lincoln was twice married, and they assumed that Bathsheba was his second wife, his
first being Mary Shipley.   Others, of whom the foremost was
Waldo Lincoln, relying upon the Nall tradition that the pioneer
left a widow whose name was believed to have been Mary, held
that there were indeed two marriages of Abraham Lincoln, one
to Mary Shipley and the other to Bathsheba Herring, but that
the order was reversed; that Bathsheba, ill ever since the birth of
her last child in 1780, died as her husband was about to remove
to Kentucky, and that he, needing a mother for his family of
small children, quickly married Mary Shipley.

In the summer of 1922, during a search for material for the
present work, a large quantity of musty papers discovered in the
basement of the old capitol in Frankfort, Kentucky, was ordered
destroyed, but was saved through the intervention of Mrs. Cannon, Secretary of the Kentucky State Historical Society. Among
other documents was found a tax list of Washington County for
1792, in which appeared the name of Bathsheba Lincoln.   She
was assessed on the same day and next in order to Mordecai
Lincoln, and the land stood in his name, as did one of the horses;
but another horse and ten cattle were listed as hers.   Hers also
was a son above sixteen, and under twenty-one, who must have
been Josiah, for Thomas was not then sixteen.

The lists for 1793 have not been discovered, but as this book
goes to press, Mrs. Cannon discovers at Frankfort, in the pile of
old records, the list of 1794.   Therein Bathsheba still is taxed in
Washington County for one horse and ten cattle.   She is recorded as having two sons above sixteen and under twenty-one,
who can be no other than Josiah and Thomas.   Thomas, who

first appears on record under his own name as over sixteen in 1795, and appears again in that class in 1796, disappears in 1797 and 1798, when he must have been in Tennessee, and reappears as above twenty-one in 1799. This gives us one more record of Bathsheba, and narrows down by a year at either end the birth-year of Thomas Lincoln. He was above sixteen in 1794 and above twenty-one in 1799; these dates with those that appear elsewhere confirm the year of his birth already arrived at, as 1778. Bathsheba was still living on Beech Fork, Washington County, and apparently with her eldest son Mordecai, until after February 3, 1801, when she signed her authorization for the marriage of her daughter Nancy or Ann to William Brum-field, Mordecai signing the bond with the prospective bride-groom. Not long afterward she removed to Hardin County to live with her daughter Nancy.

I am indebted to the Honorable L. S. Pence for another inter, esting item. In 1797 a Washington County road is officially described as running from the home of the Widow Lincoln and down the same bank, to the Beech Fork.

These discoveries completely revolutionize all theories hitherto held concerning the alleged two marriages of the pioneer Abra-ham Lincoln. No vestige of proof has been found that his mar-riage in 1770 was not to Bathsheba. She was Abraham's wife in 1780 and 1782 and accompanied him to Kentucky. She it was who wept over his murdered body, and buried it at Long Run, and brought up her fatherless children in Washington County. She it was whom the grandchildren remembered as living to a great age, though not as great as her grandchildren believed, and who died in 1836, and is buried in Mill Creek Cemetery in Hardin County, where she had spent her last years in the home of her daughter, Nancy Brumfield.

The children of Abraham and Bathsheba (Herring) Lincoln were:

(1) Mordecai Lincoln, born about 1771. He married Mary, daughter of Luke Mudd. The certificate of their marriage is at

Bardstown, Kentucky. The ceremony was performed by Reverend William de Rohan, a Roman Catholic priest, and a considerable number of their descendants have been and are of that faith. They had three sons, Abraham, James and Mordecai, and three daughters, Elizabeth, Mary Rowena and Martha. Mordecai, the father, served as sheriff of Washington County, and it is said that he was a member of the Legislature, but this is not true. He removed to Hancock County, Illinois, and died in 1830.

(2) Josiah Lincoln, born about 1773. He married, February 28, 1801, "Caty" or Catherine, daughter of Christopher and Barbara Barlow. From Kentucky he moved to Indiana and died in 1836, leaving two sons, Thomas Lincoln, of Milltown, Indiana, and Jacob, who moved to Missouri, and four daughters.

(3) Mary Lincoln, born in 1775 or 1776, who married Ralph Crume of Nelson County, Kentucky.

(4) Thomas Lincoln, born January 6, 1778, and died January 17, 1851. He married Nancy Hanks, June 12, 1806. They became the parents of Sarah, Abraham and Thomas. The last named died in infancy; the first lived to young womanhood, married and died at the birth of her first child. The second child of Thomas and Nancy was Abraham Lincoln, President of the United States.

(5) Nancy Lincoln, born March 25, 1780; married January 12, 1801, William Brumfield of Washington County, Kentucky, died in Hardin County, Kentucky, October 7, 1843, or October 9, 1845.

It was an honest, virtuous family. In it are to be discovered few brilliant men; but the record is an honorable one all the way from Hingham in New England, and quite possibly from Hingham in Old England, down to Nolin Creek where the most illustrious member of the family was born.

CHAPTER IV

IT was affirmed by Herndon and other of Lincoln's associates that the president was always reticent about his mother's family. Herndon held them in little esteem, and said, in an unpublished letter, that the Hanks family must have been about the lowest family on earth. This was an extreme and harsh judgment. The Hanks family was not of the same social standing as the Lincolns, but it was not a vicious family. It had many respectable members, and was, on the whole, virtuous and law-abiding, though generally shiftless.

Mrs. Caroline Hanks Hitchcock, in a little book entitled *Nancy Hanks,* accords this humble family nothing less than apotheosis. She derived the name from the Egyptian "Ankh," which means "living image," or as she prefers it, "soul." If the tomb of Tut-Ankh-Amen had been discovered when she wrote, she must surely have acclaimed his middle name as proof of his distinguished right to a place among her progenitors. She traced the triumphal march of this regal clan along the Roman roads to Stonehenge, in Druid England, and so to Plymouth Rock and then through Virginia into Kentucky.

The truth is that the Hanks family was not nearly so bad as Herndon affirmed, and not nearly so illustrious as Mrs. Hitchcock declared. The Kentucky branch of it was a poor, thriftless, generally illiterate and highly migratory family, such as constituted a large proportion of the population of the backwoods in the latter part of the eighteenth century.

Benjamin Hanks and his wife Abigail sailed from London about 1699, and landed at Plymouth, Massachusetts. Later they settled at Pembroke, and there eleven of their twelve children were born. Benjamin's wife, Abigail, died in 1725, and he married Mary Ripley, of Bridgewater, and moved to Easton, where his twelfth child, Jacob, was born.

The third child and second son of Benjamin and Abigail Hanks was William, born February 11, 1704. All the other children are later accounted for. They lived in New England and their marriages are of record. William may have died in youth or moved in any direction. Mrs. Hitchcock believed, on what reason does not appear, that he sailed to Virginia and settled near the mouth of the Rappahannock. There, she believed, he became the father of five sons, Abraham, Richard, James, John and Joseph. "All these sons with the exception of John, moved to Amelia County, where they bought large plantations near each other." Of these sons, as she affirmed, the youngest, Joseph, was the father of Nancy Hanks, mother of the president. He was born, as she believed, near the mouth of the Rappahannock, married in Amelia where Nancy was said to have been born, removed to Kentucky and died in Nelson County in 1793. Thus in four generations from Plymouth to the woods of Kentucky, she traced the lineage of Nancy Hanks Lincoln.

With four generations, it is possible to be mistaken in only three transitions, and Mrs. Hitchcock was in error in every one of the three. There was a William Hanks near the mouth of the Rappahannock, though her book did not discover him, and he had a son William; neither of these two Williams was the son of Benjamin Hanks of Plymouth. The alleged Joseph Hanks who sold land in Amelia County in 1747 was not the Joseph who died in Nelson County in 1793. The Joseph Hanks who died in 1793 was not the father of Nancy Hanks, the mother of the president.

This was not the full extent of Mrs. Hitchcock's creative genius. The Hankses in Amelia County, she affirmed, were friends of the Berrys, the Mitchells, the Thompsons and the Lincolns; and each of these families had a marriageable son. In Lunenburg, the second county south, was Robert Shipley, who, as Mrs. Hitchcock for some reason believed, had five marriageable daughters. A son of each of these five families as she declared, rode past the homes of all the girls residing in nearer neighborhoods and each made love to a daughter of Richard Shipley, who distributed his female children among these five notable families. Then, as she affirmed, all these five families, the Lincolns, Hankses, Thompsons, Mitchells and Berrys, moved together into Kentucky where in due time Thomas Lincoln married his first cousin, Nancy Hanks, then resident in the home of her kind Uncle Richard Berry.

Mr. Shipley may have had five daughters, or even ten, five of them wise and five amateur genealogists, but thus far not a scrap of evidence has been adduced to prove that he had even one little ewe lamb of a daughter. The Thompsons and Mitchells were indeed residents of Amelia County, but they have nothing to do with the case. Amelia County is a little south of the middle of Virginia. The Hankses were in the extreme northwest corner of the state; the Berrys, later of Washington County, Kentucky, were in the extreme south portion close to the North Carolina line, and the Lincolns, coming across the pan-handle of Maryland from Pennsylvania, had followed up the Shenandoah and were walled in on both sides by high mountain ranges and separated by long distance from both the Hankses and the Berrys. The United States Census for 1790, including enumerations in 1782 and 1785, contains no name of Lincoln, Berry or Hanks as living in Amelia County. It was vital to Mrs. Hitchcock's story that at least the Hankses should have been resident in that county, but when she got there, the record was bare. Fortune favored her. There were in Amelia County three families of the name of Hawks, a name which, when carelessly written or dimmed by processes of time, resembles that of Hanks. All was fish that came to her net. She was able of these stones to raise up children unto the Hanks family of Massachusetts of which she was a member.

The Hanks family in Virginia has been the despair of genealogists. The family kept no records; generations overlap and names are often repeated. Many of the ordinary sources fail. No record has been discovered of a Hanks holding office in the

militia or in civil life in Colonial Virginia. No Hanks is on
record as receiving land for service in the Revolution or the
French and Indian War. We still are uncertain of the original
immigrant, but this is certain, that he was not a descendant of
Benjamin Hanks, of Plymouth; the Hankses were in Virginia
before Benjamin arrived in Massachusetts. The original immigrant was not the John Hanks shown in the General Index of the
Land Office in Richmond as obtaining a grant in 1767; he was
John Hucks. The progenitor of the president's family may have
been Thomas Hancks, who came over as an indentured servant
of Thomas Fowke, of Westmoreland. He secured a patent for
his free hundred acres in Gloucester County, February 16, 1653,
and ten years later obtained two grants of five hundred and
thirty and five hundred and twenty-seven acres in New Kent
County. He may be presumed to have been the same who, as
Thomas Hankes, on October 8, 1667, obtained three hundred
additional acres. Thus far we have discovered no other Hanks
who obtained land at so early a date. If he lived and left a son,
that son was probably William, of whom we shall presently hear.
We have no record of William's immigration, and if he was born
in Virginia we do not know at this date any other Hanks than
Thomas, who might have been his father. However, later discoveries may disprove this conjectural relationship.

I am able to give, however, and for the first time, the true
story of that branch of the Hanks family from which President
Lincoln descended, beginning the documentary history on Saint
Valentine's Day in 1679, when William Hanks, who may have
been a son of the aforementioned Thomas, became the father of
a son, also named William. The wife of the elder William was
Sarah, who had been a widow named White. She and William
Hanks, Sr., were married about June, 1678. They lived in Rappahannock County, and in that part which in 1692 became Richmond County—not the county in which the city of Richmond
is located, but a rural county, north of the Rappahannock and
toward the Potomac. In 1695, William Hanks, Sr., bought from
William Woodbridge one hundred acres of land called "the In-

dian Town branch," located in the North Farnham Parish, the first certain home of the president's Hanks ancestors in America. There they lived for three generations. William Hanks bought some fourteen additional pieces of land as years went by. He and Sarah had three sons, besides Richard White, son of Sarah by her previous marriage. The eldest son William married, July, 1711, Hester Mills, and had seven children. The second son Luke married about 1718, and his wife Elizabeth bore him three children. Some of their descendants are found later in Western North Carolina, where they form the basis of a stupid story connecting the name of John C. Calhoun with the Lincoln family, and where a monument, based on this foolish myth was erected in 1923 to mark the alleged birthplace of Nancy Hanks, the mother of President Lincoln.*

John Hanks, youngest son of William and Sarah, married, about June, 1714. He and his wife Katherine had nine children. She survived her husband and died apparently in January, 1779. Her second son Joseph was appointed, February first, administrator of her rather good estate.

Joseph Hanks, son of John and Katherine, and great-grandfather of Abraham Lincoln, was born in North Farnham Parish, December 20, 1725. His wife's name was Ann, and he called her Nannie. Her maiden name has not been discovered. Their five sons and four daughters were probably all born in Richmond County, but the only date discovered is the birth of one daughter Betty, March 4, 1771.

The final papers in the estate of Katherine Hanks were filed in 1782. Joseph Hanks probably was there for the final accounting, but some time in 1781, apparently, he collected a portion of the money due him and followed up the valley of the Potomac to Patterson's Creek in the county of Hampshire, which is now in West Virginia. The United States Census of 1790 shows Joseph Hanks resident there in 1782 with a family of eleven, all white. This is precisely the size of his family at that time, and the

---

*For a complete discussion of this tradition, see my *The Paternity of Abraham Lincoln.*

3

census enumerations of all the thirteen colonies having been diligently searched, it is found that not only does this family precisely meet the numerical requirements, but there was not, so far as the census shows, any other Hanks family that approximated this result.

The Patterson Creek Valley was reasonably fertile, and the region still was sparsely settled, the neighborhood of this creek showing in 1782 only thirty-two families, much the smallest of the fifteen lists in Hampshire County. Joseph Hanks was not crowded out. On March 9, 1784, Joseph Hanks mortgaged his farm of one hundred eighty acres to Peter Putnam, a resident of Hampshire County, but not a near neighbor, for twenty-one pounds, nine shillings. This was a pitiful sum. The Lincolns sold their farm for five thousand pounds. To be sure, Virginia money was not quite so badly depreciated in 1784 as in 1780; but why did the Hanks family mortgage their home for a paltry amount of ready cash, abandon it without further deed, and leave Virginia? They had lived there less than three years. They left in 1784. That was the year of Nancy's birth.

The family of Joseph Hanks disappears from Hampshire County records with his mortgage in 1784. The very next year we find his family in Nelson County, Kentucky, and there he resided until his death in 1793.

The will of Joseph Hanks has attained to a distinction which that humble but honest citizen could never have imagined. It has become the corner-stone of a considerable body of literature, and must be quoted in full. It is preserved at Bardstown, Kentucky:

In the name of God, Amen, I Joseph Hanks of Nelson County State of Kentucky being of sound Mind and Memory, but weak in body and calling to Mind the frailty of all Human Nature do make and Devise this my last Will and Testament in the Manner and Form following To Wit
Item I Give and bequeath unto my Son Thomas one Sorrel Horse called Major.
Item I Give and bequeath unto my son Joshua one Grey Mare called Bonney.

Item I Give and bequeath unto my son William one Grey Horse called Gilbert.

Item I Give and bequeath unto my Son Charles one Roan Horse called Dove.

Item I Give and bequeath unto my Son Joseph one Sorrel Horse called Bald. Also the Land whereon I now live containing one hundred and fifty Acres.

Item I Give and bequeath unto my Daughter Elizabeth one Heifer Yearling called Gentle.

Item I Give and bequeath unto my Daughter Polly one Heifer Yearling called Lady.

Item I give and bequeath unto my daughter Nancy one Heifer Yearling called Peidy.

Item I Give and bequeath unto my Wife Nanny all and Singular my whole Estate during her life, afterwards to be equally divided between all my Children. It is my Will and Desire that the whole of the Property above bequeathed should be the property of my Wife during her Life. And lastly I constitute ordain and appoint my Wife Nanny and my Son William as Executrix and Executor to this my last Will and Testament.

Signed Sealed and Delivered
In Presence of Us this eighth
day January one thousand seven
hundred and ninety three.
Isaac Lansdale
John Davis
Peter Atherton

                                            his
                            Joseph   x   Hanks
                                          mark   (Seal)

At a Court begun and held for Nelson County on Tuesday the fourteenth day of May 1793.

This last Will and Testament of Joseph Hanks dcd was produced in Court and sworn to by William Hanks one of the Excutors therein named and was pro ved by the Oaths of Isaac Lansdale and John Davis subscribing witnesses thereto and Ordered to be Recorded.

                Teste
                    Ben Grayson Co. Ck.

Of the Hanks brothers we need only remind ourselves that Joseph established himself for a time in Elizabethtown and worked as a carpenter with Thomas Lincoln, and that William became the father of John Hanks, who later split rails with Abraham Lincoln. We have much more concern with the Hanks sisters, and with the family into which two of them married.*

Where was this first Kentucky home of little Nancy Hanks? Not in Washington County, certainly, where the Hankses never lived, but in Nelson, an immense county, which since has been diminished in area by the erection of several other counties. Joseph's will was probated in Nelson County; and it was within Nelson County, even within its present restricted borders, though just across from Larue, that Joseph Hanks died and little Nancy shed tears, alas, not the first bitter tears of her childhood, beside his grave.

The Joseph Hanks farm was part of an entry of one thousand acres by Joseph Barnett, October 3, 1783. This passed to John Lee, who, on February 28, 1787, made a contract to sell one hundred fifty acres of it to Joseph Hanks "as soon as deed can be obtained from Joseph Barnett." Apparently the deed was never made. A year after the death of the elder Joseph Hanks, his son and namesake assigned his interests to his brother William, and went back to Virginia. William Hanks traded it to Joseph Nevett. William is the only Hanks who had land on a Virginia patent, his entry being June 12, 1784, for one thousand acres of land on Rough Creek in Grayson County, which he paid for in whole or in part by an exchange of his interest in the land which his father had held by a precarious title on Rolling Fork. Some years afterward, Joseph Hanks having returned from Virginia, and his assignment to William being of doubtful legality, he quit-claimed his title to the farm "for a chunk of an old horse that would of traded for about $15." This is the lordly domain about which

---

*Miss Tarbell in her recent book, *Following the Footsteps of the Lincolns,* gives in some detail, and in entire good faith, the methods by which Mrs. Hitchcock is supposed to have obtained information of the Hanks family through two of its Illinois branches, the descendants of Joseph in Adams County and the descendants of William in Macon County. I also am acquainted with representatives of these two branches of the Hanks family, and they are very good people. I will venture the opinion that in matters relating to their family history back of the third generation, they obtained more information from Mrs. Hitchcock, such as it was, than they were able to give to her.

Mrs. Hitchcock writes, where the Hankses and their illustrious cousins went merrily hunting and fishing and hawking in right royal fashion.

In the rotunda of the new capitol building at Frankfort stands a fine bronze statue of Abraham Lincoln. One day a Kentucky farmer entered the building and regarded the statue with particular interest. The custodian spoke to him, and the visitor said that Lincoln was a cousin of his; he gave his own name as Sparrow. A reporter for a Frankfort paper, short of material for his column of political and legislative gossip, made note of the incident. I was in Frankfort a few days later, doing research work in the library of the Kentucky Historical Society, and my attention was called to the paragraph by the Secretary of the Society. I had visited Kentucky many times, and had traversed repeatedly the area inhabited by the Lincoln family, and had never encountered a Sparrow. So far as I am aware, no other Lincoln biographer had ever interviewed one of Lincoln's relatives of that name.*

But there was something of deeper interest in the incident. This man knew himself to be related to Lincoln. How did he know it? Through what connection did he trace his own more or less remote cousinship? Was it possible that the Sparrows had any considerable body of consistent tradition, any possible record, bearing on the life-story of Abraham Lincoln? Where were these Sparrows? How had they managed to keep themselves so long in hiding?

---

*For invaluable assistance in the making of this chapter, I am indebted to Mrs. Jouett Taylor Cannon, Secretary of the Kentucky State Historical Society; to Honorable William H. Townsend of Lexington, whose birthplace was in Anderson County, and who visited his old neighbors, the Sparrows, on my behalf, and subsequently took me there and introduced me to them; and to the Misses Mary and Martha Stephenson, of Harrodsburg. Miss Mary has dug deep in old records of Mercer County, recovering for me the marriage bonds and other records of the entire first generation of the Sparrows, and her sister, Miss Martha, like Mary, has chosen the good part. Records that had not seen the light for a century have been discovered. By the courtesy of Honorable Ben Casey Allin, County Judge, I have been permitted to reproduce these records in photostat. I was able subsequently to visit the Sparrow family in person, and later to make still another journey to the region of their first settlement in Kentucky.

The answer proved a simple one, the Sparrows had hidden from the biographers by staying where they were. Less migratory than the Lincolns and the Hankses, the Sparrows still cultivate the soil which the pioneers of their name wrested from the wilderness. A virtuous legislature, bent upon making two Democratic counties where formerly there was one, cut off that portion of Washington which adjoined Anderson and contained a heavy Republican population that occasionally enabled the entire county to go Republican. This section had originally belonged to Mercer, and was that in which the Sparrows resided. The Republican vote of this section was easily absorbed by the heavy Democratic majority of Anderson, where it is never considered worth while to nominate a Republican ticket. The happy result is that both counties are now "safe for Democracy." That part of Anderson County is known as the "cut-off." It is remote from the railroads, and is a picturesque and reasonably fertile section of Kentucky.

If it were determined to gather in one place as many as possible of the blood relations of Abraham Lincoln in the shortest possible time, the place of their most expeditious assembly would be the old New Liberty Church, formerly known as the Sparrow Union. On the Sunday observed as Memorial Day in 1923 and again in 1924, perhaps a thousand people gathered there for the decoration of the graves of the soldiers, a majority of them Confederate, but a number of them Union, buried in the adjacent burial-ground.* Of those one thousand people, some of them inside the old but well-preserved, weatherboarded, log meeting-house, and the rest under the spreading oak trees, perhaps five hundred were related to Abraham Lincoln.

When, in that part of the county, a man named Sparrow is arrested, a matter of infrequent occurrence, for the Sparrows generally are law-abiding, religious people, it is impossible to secure a jury not related to the defendant; a change of venue is

---

*In the South, Decoration Day is celebrated on Sunday; and other graves than those of soldiers receive this beautiful annual tribute.

therefore taken to some part of the county where the Sparrows have nested less abundantly, and a man of that name can be tried before a jury not composed of his own cousins.

The Sparrow neighborhood is at least sixteen miles from the county-seat, Lawrenceburg, and has its own local column in the county paper, the *Anderson News*. I have seen copies of this interesting periodical, containing a half column or more of local news, births, marriages, and week-end visits, and most of them related to the doings of one family. One such issue contained twenty items, and every one of the twenty named one or more members of the Sparrow family.

These Sparrows are intelligent, honest and capable people, living on their own farms, and living reasonably well. They are much inbred, and show, as far as I have noted, no signs of physical or intellectual deterioration. I have met one strong, erect young man of twenty-one who is descended by four distinct lines from the grandmother of Abraham Lincoln. I have met also a husband and wife, both of them first cousins of Abraham Lincoln.

These people have read few if any books about Lincoln. They know nothing about any controversies concerning his parentage. They have not seen or communicated with the Hankses for a hundred years. They have never been interviewed, except for this work. But as soon as they are asked about their family connections, they tell their direct and consistent story; they all know themselves to be related to Abraham Lincoln, and they know how that relationship exists. If they produce a shoe-box full of family portraits, there is a picture of Lincoln among them. It belongs there; he is of their kin.

The family Bibles of these people go back to where they join to official records in Anderson and Mercer Counties, and the records confirm the traditions.

Here is an invaluable body of testimony, never before discovered.

The Hankses and the Sparrows were intimately related, and Nancy Hanks, the president's mother, was oftener called Sparrow than Hanks. A knowledge of the Sparrows is necessary to our knowledge of the Hankses and the Lincolns. What is there to be known about them? The records are surprisingly clear, and of considerable importance.

With much labor I have discovered the nest of the Sparrows in Mecklenburg County, Virginia, and, as has often been the case, I have found an embarrassment of riches. For I wanted one James Sparrow, and I found a James Sparrow and a James R. Sparrow and a James B. Sparrow and a James Bowling Sparrow and a James Bowling and a James W. Sparrow. There were two families of these Sparrows, James Wright Sparrow and James Bowling Sparrow, cousins, being the respective fathers. James Wright Sparrow's middle name, Wright or Right, or initial W. or R., as the spelling might be preferred, appears not to have been used except when necessary to distinguish between him and James Bowling Sparrow. The census of 1790 gives us James B. Sparrow with a family of eight and James R. Sparrow with a family of ten, all white. Either family is large enough for our requirements, but the one that chiefly concerns us is James Wright Sparrow. The two families are both missing from Virginia after 1788, and almost immediately we find them both in Mercer County, Kentucky. At first their home was in the extreme southern part of Mercer County as it then was constituted, in what is now Boyle County. Their land was on the waters of Chaplain's Fork, toward Doctor's Fork, and not very far from the battle-field of Perryville.

James Sparrow died in Mercer County, Kentucky, in 1789. His will is of record thus:

The noncupative will of James Sparrow, Decd., was produced in Court, Oct. 27, 1789, in the words and figures following:
In the name of God, Amen, I james Sparrow of Mercer County, Caintucky, and province of Virginia, being of perfect mind and memory, do make this my last Will Testament and dispose of what little afects God has blessed me with in Mercer following, that is to say lawful Debts to be paid faithfully discharged out

of my personal estate to my well beloved wife. I leave the rest of my personal estate to rease the childering and support herself and my land is to be divided first One hundred for my eldest son hendry, then the other three hundred to be divided equally to the other fore sons, Thomas, James, Peter and Dinny Sparrow. This is my last will and Testament here given under my hand this 18th day of May 1789.

And the same was proved by the oaths of Josiah Campbell, Henry Sparrow, and Judith Sparrow and Susannah Campbell to be the noncupative will of the said James Sparrow Deceased and ordered to be recorded.

This James Sparrow who died in 1789 in Mercer County was James W. or James R. Sparrow, formerly of Mecklenburg County, Virginia, where the parents of Henry Sparrow were living when the latter was born in 1765, and where Henry was living when he enlisted in the Revolutionary War in the spring of 1781. Henry was twenty-four years of age when his father died, and, as the will affirms, he was the eldest son. On his father's death, Henry became the head of the family, and when Biddy, or Bridget, was married to John Daniel, by the Reverend John Bailey, March 5, 1790 (bond March 2, 1790) Henry signed as "Guardian." His mother's name was Mary, and she lived for some years after the death of her husband. The son, James, died, and it must have been his wife, "Nancy Sparrow, widow," who in 1800 married John Elliott. We are chiefly concerned with Henry and Thomas.

In 1872, Ward Hill Lamon, in his *Life of Lincoln,* gave the first real information concerning the antecedents of Nancy Hanks. He gave it bluntly, and unsympathetically, but he did it truthfully:

Nancy Hanks was the daughter of Lucy Hanks. Her mother was one of four sisters—Lucy, Betsy, Polly and Nancy. Betsy married Thomas Sparrow; Polly married Jesse Friend, and Nancy, Levi Hall. Lucy became the wife of Henry Sparrow, and the mother of eight children. Nancy the younger was early sent to live with her uncle and aunt, Thomas and Betsy Sparrow.

Nancy, another of the four sisters, was the mother of that Dennis F. Hanks whose name will be frequently met with in the course of this history. He also was brought up, or permitted to come up, in the family of Thomas Sparrow, where Nancy found a shelter.*

Lamon was not loved for this statement, but no one was prepared to deny it. When it was known that John G. Nicolay and John Hay, former secretaries of Abraham Lincoln, were engaged upon a *Life of Lincoln,* not a few readers waited with keen interest for their version of this story. The work which they produced ran for several years through the pages of the *Century* magazine, and was then published in ten thick volumes. It is a work which will be of permanent value to the Lincoln student. But it suffers marked limitations, one of which is the fact that it was written under the blue-pencil of Robert Todd Lincoln. He furnished his father's two secretaries with his father's official and private papers on condition that he should see and approve whatever they were to print. After some years of hard labor, the first part of the work was sent to Mr. Lincoln with this letter from John Hay, which is eloquent as to the feeling under which the two secretaries had done their work:

Cleveland, Ohio, January 27, 1885.

Dear Bob:—

Nicolay tells me he has laid before you or is about to do so, the first volumes of our history, containing the chapters in which I have described the first forty years of your father's life. I need not tell you that every line has been written in a spirit of reverence and regard. Still you may find here and there words and sentences which do not suit you. I write now to request that you will read with a pencil in your hand, and strike out everything to which you object. I will adopt your view in all cases, whether I agree with it or not.†

That Robert T. Lincoln made corrections, the later letters show, but even if he never made any, the work was produced

---

*Lamon: *Life of Lincoln,* p. 12.

†*Life and Letters of John Hay,* by William Roscoe Thayer, ii, pp. 24-25.

under the possibility of his doing so, and the authors had this fact constantly in mind.

What did Nicolay and Hay say on this delicate subject, knowing that for every idle word they would have to give account to Robert T. Lincoln?

They repeated the Lamon statement, but with less of detail. They named Nancy Hanks' mother, Lucy, and in the same sentence named her sisters and her sisters' husbands, grouping the sisters first and the husbands in a following clause. The paragraph so ended that the casual reader might hardly be expected to sort out and pair off the sisters and their husbands, or to notice that nothing was said of Lucy's husband, while, on the other hand, no critic could charge the authors with evading, or misrepresenting the unpleasant fact. Seldom in all his career did John Hay better illustrate his diplomatic skill, while preserving his complete regard for the truth:

Mrs. Lincoln's mother was named Lucy Hanks; her sisters were Betty, Polly and Nancy, who married Thomas Sparrow, Jesse Friend and Levi Hall. The childhood of Nancy was passed with the Sparrows, and she was oftener called by their name than her own. The whole family connection was composed of people so little given to letters that it is hard to determine the proper names and relationships of the younger members amid the tangle of traditional cousinships.*

We may assure ourselves that no paragraph in the entire ten volumes cost John Hay more thought than this one, or was reviewed with more care by John G. Nicolay. Nor can there have been any paragraph over which the newly sharpened pencil of Robert T. Lincoln was longer or more thoughtfully poised.

But it was approved by him in January, 1885, and it was published in the *Century* in November, 1886; and when the ten volumes appeared, it was not changed. It is certainly to the credit of John Hay, as it is also to that of Robert T. Lincoln,

Abraham Lincoln: A History, i, p. 24.

that no attempt was made to disguise this unpleasant truth. They were disposed not to make it prominent, but they were both too honorable to deny or omit it.

No one can imagine that Robert T. Lincoln enjoyed that paragraph, but it was true, and he knew it, and it was stated as delicately, perhaps as vaguely, as so bald a fact could be stated.

And that is where it ought to have been left. I did not covet the task which has been thrust upon me by those who, some of. them having a zeal without knowledge and concerning others of whom something not so gentle would need to be said, have undertaken to establish a wholly different story.

That story is based upon the fact that Joseph Hanks, in his will, names three of these sisters but does not mention a daughter Lucy; and even Waldo Lincoln, in his new *History of the Lincoln Family* affirms that her existence has not been proved.* It is necessary now to prove it.

The simple question involved, is, was Nancy Hanks, the president's mother, the daughter or the granddaughter of Joseph Hanks? President Lincoln answered this question in his campaign biography furnished to John Locke Scripps in 1860. Writing of his flat-boat journey to New Orleans in 1831, with John Hanks, he said:

He is the same John Hanks who now engineers the "rail enterprise," at Decatur, and is a first cousin of Abraham's mother.

John Hanks was born February 9, 1802, and died July 12, 1890, being the son of William and Elizabeth (Hall) Hanks and the grandson of Joseph and Ann Hanks.† If the president's mother had been a daughter of Joseph Hanks, she would have been John Hanks's aunt, and not his first cousin.

Again brief reference must be made to a little book entitled *Nancy Hanks,* by Mrs. Caroline Hanks Hitchcock. That book

---

History of the Lincoln Family, p. 340.

†Elizabeth Hall, who married William Hanks, was a sister of Levi Hall who married Nancy Hanks. Their father was James Hall, and when he died their mother married Caleb Hazel, Lincoln's teacher.

announced that its author had prepared a complete genealogy of the Hanks family, which was soon to appear. That was twenty-five years ago. The genealogy has not appeared, and Mrs. Hitchcock did not possess in 1899, and does not possess, material for a complete and trustworthy work of that character. Miss Ida M. Tarbell furnished the Introduction to Mrs. Hitchcock's book, and proclaimed that Mrs. Hitchcock had forever removed the stain which wicked men had cast upon the lineage of Lincoln's mother.

Ten years went by, and James Henry Lea had ready for publication the results of J. R. Hutchinson's investigations into Lincoln's English lineage, and his own inquiries into the American line. But of the Hankses he knew little, if anything, except what he learned from Mrs. Hitchcock. Some of her conclusions staggered him, but he had no other source of information, so he accepted all he could, then shut his eyes and accepted some more. The results of his attempt to combine truth and Mrs. Hitchcock's story are painfully evident, as he is now and then driven to bigamy.

Laying to one side Mrs. Hitchcock's little book, let us find our material in the more formal work of Lea and Hutchinson:

Robert Shipley, an Englishman, is said on the authority of Mrs. C. H. Hitchcock, to have come to America about the middle of the eighteenth century and to have settled in Lunenburg County, Virginia. He was probably the father of two sons, Robert Shipley, Jr., and Edward Shipley. There were also five daughters, who do not appear in the Virginia records. . . .

Mary Shipley married Abraham Lincoln, of Rockingham County, Virginia, before 1763, and died in Virginia before 1779. . . .

Lucy Shipley married Richard Berry, of Rockingham County, Virginia, who removed to Kentucky about 1789, and lived at Beechland, near Springfield, Washington County. They were the foster parents of the orphaned Nancy Hanks, whose legal guardian Richard Berry became, and from whose home she was married to Thomas Lincoln, he becoming the surety on the marriage bond. It is this Aunt Lucy—Berry, not Hanks—who was mistaken by the first hasty historians as the mother, Lucy Hanks, and so helped to give credence to the foul fable of false birth so industriously fomented by the enemies of the president. . . .

Sarah Shipley married Robert Mitchell, who removed to Kentucky in 1789. . . .

Elizabeth Shipley married Thomas Sparrow. They removed with the rest of the family to Kentucky and settled in Washington County. In 1817 they rejoined Thomas and Nancy (Hanks) Lincoln at Gentryville, Indiana, where both parents succumbed to a fatal malarial epidemic in October, 1818, having had a daughter Nancy Sparrow (confused with Nancy Hanks by some of the earlier biographers) who married Charles Friend, brother of Jesse Friend, who married Polly Hanks, daughter of Joseph. Charles and Nancy (Sparrow) Friend were the parents of the irresponsible and unreliable Dennis Friend, one of the President's youthful associates, who, assuming the name of Dennis Hanks, did much to complicate the already difficult problem of the Hanks genealogy, which the mendacity of his declining years still further confused.*

There is at least one true statement in the foregoing, which is that the five daughters of Robert Shipley do not appear in the Virginia records. There is also another true statement, which is that Polly Hanks married Jesse Friend. She is the only one of the four Hanks sisters who has been permitted to live with her own lawful wedded husband in the biography of the last twenty-five years. Polly, or Mary, Hanks and Jesse Friend were married in Hardin County, December 10, 1795, by Reverend Josiah Dodge, and no one disputes that date.

We have no concern with the Mitchell family, who think they trace a Shipley ancestry through a middle letter "S" in one of their family names, and who may or may not be correct in their conjecture that their ancestor Robert Mitchell married a woman named Shipley.

All the rest of the foregoing genealogy so far as it relates to Lincoln, is false, and the original inventors of it must have

---

*The Ancestry of Abraham Lincoln, pp. 105-108, passim.

known that it was false. Mary Shipley, if there was any such woman, did not marry Abraham Lincoln. Lucy Shipley did not marry the Richard Berry of this genealogy; his wife was Rachel. That same Richard Berry did not sign Thomas Lincoln's marriage bond; he had been dead eight years. It was his son who signed the bond, and his wife was not Lucy Shipley but Polly Ewing. Elizabeth Shipley did not marry Thomas Sparrow, and Thomas Sparrow and his wife did not have any children, and the mother of Dennis Hanks was not Nancy Sparrow Friend. But just here we find one other true statement: Dennis Hanks was the son, albeit the illegitimate son, of Charles Friend; and he concealed the name of his father from even the close cross-questioning of William H. Herndon, who thus wrote concerning him:

Dennis Hanks, still living (1889) at the age of ninety years in Illinois, was the son of another Nancy Hanks—the aunt of the president's mother. I have his written statement that he came into the world through nature's back door. He never stated, if he knew it, who his father was.*

The people who invented this Shipley genealogy for the glorification of the Hanks family found out who Dennis Hanks's father was, and learned the truth. I have a signed and sworn statement from Charles Friend, grandson of the original Charles Friend, attesting this relationship, and I have similar documents from grandsons of Dennis Hanks, and a further affidavit, made in 1892 by the Hall family when they sold the Lincoln cabin at Farmington for exhibit at the World's Fair, which shows their relationship to the family; for this Nancy Hanks, the daughter of Joseph, after the birth of Dennis, married Levi Hall. We have this relationship trebly attested by the Hankses, the Friends and the Halls. And now the question arises, how did the originators of this piece of fiction learn who was the father of Dennis Hanks and not learn who was his mother? The answer is that they did learn, and that they deliberately invented another moth-

---

*Herndon's *Lincoln*, i, 13.

er, and another grandmother, and a false marriage to conceal the truth.

Both Lea and Hutchinson and Miss Tarbell are guiltless of intentional wrong in this matter, though they erred sadly in broadcasting misinformation which they had not investigated; and I do not think Mrs. Hitchcock invented it. I do not know who was the original and responsible prevaricator, though I might possibly entertain a conjecture concerning persons no longer living; but this I know, and the knowledge has cost me much labor, that this fabric of falsehoods could not have originated innocently.

There is not room in this chapter for the laborious and complicated investigation which I have been compelled to make. This is the sum of it:

Joseph Hanks had four daughters, one more than was mentioned in his will.

The Nancy who was therein named was not the president's mother, but her aunt, who on May 15, 1799, gave birth to Dennis Hanks, the father being Charles Friend.*

She subsequently married Levi Hall and became the mother of a family still resident partly in Illinois and partly in Missouri. Levi and Nancy Hall migrated to Indiana just in time to be carried off by the same epidemic that took away Nancy Hanks Lincoln and her other aunt and uncle, Thomas and Elizabeth Hanks Sparrow.†

It was regarded as highly important for the purposes of the inventors of this genealogy to discredit Dennis Hanks, and rid

---

*Charles Friend was responsible for the sorrow also of a Nancy Riley, who on February 8, 1803, caused his arrest for the paternity of her bastard son, born November 7, 1802. He later married (November 19, 1804) Sallie Huss, daughter of Edward Huss, and joined the Little Mount Baptist Church, and there is buried.

†There are five graves in the enclosure with the Nancy Hanks monument in the State Park near Lincoln City. They were identified on the testimony of Dennis Hanks. He was not taken to the spot, but described it with quite remarkable accuracy, saying that his mother and her husband, Nancy and Levi Hall, his foster-parents, Thomas and Elizabeth Sparrow, and his cousin, Nancy Hanks Lincoln, were buried in a group of five graves apart from the others in the little cemetery.

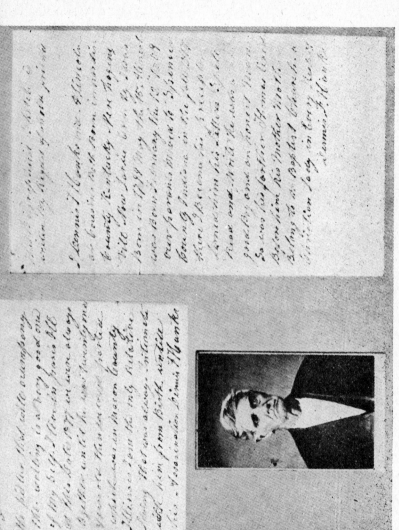

DENNIS F. HANKS

Portrait and autobiographical sketch photographed for this work

the noble Hanks family of so troublesome a member. Even Waldo Lincoln in his recent book tells us that "Dennis Hanks appears to have gone out of his way to calumniate both Nancy and her husband."* I find no evidence of this. Dennis could lie a little when necessary, but as a liar he was not in the same class with the people who gave to Mrs. Hitchcock her ready-to-wear genealogy.

These gifted inventors could not stop with the results above cited. They must at all hazards get rid of the Nancy Hanks who was named in Joseph Hanks's will in order to short-circuit one generation and move the president's mother into that place as the heiress of the pied heifer. Their first step was to create a new mother for Dennis Hanks; their next was to provide a new wife for Levi Hall:

Elizabeth Hanks (Betsy) married Levi Hall, brother of Elizabeth Hall, wife of William Hanks, removed to Spencer County, Indiana, soon after her brothers and sister, Nancy Lincoln, and died shortly and buried beside them. They had three children: 1. Squire Hall, married Matilda Johnson, daughter of Daniel and Sarah (Bush) Johnston, and had nine children; 2. William Hall, married Mary Ann Hanks, daughter of Joseph and Mary (Young) Hanks; 3. James Hall, married Caroline Hanks, sister of the last named.†

It is difficult to carry through so elaborate a scheme of invention and not collide with a fact; and it is not strange that six pages later this record is contradicted, and Elizabeth appears wedded to her own proper husband, a clear case of literary bigamy. The Hitchcock story breaks down of its own weight. We will dwell no longer on Nancy, the wife of Levi Hall, but pass on to discover the true husband of Elizabeth.

Deep down in the dust of old records in Mercer County we have the proof we seek. The marriage bond of Thomas Sparrow

*History of the Lincoln Family, p. 338.
†The Ancestry of Abraham Lincoln, p. 122.

and Elizabeth Hanks bears date of October 17, 1796. And that disposes of several falsehoods.

And now we come to the crux of the whole matter, the existence and character and life history of Lucy Hanks. There was such a woman, the eldest daughter of Joseph Hanks, the mother of Nancy Hanks, the mother of President Lincoln. The reason she is not named in her father's will is that he disinherited her. But was the moral standard of the Hanks family so high that Joseph Hanks, an old man on the verge of eternity, should have refused to forgive his eldest daughter for an offense committed many years before? For Lucy Hanks gave birth to her daughter Nancy in 1784, and Nancy was nine years old when her grandfather died in 1793.

No; the standard of the Hanks family was not so high as that; and no family should have a standard of that character. But the birth of Nancy was not the last time that Lucy caused her parents anxiety; and though she had been married two years, and was behaving like a perfect lady in 1793 when her father died, and though her brothers and sisters had become reconciled to her and continued on terms of friendship becoming their relation, Joseph Hanks did not forget the sorrows of those seven years between the birth of Nancy and the marriage of Lucy. Only three daughters are named in the will of Joseph Hanks. Joseph Hanks did not forget her. To each of his other daughters he gave a heifer; but he did not mention Lucy.

Lucy Hanks was born in Virginia about 1765, and came to young womanhood in the period of license and revolt that accompanied the close of the Revolutionary War. When she was about nineteen, she became the mother of a child, named Nancy. The name of the child's father is unknown, but President Lincoln believed him to have been a planter of standing and unusual ability.*

Lucy must have continued to reside in the home of her parents

---

*The story is told in the much discussed buggy-ride narrative in Herndon, i:3.

after the birth of her little girl, and until some time after the removal to Kentucky. But long before the death of her father and
mother she had left home. Whether her parents turned her out
or she left against their will we do not know. But we do know
that she continued her wayward life.

The early Kentuckians were highly litigious, but most of their
litigation was in civil suits or was concerned with minor cases
of assault and battery or slander. The Grand Jury that met at
the quarterly courts, in which the county magistrates sat *en banc*,
were often hard put to it to earn their *per diem* and mileage, and
usually finished their work in a fraction of a day. There was
one matter which could always be relied upon to furnish them
occupation: the indictment of the road-surveyors. Every grand
juror knew that the supervisor of the road over which he had
ridden to the court-house deserved anything short of hanging.
Having been familiar with those roads for the past forty years,
I vote to sustain the indictments against the road-surveyors. At
one session of the Grand Jury there would have been nothing
else than the roads to occupy its attention save for the misbe-
havior of Lucy Hanks; and I am reluctant to tell about it. But
it is necessary that this story be so told that it shall not have to
be told again.

The record reads:

Mercer Court of Quarter Sessions, November 24, 1789. Lewis
Homes, Joseph Davis, John Berry, David Prewett, James Har-
rod, John Haggin, John Mahan, Geo. Bohannan, John Robinson,
Henry French and Parmeneas Briscoe were sworn a Grand Jury
of inquest for this county, and having received their charge, retired out of court to consult what presentments they could make.

The Grand Jury returned into court, and made the following
presentments, viz:

The surveyor of the road from Harrodsburg to George Buck-
hannon's.

Lucy Hanks for fornication.

The overseer of the road from the county line to Chaplin's
Fork.

And having nothing further to present were discharged.

Ordered that the Clerk issue summonses against these persons this day presented by the Grand Jury.*

There is no record that the sheriff served the summons upon Lucy. On March twenty-third, she not having appeared in court, an alias summons was ordered to be issued.

Still she did not appear. Neither Lucy nor the county officials could ignore the matter much longer. By the May term of court, Lucy must have appeared and been publicly branded with an unpleasant name.

And then—

We have reached an exciting moment in this drama, and we have no orchestra to strike the cymbals or blow the bugles. But there enters quietly upon the stage at this juncture a new and important character, almost a hero.

Henry Sparrow was born in Mecklenberg County, Virginia, October 9, 1765, and was half-way between twenty-three and twenty-four when Lucy Hanks came into unpleasant publicity. He had been a soldier in the Revolutionary War, serving in Captain Thomas Shipp's company of Colonel William Mumford's regiment. He had come with his parents, James W. and Mary Sparrow, from Virginia to Kentucky, and since the death of his father, May 18, 1789, six months before the indictment of Lucy Hanks, had been caring for his widowed mother, his sister and younger brother.

He believed in Lucy, and offered to marry her.

---

*Order Book No. 1, p. 415. I have already referred to the affirmation of my friend, Mr. Waldo Lincoln, that no proof has yet been adduced that such a person as Lucy Hanks existed. Miss Tarbell, in her delightful book, *Following the Footsteps of the Lincolns,* issues this friendly challenge: "If now Doctor Barton can establish beyond dispute the place of Nancy Hanks in her family, he will have relieved future Lincoln biographers of much bewilderment and disgust—but his chain must be faultless." (p. 88). It is partly because of the natural reluctance of these and other friends to give up the Hitchcock story, and because I am warned that nothing short of positive proof will be accepted, that I am compelled to adduce this evidence, which under some circumstances it might not be necessary to print.

On April 26, 1790, Henry Sparrow and his brother-in-law, John Daniel, husband of Biddy Sparrow, rode to the court-house and gave bond for a license of marriage between Henry Sparrow and Lucy Hanks.

No one appeared as Lucy's "guardian" nor was that formality required. John Daniel certified that she was of legal age.

But Lucy herself furnished a certificate.

It is her sole literary monument, on a bit of paper about four by five inches:

I do sertify that I am of age and give my approbation freely for henry Sparrow to git out Lisons this or enny other day.
given under my hand this day
                    Apriel 26th, 1790.
                              Lucey Hanks
        Test:
        Robert Michel
        John bery.

Do not judge her spelling uncharitably. She stumbled over the word "approbation," beginning to spell the last syllable with an *s* but changing it properly to a *t*. The wonder is not that she spelled so badly but that she could do so well. Her father and her brothers could not write, and neither could her husband or any of her husband's brothers; but she wrote with a flourish.

And so the license was duly issued for the marriage of Henry Sparrow and Lucy Hanks.

When, therefore, the County Court of Quarter Sessions assembled for its May term, the following entry was made:

The Commonwealth plaintiff, against Lucy Hanks, deft.
Upon a presentment.
For reason appearing to the court the suit is ordered to be discontinued.

I should like to know, for I do not know, why John Berry was witness to Lucy's consent to the marriage, and why his brother, Richard, sixteen years later, was surety when Lucy's daughter Nancy married Thomas Lincoln. John Berry, who lived and died on Doctor's Fork, in Mercer County, was on the Grand Jury that indicted Lucy, and was evidently concerned that she should not be prosecuted. I do not know why this family was interested in the matter; I know only what the records show.

Now follows an interesting little bit of unwritten history, and he who knows what should be written may write it. Henry and Lucy were not married for nearly a year.

I can imagine Henry's saying to Lucy that, while he had faith in her, it would be well under all the circumstances if she should prove to the community that she could live a single and virtuous life. I can imagine that Lucy herself preferred the postponement, saying that she deeply appreciated the knightly offer of Henry Sparrow, and his act that resulted in the quashing of the indictment against her, but that she wanted to prove to the world that she was worthy of his confidence and to marry as a woman of established and virtuous reputation. I leave it to others to write in this missing page of history. All that I venture to record is that the license was issued April 26, 1790; that the case against Lucy was dismissed on the opening day of the May term of court in the same year, and that, on April 3, 1791, after almost a year of probation in which we have good reason to believe that Lucy remained true, Henry Sparrow and Lucy Hanks were duly married by the Reverend John Bailey, a well-known Baptist preacher.

This is not as pretty a story as that told by Mrs. Hitchcock and the rest; but now we come to the part that is finely well worth telling. Henry Sparrow, who sheltered Lucy behind the protection of his honest name, lived to be assured of the wisdom of his course. Lucy Hanks was a young woman of superior intelligence and unusual strength of character, and she made him a good wife. They became the parents of eight children, James,

ABRAHAM LINCOLN'S LOST GRANDMOTHER
Her one existing autograph. Discovered by the author

Thomas, Henry, George, Elizabeth, Lucy, Peggy and Polly. All these lived to maturity and married and bore children, and their seed are mighty in the earth. They all know that their great- or great-great- or great-great-great-grandfather married Lucy Hanks and that she had a daughter Nancy Hanks, but they have never heard that there was a scandal about it; they suppose that Lucy had been married before. In the days of the Civil War, some of their descendants entered the southern army, but some of them, and among them Henry's son Henry, voted and talked and prayed for the Union and for Henry's nephew, Abraham Lincoln; and Henry was in a position to influence his neighborhood, for he was minister of the Sparrow Union Church.

And this is the happy and rather fine ending of a somber story. Elizabeth Sparrow made a true mother to Nancy, and when there were visits back and forth, as there were, Elizabeth stood in the relation of mother to Nancy, while Lucy was known as her aunt. Lucy soon had her arms full of other children, and she made them a good mother. She brought up her children in honesty and simple virtue. They are industrious, law-abiding, God-fearing people unto this day.

Henry and Lucy lived together as husband and wife about thirty-four years. She died apparently in 1825, aged about sixty. He again married, on bond issued July 31, 1827, Rhoda, sister of Jacob Johnston, and appears to have survived her. In his later years he drew a pension as a Revolutionary soldier, and his last voucher was signed by mark, September 17, 1840.

And Lucy lived so worthily and well that every trace of scandal against her disappeared, and her children rose and her children's children's children still rise, and call her blessed. All her children grew up worthily, and two of them, Henry and James, became ministers of the Gospel.

Let him who has done more for posterity than Lucy Hanks, cast the first stone.

Now we are able to tell the true story of the life of Nancy

Hanks. She was born in 1784 on Mike's Run, a small tributary (the mortgage calls it a "drean" or drain) of Patterson's Creek, in what is now Mineral County, West Virginia. Her family removed in the very year of her birth and settled in Nelson County on Rolling Fork of Salt River, about two miles upstream from the present village of Athertonville, and on the opposite side from where in after years she lived, the wife of Thomas Lincoln, on Knob Creek. There is every reason to suppose that in the early part of the family's residence in Kentucky, she and her mother lived with Nancy's grandparents, Joseph and Ann Hanks. Joseph Hanks, as we know, died in 1793. When, in the following year, Joseph Hanks, Jr., to whom the farm had been left in his father's will, subject to a life use by Ann, the widow of Joseph, conveyed his interest to his brother William, two names were signed (with mark, of course) to the deed. Both signatures bear the name Hanks, but the first part of the name below that of Joseph is illegible. It can hardly be doubted that it is the name of Ann Hanks, the mother. Apparently she did not die on Rolling Fork, but, grief-stricken and perhaps with deeper sorrow, went back to Virginia and died among her old neighbors, some of whom may have been relatives. In that year as we know, Joseph went back to Virginia, and after a few years returned to Kentucky. By that time his mother probably was dead.

As Nancy's Uncle William and Aunt Elizabeth (Hall) Hanks came into immediate possession of the farm, it is probable that for a time Nancy lived with this aunt and uncle; and then it appears almost certain that she went for a few months to her own mother, Lucy, who had married Henry Sparrow. But this was not an ideal arrangement, and when Thomas Sparrow married Elizabeth Hanks in 1796, she went to live with them.

Nancy was not less than twelve years of age when she went to live with this uncle and aunt. As the years passed, and no children were born to them, they clung to her with a closer affection. Her own name of Hanks, which had begun to fall away from

MARRIAGE BOND OF HENRY SPARROW AND LUCY HANKS
Discovered at Harrodsburg, Kentucky, by the Misses Mary A. and Martha
Stephenson

her while she lived in the home of her mother Lucy Sparrow, dropped farther out of sight. As Nicolay and Hay tell us, she was oftener called Sparrow than Hanks. In after years, when she had come to fame as the mother of Abraham Lincoln, her Hanks cousins united in declaring that Henry Sparrow was her father, and that her name was not Hanks. Dennis has been held up to scorn as a man devoid of honor, and even Waldo Lincoln accuses him of going out of his way to calumniate the mother of the president. On the very contrary, Dennis Hanks, sorrowfully admitting that he was "base-born," lied like a gentleman to protect his cousin from like reproach.

Nancy was in the home of Thomas and Elizabeth Sparrow when they learned of the misfortune that had befallen Elizabeth's youngest sister, Nancy. The tax lists show that Thomas Sparrow was living in Mercer County in 1797, 1798 and 1799. In 1801 Thomas and Elizabeth, with Nancy, moved to Nolin Creek, and then, if not earlier, took the little waif, Dennis, as their son. In 1803 they moved back to Mercer and remained till 1805.* In May, 1806, Thomas Sparrow bought land on the South Fork of Nolin, apparently the same farm he had previously rented in Hardin County. His name appears on the Hardin County tax lists regularly from 1806 until 1817 when he and Elizabeth, and Dennis Hanks their foster son, removed to Indiana to be near their foster daughter, Nancy Hanks Lincoln; and there in a very few months Thomas and Elizabeth died.

Although neither Thomas nor Elizabeth could read, they sent Dennis to school in the old Baptist meeting-house on Nolin, and he became, according to the standards of the Hanks family and

---

*My clue to a residence of Nancy Hanks in Mercer County came through an autobiographical letter of Dennis Hanks, which is quoted in the appendix to this volume, stating that Thomas and Elizabeth Sparrow, who reared him as a foster son and Nancy Hanks as a daughter, removed from Nolin Creek in Hardin County and spent three years in Mercer, returning afterward to the same farm in Hardin County. Most biographers openly flout Dennis Hanks, but in so doing leap out of the frying-pan to more inaccurate authorities, but I have found him usually truthful. Following this clue, I found the information correct, and it led to important discoveries in Mercer County, which has not hitherto been explored for Lincoln material.

the neighborhood, a well educated man. He was by far the most literate of the Hankses of his generation. His spelling was erratic, as was the spelling of nearly every one else, and his grammar displayed strong individuality, but he expressed himself in good, forcible and intelligible language. These foster parents gave to Nancy educational advantages quite superior to their own. They sheltered her and brought her up virtuously and religiously. To her relatives she seemed a young woman of liberal education; her attainments in knowledge and character are greatly to her credit, and to the credit of these foster parents.

When Thomas and Elizabeth Sparrow, accompanied by their two foster children, returned to Mercer County in 1803, Nancy had become a young woman, capable of earning her own living. She was a skilled seamstress, and sometimes assisting her aunts and at other times working for neighbors and friends, she left wherever she lived a tradition of industry, intelligence and virtue. Cruel aspersions on her character were circulated after her son became famous, but not one of these originated in any place where she had ever lived, nor can any tradition be discovered, taking its rise among those who knew her, save those that proclaim her a young woman of marked ability and of high moral character, a woman fitted in mind and heart to be the mother of her illustrious son.

The wedding company is assembling at the Berry house on Beech Fork. Some friends have come in ox-wagons, but most of them on horseback. The horses from a distance have been turned into the pasture lot, but those that have come no farther than from Springfield, a matter of seven miles, have been relieved of their saddles and are tethered by their bridle-reins to the swinging limbs of the beech trees. They stamp their feet, and switch their tails, for it is fly-time, but they seldom break loose, and if one should, he would not wander from the others.

Let us join the company, and attend the wedding, never doubting our welcome, whether friend or stranger.

The wedding will occur about sunset, and the feast will be served by early candle-light. As we approach the house, we meet groups of men, lounging, discussing the "craps," talking about the corn and wondering whether it will be "knee high by the fourth of July," as by rhyme and reason it ought to be. The men are dressed mostly in hunting shirts and buckskin breeches, but here and there is one fashionably clad in jeans.

The woman are gathering in the house and on the porch. Some of them wear the fabrics Ann McGinty taught them to spin, of nettle-lint and buffalo-wool, but others are dressed in linsey-woolsey, for there are areas where a liberal bounty for scalps has made these neighborhoods nearly free from wolves and so available for sheep. There are fields that regularly are sown with the blue-blossoming flax. Scratchy garments it makes, for the means of ridding the thread from fiber are only partly effective; but there is evident advance in the matter of clothing, and even some approach to what seems luxury of attire.

From the cook-house come appetizing odors. The sun shines bright in the old Kentucky home; 'tis summer, the darkies are gay. Around behind the shed the musician is testing his home-made cat-gut with strains of *Turkey in the Straw*, the *Money-musk* and *Hey, Betty Martin, tip-toe, tip-toe*. The sawed floor (no puncheons) of the Berrys will resound with merry footfalls to-night. Even the Reverend Jesse Head will not find it easy to keep his feet still.

Yonder comes the parson. A few years later, he owned at one time two or three horses; for a circuit-riding preacher had need to be a good judge of horse-flesh, and on occasion capable of driving a profitable trade. But at this time he owned only an old gray mare, easily recognized at a considerable distance. There is a little hush in the conversation as he approaches, and one of the Berry brothers goes to the fence to meet him, and take his horse. The preacher 'lights and lifts his saddle, looking well to the back of his beast, to see that it does not scald in this hot weather. This done, he moves toward the house, walking with

4

authoritative step. He is tall, lean, wiry, with strong Roman nose, high cheek-bones and red hair. He is said to fear God, but he fears no Calvinist, or any other man. He greets his neighbors with cheerful and unaffected interest in their concerns. He is a man some people do not love, but whom every one respects, a hard-hitting, devil-fighting circuit-riding parson, striving mightily to save the wilderness from godlessness and savagery. Well may this company rise up and do him honor. It is the twelfth of June, 1806; Jesse Head was thirty-eight years old day before yesterday. He has been preaching now since he became a man, and he is to preach for many years to come. He has no reason to suppose that this wedding which he has come to solemnize is to be any different from those to which he is accustomed; but the great events of life do not come to us labeled.

The sun nears the horizon, and the company moves in a little nearer to the house. It is almost time for the ceremony. As the guests converge, they meet and greet the relatives of the bride and groom. The Lincolns are fairly well known, for Mordecai and Josiah live near by, and Mary and Nancy, though married and living some distance away, are not forgotten. Not so the aunts and uncles of the bride. They are strangers to nearly all the company, and must be introduced.

And now I wonder if I do not see two other guests, approaching the ford from the other side, and preparing to cross Beech Fork. Their horses dip their feet in the water and splash cheerfully, for the day has been warm and the water is pleasant. They pause as they enter the stream, and the horses drink and are refreshed. The man and woman talk together in a rather low tone, a tone of eager anticipation tinged with a little solicitude on her part, and one of calm assurance on his. They cross the stream and ride up to the fence. They heed the invitation to 'light and lift their saddles. They dismount and the woman goes to the house, while the man, accompanied by one of the hosts, leads the horses out to the pasture lot, and turns them loose for a roll and a feast of grass. Then he washes his face at the spring, makes a proper toilet, and mingles for a time with the men, and in due season joins his wife.

They are there during the ceremony—I am almost sure of it—and they have good right to be there. Have they not ridden twenty miles to be present?

They are a well-looking couple, each about forty-two, he substantial and reliable, she of rather unusual vivacity and charm, holding her youth well into middle life. After the ceremony, we shall meet them.

They are introduced as another uncle and aunt of the bride, from over in Mercer County, Mr. and Mrs. Henry Sparrow.

Yes, they have good right to be present.

CHAPTER V

NANCY HANKS LINCOLN sat in her splint-bottomed chair in the cabin on the Sinking Spring farm, and rocked her baby with quiet satisfaction The chair was without rockers, and its front legs came down hard upon the earthen floor, but the baby appeared to enjoy it. As she rocked, she sang. She knew the old ballads which had come down by tradition in the literature of the illiterate. Some of them harked back to Old England. There was a ballad of Lord Bateman and the Turkish Lady, and another of the Cruelty of Barbara Allen. There was the song of Fair Eleanor (Nancy pronounced the name "Ellender") and the Brown Girl. The hero loved Fair Eleanor, but the Brown Girl she had lands and gold, Fair Eleanor she had none, so he riddled his riddle on maternal advice, and brought the Brown Girl home. He was bold about it, and he rode past Fair Eleanor's abode, and "he tingled at the ring," and invited Fair Eleanor to the wedding. She braved all the peril and the gossip, and she went. "Is this your bride?" Fair Eleanor said. "She seemeth me plagued brown; and you might have had as fair a maid as ever the sun shone on." The Brown Girl did not enjoy this comment on her personal appearance. She had come prepared to defend herself against any such aspersion. The Brown Girl she had a little slim knife, and it was keen and sharp; she reached around the corner of the table, and pierced Fair Eleanor's heart. When the hero saw Fair Eleanor dead, he drew his sword, cut off the Brown Girl's head "and slung it ag'in the wall." Then he stabbed himself to death. Those old songs were based upon the theory that two's company and three's a crowd. They were good and gory and had abundance of melodrama, and they thrilled the hearts of shrill-voiced maidens all the way from Merry England to Virginia and over the mountains to Kentucky. They were better than many of the modern triangles, for at the end all three of the characters were decently dead, and the funeral may be presumed to have been conducted in accordance with the hero's dying instructions:

> And bury Fair Eleanor in my arms,
> And the Brown Girl at my feet.

Also she sang of the Romish lady, brought up in Poperie, and this was one of the songs which Abraham remembered and tried, though not very successfully, to sing.

She sang religious songs, such as abounded in the country. Many of them were "family songs" in which the successive stanzas varied only in the substitution of the words "fathers," "mothers," "preachers," and so on:

> Brothers, bear your cross;
> It will onlye make you richer,
> For to enter in that bri-*ight* kingdom by and by.

In singing songs containing such words as "only" the second syllable pronounced the "y" with the long sound, just as the high-priced soprano pronounces "wind," meaning the atmosphere in motion, to rhyme with "mind." They had their conventions in singing in Nancy's day, just as they have them now. The word "bright" had a curious syncopation that came in the middle of the word; you could see the brightness increase as the word was carried over the beat:

> For to enter in that bri-*ight* kingdom by and by.

There was another hymn whose syncopation had a lift that was almost physical:

> You may bury me in the east,
> You may bury me in the west,
> And we'll all ri-*ise* together in that morning.

There was another which Mr. Sankey heard, and spoiled it by making its minor over into the major mode and giving it the tempo of a jig:

> Jesus is a rock in a wearye land,
> A wearye land, a wearye land;
> Jesus is a rock in a wearye land,
> A shelter in a time of storm.

As Nancy sang it, you could feel the weariness of the journey till your very bones ached, and you felt also the security of the shelter.

Sometimes Nancy sang long religious ballads, such as *Wicked Polly*. She'd go to parties, dance and play, in spite of all her parents would say: "I'll turn to God when I get old, and He will then receive my soul." But it did not happen that way. Stricken down in the midst of her frivolity, she called her mother to her bed, her eyes were rolling in her head: "When I am dead, remember well, your wicked Polly screams in hell."

Nancy sang such songs as these. Americans are said to take their pleasures sadly; the people of Nancy's locality and generation may be adjudged to have taken their religion in that fashion; but if they got more joy out of it in that way, who shall deny them the comfort of their lugubrious satisfaction? And who shall blame them if in times of religious excitement they went to the other extreme? A distant and superficial judgment might be that such a religion was worse than none; but that is not the judgment of one who has observed that type of religion in all its variant moods.

The baby slept, and Nancy laid him down and prepared supper for her husband and little Sarah. "Hog and hominy" had come to replace the primitive dependence upon game, and there was corn bread, and very rarely any other.

You should have seen Nancy bake bread. She stirred the meal in a wooden bowl, putting in nothing in addition to the meal but water and a pinch of salt. She scooped out a handful of the mush, turned it over and over in her palms, and put it into the open-hearth oven with a good cast of her hand and fingers on the top of each pone. Five or six of these pones made an ovenful, and they were good.

While the pones were baking, you might have seen Nancy at her spinning-wheel. Of all arts ever invented to display the grace of the female form, in step and gesture and skill of eye and hand, there never has been anything to compare with spinning. It would be worth a journey to Nolin Creek just to see Nancy spin.

You watch Nancy as she goes to her cupboard, and you wonder with what dishes she will set her table, and whether, indeed, she has any dishes except perhaps wooden ones that Thomas has made for her. But I will tell you what she had, or part of it; for in addition to whatever she may previously have owned, her stock had been increased before the birth of Abraham and since the death of Thomas McIntire. Thomas Lincoln attended the auction sale of McIntire's personal property and made two rather large purchases. He bought a "Dish and Plates" for $2.68; and a "Bason and Spoons" for $3.34. These were not trivial sums in 1807. Nancy's cupboard was fairly well supplied with crockery and pewter.

Nancy was nothing less than proud of her table-wear when the preacher spent the night with them. The Severns Valley Baptist Church in Elizabethtown is the oldest church of that communion in the State of Kentucky. Hodgenville was a Baptist settlement also, one of its founders being a Baptist preacher. For him Nolin Creek is supposed to have been named; for he wandered away and is supposed to have been killed by the Indians; and when the hunting party came back, they sadly said, "No Lynn." So you must not accent the name *"Nolin"* on the first syllable; that is not the proper way. Say "No-lin" just as if you were saying "No Lynn." They often spell it that way. In 1803, the Severns Valley Church established a branch on Nolin. Reverend Josiah Dodge preached there once a month, which was as often as any Baptist preacher was expected to preach in any one place in that day. When Brother Dodge rode over to Nolin or to the nearer church on South Fork and having preached a matter of two hours, spent the night with Brother and Sister Lincoln, he may have had hog and hominy for supper. But in the morning, he was wakened by a smothered squawk, and the flutter of feathers pulled down through leafy boughs, and the sharp stroke of an ax against the block. When he rose and went down to the Sinking Spring to wash his face, he saw a rooster's head at the block, and knew what he was to have for breakfast.

Nancy did not sit down at the table with the men. She attended to the processes under way on the hearth, and from time to time brought on more pone or bacon and whatever else there was to eat. Little Sarah did not have a high chair. She stood in a chair that was placed with its back to the table. With one hand she held to a chair-post and in the other she brandished one of the spoons from the McIntire sale.

The Sinking Spring farm had one picturesque feature, the spring. It was in a cave. Behind it the hill made a low bluff. In front the ground was nearly level, and the spring was reached by climbing down several steps. The water did not rise to the surface of the ground, but flowed away through a subterranean channel.

The site was pleasant and the water was good, but the soil was not fertile. It was hard to make a living there. Thomas Lincoln had paid two hundred dollars for the farm, and was to have made a small additional payment when the deed was delivered; but the deed was not delivered, and the suit followed. Thomas won his suit, but probably could not collect the money he had paid nor be sure of getting a good title. The land was sold, and bought in by Mather who paid seventy-eight dollars for it. Why Thomas, who had already invested much more than that in the farm, did not raise the bid and get a court-title to the farm we do not know.

Three crop seasons and two winters the Lincolns lived on Nolin Creek, and then removed to the Knob Creek farm, where Abraham stayed from the time he was three until he was seven.

The birthplace of Lincoln, the cabin on the South Fork of Nolin Creek, has an interest which belongs to no other home of the future president; but the home of his earliest memories was that on Knob Creek.

Thomas Lincoln appears to have owned or occupied five houses in what was then Hardin County. The first of these, purchased before his marriage and not occupied by him afterward, was located on Mill Creek.* This farm consisted of 238 acres, and was purchased by Thomas Lincoln from Doctor John Toms Slater, September 2, 1803. It was paid for in cash, or its equivalent, the consideration being one hundred and eighteen pounds. The same farm, measured at two hundred acres, was sold by Thomas and Nancy Lincoln to Charles Milton, October 27, 1814.

-----

*Until the publication of *The Paternity of Abraham Lincoln,* these transactions were confused by all authors who wrote of them. Lamon assumed that this was the Knob Creek farm, and so did Herndon. Other authors assumed that this was the Nolin Creek farm, and that Thomas Lincoln had been improving it for three years before his marriage, and that during his residence, with Nancy, in Elizabethtown, he was building the house where Abraham was to be born. A complete record of Thomas Lincoln's ownership of this property is given in *The Paternity of Abraham Lincoln.* Miss Tarbell, who thought her finding of the Slater sale to Lincoln to have been an original discovery, supposed this to have been the farm where Lincoln was born. She tells us that Thomas Lincoln "moved to the farm he had bought in 1803 on the South Fork of Nolin Creek, in Hardin County, now Larue County, three miles from Hodgenville, and about fourteen miles from Elizabethtown. Here he was living when, on February 12, 1809, his second child, a boy, was born. The little new comer was called Abraham." (Vol. i, p. 14.) Most authorities have followed either Lamon in assuming that the farm purchased by Thomas Lincoln and sold to Milton was the Knob Creek farm, or Miss Tarbell in assuming that it was the Nolin Creek farm. All are wrong. The Mill Creek farm has been identified, and it is many miles from either of the others. Nancy Hanks never lived upon it. Thomas Lincoln may have lived here for a time before his marriage, or he may have worked it in desultory fashion in 1803 and 1804, while boarding with his sister Nancy Brumfield. For further information reference may be made to my address before the Filson Club of Louisville on *The Lincolns in Their Old Kentucky Home.*

The next home of Thomas Lincoln in Hardin County was the cabin in Elizabethtown, which in 1865 and subsequent years was shown in steel engravings and other reproductions as the birthplace of Abraham Lincoln. Of this cabin Lamon wrote in 1872, basing his statements on Herndon's visit to Kentucky in 1866:

Lincoln took Nancy to live in a shed in one of the alleys in Elizabethtown. It was a very sorry building, and nearly bare of furniture. It stands yet, or did in 1866, to witness for itself the wretched poverty of its early inmates. It is about fourteen feet square, has been three times removed, twice used as a slaughter house and once as a stable. Here a daughter was born on the tenth of February, 1807, who was called Nancy during the life of her mother, and after her death, Sarah.*

The foregoing is correct, except that the little girl was Sarah, and never called Nancy, and that the occupancy of a cabin fourteen feet square is no certain proof of wretchedness. The house is no longer standing. Its site is disputed; but has been identified with reasonable certainty.†

In the spring or early summer of 1808, Thomas and Nancy Lincoln, with little Sarah, moved from Elizabethtown, and are believed to have lived for a few months on the farm of George Brownfield, near Buffalo, in what is now Larue County. The site of their cabin has been identified. It is in the "plumb-orchard," a grove of wild crab-apples.‡

Life of Lincoln, pp. 12-13.

†Here again, as in very much that relates to matters in Hardin County, I acknowledge my debt to Reverend Louis A. Warren, in company with whom I have visited, and in some instances repeatedly, these and all other sites relating to Lincoln in Hardin County.

‡The discovery of this home was made in the search for information at the time the government took over the Lincoln farm. I have given the facts, as that investigation appeared to establish them, and as I received them from Honorable L. B. Handley, attorney for the Lincoln Farm Association. The spot was identified for me by Honorable Richard Creel, Judge of Larue County. For the affidavits concerning this and kindred matters, I refer the reader to the appendices of *The Paternity of Abraham Lincoln*. I am endeavoring to repeat in this volume only what is essential to a continuous narrative. *The Paternity of Abraham Lincoln* and *The Soul of Abraham Lincoln* both contain important matter which I must not undertake to duplicate here.

In this cabin they were tenants while Thomas Lincoln worked as carpenter and farm laborer for the man who owned the cabin. When they moved from here, in the autumn or early winter of 1808, it was to the humble home near the Rock Spring or Sinking Spring, which the birth of their son in the following winter made forever illustrious.*

The removal of Thomas Lincoln from Nolin Creek to Knob Creek appears upon the face of it an unimportant shifting of a migratory family from one farm to another in the same county. Viewed only as a removal of twelve miles, it is not surprising that its significance has been overlooked by students of the life of Lincoln. But he who journeys over the roads, and becomes acquainted with the environment, discovers that the transfer from the one rough farm to the other a little less rough was an event of considerable importance.

The two farms were in the same county, and lawsuits or trade called Thomas Lincoln occasionally to the county-seat, Elizabethtown; but except when he had business in court, which was not very often, he found it easier to go to Bardstown, the county-seat of Nelson County; for the distance was the same, and the road to Bardstown was better. Except for his small amount of official business, as his lawsuits over the title to his farms, and his appointment as road "surveyor," he had little to take him back to his own county-seat, and not much more to take him to his old neighborhood on Nolin. An epoch in the life of the Lincolns ended with this short migration.

This removal transferred the family across Muldraugh's Hill, which is not a hill, but an escarpment facing the Blue Grass region. It extends from West Point, in the southwest corner of Jefferson County near where Rolling Fork enters the Ohio River, southeastward to the vicinity of Brodhead, Rockcastle County, thence northeastward to the Ohio River west of Vanceburg, Lewis County.

---

*The purchase of the farm was December 12, 1808, but the Lincolns may have been living there a few weeks earlier.

Knob Creek is in the hills, but it is a short stream which quickly finds the Blue Grass. Thomas Lincoln changed his outlook on life by this migration of a dozen miles.

The Lincoln farm was situated in the forks of Knob Creek. There were three fields, lying in the rather fertile valley. Thomas Lincoln made no attempt to cultivate the hillslopes of his farm, the three little fields affording him sufficient labor. The house stood on the opposite side of the road from the large house afterward erected and still standing, and the site may still be found.

It was while living on Knob Creek that Abraham Lincoln first went to school. The site of the schoolhouse has been identified for me by Francis X. Rapier.*

This is his statement to me:

My father, Nicholas A. Rapier, born in 1820, moved to Knob Creek about 1842 or 1843. The Lincoln farm remained in our family until twelve or fifteen years ago. I was born on the Knob Creek Lincoln farm. The Lincoln house was still standing in my childhood, but was not used as a house. The house which our family occupied is on the right as one goes down the creek toward Athertonville and New Haven. The two creeks meet in the middle of the farm. The road crosses a bridge where the creek comes in from the left. Just this side of the bridge, that is, on the side nearer Muldraugh's Hill, is a large farm gate. A little distance inside that gate is a slight elevation where the house stood. That little elevation has always been used as a feeding place for cattle, being a little above the bottom land, and hence more dry. That doubtless was the reason why the spot was selected for a house; and as it was used as a barn in my father's ownership, the stock gathered there, and the spot continued to be used as a feeding-place after the old shed disappeared. The gate shows the general course of the short path from the road to the front door of the house.

This road was a part of the old Louisville and Nashville turnpike, and my father fed stage passengers. Thomas Lincoln's

*Mr. Rapier, who had not previously been interviewed, made this interesting statement to me in 1920, and I wrote it at the time, and have confirmed his statements on the testimony of other old residents of the locality.

cabin was then just a cattle shed. But we were in no uncertainty about it.

I have never been interviewed by any writer of books about Lincoln. But I was born across the road from the cabin where he lived, and talked with all the men who knew him and were living when Lincoln became famous; and I presume that I am nearer to accurate sources of knowledge of the life of the Lincoln family while living on Knob Creek than any one else.

The schoolhouse was a mile and a half from the Lincoln home. It is on the left as you drive into Athertonville, just as you pass the first house, on a little elevation about a hundred yards up a little run or "holler."

Old man Austin Gollaher lived not far away from us. We had a good well, and he liked to drink the water. He came to our house almost every day. He wore trap-door trousers and coarse white shirts with knit suspenders. I seldom saw him with a coat. He was the only man I ever knew who attended school with Abraham Lincoln.

He said Lincoln attended very little. All the boys at that time used to wear just one long garment in the summer time: the darkies still run around in their shirt-tails, and in those days all the boys wore long tow shirts. But in school, trousers were expected, and Austin said Abe had his first pair of pants when he went to school. But he said Abe did not have a hat. Hats were about the hardest garments to get. Coonskin caps were common, but the boy who had a wool hat was in style, and Gollaher was quite certain that when Abe first came to school he was shy a hat. His impression was that Abe had no school book of his own; but that was not so uncommon. He knew Abe best of any one who was living here after Lincoln became famous, but of course what he remembered had happened many years before, and there was not a great deal that he could really tell. He liked to talk of it, however, and I have heard him tell his story many times.

Austin Gollaher gained considerable celebrity in his old age by his claim to have saved the life of the boy Abraham Lincoln. The story has been published in several Lives of Lincoln, perhaps the best version, though not one of the earliest, is that recorded by D. J. Thomas in an interview with Austin Gollaher:

"Yes," said Mr. Gollaher, "the story that I once saved Abraham Lincoln's life is true, but it is not correct as generally related.

"Abraham Lincoln and I had been going to school together for a year or more, and had become greatly attached to each other. Then school disbanded on account of there being so few scholars, and we did not see each other much for a long while. One Sunday my mother visited the Lincolns, and I was taken along. Abe and I played around all day. Finally, we concluded to cross the creek to hunt for some partridges young Lincoln had seen the day before. The creek was swollen by a recent rain, and, in crossing on the narrow footlog, Abe fell in. Neither of us could swim. I got a long pole and held it out to Abe, who grabbed it. Then I pulled him ashore. He was almost dead, and I was badly scared. I rolled and pounded him in good earnest. Then I got him by the arms and shook him, the water meanwhile pouring out of his mouth. By this means I succeeded in bringing him to, and he was soon all right.

"Then a new difficulty confronted us. If our mothers discovered our wet clothes they would whip us. This we dreaded from experience, and determined to avoid. It was June, the sun was very warm, and we soon dried our clothing by spreading it on the rocks about us. We promised never to tell the story, and I never did until after Lincoln's tragic end.

"Abraham Lincoln had a sister. Her name was Sallie, and she was a very pretty girl. Sallie Lincoln was about my age; she was my sweetheart. I loved her and claimed her, as boys do. I suppose that was one reason for my warm regard for Abe. When the Lincoln family moved to Indiana, I was prevented by circumstances from bidding good-by to either of the children, and I never saw them again."*

If this story is authentic, it entitles Austin Gollaher to our very warm thanks. But Newton Bateman, in his *Biographical Encyclopedia of Illinois,* reminds us that Dennis Hanks claimed to have performed this brave deed; and added: "Austin Gollaher, a school- and play-mate of Lincoln's, has also made the same claim for himself—the two stories presumably referring to the same event."†

Early Life of Lincoln, by Ida M. Tarbell, pp. 45, 46; also her *Abraham Lincoln,* i, pp. 14, 15.

†Revised edition, Vol. I, p. 219.

In June, 1886, Honorable A. M. Brown, of Louisville, who had a sister living in Larue County, went at the request of Colonel R. T. Durrett to interview Austin Gollaher, and wrote out the account of his interview on June 17, 1886. The manuscript is now in the Durrett Collection in the Library of the University of Chicago.*

Mr. Brown was impressed with the sincerity of Gollaher, whom he described as an evidently honest and a well-preserved old man. He noted, however, that Gollaher stated that it was in 1812 that he saved the life of Abraham Lincoln, and that at that time Abraham was three years old and Austin five. He also ascertained that the Gollaher family did not reside in Hardin County until 1812, and that Gollaher's memory of the removal of the Lincolns was that when they left Knob Creek they first moved into another part of Hardin County and thence, subsequently, to Indiana. It is interesting to note how Gollaher's memory improved in later years to the point where he thought that his mother was among those present at the birth of Lincoln, and his own knowledge of the date of the Lincoln removal from Kentucky seemed to him sufficiently clear to enable him to correct the historians.

Let the reader think back to his own school-days, and recall, if he can, some boy who attended school more or less irregularly for two or three terms and with whom he occasionally played, whose family moved into the neighborhood when he was three and moved away when he was seven, and was not heard from afterward for something like fifty years. Just how much could the reader, relying solely upon his own unaided memory, add to a biography of that boy?

Austin Gollaher bore a good reputation for truthfulness, and I, who never knew Mr. Gollaher, have a distinct impression that he tried at first to tell what he actually remembered about Lincoln. But as he grew older, he was pressed by different inter-

*To this collection I am indebted for much important assistance.

viewers to remember additional details, and if he did not supply those details the interviewer sometimes did.*

Austin Gollaher's memories of Lincoln's life as a pupil in a Kentucky school were very meager. Abraham attended irregularly; the school was cut short because the number of pupils was small. It was not, of course, a free school, but a subscription school, and there was little to make it profitable for the teacher, and not much more to make it profitable for the pupils. The boys can not have seen each other very frequently. A survey made about the time the Lincolns were leaving shows the location of the home of nine neighbors of the Lincolns, nearly or quite all of them nearer than the Gollahers. I have traveled the road between the two homes, and it can not be less than three miles from one house to the other. Three miles in a rough and wooded country is not a short distance.

This may be as good a place as any to comment upon the testimony of men and women who knew Lincoln personally, and whose recollections form invaluable material for the historian. Their testimony is not to be regarded lightly. The reminiscences of a person who actually knew Lincoln at any stage of his career are worth gathering and are entitled to careful consideration. Innumerable such persons have contributed to this work by personal narration and by correspondence. Most of the people who knew Lincoln and who tell their experience to a biographer endeavor to tell their story truthfully. But one has frequent occasion to recall the comment of Falstaff, on the lack of veracity in old men.

The old man or woman who recalls for publication his memo-

---

*J. Rogers Gore, who lived for some years in Hodgenville, gathered up the entire tradition of the neighborhood and for the sake of unity put it all into the mouth of Gollaher. His book, *The Boyhood of Lincoln,* presents this tradition, and does not intend to represent that Gollaher personally knew all that he is credited with saying in that book. In fact, he could not have known any very large fraction of what the book tells. The book belongs in the class of rather highly imaginative historical fiction rather than history, and gathers up in readable form the gossip of later years. I have talked with Mr. Gore, who has told me in detail of his many conversations with Gollaher.

ries of Lincoln is under very strong temptation to enlarge somewhat upon his actual recollections. Time itself tends to the
enlarging of the story. The questions of interviewers suggest
details which are unconsciously filled in. Above all, there is a
tendency to add details appropriated from what one has heard
or read.

I could name certain very respectable persons whose published
reminiscences of Lincoln are well known, some of these persons
still living and more of them dead, of whom it would be safe to
say that the Lincoln they describe is only in minor part the
Lincoln they personally knew; the outline furnished by their own
actual memory has been filled in with detail and color borrowed
from their reading or from the stories of others.

It would greatly simplify the task of the historian if he could
say, "John Doe knew Lincoln; John Doe is a truthful man; John
Doe relates this incident; I will therefore record it, and cause it
to be written down as accredited history." Too largely have
histories and biographies been made in this fashion. John Doe
did indeed know Lincoln, and John Doe is a truthful man. But
John Doe did not make record of his interviews with Lincoln at
the time, nor did he then count them of particular significance;
and many years went by before they seemed to him important
enough to print. Meantime, John Doe told his reminiscences a
good many times. At first he related them to friends in conversation. Year by year as he told them, and his friends showed
interest, additional details occurred to him, not quite all of them
imaginary. When men who had known Lincoln more intimately
or in matters of larger public interest died, John Doe found himself the object of increasing attention. Representatives of the
press called upon him, and photographed him, and put his story
into more readable shape. He read his own enlarged story as it
appeared in print, and easily believed it in its more pleasing form.
Subsequent interviews imposed additional demands upon his
memory. John Doe knew Lincoln; John Doe is a truthful man;
I am greatly indebted to John Doe and to his friend, Richard

Roe, who also knew Lincoln. But the task of the biographer is not finished when he has collected their statements and those of other men like them. There still remains the serious task of critical historical judgment, analysis and construction.

Ex-President Eliot, of Harvard, has published a book of essays and addresses prepared by him between the ages of eighty and ninety. In one of these he deals with the defective character of our education in the training of the perceptive faculties. He says that the average American, young or old, rich or poor, educated or uneducated, can not see straight or hear straight, or think straight, and can not relate with reasonable accuracy one hour afterward a conversation in which he has participated or an incident which he has witnessed. If this be true, and I think it is, what historian or biographer can be saved? For history and biography are based on testimony gathered for the most part many years after the events described, and after those events have come to take on quite other significance than at the time was understood. The answer is that historians and biographers have reason to be more careful than many of them are or have been; and that much history deserves the stinging definition of Voltaire, "a lie agreed to."

I may illustrate the ease with which a Lincoln biographer can fall into error. In 1922 I delivered before the Chicago Historical Society an address on *The Influence of Chicago upon Abraham Lincoln.** As part of the preparation I compiled a list of Abraham Lincoln's known visits to Chicago. I now could add a few visits to the list then made, but it was for the purposes of my lecture an adequate as it was also an instructive list. Among other things, I published in the Chicago daily press a statement that I was preparing this address and requested all persons who had seen Lincoln in Chicago to write to me. I had many interesting letters, and received some valuable information. But many people told me of seeing Lincoln in Chicago on dates when I knew he was elsewhere. For example, a number pro-

*This address has been published by the University of Chicago Press.

fessed to have seen him at the Republican Convention in 1860, a convention which he did not attend.

Dwight L. Moody was accustomed to tell, and his son relates in his *Life* of his father, how Lincoln addressed Moody's Sunday-school when Lincoln was on his way to his inauguration, in February, 1861. But Lincoln did not pass through Chicago on his way to his inauguration. Bishop Charles E. Cheney, of the Reformed Episcopal Church, in an address in Memorial Hall, on Lincoln's Birthday in 1914, related that he preached in St. James Church on Christmas Day in 1860 and that Lincoln was present. But Lincoln spent that last Christmas before his inauguration in his Springfield home.

If Chicago ever had two truthful citizens, they were D. L. Moody and Bishop Cheney, but both were mistaken. On Sunday, November 26, 1860, Lincoln attended St. James Church with the family of Honorable Isaac N. Arnold, and on the afternoon of the same day spoke in Mr. Moody's North Market Mission. So I learned from the *Chicago Tribune* of Monday, November 27, 1860, and it was correct.

For ordinary purposes, the mistakes of Mr. Moody and of Bishop Cheney were unimportant. The incidents as they related them were correct, except as to the date. But for the purposes of the historian an accurate use of dates is highly important, as well as exceedingly difficult.

If these two unusually intelligent and honest men could be mistaken in a matter of this character, there is great need to scrutinize carefully recollections submitted as sources of history. Yet I will not say in my haste that all men are liars; in general a tradition has in it a kernel of truth. This book contains many such kernels, separated with some difficulty from their husks of exaggeration and unintentional misrepresentation.

Thomas Lincoln's new outlook into the world was toward the prosperous settlements of the Roman Catholics in the neighborhood of Bardstown. Edward Eggleston has reminded us how frequently the first teachers of frontier schools were Irishmen. Abraham Lincoln's first school-teacher was an Irish Catholic.

"Before leaving Kentucky, he and his sister were sent, for short periods, to A B C schools, the first kept by Zachariah Riney, and the second by Caleb Hazel." So wrote Abraham Lincoln for John L. Scripps, in 1860. His earlier autobiography, written in 1859 for Jesse W. Fell, told of his schooling in Indiana, but said nothing about these two brief periods of instruction in Kentucky.

The schools which Lincoln attended were "blab-schools." The pupils were required to study aloud, as an evidence that they were studying at all.* Text books were very few, a majority of the pupils having only a speller. Dilworth's speller was used at the first, then Webster's *Old Blueback*.

Not all the children of the neighborhood attended school. If a boy who was not in school passed within earshot of the schoolhouse and cried "School-butter" he had need to be fleet of foot to escape punishment at the hand of the pupils. Just what the phrase meant, no one appears to know, but it was the common insult and challenge, the appeal to the "town and gown" hostility that manifests itself all the way from Knob Creek to Cambridge and Heidelberg. The cry of "Hey Rube" in a circus does not more quickly rally all employees of the show to fight the outside populace than did the cry of "School-butter" rally the students to punish the unlearned and insolent of the world that lay extra-mural to the frontier school.

Lincoln was too small to have participated in any of these class struggles of his first school experience, and too young also to have had a share in the occasional attempts of the pupils to lock the teacher out. Indeed, we know almost nothing of his school experiences while a boy in Kentucky.

Nicolay and Hay say of these early years:

---

*For further facts about primitive Kentucky schools, based in part upon the author's personal experience as a teacher in schools in the hills of Kentucky, the reader is referred to *The Soul of Abraham Lincoln*.

Of all these years of Abraham Lincoln's childhood, we know almost nothing. He lived a solitary life in the woods, returning from his lonesome little games to his cheerless home. He never talked of those days to his most intimate friends. Once, when asked what he remembered about the war with Great Britain, he replied, "Nothing but this. I had been fishing one day and caught a little fish which I was taking home. I met a soldier in the road, and having always been told at home that we must be good to soldiers, I gave him my fish!" This is only a faint glimpse, but what it shows is rather pleasant—the generous child and the patriotic household. But there is no question that these first years of his life had their lasting effect upon the temperament of this great mirthful and melancholy man. He had little schooling. He accompanied his sister Sarah* to the only schools that existed in the neighborhood, one kept by Zachariah Riney and the other by Caleb Hazel, where he learned his alphabet and a little more. But of all those advantages for the cultivation of a young mind and spirit which every home now offers to its children, the books, toys, ingenious games, and daily devotion of paternal love, he knew absolutely nothing.†

Life in the Knob Creek cabin proceeded along a line so well defined by the conditions of frontier life, and so familiar to those who have known life of that character that we have no uncertainty concerning its essential details. Thomas Lincoln annually scratched the surface of his three little fields, the largest of which contained seven acres, using a wooden plow shod with iron. His main crop was corn; but he had some beans, and he dropped a pumpkin seed into every third hill of corn. Abraham when a small boy was taught the art of corn-dropping, and instructed to remember the pumpkin seed in the third hill. The corn was cultivated with a "bull-tongue" plow, Abraham in his last year in Kentucky riding the horse to plow between the corn-

---

*Nicolay and Hay fell into the error of saying that she was sometimes called Nancy. They suggest that she was named for her mother and that she took her stepmother's name after her mother's death. I have discussed this question in *The Paternity of Abraham Lincoln*. Her name was Sarah, first and always. The name Nancy came to her from the torn page in the family Bible, her own name having been lost in the part that was worn off, and her mother's name mistaken for hers.

†*Abraham Lincoln: A History*, i, p. 27.

rows.   Thomas also planted some potatoes and a few onions, and Nancy may have had a small garden and a few flowers.

Thomas Lincoln was a good judge of horses.   The Estray Books contain for the most part stereotyped notices to the effect that John Smith took up as an estray at his farm on Bull Skin Creek, a bay mare, or a brindle cow.   When Thomas Lincoln reported an estray, he measured the height in hands, and looked at the teeth for age, and noted all the marks and brands.   He was never without horses after his coming of age, and on Knob Creek he owned a stallion and several brood mares.

He attended the auction sale of the personal property of Jonathan Joseph in 1814.   Three heifers were sold at auction, and Thomas Lincoln bought the best one, as judged by the price. He habitually attended auctions, and with sufficient money in his pocket to be a successful bidder, and his purchases were sensible.

With one possible exception:

On July 19, 1814, he attended the auction sale of the estate of Thomas Hall and made several purchases.   A sword which he bought is easily accounted for; he wanted to make it over into a drawing-knife.   But he bought a "truck-waggon" for 8½ cents. What kind of wagon could he have bought for that price?   No kind of wagon, so far as I know, but a toy.   Abraham was then five years and five months of age.   I imagine Abraham was the happiest lad on Knob Creek that night.

These are trivial incidents; but they afford us little flashes of light on the boyhood of Lincoln; we have very meager material at the best, and much of it none too reliable.   Let us therefore be glad of these unimportant records that assist us in rescuing from oblivion a little of the childhood of our great president.

While actual details are lacking, we have no difficulty in supplying the essential facts of the life of the Lincoln family on Knob Creek from our knowledge of the nature of the farm and of frontier life of the period.   We know with reasonable accuracy how Abraham Lincoln lived in his childhood, and the conditions of life in the home of his father and mother.

It is not probable that Nancy Lincoln had a button to her back. Her dresses were of linsey-woolsey and they were put on and removed without any needless enlarging or closing of the aperture at the neck. One or two pins may have been used at the throat, but pins were a luxury. Nor did she possess a hair-pin. She probably wore a horn-comb, and it may have been ornamental. In that region, the hair of a woman is always slipping from its one mooring, and coming loose. The owner must frequently remove her back-comb, run it through her hair a few times, coil up the hair again, and refasten it with her comb. A woman in the hills of Kentucky never starts any new occupation without first winding herself up in this fashion.

Cows were cheap. A good cow and calf could usually be bought for ten dollars. Feed for cattle cost nothing from early spring until late in the fall; for the cattle ranged freely in the woods, but usually came home at night to their calves. When they did not come home, some one had to hunt for them; and that was likely to be a wearisome quest. Nancy milked the cows until Sarah was old enough to relieve her of this duty; does not the word "daughter" mean "milker"? This is the way Sarah milked. First of all, she drove the cow into a fence-corner, and then led the calf out of the pen, and permitted the calf to begin its meal. This induced the cow to let down her milk. The prospect of a speedy meeting with the calf was a strong induce-ment to the cow to come home at night; one cow with a young calf could usually be depended upon to lead the entire herd to the fence at milking time. When the milk was ready to flow freely, Sarah led the protesting calf back into the pen or shed, and pro-ceeded to secure the family's share of the milk. She did not use a milking stool, but stood and with her right hand milked into a gourd which she held in her left hand. Now and then she stopped to empty the gourd into a bucket placed in an adjacent fence-corner, safe from the danger of being kicked over. After she had obtained as much milk as she deemed equitable, she brought back the calf; and the calf had the rich strippings, while the mother contentedly licked her offspring. This was a happy hour for both cow and calf; for there was no reason to lead the calf away abruptly; and the calf continued to enjoy the cow, and the cow likewise enjoyed the companionship of the calf for perhaps an hour.

Of duties inside the house, we also know the daily routine.

Thomas worked his little farm, not industriously, but with sufficient labor to produce each season a little crop of corn; now and then he cheerfully went by invitation to do an odd job of carpenter work; but Nancy worked at home every day. If Thomas had sheep, she carded, spun and wove. In the absence of wool, she knew the uses of buffalo-wool. The chafing-dish was unknown to her, but she was on terms of intimate friendship with its predecessor, the skillet. She laid hold of the spindle and her hands knew the distaff. She ate not the bread of idleness. But let no one suppose that Nancy was overworked. Women had plenty of spare time until the invention of the sewing-machine and other labor-saving devices for women. Not till these came to lighten their toil were they worked and worried into nervous prostration by the burden of their house-work. Nancy was able to finish all her necessary work early in the afternoon; and, having no rocking-chair, she held her baby in her arms as she sat in a low splint-bottomed chair whose front legs thumped the puncheon floor, if indeed, the Knob Creek cabin had such a floor. There was a certain unhurried spirit about the labor of the pioneer household, a spirit which we have quite lost in these more leisurely times. The pioneer did not fret because he could not cut down the whole forest in a single year. He accepted his situation, and when his day's work was done, he rested and visited and took life as comfortably as he was able. Nancy knew what to do in her hours of ease; we work very hard to attain a leisure which we do not deserve and do not know how to use.

Nor was life in those conditions devoid of a certain simple luxury. Now and then Thomas cut down a bee-tree, and then the family had honey, some of which was kept in a crock against the time of need. Occasionally he did a day's work in Bardstown and took his pay in unbolted wheat flour. Who that has never lived long on hoe-cake and corn-pone with sorghum molasses (a plural noun) for "long-sweetening" can know the sheer delight of hot biscuit and honey? And there was wild turkey, and in time there were chickens to fry. The creek furnished fish. The Knob Creek farm provided a reasonably sure living with a minimum of physical exertion.

Nor were occasions of special festivity lacking. There were corn-huskings and frolics and raisings and weddings and camp-meetings and funerals. And there was the monthly preaching service.

Besides all this, the Knob Creek farm was on the main road from Louisville to Nashville. Travelers went by every day, and sometimes stopped and talked. There was a mill on Knob Creek as early as 1797, and that was an important social center. Moreover, Caleb Hazel, father of Lincoln's school-teacher of the same name, kept a tavern, where he provided things to eat and also to drink. Sometimes he paid his license, and sometimes he paid his fine.

Life on Knob Creek was not so dull as has been imagined. Compared with Nolin Creek, the Knob Creek farm was located on Main Street of the Kentucky wilderness.

The Knob Creek farm was more fertile and more easily tilled than that on Nolin Creek; and here Abraham had his first experience in riding a horse to plow corn. The farm was subject to sudden rise of water, which sometimes flooded the valley almost without warning when a heavy storm broke over the hill, and the plain would be submerged when there had been little or no rain at the cabin. One such storm came just after corn-planting and seemed to wash all the seed and soil away, and to leave instead only sand and clay.*

*On my last visit to Knob Creek, in June, 1923, the bridge on the main road through the Lincoln farm had been washed out by one of these freshets, and we had to ford Knob Creek twice on Lincoln land.

The nature of the claim of Thomas Lincoln upon the Knob Creek property is disclosed in the papers of the eviction suit. He bought the land, thirty acres, from George Lindsey, but as yet did not have a deed. He and Lindsey continued as defendants in the Hardin County Court while suits against the other alleged squatters were transferred to Nelson County on change of venue, the plaintiffs alleging that they could not obtain justice in Hardin. In a bill of exceptions it is stated that Lindsey was Lincoln's landlord and was absent in Breckenridge County; and that Lincoln as tenant had papers served upon him. This means that the title stood in the name of Lindsey, and that Lincoln occupied it as tenant subject to Lindsey's ability to give clear title, the balance of purchase money to have been then paid. Lincoln paid taxes on this farm; and the papers in the suit indicate plainly that he was considered the owner of that small part, thirty acres, of the land in controversy. It is further of record that Lincoln, being sued as a trespasser, won his suit,* which he could hardly have done if he had not had valid title to the land. Evidently there were several small purchases, ten of them being indicated upon a plat which was introduced as evidence, and which is preserved, these being portions of a much larger tract owned under a conflicting patent by parties resident in Philadelphia.

This suit, instituted January 1, 1815, and decided June 9, 1818,† shows that the farm was a part of a tract of ten thousand acres, surveyed in 1784, and patented in 1786 by Thomas Middleton. Lincoln and the other alleged squatters who were sued at the same time, were successful, but Lincoln had already removed from Knob Creek to Indiana, alleging as one of his reasons for removal the uncertainty of land titles in Kentucky.‡

---

*For the records of this suit I am indebted to Honorable George Holbert and Reverend Louis A. Warren.

†See the chapter on Thomas Lincoln in *The Paternity of Abraham Lincoln*. The records are in Civil Order Books E and F, Hardin County Court.

‡It is necessary to remind the reader that all that Lamon has told us about the title to this farm is incorrect; and that other authors have not helped to clarify his errors. Lamon utterly confused the several Lincoln farms in Kentucky, and those who have since attempted to correct his errors have not improved upon his conjectures.

On the whole the Knob Creek farm was a desirable one, save for the uncertainty about the title. Doubtless the place was visited by agents of the Philadelphia claimants, and then came vague rumors, followed by actual litigation. Thomas Lincoln stood better with the Hardin County juries than did the people in Philadelphia; but his tenure was uncertain; so he loaded his goods into his flatboat, and set forth to discover Indiana.

If Thomas Lincoln had launched his flatboat on Nolin Creek, he would have followed the meanderings of that stream and Green River two hundred fifty-six miles to reach the Ohio, and would have entered that river forty-six miles, by the Ohio channel, below the landing for their home in Indiana. He would not have made his way up-stream to the same place, nor is it very likely that he would have landed in Indiana, for settlements were more abundant below the mouth of Green River, toward the mouths of the Wabash, Cumberland and Tennessee; he would have been rather more likely to float on to Missouri and have made his home in that state, as many Kentuckians did, among them Daniel Boone. But when he floated away from his Knob Creek farm, he had only forty-two miles, instead of two hundred fifty-six, to sail until he reached the Ohio, and then about fifty miles to Thompson's Ferry in Perry County, Indiana. If Thomas Lincoln had continued to live on a stream whose mouth was so far from the Ohio, would he have gone out of Kentucky in that way at all? If so, he certainly would not have made his home where he did in Indiana, and in either event the whole story of Abraham Lincoln's life would thenceforth have been materially modified.*

Of Abraham Lincoln's life in this environment few authentic traditions remain. The years were uneventful. The labored efforts of later decades to fill in this gap bear on their face the marks of invention. But these were not lost years in Lincoln's life. I have seen much of the life of boys and girls reared amid

---

*I am indebted to the United States Geological Survey and to the Kentucky Geological Survey for these measurements and related data.

such surroundings, and have no difficulty in thinking of Lincoln's boyhood as a period fruitful of good.

It is sometimes assumed that life amid beautiful scenery is inspired from infancy by the charm of such surroundings. If this were true, all people born on Knob Creek should have been poets, for the scenery, while not majestic, is attractive and picturesque. But my own observation does not wholly sustain the opinion that features of natural beauty inevitably inspire the souls of those who reside among them. Most people I have known who spend their lives amid mountains accept their situation with stolid patience. A hill is not something to be admired, but something whose climb is to be avoided if possible. Such people do not ascend a hill to behold a sunset. It would be difficult to conjecture what natural phenomenon, as eclipse or comet, would induce the average mountaineer to climb a hill. History may almost be said to have been made by the disinclination of humanity to climb hills; mountain ranges hardly less than oceans are effective national boundaries. But now and then a mountain lad feels from his childhood the companionship of the hills.

I remember riding many years ago along a valley in the Kentucky highlands, beside a stream that wound past the base of a prominent and exceptionally high mountain. Between the road and the hill, in a place where the valley widened a little, stood a cabin. A little distance up the road from the cabin, in a place where the clearing gave a good view, stood a boy of nine or ten. The sun was coming over the range of hills, and, shining through a notch it lit up his face. He was looking at the hill, and talking to it in a sing-song chant which he had composed:

> "Oh, Mountain, big and high:
> I'll stand on you and I'll touch the sky!"

He chanted this over and over, pausing each time to listen to the echo of his own voice. The road was little traveled, and the boy talked to the mountain with no expectation of intrusion. As he saw a stranger approaching he ceased his chant and slipped away into the woods with evident embarrassment. The traveler wanted to stop and talk with him, but the boy would not come. He felt ashamed that he had been overheard in his dialogue with the high hill in whose shadow he dwelt.

I do not remember any other incident of precisely this character, either in the Kentucky hills or in any other mountainous regions which I have visited. That boy had in him something unusual.

Abraham Lincoln may not have done that sort of thing when he lived on Knob Creek; but his surroundings there were more calculated to inspire such moods than any in which he ever lived elsewhere. Much more romantic than Nolin, Knob Creek was a place to stir the boyish imagination. In some fashion, the strength of the hills became his in those years in the Knob Creek cabin. When, now and then, I recall the chant of that mountain boy, I am somehow reminded of Lincoln on Knob Creek. Child that he was, and with a narrowed horizon walled in by almost insuperable heights that shut him from contact with the outer world, save as that world plodded along the rough road down Muldraugh's Hill and along the creek, he was not wholly out of touch with the beginnings of imagination and aspiration and nascent achievement. There was more in that environment than on Nolin to answer his own inward strivings. Already there was the beginning of the answer to America's call, as interpreted by Sam Walter Foss:

"Give me men to match my mountains!"

We can not suppose that the Lincoln family left Knob Creek without a final round of visits from their relations. Thomas and Elizabeth Sparrow and Levi and Nancy Hall and Jesse and Polly Friend must all have come to hear Thomas Lincoln's account of the Indiana he had visited and to which he and his family were about to migrate. And it is not to be doubted for a moment that Henry and Lucy Sparrow rode over from Doctor's

Fork to Knob Creek and spent a night before the final removal.
The outward relations between Lucy and her daughter were
those of aunt and niece, and Abraham did not suspect that this
woman of fifty years sustained toward his mother any closer
relation than did her Aunts Polly and Nancy, nor as close as
her Aunt Betty. But Lucy and Nancy knew. And when Lucy
looked at this lad of seven and commented on his growth since
her last visit, and the progress he was making at school, her
heart must have given a significant leap; for she knew that he
was her own grandson. Both she and Nancy kept these things
and pondered them in their hearts.

CHAPTER VI

LINCOLN'S KENTUCKY

THE Kentucky which Abraham Lincoln knew was limited in area. It comprised parts of three counties—Hardin, Nelson and a little of Washington. The removal to Knob Creek from Nolin turned the face of the Lincoln family toward the nearer counties in the edge of the Blue Grass. Both Thomas and Nancy had lived in Washington County, and she had lived in Mercer, and they had friends in Nelson and their friends were near at hand. The four villages, all county-seats, which Abraham Lincoln is likely to have visited in his childhood are Elizabethtown, Bardstown, Harrodsburg and Springfield. He probably did not go many times to any one of them. However, county court day was and is a notable day in Kentucky county-seats. The business of the court is a minor though a genuine interest. The event has commercial and social importance. Thomas Lincoln was a man too socially inclined not to visit the county-seats within easy reach on monthly court days, and swap a story or a horse with some distant acquaintance.

When Abraham was old enough to stick on behind his father, he doubtless sometimes rode with him to some of these gatherings. The primitive log court-house in the middle of the huddled little town must have seemed to him a great building, and the village itself a city. The crowd that moved around the court-house square and shuffled in and out of the court room must have impressed him deeply. The boy who is reared in isolation and emerges now and then to behold on one acre of land more people than he knew existed on earth, has a new vision

97

of the significance of collective humanity and of social psychology.

The life of the pioneer in Lincoln's boyhood was one of approach to isolation. Distances were great and houses were far apart. The settlements were small, and even the cities were villages. In 1800 Pittsburgh had only 1,565 inhabitants; Lexington, the metropolis of the new region, had 1,797, of whom 439 were slaves; Frankfort had 628 including 260 slaves; and Nashville 355, of whom 141 were slaves. The county-seat towns had only a court-house, a jail, a blacksmith shop, one or more primitive log taverns, two or three stores and perhaps a dozen or a score of cabins.

Of the strong individualism of the pioneer Senator Beveridge writes:

These American backwoodsmen, as described by contemporary writers who studied them personally, pushed beyond the inhabited districts to get land and make homes more easily. This was their underlying purpose; but a fierce individualism, impatient even of those light and vague social restraints which the existence of near-by neighbors creates, was a sharper spur. Through both these motives, too, ran the spirit of mingled lawlessness and adventure. The physical surroundings of the backswoodsman nourished the non-social elements in his character. The log cabin built, the surrounding patch of clearing made, the seed planted for a crop of cereals only large enough for their household's need—these almost ended the backwoodsman's agricultural activities, and the habits of regular industry which farming requires.*

But the Kentucky pioneers were also social and gregarious. They wanted plenty of room, and the usages of society sat lightly on them, but they sought opportunity for friendly association; and their large family connections, widened by intermarriage, gave to kinship the basis of a strong bond of attachment.

Kentucky was originally the western end of Virginia's west-

---

*Life of John Marshall, i, p. 29.

ernmost county of Fincastle. In December, 1776, Kentucky County was divided from Fincastle, and formed into a separate county, having its county-seat at Harrodsburg. About November 1, 1780, this county was divided into three,—Jefferson, Lincoln and Fayette. Kentucky was admitted to the Union as a state June 1, 1792. By this time there were fourteen counties, and their number grew. Washington was formed in 1792, and in the same year the legislature erected Hardin County. Both of these had formerly been parts of Nelson, and, prior to that, parts of Jefferson. Hardin County as originally formed contained not only its present territory but that included in twelve other counties in whole or in part. That is why one must search in several different county-seats for records relating to the same piece of land.

Kentucky was a land of conflicting land titles. Virginia sold her public land with no official survey. A fee was paid for the privilege of "taking up" a given number of acres, and a warrant was issued, directed to the surveyors to measure off that amount of land and certify it to the land office as satisfying the conditions of the warrant. This left the owner of the warrant at liberty to select any land which he might find, and have it surveyed and entered as his. Professor Shaler says: "To this day one can, if he please to pay the costs, patent any land that lies in Kentucky, and repeat the same process on the same area each year."

There would appear to be no good reason why any man who desires it should not obtain a patent to the court-house in Louisville or the race track at Lexington. He might have some difficulty in proving that his claim was prior to that of the occupants or others, but his patent would give him title against any subsequent adventurer.

At this moment, as Professor Shaler again informs us, there are hundreds of thousands of acres of land in Kentucky that have never been patented and on which no taxes are collected.

5

The old surveys did not always join. On the other hand, they often overlapped.

The advantages of the Virginia plan were large. The plan virtually authorized any man who paid a moderate fee to go out and find his land and send in a description of it, and feel assured that he could hold it if his claim was a good one. It facilitated rapid settlement of the new territory. Kentucky would have developed much more slowly had Virginia held her land off the market until it was officially surveyed and divided.

But on the other hand, the disadvantages were grave. To this day lawsuits abound that have their origin in these overlapping surveys.

Twice at least, on Nolin Creek and on Knob Creek, Thomas Lincoln paid money for farms and was later sued as a trespasser by the owners of large tracts inclusive of his small holdings.

Thomas Lincoln knew that in Indiana, just across the Ohio, it was not thus. There the land was surveyed by the United States Government into sections a mile square, and these sections were divided into four farms of one hundred and sixty acres each. A patent from the government meant a guarantee of possession, and not the probability of a lawsuit.

Abraham Lincoln, therefore, in giving his father's reasons for leaving Kentucky, mentioned prominently among them the uncertainty of land titles in Kentucky. In the light of preceding chapters, for the first time we know what Thomas Lincoln had suffered from overlapping titles in Kentucky.

The Kentucky of Lincoln's childhood was haunted by the shuddering fear of savages. We who look back more than a hundred years and have before us the map of the country, know that before 1800 Kentucky, which was a common hunting-ground for many tribes but the home of none, had been permanently cleared of resident hostile Indian tribes, but the early settlers did not know this. To them the forests were possible hiding-places for innumerable ferocious savages, pushed back, indeed, by the advancing pressure of immigration, but never an impossible distance away, and in number overwhelming as compared with any possible number of white men in any one neighborhood. There were frequent attacks and some bloody battles. The fear of Indians continued long after there was any need of it and boys were brought up on Indian stories. Often in his childhood Abraham heard the story of how his grandfather was killed, and how his father, Thomas, then a little child, had been with him at the time.

This story and others like it were told by the fire at night. Whenever strangers stayed over night in the Lincoln cabin, Indian stories were exchanged. Abraham heard this and other tales of murdering and scalping. The forest, infested with savages, never an impossible distance removed, had its marked and permanent influence upon the life of the boy.

The Durrett Collection has an original list, dated March 10, 1795, of a popular subscription to pay for scalps of Indians killed near Louisville, and along the road to Shepherdsville, a road familiar to the Lincolns. The last Indian battle was long past; but the fear of savages remained, and in that year there were alarms in many counties of Kentucky.

Lincoln's Kentucky was in the hills, but not in the mountains. It bordered hard on the Blue Grass, but was not of it. Geographically and socially he was of the highlands.

He saw almost nothing of slavery in his own childhood. Herndon says there were not fifty negroes in Hardin County at the time of Lincoln's birth. This is a mistake; there were several hundred negroes there.* In 1816, the year of Lincoln's removal, 1,238 slaves were listed on the tax lists of Hardin County. Herndon's estimate would have been more nearly correct if he had multiplied it by 24. Washington County in 1811 had 974

---

*In *The Paternity of Abraham Lincoln* I have cited the very interesting Hardin County Case, which went up to the Supreme Court, of Enlaws Heirs vs. Enlaws Executors, in which a slave woman named Nancy figured prominently.

negroes above sixteen years of age, perhaps a total population of 1,500 negroes, in a county with 1,827 white males above twenty-one. Here was nearly a slave to each possible male owner. Still, these slaves were not owned by the immediate neighbors of the Lincolns. If Lincoln on any childhood visit to friends in Washington County saw anything of slavery, he saw it in its mildest form.

The Kentucky of Lincoln's childhood was agitated by anti-slavery discussions. Slavery existed in that state when it was a county of Virginia, and already had its slaves when it became a state. Washington, Hamilton, Jefferson, Franklin, Adams, Madison and Monroe all lamented the existence of slavery in America and many hoped for its gradual decrease and ultimate abolition. When a Constitutional Convention was called in Kentucky in 1792, a movement to prohibit slavery within the bounds of that state began. This movement* was led by Reverend David Rice, the father of Presbyterianism in the West. He moved from Virginia in 1783, and was a leader in the organization of churches and in advancing the causes of education and of freedom. Just before the Constitutional Convention was called, he issued a pamphlet, entitled *Slavery Inconsistent with Justice and Good Policy*. He spoke freely of slavery's infringement of personal rights; of the degradation which it brought to womanhood; of its deprivation of religious and moral instruction; of its violent separation of families; of the encouragement which it gave to idleness and vice, particularly among young men; of the comparative unproductiveness of slave property and of the growing danger of servile insurrection. He answered the familiar arguments from Scripture in favor of slavery, and proposed that the coming convention should forever end slavery in Kentucky. He himself was a delegate to the Convention, and taking the floor he advocated abolition in a notable address. He said:

Holding men in slavery is the national vice of Virginia, and

*See *The Anti-Slavery Movement in Kentucky Prior to 1850,* by Asa Earl Martin. Published by the Filson Club, 1918.

while a part of that state, we were partakers of the guilt. As a separate state we are just now come to the birth; and it depends on our free choice whether we shall be born in this sin, or innocent of it.

Of the forty-five members of this Convention, seven were ministers. There were three Presbyterians, three Baptists and one Methodist. To their lasting honor be it recorded that all seven voted against slavery. Among them was Reverend John Bailey, the Baptist preacher who married Henry Sparrow and Lucy Hanks.

At that time there were only fifteen thousand slaves in Kentucky, and few people realized the seriousness of the evil which slavery entailed; but foremost of those who did realize the evil and courageously oppose it were the ministers.

The Severns Valley Church, the first Baptist Church of Elizabethtown, to which the Bush family belonged, and which Thomas and Nancy Lincoln probably attended while living in Elizabethtown, has the following of record:

January 23, 1796. *Quare*. is slavery oppression or not? The quare being taken up was answered in the affirmative; it was oppression.

Feb. 27, 1796. Question. Can we as a Church have fellowship with those that hold the righteousness of perpetual slavery? It was answered in the affirmative; that we could not.

April, 1796. Resolved that whereas the Church having taken into consideration Respecting Slavery that if any member has got Slaves or shall purchase hereafter any Slaves shall have the time that they shall serve to make satisfaction for his or her raising or purchase to his or her Master or Mistress either in the Church or belonging to any other provided there should not be a sufficiency of Brethren that shall be deemed by the Church to be Judges of the business but if Said Slaves shall not behave himself as a dutiful servant ought to do, that the sd Master or Mistress Shall dispose of Sd disobedient Slaves as they may judge expedient themselves."

The Nolin Church was separated from the Severns Valley Church on March 13, 1803. Already there had been separate preaching appointments, but one organization. From that date there were two organizations, both under the pastoral care of Reverend Josiah Dodge.

While Thomas and Nancy doubtless rode around to monthly preaching appointments when the weather was favorable, and did a great deal of their visiting of friends on these various pilgrimages, Thomas, certainly, and Nancy almost as certainly, had a local church membership; for when Thomas joined the Little Pigeon Baptist Church in Indiana, he brought his letter from Kentucky. Unfortunately, the record does not name the local church which issued the letter. To what church did Thomas and Nancy belong?

It can hardly have been the Severns Valley Church, for their residence in Elizabethtown was brief; moreover, the records of this church are extant and their names do not appear on the roll. Neither was it probably the Nolin Church. They must have attended services there, but this church was located four miles from the Sinking Spring farm, and farther from the Knob Creek farm. The nearest church to the Sinking Spring farm was the South Fork Baptist Church, organized in 1804. Its oldest records are in existence* and do not show the names of Thomas and Nancy Lincoln as members. At the time Thomas and Nancy established their home on Sinking Spring farm, the South Fork Church was torn by dissensions over slavery. The records show that on the third Saturday in July, 1808, just about the time the Lincolns were removing to this locality, fifteen members—a large section of the church—were "rent off from the Church on account of slavery." Of these fifteen were Isaac Friend and Jesse Friend.† The church to which this antislavery contingent apparently transferred their membership was the Little Mount Church, about three miles eastwardly of

---

*They are in possession of Honorable Otis M. Mather, of Hodgenville, one of the most reliable of my correspondents, from whom I have much valuable material on early Hardin County.

†Caleb Hazel was a member, and did not withdraw in the slavery dissension.

Hodgenville, toward Muldraugh's Hill. The records of this church are not known to exist. The organization and building have both disappeared. But we know that the Friends became members of the Little Mount Church. A bequest of Charles Friend, father of Dennis Hanks, preserved the cemetery, and there are inscribed stones as early as 1812, and others doubtless older. This was a reasonably convenient church for the Lincolns while living on the Sinking Spring farm, and much the most convenient for them while living at Knob Creek. There was a meeting-house on Knob Creek, with regular or occasional preaching, but, so far as I have been able to learn, no church organization. I am confident, therefore, that the church home of the Lincolns was the Little Mount Church, a Primitive Baptist anti-slavery Church; and that in its little graveyard Abraham Lincoln's little brother Thomas was buried.

In the first quarter of the nineteenth century the churches somewhat abated their opposition to slavery. The question was a divisive one, and its discussion was attended with increasing difficulty. The Methodist Church in 1804 ceased to memorialize legislatures for the abolition of slavery; and in 1808, it went further by removing all restrictions against its members' holding slaves. The Presbyterians, too, became less certain that it was advisably to "disturb the peace of Zion" by agitation of this subject. The agitation never died down; but it was the Baptists who formed the first anti-slavery body in Kentucky—the Kentucky Abolition Society, composed largely of members of the "Baptized Licking-Locust Association, Friends of Humanity," but embracing also some members of other communions.

Agitation against slavery in Kentucky measurably subsided. Henry Clay, who vigorously opposed slavery in 1799, ceased to stand strongly against it. Churches wearied of divisive controversy and counseled peace when there was no peace. Opposition to slavery did not wholly disappear; and in time it broke forth with new vigor in the preaching of John G. Fee, the fearless orations of Cassius M. Clay, and in the movement which led to the establishment of Berea College. There was some prospect that if slavery was let alone in Kentucky, it would break down of its own weight; and the opinion of Professor Shaler is familiar— that "if there had been no external pressure against slavery, there still would have been a progressive elimination of the slave element from the population, by emancipation on the soil, by the sale of slaves to the planters of the Southern States, and by their colonization in foreign parts."

The question was alive in the first decade of the nineteenth century, and the Lincoln family can not have escaped the discussion of it.

The Kentucky of Lincoln's experience was a religious community. The Hodgenville community was a Baptist settlement. Preaching services were held monthly, and the Lincolns doubtless attended their own and other church services from the time that Abraham had to be taken in his mother's arms.*

Dennis Hanks wrote truthfully to William H. Herndon: "William I have seen a Book which states that Lincolns was Quakers. I say this is a mis take they was Baptist."†

I, who rode through these mountains in later years, with my wardrobe in one saddle-bag and my library in the other, should like to pay my tribute of respect to the mountain doctors and the mountain preachers, hard-riding, sturdy ministers to men's bodies and souls. There was much in the religion of the backwoods which personally I did not enjoy, and much in the character of its preaching which was foreign to my own training and belief; but increasingly as I lived there I respected the men who rode their circuits and preached the vehement evangel of the hill country.

The religion of the Kentucky hills was boisterous and emotional. The doctrine was a rigid predestinarianism. Hell fire was preached with great fervor. Camp-meetings were held in

---

*Of the religous conditions of Lincoln's childhood and subsequent years I have treated fully in *The Soul of Abraham Lincoln*.

†This letter bears date of April 2, 1866. The original is in the Gunsaulus Collection in the Library of the University of Chicago.

the autumn, and were wide-reaching in their fervor and spiritual results. A religion less gentle or more refined would not have served so well the rude conditions of the frontier.

The doctrine of hell fire as the pioneer preachers proclaimed it was a very wholesome one; nothing less virile would have met the requirements of the situation. But it was preached for the admonition of the living, and held with all possible charity for the dead. The doctrine of predestination helped in the application of a broader charity than might otherwise have been possible. When I was preaching in the mountains of Kentucky, and had to share with a primitive Baptist preacher the funeral of a man killed in a drunken brawl, I always felt that his theology fitted the requirements of the situation quite as well as my own. I preached very little about hell, but these older men preached it mercilessly for the living and found great comfort for the dead in the sovereign grace of God. If this dead man was one whom God had chosen as of his elect, nothing could frustrate his grace. Only incidentally was it a matter of this man's repentance, but there was time for that. Between the time the bullet left the gun and the time it reached his heart, if he truly repented, that was time enough for God. What right had we to limit the pardoning grace of God? As for the living, let them take warning from this tragic ending of this, which might have been a useful life. As for the dead, let us believe that:

> Between the saddle and the ground,
> He pardon sought and pardon found.

The Methodists, and even the Disciples, had got into Hardin County in Lincoln's time, and while the Lincoln household was consistently Baptist, it was aware of the general influence upon the life of the community of these other denominations. The Little Mount Church was conveniently near; there was a meeting-house on Knob Creek; and the monthly meetings were events of social as well as religious importance.

The period of the Revolutionary War was one of great difficulty for all American churches; and was followed by a number of years in which godlessness, infidelity and immorality were rife. The westward movement did not of itself improve the moral tone of the period. Many religious people moved west, and some of them transported their religion with them. Some Virginia churches were seriously weakened by the migration to Kentucky; and many of the ministers, especially the young, hardy and adventurous, joined in the migration. But the conditions of pioneer life were hard upon the institutions of organized religion. Imlay wrote in 1792:

There is a number of people who have so long been in the custom of moving, farther and farther back as the country becomes settled, for the sake of hunting, and what they call range for their cattle . . . that they seem unqualified for any other life.*

Francis Bailey, in 1797, described the people of the migratory sort as "a race of people rough in their manners, impatient of restraint, and of an independent spirit, who are taught to look on all men as their equals, and no further worthy of respect than their conduct deserves."†

For several years, life on the frontier was rude and largely irreligious. But it was not wholly so in the period of Lincoln's boyhood. In 1800, a great revival of religion spread over the settlements and continued with intervals of partial cessation for a half-dozen years. Baptists, Methodists and Presbyterians joined in movements of far-reaching significance; and other denominations were born. The Cumberland Presbyterians, the "New Lights," the Disciples of Christ and the Shakers, all these came into being in Kentucky at about this time.

The revival was accompanied by physical exercises, by "fall-

*Imlay: *Topographical Description of the Western Territory of North America,* London, 1792, p. 149.

†Francis Bailey: *Journal of a Tour in the Unsettled Parts of North America, 1796-1797,* (London, 1856), p. 217. Theodore Roosevelt's *The Winning of the West,* contains an excellent description of social and religious life on the frontier.

ing," "the jerks" and by dancing and leaping. The camp-meeting came into existence; and its influence was wide-spread.

The Baptist Church was always strong in Kentucky. In 1800 there were in that new commonwealth one hundred six churches, with a total membership of five thousand. The Methodists were much fewer in number; but their system of circuits gave them a notable advantage as propagandists of their faith, and they rode, singing and shouting, far back into the wilderness.

The great revival was preceded by a period of depression, out of which came a deepening earnestness. Then came the message of the preachers, sternly rebuking sin and worldliness, portraying the terrors of an endless hell, and calling on men to repent and believe the Gospel.

People flocked together wherever religious interest was aroused. Isolated, and starved for social contacts, they sought out the places where meetings were announced; and when conviction came, it came with mighty power. Those people who went to camp-meetings to scoff were not infrequently taken with "jerks" and found no relief till they cried out in agony of spirit for forgiveness and peace. Drunkards, profligate men and women, and people notorious for vicious habits were seized with conviction and cried out for mercy.

The Baptist churches doubled their membership. The Methodists in a single year, 1801, within the bounds of the Western Conference, added 3,250 members, and in the following year, 1802, they added 3,000 more.

When Thomas Lincoln and Nancy Hanks were married in 1806 the intensity of this revival had abated and a reaction set in. But the wilderness had been evangelized; and a new spirit of reverence and religious earnestness was there.

The Kentucky of Lincoln's childhood was young. The men and women who had come over the wilderness road were largely young people, strong, resolute, courageous and full of the spirit of adventure. A majority of them had come from Virginia; and there was continuous travel back and forth through Cumberland Gap, keeping the new state in touch with the mother-state. But the wilderness population had a life of its own, independent, self-contained and virile.

Lincoln's Kentucky was a horse-racing, whisky-drinking community, with poverty as a check upon great excess in either gaming or drinking. There is record of a member of the Baptist Church in Elizabethtown being expelled for riding around the racetrack, which shows how sternly horse-racing was fought by the religious interests. But every one who owned anything owned a horse, and there were few better judges of horse-flesh than the preachers.*

Lincoln's Kentucky was a land of superstition. The backwoods abounded in superstitions. Few people now are free from superstition in some form, and in Kentucky, in that day, no one pretended to be free from it.† It was a region in which witches were understood to exist; a land of "haunts" and ghosts, and omens and warnings and "bad signs." Lincoln grew up amid superstition from which none of his neighbors was free. He inherited some of these superstitions and never outgrew them.

Not only did Lincoln spend his childhood in the midst of these primitive conditions, but he was in all essentials a part of his environment. He had in him dormant qualities which were

---

*I did my first preaching in the hills of Kentucky and Tennessee and write with a very tender feeling for a good horse. I have never yet convinced myself that there is special virtue in taking other people's dust.

†Reference may be made to *Kentucky Superstitions*, by Daniel Lindsey Thomas, Ph.D., late Professor of English at Center College, Danville, Kentucky, and President of the Kentucky Branch of the Folk-Lore Society; and, Lucy Blayney Thomas, M. D., a teacher at Nashville, Tennessee. This volume contains nearly four thousand "superstitions" that have been located in Kentucky—3954, to be exact. Not all of the instances cited deserve to be called superstitions, and not all by any means are distinctive of Kentucky. But the present author has found the greater part of these superstitions in various parts of Kentucky, and many of them elsewhere. The collection of such a body of what, under any possible flexibility of interpretation, may be called superstitions is arresting. Moreover, all these are given as now current. Most of them, and perhaps some others, were current in primitive days.

later to lift him above these conditions, but he was not in his childhood superior to the life around him. He was to the manner born. Later he came to think meanly of his poverty-stricken youth; but at the time his was the life of a normal backwoods boy, and he was the logical product of the life in the midst of which he lived.

CHAPTER VII

THE seven years of Lincoln's childhood belong to Kentucky. Twice seven were the years of his boyhood in Indiana.

Abraham Lincoln appears to have inherited from his father his life-long interest in waterways. Thomas Lincoln made one or more trips to New Orleans. On one of these journeys he was in the employ of Isaac Bush; and it is said that Isaac's intimate knowledge of Thomas stood the latter in good stead some years later when Thomas Lincoln returned to Kentucky and laid suit to the hand of Sarah Bush Johnston; her male relatives favored the match. Having learned how to build and navigate a flat-boat, Thomas Lincoln built one for himself in the fall of 1816, and launched it upon the waters of the Rolling Fork of Salt River, near the mouth of Knob Creek. The Rolling Fork has long been noted for its distilleries. Thomas Lincoln was no drunkard, neither was he a total abstainer. He procured four hundred gallons of corn whisky, and loaded it upon the flat-boat with his tools and the greater part of his household goods. He floated safely down Salt River to the Ohio, but on the larger stream he suffered shipwreck. His home-made craft capsized, and landed his cargo in the river. Recovering his tools, and most of his whisky, he continued his journey to Thompson's Ferry in Perry County, Indiana. There he left his property in the care of a settler named Posey, and set forth on foot to discover a site for a home. He had some acquaintance with a man named Thomas Carter who lived on Pigeon Creek, and he inquired the way to Carter's house.

The spot which Thomas Lincoln selected for a home is a slight elevation within the bounds of the present village of Lincoln City. The public school now stands immediately adjacent to the site of his cabin.*

The soil was reasonably fertile, but it lacked a good well. The land was heavily timbered. Thomas Lincoln selected his farm, marked its corners by chopping and piling some brush, and, warned by his experiences in titles in Kentucky, he walked to Vincennes and filed his claim.†

At the time the Lincoln family moved to this farm, there were only eight other settlers in the vicinity. Gentryville, of which town we hear much in the story of the boyhood of Lincoln, did not as yet exist. The new home was in the heart of the virgin forest, eighteen miles from Thompson's Ferry, where Lincoln had landed his mixed cargo and stored it in the home of Posey. Thomas Lincoln walked back from Vincennes to Knob Creek, and informed the family of his selection of a site for a home. His title, when he paid up, would be from the Government of the United States, with no more lawsuits about ownership or conflict of claims.

The journey from Knob Creek to Spencer County, Indiana, is not a long one. As traveled through the woods, and with detours for hills and fords, it was less than a hundred miles. If the family spent their first night with relatives near Elizabethtown, they had not more than three or four additional nights to spend upon the way. The journey can not have been a very

---

*The cabin was standing within the memory of men now living. After the house disappeared the site was marked by a cedar tree. A tablet now occupies the site of the permanent Lincoln home. It is probable that the school will be removed, and the home site transformed into a park by the State of Indiana.

†The entry of the land was made a year later, on October 15, 1817. The land is the Southwest Quarter of Section 32, Township 4, South of Range 5 west, in Spencer County, Indiana. He subsequently relinquished his claim upon the east half of this quarter-section, and paid for the remaining eighty acres. The land was purchased under the "Two dollar act" and the patent was not issued until June 6, 1827. It was signed by John Quincy Adams as President and George Graham as Commissioner of the General Land Office.

hard one. Thomas and Nancy each rode a horse, and each one had a child and a bundle of bedding and of household belongings upon the horse with the rider. Abraham was seven; Sarah was nine. There had been a little son Thomas, two years younger than Abraham, but he died in infancy. Four persons made the company. What livestock they had other than horses is not known, but it is to be presumed that there were one or more cows and possibly a few young hogs. Abraham and Sarah did not ride all the way. Part of the time they walked, for their own enjoyment and for the comfort of the horses.*

The family arrived at the home of Posey, where they borrowed a wagon, loaded in their additional belongings, and in due time came through the unbroken forest to what was to be for fourteen years the home of Abraham Lincoln.

Then followed what Lincoln later described as "pretty pinching times." The first winter was spent in what Dennis Hanks described as a "half-faced camp." It was a shed of poles, with the front facing the south, and the rear wall supported by the hill out of which room for the home had been dug. It was a cheerless place in which to spend a winter;† but there was no lack of firewood, and the supply of corn-bread and bacon held out till spring.

This poor shed was only the temporary home of the family,

---

*Lamon opines that Lincoln borrowed the horses from his brother-in-law, Ralph Crume; but Thomas Lincoln was the owner of four horses in 1816, and also of cows and other livestock.

†It is interesting to note and record that, as the first winter of the Lincolns in Illinois was "the winter of the deep snow" with its attendant hardship to man and beast, and its pathetic slaughter of wild game, the year of their removal from Kentucky to Indiana was one of severity. No records exist of the suffering of the Lincolns on account of the unusual climatic conditions of that year, but throughout the country it was a season of violent changes. In Salem, Massachusetts, according to Perley's *Historic Storms of New England,* the weather about May twenty-third was the hottest in ten years, rising to 101 in the shade, and on June fifth it was 92; but next morning it was 43, a drop of 49 degrees in one night, and there were snow flurries in parts of Massachusetts. On June seventh, there was snow in the suburbs of Boston, and a foot or more of snow fell in Williamstown. On June twenty-second and twenty-fourth, the thermometer ranged from 93 to 101 in Salem, and then came more cold weather. We have no such detailed record of the weather in Kentucky, but we know that throughout the country the year 1816 was remembered as "eighteen-hundred-and-froze-to-death."

though it appears to have been kept somewhat steadily in use. The reports of the Lincolns to their Kentucky kinsfolk can not have been very depressing, for there soon followed an exodus of Sparrows and Hankses to the new land of promise. When the Lincolns moved into their permanent home, Thomas and Elizabeth Sparrow came on and occupied the camp until they had a home ready; and afterward there came Levi Hall and Nancy his wife, and there were other families moving from Kentucky who successively rejoiced in the poor shelter of the half-faced camp.

The home which Thomas Lincoln built was of hewn logs and about eighteen feet square. It had a low loft reached by means of pins driven into the logs in the corner. The earth was its floor and it had neither window nor door at the beginning. These luxuries came later.

Game was abundant, and the settlers were not too far from their former homes in Kentucky nor from the river to procure corn until they could raise some of their own. Wheat was scarce in the beginning, and it was long before it became plenty; but there was no lack of corn-bread.

The first great sorrow in the life of Abraham Lincoln occurred two years after the removal of the family to Indiana. The "milk-sick" visited the settlement, and claimed a number of victims. Thomas and Elizabeth Sparrow, who had been Nancy's foster parents, died. Levi and Nancy Hall also died. Thomas Lincoln sawed out lumber for their coffins, and gave them decent burial according to the standards of the time and place. A few days later Nancy Hanks Lincoln died. The date of her death was October 5, 1818. Again Thomas, aided by Abraham, brought the whip-saw into requisition, and the mother of the future president was laid to rest beside the Sparrows and the Halls.*

---

*The land which includes the cemetery where the body of Abraham Lincoln's mother is buried is now a state park. The situation is beautiful, and the grave is well marked and receives adequate care. The knoll where

Of the last sickness of Lincoln's mother, we have one testimony from an eye-witness, as it was given in Herndon:

She struggled on, day by day, a good Christian woman, and died on the seventh day after she was taken sick. Abe and his sister Sarah waited on their mother, and did the little jobs and errands required by them. There was no physician nearer than thirty-five miles. The mother knew she was going to die, and called the children to her bedside. She was very weak, and the children leaned over while she gave her last messages. Placing her feeble hand on little Abe's head, she told him to be kind and good to his father and sister; to both she said, Be good to one another, expressing a hope that they might live, as they had been taught by her, to love their kindred and worship God.*

According to the custom of Kentucky Baptists then and now, the burial of these early settlers in the Pigeon Creek neighborhood was not accompanied by funeral services.† Not simply the absence of ministers but a distinct and well established custom, still persisting, postponed the funeral for several months. There was nothing unusual about the delay in the funeral of Mrs. Lincoln.

---

the grave is located is sightly, and the surroundings are appropriate, but the area owned by the state should be increased, and the approach improved. The first marker above the grave of Lincoln's mother was erected by local subscription, headed by Joseph D. Armstrong, as stated in a paper by his daughter, Miss Ida D. Armstrong of Rockport, Indiana, before the Southwestern Indiana Historical Society, October, 1923. When this stone was removed for a larger one, the little marker was broken up and carried away by relic hunters. The second marker, which now stands at the foot of the grave, was erected in 1879, the gift of Clement Studebaker, Sr., of South Bend. The present monument was dedicated October 1, 1902. In 1907 the property was transferred to the State of Indiana. A suitable iron fence was erected around the graves of Nancy Hanks Lincoln and the four relatives who lie buried with her. The five graves are not all in one row, but are in one row of three graves and another of two. Soil where a grave has been dug and filled can rarely, if ever, be replaced in such manner as to mislead an experienced grave-digger who has occasion to remove the upper layers or to re-excavate the grave. The erection of the fence and the laying of a walk compelled such disturbance of the top layers of soil. The three graves in one row are those of Nancy Hanks Lincoln and her foster parents. Thomas and Elizabeth Hanks Sparrow; the two graves at the foot of these three are those of Nancy's aunt, Nancy Hanks Hall and her husband, Levi Hall.

*Herndon's *Lincoln*, 1st ed., p. 27.

†The subject on which so many writers have gone astray has been considered at length in *The Soul of Abraham Lincoln*. Reference to that book makes extended treatment of the subject here unnecessary.

Some months after the death of Nancy Hanks, a funeral service was held. Reverend David Elkins,* a Baptist preacher from Kentucky, preached, and probably included the Halls and Sparrows and other deceased neighbors in the same funeral discourse.

A little more than a year after the death of his first wife, Thomas Lincoln went back to Elizabethtown, and courted Sarah Bush Johnston, whom he had known before her first marriage. She was the widow of Daniel Johnston, jailer of Hardin County.†

Thomas Lincoln and Sarah Bush Johnston were married in Elizabethtown, Kentucky, December 2, 1819. Although she was a poor widow, with three children and in debt, she was not without a substantial marriage portion. She had bed-clothes

---

*Reverend David Elkins, who preached the funeral sermon at the grave of Abraham Lincoln's mother, Nancy Hanks Lincoln, was born in South Carolina, and served as a private in the Second South Carolina Militia in the War of 1812. His enlistment was October 17, 1814, and his discharge, March 9, 1815. He was then a resident of the Richland district, South Carolina, and later migrated to Kentucky. He appears in Spencer's *History of Kentucky Baptists,* first as minister of Good Hope Church in Taylor County. About 1820 he united with the Separate Baptists of Nolynn (Nolin) Association. These were anti-slavery. Spencer says:

"He was a man of extraordinary natural intellect, but was uncultivated, being barely able to read. He was extremely poor as to this world's goods, and what was worse, he was very indolent and slovenly in his dress. Yet it pleased the Lord to use him to good account, especially in the early days of his ministry. . . . His reputation was somewhat sullied in his later years, perhaps from too free use of strong drink."

He was minister in Indiana of the Rock Lick church and later of the Spice Valley Baptist Church. He removed to Lawrence County in the 'forties, and died in 1857, and is buried in a nearly abandoned cemetery three miles west of Mitchell. Citizens of that town are proposing to erect a monument over his grave, which now has only the government marker with the inscription, "David Elkins, 2nd South Carolina Militia, War of 1812."

†The story is told that when Thomas Lincoln proposed to Sarah Bush Johnston she said to him that she could not accept immediately, because she was in debt. He obtained a list of her creditors, paid the bills, produced the receipts for her inspection and renewed his proposal. She accepted. This story is not new; but I should like to add that members of the Bush family, including S. H. Bush, an aged member of the Elizabethtown bar, a former Confederate soldier, and a nephew of Sarah Bush, related the story to me in detail. The Bush family show no sensitiveness concerning the story, but tell it rather with pride that she married a man of sufficient resource and resolution to meet an emergency of that kind. The Hardin County records show that Daniel Johnston left her poor. She did better in her second marriage than in her first.

and cooking utensils and furniture such as the humble home on Pigeon Creek had never known. Thomas Lincoln borrowed from his brother-in-law, Ralph Crume,* a four-horse wagon, into which Thomas loaded his bride, her three children and her belongings, and made his return journey to Spencer County. In due time they arrived, and the new mother took up her responsibilities.

What Sarah Bush Lincoln found on her arrival may or may not have surprised her. She knew the lot of pioneers, and there is no reason to suppose that Thomas Lincoln had attempted to deceive her. At the same time she must have felt some contrast between his readiness in Elizabethtown to produce money and pay off her small indebtedness and the manifest poverty of the home as she found it. The cabin was windowless and floorless, and the furniture was of the most primitive sort. There were two unkempt children, Sarah, aged twelve and Abraham aged ten. There was yet another, for Dennis Hanks, since the death of the Sparrows, lived with the Lincolns.

There was call for a gourd of soft soap, and plenty of water. The children were scrubbed and better clad. The home took on new character at once. Thomas Lincoln had to saw out lumber for a floor, and plane the boards. He bought lime and mixed whitewash, and used it where Sarah directed. Dennis Hanks, who remembered her coming and the revolution which it wrought, said that Aunt Sarah "certainly had faculty." She transformed the home of the cheerless widower and his two motherless children into a spot of pleasant associations and happy memories. Her own three children, John, Sarah and Matilda, lived in perfect accord with the children already there. It was a good day for Abraham Lincoln and the world that brought Sarah Bush Johnston to the rude cabin of Thomas Lincoln. It was equally a good day for Sarah and her fatherless children.

Of Sarah Bush, her granddaughter, Mrs. Harriet Chapman,

---

*It is the loan of Crume's wagon to meet this matrimonial emergency which careless biographers have confused with the original migration.

daughter of Dennis Hanks, wrote: "My grandmother is a very tall woman, straight as an Indian, and was, when I first remember her, very handsome, sprightly, talkative and proud. She wore her hair curled till gray; is kind-hearted and very charitable, and also very industrious."

Herndon spent a day with her in 1865, and was much impressed by her character and her love for her stepson, Abraham. To this visit we owe some of our best and most authentic traditions of Lincoln's boyhood.

The Southern Indiana of Lincoln's boyhood was a transplanted section of Kentucky. The social life, the religious environment, the superstitions, the schools, were all of the same sort with which the family was familiar. Moreover, it was not so far away as to forbid occasional return, and more frequent visits from old neighbors as they came over the river and toward the West, looking for better locations than those they had possessed in Kentucky. The urge that was in the patriarch Abraham, sending him forth not knowing whither he went, was in the blood of the American pioneer.

Abraham Lincoln attended school in Indiana. His first teacher was Andrew Crawford, his second a man named Sweeney, and his third was Azel W. Dorsey. The school which Lincoln attended was one and one-fourth miles from the home. Like the Kentucky schools, it was a "blab" school.* The system of silent study was beginning to be recognized, but how was the teacher to know that a boy was studying unless the boy kept repeating his lesson aloud as he studied? And how was he to be persuaded to continue his industrious application to his spelling book unless the teacher passed about the room, whip in hand, and gently or otherwise whipped those who were silent?

Abraham's schoolmates in after years remembered that he had

---

*The blab schools had not passed entirely out of Southern Indiana when George Cary Eggleston had the experiences which furnished his brother Edward Eggleston the material for his *Hoosier Schoolmaster.* This was about 1858. There were few of any other kind forty years earlier. See *The First of the Hoosiers,* by George Cary Eggleston; being reminiscences of Edward Eggleston.

been an apt pupil, eager to learn, and that he quickly surpassed his companions. His sister Sarah, who accompanied him, was also a bright pupil, of good mind, and was more industrious than her brother. For while Abraham loved books, he did not love hard work; and when study became work, he became for a time less eager for learning, and gave himself to fun.

Of Lincoln's school-days in Indiana, the most definite memories appear to be those of the school kept by Andrew Crawford. This teacher endeavored to impart not only the education contained in books, but the principles which underlie the usages of polite society. One pupil was required to go out-of-doors, and to be met at the door by another pupil who inquired his name, and then escorted him about the room, presenting him to the pupils one by one.

In his first schools Abraham used only the spelling book. It was the custom in that day for a pupil to spell the book through several times before he began to read. He knew how to spell "incomprehensibility," a "word of eight syllables, accented on the sixth" long before he could read that interesting statement that "Ann can spin flax." At first he used Dillworth's Speller, then Webster's *Old Blueback*. After long and faithful use of the speller, he learned to use the reader, and in time became familiar with Murray's English Reader, which he believed to have been the best text-book ever supplied to an American boy. Having used it as a text-book, I am inclined to agree with him.

The whole of his schooling, as he has informed us, was less than a year. What he has told and what is otherwise known of his teachers has caused some authors to question whether his teaching was of any considerable value to him; whether, like George Bernard Shaw, he was not one of those whose education was interrupted by his schooling. But I know the kind of schools Lincoln attended, and in spite of their grave limitations I have a high sense of their value. Even the discipline of those schools, severe as it was, and combining "lickin' and l'arnin'" with a liberal allowance for the licking, was not without its worth. If the teachers were ignorant, so were the pupils and their parents; if the teacher could cipher to the rule of three, that was quite as far as most of the pupils had any occasion to go. The school-houses were bare, log buildings, with the cracks unchinked. They were built upon slopes high enough at one end for hogs to rest under the floor, and fill the place with fleas,—a situation only partly remedied by the pennyroyal which the pupils brought in by the armful and tramped upon in the aisle. The benches were of puncheon and had no backs, and it was thought a needless concession to the love of luxury to saw off the legs where they projected upward through the surface of the seat. But the children departed from those schools a little less ignorant than they were when they entered.

The books that Lincoln read and re-read in his boyhood had a marked influence upon his life. There was the Bible, first of all, the basis of his pure literary style, and the foundation of his system of righteousness expressed in law. There were *Pilgrim's Progress* and Æsop's *Fables*. There was Weems' *Life of Washington*, at which people smile, but which did good to Abraham Lincoln and many another lad. There was *Robinson Crusoe*, and a History of the United States. If we could substitute a better *Life of Washington* and a modern History of the United States, it would be for the profit of any American boy if he were shut up with these half-dozen books and no others until he thoroughly mastered them. They were an almost ideal selection. To this short list he later added Franklin's *Autobiography* and Weems' *Life of Marion*.

It has become common to refer mirthfully to Weems' *Life of Washington*, and in truth it has no great merit as critical biography; but it is quite as good in that particular as many more pretentious works, including some Lives of Lincoln. Even the story of the cherry-tree and the little hatchet has this to be said in its favor, that such a story could not easily have come into current circulation and belief in the immediate vicinity of Washington's home if he had not borne in boyhood as in manhood the reputation of being truthful. Lincoln read this pompous and highly colored book with none of the disdain of the modern critic. In 1861, in addressing the Senate of the State of New Jersey, he said:

May I be pardoned if, upon this occasion, I mention that away back in my childhood, the earliest days of my being able to read, I got hold of a small book, such a one as few of the younger members have ever seen—Weems' *Life of Washington.* I remember all the accounts there given of the battle-fields and struggles for the liberties of the country, and none fixed themselves upon my imagination so deeply as the struggle here at Trenton, New Jersey. The crossing of the river, the contest with the Hessians, the great hardships endured at that time, all fixed themselves on my memory more than any single Revolutionary event; and you all know, for you have all been boys, how these early impressions last longer than any others. I recollect thinking then, boy even though I was, that there must have been something more than common that these men struggled for.

Abraham Lincoln became the owner of Weems' *Life of Washington* through an accident. He borrowed the book from Josiah Crawford, a neighbor reputed to have been close-fisted. The book was placed upon a little shelf below an unchinked crack between the logs of the Lincoln home and was damaged by rain. Lincoln offered to pay for it, and had to pull fodder three days at twenty-five cents a day to purchase the book.

Crawford has been unjustly blamed for his part in this transaction. It was his right to receive compensation for the book, and seventy-five cents was a fair price, and twenty-five cents was not an oppressive wage. Abraham often worked for less. Abraham had cause to dislike Crawford, but not for his collection of an extortionate price for his damaged book. And Abraham then owned and prized the book.

Studying by the fire at night, or by the light of pine knots, and lying in the shade in the daytime with a corn pone in one hand and a book in the other, Abraham Lincoln made the ac-

SNAPSHOTS OF GENTRYVILLE

Site of Lincoln home
Main Street

Little Pigeon Church
Grave of Lincoln's sister

quaintance of a few highly desirable books, and he profited by the reading of them.

At school Abraham was a leader. He stood well in his studies. He was a good reader, an excellent speller, a good penman, and was able to compose well. Very early he had a desire to write out his opinions on many topics; and his essays attracted attention at once. He won the respect of his teachers and also of his fellow-students. His habitual and well-known fairness caused him to be chosen to decide mooted questions, and his decisions were accepted without appeal. Altogether it is an attractive young giant who emerges from our study of the conditions of Lincoln's boyhood. He was rude and uncultured; but he had a good mind, a warm heart, a love of justice and fair play, and a high sense of honor that won for him the lasting respect of those who knew him.

While Lincoln was a boy in Indiana he had two important social centers, the mill and the general store at Gentryville.* He loved to go to mill, and he loved to loaf in the country store. He liked the conversation, the discussion, the attempts to settle the problems of the universe. He participated in all this with great satisfaction to himself, and to the joy of his companions. He was a good story-teller, a clever debater, a jolly companion.

Abraham Lincoln in his mature years thought, spoke and moved slowly. He inherited on both sides the deliberate and almost lazy movement of the Kentucky hill-dweller. But in one particular he exhibited very rapid development. In his eleventh year he suddenly shot up in stature until he overtopped all his companions. This rapid growth made him tired, and he never recovered from the effort. On this abrupt change, David Turnham wrote to Herndon:

As he shot up he seemed to change in appearance and action. Although quick-witted and ready with an answer, he began to exhibit deep thoughtfulness, and so was often lost in studied re-

---

*I have discovered no local tradition in Gentryville that Lincoln was ever a clerk in the store there, and I do not credit the statement.

flection. We could not help noticing the strange turn in his
actions. He disclosed rare timidity and sensitiveness, especially
in the presence of men and women, and, although cheerful
enough in the presence of the boys, he did not appear to seek our
company as earnestly as before.*

Among the incidents of Lincoln's boyhood which reach us
practically at first hand, and may therefore be presumed to be
reliable, is one which his stepsister Matilda Johnston, later the
wife of Squire Hall, related to Herndon.

When Lincoln was well grown, he undertook one autumn the
clearing of a piece of woodland so far from the house that it
was his custom to take his lunch and spend the day. Matilda,
youngest child of Mrs. Lincoln, liked to go with him, but her
mother forbade her. One morning she stole away, and slipping
through the bushes, came up behind Abraham as he went, singing, to his work. She crept up behind, and with a cat-like leap,
landed with one hand on each of his shoulders and her knees in
the middle of his back. That trick, familiar to school-boys, enabled her to land Abraham on his back before he could turn
around or in any way guard his fall. As he fell, his ax cut a
wound in her ankle. He staunched the flow of blood with bits
of cloth torn from his shirt and her clothing; and when she had
ceased or nearly ceased crying, he asked:

" 'Tilda, what are you going to tell mother about getting hurt?"

"I'll tell her I did it with the ax," she sobbed. "That will be
the truth, won't it?"

"Yes, that's the truth, 'Tilda," replied Abraham, "but it's not
the whole truth. Tell the whole truth, 'Tilda, and trust your
good mother for the rest."†

Incidents such as this illustrate the reasons for Abraham's
popularity in his youth. He was manly, courageous, truthful,
sympathetic and honest. No incident comes to us from those
years that shows him in any act of meanness or dishonesty.

---

*Herndon's *Lincoln,* 1st Ed., i, p. 25.
†Herndon's *Lincoln,* i, p. 34.

Some of the most interesting of the recollections of Lincoln that were given to Herndon in 1865, were those of Mrs. Allen Gentry, formerly Katie Roby. She attended school with Lincoln, and was about three or four years his junior. While she took pains to explain that they were never lovers, there was between them a boy-and-girl attachment.

She told how one day at a spelling match, when she and Lincoln were on opposite sides, she hesitated over the word "defied," not feeling sure whether to spell it with an "i" or a "y." Lincoln, seeing her hesitation, generously helped her by holding up one finger to his eye.

When Lincoln was about to sail down the Ohio River on his flat-boat, she sometimes strolled down to the river with him in the evening, and he and Katie dangled their bare feet in the water and watched the sun go down and the moon come up. On one such evening he explained to her that the sun did not really set nor the moon rise, but that the earth revolved and made these other bodies appear to move around it. Such knowledge seemed to her quite wonderful, indeed, incredible; for the people among whom Lincoln spent his youth, including the ministers, believed the earth to be flat and stationary, and the sun to move around it once in twenty-four hours. Katie never forgot the vast learning of Abraham.

She took careful account of his appearance, and it is to her we owe our best description of the Lincoln of that date.

At the end of his seventeenth year he weighed about one hundred sixty pounds, was tough, wiry, vigorous and strong. His body was slender, and his head seemed small in proportion to his great height. His legs and his arms were extraordinarily long, and his hands and feet very large. She said:

His skin was shriveled and yellow. His shoes, when he had any, were low. He wore buckskin breeches, linsey-woolsey shirt and a cap made from the skin of a squirrel or coon. His breeches were baggy, and lacked by several inches meeting the tops of his shoes, thereby exposing his shin-bone, sharp, blue and narrow.

Certainly he was not handsome; but he was tall, kind and brave; and both the boys and girls admired him.

By the time he was seventeen, Lincoln had attained his great stature. He had used the ax from the time of his arrival in Indiana, and could sink it deep in the log. He could plow, reap and do all manner of rough work, and was sometimes employed by neighbors. He was in demand in hog-killing, and for this hard, none too pleasant work received what now seems a poor stipend; but it was a time when money was hard to get, and a very little of it purchased a considerable amount of muscular toil.

He shared in the merry-making of the neighborhood, and showed no refinement of taste higher than his neighbors. Too much has been made of a certain rude country prank which he and others are alleged to have performed at a wedding, and some coarse articles that he wrote about it.* Jokes at weddings are not very refined even now, and such as were then performed were part and parcel of rude frontier life. The pioneer was rough and coarse-grained, and the objects of his mirth were elemental. They were coarse but not degenerate. The author finds no good reason to reproduce here any of the crude lines written by Lincoln in this period; they are easily accessible for any who want them, and there is no occasion to suppress them. Neither is it necessary to take them too seriously. They represent the characteristic humor and satire of the period and the place. Lincoln was as refined as his boyhood neighbors, and at that time not much more so.

---

*It may be worth while to record that the practical joke described in the verses which Herndon unwisely printed probably never occurred. After the appearance of Herndon's book, inquiry was made in Indiana, and what was declared to be the original manuscript of Lincoln's doggerel was then in possession of Edmond Grigsby, of Rockport, Indiana. A newspaper obtained possession of a copy, and before printing the *Chronicles* sent a reporter to interview Elizabeth Grigsby, or "Aunt Betsy" as she was known. She was asked about the manuscript, and declared that it was true that Lincoln wrote the verses, but that there was no intention of giving the impression that the event really occurred. "Yes, they did have a joke on us," said Aunt Betsy. "They said my man got into the wrong room, and Charles got into my room. But it wasn't so. Lincoln just wrote that for mischief. Abe and my man often laughed about that."

Thomas and Nancy Lincoln were religious people, and Sally Bush, who later came to the home, was also religious. The assumption that Thomas Lincoln was dragged into church membership by his second wife, does not appear to be well-founded. When he first reached Indiana, there was no church on Pigeon Creek.* When he united with the Little Pigeon Church, his membership was by letter, while that of his wife was "by experience."

It was Thomas Lincoln's custom to "ask a blessing" at the table. On one occasion when the meal consisted wholly of roasted potatoes, Abraham looked up from the potatoes to his father and remarked, "Dad, I call them mighty poor blessings."

Thomas Lincoln became a prominent as well as a consistent member of the Little Pigeon Church.

The records of the Little Pigeon Church contain this record of the uniting of Thomas and Sarah Lincoln:

June the 7 1823
The church met and after prayer proceeded to busyness.
1st Inquired for fellowship.
2nd Invited members of sister churches to seats with us.
3rd Opened a dore for the Reception of Members.
4th Received Brother Thomas Linkhon by letter and
5th the case of Sister Elizabeth White coled for & refires and the Brother and the brother that was to bare a letter to his aquited.
6th The church appoints Messengers to Represent them at the next asiation: Yong Lemare Charles Harper & Wm Stark and the Clirk to prepare a letter to be inspected At our Next Meting—
7th Received Brother John wire by Relation And Sister ——— Linkhon and Thomas Carter by Experance.

A few days later Abraham Lincoln doubtless saw his stepmother immersed in the waters of Little Pigeon Creek.

---

*Honorable Thomas B. McGregor, Assistant Attorney General of Kentucky, first called my attention to the Pigeon Creek records, which I later examined and copied. I acknowledge the courtesy of the clerk of the church, Mr. Lewis Varner, in being permitted to copy these records.

Baptisings in those days were noisy events; and it was con
sidered desirable for the candidate to "come up a-shouting." But
we can imagine that Sarah Bush took the experience calmly, and
with a deep realization of its meaning.

The Lincolns were active members of the church. Thomas
Lincoln was an officer, and is of record as a contributor. There
are several records such as this:

We the under Signed Refereas being Conveaned at the meting
house on the 20th of February in 1830 in order to Settle A difficulty between Sister Grigsby & Sister Crafford first chose
brother T. Lincoln moderator & Bro. Wm. Bristow Clk. not
being one of the body qualified and agreed to deside on all
points by a Majority third after a long patient Investigation on
the above case on motion The referees agrees that the Charge
is In legal therefore agrees the defendent is aquited.

Attest: T. Lincoln mod.
    Wm. Bristow Clk.   A. Guntraman
                                  R. Oskins
                                  I. Oskins
                                  D. Turnham.

The name of Thomas Lincoln appears frequently on the record
book of the Little Pigeon Church. Thomas was often moderator
of church meetings, and sometimes a messenger to other
churches. He was appointed to arbitrate disputes between members. At no time is there any indication that he and his wife were
not acceptable members of the church, and loved by most of their
neighbors. We know, however, that the Lincolns and the Grigsbys were not always at peace. Abraham's sister Sarah married
Aaron Grigsby, and died at the birth of her first child. Abraham,
and apparently the other members of his family, disliked the
Grigsbys, evidently for some reason associated with the death of
Sarah. When the Lincolns were preparing to leave Indiana for
Illinois, they requested their church letters, that they might unite
with a church in their new home state. These letters were
granted at a meeting of the church November 12, 1829. There

was no opposition. But two months later, on January tenth, this entry appears:

Inquired for fellowship and Sister Nancy Grigsby informed the church that she is not satisfied with Br. and Sister Lincoln. The church agreed and called back their letters until satisfaction could be obtained. The partys convened at Wm. Hoskins and agreed and settled the difficulty.

So Thomas and Sarah Lincoln left Indiana with their church letters in due form, commending them to any other Primitive Baptist Church.

The Primitive Baptist Church in Lincoln's day was not a startlingly progressive organization. The records of Little Pigeon, in the time of the membership of the Lincolns, show more than one vote in which the church declined all responsibility for missionary organizations and "track societies." To this day that church, and the other churches of that communion in the Little Zion Association, have their monthly preaching appointments instead of weekly services. They have grown somewhat more progressive with the passage of the years; but in Lincoln's day they stood for the good old Two-Seed, Hardshell, Anti-Missionary, Predestinarian gospel, and he was not much of a preacher who could not be heard a mile.

The woods of Kentucky and the woods of Indiana are much alike. But Spencer County has one thing adjacent to its woods which the Knob Creek neighborhood did not have, and that is the Ohio River, a mighty artery of the nation's life and a potent influence in the life of Lincoln. The significance of this fact must not be overlooked. In his later boyhood Lincoln was engaged as a ferryman, at the mouth of Anderson's Creek, at the present village of Troy. This was a task which must have been an education to him. Low water tied up all sorts of traffic, and even when the traffic moved, it was deliberate. Lincoln had occasion to meet and know many types of life as he wrought at his task as a ferryman.

6

When he was nineteen, he made a voyage on a flat-boat to New Orleans. It must have been an illuminating journey. He received eight dollars a month and his return transportation; but what he learned must have been worth to him much more than the money, although at the time the money doubtless seemed the more desirable. He was later to make another voyage, from Illinois, and we know some convictions concerning human freedom that grew stronger as he made that journey.

For several months in the latter part of 1826, Abraham worked for James Taylor of Posey's Landing, near where the Lincoln family had first entered Indiana ten years previously. Taylor was a merchant, operating a "bank-store" which, located on the river bank, supplied both river trade and that of the farms. He also operated a ferry across Anderson's Creek. Lincoln does not appear to have worked in the store; Taylor was assisted there by his son Green. Lincoln's task was to operate the ferry.

Near the same point was a ferry across the Ohio River, operated by John T. Dill. Apparently there was a somewhat sharp distinction between the right to navigate a ferry across Anderson's Creek, which was an Indiana concession, and that which permitted the operation of a ferry across the Ohio; for by the original Act admitting Kentucky to the Union, the Ohio River to low-water mark on the opposite shore, lies within the jurisdiction of Kentucky.

In the spring of 1827, Lincoln built for himself a flat-bottomed boat, and now and then did a little business on his own account. He was able at times to earn an honest penny by rowing passengers out from the Indiana side to steamers halted by signal. Secretary Seward was accustomed to tell a story about an entire dollar which Lincoln received from two appreciative passengers for a service of this character. A dollar for less than a day's work seemed fabulously large to a young man accustomed to work for something like sixteen cents a day.

The river ferryman, John T. Dill, did not enjoy having Lin-

coln engage in this traffic; and apparently Lincoln did not
solicit custom when Dill was on the Indiana side of the river.
But if a steamer had been hailed and was approaching, and
Dill was on the other side of the stream, that was Lincoln's
opportunity, and he improved it.

One day when Lincoln was in his boat, Dill hailed him from
the Kentucky side, and Lincoln rowed to the shore, where he
was seized by Dill and his brother, the brother having hidden
till Lincoln was within reach. They accused him of taking their
business away from them, and threatened to duck him in the
river. Perhaps they felt some misgivings as to whether even the
two of them were safe in an undertaking of this character. For
whatever reason, they offered to modify the plan if Lincoln
would go with them to the house of a magistrate and have the
matter settled according to law. Lincoln readily consented, and
the three went together to the house of Squire Samuel Pate, only
a few hundred yards away.

There the Dills entered complaint, and swore out a warrant.
This was issued and served upon the defendant, present in court,
and the case of the Commonwealth of Kentucky against Abraham Lincoln was called. Both parties announced themselves
as ready for trial.

The complaining witnesses introduced their evidence. The
defendant had transported passengers from the Indiana shore
to steamboats on the Ohio River, though having no license to
operate a ferry on that stream. The river belonged to Kentucky, and John T. Dill held a license to operate a ferry across
the Ohio River from the Kentucky shore to the mouth of Anderson's Creek.

The defendant admitted the facts as alleged, but denied having violated the statute or having infringed upon the rights of
the authorized ferryman. The ferry license authorized John T.
Dill to convey passengers across the Ohio River, and gave him
the exclusive right of doing this for pay between the points
specified. But it did not forbid others than the ferryman to
transport passengers to the middle of the stream.

He told the magistrate that he had not intended to violate the law and did not think that he had done so. He had not claimed the privilege of "setting persons across the river," but had rowed them out to midstream. He stated that as the ferry-boat could not always be on the Indiana side when a steamer was approaching, and as steamers would not be delayed, it seemed but right that passengers who were awaiting the steamer should have opportunity to hire a boat to convey them to the steamer when it arrived.

Squire Pate was impressed by the evident sincerity of the young man, and began to examine with some care the copy of the Statutes of Kentucky which he owned. He stated at length that Dill unquestionably held the lawful and exclusive right to "set a person across" the river; but the court was of opinion that that right did not preclude an unlicensed person from rowing passengers to the middle of the stream. The defendant was therefore acquitted.

The Dill brothers, much disgruntled, went their way, and Lincoln sat on the ample porch and talked with Squire Pate. The squire told Lincoln that many difficulties arise because people do not inform themselves concerning the statutes, and said that every man ought to know something about law.*

Squire Pate had built his new hewn-log house with one of its rooms of unusual size, with special reference to use as a magistrate's court room, and once a month he cleared his monthly docket. Lincoln rowed across the river more than once to attend these trials, and grew increasingly interested in court procedure. There would appear to be reasonable probability that this case had an important influence in turning Lincoln's attention

---

*My knowledge of this interesting case comes to me from Honorable William H. Townsend, who has discovered these facts and corroborated them by evidence obtained from the descendants of Squire Pate, who still lives in the house where the case of the Commonwealth of Kentucky against Abraham Lincoln was tried. Very appropriately, Mr. Townsend owns the copy of the *Revised Statutes of Indiana* which belonged to David Turnham, and which Abraham Lincoln studied after this experience. Mr. Townsend is relating this and much other important information in his *Abraham Lincoln, Litigant,* to be published about the time of publication of the present work.

to the law. He borrowed a copy of the Indiana Statutes from David Turnham, and afterward borrowed other books from Judge John Pilcher.

Stern as were the conditions of frontier life, they did not obliterate any of the essential joys of living. Hope was strong in the hearts of the pioneers, and love and labor were the common lot. There was little time for romance, but there was rough and hearty and generally wholesome merry-making, and now and then a dream of something beyond.

As near a day-dream as has come to us of Abraham Lincoln is the following, which has found a place in various collections of Lincoln's stories and sayings, and which was recorded by T. W. S. Kidd, editor of *The Morning Monitor,* of Springfield:

Did you ever write out a story in your mind? I did when I was a little codger. One day a wagon with a lady and two girls and a man broke down near us, and while they were fixing up, they cooked in our kitchen. The woman had books and read us stories, and they were the first I had ever heard. I took a great fancy to one of the girls; and when they were gone I thought of her a great deal, and one day when I was sitting out in the sun by the house I wrote out a story in my mind. I thought I took my father's horse and followed the wagon, and finally I found it, and they were surprised to see me. I talked with the girl and persuaded her to elope with me, and that night I put her on my horse, and we started off across the prairie. After several hours we came to a camp; and when we rode up we found it was the one we had left a few hours before, and we went in. The next night we tried again, and the same thing happened—the horse came back to the same place; and then we concluded that we ought not to elope. I stayed until I had persuaded her father to give her to me. I always meant to write that story out and publish it, and I began once; but I concluded it was not much of a story. But I think that was the beginning of love with me.

It was unfortunate for Lincoln that in all his childhood and youth he did not fall under the direct influence of an educated minister who might have encouraged his love of learning and given it some measure of direction. The preachers whom the Lincoln family heard were nearly all Baptists, earnest and unlettered men, who plowed corn and preached with equal perspiration and other evidence of hard work, and who did good, but had no learning or love of it. Lincoln is alleged to have mimicked the preachers of his boyhood. Their mannerisms invited mirthful mimicry. Their cultivated whine, their periodic and professional expectoration, their dogmatism, their appeal to the terrors of hell fire, all invited the imitation of a frolicsome boy. They appear to have done him no harm, and their preaching and his home doctrine made him a predestinarian, or as Herndon declares, a fatalist, to the day of his death. But his love of learning was not strongly assisted by the ministry of the backwoods. One Baptist preacher, Aaron Farmer, commended an article of Abraham's on Temperance, and is said to have sent it for publication to an Ohio newspaper; but this incident was exceptional.

Of Abraham's conduct in the years of his boyhood, Dennis Hanks, his constant companion, wrote to Herndon, June 13, 1866:

Abe was a good boy—an affectionate one—a boy who loved his parents well and was obedient to their every wish. Although anything but an impudent or rude boy, he was sometimes uncomfortably inquisitive. When strangers would ride along or pass by his father's fence, he always—either through boyish pride or to tease his father—would ask the first question. His father would sometimes knock him over. When thus punished, he never bellowed; but dropped a kind of silent, unwelcome tear as an evidence of his sensitiveness or other feelings.*

In Indiana as in Kentucky the principal crop of the pioneer was corn. It began to be an article of food as soon as the ears were ready for roasting. A little later the kernels were utilized for hominy; and as they matured a little more they were gritted against a sheet of tin, perforated and attached to a board. Hand-

---

*Herndon's *Lincoln*, i, p. 22.

mills were in many homes, and were utilized for the grinding of corn in small quantities. But the food for the greater part of the year had to be ground in the public mill and prepared as hoe-cake or corn pone. This made the local mill an important adjunct to the home. When the streams were flowing well, the small dull stones were driven slowly round by water-power; but when water failed, the horse that brought the grist to mill was the power that turned the mill. Hitched to a long sweep, the horse walked round and round, the stone making one revolution each time the horse completed the larger circle. It was a painfully slow process. The boy who had ridden to mill on his sack of corn and who hoped to ride triumphantly home upon the same bag filled with meal, had no fondness for the weary task of whipping his reluctant horse around the dusty circular path.

One day Abraham rode his father's gray mare to mill. The miller's name was Gordon, and the mill was several miles away. Abraham was late in arriving; and if there had been any water in the pond, it had flowed through the race and over the wheel before his turn came. He had to hitch the old mare to the sweep, and drive her around the course, a task which he enjoyed as little as the mare. Seeking to shorten a little the period of this distasteful labor, he urged the old mare on by clucking and whipping until the mare rebelled and kicked back at him with her unshod hoof. "Get up, you old hussy," he began to say, and accompanied the first word with the use of the whip. He had just said "Get up" when the kick came. The blow knocked him senseless and apparently dead. Gordon sent word to Thomas Lincoln, who came with his wagon and conveyed the insensible boy home. All night he lay, and gave no sign of life; but as dawn came in, his consciousness struggled slowly back, and the first sign of it was his utterance of the words, "you old hussy!"

In later years he pondered long over this incident. His mind resumed its normal activity at the precise point where consciousness had been interrupted. The suspended thought and the uncompleted sentence were completed automatically under the impulse of his previous intent. Lincoln never ceased to think this one of his notable experiences; and it gave him material for thoughtful consideration of the nature and operation of the human intellect.

Lest we seem to exalt unduly the Lincoln of this period, let it be recorded that he did not love work. Some of his old neighbors, including one or two of his employers, were sufficiently unawed by his subsequent greatness to say frankly that he was lazy. He could work hard, and on occasion did so; but his work was interrupted by his love of story-telling, his fondness for gossip with any one who passed along the road, and by periods of deep meditation and abstraction. John Romaine said of him in 1865:

He worked for me, but was always reading and thinking. I used to get mad at him for it. I say he was awful lazy. He would laugh and talk, crack his jokes and tell stories all the time; but he didn't love his work half as much as his pay. He said to me one time that his father taught him to work, but he never taught him to love it.*

The women liked to have him about. While he was not observant of trifling jobs that needed to be done, he was always obliging, and ready to bring a bucket of water from the spring, or take a hand at the churn. But one of these women admitted that "Abe was no hand to work like killing snakes."

Though he did not like to work, he did like to read. He borrowed newspapers from William Wood and learned about the life of the world as it then was lived outside Gentryville. But as for manual labor, we may accept the statement of John Romaine that he was "awful lazy" and liked his pay much better than he liked work.

The Lincoln family is nearly ready for its next migration. For all of them it will mean a permanent removal from Indi-

---

*Herndon's *Lincoln*, 1st Ed. i, p. 42.

ana, more complete than their removal from Kentucky fourteen years previously. For Abraham it will mean more; for this up-rooting from his boyhood soil in Indiana coincides with his arrival at the age of manhood.

It meant much to Abraham Lincoln to spend the years of his adolescence in Southern Indiana. He was on free soil, protected from slavery by the Ordinance of 1787, yet he was not detached from the social and political and religious environments of his Kentucky childhood. There was in the transfer of the family from Kentucky to Indiana a wholesome step in evolution toward his predestined greatness, but not too violent a wrenching away from what he had previously known and believed. Indiana was a good place for him in those obscure years.

And now, Indiana sends him forth, a tall, strong, awkward youth, who has not yet been seriously in love, who has not united with any church, who has not cast a vote, but who has in him the promise and potency of large achievements. He is intelligent, courageous, sympathetic. He can read and write and spell, and he can cipher to the rule of three. He can write essays and declaim stump speeches and command respect for his power of arm and strength of character.

Indiana does not know that she has been sheltering and training a future leader of the nation, but no state ever knows that. Indiana has done well by him, and will one day discover of what sort is this raw-boned youth who is about to leave her for a new home, and will make a shrine of the place where he lived, and will seek out the lovely spot where Nancy Hanks lies buried, and erect a monument on the soil where he wept in boyhood over the grave of his mother.

CHAPTER VIII

THE childhood of Lincoln belongs to Kentucky, and his youth to Indiana; but the whole of his manhood, until his inauguration as president, belongs to Illinois. Less than three weeks after his twenty-first birthday, Abraham Lincoln set out for Illinois, and never left that state for residence elsewhere until he departed for Washington, on February 11, 1861.*

The autumn of 1829 brought to Spencer County a recurrence of the "milk-sick." Cattle and human beings died. The fatality was less than it had been eleven years previous, but the fear was great. No member of the Lincoln family or of their immediate kin perished in this outbreak, but they lost some of their live-stock. They were discouraged and alarmed. Moreover, they were of a migratory disposition. John Hanks had gone to Illinois some years earlier, and his reports and those of others who had made their homes there were very attractive. Dennis went to Illinois to visit John and spy out the land, and his report was favorable. The Lincolns and their kin were ready to move.

Thomas Lincoln had entered one hundred sixty acres of land when he first came from Kentucky to Indiana. He had reduced that venture to an eighty-acre tract, applying upon the half which he retained the whole of his payment. Still he owed the

---

*Reference may be made to my address on *The Influence of Illinois in the Development of Abraham Lincoln* delivered before the Illinois State Historical Society and published in its Transactions for 1921; also to my address on *The Influence of Chicago upon Abraham Lincoln* delivered before the Chicago Historical Society, and published by the University of Chicago in 1922.

government more than he was likely ever to pay toward the completion of his purchase at two dollars an acre. He sold his land to James Gentry, and his stock and grain to David Turnham. He had recently disposed of a town lot in Elizabethtown, which had come to him on his marriage with Sarah Bush Johnston. He was able to pay up his bills and to leave Indiana with more personal property than he brought to it.

On the first day of March, 1830, the family of Thomas Lincoln left their home in Spencer County, Indiana, and started for Illinois. The company included Thomas and Sarah Lincoln, Abraham Lincoln, John D. Johnston, son of Sarah Lincoln by her former husband, Dennis Hanks and his wife Sarah, a daughter of Sarah Bush Lincoln, Squire Hall and his wife Matilda, the other daughter of Sarah Bush Lincoln, and enough small children, grandchildren of Mrs. Lincoln, to make the entire party thirteen.*

These people and their belongings were loaded into a wagon drawn by two yoke of oxen. Abraham drove the oxen a considerable portion of the journey. Long afterward he described the experience which he remembered vividly:

He said the ground had not yet yielded up the frosts of winter; that during the day the roads would thaw out the surface and at night freeze over again, thus making traveling, especially with oxen, painfully slow and tiresome. There were, of course, no bridges, and the party were consequently driven to ford the streams, unless by a circuitous route they could avoid them. In the early part of the day the latter also were frozen slightly, and the oxen would break through a square yard of ice at every step.

---

*Mrs. Harriet Chapman, daughter of Dennis Hanks, accompanied this party. She was a little girl at the time. She made oath in 1912 that there were three covered wagons, two drawn by oxen and one by horses, but other accounts speak of only one wagon. She gave the names of the members of the party: Thomas Lincoln and his wife Sarah; Dennis F. Hanks and his wife Elizabeth (Johnston) Hanks and their children, John, Sarah Jane, Nancy and the affiant, Harriet Hanks; Squire Hall and his wife Matilda (Johnston) and one child named John Hall; Abraham Lincoln and John D. Johnston. In this company of thirteen Thomas Lincoln could write his name, but the only ones who could have written any account of the journey were Abraham Lincoln and Dennis Hanks.

Among other things which the party brought with them was a pet dog, which trotted along after the wagon. One day the little fellow fell behind and failed to catch up till after they had crossed the stream. Missing him, they looked back, and there, on the opposite bank, he stood, whining and jumping about in great distress. The water was running over the broken edges of the ice, and the poor animal was afraid to cross.

It would not pay to turn the oxen and wagon back and to ford the stream again in order to recover a dog, and so the majority, in their anxiety to move forward, decided to go on without him. "But I could not endure the idea of abandoning even a dog," related Lincoln. "Pulling off shoes and socks, I waded across the stream and triumphantly returned with the shivering animal under my arm. His frantic leaps of joy and other evidences of a dog's gratitude amply repaid me for all the exposure I had undergone."*

This is practically the only incident preserved to us of a notable migration. The journey occupied two weeks. To the thirteen occupants, old and young, of the big prairie schooner, it was too much akin to the life they knew and understood to leave many very permanent impressions. Lincoln afterward told his friends that as they passed through Vincennes he saw a printing press for the first time.† He also related that as they passed through Palestine he saw a juggler performing tricks of sleight of hand. One night near the middle of March they came to Decatur and camped in the court-house square. In 1856, Lincoln was able to identify the exact spot where the wagon had stood, and the site is now indicated by a tablet. They had come to Decatur from the

---

*Herndon's *Lincoln,* i:59

†In June, 1923, accompanied by Honorable William H. Townsend, of Lexington, Kentucky, and his brother-in-law, Mr. Cleveland D. Johnson, of Kansas City, I traced the Lincoln route from Springfield, Kentucky, to Springfield, Illinois. Our journey by automobile occupied three and one-half days, and our mileage was six hundred and eighty-seven. We followed the route laid down in two official investigations, that of Mr. C. M. Thompson for the Illinois State Historical Library, and that of Messrs. Joseph M. Cravens and Jesse W. Weik for the governor of Indiana. We ferried across the Ohio, the Kentucky and some other rivers.

south, their route being not far from the main line of the Illinois Central Railroad.*

The next day they journeyed westward to the home of John Hanks,† who had already located in Macon County. He had cut logs for a new home located on the Sangamon River about ten miles west of Decatur. Thomas and Abraham Lincoln, Dennis Hanks, John D. Johnston and Squire Hall soon had the logs built into a cabin. There the entire company of thirteen made their first home in Illinois. They broke ten acres of prairie ground and raised a crop of sown corn that same year. They cut down trees and made rails with which the ten acres were fenced. These rails, according to the testimony of Abraham Lincoln himself, were the ones that afterward became famous. They were not, however, the only rails that Abraham Lincoln split in Macon County. He and John Hanks split three thousand rails for Major John Warnick, Sheriff of Macon County, and Abraham procured his first new clothes after the attainment of his majority by the splitting of four hundred rails for every yard of brown jeans dyed with white walnut bark, that would be necessary to make him a pair of trousers. For a man of his height this was no small contract, and apparently, he did not at that time procure the rest of his suit.

Having provided for his father and stepmother, Lincoln now

---

*Henry C. Whitney relates that he was in Decatur with Lincoln in 1856, when the latter pointed out the precise spot where the wagon halted for the night. The place is now marked by a tablet.

"Lincoln walked out a few feet in front, and after shifting his position two or three times, said, as he looked up at the building, partly to himself and partly to me: 'Here is the exact spot where I stood by our wagon when we moved from Indiana twenty-six years ago; this isn't six feet from the exact spot.' . . . I asked him if he, at that time, had expected to be a lawyer and practice law in that court-house; to which he replied: 'No, I didn't know I had sense enough to be a lawyer then.' He then told me he had frequently tried to locate the route by which they had come; and that he had decided that it was near to the main line of the Illinois Central Railroad."

†Herndon in his account of this journey speaks of him as "John Hanks, son of that Joseph Hanks, in whose shop at Elizabethtown Thomas Lincoln learned what he knew of the carpenter's art." Nicolay and Hay make this same mistake. John was the son of William Hanks and nephew of this, the younger Joseph.

left the paternal home. For a year he worked at odd jobs obtained from various settlers in Macon County. He split rails, he worked in the harvest field and took a general share in the rough work of a new community.

Freed from the restraints of home life, Lincoln at this time made some independent adventures into society. One still may hear tales in the vicinity of Decatur of Lincoln's attentions during those twelve months to the girls of the settlement. These little gallantries were all innocent enough, but they have served to preserve the names of one or two of the young women of the neighborhood. Polly Warnick, daughter of Major Warnick, the Sheriff of Macon County, lived on a large farm on the opposite side of the river from the Lincolns, and Abraham paid her some little attention. Major Warnick is said not to have favored the match. Polly had suitors in abundance who owned land or had political influence; and Lincoln belonged to a poor family lately arrived and without brilliant prospects. If Lincoln cared for her or she for him beyond a pleasurable and passing interest in each other, there is no record of it. And it did not last long. The records of Macon County show that on June 17, 1830, license was issued for the marriage of Joseph Stevens and Mary Warnick. But Joseph Stevens boasted to the end of his life that he and Abe Lincoln had been rivals for the affection of Polly, and that in the contest Abe came out at the little end of the horn.

John Hanks, who was his closest companion at this time, informs us that Lincoln made a political speech in or near Decatur. A man by the name of Posey visited the locality and delivered an address. John Hanks declared that Abraham could do better. Abraham ascended a box or stump and delivered an address on the navigation of the Sangamon River. That subject interested the people of Macon County more than almost anything else which he could have talked about. John recorded that Posey himself was impressed by it and called Abraham aside to inquire how he had learned so much. Abraham told him what he had read, and Posey encouraged him to persevere in his studies. Several old settlers resident in and about Decatur in after years professed to have heard this first political speech of Abraham Lincoln. It is affirmed that so far as he discussed national issues, he spoke in praise of Andrew Jackson. This may or may not be true. It would have been natural, considering Lincoln's background and environment. But he wisely refrained from much discussion of national issues, of which he knew but little and his audience cared less. "His subject was the navigation of the Sangamon," says John Hanks, and other men who professed to have heard the speech agreed with him.

The winter of 1830-1 was long remembered in Illinois as "the winter of the deep snow." Lincoln's canoe upset as he was crossing the Sangamon River, and his feet froze. For two weeks he lived in the home of Major Warnick while his feet were healing.

"The winter of the deep snow" was for a whole generation a dividing point in Illinois history. The snow fell, not, as it seemed, in flakes, but in shovelsful. The snow was followed by bitter cold weather—twelve or more degrees below zero—and the settlers were imprisoned for weeks. Livestock perished; and wild game has never been so plentiful in Illinois since. In later years when old settlers compared early experiences, no one was thought to have anything really worth recounting unless he came to the prairies in time to participate in the experiences of that terrible winter.*

*For matters relating to the life of Lincoln in Illinois I am indebted to the unfailing kindness of Mrs. Jessie Palmer Weber and Miss Georgia L. Osborne, of the Illinois State Historical Society, and Miss Caroline McIlvaine, of the Chicago Historical Society.

CHAPTER IX

A WIZARD OF FINANCE
1831-1832

ABRAHAM LINCOLN sat in the large and comfortable house of
Major Warnick awaiting the healing of his frozen feet. It was
such a home as he had seldom if ever occupied even for a single
night, and it offered a sorrowful contrast to the cabins of Thomas Lincoln. If, as the local tradition affirms, he was casting
longing looks at Polly Warnick, and knew that she had a landed
suitor ready to marry her, he could hardly blame Major Warnick for preferring the other man.

Abraham Lincoln was not a man who counted leisure time
wasted. He had enough to eat and no pressing duties awaiting
his attention. The snow was too deep for unnecessary work.
With his feet encased in huge moccasins extemporized from
deerskins, he shuffled over the floor to the fireplace, and, with
his chair tipped back against the wall, or laid face-downward on
the floor with its tilted back as the hypothenuse of a convenient
triangle for the support of his own back stretched partly along
the chair and partly on the floor, he alternated two of his favorite
positions and read from a volume of the Statutes of Illinois
which Major Warnick, in his capacity of sheriff, had in his possession.

What was he to do when his feet healed, and the snow melted
and another spring appeared in the valley of the Sangamon? He
had come to Illinois with his father, having no plan beyond this,
that he would see his father and stepmother established in a new
home, and then make his own way in the world. For nearly a

year he had been pursuing this course. What had he to show for it, and what was he to do next? These questions troubled Abraham Lincoln as little as most men, but they troubled him.

For two weeks he was confined to the house. Outside, as he looked through the windows, the snow was piled high. Roads began to be broken, but it was no time for unnecessary travel. Decatur was nine miles away, and the crowded cabin of Thomas Lincoln was three miles distant and across the river. He sat down, or lay down, in the comfortable Warnick home, and waited with less impatience than some men would have displayed, for the passing of the bitter cold and the melting of the snow. What was he to do next?

He might take up land, as John Hanks had done, and as Dennis Hanks and John D. Johnston professed to intend to do; but he did not enjoy manual labor. It was not simply that toil was irksome to him, though that was true, but he disliked the isolation and monotony of farm work. Two tendencies within him prevented his seeking a farm of his own as a home for himself and Polly Warnick or some other Macon County girl. One was his disinclination to farm labor; the other was the stirring of a consuming ambition. He remembered his political speech of the preceding summer. The approval with which it was greeted was pleasant to remember as he sat in Major Warnick's home and wondered what he was to do when he was able to go to work again.

One thing was certain, he must finish his contract of three thousand fence-rails which he had agreed to split for Major Warnick. It would require most, if not all of those rails, to pay for his board. And there would be occasional jobs until spring. Then he must depend on such labor as he could pick up in aid of one farmer or another. He was determined not to go back to his father's over-populated cabin; and he was equally disinclined to begin with the virgin prairie and devote the years of his life to the making of a farm for himself. What was he to do when the snow melted? He did not know. Abraham Lincoln was the

least impatient of the prisoners of the deep snow, but he sometimes wished he knew.

Destiny chooses strange heralds.   Most of us, if we were to
think back over the changes in our lives, would recall some incident which at the moment seemed trivial, or some person apparently insignificant, that served as the messenger of a new dis-
pensation.   One day after Lincoln's feet had healed, John Hanks
rode over to where Abraham was then making his temporary
home, and asked him to ride to Decatur and meet a remarkable
man then stopping at the tavern in that place.   That man was
Denton Offutt.

Now the curtain rises on one of the most important scenes in
the early life of Abraham Lincoln, his interview at Decatur with
Denton Offutt.   Abraham Lincoln, his second cousin John
Hanks and his stepbrother John D. Johnston sat down with this
merchant prince of the Sangamon, and discussed the future prosperity of that region, whose destiny Offutt appeared to hold in
his keeping.   Offutt had come from Lexington, Kentucky, and
possessed the self-confidence and courtesy that belonged to a
Kentuckian who assumed a position in the higher social strata
together with the camaraderie that insured immediate acceptance
among the common people.   What the people of Illinois needed
was markets for their produce, he affirmed.   The prairies were
capable of producing enormous crops, but for them there was
no natural outlet save by the rivers, whose use was undeveloped.
He proposed to buy cargoes of grain and pork in Illinois and
market them in New Orleans, and to promote in connection with
this central line of business a group of related enterprises that
would bring wealth to all who participated in the venture.

John Hanks had had a preliminary conversation with Offutt
and was impressed, but desired to confirm his own favorable
judgment by the concurrent approval of Lincoln and Johnston.
That approval was not delayed.   They all approved.   Offutt appeared to them a man of vision and enterprise, and they could
not fail to trust him.

It was John Hanks and not Lincoln, of whom Decatur had heard, and so informed Offutt, as a capable riverman; and it was Hanks who told Offutt that he had two friends, Abraham Lincoln and John D. Johnston, both of whom had accompanied him on one of his voyages to New Orleans, and who might be persuaded to go again. These three, all experienced, and knowing one another and capable of working well together would make, with Offutt, a complete crew. Offutt did not pretend to understand river navigation. But he knew or was supposed to know business. He knew the prices at which corn and pork could be bought along the Sangamon, and the prices at which these commodities could be sold in New Orleans. He wanted three men to handle his boat. Such men were not as plentiful in Macon County, Illlinois, as they were in Spencer County, Indiana. He was glad to meet Hanks and thus secure one man; but when he found himself able through Hanks to secure two other experienced hands, whose knowledge of river navigation he was able to add to his own business ability, he was greatly pleased. After negotiation, he employed the three at a wage of fifty cents a day, and a bonus of sixty dollars each, a liberal sum as they estimated, and one he felt able to promise.*

Offutt informed them that he would procure a flat-boat at Beardstown and have it ready at the mouth of Spring Creek, near the little town of Springfield.

Springfield at that time had not conceived the ambition to be the capital of Illinois; but it had lately become a county-seat; it was one of a number of aspiring river towns, a large proportion of which have now disappeared from the map, each one of them pinning its hope of fame to the navigability of the Sangamon. The boat would be ready near Springfield by the ides of March; the three Macon County men were to be on hand to navigate it.

It may be that we ought to revise our judgment of men of

---

*This is the wage as stated by John Hanks. Lincoln once spoke of himself as working on a flat-boat for ten dollars a month; but he was apparently speaking in round numbers and in contrast with more affluent earnings.

Offutt's type, at least to the extent of doing justice to their influence in wakening ambition in the lives of other men. The
evil that such men as Offutt do lives after them in the empty
pockets and disappointed hopes of those who lend them money;
the good is often interred under the imprecations of their creditors. The Colonel Sellers of Mark Twain's *Gilded Age,* the
"Get-Rich-Quick-Wallingford" of more recent literature and
other men of their kind, face a day of retribution in the wrath of
those who too readily confide in them. But meantime something
ought to be said of those men whom these promoters waken from
lethargy or indecision and to whom they bring new impulse and
vision. If we are to give the devil his due, Denton Offutt deserves a more gracious word than the biographers of Lincoln
have accorded him. Other people may have had occasion to
speak ill of him, but to Abraham Lincoln he was a generous
friend, and one who blazed for him a highway into larger things
than Lincoln himself at the time could well have understood.

It has been the custom of Lincoln's biographers to speak in
terms of disrespect of Denton Offutt, and some of them have
snuffed him out with a contemptuous phrase. He was a noisy
braggart, a vain and shallow pretender, a wild and reckless spec-
ulator who did not disdain fraud when it served his ends, a man
"windy, rattle-brained, unsteady and improvident." All this,
and more to the same effect, we learn from various accounts of
him. People trusted him to their sorrow, for he borrowed more
money than he could well repay, and enticed those who trusted
him into unprofitable ventures.

All this may be true, and it is too late to deny any of it. But,
on the other hand, if we are to believe what comes to us on equally reliable authority, he was quick-witted, far-sighted, and had a
clear head for business as well as a warm heart for friendship.
Toward Lincoln, his attitude was one of generous appreciation.

For our knowledge of this second and more eventful of Lincoln's journeys to New Orleans, we are indebted to the recollections of John Hanks, who gave them in detail to Herndon in

later years. When the time arrived for the three men from Macon County to join Offutt near Springfield, the country was so flooded by the melting of the snow that it was not found practicable to make the journey overland. They procured a canoe and paddled down the Sangamon to Judy's Ferry, five miles east of Springfield. Only Hanks and Lincoln made the canoe voyage; Johnston had preceded them and he joined them at that point. Together they searched for Offutt and the boat that was to have been ready for their use. Neither Offutt nor the boat appeared, but inquiry disclosed the whereabouts of Offutt. The voyagers walked to Springfield, and found Offutt greatly enjoying the hospitality of the Buckhorn Tavern, whose cheerful host, Andrew Elliott, knew how to make his place attractive to men of Offutt's proclivities. The Buckhorn was the best of Springfield's two or three taverns, and Offutt was a man who appreciated the best and paid for it when he had the money. When he was out of money, he still had the best of entertainment which the place where he happened to sojourn afforded; his face and his ready speech secured him ample credit.

Recalled by the presence of the three men to his contract, Offutt proposed to them that they should build the boat, and receive additional wages while doing it. Reassured, the men returned to the shores of the Sangamon and began cutting down trees on Congress lands. Offutt arranged with William Kirkpatrick, who owned a saw-mill at Sangamontown, to saw the logs into lumber of the proper dimensions.

First of all, the navigators erected a shanty for their own shelter. They elected Lincoln cook, and he is said to have esteemed it a compliment. Diligently they labored, cutting down trees, rolling them to the water, floating them to the mill, and after the lumber had been sawed, fashioning it into a boat such as all of them had known on the Ohio. They were diligent because the river was falling, and they wanted to utilize the high water.

Four weeks were expended upon the construction of the boat, and when it was completed, Offutt bade farewell to his congenial friends at the Buckhorn, and was present when the new vessel slid from her ways into the welcoming waters of the Sangamon. There was oratory such as was deemed appropriate to the occasion; and it is declared by John Hanks that when the speechmaking entered the political field it was in praise of the Whig Party and of Andrew Jackson. That was surely a strange combination, but the strangest feature of it, and the one on which we shall have occasion to comment briefly, was that the Whig Party should have had any share in this celebration.

Some day it will be the task of some keen historical student to go minutely into a study of the political conditions of that period, and answer, if he can, how and why did Abraham Lincoln become a Whig? We shall later propound that question when we observe Abraham Lincoln entering politics. For the present we are concerned with the oratory that accompanied the launching of the flat-boat. Herndon, deriving his information in part from Lincoln himself, but mostly from John Hanks, wrote of this event:

Within four weeks the boat was ready to launch. Offutt was sent for, and was present when she slid into the water. It was the occasion of much political chat and buncombe, in which the Whig Party and Jackson alike were, strangely enough, lauded to the skies. It is difficult to account for the unanimous approval of such strikingly antagonistic ideas, unless it be admitted that Offutt must have brought with him some substantial reminder of the hospitality on draught at the Buckhorn inn.*

That is an inadequate explanation, and Herndon should have known it. He was far from being a stranger to such entertainment as the Buckhorn afforded; that very bar was familiar to his youth. But Herndon was never drunk enough to have lauded the Democratic Party.

Here is a conjecture which possesses at least the merit of originality:

---

*Herndon's *Lincoln*, i:73.

It is that whatever of laudation the Whig Party received at the launching of the flat-boat was contributed by Offutt himself. Certainly John Hanks did not praise the Whig Party; he was advertised throughout the nation in 1860 as an old Democrat who was to vote for Lincoln, and so far as we know he was the only Hanks who did so. Neither Abraham ·Lincoln nor John D. Johnston inherited through Thomas Lincoln any other politics than those of Andrew Jackson, as interpreted in the Indiana woods by men born in Kentucky. But Denton Offutt was from Lexington, the home of Henry Clay. Did he on the day of the launching go into a panegyric of that statesman, and did he on the long days of the voyage relate to the eagerly listening Lincoln such knowledge as he had of the idol of the Whig Party who was destined to become Lincoln's own idol?

We are to thank Offutt for leading Abraham Lincoln a mile or more along the highway out of obscurity toward his life mission; are we to thank him for going not one mile but twain, and for the beginning of those reflections that made Lincoln a Whig?

In another chapter we must return briefly to this question in its wider implications. We now climb down the muddy bank of the Sangamon and prepare for the journey to New Orleans.

The boat was built flat on the bottom, save for a bow and stern that took an obtuse upward angle. There was an attempt to add to the river current auxiliary power by means of a sail made of planks and cloth, a feature which is said to have excited the mirthful contempt of river-wise Beardstown, which lies at the junction of the Sangamon and Illinois. It is not likely that the sail was of material assistance. The cargo consisted partly of grain, but more of pork in barrels, and some live hogs.

One incident ought to be recorded before the boat casts off, which is that, shortly before they left, the crew attended a performance given by a strolling magician, and that he cooked eggs in Abraham Lincoln's low-crowned, wide-brimmed felt hat. Lincoln loaned the hat with real or feigned reluctance, explaining his hesitation on the ground that he did not greatly value the hat but had respect for the eggs. Abraham Lincoln had left behind him the days of the coonskin cap. He was still a long way from the enormous stove-pipe hat of his professional career, but his raiment was in the process of evolution.

The log of this eventful voyage is somewhat as follows:

About March 1, 1831, just a year after his entrance into Illinois, Abraham Lincoln and John Hanks launched their canoe on the swollen water of the Sangamon and were floated by the melting flood of the deep snow to Judy's Ferry. About the middle of April they launched their flat-boat. John Hanks did not accompany the boat all the way to New Orleans. By the time they reached St. Louis his concern for his family caused him to leave the party, and he walked back to Decatur. The boat made good progress down the Mississippi. It tied up for a day at Memphis, and made short stops at Vicksburg and Natchez. Early in May it tied up to the levee in New Orleans. Here Offutt and his two assistants spent a month, disposing of their cargo to good advantage, and having ample time to view the sights of the city already slightly familiar to Lincoln. In June they boarded a river steamer and returned up the river to St. Louis, where Lincoln and Johnston left Offutt and made their way to Coles County, where Thomas Lincoln had removed, one year's residence in Macon having convinced him that that county was unhealthy. About a month Abraham waited at his father's farm in Coles County, Thomas Lincoln's permanent and final home on earth. While there Abraham whipped a bully named Daniel Needham. In August he left his father's home for the last time, except for short and infrequent visits.

This outline has omitted two or three significant incidents, which call for brief mention. One of these is recorded by John Hanks as having occurred while the crew of the boat were in New Orleans, where Lincoln spent nearly a month. There Lincoln saw slaves chained and exposed for sale. The familiarity of the bidders in handling and examining a mulatto girl roused his deep resentment, and the whole system seemed to him wicked and debasing. John Hanks declared many years afterward that Lincoln said then and there that if he ever got a chance to hit that institution, meaning slavery, he would hit it hard. We may not trust implicitly to the accuracy of John Hanks' verbal memory, but we know from other sources that what Lincoln saw of slavery upon this voyage made an indelible impression upon his mind. Lincoln was not without prophetic intimations of his own coming power. It is not impossible that he said what John Hanks declared that he said. In due time he had his chance to hit that institution, and he did hit it hard.

In giving a measure of credence to this story, however, we remember that if the incident occurred as John Hanks told it, John could not have been a witness of it. John Hanks did not, on this journey, go all the way to New Orleans.* The trip had been delayed a month by the necessity of building the boat, and had encountered some other delays, and Hanks considered that. having a family, it was better for him not to be away from home so long; and he left the boat at St. Louis, on the way down, and walked home. But Herndon relates that he himself often heard Lincoln refer to this trip as one on which his experiences deepened his hostility to slavery; and the remark is one that he may have made to John as they talked matters over after his return. Granting that the story has lost nothing in the telling, it is not inherently improbable. We have an account from Lincoln's own pen of a journey made just ten years later to a point not so far south, and of its effect upon him. Writing some fourteen years after the event to his friend, Joshua F. Speed, of Kentucky, Lincoln said:

In 1841, you and I had together a tedious low-water trip on a steamboat from Louisville to St. Louis. You may remember, as I do, that from Louisville to the mouth of the Ohio there were on board ten or a dozen slaves shackled with irons. The sight

---

*Lincoln is specific on this point: "Hanks had not gone to New Orleans, but having a family, and being likely to be detained from home longer than was first expected, had turned back at St. Louis." *Autobiography* furnished to J. L. Scripps in 1860.

was a continual torment to me, and I see something like it every time I touch the Ohio or any other slave border. It is not for you to assume that I have no interest in a thing which has, and continually exercises, the power of making me miserable.

What Lincoln remembered to have seen of slavery in Kentucky in the years of his childhood had little in it that was repellent; but when he saw it in its full possibility of degradation of both black and white, it is little wonder that his soul was roused in righteous protest.

Another fact that is not to be overlooked is that, while the voyage appears to have been a prosperous one, it completely satisfied Offutt. His career thenceforth was destined to be on land rather than on the rivers. He determined to establish a vast commercial enterprise at a town well located and conduct his operations from that center, leaving the boating to those who had greater fondness for water.

A third fact is that Lincoln and Offutt found themselves increasingly attached to each other, and each found in the other a companion who might be of material advantage to him. Lincoln himself was apparently proud when in later years he remembered Offutt's liking for him. When he furnished John Locke Scripps his campaign autobiography, he wrote:

During this boat enterprise acquaintance with Offutt, who was previously an entire stranger, he conceived a liking for Abraham and believing he could turn him to account, he contracted with him to act as clerk for him on his return from New Orleans, in charge of a store and mill at New Salem, then in Sangamon, now in Menard County.

And finally, we must write into the log a date very near the beginning of the voyage, the nineteenth of April. That has been a notable day in American history. On April 19, 1775, was fired the shot heard round the world. On April 19, 1861, was shed the first blood of the Civil War. On April 19, 1831, the flatboat commanded by Denton Offutt and manned by Abraham Lincoln, John Hanks and John D. Johnston, stuck on the dam of Rutledge mill at New Salem.

CHAPTER X

ABRAHAM LINCOLN stood at his watch at the steering-oar of the flat-boat that was conveying him and Denton Offutt and John Hanks and John D. Johnston down the Sangamon to the Illinois, down the Illinois to the Mississippi and down the Mississippi to New Orleans. He watched the shore, the current and the passing river craft. He also watched the flotsam of the river. The high floods that followed the deep snow carried in their current an unusual quantity of drift. The waters were subsiding. Much that floated down had caught in the branches of low-growing trees, or stranded on muddy banks. There is a fascination in river drift. The plank-and-cloth sail of the flat-boat proved no material aid to navigation, so the boat floated about as rapidly as the logs and branches. Some of the logs were recognizable by reason of projecting knots or upstanding stubs of limbs that took on a grotesque appearance of personality. Some of the pieces of drift became old friends. They would disappear for days, and then reappear many miles farther down the stream as eddying currents drifted them near to the boat again.

Abraham Lincoln came to feel a strange kinship with these floating logs. He thought it out in phraseology which he afterward remembered, and now and then repeated to his friends:

He assured those with whom he came in contact that he was a piece of floating driftwood; that after the winter of deep snow he had come down the river with the freshet, borne along by the swelling waters, and, aimlessly floating about, he had accidentally lodged at New Salem.*

But there are distinctions even in river driftwood.

There is a somewhat recent story which takes the character of a fable, that has made its way through newspaper columns on this wise:

A Dead Rat and an Apple Core were flung into the Mississippi at St. Paul, and, drifting together, started a voyage down the great Father of Waters. Much of the time they floated apart, but occasionally they met, and sometimes were for hours or even days within hailing distance of each other. They sailed together past Dubuque, encountered each other again at Alton, and after a long period of absence met again below Cairo. At Memphis they were caught in the churning wake of a steamboat, and washed under a wharf, where for some time they bobbed up and down together among the piles. As the steamer backed out into the stream, and its wash leveled down, they floated free again. Then, and for the first time, the Apple Core spoke, and said, cheerfully, "We are having an eventful voyage." But the Dead Rat lifted its aristocratic nose in scorn at this approach to familiarity, and asked, "Where do you get that 'we' stuff?"

Abraham Lincoln never heard this story, and the modern slang of it would have been unfamiliar to him; but he was not too fastidious to have enjoyed hearing and telling this modern Æsopian tale, and he would have instantly recognized its moral.

He was a piece of driftwood. But driftwood is not all alike. John Hanks and John D. Johnston floated down the same stream and stuck on the same dam with Lincoln. Neither John Hanks nor John D. Johnston impressed Denton Offutt as a man with whom he would like to negotiate a permanent relationship.

But what would have happened to Abraham Lincoln if there had been no dam at New Salem? The flat-boat would have floated more or less proudly past that enterprising settlement,

*Herndon, i, 79.

nor dropped anchor till it reached the farm of Squire Godbey, several miles below, where there were live hogs to load. But there was a dam at New Salem, and Abraham Lincoln lodged there on the nineteenth day of April in the year of our Lord, 1831.

Leave the boat for a moment, with its snub-nose pushed out over the dam, waiting for some one to bring a borrowed auger from the mill for Abraham Lincoln to accomplish the boring of a hole which, by means which no one quite understands, is to let out the bilge water and enable the boat to float free over the dam. And consider for a moment the significance of that dam at this moment in the career of Abraham Lincoln.

If any event in human history had occurred otherwise than it did, very many subsequent events, some of them very remote, would have happened far otherwise than they did, or would not have happened at all. If Arlotta, the tanner's daughter, had remained at home on a particular morning to prepare her father's noonday meal, instead of going with the other maidens of Falaise to wash the family linen in the village brook there would have been no William the Conqueror, and the whole history of Europe since 1066, and that of America from the time of England's first explorations of the coast, would have been profoundly modified. If Concord Creek had proved in the summer of 1828 a stream with as good a flow of water as appeared certain in the spring of that year, the Reverend James M. Cameron would have been content with the little mill he established there, and he and James Rutledge would not have founded the city of New Salem.

James M. Cameron was born in Kentucky in 1791, a son of Thomas Cameron and his wife Nancy Miller, who was a sister of Mary Ann Miller, wife of James Rutledge. Rutledge was ten years older than Cameron, but still was by marriage Cameron's uncle. Cameron was a Cumberland Presbyterian, product of the revival preaching of Reverend James McGready.*

---

*The founder of the Cumberland Presbyterian Church spelled his name McGready. James McGrady Rutledge and the Rutledge family, generally, adopted the shorter spelling.

The Cumberland Presbyterian system combined the Presbyterian form of government with a rejection of the Presbyterian Calvinistic theology. It also emphasized the spiritual as over against the intellectual qualities of the older Presbyterial faith as essential to the preaching of the Gospel. Of this faith Cameron became a preacher. Cameron was a man of great physical strength and of upright life.*

James Rutledge was born in South Carolina, but, moving westward, came under the same religious influence which determined the career of Cameron. He was married to Mary Ann Miller by Reverend James McGready, January 25, 1808. Rutledge was a man of distinguished family connections, a man of generous nature and impulsive kindness, given to hospitality, and sincerely religious.† Cameron and Rutledge both entered land on Sand Ridge in that part of Sangamon which is now Menard County, Illinois, February 8, 1828, and Cameron began his mill on Concord Creek. The neighborhood was attractive. The people were nearly all Cumberland Presbyterians, the old Concord Church having already been established by Reverend John McCutcheon Berry, father of the worthless William F. Berry who was later Lincoln's partner. The church was located, not where the building now stands, but more than a mile from there, on the farm of McGrady Rutledge, a nephew of James. The neighborhood seemed ideal to these devout people, and they would have been content to live and die there if the water of Concord Creek had proved adequate.†

*After the failure of New Salem, Cameron and his family moved to Fulton County, Illionois, and thence to Iowa. They went to California in 1849. Mrs. Cameron died there in 1875, and her husband in 1878.

†James Rutledge died December 3, 1835, in the Cameron house on Sand Ridge, which, as also his own house and farm in that locality, had become the property of John McNamar. His widow and her children moved to Fulton County, Illinois, and later to Birmingham, Iowa, where she died aged ninety-one, December 26, 1878, in the home of her daughter, Nancy Rutledge Prewitt. Mary Ann (Miller) Rutledge was born October 21, 1787.

‡John McCutcheon Berry was born in Virginia, March 22, 1788. He was a soldier in the War of 1812. He was licensed to preach by Logan Presbytery in Tennessee in 1819, and ordained by the same body in 1822. He removed to Illinois immediately after his ordination, and settled in the Rock

But the summer of 1828 proved to their sad satisfaction that Concord Creek was no place for a mill; and so, holding to their farms on Sand Ridge, Cameron and Rutledge entered a new tract of land, July 29, 1828, and there projected their ambitious scheme.

This new venture had nothing less than the damming of the mighty Sangamon itself, and establishing upon its banks a new and ideal community, with a Biblical name, being indeed no other than the ancient name of Jerusalem.

Considerations of utility had their place in the selection of the site of New Salem, but neither Cameron nor Rutledge could have been blind to the beauty of the spot. The Sangamon flowing through level meadows varied with forests of oak, ash, hickory and basswood, winds a portion of its way between bluffs that on one side reach a height of a hundred feet. The stream, flowing northwesterly, makes a westward bend and strikes this bluff and is deflected in an abrupt northward turn, then winds around so that with an inflowing tributary it leaves a promontory which is virtually a peninsula. This elevation is two hundred and fifty feet wide where it fronts the stream, and gradually widens until it finds the upland level of the surrounding country. Beautiful for situation, and a joy to the beholder, was this new Mount Zion on the sides of the north, the city of a new hope.

To dam the Sangamon was no small undertaking. First of all, an act of the Legislature must be secured, permitting the construction of a dam. This proved not to be a difficult undertaking, and was accomplished with surprising promptness. Then a thousand wagon-loads of rock must be hauled and sunk in log cribs. Even at the low cost of labor in those days, it was a

---

Creek precinct in 1822 or 1823, organizing the Concord Church almost immediately. In 1838 he organized the Rock Creek Church, and became its pastor also. The original members were James Pantier and his wife Eliza (Armstrong) Pantier, William and James Rutledge, and their wives, Samuel Berry and his wife. Cameron is not known to have held a regular pastorate, but exhorted at meetings conducted by the other ministers, and on occasion himself preached. Reverend John M. Berry sorrowed deeply over his wayward son.

large task. But it was accomplished by those two men of courage and hope, and a saw- and grist-mill was erected on the new dam.

On October 23, 1829, after a full year of strenuous toil, the town was surveyed, and on Christmas Day of the same year a post-office was established with New Salem as a place to be recognized, even in Washington.

And so it came to pass that, when that piece of human drift-wood that bore the name of Abraham Lincoln came floating down the Sangamon on the spring tide of 1831, New Salem was on the map of the world, and the Rutledge dam was a reality which not even a boat of as flat a bottom and light a draft as that which Lincoln navigated could dispute or ignore.

The whole population of New Salem is said to have assembled to witness the predicament of the flat-boat, and to have been impressed with the ingenuity of Lincoln, who, with his trousers rolled up "about five feet," as Rowan Herndon affirmed, em-ployed this effective method by which the boat at length floated over. The affair occupied no little time, and afforded oppor-tunity for the beginning of pleasant acquaintanceships.

As Lincoln and Offutt discussed the matter on their month's voyage down-stream, and their month's sojourn in New Orleans, and their week's journey by steamer up to St. Louis, it became evident to Offutt that river life was too monotonous for a man of his active temperament. He determined to establish a center from which his genius could radiate, and on occasion move up and down the Sangamon, but not the length of the larger streams. And if he did this, he must have an associate who would attend to the home base while he moved freely about, conducting the large enterprises that became so great a man. And of all the places that he had seen, there was none that appeared to offer so promising a future as New Salem, and no man who appeared to combine so many of the qualities that he required as Abraham Lincoln.

Lincoln participated in all this discussion, and was deeply im-pressed by the sagacity and ability of Offutt. The plan was

THE SANGAMON AT NEW SALEM
Photograph by Herbert Georg

wholly to his liking. So he tarried for a month with his father and stepmother in Coles County, and then walked back to New Salem, where he expected to meet Offutt and his goods.

But as Offutt had been detained in Springfield, so was he detained in St. Louis. The goods were not at New Salem when Lincoln arrived. This did not distress Lincoln. He was fully equal to any emergency that called for leisure. He settled down to wait for the goods, and to become acquainted with New Salem and its population.

From the point of view available from our knowledge of his subsequent life, it is now easily possible to see that Lincoln was moving through a series of experiences each one of which was advancing him toward the high destiny of his ultimate greatness. But it is not to be assumed that this was apparent even to himself at the time when these experiences occurred.

The plastic material of his life was in process of formation, and even the mold in which the Lincoln of history was to be cast was in process of making. But the mold was not the man. While Lincoln fitted into his environment, and took shape from it, he was, like every strong man, master of the forces that determined the influence of his environment. Personality is still the determining factor in history.

While Lincoln waited for Offutt at New Salem, the August election occurred. He was a new arrival, but according to law and custom was entitled to vote, and vote he did. It was Lincoln's first vote. He voted for James Turney for Congress. Turney then or later was a Whig; and he was defeated by Joseph Duncan, who was then a Democrat, but some years later following his election as governor of Illinois, he became a Whig. Lincoln voted for Robert Conover and Pollard Simmons for justices of the peace, and for John Armstrong and Henry Sinco for constables.

This election was held in the house of John McNeil August 1, 1831, and it is a remarkable fact that McNeil did not vote, either at that or any subsequent election at New Salem, so far as the preserved election returns show. Mentor Graham, the schoolmaster, was clerk of the election, and he needed help. He asked Lincoln if he could write, and Lincoln replied that he was able to "make a few chicken-tracks." He served as assistant clerk at that election, and at practically every subsequent election in New Salem, except elections where he was himself a candidate. There were always two and some times three elections a year, in April, August and November. Local officers were elected in the spring; the legislative election was held in the summer; and the national election occurred in November. In several of these elections appeared the names of Mentor Graham* and Abraham Lincoln as clerks, and their oaths were acknowledged before Bowling Green, Justice of the Peace.

No device would have been less popular in New Salem than the Australian ballot. Every man walked up to the polls and announced orally the names of the candidates for whom he voted. As he left, the judge of election shouted in the ears of all men that John Doe had voted for John Smith for governor, John Jones for secretary of state, John Brown for state treasurer, and so on. These votes were visibly recorded as cast. There were no printed ballots.

And New Salem voted. All except John McNeil, who, probably not to be confronted with unnecessary documentary evidence of a name about which he did not feel wholly comfortable, somehow escaped voting. John McNeil was partner with Samuel Hill in one of New Salem's stores. John McNeil was saving money. Whenever any one had anything to sell and needed money badly, John McNeil had money to pay for it at a bargain price. He was fast accumulating more than he counted prudent to hold under an assumed name. He was a prudent man, and he did not record his name on the election sheet. So though the election was held in the house of John McNeil, John McNeil did not vote.

*He invariably signed it Mentor Graham; not Minter, as it is sometimes printed, nor Menton, as Nicolay and Hay give it. In the Appendix are the complete Election Returns from the New Salem precinct.

New Salem voted. It mattered little whether Andrew Jackson was running for the presidency or Jack Kelso was running for constable, New Salem did its enthusiastic duty at the polls. It is practically possible to determine just who was resident in New Salem in any year by the election lists. We can learn just when Doctor Allen moved in and when Hardin Bale moved out by a study of these documents, duly certified by Mentor Graham and Abraham Lincoln. Except that we seek in vain to determine just when John McNeil went back to New York State and when he reassumed his real name. We must look elsewhere for that information, for John McNeil was too cautious to vote. He was saving money and investing it discreetly. He was not indulging in any bad habit, and certainly not in any expensive habit. And, though he had entered his land in the name of John McNeil, he was considering whether it would not be better to change it soon and resume his correct name. You will search the polling lists in vain for his name. But the rest of New Salem's adult male population is on record there.

While Lincoln waited for the arrival of Offutt, he had opportunity to use his knowledge of navigation. A Doctor Nelson who had been for a short time a resident of New Salem, loaded his household goods upon a boat and started down the river, his ultimate destination being Texas. He desired and obtained Lincoln's service as pilot as far as the mouth of the Sangamon. The river still was reasonably high, and the task of navigation was not difficult. Lincoln piloted the boat as far as Beardstown, was paid off, and honorably dismissed.

Good fortune further awaited him, for he found at Beardstown that Offutt's goods had arrived from St. Louis. He started walking back to New Salem expecting to convey the message to teamsters who had been engaged to transport the merchandise, but met the wagon as he journeyed, the drivers having already been notified. So he returned to New Salem with satisfaction.

Soon Denton Offutt arrived. On July 8, 1831, he took out

his license to sell goods in New Salem. On September 2, 1831, he purchased a lot as a site for the erection of his store, and he and Lincoln went to work at once to construct a building. The consideration named in the deed was ten dollars, which was a fair price for the lot.

Then the career of Lincoln and Offutt as merchants became a reality, and Offutt added one enterprise after another until he rented the Rutledge mill, and seemed likely to acquire a monopoly of all the business in New Salem. Some men of Offutt's type become great captains of industry, and, having accumulated millions, go about like roaring lions seeking what they may endow; others become bankrupts and are accounted visionaries and perhaps frauds. Offutt was a promoter. Some people did not believe in him, but Abraham Lincoln was not one of them.

In those days a new arrival in a frontier town was expected early to define his status in the matter of physical strength. Lincoln was tall, muscular and strong. He did not like to work, but he was capable of arduous labor when occasion arose. He did not like to fight, but when he fought he was a dangerous antagonist. Offutt had seen enough of Lincoln's physical strength to give him occasion to boast about it. He informed William Clary, who kept a saloon near the Offutt store, that Lincoln could outrun, outlift and outwrestle any man in the community. Clary represented a group of men known as the "Clary Grove boys," named for a strip of timber about six miles distant from New Salem. The champion of the group was one Jack Armstrong, the man for whom Lincoln had already voted as constable. Clary and Offutt made a bet of ten dollars on a wrestling match between Lincoln and Jack Armstrong. Lincoln is said to have been reluctant to engage in the match, but he found himself committed to it by the boastfulness of his employer. He soon outmastered Armstrong, and when the latter attempted to win by a foul, Lincoln picked Armstrong up bodily and threw him heavily upon the ground. There was some danger that he might have to fight the whole Clary Grove contingent in consequence of this act, but his strength, courage, fairness and good nature won for him the admiration of the crowd, including his contestant, and Lincoln became the popular hero of the Clary Grove boys. They became his followers and most enthusiastic supporters. Hannah, Jack Armstrong's wife, and the pre-matrimonial mother of Bowling Green, became a sincere friend of Lincoln, and he later had occasion to reward her well.

Lincoln participated in several wrestling contests in New Salem, but not, so far as is known, in any fights. He was referee in wrestling matches, and his decisions were accepted on both sides as fair.

The early spring of 1832 still further increased Lincoln's popularity by his successful piloting of the steamboat *Talisman* up the Sangamon from Beardstown to Springfield. Captain A. Vincent Bogue, of Springfield, went to Cincinnati, where he procured the steamer, and her ascent of the Mississippi and the Illinois was hailed with delight. The prosperity of Springfield, New Salem and other towns along the Sangamon was believed to depend on the navigability of the river. The actual ascent of the Sangamon River by a steamboat was expected to prove beyond possibility of doubt, not only that the river was navigable, but that all towns located upon it had before them a career of great prosperity. A number of citizens of Springfield and other Sangamon towns went down to Beardstown to meet the vessel as she came from the Illinois into the Sangamon. Some of these carried axes with long handles to cut away the branches of trees along the banks of the Sangamon. Lincoln accompanied the group, and having acquired a reputation as a navigator of rivers, he and Rowan Herndon were employed as pilots. At the rate of about four miles a day the *Talisman* ascended the narrow stream. Like Lincoln's flat-boat, she stuck at the Rutledge dam, but tore away a part of it and got across. The damage done at the dam raised a vigorous protest from Cameron and Rutledge, but it does not appear to have disturbed their kindly relations with Lincoln. The vessel found safe anchorage at Springfield, or at the point where the Sangamon most nearly approached that city. Celebrations were held, and the river towns indulged in a boom. A great ball was given in Springfield to the captain of the *Talisman* and his right good crew.* The *Talisman* succeeded in making her way back down the river, but had a warm controversy on hand with Rutledge and Cameron for damage done to their dam.

The attempt to prove that the Sangamon was a navigable stream succeeded theoretically but failed practically. The people of Springfield shouted themselves hoarse and declared that henceforth that city "could no longer be considered an inland town." Captain Bogue accepted with satisfaction all the honors thrust upon him. He knew they were the last that would ever accrue from that source. He remained in Springfield while the feasting lasted, and then prudently sailed his boat back downstream, and left the subsequent navigation of the Sangamon to other adventurers, of whom there were not many.

Lincoln earned forty dollars and considerable glory by his share in this apparently successful undertaking. He walked back from Beardstown to New Salem with his money in his pocket, richer in purse and reputation than he had been before since his arrival at the village. But the *Talisman* never came back up the river. Not long afterward she was burned at the dock in St. Louis. Suits in attachment were filed against Captain Bogue, who prudently disappeared. One other attempt to navigate the river was made, this one by the steamboat *Utility*. She did not succeed in getting above the dam, but remained at New Salem and was sold and broken up. Gradually it became clear even to the most optimistic proponent of the thesis that the Sangamon was a navigable stream that this claim must be abandoned. Lincoln and Rowan Herndon, with their forty dollars apiece, were the only men who made any money out of the navigability of the Sangamon. But a note which Lincoln gave to Captain Vincent

---

*Herndon says that Lincoln was not invited to the ball.

A. Bogue, on which Lincoln was afterward sued, raises a question whether Lincoln did not subscribe to the enterprise more money than he got out of it.

During Lincoln's employment by Offutt it appears that his work was largely at the mill.   In the announcement of his candidacy for the Legislature, March 9, 1832, he said:

From my peculiar circumstances, it is probable that for the last twelve months I have given as particular attention to the stage of the water in this river as any other person in the country.   In the month of March, 1831, in company with others, I conceived the building of a flat-boat on the Sangamon, and finished and took her out in the course of the spring.   Since that time, I have been concerned in the mill at New Salem.   These circumstances are sufficient evidence that I have not been very inattentive to the stages of the water.

His future hopes, commercial and political, depended upon the navigability of the Sangamon.

Misfortunes never come singly.   Importunate creditors began to press the optimistic Offutt, and he had no money to pay them. Whatever his qualifications in the sphere of finance, they were not such as fitted him to settle down to the keeping of a country store, and Lincoln, to whom he had trusted local matters, was not a successful merchant.   There were too many stores in New Salem for its population and that of Offutt, located near the expected steamboat wharf, was farthest from the main source of revenue, if New Salem had to depend on commerce from the landward side.   There came a sad day when Offutt had to confess that he could not meet his bills.   His creditors took over his stock; Cameron and Rutledge took back their mill, and Offutt departed, never to return to New Salem.

Doubtless his competitors and other wise men of New Salem were ready to affirm that they had felt sure all the time that Offutt was too much of a braggart to be a good business man. Offutt's name after his downfall was held in little regard in New Salem.   In the day of his glory it might have stood against all competitors, but after his failure there was none so poor to do him reverence. But Lincoln parted from him in real sorrow. Whatever losses others had suffered through trusting him, Lincoln knew that Offutt had rendered him a lasting service. He had given Lincoln a larger vision of life and inspired him with a new confidence in his own powers.

Offutt was heard from in New Salem now and again. He went south, and devoted his energies to the training of wild and refractory horses. He gave public exhibitions of his own skill in subduing horses brought to him, and then imparted the secret to farmers at five dollars each, requiring an oath not to reveal the secret. It was said that he had a magic word that he whispered in the horse's ear. A modern psychologist might explain the potency of this word by the reflex action upon the farmer, giving him new confidence which the beast felt and submitted to. It was said that Offutt went from town to town, and appearing on the street, wore over his well cut coat a sash that decorated his right shoulder and fastened with a rosette under his left arm. Wherever he went, he was a life-sized advertisement of Denton Offutt.

It is pleasant to be able to add one authentic incident to those on record concerning Denton Offutt. In the year 1856 a young man from Petersburg named Thomas W. McNeeley, went south to teach a select school on a Mississippi plantation. On a Saturday he went with his employer to the town of Woodworth some miles away, a part of the attraction being the exhibition advertised to be given by a tamer of wild horses. Each planter who had a vicious horse took him to town, and the tamer had remarkable success with them all. He used his whip and spur very sparingly; but began with a little preliminary petting, then whispered something in the horse's ear and mounted. The planters knew their own and each other's horses and knew that whatever Offutt's secret might be, there was no question about his control over the animals he rode. Five-dollar notes in considerable numbers went to his hospitable pockets, and Offutt imparted his secret to each man who paid him. Whether the farmers got their money's worth may have depended on whether they approached men and horses with the same happy assurance that characterized Offutt.

After the exhibition was over McNeeley sought Offutt, whose name he had often heard, and told him that he was from Petersburg, and knew many people whom Offutt had known. Offutt expressed great delight in meeting him, and inquired about his old neighbors, and especially about Lincoln, of whom he had heard now and then. McNeeley told him that Lincoln had become quite a famous man in central Illinois, and Offutt was quite ready to believe it. He sent a verbal message to Lincoln. Soon after his return to Petersburg, the young man had occasion to ride over to Springfield, and seeking out a friend who had an office in the court-house he asked for an introduction to Lincoln. Lincoln welcomed news from Offutt, and greatly enjoyed the story of Offutt's performance. The young man still had his message to deliver, and, as he talked with Lincoln, he had a growing reluctance to deliver it; for he began to fear that Lincoln would be displeased with a message that reflected on his own profession. Said he:

"Mr. Offutt gave me a message to deliver to you, but I hardly know whether I ought to deliver it or not."

"Tell it to me," said Lincoln. "Tell it just as Offutt said it."

"He told me to say to you, 'Tell Lincoln to get out of his rascally business of politics and law, and do something honest, like taming horses.'"

Lincoln laughed immoderately at this word from his old friend:

"That's Offutt," he said. "That's just like Offutt."

Lincoln, out of employment, or soon to become so, decided to enter politics. That was a simple matter in 1832. One had no need to wait for nomination by convention; nor did a man feel shame in publishing in the local newspapers an announcement that he was a candidate. A candidate was expected to declare his convictions, and it was the custom to issue a circular setting forth the candidate's principles. This Lincoln proceeded to do in a circular probably printed in Springfield, and bearing date of March 9, 1832. In this declaration of principles he undertook to discuss the leading questions of the day as understood by his constituents. Although he had been reared a Jackson Democrat, he favored national banks, which was a distinctive test of the Whigs. Yet one does not discover in his political career any indications that his principles at this time were those which distinguished the Whigs from the Locofoco Democrats. He favored a high protective tariff, and of course, was an ardent advocate of internal improvements and river navigation. This was Lincoln's strong point. He favored a law against usury; but considering that men who had the most need of money could not obtain it unless they paid usurious interest, he wrote this amazing paragraph:

In cases of extreme necessity, there could always be found means to cheat the law; while in all other cases it would have its intended effect. I would favor the passage of a law on this subject which might not be very easily evaded. Let it be such that the labor and difficulty of evading could only be justified in cases of the greatest necessity.*

From this and other portions of his circular, it is evident that Lincoln had not thought through all, or perhaps any, of the questions which in this first political pronunciamento, he felt compelled to discuss. The remarkable fact is, not that his letter announcing his candidacy was a crude performance, but that it was not far more crude. It can but surprise us to remember that this uncouth backwoodsman, barely twenty-three years of age, who

---

*John McNeil, subsequently known by his true name of John McNamar, later professed to have assisted Lincoln in preparing this circular. I think the statement not wholly untruthful, and it is my opinion that this paragraph on money shows the influence of John McNamar.

less than a year before had stepped off a flat-boat into New Salem, should have announced himself as a candidate for the General Assembly. He proclaimed himself as in favor of education, which he called the most important subject before the people. He believed that every man, no matter how poor, should be able to procure for himself and his children at least sufficient education "to read the Scriptures and other works both of a moral and religious nature." The concluding paragraphs of his address are the most personal and most interesting part of this strange but remarkable document. They have in them real promise of the Lincoln of the future.

But, fellow-citizens, I shall conclude. Considering the great degree of modesty which should always attend youth, it is probable I have already been more presuming than becomes me. However, upon the subjects of which I have treated, I have spoken as I have thought. I may be wrong in regard to any or all of them; but, holding it as a sound maxim that it is better only sometimes to be right than at all times to be wrong, so soon as I discover my opinions to be erroneous, I shall be ready to renounce them.

Every man is said to have his peculiar ambition. Whether it be true or not, I can say, for one, that I have no other so great as that of being truly esteemed of my fellow-men by rendering myself worthy of their esteem. How far I shall succeed in gratifying this ambition is yet to be developed. I am young, and unknown to many of you. I was born, and have ever remained, in the most humble walks of life. I have no wealth or popular relations or friends to recommend me. My case is thrown exclusively upon the independent voters of the county; and, if elected, they will have conferred a favor upon me for which I shall be unremitting in my labors to compensate. But if the good people in their wisdom shall see fit to keep me in the background, I have been too familiar with disappointments to be very much chagrined.

But hardly had Lincoln announced his candidacy for the Legislature when an event occurred which, if it did not modify, at least postponed his adventure into politics.

CHAPTER XI

THIS earth has no nook or cranny where savagery may lurk secure from the ultimate inrush of progress. Civilization advances upon savagery with a pistol in its belt and a pill-box in its pocket, a Bible in one hand and a bottle of rum in the other. Savagery has its choice, but it must be civilized by the one method or the other, or move beyond the borders of the map. This is a painful process, often fatal to the savage and demoralizing to the man who undertakes to civilize him. What Kipling calls "the White Man's Burden" is indeed a burden. It is the burden of making the world safe for civilization; and that process goes on more rapidly than the process of making civilization safe for the world. All in all we pay a high price for what we call culture. Said Thoreau, "We exterminate the deer, and we cultivate the hog." That is only a part of what we do.

The American Indian is the most picturesque savage on the face of the earth. The French managed to live among the Indians more successfully than the English and Americans have even yet learned to do. From the beginning the English immigrants regarded the Indians with terror and hatred; and the story of their relationships has been long and bloody, and it does not make pleasant reading.

Black Hawk was in many respects a truly noble red man. He compels the reluctant admiration of the student of history. Long after the white man had settled in Southern Illinois, scorning the treeless prairies of the northern portion of the state, Black

Hawk lived secure in the Rock River country, and came and went, and believed that territory to be his own. He had what Fitz Greene Halleck attributed to Red Jacket—

"Love for thy land as if she were thy daughter,"

without possessing to quite the same degree Red Jacket's

"Hatred of missionaries and cold water."

The time came when Black Hawk and the white man could not equally own the Rock River country, and then came the trouble.

Black Hawk, whose Indian name as given in his *Autobiography* was Ma-ka-tai-she-kia-kiak, was born in 1767, on the north bank of the Rock River, about three miles above where it empties into the Mississippi. Illinois has few spots more beautiful. Black Hawk was a full-blooded Sac Indian, five feet and eleven inches tall in his moccasins, rather broad and very powerful, but slender, weighing only about one hundred forty pounds. He had a high forehead and a Roman nose, high cheek-bones and a sharp chin. The height of the forehead was emphasized by the plucking of the hair from the entire scalp except the scalp-lock, in which he wore a bunch of eagle feathers. His mouth was full, and tended to remain open. At fifteen he distinguished himself by wounding an enemy, and thenceforth became a brave, and was permitted to paint and to wear feathers. In 1783 he took his first scalp, and had a share in the scalp-dance. From this time on he kept his tomahawk red.

By the Treaty of 1804, the Illinois lands of the Sacs were ceded to the United States Government. Black Hawk maintained that the Indians who signed this treaty had no authority to do so. Moreover, he maintained, his reason taught him that land could not be sold: the Great Spirit gave it to his children for their equal enjoyment. Black Hawk, if he were now living, could find many men of learning who would share his view. The

Indians removed beyond the Mississippi, but were accustomed to return every year, to follow up the Rock River, and spend some time at their old village near its mouth. There was the grave of Black Hawk's daughter; and there he mourned long for her.

"The white people brought whiskey to our village," said Black Hawk in his *Autobiography,* "they made our people drunk and cheated them out of their horses, guns and traps. I visited all the whites and begged them not to sell my people whiskey. One of them continued the practise openly; I took a party of my young men, went to his house, broke in the head of the barrel, and poured out the whiskey. I did this for fear some of the whites might get killed by my people when they were drunk."*

The white people also had their grievances, and very real ones. They were endeavoring to make homes on land which they had preempted from the government, to which it had been conveyed by treaty from the Indians. And when the break came, it was bloody and cruel.†

The year 1831 brought increasing friction between the Indians and white men. In the spring of 1832 it became evident not only that Black Hawk would return to the lands from which the treaty and subsequent orders had prohibited his occupation, but that he was organizing for war. On April 16, 1832, Governor John Reynolds issued a call for the militia of the State of Illinois to rendezvous at Beardstown on the twenty-second. The governor himself, proud of a military career and the popular soubriquet of "the Old Ranger," accompanied the expedition whose purpose was to move from the southern and central portions of the state, where the population chiefly was, into the Rock River country, and to drive the Indians back to their

---

Autobiography of Black Hawk, p. 73.

†This work attempts no history of the Black Hawk War. Its story has been written by others. Honorable Perry A. Armstrong wrote it in a spirit of sincere appreciation of the Indian's wrongs, suffered at the hands of the white man. A more discriminating work is that by Frank E. Stevens. *The Autobiography of Black Hawk,* in which the editor, J. B. Patterson, modestly called himself the amanuensis, must owe not a little to the editor; but it is a work of remarkable interest.

reservation across the Mississippi. Black Hawk came for war, and he began at once his movement up the Rock River. The troops gathered at Dixon, where the pioneer John Dixon had a ferry. The first fight was at Stillman Valley, and resulted in the killing of eleven white men, and the precipitate retreat of the rest back to Dixon. Then came the Indian Creek massacre, and the captivity of the Hall sisters, and the attack on Apple River. In the first conflicts the Indians had matters their own way. The stories of their atrocities terrified the settlers, and gave to Illinois a fright that was hardly less than a panic. But the war had begun, and it could have but one end.

The events connected with the Black Hawk War appear small through the mists of the years. A forlorn band of Indians undertook a completely hopeless attempt to win back their land by bloodshed, and they went down to inevitable defeat. It might seem to us that no community living a day's march outside the actual field of probable encounter need have disturbed itself greatly over a situation that must so soon be settled and in the only way in which it could be settled. But that was not as matters looked in Illinois in 1832. The settlers confronted what seemed to them the most terrible uprising of Indians since the massacre at Fort Dearborn. All their hereditary fear and hatred of the Indians awoke. All the savage instincts which lie dormant in the civilized breast broke forth with the first suggestion of actual conflict with savages. The volunteers were filled with valor and were ready to bring back the scalps of as many savages as might be.

Abraham Lincoln had returned from New Orleans, and had taken up his abode in New Salem, and distributed his hand-bills announcing himself as a candidate for the Legislature when the proclamation of the governor turned his thought toward a different kind of employment and another sort of glory. He volunteered immediately, and so did a considerable number of his associates in and about New Salem. The Clary Grove gang was there almost to a man. An election was held for captain. Will-

iam Kirkpatrick, the man for whom Lincoln had worked in a
saw-mill as the Offutt flat-boat was in process of construction,
and who had treated Lincoln ungenerously in the matter of the
furnishing of a cant-hook to lighten his labor, was a candidate.
Lincoln entered the lists against him, and had the great joy of
winning. No victory in later life ever gave him so much satisfaction. Lincoln's first sergeant was Jack Armstrong, his early
rival in New Salem, and ever since his thrashing, Lincoln's firm
friend.

In the Black Hawk War Lincoln may have met Captain Zachary Taylor, whom later he warmly supported as president of the
United States. He certainly met Major Robert Anderson, who
later came into prominence as the defender of Fort Sumter.
Persistent tradition declares that he was mustered into service by
a young officer in the Regular Army, Lieutenant Jefferson
Davis. This tradition has been repeated so often it is almost
cruel to deny it. Lincoln himself is said to have come to think
that it might be true. On May ninth, Lincoln's company was sworn
into the service of the United States Government by General
Henry Atkinson.* Twenty days later, when he again enlisted,
and was sworn in at Ottawa, it was Lieutenant Robert Anderson who administered the oath.

The end of the Black Hawk War came in the battle of Bad

*Mr. Stevens in his book on the Black Hawk War reluctantly disproved
the Jefferson Davis story, saying that he gave it up with great regret, as
his early home was in Dixon and he had heard and believed that story all
his life. I was born in the same county. The "army trail" through Knox
Grove was still visible in my boyhood. Abraham Lincoln and his company,
on their first night out of Ottawa, May twenty-seventh, camped a little south
and east of my birthplace. Shabbona, the devoted friend of the white man,
camped often on Bureau Creek on the land of my grandfather; and my
father as a boy participated in one wolf-hunt with Shabbona, and once afterward, meeting him in Chicago, went with him to buy fish-hooks, and fished
with him in Chicago River. Stories of the Black Hawk War were abundant
in my youth, three years of which were spent on the site of Stillman's
first battle. I would be very glad to believe, what I heard a hundred times
in my youth, that the first time Abraham Lincoln had occasion to make oath
that he would support the Constitution of the United States, the oath was
administered by Jefferson Davis. But even though the oath was administered by another officer, Abraham Lincoln kept his promise, and Jefferson
Davis discovered the fact.

Axe in Wisconsin, August 1, 1832. The Indians were surrounded and defeated with great slaughter. Black Hawk escaped, but later was captured. The Indians were forever driven from the Rock River country. Illinois became the undisputed land of the white man.

Black Hawk made two journeys to the East. He witnessed a balloon ascension in New York City and had a reception at Philadelphia and another in Washington. Thoroughly impressed with the vastness of the country and the impossibility of the Indians driving the white man out of it, he returned to Iowa where a reservation had been assigned to him, and was released from imprisonment. He died in October, 1838. It had been well for him if he had continued to remember the earnest protest which he made in earlier years against the white man's furnishing liquor for the Indians. Black Hawk now and then in his later years was the worse for drink. In his last days his relations with the white man were friendly, but he never forgave his Indian associate Keokuk for not standing by him in his fight against the white man. Black Hawk's widow, Singing Bird, did not long survive her husband.

Lincoln's military experience was brief. His election as captain was confirmed at Beardstown, April 21, 1832. His company formed a part of the fourth regiment of mounted volunteers in General Whitesides' brigade. They moved from Beardstown to Rock Island, and thence up Rock River to Dixon, and thence to the site of Stillman's battle and defeat in Ogle County. Returning to Dixon, they were marched south to Ottawa at the mouth of Fox River, where, their term of enlistment having expired, the company was disbanded on May 27, 1832. Lincoln immediately reenlisted as a private in Captain Alexander White's company, where his name appears on the roll as of May twenty-sixth. For some reason Lincoln did not go out with this company but on the following day he enrolled in Captain Elijah Iles' company for a period of twenty days. On June sixteenth, this company was mustered out. On the same day, Lincoln reenlisted in

Captain Jacob M. Earley's company. He was honorably discharged and mustered out at Whitewater, Wisconsin, July 10, 1832.

Lincoln was not in any battle. His company arrived at Kellogg's Grove on June twenty-fifth, shortly after a skirmish in which five men were killed. He helped to bury these men. As a disciplinarian he was not a pronounced success. He was once arrested and deprived of his sword for a day for firing his gun within fifty yards of camp. On another occasion he was compelled to wear a wooden sword for two days because some members of his company broke into the officers' quarters, and consumed a quantity of liquor and were unable to march with the regiment on the following morning. He himself afterward told amusing stories of his own ignorance of military terms. Many stories, supposed to be amusing, are related of this campaign, but most of them are spurious. He was not a great soldier; but he was popular both as officer and private.

The only incident which has come down to us out of Lincoln's military experience which shows the full quality of his manhood, relates to a friendly Indian, said to have been Shabbona, who had come to the camp with a pass from General Cass. Lincoln's men held to the theory that the only good Indian was a dead one, and proposed to kill this visitor. Lincoln intervened and saved the life of this virtuous and heroic chief, beloved as the white man's friend. The undisciplined hatred of the militia nearly cost him his life, but Lincoln's humanity and courage saved it. The story appears to be well authenticated, and it is characteristic of Lincoln. It deserves to be true, and there is good reason to believe that it is true.

On the night preceding his final discharge, Lincoln's horse, a borrowed one, was stolen, and he was obliged to walk from Whitewater, Wisconsin, to Dixon, and thence to Peoria, except as now and then he was helped by a ride of a mile or two by some more fortunate friend. At Peoria, he and a comrade, who appears to have been Major John T. Stuart, of Springfield, bought a canoe, and paddled down the Illinois River to Havana, where they sold the canoe, and walked, Stuart to Springfield and Lincoln back to New Salem.

The Black Hawk War does not appear to have been one of the great turning points of Lincoln's career. It was soon over, and he went back to New Salem, and took up his then uneventful career just where he had left it. His military experience did not measurably enhance his political popularity, nor did it open for him any other avenue into life than those that were already available.

But the war was not without advantage to him. He made friends who continued to be his associates in subsequent years, including his first law-partner, John T. Stuart. He learned something of the handling of troops, and of the difficulties of providing them with munitions and supplies. In the Civil War his scant but suggestive military experience came to him and sometimes made him wiser than his generals. It was a small and short war, and at the time it did not seem greatly to have affected the career of Lincoln; but it had its value in his training.

Lincoln never pretended that his enlistment and service in the Black Hawk War was conclusive evidence of his patriotism. Of that patriotism he was able to give other and larger proof. He was young, strong, free and unemployed when the call for volunteers came, and he did his duty. Years afterward, in Congress, he made a speech in which he talked humorously of his military bravery, and told of the blood he had lost through mosquito bites in his experience as a soldier. The experience was good for him. It gave him new proof of his power to command the admiration and loyal support of men. It gave him employment for a few weeks when he was out of work. It sent him back to New Salem in time for the election which was to determine whether his first venture into politics would be as successful as his first appearance as a military leader. For Lincoln was still a candidate for the Legislature. One only reference to his campaign appears to have been made in the Springfield papers, and that was a statement that Captain Lincoln was serving with his company in the war, and had left the issues of the campaign in the hands of his friends. That was a safe place in which to leave them, even if he could not win his first election. In the long run, Abraham Lincoln ran little risk in trusting his future to the people.

CHAPTER XII

POLITICIAN AND POSTMASTER
1832-1833

It is interesting to note that the popular opprobium which gathered about the memory of Denton Offutt in New Salem did not attach itself also to Abraham Lincoln, Offutt's clerk. Lincoln was still popular in New Salem. That is a significant fact. It speaks much for his qualities of solid worth that his association with the now discredited Offutt did not cause New Salem to suggest to him that he pack his few belongings and leave when Offutt left. New Salem and its Clary Grove suburb had effective ways of making a suggestion of this character. New Salem liked Lincoln, and Lincoln liked New Salem. He cast about for employment. The commercial condition of New Salem offered him no immediate opening as a storekeeper, and the river gave him no promise as a navigator. It was less than a year since he first had seen New Salem, and he had no acquaintance in the legislative district outside of that microscopic municipality, but he unblushingly announced himself a candidate for the Legislature. Those do greatly err who believe that at any period in his career Abraham Lincoln was handicapped by modesty.

Rudyard Kipling in an address at Oxford in 1924, cautioned the Rhodes scholars then there assembled against the infection of weak souls with "the middle-aged failings of toleration, impartiality or broad-mindedness." There were no such symptoms of premature senility in New Salem. It was a place of opinions, not held in the poise of static toleration, but fought for in the free arena of public discussion. New Salem did not want its candidates to be modest.

As has already been noted, Lincoln announced himself a candidate for the Legislature on March 9, 1832. His absence from New Salem on account of the Black Hawk War covered the period from about April nineteenth to an unknown date in the end of July. The election for which he announced himself a candidate took place August sixth. Lincoln had little time for electioneering. He probably had not lost anything of his political popularity by his military career, although to his credit it deserves to be said that he never afterward attempted to make political capital out of his military experience, and that he never assumed for political effect or traded in his title of captain.

His first political speech was at Pappsville, following an auction sale. The speech was interrupted by a fight, and Lincoln left the platform to interfere on behalf of one of his friends who was getting the worst of it. Lifting his enemy bodily, he flung him flat upon the ground, remounted the platform, and finished his speech. This incident helped him more than any oratory could have done. A few days later he made a speech at Springfield with Major John T. Stuart as a candidate with him on the same ticket.

Lincoln's opponent in this election was Reverend Peter Cartwright, an able itinerant Methodist preacher, and a politician of experience and ability. Lincoln was defeated, and he afterward said it was the only time in his life when he was defeated by a direct vote of the people. The surprising fact is, not that Lincoln did not succeed in his first political venture, but that he should have run so well against so able and so justly popular an opponent. Although Lincoln was a Whig, if his political status could be defined at that period of his development, and Lincoln's friends at New Salem and Clary's Grove were Democrats, he received two hundred and seventy-seven out of the two hundred and ninety votes cast at New Salem, and he laid the foundation for subsequent political success.

The morning of the seventh of August, 1832, found Lincoln a defeated candidate for the Legislature. His career as a military

hero was also at an end. His commercial venture with Denton
Offutt had terminated disastrously. Lincoln was out of employment. He sought again to become a clerk in a retail store.
There were no vacant clerkships. The small stocks of merchandise in New Salem, however, changed hands with rapidity, and
though he might not be a clerk, he easily found opportunity to
become a proprietor. Two of the Herndon brothers, cousins of
his subsequent law partner, owned a store in New Salem. One
brother sold his half interest to William F. Berry. The other
brother, Rowan Herndon, who had been Lincoln's co-partner as
a pilot on the *Talisman,* became dissatisfied with Berry as a partner, and sold his interest to Lincoln, who gave his note in payment
of the purchase price. Another store, owned by the Chrisman
brothers, had failed, and James Rutledge had taken a portion of
their stock of groceries on a debt. This stock was purchased by
Berry and Lincoln, who gave their note in payment. A little
later, Reuben Radford, another merchant, incurred the enmity
of the Clary Grove boys, and found it profitable to move. Berry
and Lincoln acquired this stock also, and gave more notes.
Berry and Lincoln ought to have made a success of their approach
to monopoly. But they still had competition in Samuel Hill, and
Berry was his own best customer in the consumption of liquor.
After a time Lincoln sold his interest in the store to Berry, accepting Berry's notes in payment. Not long after this Berry dropped
out of the business and later died insolvent. Lincoln assumed
the debts of the firm, and it was many years before he succeeded
in paying them.

The Offutt failure must have had a depressing effect upon
nearly every one in New Salem. That and the hopelessness of
expecting the navigation of the Sangamon, must have warned
some far-visioned men that the town was doomed. One man
appears to have appreciated the danger. That was John McNeil,
the thrifty partner of Samuel Hill. Their store had been in
operation for three successful years, doing business at a profit of
about seventy-five per cent., and John McNeil had saved his share

of the money. Trade had fallen off with the advent of Offutt's competition; and McNeil saw that even with Offutt out of the way, business was not likely to be what it had been. He told his partner that he had left his aged parents in New York State, and felt it his duty to return to them. He sold out his half of the store to Hill, and sold while the price was good. John McNeil was accustomed to do things that way.

Rutledge and Cameron took back the mill, and they were pressed for working capital. They had to sell either their interests in New Salem or their farms on Sand Ridge. They chose the latter, and chose unwisely. There was one man who had ready money to assist men in the situation of Cameron and Rutledge. That man was John McNeil. He bought both farms at rock-bottom prices and provided the money with which the founders of New Salem kept afloat a little longer their hopeless enterprise.

John McNeil did not go to Bowling Green to have him make out the deeds. Abraham Lincoln had begun to study law, and would do it cheaper. To him, and thereafter to others, John McNeil had now to make an explanation.

His name, he told Lincoln, was not McNeil but McNamar. He had left home when his father failed in business, and had changed his name to prevent his unfortunate relatives finding him and hindering him, by their appeals for assistance, in his ambition to become rich. He was rich now; for he had accumulated ten thousand dollars in three years, and he proposed to resume his true name, go back to New York State, find his parents and return with them to New Salem. He wanted the deeds made out to John McNamar.

We shall have occasion in due time to relate the story of Ann Rutledge. The point which now should be definitely fixed in mind is that according to legal papers in which his name appears, John McNamar was living in New Salem under the name of McNeil as late as November 4, 1831. Cameron became hard pressed for money and sold his Concord land to "John McNamar, Jr.," December 9, 1831. The same enterprising man, John McNamar, bought the Rutledge farm at Sand Ridge, at a bargain price, July 26, 1832. The change of name appears to have been held in confidence after the first and until the second deed. Soon after the second purchase McNamar left New Salem. He was careful afterward not to be too certain about the date, saying, "I left the county in 1832 or 1833—I returned in 1835." He left in the summer or early autumn of 1832. We now know within five weeks the time when McNamar resumed his lawful name. It was between November 4 and December 9, 1831. After the date of December 9, 1831, Abraham Lincoln knew and the Rutledge and Cameron families knew, and by July 26, 1832, all New Salem must have known, that John McNamar had been living among them under an assumed name; but by the time this knowledge had become public, John McNamar's concern for his parents had tardily occurred to him, and he had ridden away to New York State to bring them back and share with them the prosperity of New Salem.

He made no haste about returning. Like the Detroit colored man who, hearing that the world was coming to an end, prepared to move across into Canada until the world got done ending, John McNamar resolved to trust no penny of his ten thousand dollars in New Salem, nor to return till its fortunes got better or worse. As for the land he owned on Concord Creek and Sand Ridge and elsewhere, that would not suffer by reason of his absence; it was steadily rising in value.

Thus John McNamar was not among those who suffered by the failing fortunes of New Salem; nor did he, like Lincoln, proceed to invest in grocery stores in that place after Offutt failed. Neither did he sell his half of the Hill stock to Lincoln. Lincoln could only give his notes; John McNamar was accustomed to sell for cash.

So Lincoln and Berry had only one competitor in the retail business in New Salem, and that one was Samuel Hill.

Lincoln's position as a merchant brought him appointment as

postmaster at New Salem. The post-office was established on December 25, 1829, with Samuel Hill as postmaster. He was succeeded by Isaac P. Chrisman, who began his duties on November 24, 1831. On the failure of Chrisman Brothers Hill again became postmaster. He grew unpopular with the women of New Salem, who claimed that he neglected them while he was attending to the sale of liquor. Lincoln's appointment grew out of a petition asking for the removal of Hill and the appointment of Lincoln. Lincoln's commission was dated May 7, 1833, and he continued to be postmaster until the office was discontinued in 1836. The business of the office was small, and the remuneration trifling, but Lincoln was in no position to despise the day of small things. Gladly he accepted the few dollars which the office paid, and when his partnership with Berry failed, he transported the post-office to the store of Samuel Hill, in which store Lincoln became a clerk.

There was not very much to transport. Lincoln was in the habit of carrying the letters in his hat. If the people to whom they were addressed were not at the post-office when the mail arrived, Lincoln provided a free rural delivery of his own. He carried the letters around to their several owners, in no wise reluctant to make a little visit and swap a story or two in connection with the process.

He was never very anxious to have newspapers called for promptly. He liked to have time to read the papers before he delivered them.

His service as postmaster gave to the community various opportunities of proving his honesty. Several incidents are related, which, however they may vary in detail from strict accuracy, have this at least to justify them, that they show how well established was Lincoln's reputation in this early day for truthfulness and honor. It was in New Salem that he acquired the popular name of "Honest Abe." That name he never lost.

CHAPTER XIII

SURVEYOR AND LAWMAKER
1834-1835

THE compensation of the postmaster of New Salem was proportionate to the responsibilities of the office. No one connected with the Post Office Department is now able to tell what remuneration Lincoln actually received for his services. But it was small, and Lincoln picked up a day's work wherever he could to help him to pay his board. He considered becoming a blacksmith, but decided instead to study surveying. Already he knew a little about law; and he was studying with an ardor greater than he had known before.

Among the friendships which Lincoln formed in New Salem, one of the most important was that of Mentor Graham, the school-teacher. From the date of the election, August 1, 1831, Graham became interested in him and directed his studies in grammar and other subjects. Kirkham's grammar is a volume which makes a modern text-book on the subject look like a treatise for the feeble-minded. Lincoln studied this volume with some protest at the beginning, but with increasing appreciation of its value. A self-educated young man who could take up and master that work with only incidental assistance deserves credit for no small power of application.

Lincoln at this time was given to writing treatises on a rather wide variety of subjects; some of these Graham read and corrected.

Partly under Graham's instructions, Lincoln obtained his knowledge of surveying. Graham taught him the rudiments of this science, and Lincoln learned as he labored. John Calhoun, at that time surveyor of Sangamon County, appointed Lincoln his deputy. Lincoln became a skilful and accurate surveyor. A number of his surveys are preserved, and the work shown in his handwriting is painstaking and neat. Both the county surveyors under whom Lincoln served were men who rose to distinction.*

Lincoln's surveying was remunerative; it enabled him to make some small payments on the Lincoln and Berry notes. But all of his fees as surveyor and his emoluments as postmaster and the small sums he received for drawing contracts and other legal papers, were less than enough to pay his very modest living expenses and to meet the notes which from time to time matured and were presented for payment. Now and then Lincoln performed manual labor in the harvest field and was very glad of the small wage which his toil brought him.

Lincoln was now in a position where he could have made a living, but he was burdened with the debts incurred through his partnership with Berry. The firm of Lincoln and Berry purchased a stock of goods from Reuben Radford, and executed the firm's note, October 19, 1833, for $379.82. This note was assigned by Radford to Peter Van Bergen. He, alone of Lincoln's creditors, declined to wait for payment, and on April 7, 1834, he brought suit.†

---

*John Calhoun, under whom Lincoln had his first opportunity as deputy surveyor, was born in Boston, Massachusetts, October 14, 1806. In 1830 he removed to Springfield, Illinois, and after serving in the Black Hawk War was appointed surveyor of Sangamon County. He was a Democratic representative in the Legislature of 1838 and an unsuccessful candidate for governor in 1846. He served as mayor of Springfield for three years, 1849-1851. In 1854, President Pierce appointed him surveyor general of Kansas, and he became a leader in political affairs in that territory, presiding at the Lecompton Convention. He died in St. Joseph, Missouri, October 25, 1859.

He was succeeded as surveyor of Sangamon County by Thomas M. Neale, who, on September 12, 1835, announced through the *Sangamo Journal* the appointment of John Calhoun and Abraham Lincoln as his deputies. Neale was born in 1796 in Fauquier County, Virginia. He removed to Kentucky, where he studied law, and in 1824 removed to Sangamon County, Illinois. He made the survey on the basis of which in 1825 the town of Springfield was laid out as the prospective county-seat of Sangamon County. He was three times elected county surveyor, and held that position at the time of his death, August 7, 1840.

†Various biographers assert that this suit was brought before Lincoln's friend, Bowling Green; but Honorable William H. Townsend discovered the original papers in the Sangamon Circuit Court at Springfield, as shown in his *Lincoln the Ligitant*.

It is generally supposed that by the time of this suit Berry was dead; but he was alive and was summoned August 15, 1834. Lincoln was summoned five days later. The note had been reduced by part payments to $204.82, of which under the assignment Van Bergen was entitled to $154 and Radford to the balance. On October 11, 1834, a horse was credited by Radford on the note, at an agreed value of $35.00. When the case came to trial Berry was able to pay the small balance due Radford, but Lincoln was not able to pay Van Bergen. Accordingly, judgment was rendered against Lincoln for $154 and costs. To satisfy this judgment the small worldly wealth of Abraham Lincoln was taken from him by process of law, his horse, saddle and bridle, and his surveying instruments—the means by which he had expected to be able to pay the debt.

But Lincoln always had friends. On the day of the sale, "Uncle Jimmy" Short, of Sand Ridge, bid in the property, and gave it back to Lincoln. With tears in his eyes, Lincoln thanked him. In time he repaid the debt in full. Years afterward, when Lincoln was president, he heard that "Uncle Jimmy" was in California and penniless. Thereupon, without solicitation, James Short received an appointment as Indian agent.

But the horse which had been taken on the Van Bergen execution was not fully paid for at the time. Thomas Watkins, of Petersburg, had sold the horse to Lincoln for fifty dollars, and of this amount ten dollars remained unpaid. Although few men in Sangamon County were better able to risk ten dollars, and few men more likely to pay it than Abraham Lincoln, Watkins brought suit against Lincoln in the court of Squire Edmund Greer. Fortunately, Lincoln was able to borrow ten dollars and to settle with Watkins before the case came to trial.

Those were anxious days for Lincoln. The weekly board-bill had to be met, and his friends in New Salem were not in position to extend him credit. It required his best efforts to find money for his daily needs, and the Lincoln-Berry obligation was a mill-stone constantly round his neck. Then and years afterward he called it "the National debt."

If John McNamar had been in New Salem, he would have had money. Whether he would have loaned it to Lincoln, and if so on what terms, we do not know. McNamar had been away since the autumn of 1832. It was said that one of the Rutledge girls had cared for him and was anxiously looking for a letter from him; but the letter did not arrive. Her parents, and for that matter, the people of New Salem generally, had come to think ill of McNamar; and they were inclined to believe that the poor excuse he had given for living three years among them under a false name was not his only reason for leaving New York State. But Lincoln knew that no letter came from McNamar to Ann Rutledge.

In 1834 Lincoln again announced himself as a candidate for the Legislature, and devoted a considerable part of the summer to his canvass. Lincoln told Herndon that it was more of a hand-shaking campaign than anything else. Lincoln, however, definitely committed himself to the Whig platform, and that in a Democratic district. He won by a very large plurality. Sangamon was a large county, and entitled to four representatives in the Legislature. Lincoln stood second among the successful candidates. It usually has been stated that Lincoln's name led the list, but Herndon shows that while Lincoln had thirteen hundred and seventy-six votes, Dawson had thirteen hundred and ninety. The error of those historians who gave Lincoln first place was in reading Dawson's total vote of 1390 as 1370. Even with this slight and unimportant correction, Lincoln's vote is surprisingly large. From this time forth he never was defeated when his request for office was made to the people.

Lincoln had to borrow money to go to Vandalia, which was then the state capital. It has been alleged that he walked to his first session of the Legislature. Instead, he rode there in the stage, and was attired in a new suit of clothes. A friend loaned him two hundred dollars, and he reached the capital reasonably well clothed, and in as good a degree of physical comfort as traveling facilities of that day permitted.

Lincoln was placed upon the Committee on Public Accounts and Expenditures. It was a position for which he was singularly ill fitted. The Assembly which he entered was composed of eighty-one members. The Senate contained twenty-six and the House of Representatives fifty-five. The most of these men had been born in Kentucky, Tennessee or Virginia. There were few Frenchmen and fewer Yankees. The French were destined almost wholly to disappear and the Yankees to increase as the northern part of the state was settled.

Vandalia at this time was a town of about eight hundred inhabitants. The Methodists and Presbyterians had meeting-houses. There were two newspapers in the town, and three taverns, besides five lawyers and four physicians. The capitol building, now the court-house, was erected while Lincoln was in the Legislature, and is a dignified colonial building with a belfry. The first session attended by Lincoln was in the Methodist Church.

This Ninth General Assembly, in which Lincoln had his first experience as a lawmaker, held two sessions. The regular session in 1834-35 was important. An extra session, called in December, 1835, devoted itself in good part to the matter of internal improvements. Lincoln made no marked impression upon this legislative body.

Perhaps the most important, and certainly the most interesting, event in connection with Lincoln's first experience as a lawmaker is that there for the first time he met Stephen A. Douglas, who was present as a lobbyist. Lincoln's first impression of Douglas had chief regard to his diminutive stature. Lincoln said of him, "He is the least man I ever saw."

8

CHAPTER XIV

LINCOLN went to school, as he said, "by littles." His two short terms of schooling in Kentucky and his three in Indiana totaled less than a year of formal instruction. When he went to Congress in 1848, and filled out a concise blank whose catch words were intended to suggest the outlines of a brief biography, he entered opposite the title "Education," the single word "Defective." But when we consider him as he was toward the end of his experience in New Salem, we are impressed not so much by the meagerness of his equipment as by the extent of his preparation for a successful life.

We can not account for Lincoln's education on the theory that he was an omnivorous reader. To his associates in Indiana he thus seemed. Probably he was never as diligent or systematic as his admirers thought. In any event he ceased to be a great reader. Herndon repeatedly declares that he read less and thought more than any man in public life in his generation.

Abraham Lincoln had lived at different periods not far from Utopian cities. In 1794 a magnificent paper city named Lystra, was projected on Rolling Fork, eight or ten miles above where Thomas and Nancy Lincoln later lived on Knob Creek. Another dazzling city named Ohiopoimingo, exceeding even Lystra in magnificence, was planned to be located in Meade County only sixty miles from the Lincoln home. When in Indiana he was not very far from New Harmony. It is not known that any of these dream cities affected him appreciably. But in Illinois he was destined to be profoundly influenced by the prairie Utopia, New Salem.   New Salem greatly encouraged his love of learning.   We can not pursue the history of Lincoln's six years at New Salem intelligently and confine our study to the financial adventures of the firm of Lincoln and Berry, or the vicissitudes of Denton Offutt and his rough-and-tumble encounters with the Clary Grove boys.   Lincoln was in an environment that gave him adequate mental stimulus and encouragement.

Among Lincoln's friends was Jack Kelso, a peculiar, unpractical genius, who bore the reputation of having a fine education. Kelso introduced him to Shakespeare, Burns and Byron.   Kelso was married but childless.   He was not fond of labor, but was a good fisherman.   Fishing was about the only job at which he worked industriously, and he rather resented it when any one intruded upon his vocation with an offer of remunerative employment.   Lincoln had no musical ability, but had an ear for rhythm.   He fished now and then with Kelso, and oftener sat with Jack and visited in the evening.   Lincoln's taste in poetry up to this time had been principally for jingles, and rhymed nonsense.   He began to appreciate some of the real beauties to be found in the writings of great poets.

Lincoln early formed the acquaintance and close friendship of Bowling Green.   Green was a half-brother of Jack Armstrong. His father had lived in Tennessee, and his mother, whose maiden name was Nancy Potter, bore him prior to her marriage to Robert Armstrong by whom she had eight children.   Bowling Green was a very large man, weighing over two hundred pounds, and had a singularly pink and white skin, his complexion being like that of a woman.   He was easy-going and hospitable, and Lincoln was much in his home.   Green and Lincoln both were inclined to be Whigs in a community where most men were Democrats.   Green was a justice of the peace, and had a few law books which he willingly loaned to Lincoln.   Lincoln for a time boarded in the home of Bowling Green.   When, somewhat later,

Green died, in 1842, Lincoln was to have delivered an address at his funeral, but was overcome by emotion and could not speak.

How Lincoln acquired his first law book is disputed. Arnold affirms that in 1832, Lincoln bought at auction, in Springfield, a second-hand Blackstone's *Commentaries* and began to study law. A few weeks of hard study, and he had mastered his elementary work, and laid the foundation of a good lawyer's education; he then resolved to make the law his profession.*

The story which survives in the neighborhood of Petersburg, is that a mover passing through New Salem stopped in front of Berry and Lincoln's store, and, having in his wagon a barrel which took up room that he needed for other purposes, offered to sell it and its contents for fifty cents. Lincoln bought it and found in it, among other contents, a badly worn set of Blackstone.

By whatever process he obtained the book, he mastered it. Sometimes he lay upon the counter with his head upon a bolt of jeans cloth, diligently perusing the book. Sometimes he lay in the shade of a tree, moving around with the shadow. Sometimes he lay upon the floor, using as a sloping support the back of a chair turned down and with its four legs in the air. When Richard Yates first met him he was lying on the slope of a cellar door, studying law. He preferred to read lying down.

In this study he was not without encouragement. In his brief canvass for membership in the Legislature, he had met Stephen T. Logan and William Butler, both of Springfield, and they had encouraged him to persevere in politics and to study law. In the Black Hawk War he had come to know Major John T. Stuart, who afterward became his law partner, and who now loaned him books. Lincoln rode to Springfield to obtain these. He borrowed them one by one, beginning to read each one as he rode homeward, and reviewing it as he rode back to exchange it for another. The number of books which he read was not

Life of Lincoln, p. 40.

large, but it included the volumes deemed requisite in that day for a law student's preparation.

Lincoln never supposed that his preparation had been ideal. He was accustomed to refer to himself as a "mast-fed lawyer." It sometimes fell to him by appointment of a judge to examine young men for admission to the bar. On such occasions he was a very lenient examiner, and was accustomed to say, "Your Honor, I think this young man knows as much about law as I did when I began to practise, and I recommend his admission to the bar."

Among the agencies which affected Lincoln during his residence in New Salem was a debating society, organized under the direction of James Rutledge, and including in its membership the literary lights of the community. Lincoln attained considerable skill as a debater and he set himself to the work of preparation of essays on a wide variety of themes, philosophical, scientific and religious.

Although one of the founders of New Salem was a preacher of the Cumberland Presbyterian faith, and the coming of the Bale family brought two Baptist preachers, Abraham and Jacob Bale, as residents of the town, and although Peter Cartwright and other Methodist preachers came frequently and preached in the schoolhouse or in the Rutledge tavern, there was in New Salem a rather strong tendency toward what was called infidelity. Paine's *Age of Reason* and Volney's *Ruins* were in active circulation. Lincoln read them, and they were not without their influence upon his thinking. Among other essays which Lincoln wrote at this time was one a portion of whose subject-matter he derived from the reading of these books. It is alleged that Samuel Hill burned this manuscript out of tender concern for Lincoln's political future, but after a thorough investigation of the evidence upon which the story rests, I do not credit this tradition. The essay was one of a number which Lincoln wrote in that period, and none of them is preserved. We have no reason to assume that their destruction involves any serious loss. If we may judge from Lincoln's extant compositions from this period, they were the rather sophomoric attempts of a young man to define his opinions, and his writings had a certain value in helping him to put his thoughts on paper; but none of them deserve to be considered too seriously.*

One of Lincoln's best friends in New Salem, and one of the strongest forces for righteousness, was Doctor John Allen, who came to New Salem from Vermont before August 28, 1831. He was a strict Sabbatarian, whose principles in this regard were strengthened by an incident that occurred on his westward journey. Coming down the Ohio River, he stopped on Saturday night and waited for the next boat. The boat on which he had been traveling sank next day with loss of life. Doctor Allen practised his profession on Sunday, but gave his fees for that day to religion and charity. He organized the first Sunday-school in New Salem, and was its superintendent. He organized a Temperance Society, which was looked upon with disfavor. Mentor Graham became a member; and for his membership in it was expelled from the New Salem Baptist Church; the same church meeting, by way of even-handed justice, expelled three other members for drunkenness.

New Salem had musical aspirations. Besides the usual backwoods music, it had copies of *The Missouri Harmony*, the most pretentious of musical books then in circulation in that region. It is of record that about this time Peoria introduced *The Missouri Harmony* into its church choir, and prided itself on having so notable a book. It contained a first part for use in singing schools and for general instruction in the art of singing by note, and "a choice collection of Psalm Tunes, Hymns and Anthems." It is recorded that Abraham, who was not musical, now and then essayed a song out of this book, and there is a legend that he sang out of it with Ann Rutledge.† But the only song men-

---

*This subject I have discussed in detail in the chapter on "Lincoln's Burnt Book" in *The Soul of Abraham Lincoln*.

†*The Missouri Harmony*, compiled by Allen D. Carden, was published at Cincinnati in 1827. I have a first edition, and it does not contain the song

tioned in connection with Lincoln's use is a mournful drinking
song called "Legacy" on which Lincoln is said to have made a
rather coarse parody.

The social life of New Salem in those days was a revelation to
Lincoln. It was far beyond anything he had known in Spencer
County, Indiana. Gentryville never supposed that it was going to become a great city. It never cherished a hope that
brought to it any such group of people as made up the population of New Salem. This mushroom village on the Sangamon,
which disappeared from the map almost as soon as it found a
place there, combined in itself during its short lifetime, those
elements which made it for Lincoln the portal to new experiences.
It had almost as many different types of people as it had log
cabins. There were preachers and infidels, earnest advocates of
temperance like Doctor Allen, and swaggering bullies of the
backwoods like the Clary Grove boys. There were men who
drifted along the river, "half horse, half alligator," not all of
them gamblers and thugs, but men who regarded the life of the
river as providing a law of its own. There were people who
made a cross instead of signing their names, and there were
others who read the classics and were at home among the poets.

"Legacy." The supplement "by an amateur" adding twenty-three pieces of
varied character to the two hundred pages of the original edition, was added
in 1835, the year of Ann's death. The Rutledge copy was printed in 1844.
There can be no doubt that this copy belonged, as it still belongs, to the
Rutledge family, but it can not have been owned by them during Ann's lifetime, or Lincoln's residence in New Salem, or the residence of the Rutledges
in Illinois. This book was for a time in my possession, kindly loaned to me
by Reverend A. M. Prewitt, son of Nancy Prewitt, Ann's sister. We are
not at liberty to suppose that Ann and Abraham sang "Legacy" out of the
earlier edition, and that its place was taken later by a new copy, for the
earlier edition does not contain this song. However, it was probably a song
that was sung in New Salem, the old tune being that now sometimes used
to the words "If I were a cassowary, on the plains of Timbuctoo." Lincoln
may or may not have composed or known the parody. The story is not
confirmed by the dates on the title pages of the book. However, the book
was in use in New Salem, and indicates some degree of musical culture.
It employed "patent notes." I have a third and completed edition printed
in 1850. The shape of the book, long and narrow, made it easily destructi-
ble; and copies now are rare. One may find the words of "Legacy" and
Lincoln's alleged parody in several Lives of Lincoln; but I do not quote
them, for the evidence of the book does not confirm Lincoln's use of it.

In all of this remarkable heterogeneity there was a strange kind of social unity. The Rutledges were known to be related to a signer of the Declaration of Independence, and there were other people in New Salem who might have some difficulty in naming their own fathers. But it was a place where, to quote the not over-nice but accurately expressive language of the period, "kin and kin-in-law did not count a cuss." It was no disgrace to be poor, and there was little to encourage a man in making any hypocritical pretense of more piety than he actually possessed.

It is an interesting question whether Lincoln made the best possible use of his educational advantages. Judged from one point of view he certainly did not. Abraham Lincoln might have obtained a college education.

Twenty-five miles south of New Salem was Illinois College, established at Jacksonville in 1830. Edward Beecher, son of Lyman and brother of Henry Ward Beecher, was its president. Of its faculty were four graduates of Yale, two of them besides the president being men of outstanding ability, Julian M. Sturtevant and Jonathan Baldwin Turner. Illinois did not possess at the time three men of finer mind or nobler character than Beecher, Sturdevant and Turner.

Besides this there were two other colleges, one Methodist and the other Baptist. McKendree College was at Lebanon, founded by the Methodists. Peter Cartwright, who was not himself a man of college education, expected to found and head a Methodist Academy, but gave up that scheme and threw himself ardently into the support of McKendree. Shurtleff College, at Upper Alton, was established by Reverend John Mason Peck, a Baptist missionary and agent for the American Bible Society, and author of the first *Gazeteer of Illinois*. Peck represented the progressive element in the Baptist church, and was bitterly opposed by the reactionaries in his own denomination, the "hard-shells" as they were called.

Lincoln knew of all these colleges. Their founders and proponents came to Vandalia seeking charters for these new institu-

NEW SALEM RESTORED
The Rutledge Tavern and the Museum
The Lincoln and Berry store
Photographed for this work

tions. Lincoln had opportunity to know these educated Christian gentlemen, to hear them preach, and to learn of the advantages offered by their respective schools. Why did not he himself go to college? The ready answer might be that he was too old or too poor, or that he lacked the necessary preparation. None of these answers is satisfactory. All these schools had preparatory departments; each of them had students entering who were as old as he. Not only had each of them students as poor as he, but it would have been an exceptional student who was any richer. Why did not Lincoln go to college?

Some of Lincoln's associates in Illinois politics were college-bred men. Some of his friends in and about New Salem were college students. William Graham Greene, his long time and intimate friend, was a student in Illinois College in 1834-35. David Rutledge was a student in Illinois College for a part of his training in preparation for his career as a lawyer. Ann Rutledge, his sister, intended to go to the Jacksonville Female Academy, now a department of Illinois College, but died shortly before the opening of school in 1835. If Lincoln had attended any college it would have been Illinois. There he would have come to know intimately Edward Beecher, Julian M. Sturdevant and Jonathan Baldwin Turner. His anti-slavery convictions would have been strengthened, perhaps prematurely developed. What would have happened if he or both he and Ann Rutledge had gone to Jacksonville to school?

Lincoln has left us no record of his own mental processes regarding this decision. We may not cherish too confident assurance that we know what he thought about it. We are certain those are wrong who suppose that Abraham made the most of every educational opportunity, if by making the most we are to understand that he would gladly have availed himself of opportunity for further schooling. He was not too old. He was not too poor. He was not definitely obligated to the support of dependent parents. He was not too remote. He could have entered McKendree or Shurtleff or Illinois, or even Knox College, which was organized and in full operation while he was selling goods at New Salem.

The most probable answer would seem to be that Lincoln had already committed himself to a political career, which seemed to promise him almost immediate reward, and a college course would have postponed his political activity.

If Lincoln had gone to Illinois College he would have required perhaps two years in the preparatory department, and four more to complete the college course. He would have been twenty-eight when he graduated. That would have been a long time to wait for the beginnings of a career upon whose threshold he seemed already to stand.

Six years Lincoln lived in New Salem. Those same six years would have won for him a degree as Bachelor of Arts, at Illinois or Knox.*

Equally interesting is the question, What would a college course have done for Lincoln? If Abraham Lincoln had entered Illinois or Knox, what could either of them have done for him? Would they have made a minister of him instead of a lawyer; and if so would that have been a change worth making? Would they have made him a more ardent and outspoken anti-slavery man, and if so would the ultimate interests of the anti-slavery cause have been furthered? They would have given him a much more liberal and reasonable theology than that which he had learned from backwoods Baptist preachers, and might have made it possible for him in consistency with his convictions to have united with the church, but would they have made him any better Christian? They would have taught him a great deal

---

*Mrs. Eleanore Atkinson in an interesting and valuable article in *Harper's Magazine* in May, 1913, said:

"Illinois College opened in the fall of 1830 as a full-fledged college, with Dr. Edward Beecher for its president, and a faculty of four graduates from the Divinity School at Yale. No allowances were made for the pioneer youth's supposed lack of advantages. The entrance requirement and the four years' work in the classic languages, mathematics, and philosophy were practically identical with those of Yale at that day. But as there was little money in that region, all these infant institutions were obliged to smooth the financial path to learning."

which he never learned and the lack of which he felt throughout his life, but would they have made him in the large sense a better educated man? If the six years which he spent in New Salem had been spent upon a college campus would he have gone forth better equipped for the great work he had to do than he was when he left New Salem penniless, burdened with debt and with his whole library and wardrobe in his saddle-bags?

These are questions we can not answer. But this we know, that, defective as was his formal instruction, Abraham Lincoln was in the larger sense of the term, an educated man.

All in all, the best thing which a college education gives to a man is his association with his teachers and fellow-students. There in the free republic of the campus he is learning how to deal with men. Lincoln learned that lesson in New Salem. New Salem has been rightly called "Lincoln's Alma Mater."

CHAPTER XV

IN THE campaign of 1834 in which Lincoln was elected a member of the Legislature, he was understood to be a Whig. The question has already been propounded, why did he become a Whig? Not, certainly, because he inherited that faith from his father; and not because the majority of his constituents in and about New Salem were Whigs. His principles as announced at the beginning were no more those of the Whigs than they were of the Locofoco Democrats. To his relatives, the Hankses, who were Democrats, he seemed "Whiggish, but not a Whig." How had he become Whiggish? And why did he become a Whig?

A possible answer to the first of these questions has already been suggested. The friendships which Lincoln found in the Black Hawk War, with men like Major John T. Stuart, may suggest the answer to the second. Whatever the reason, Lincoln's choice of a party was deliberate and honest.

In 1834, Lincoln sought and obtained the support of Democrats as well as Whigs. Lamon affirms that he did this with the consent of Whig leaders such as John T. Stuart and Ninian W. Edwards.* But after 1834 the increase in the Whig vote in Sangamon County showed that Lincoln had made no mistake. The split in the Democratic Party between "Whole-hog" and the "Locofoco" factions, resulted in a delivery of the county to the Whigs in 1836.

On June 13, 1836, Lincoln published in the *Sangamo Journal*†

Life of Lincoln, p. 155.

†As there must be frequent mention of this newspaper under its several titles, and of the river and county bearing the name of Sangamon, I am giving, in the Appendix, a note on the name and the newspaper.

the announcement of his candidacy for reelection to the Legislature, to be chosen in August of that year. His platform was short, and again definitely committed him to the principles of the Whig Party. He also announced himself as in favor of the distribution of a portion of the proceeds of the public land among the several states, in order that they might be able to carry out their schemes of public improvement without borrowing money.

This campaign was much more exciting than either of the previous contests in which Lincoln had engaged. Party lines were beginning to be drawn more tightly, and personal abuse became a more marked characteristic of the contest. For the first time Lincoln was made the subject of an attack, the precise character of which is not known. But the method of his meeting the attack is known. He addressed an open letter to the man who had claimed to know facts that would discredit Lincoln. The letter was so manly, so thoroughly characteristic, and proved so unanswerable that it deserves to be recorded here. The man addressed never came forward with his charges against Lincoln, and the latter was left triumphant:

New Salem, June 21, 1836.

Dear Colonel.

I am told that during my absence last week you passed through the place and stated publicly that you were in possession of a fact or facts which, if known to the public, would entirely destroy the prospects of N. W. Edwards and myself at the ensuing election; but that through favor to us you would forbear to divulge them. No one has needed favors more than I, and generally few have been less unwilling to accept them; but in this case favor to me would be injustice to the public and therefore I must beg your pardon for declining it. That I once had the confidence of the people of Sangamon County is sufficiently evident; and if I have done anything, either by design or misadventure, which if known would subject me to a forfeiture of that confidence, he that knows of that thing and conceals it is a traitor to his country's interest.

I find myself wholly unable to form any conjecture of what fact or facts, real or supposed, you spoke; but my opinion of your veracity will not permit me for a moment to doubt that you at least believed what you said. I am flattered with the personal regard you manifested for me; but I do hope that on mature reflection you will view the public interest as a paramount consideration and therefore let the worst come.

I assure you that the candid statement of facts on your part, however low it may sink me, shall never break the ties of personal friendship between us.

I wish an answer to this, and you are at liberty to publish both if you choose.

Very respectfully,
A. Lincoln.

Colonel Robert Allen.

To this campaign also belongs the famous incident of his reply to George Forquer. Forquer had been a Whig, but had changed politics, his change occurring simultaneously with his appointment as Register of the Land Office. Forquer had attained further celebrity in local circles by his purchase of a lightning rod, the first or one of the first in Springfield. It was an object of great interest. Forquer was well known and a man of ability. His attack upon Lincoln at a great mass meeting was ingenious. It made its impression upon those who heard, and Lincoln was at considerable disadvantage when he arose to answer this opponent. Joshua F. Speed has told the story. He later became one of Lincoln's most intimate friends. At this time Lincoln was little known to him, but the impression made upon him was lasting:

"I was then fresh from Kentucky," says Mr. Speed, "and had heard many of her great orators. It seemed to me then, as it seems to me now, that I never heard a more effective speaker. He carried the crowd with him, and swayed them as he pleased. So deep an impression did he make that George Forquer, a man of much celebrity as a sarcastic speaker and with a great reputation throughout the state as an orator, rose and asked the people to hear *him*. He began his speech by saying that this young man would have to be taken down, and he was sorry that the task devolved upon him. He made what was called one of his 'slasher-gaff' speeches, dealing much in ridicule and sarcasm. Lincoln stood near him, with his arms folded, never interrupting him. When Forquer was done, Lincoln walked to the stand, and replied so fully and completely that his friends bore him from the court-house on their shoulders.

"So deep an impression did this first speech make upon me that I remember its conclusion now, after a lapse of thirty-eight years. Said he:

" 'The gentleman commenced his speech by saying that this young man would have to be taken down, and he was sorry the task devolved upon him. I am not so young in years as I am in the tricks and trade of a politician; but live long or die young, I would rather die now than, like the gentleman, change my politics and simultaneous with the change receive an office worth three thousand dollars a year, and then have to erect a lightning-rod over my house to protect a guilty conscience from an offended God.' "

This was one of Lincoln's most famous campaign replies, and his reputation was vastly enhanced by it.

The election of 1836 resulted in the choice of a notable delegation from Sangamon County. A new apportionment had been made, and that county's delegation, the largest in the state, consisted of nine men. The candidates elected were Abraham Lincoln, John Dawson, Daniel Stone, Ninian W. Edwards, William F. Elkins, R. L. Wilson, Andrew McCormick, Archer Herndon and Job Fletcher. Each of these men stood over six feet in height. They were known as the "Long Nine." They went to Vandalia determined to move the capital to Springfield. They were ready to swap votes with any delegations which were not striving for the capital, but that wanted other concessions for their own localities. The extent of the log-rolling had probably lost little in the telling, but it seems quite certain that Lincoln and his associates traded votes on the general theory that anything not positively dishonorable was justified if necessary to secure the removal of the state capital. The effort was successful. Springfield became the capital city of the state. It became popular after that, to charge all the bad legislation of the Tenth and subsequent Assemblies to the influence of the "Long Nine."

Of this session of the Legislature one incident is remembered in which Lincoln appears in an undignified light. In a close contest in which his side was evidently about to be defeated, Lincoln and Joseph Gillespie, another Whig, jumped out of the window of the church* in which the Legislature was sitting and so broke the quorum. This was not corrupt or dishonorable, but it was undignified. Lincoln afterward regretted that he had participated in this arrangement.

It is rather remarkable that we have so little information concerning Lincoln's activities as a member of the Legislature and a parliamentary debater. He was a member of important committees, and chairman of some, but his speeches were not reported. In December, 1840, he made a speech in support of a motion which he introduced as chairman of the Finance Committee. Evidently the excessive expenditure for printing appeared to him a matter of party politics, and was one concerning which Lincoln wished an investigation. Simeon Francis, owner of the *Journal,* which presumably had not been awarded the printing contract by a Democratic administration, was doubtless more than willing to print an outline of Lincoln's speech. I have no doubt Lincoln himself prepared this summary of his argument:

Mr. Lincoln offered for adoption a resolution raising a select

---

*Although Herndon, and others who ought to have known, assert that Lincoln was humiliated when he remembered this incident, it is of interest to note that his associate in this adventure, Honorable Joseph Gillespie, remembered it, and thought that Lincoln remembered it as an unimportant event. "It is doubtful whether either one of them ever attached any importance to it," says Gillespie's daughter. (*Joseph Gillespie,* by his daughter, Mrs. Josephine Gillespie Prickett; *Transactions of the Illinois State Historical Society for 1912,* p. 105.) I find most contradictory accounts of this incident current in Vandalia, some persons denying that it ever occurred, and others proudly pointing out the window through which Lincoln and Gillespie escaped. It may be noted also that Gillespie remembered it as having occurred in Springfield.

committee, to inquire into the causes which have produced so
large an expenditure for public printing, and to report a bill for
the purpose of reducing the expenditure of that item, if in their
opinion it can be done without detriment to the public good.

Mr. Lincoln said he did not offer the resolution by way of
attack upon the public printer, or any one else. He was in possession of no fact which would justify him in so doing. He did
not expect that more was printed than was ordered, or more was
charged for it than the law allowed. He was disposed to believe, if there was any fault, it was at our own door. He had
just read the message of the Governor of Indiana, in which he
called the attention of their legislature to the enormous expenditure of twelve thousand dollars for public printing. Thus it
would seem in our sister state, with a population doubling ours,
twelve thousand dollars was called an enormous expenditure,
whilst we, with only half the population and doubly more embarrassed, were paying twenty thousand for the same object.
To remove all suspicion of his having the management of this
committee for the purpose of making a party matter of it, he desired that the chair would not appoint him upon the committee.

The state just at this time was in the midst of a mania for speculation. Not only individuals, but the state government went
mad on the scheme of internal improvements. Money was borrowed with the utmost recklessness, and squandered upon proposed railroads and canals, some of which have never yet been
built. Lincoln was a member of the Committee on Finance. He
declared it was his ambition to be "the DeWitt Clinton of
Illinois." No suspicion of personal dishonor attaches to Lincoln
through all this period of wild legislation. He did nothing to
enrich his own pocket. He sincerely believed that the extravagant measures which the State Legislature adopted were for the
well being of the state. He and his associates were mistaken.
The day of disaster was not far away.

In all these matters of finance, Lincoln was as wise as his
associates, and no wiser. It is pleasant to turn from this record
of mistaken zeal to another in which Lincoln took a brave stand
on a moral issue. The slavery question was exciting violent de-

bate. In 1837, Elijah P. Lovejoy was killed by a mob at Alton, and the press upon which his anti-slavery paper was published was destroyed. This murder excited little official protest at the time. On the contrary, the anti-slavery advocates were quite generally condemned as those whose agitation had produced this not unnatural reaction. The pro-slavery vote in Illinois was too large and influential for politicians needlessly to offend. On March 3, 1837, the Illinois General Assembly passed the following resolution in condemnation of abolition societies and their doctrines:

Resolved by the General Assembly of the State of Illinois:
That we highly disapprove of the formation of Abolition societies, and of the doctrines promulgated by them.
That the right of property in slaves is sacred to the slaveholding states by the Federal Constitution, and that they can not be deprived of that right without their consent.
That the General Government can not abolish slavery in the District of Columbia against the consent of the citizens of said district, without a manifest breach of good faith.
That the governor be requested to transmit to the states of Virginia, Alabama, Mississippi, New York and Connecticut a copy of the foregoing report and resolutions.

Lincoln was one of the few members of the General Assembly who did not vote for these resolutions. He sought to discover what other members would join in with him in a protest against these resolutions and at the same time in a protest against intemperate abolitionists, and he found but one such member. These two members of the General Assembly, Abraham Lincoln and Dan Stone, joined in placing upon the record of that body this righteous protest, being Abraham Lincoln's first public testimony against slavery on both economic and moral grounds:

Resolutions upon the subject of domestic slavery having passed both branches of the General Assembly at its present session, the undersigned hereby protest against the passage of the same.
They believe that the institution of slavery is founded on both

injustice and bad policy, but that the promulgation of abolition doctrines tends rather to increase than abate its evils.

They believe that the Congress of the United States has no power under the Constitution to interfere with the institution of slavery in the different states.

They believe that the Congress of the United States has power under the Constitution to abolish slavery in the District of Columbia, but that the power ought not to be exercised unless at the request of the people of the district.

The difference between these opinions and those contained in the above resolutions, is their reason for entering this protest.

Dan Stone,
A. Lincoln,
Representatives from the County of Sangamon.

It must not be assumed from this protest that Lincoln was announcing himself as an abolitionist; on the contrary, he was much opposed to abolition agitation, and took pains to say in this protest that "the promulgation of abolition doctrines tends rather to increase than abate" the evils of slavery. The protest was honestly, but very shrewdly drawn. One of Lincoln's chief concerns then and for many years afterward was to avoid being known as an abolitionist. But he and Dan Stone were unwilling to go with a multitude to do evil, or to permit the murder of Lovejoy to pass with a censure of the men who loved freedom enough to die for it and no word of condemnation for the system which these abolitionists, wisely or unwisely, were opposing. He registered his honest and his abiding conviction that "the institution of slavery is founded on both injustice and bad policy." From that position thus early taken, Abraham Lincoln never receded.

It would perhaps be but fair to add that the standards which obtained in Illinois politics were the more favorable to the advancement of Lincoln because the mistakes of politicians in his day, in which mistakes he participated, were so largely the mistakes of the whole body of the people and of Lincoln's constituents, that a public official was not too summarily condemned to oblivion for his errors of judgment. Governor Ford comments on this matter with characteristic severity, condemning the "Long Nine" whose log-rolling in connection with the removal of the capital from Vandalia to Springfield cost the state, as he maintained, more than the value of all the real estate in the vicinity of Springfield, and he records the names of those members of the House of Representatives who voted for the disastrous "internal improvement system." He was especially unhappy when he considered how many of these men, who, as he believed, ought to have been retired by the people, were continued in office. Ninian W. Edwards and others were "since often elected or appointed to other offices, and are yet all of them popular men. . . .Dement has been twice appointed Receiver of Public Moneys. . . . Shields to be Auditor, Judge of the Supreme Court, Commissioner of the General Land Office, and Brigadier General in the Mexican War. . . . Lincoln was several times elected to the Legislature and finally to Congress, and Douglas, Smith and McClernand have been three times elected to Congress, and Douglas to the United States Senate. Being all of them spared monuments of popular wrath, evincing how safe it is to be a politician, and how disastrous it may be to the country to keep along with the present fervor of the people."*

We need not claim for Lincoln in these matters wisdom superior to that of his associates, but may remind ourselves that his errors of judgment were not only shared by his associates in office, but that they did not prevent his repeated reelection, much to the disgust of Governor Ford, who counted him one of the "spared monuments of popular wrath."

Into this state, whose early political affiliations were with the South, Abraham Lincoln entered at a period when conditions were ready for a significant change; and he came into a position of commanding leadership just when that change was ready to occur.

History of Illinois, pp. 195, 196.

CHAPTER XVI

ANN RUTLEDGE
1834-1835

HONORABLE ISAAC N. ARNOLD, whose *Life of Lincoln* is a valuable source of information, reminds his readers that Lincoln was unlike Washington in that the latter very early manifested a fondness for women, and that Lincoln became a lover at a much later period in his young manhood. He quotes Washington Irving, who said concerning Washington that "Before he was fifteen years old, he had conceived a passion for some unknown beauty, so serious as to disturb his otherwise well regulated mind, and to make him really unhappy." Arnold says, "Lincoln was less precocious than Washington, or perhaps his heart was better shielded by the hard labor to which he was subjected."

As a schoolboy in Indiana, Lincoln showed some fondness for girls who lived in the neighborhood, but he had nothing that can properly be called a love-affair. This volume has already noted that there seems to have been a kind of boy and girl attachment between him and Katie Roby, who afterward became Mrs. Allen Gentry, and has also mentioned his attentions, such as they were, to Polly Warnick.

When Lincoln first arrived in New Salem he boarded in the home of Reverend John M. Cameron, who had eleven daughters. From this interesting environment Lincoln escaped unmarried. There appears to have been safety for Lincoln's heart in the number of the Cameron girls. John McNamar also boarded at the Cameron home, and he also escaped without embarrassing entanglements. The Camerons and Rutledges agreed in their religion but disagreed in politics. Rutledge was a Whig; Cameron was a Democrat. The Cameron girls made fun of Lincoln, calling him "old plain Abe." When Lincoln had fever and ague, Mat Cameron brought him water. Lincoln told her that if she kept him well supplied with water when his fever was on, he would remember her with a remunerative office when he became president. But not even in this mirthful fashion did he offer to reward her with his heart. When, later, he transferred his boarding-place to the Rutledge tavern, he took his heart with him, and the eleven Cameron girls also were heart-whole and fancy-free.

James Rutledge, uncle of John M. Cameron, had nine children, of whom the third was a daughter, Ann Mayes Rutledge. She was born in Kentucky, January 7, 1813, and was nineteen years old when she first met Lincoln.

Tradition has endowed her with every possible grace possessed by young womanhood. She had auburn hair, and a fair complexion. Her face must have been attractive, and all that we know of her is to her credit. Her youngest sister, whom I knew personally, was a woman of attractive personality, even in her more than ninety years.* She possessed vivacity, intelligence, and a gentle and affectionate disposition, all of which qualities appear to have been equally present in her older sister Ann.

Ann Rutledge did not lack for lovers. At least two men besides Lincoln sought to win her heart. One of them was Samuel Hill, proprietor of the store in which Lincoln was a clerk after the failure of the firm of Berry and Lincoln. She preferred the clerk to the proprietor; and such information as I have been able to obtain leads me to believe that she manifested good sense in that choice. It was, however, a second humiliation which Hill received at the hand of Lincoln, for he lost the post-office in response to a petition circulated by the women of New Salem,

---

*Sarah Rutledge Saunders, youngest child of James and Mary Ann Rutledge, was born in the Rutledge Tavern at New Salem, October 20, 1829. As stated in the text, she died at Lompoc, California, May 1, 1922. She was a woman of clear mind, strong character and abiding faith. To the end of her life she was a devout Cumberland Presbyterian. Her numerous friends know her as "Aunt Sallie" and she liked the name.

and he lost the hand of Ann Rutledge. However, Samuel Hill did not long grieve for her, for on July 28, 1835, he married Parthenia Nance. Parthenia did not cherish lasting resentment against her husband for first having loved Ann Rutledge, and in her old age she bore witness that Ann was a gentle and likable girl. But she treated with good-humored scorn the story of Ann's beauty. "She was not beautiful," said Mrs. Hill. "To begin with she had red hair."

The other lover of Ann Rutledge, if he can be said ever to have loved anything except money, was John McNamar, who entered New Salem in 1829 as has already been stated, and for nearly three years bore the name of John McNeil. In 1832 he returned to New York State, professedly to relieve the poverty of his parents and bring them with him back to New Salem. The three years of silence which followed he later explained by three weeks of sickness which befell him in Ohio as he was on his way home. It was perhaps as good an explanation as the others that he gave.

Arriving in New York State, he found his father, John Mc-Namar, Sr., near death, and he died soon afterward. In the autumn of 1835, McNamar returned to Illinois, bringing with him his widowed mother, who did not long survive. He buried her in the old Concord graveyard, about two miles from his home. Two fresh graves were there, those of Ann Rutledge and her father. When, some years later, there was a question as to the graves, he was unable to identify any of them. He had never visited either Ann's grave or his mother's.

In the early part of his residence in New Salem, when Ann Rutledge was a girl of seventeen, John McNeil, as he was then known, professed to love her, and she returned his affection. If we are to believe the Rutledge family, her father, as soon as he knew that McNamar had been masquerading under a false name, became convinced that he could not be trusted, and disapproved the match; Ann for a little time after his departure cherished her affection for him, but not hearing from him, gave him up utterly, and later accepted Abraham Lincoln with all her heart. If we are to believe McNamar, Ann still loved him more than she loved Lincoln, and, distraught because she could not give to Lincoln her whole heart, worried herself into brain fever from which she died.   The silly part of the reading public believes the latter.   I believe the former.

If Ann Rutledge died of a broken heart for love of McNamar, there was no possible way for him to have known it, and he is our sole source of information to that effect.   If he won the heart of Ann Rutledge and broke it, he should at least have had the decency to keep the fact to himself.

Early in 1834 the affairs of the Rutledges and Camerons became so involved that they had to move from New Salem. They had sold their farms on Sand Ridge, and the Cameron house, a double log structure, stood vacant. They moved back to that farm, both families, and there lived in one house till the spring of 1836.

Those were hard times for the Rutledge family. Those of the children who could secure employment did so. Ann worked for a time in the home of James Short. It was on Lincoln's visits to Ann that Short formed the favorable judgment of Lincoln that led him to redeem Lincoln's horse and surveying instruments at the Van Bergen sale.*

Abraham Lincoln and Ann truly loved each other. For thirty years after her death no man is known to have alleged that any shadow of her former regard for McNamar came between them; and then the affirmation was made by the one man who, above all others, should have been silent.

Poor as the Rutledges were, their ambition was unconquered. They did not permit their son David to give up his course in Illinois College; and they encouraged Ann to expect that she might go in the fall of 1835, to the Female Academy in Jacksonville.

The last sister of Ann Rutledge, Mrs. Sarah Rutledge Saun-

*Lamon, *Life of Lincoln*, p. 163.

ders, died in Lompoc, California, May 1, 1922. For some years before her death I was in correspondence with her, and, in the summer of 1921, I went to California and visited her and made a photograph of her. She was at that time in bed with a broken hip, but was able to be lifted, and I lifted her into a wheeled chair, rolled her out into the sunshine and made a picture of her, the last that was taken, as I suppose, for from that bed she did not arise thereafter, except for a few moments at a time to rest, and this at infrequent and lengthening intervals.

I learned from "Aunt Sally" that she had one letter addressed to Ann, the only letter the family had that she received from any one, and perhaps the only one that was addressed to her by any member of her own household. This letter she loaned to me, with the privilege of use. To my great delight, I found it had an important bearing upon the question of Ann's plans for an education. The letter was written to her from Jacksonville, where her brother David was in college, and it dealt directly with her own purpose to go there the next autumn, and he encouraged the plan. It was really three letters in one, all on the two sides of one sheet, with room still saved for the address. The main letter was to David's father, James Rutledge. The first postscript was to Ann. The second postscript was to James Kittridge, concerning the district school at Sand Ridge, where the Rutledges had their farm. The letters are in the stiff and formal language of the time. Postage cost a good deal, and David had opportunity to save postage by sending this letter by a schoolmate. The letter to his father read thus:

College Hill, July 27, 1835.

Dear Father:—

The passing of Mr. Blood* from this place to that affords me an opportunity of writing you a few lines. I have thus far enjoyed good health, and the students generally are well. I have not collected anythings of Brooks, except that I agreed to take

---

*This was Charles Blood who later became a well known Presbyterian minister.

his paper as I thought that that would be better than nothing at all, though he says he could pay the order in about two months. L. M. Greene is up at home at this time trying to get a school, and I had concluded to quit this place and goe to him until the commencement of the next term, but I could not get off without paying for the whole term, therefore I concluded to stay here.

If Mr. Blood calls on you to stay all night, please to entertain him free of cost, as he is one of my fellow students and I believe him to be a good religious young man. I add nomore, but remain yours with respect untill death.

D. H. Rutledge.

To James Rutledge.

It will be noted also that a year's subscription to a newspaper, though not greatly prized, was considered better than nothing, and that an editor's promise to pay in two months was not rated highly.

The Greene brothers, to one of whom this letter makes reference, were friends of David Rutledge, as they were of Abraham Lincoln, and their home-coming for vacation teaching must have been a matter of general comment.

The second postscript had to do with school teaching. McGrady Rutledge, a nephew of James and cousin of David, had been asked to secure the teaching of the Sand Ridge school for another student named Porter. The Sand Ridge school was near the Rutledge farm, though several miles from New Salem. I quote, out of its order, the second postscript, which is to James Kittridge:

P. S.—I wish you to send McGrada's letter to him immediately as it requests him to attend to the school on Sand Ridge for Mr. Porter and also I want intelligence to come the next mail concerning it. I add nomore.

D. H. Rutledge.

James Kittridge.

David spelled "nomore" as a single word, and that was the way it was pronounced in formal discourse, a kind of "Amen."

It was a word sometimes uttered with great solemnity in sermons, a word of two syllables, accented on the second.

The first postscript is the part of the letter of the greatest interest. It reads:

To Anna Rutledge:
Valued Sister. So far as I can understand Miss Graves will teach another school in the Diamond Grove. I am glad to hear that you have a notion of comeing to school, and I earnestly recommend to you that you would spare no time from improving your education and mind. Remember that Time is worth more than all gold therefore throw away none of your golden moments. I add nomore, but &c.

D. H. Rutledge.

Anna Rutledge.

This letter is in full accord with the Rutledge tradition. Ann Rutledge and Lincoln were engaged to be married, and she desired to wait at least a year to attend the Jacksonville Female Academy. This, the only girls' seminary in Jacksonville in 1835, was merged with Illinois College in 1903. Ann had written or sent to her brother an inquiry concerning the school, and of her hope to be a student there in the fall of 1835, according to the Rutledge tradition. Lincoln, as he and Ann dreamed over the matter together, was to have entered Illinois College, at least for a year.

Ann Rutledge must have been sick when her brother wrote this letter. It was dated July 27, 1835, and she died August 25, 1835, after a sickness of about six weeks. Lincoln was not living in the house in which she died. He went over, riding from New Salem to Sand Ridge, and visited her once during her illness. What they said to each other no one knows.

No one remembers the funeral of Ann Rutledge. "Aunt Sally" had an impression that her cousin, Reverend John Cameron, conducted the service, though it is quite as likely to have been Reverend John M. Berry.

What would have happened if Ann Rutledge had lived, and

she had gone to the Jacksonville Female Academy in the autumn of 1835, and Abraham Lincoln at the same time had entered Illinois College?

I do not think that Ann Rutledge planned to go to Jacksonville unless Lincoln also went. She had had one love-affair that ended unhappily, and she was not likely to go away deliberately and leave her lover for a year. The Rutledge tradition appears to me to have every appearance of probability, that the plan of Ann to attend the Female Academy was thought out jointly by Abraham and Ann, and had joined to it his plan for at least a year of study at Illinois College.

The death of Ann Rutledge from malarial fever, in the summer of 1835, was followed a few weeks later by the death of her father, who died of the same disease. The sorrowing family remained through the winter in the Cameron home. John McNamar returned to Illinois soon after the death of James Rutledge. His generous heart forbade him to turn out the widow and her orphaned children before spring.

John McNamar, having performed his final filial duty in the burial of his mother, settled down and added farm to farm until he had a large estate. He made his home in the Cameron house, and across the road he erected ample barns. In time the log house gave place to one of brick; and his was known as one of the best farms in the county. He was elected county assessor, and his assessments were just and fair. He had a good sense of values. He paid his honest debts, and had no bad or expensive habits. In the latter part of February, 1879, he died on his farm, in the same dooryard where Ann Rutledge died, the local paper containing his obituary bearing date of March first of that year. His widow said of him that he was an honest man, but utterly destitute of sentiment. He was twice married. So far as I have been able to learn, he had no prejudice against ministers or religion, but ministers were expensive; men sometimes in the excess of matrimonial generosity, paid them as much as five dollars for a wedding fee, while justices of the peace were content with two dollars. John McNamar was married to Deborah S. Latimer, February 15, 1838, by William Armstrong, justice of the peace. After the death of Deborah he was married to an excellent widow, Eliza McNeal, April 17, 1855, by Jacob Garber, justice of the peace. By these two marriages John McNamar may have saved six dollars. He was not a sentimental man.

William H. Herndon was a diligent if not always a discriminating gatherer of facts regarding Abraham Lincoln. When his book states a fact, within the range of Herndon's own observation, it is reliable; when he quotes an interview, he does it faithfully. But when he draws an inference, he is often wrong Herndon was a man of emotional temperament, and his habits rendered him yet more emotional at times. In his later years it was his custom to drive over to Petersburg when court was in session, and pick up a few dollars as associate counsel for younger lawyers. Herndon boarded with his brother-in-law on these visits, and had to pay only for what he drank. On one of these trips he determined to visit John McNamar and learn whether he knew anything about the location of Ann Rutledge's grave. Herndon's brother-in-law drove Herndon to McNamar's farm on Sunday morning, October 14, 1866, as Herndon informs us, not omitting even the hour of his arrival. Services were in progress at the Concord Church, and thither they ultimately had to go to find some of the Berry sons who could identify Ann Rutledge's grave. McNamar could not assist them in the matter.

But he modestly told Herndon that Ann Rutledge loved him more than she ever loved Lincoln, and died of a broken heart for love of him. He pointed through the window at a currant bush in the dooryard, and said it marked the site of the log house where Ann Rutledge died. He intimated that it was the tenderness of his sentiment regarding Ann which led him to buy the farm where she had died.

Ann Rutledge did not die at New Salem. She died on the Cameron farm which then belonged to McNamar. She was never buried in the present Concord churchyard, the alleged photographs of her original grave being of another grave in the newer Concord Cemetery.*

The old Concord Cemetery, where the Rutledges, Armstrongs, Berrys, Pantiers and their neighbors are buried, is a measured acre of ground on the McGrady Rutledge farm. There stood the original Concord Church. The site is now completely overgrown, but many of the tombstones are erect and legible. It is well fenced and secure from cattle, whose rubbing quickly overturns grave-stones; and it is almost never visited by men. The curious go to the Oakland Cemetery in Petersburg, where reposes the handful of dust that in 1890 was removed thither as the body of Ann Rutledge. But more of Ann Rutledge than the covetous undertakers were able to scrape up and remove, remains in God's acre where the old Concord Church once stood, and which is now a sanctuary for the birds and the home of memories.

William H. Herndon visited John McNamar, as he particularly tells us, at half-past ten on Sunday morning, October 14, 1866; and on the same drive visited the site of New Salem. He did not waste any time in the publication of the information which he had received. On Friday evening, November 16, 1866, he delivered a lecture in the old Court-house in Springfield, on *"Ann Rutledge, New Salem, Pioneering, and the Poem 'Oh, Why Should the Spirit of Mortal be Proud.'"* The *Register,* Democratic newspaper, did not announce the lecture before nor comment on it after its delivery. The *Journal,* whose job department printed it in a broadside in its newspaper type, did not admit it to its columns, and merely said that as it was in print, no comment upon the lecture was necessary.

About a dozen people, so I am told, came out to hear that free lecture; and next day Springfield was ablaze with wrath. Lincoln left no blood relatives in Springfield; that town belongs to Mrs. Lincoln's nieces, not one of whom had ever heard of Ann Rutledge.

---

*Concerning the removal of the body of Ann Rutledge from the old Concord cemetery, see the Appendix.

THE GRAVE OF ANN RUTLEDGE
Petersburg, Illinois

The original grave
Old Concord Cemetery

Rutledge lilac bush
McGrady Rutledge farm

9

Not very far away, in a lonely home on Washington Street in Chicago, in one of those new white-front houses facing south between Elizabeth and Ann, a woman already crazed by her grief, read in the newspaper that her husband had so deeply loved Ann Rutledge (whose name she could barely recall as a youthful and long dead sweetheart of her husband) that he had never loved the mother of his children.

On whose testimony has the world accepted this libel on the character of Abraham Lincoln, this wicked stab into the broken heart of his widow? On the sole testimony of John McNamar.

Subsequent versions of the story have done little save to make it worse. Now it has come to pass that the ring which Lincoln gave to Mary Todd, the only ring he ever gave to any woman, has been plucked from her hand to adorn the hand of Ann Rutledge; its motto, "Love is eternal," transferred from Mary Todd who wore it to the grave is given over to Ann Rutledge who never saw it. It is high time to recall the sentimental interest of the American people to some appreciation of the truth.

I sat beside the bed of Aunt Sallie Saunders. She said my questions brought back to her memory things she had not thought about for half a century. From time to time I left her, and in an adjoining room, wrote down on a portable typewriter the substance of what she told me. I read it to her, section by section, and each time it reminded her of something else. When it was finished I read it and she signed it without glasses.

"Where did Ann die?" I asked toward the end.

"Didn't she die in the old tavern at New Salem?" she asked.

"No; think again about the house as you remember it; it was not the tavern."

"It was a double log-house with an open porch between, much like the tavern. I was only a little girl of six. No, it was not the tavern. It was not our house. The owner came back, and after father's death, we could not pay the rent. He turned mother out; and we had to move to Iowa and begin all over again. Mother had a hard time. I remember how sad and how brave she was."

"Think again, and see if you can remember whose house it was."

"Do you know?"

"Yes, I know who was the owner at the time of Ann's death, but I should like you to remember if you can."

She thought a little while, and then said:

"It was John McNamar! He was the man who turned mother out!"

CHAPTER XVII

LAWYER AND LOVER
1836-1839

LINCOLN sorrowed over the death of Ann Rutledge. The stories of his frenzied grief are doubtless exaggerated; but Lincoln's temperament was such that at times emotion controlled it. His grief was of a character that deeply impressed the men of his acquaintance.

But none of the women of New Salem thought of his sorrow as likely to last forever. With great promptness, and not wholly without his knowledge and cooperation, they set about finding him a suitable wife. Lincoln was now engaged in his campaign for reelection; was supported by both Whigs and Democrats, and was regarded as sufficiently established in his career to justify popular interest in his domestic affairs. This story would not shock us greatly if it were not for the popular impression that Lincoln held the memory of Ann Rutledge in such perpetual regard that he could love no other woman. Lincoln did love Ann Rutledge; but she was dead, and he had no thought of remaining single, as we shall presently discover.

Before we take up the story of Mary Owens, there is one other fact of large significance as to Lincoln's supposed life-long devotion to Ann Rutledge's memory, a devotion that, according to Herndon, kept Lincoln from ever loving any other woman. When in 1841-1842, Lincoln was in the throes of his uncertainty whether or not to marry Mary Todd, he unburdened his heart to Joshua F. Speed. The pent-up reservoir of Lincoln's habitual reticence broke its dam, and Lincoln talked to Speed as men rarely talk with each other about the most intimate details of his love and doubt. If, as has been assumed, the reason for Lincoln's uncertainty was that he could not give his heart to Mary Todd on account of its being buried with Ann Rutledge, Speed would have known about it to the last detail, and the letters of Lincoln to Speed and of Speed to Lincoln would have contained inevitable references to it, as to his superficial interest in Sarah Rickard. Not only is there no slightest suggestion of this situation in the correspondence, but when, in 1866, Herndon's lecture was delivered, Speed declared that it "was all new to him." It was new to Speed for only one reason, namely, that it was not true.

Mary S. Owens came to New Salem only a few months after the death of Ann Rutledge. She came intending to look Lincoln over with a view to marrying him, and Lincoln knew that she was coming with that thought in her mind, and himself consented to her coming. Before she came, he more than half promised to marry her, and he set forth at once to cultivate her friendship with a view to their probable matrimony. Mary Owens was cousin to a considerable fraction of the population of New Salem, and her married sister had lived there through the whole of the Ann Rutledge incident. The female relatives of Mary Owens talked to her of little else than Lincoln and of what he had said and done since he became a resident of the town. She had a good mind and a good memory; she preserved all of Lincoln's letters, and she treasured in her heart the memories of his courtship and the gossip of her friends. As she recalled these things in later years, she was unable to remember that she had ever heard herself spoken of as the successor of Ann Rutledge in the affections of Lincoln, or that any one had ever spoken of Ann Rutledge except as a girl of the village whom Lincoln had liked and who had died.

Ann Rutledge died August 25, 1835. In the following summer Mrs. Bennett Able of New Salem, told Abraham Lincoln that she was going on a visit to her old home in Kentucky, and she proposed to Lincoln to bring her sister Mary back with her on condition that Abraham should marry her. Mary Owens had spent a month in New Salem in 1833, and Lincoln remembered her as a handsome and attractive woman. He told Mrs. Able that if she would bring Mary back with her he would marry her. This, of course, was understood to be a joke, but it was not wholly a joke. Lincoln was twenty-seven years old and a member of the Legislature. Mary Owens was between four and five months older; she was born in Green County, Kentucky, September 29, 1808. When Mrs. Able told her sister Mary of the contract she had entered into, and Mary accepted the proposition and returned with her sister, Lincoln also knew that the arrangement was less than half a joke on Mary's side.

Ann Rutledge had auburn hair, was delicate and slender, and had a limited education. She was a Presbyterian of the Cumberland group. Mary Owens differed from her in these and other respects; she was tall and large, had dark curling hair, and inherited wealth. She was reared a Baptist, and herself belonged to that church. But her father was a man of wealth and influence and had sent her to a Catholic convent where she received an education well in advance of other women in New Salem. She had an excellent mind and keen wit. She was pleasing in her address, and her manners showed cultivation. She was a good reader, had a cheerful disposition, and was rather brilliant in conversation. She had a little dash of coquetry in her intercourse with young men, but still she held them at a distance. She had just passed her twenty-eighth birthday, and she was well aware that it was time for her to marry, but she did not intend, having gone so far through the woods, to cut a crooked stick. She intended to select her husband with care.

We know very little about the Ann Rutledge incident. If Lincoln wrote any letters to Ann they were not preserved. If there is any other documentary proof of their love-affair, it is unknown. We know that much that has been told about it is unreliable. It is not so with the Mary Owens courtship; we have Lincoln's letters to her, preserved and loaned to Herndon who copied them verbatim and published them. We have her own story of the courtship, also, and, unfortunately, we have Lincoln's account of it. He wrote this narrative to Mrs. O. H. Browning on April 1, 1838. In all essential particulars his story agrees with that of Miss Owens. From this threefold record we have no difficulty in making a correct narrative of the affair.

When Mary Owens arrived in New Salem in the fall of 1836, Lincoln began immediately and paid her more ardent attention than he had ever paid any woman before. She made her home with her sister, Mrs. Bennett Able, who lived just outside the corporate limits of New Salem. She had a habit of going in the afternoon to visit some cousins and meeting Lincoln by appointment there, and they walked home together in the evening. They saw each other almost constantly, and Lincoln began to feel somewhat surfeited. His habitual indecision came over him. He began to eye critically the woman who seemed to him almost too willing to be his wife. He noticed how large she was, and that she had passed her first youth. He began to consider that before many years she would be old and fat. On the other hand she was a woman of fine character, excellent education, good social standing and considerable wealth. He hesitated; he was already committed, but he was inclined to withdraw.

While he was in this state of indecision, Lincoln went to Vandalia to attend the winter session of the Legislature. He wrote to her from Vandalia under date of December 13, 1836, telling her that he had been ill and was depressed, and was disappointed in not hearing from her. He told her of the prospects of removal of the state capital. He was impatient at the thought of remaining ten weeks at Vandalia, and hoped she would write him as soon as she received his letter. Their correspondence during this absence did not, however, bring about an engagement, and Lincoln was soon busy with his plan for the removal of the seat of government to Springfield; and then followed other matters.

Lincoln returned from Vandalia at the close of his second term in the Legislature a popular and successful man. He had managed the log-rolling of the Long Nine so successfully as to secure the removal of the state capital from Vandalia to Springfield. New Salem received him with evidence of popular approval.

But there was not much left of New Salem. Situated as it was on a peninsula, approachable only from the west and from the river, it was on the road to nowhere. When the river failed, the town began to disappear. A new town, Petersburg, grew up two miles away, and in due time became the county-seat of a new county, Menard. New Salem, as Lincoln expressed it, "winked out." Even the post-office was discontinued. Lincoln was its last postmaster.

If New Salem had to "wink out" its expiring wink came at an opportune moment for Lincoln. He was so constituted as not willingly to make any new ventures, and he might not have consented to a removal of his few effects to Springfield with the risks of that new venture if New Salem had continued to live, and he had been able to continue there in a practise of law that would have yielded him a living, and the assurance that as long as he chose to do so he could return to the Legislature.

On his return from Vandalia to New Salem, and before his departure for Springfield, Lincoln saw more or less of Mary Owens, but their meetings were unsatisfactory and led to a break, which, however, did not end the matter.

An incident occurred which was alleged to have been the basis of their rupture. Miss Owens, writing in 1866 under her married name as Mrs. Jesse Vineyard, denied that a certain story as circulated in the vicinity of New Salem was strictly accurate, at least so far as its having been the direct cause of her break with Lincoln. Apart from that feature, the story appears to have been substantially correct. One day she and Mrs. Bowling Green were climbing the hill to the Able house. It is a steep climb, as I can testify, and Mrs. Green was carrying a baby as fat as its father. Lincoln walked along, talking and joking, and paying no attention to the heavy load which his friend's wife was carrying. Miss Owens did not fail to notice Lincoln's neglect.

These unsettled conditions in Lincoln's love-affairs affected his state of mind in the period when he was leaving New Salem behind and transferring his residence to Springfield.

In March, 1837, just a few days after his and Dan Stone's protest, Lincoln was admitted to the practise of law. The state capital had been removed from Vandalia to Springfield. Lincoln, as we shall later remind ourselves, had no small part in effecting this transfer. Springfield offered him an opportunity such as New Salem could not possibly afford. Lincoln left New Salem, and established an office in the capital city of the state. There we shall presently find him, and shall continue the narrative of his fortunes. Before doing so we pause to consider some special topics which relate themselves to this part of his career.

Lincoln arrived in New Salem in April, 1831, alone, without money and except for Offutt without friends. He left in March, 1837, poorer than when he arrived. He was not only without money but he was heavily in debt. He had not achieved any large success in any undertaking.

But he had won friends, and they were true and loyal. Few men have had more friends than Lincoln, or utilized them more freely. He had physical strength, which was ever an element in his power with men. He had an education, such as it was, and it was of a kind not to be despised. He had character. He was honest, generous, just and kind. He had qualities which caused men to say of him that he would some day be a great man; and sometimes he himself believed it. But there were other times when the future looked blank or black to him. As he rode out of New Salem on his borrowed horse to begin in Springfield his uncertain career as a lawyer, his own hope for the future was neither bright nor certain. But we know that there were even then in Abraham Lincoln qualities destined to win recognition. The recognition came, and when it came he was prepared for it.

It was a solemn day for Lincoln when he bade farewell to his friends in New Salem and departed to become a resident of Springfield. He had come to New Salem as he himself said "as a piece of driftwood floating down the Sangamon." There he had found shelter and companionship and a widened horizon. He was going forth to face he knew not what. Lincoln shrank from the necessity of making decisions. In deciding to leave New Salem he knew that he was entering upon a new epoch, and he did not face it with wholly pleasant anticipations.

On the other hand, Springfield offered to Lincoln exceptional opportunity. Its politicians were very grateful to him for his share in the removal of the capital. They promised him assistance if he would move thither. Lincoln had just procured his license as a lawyer. His old friend and comrade, Major John T. Stuart, offered to take Lincoln in as a partner. So Lincoln packed all his belongings into a pair of saddle-bags, borrowed a horse, and rode to Springfield.

We are fortunate in possessing an account of his arrival in Springfield. His friend, Joshua Fry Speed, thus told the story of his arrival:

He had ridden into town on a borrowed horse, with no earthly property save a pair of saddle-bags containing a few clothes. I was a merchant at Springfield, and kept a large country store, embracing dry-goods, groceries, hardware, books, medicines, bed-clothes, mattresses—in fact, everything that the country needed. Lincoln came into the store with his saddle-bags on his arm. He said he wanted to buy the furniture for a single bed. The mattress, blankets, sheets, coverlid, and pillow, according to the figures made by me, would cost seventeen dollars. He said that perhaps was cheap enough; but small as the price was, he was unable to pay it. But if I would credit him till Christmas, and his experiment as a lawyer was a success, he would pay then; saying in the saddest tone, "If I fail in this I do not know that I can ever pay you." As I looked up at him I thought then, and I think now, that I never saw a sadder face.

I said to him: "You seem to be so much pained at contracting so small a debt, I think I can suggest a plan by which you can avoid the debt, and at the same time attain your end. I have a large room with a double bed up-stairs, which you are very welcome to share with me."

"Where is your room?" said he.

"Upstairs," said I, pointing to a pair of winding stairs which led from the store to my room.

"He took his saddle-bags on his arm, went upstairs, set them on the floor, and came down with the most changed expression of countenance. Beaming with pleasure, he exclaimed:

"Well, Speed, I'm moved."

Thus was Lincoln furnished with a roof above his head, and his partnership with Stuart afforded him a law office. But that did not guarantee him food and clothing. Fortunately, this also, was provided. William Butler, State Treasurer and a most astute politician, had taken a liking to Lincoln during his first campaign for the Legislature, and had seen much of him in Vandalia. He was of those who encouraged Lincoln to remain in Sangamon County and run again, not doubting that two years later, if his influence continued to grow, he could be elected to the office for which he was in the beginning defeated. Butler was a hospitable, warm-hearted Kentuckian.*

William Butler took Lincoln into his home, and not only boarded him, but on occasion loaned him money for clothing. Lincoln made payments as he could, but the system of accounting was rather loose and irregular. Lincoln had a home with the Butlers for five and a half years from the time of his arrival in Springfield in March, 1837, until he married Mary Todd, November 4, 1842.

Lincoln deserves great credit for his own part in his making; but those who know of the beginnings of his life in Springfield, are disposed to say that there has never been adequate recognition of the assistance which in those days Lincoln received from his friends. "No man had more or better friends than Abraham Lincoln," said one of these men, "and no man was more willing to accept the kindness of his friends; but he deserved it and justified their faith in him."

---

*His grandson, William J. Butler, who has given me much information, has fighting-cocks descended from those which his grandfather owned, and some of them trace their lineage farther back to the fighting stock of Andrew Jackson and George Washington.

Lincoln's partnership with John T. Stuart formally began on April 27, 1837, and continued until April 14, 1841. This was the first of three law partnerships of Lincoln. The business of the office of Stuart and Lincoln was primarily politics, and incidentally was law. In this respect it did not differ greatly from other law offices in that city. When Blackstone declared the law to be a jealous mistress, he did not know how much flirting with politics an Illinois lawyer might do unrebuked.

When Lincoln entered Stuart's office, Stuart was just recovering from the effects of a campaign for Congress, in which he had been defeated. His main interest at the time was in preparing for the next canvass, in which he was finally successful, defeating Stephen A. Douglas. Stuart was giving the office only incidental attention. He desired Lincoln as a partner largely that Stuart might be free to give more time to politics. Lincoln did not enjoy this, but it was good for him. Herndon says of the beginnings of Lincoln's partnership:

In consequence of the political allurements, Stuart did not give to the law his undivided time or the full force of his energy and intellect. Thus more or less responsibility in the management of business and the conduct of cases soon devolved upon Lincoln. The entries in the account book of the firm are all in the handwriting of Lincoln. Most of the declarations and briefs are written by him also. This sort of exercise was never congenial to him, and it was the only time, save for a brief period under Judge Logan, that he served as a junior partner and performed the labor required of one who serves in that rather subordinate capacity. He had not yet learned to love work. The office of the firm was in the upper story of the building opposite the northwest corner of the present court-house square. In the room underneath, the county court was held. The furniture was in keeping with the pretentions of the firm—a small lounge, or bed, a chair containing a buffalo robe, in which the junior member was wont to sit and study, a hard wooden bench, a feeble attempt at a bookcase, and a table which answered for a desk.

Stuart had need of all the time he could spare from his office if he intended to defeat Stephen A. Douglas. Illinois at that time had but three congressional districts. Sangamon County was included in the third, which was made up of the twenty-two northernmost counties. In the spring and summer of 1838, Stuart and Douglas rode together from town to town, all over this great district, speaking six days a week. The election occurred in August, 1838. Stuart, the Whig candidate, won by a majority of fourteen. The total vote cast was thirty-six thousand. This election foretokened the coming power of Illinois as a possible Whig state. The growth of the northern end in population bid fair in time to transfer the state from the Democratic to the Whig column. This campaign was far more interesting to Stuart than the routine business of his law office. Lincoln, too, had much more fondness for the excitement of the political arena than for the drudgery of officework. Lincoln needed the discipline, however, and though it was irksome, it did him good.

The first months of Lincoln's life in Springfield were very lonely months. His social position was not what it had been at New Salem. When the Legislature was in session, he was a member of the lower House, but that was a less inspiring occupation than it had been. No longer was there any occasion for exciting manipulation such as the Long Nine had displayed in the removal of the capital. No longer was there the same occasion for the display of Lincoln's imaginary talent as a financier and a promoter of wild schemes of local improvements. The panic of 1837 was bringing men to a serious consideration of the folly of their wild speculation. Lincoln had occasion with the rest to sit down and consider the unwisdom of much that had been done.

Whatever of society New Salem boasted, Lincoln belonged to it. If he flattered himself that Springfield, being grateful to him for his share in removing the capital, would receive him socially with open arms, he was mistaken. A few politicians remembered his share in that achievement, and a little group of his friends were willing to stand by him and enable him to get a start, but

Springfield had its aristocracy, and Lincoln did not as yet belong to it. Later he came to be a prominent figure in its legal and social life. But his first feeling was one of isolation. He felt his poverty as he had never felt it before, and he was weighed down by his debts and the apparent hopelessness of his paying them.

Added to his other occasions for discomfort was the fact that his relations with Mary Owens still hung fire. At times he greatly desired her, but his almost fatal habit of indecision had now to meet her very serious questioning whether Lincoln with all his good qualities and his undoubted ability could make any woman happy.

While matters were in this state, he wrote to her on May 7, 1837, a letter revealing his depression, loneliness, consciousness of poverty and pathetic indecision. He said:

I am often thinking about what we said about your coming to live at Springfield. I am afraid you would not be satisfied. There is a great deal of flourishing about in carriages here, which it would be your doom to see without sharing it. You would have to be poor, without the means of hiding your poverty. Do you believe you could bear that patiently? Whatever woman may cast her lot with mine, should any ever do so, it is my intention to do all in my power to make her happy and contented; and there is nothing I can imagine that would make me more unhappy than to fail in the effort. I know I should be much happier with you than the way I am, provided I see no signs of discontent in you. What you have said to me may have been in the way of jest, or I may have misunderstood it. If so, then let it be forgotten; if otherwise, I much wish you would think seriously before you decide. What I have said I will most positively abide by, provided you wish it. My opinion is that you had better not do it. You have not been accustomed to hardship, and it may be more severe than you now imagine. I know you are capable of thinking correctly on any subject, and if you deliberate maturely upon this before you decide, then I am willing to abide by your decision.*

_____

*These letters, with that to Mrs. Browning, are in all editions of Lincoln's Works, and need not here be reprinted in full.

This was a very strange love-letter in which Lincoln at once professed his affection and told her why she should not marry him. By this time Mary herself was hesitating. She was not yet ready to throw Lincoln over, but she was by no means convinced that he would make an acceptable husband.

During this whole period Mary Owens had been doing some thinking of her own. She noticed that when she and Lincoln were riding together on horseback in company with a group of friends, and they came to a dangerous ford, the other young men looked after their partners and saw them safely across, but Lincoln rode on ahead and let her come through as best she could. She had heard of his tender heart, and how he dismounted once to release a mired pig from a mud-hole, and she liked it little that he showed no concern for her safe transit. She chided him for his neglect, and he seemed to her obtuse; he merely laughed and said that she was "smart enough to get over alone." So she was, and she also was smart enough to want a husband who cared whether she got over safely or not.

One day in midsummer Lincoln rode to New Salem and saw Mary. Their visit brought him no nearer to a decision. That night at Springfield he wrote to her as follows:

Springfield, August 16, 1837.

Friend Mary: You will no doubt think it rather strange that I should write you a letter on the same day on which we parted, and I can only account for it by supposing that seeing you lately makes me think of you more than usual; while at our late meeting we had but few expressions of thoughts. You must know that I cannot see you or think of you with entire indifference; and yet it may be that you are mistaken in regard to what my real feelings toward you are. If I knew you were not, I should not trouble you with this letter. Perhaps any other man would know enough without further information; but I consider it my peculiar right to plead ignorance, and your bounden duty to allow the plea. I want in all cases to do right, and more particularly so in all cases with women. I want at this particular time, more than anything else, to do right with you; and if I knew it would be doing right, as I rather suspect it would, to let you alone, I would do it. And for the purpose of making the matter as plain as possible, I now say that you can now drop the subject, dismiss your thoughts (if you ever had any) from me forever, and leave this letter unanswered, without calling forth one accusing murmur from me. And I will go even further, and say that if it will add anything to your comfort or peace of mind to do so, it is my sincere wish that you should. Do not understand by this that I wish to cut your acquaintance. I mean no such thing. What I do wish is that our further acquaintance shall depend upon yourself. If such further acquaintance would contribute nothing to your happiness, I am sure it would not to mine. If you should feel yourself in any degree bound to me, I am now willing to release you, provided you wish it; while, on the other hand, I am willing and even anxious to bind you faster, if I can be convinced that it will, in any considerable degree, add to your happiness. This, indeed, is the whole question with me. Nothing would make me more miserable than to believe you miserable—nothing more happy than to know you were so.

In what I have now said, I think I can not be misunderstood, and to make myself understood is the only object of this letter.

If it suits you best to not answer this, farewell. A long life and a merry one attend you. But if you conclude to write back, speak as plainly as I do. There can be neither harm nor danger in saying to me anything you think just in the manner you think it.

My respects to your sister,

Your friend,
Lincoln.

Women do not enjoy this kind of love-making. Mary Owens did not want Abraham Lincoln to tell her that she was at liberty to marry him if she thought it would make her happier. She wanted to be loved ardently and wooed earnestly. When, therefore, Lincoln sought to end the affair one way or the other, by a definite proposal of marriage, and though he hoped that he had done it so coldly that she would refuse him, he was surprised and pained beyond all expectation to find that she did that very thing. He proposed a second time, and again she refused. He made a third proposal, and the third time was re-jected.

In Lincoln's letter to Mrs. Browning he said:

I was mortified, it seemed to me, in a hundred different ways. My vanity was deeply wounded by the reflection that I had so long been too stupid to discover her intentions, and at the same time never doubting that I understood them perfectly; and also that she, whom I had taught myself to believe nobody else would have, had actually rejected me with all my fancied greatness. And, to cap the whole, I then for the first time began to suspect that I was really a little in love with her. But let it all go! I'll try and outlive it. Others have been made fools of by the girls, but this can never with truth be said of me. I most emphatically, in this instance, made a fool of myself. I have now come to the conclusion never again to think of marrying; and for this reason —I can never be satisfied with any one who would be blockhead enough to have me.

It would seem to be reasonably plain that if Lincoln had sum-moned himself to a resolute determination to marry her whether or no, he might even yet have had her. She remained with her sister until the following April, apparently not quite willing to consider the incident closed. Had Lincoln ridden over from Springfield on any day in the winter of 1837-8, and told her that he loved her and would not take no for an answer, it is not likely that she would have refused him.

After Mary Owens* had gone back to Kentucky and to the stepmother from whose domination marriage with Lincoln would have relieved her, Lincoln met Mrs. Able in Springfield one day, and said to her, "Tell your sister she was a great fool not to stay here and marry me."

Miss Owens was not at all certain that she had decided un-wisely. She married a Kentuckian, made her home in Missouri, and when the Civil War broke out she sided with the South. Her

*Mary S. Owens was born in Kentucky, September 29, 1808; married Jesse Vineyard March 27, 1841; removed to Weston, Mo.; had five children, and she died July 4, 1877.

sons served in the Confederate Army. But she remembered Lincoln as having been in many ways congenial, both personally and in that earlier day, politically. She wrote concerning him in 1866 that she regarded him as one of the kindest and best of men, and counted it an honor that he had offered to marry her and that he had repeated his proposal the second and even the third time. She felt sure that if she had married him he would have been an honorable and true husband, but she could not overlook what she regarded as his bad breeding and his inattention. She said she never believed that it had proceeded from any lack of goodness of heart, but his training had been different from hers. She summed up her reason for refusing the hand of Abraham Lincoln in this sentence: "Mr. Lincoln was deficient in those little links which make up the chain of a woman's happiness."

Lincoln was gaining in personal acquaintance and influence. He had come to be recognized as leader of the Whig Party in the House of Representatives. His associates among the Whig leaders were men of ability. His partner, John T. Stuart, was foremost among them. Closely associated with him was O. H. Browning, later United States Senator. There also were Colonel John J. Hardin, Jesse K. Dubois, Ninian W. Edwards, and Edward Dickinson Baker, after the last of whom Lincoln named one of his sons. The Democrats were represented by William L. D. Ewing, who twice defeated Lincoln as Speaker of the House; John Calhoun, former surveyor, under whom Lincoln had served as deputy, a man of character and ability; Lyman Trumbull, who was chosen for United States Senate in 1855 in Lincoln's stead; James Shields, with whom Lincoln later had his famous approach to a duel, and Ebenezer Peck, who introduced the convention system into Illinois politics. Besides these must be mentioned a young man, who, like Lincoln, had but newly arrived in Springfield, and of whom we shall find much to say hereafter, Stephen Arnold Douglas.

Among these men on both sides of the political fence, Lincoln was recognized increasingly as a leader to be reckoned with.

Lincoln did not spend the major part of his time in Stuart's law office. Speed's store was his headquarters. There gathered a group of men, largely lawyers more interested in politics than law, but including in its personnel men of other vocations and of no vocation at all. They discussed politics, religion and all other questions. There statesmen and near-statesmen and aspiring orators talked things over.

A few months after Lincoln's arrival in Springfield, a second bed was installed in Speed's large room above the store. It was occupied by Charles R. Hurst and William H. Herndon. Herndon was son of a Springfield tavern keeper. The father was a Kentuckian and a pro-slavery Democrat. The son had been sent to Illinois College. The murder of Lovejoy at Alton raised the anti-slavery sentiment of Illinois College to white heat. Herndon's father, learning that his son had become a hot abolitionist, withdrew him from school and cast him upon his own resources. Herndon had worked for Speed as a clerk before going to college, and on his return to Springfield he reentered Speed's employ and continued to be his clerk for several years. Herndon later studied law, and in time became Lincoln's partner. At this time, however, he was simply Speed's clerk, and a hot-headed abolitionist.

This group of four young men formed the nucleus of a literary society. In this Lincoln continued to exercise his gifts. His literary style began to change from the florid character of his earlier years, and to take upon itself some nearer approach to that clear, simple, straightforward quality which subsequently became its most outstanding characteristic.

Late in the year 1837 Lincoln delivered an address before a larger and more pretentious society, known as the Young Men's Lyceum. It was entitled, *The Perpetuation of our Free Institutions*. This met with so much favor that it was printed in the *Sangamo Journal* and greatly enhanced Lincoln's reputation as an orator. It is contained in all the editions of the works on Lincoln, and may be studied by those who wish to study his style at the height of his sophomoric period.

ABRAHAM LINCOLN'S FIRST PORTRAIT
From a daguerreotype owned by Robert T. Lincoln

Somewhat better in its method of treatment, and much more restrained in its diction, was his Washington's Birthday address delivered on February 22, 1842, before the Washingtonian Temperance Society. This is the address, well known to all students of Lincoln's life, which the newspapers discover now and then and quote as a newly found document containing Lincoln's tribute to Washington. That address shows considerable ability, and has some admirable paragraphs. Speaking on a patriotic anniversary, and on behalf of temperance he said:

When the victory shall be complete, when there shall neither be a slave nor a drunkard on the earth, how proud the title of that land which may claim to be the birthplace and cradle of those revolutions that shall end in that victory!

Thus early did Lincoln commit himself, though not yet as an abolitionist nor as a prohibitionist, but as a lover of sobriety and freedom, to a program whose avowed end was the elimination both of drunkenness and of slavery.

Two incidents may here be recorded as indicating Lincoln's growing popularity as a political speaker. The first is from the campaign of 1838, in which Lincoln again was chosen a member of the Legislature. The second is from the campaign of 1840, which was Lincoln's last active canvass for the Legislature, and the period of excitement of the Log Cabin and Hard Cider campaign. In the campaign of 1838, Lincoln more than once engaged in joint debate with a prominent orator known as Colonel Dick Taylor. Taylor had a personal fondness for fine clothes and other adornment, but in his campaign speeches he was accustomed to hide his jewelry. A part of his argument was an appeal to his horny-handed neighbors on behalf of democratic simplicity, and a protest against the lordly ways and aristocratic pretentions of the Whigs. On one occasion while Taylor was in the midst of his address, Lincoln slipped up to his side and jerked his vest open, revealing a ruffled shirt front and a heavy gold watch-chain and seal. The audience roared and the speaker continued his address amid great confusion.

When it came Lincoln's turn to speak, he reviewed Taylor's indictment against the Whigs, and described Taylor himself as riding in a fine carriage, flourishing a gold-headed cane, and wearing kid gloves, a massive gold chain with a large gold seal and a ruffled shirt. He then described his own claim to aristocracy, and told how not many years before he had been working on a flat-boat at eight dollars a month, possessing only one pair of breeches, which were of buckskin which shrank until they grew so short that they left a permanent blue streak around his legs.

This address was received as an effective rejoinder to Taylor's charge that the Whig Party and its candidate represented wealth and aristocracy.

The capacity of Lincoln for controversial argument found illustration in his first year in Springfield. At the August election of 1837, one General James Adams was a candidate for election as "Probate Justice of the Peace." Just before the election a handbill was circulated through Springfield charging the general with having acquired title to a ten-acre lot of ground near Springfield by the defrauding of a widow, and the forging of the name of her deceased husband. The author of the handbill did not sign his name, but authorized the editor of the *Sangamo Journal,* in whose office the handbill was printed, to furnish the name of the author to any one who might call for it. Individuals were not long in learning that Lincoln was the author of this vigorous denunciation, and the editor a few days later made definite announcement of this fact in a signed card published in the *Journal.*

Then ensued one of the fiercest of newspaper controversies. Lincoln was attorney for the widow, and Adams knew that Lincoln had obtained all the facts in her possession. He replied to Lincoln in articles many columns in length, denouncing Lincoln's attack upon him as a conspiracy. Lincoln used plain speech, declaring that certain statements of Adams were "false as hell." At length the *Journal* published an editorial, which

Lincoln doubtless wrote, and followed it with a copy of an indictment found against Adams in Oswego County, New York, in
1818, charging him with the very same offense, the forgery of
a deed.

This settled the status of Adams, and it did much to establish
that of Lincoln as an antagonist to be feared. It also did something to increase Lincoln's confidence in himself as a writer.
From this time on the *Journal* was virtually his paper. The editor, Simeon Francis, was his warm personal and political
friend, and Lincoln wrote many of the editorials from this time
until 1860.

Gradually Lincoln emerged into the social life of Springfield.
He was recognized as a man of coming political power, and one
who, while lacking in social graces, would give to some young
woman a social prestige worth thinking about. Almost immediately on his arrival in Springfield he was toasted at banquets
for his share in bringing the capital of the state to that city. Before very long he was invited to parties and balls. He habitually
attended these events. Young women were always interested in
him, though they were inclined to resent his habit of withdrawing
groups of young men who gathered about him and listened to
his stories. He danced rarely, and not very gracefully. Still he
had a certain dignity of his own, and there was a kind of grace
that inhered in his very awkwardness. In a pleasant social environment he responded to the stimulus of congenial companionship, and almost forgot his great hands and feet. He never
was what was called a ladies' man. But he had a touch of native
courtesy which was the normal expression of a genuinely kind
heart, and women admired him, even though they sometimes
poked a little fun at him. In the early days of his residence in
Springfield we find his name prominent among the social leaders
of that city. The local papers mentioned him frequently at social
gatherings. A printed invitation is preserved in the library of
the Chicago Historical Society of a cotillion party at the American House at seven o'clock P. M., on December 17, 1839. The

invitation is signed by sixteen "managers." Among them are Ninian W. Edwards, John A. McClernand, Joshua F. Speed, James Shields, Stephen A. Douglas and Abraham Lincoln.

On this wise did the lonely lawyer emerge from isolation into growing prominence in Springfield. It was an experience far from being cheerful, but it had its value; and Lincoln moved steadily forward and upward to a position among the most prominent of Springfield's influential men, and toward a place of commanding leadership in the political life of the state of Illinois.

CHAPTER XVIII

MARY TODD
1839-1842

ALTHOUGH Lincoln's removal to Springfield put some miles of distance between him and his old neighbors and supporters, he did not lose their friendship or political support. He was a candidate for the Legislature in 1838, and again was elected. He was a candidate for speaker of the House and was defeated by a small majority. This session of the General Assembly was the first to experience a reaction against the unwisdom of the financial schemes of the preceding years. Lincoln was compelled to acknowledge that he was no financier, and his efforts to extricate the state from its embarrassing condition afford evidence, if any were needed, of that fact. We can find little to commend in Lincoln's contribution to the financial conditions of Illinois during the period when he was a member of the Legislature. Two facts, however, are to be remembered to his credit. One is that he was desperately poor and continued to be poor throughout all those years in which it was possible for a member of the General Assembly to be paying off his debts and providing for the future. The other is that while some of Lincoln's associates advocated repudiation as the only way out of the intolerable situation, Lincoln as a member of the Finance Committee steadfastly opposed it. He saw no better way out of it, but he believed that Illinois must keep her promises.

Lincoln was a candidate as elector on the Whig presidential ticket in 1840, but was not permitted to serve. Illinois, true to form, went Democratic. Douglas stumped the state for the

Democrats and added to his prestige. Lincoln made a number of campaign speeches for the Whigs. Only one of them is preserved. It is in the florid style to which Lincoln was addicted in this period of his career, and which he subsequently outgrew. It was, however, the style of oratory which his audiences enjoyed. Although he was not chosen on the presidential electoral ticket, he was a successful candidate for the Legislature. Again, he was the candidate of his party for the speakership and had thirty-six votes, but Ewing, candidate of the Democratic members, had forty-six, and Lincoln never became speaker of the Illinois House of Representatives.

In the campaign of 1840, Lincoln crossed swords with Jesse B. Thomas, a prominent Democratic politician. Lincoln engaged in a debate with him at a meeting held in the Presbyterian Church of Springfield. Subsequently Thomas delivered an address in the court-house in which he denounced the Long Nine and held them up to ridicule, reflecting most severely upon Lincoln. Lincoln was not present at the beginning of the address, but the strictures of Thomas were so severe that some of Lincoln's friends stepped out and informed him, and he hurried to the meeting and heard the closing portion of Thomas' speech. Lincoln was thoroughly aroused, not so much by the argument as by the ridicule. When Thomas closed, he stepped to the platform and made answer to Thomas' address. He did not stop with argument; he disclosed a wholly unsuspected power of ridicule, sarcasm and mimicry. He imitated the mannerisms of Thomas, and held him up to scorn. So severe was his castigation, so unlike anything that his friends had ever seen or suspected in Lincoln, that all who heard him were amazed. The crowd yelled and cheered, and Lincoln, thus encouraged, went still farther with his scathing ridicule. Thomas writhed under the pain of this experience and finally gave way to tears. Herndon says of this incident, which was known as "the skinning of Thomas":

The whole thing was so unlike Lincoln, it was not soon forgotten either by his friends or enemies. I heard him afterward say that the recollection of his conduct that evening filled him with the deepest chagrin. He felt that he had gone too far, and to rid his good nature of a load, he hunted up Thomas and made ample apology. The incident and its sequel proved that Lincoln could not only be vindictive but manly as well.

In 1842, Lincoln for the first time in his life met a former president of the United States and found himself at ease in his presence. Martin Van Buren, who had just finished his term as president, made a tour of the West. In July his party reached Rochester, six miles from Springfield, and, the roads being bad, remained there for the night. A large delegation of politicians, mostly Democrats, went out and spent a merry evening with Van Buren and his fellow-travelers, taking with them from Springfield such refreshments as they supposed appropriate and which they thought the facilities of Rochester might lack. Lincoln, though a Whig, accompanied this party, and shared in the festivities. Van Buren was an accomplished story-teller and had a fund of reminiscences; but Lincoln distanced all competitors in the exchange of stories. The fun continued until after midnight, and Van Buren declared his sides were sore from laughing. Thus did Lincoln move forward in his relations with men.

Shy as Lincoln was in the presence of women, he was less so in 1840 than in 1830. His experience in Springfield and on the circuit had given him wider relationships with men and women both. County-seat society was at its best during court sessions, and Lincoln shared increasingly in these enjoyments. On one of these journeys he was invited to play "Muggins." He did not know how the game was played; no man was expected to play it more than once. He was seated in a ring, face to face with an attractive girl, and charged under penalty to look her steadily in the eye and do exactly what she did. She produced two dinner plates, gave him one of them, and kept the other. Holding the plate on her knee with the left hand, she rubbed the index finger of her right hand upon her plate, and then rubbed the same finger upon her cheek, forehead or chin. This was done repeatedly, the rubbing of the plate alternating with the rubbing of the face. It was the duty of the young man to follow all her movements, touching his plate whenever she touched hers, and rubbing his finger on his face when she rubbed her finger on her face. If he failed to look her steadily in the eye, or to follow any of her movements, he had to pay a forfeit. The young man did not know it, but while the plate in her lap was clean, the plate on his knee had been smoked above a candle. Lincoln won the game. That is to say, he did not fail steadily to look her in the face and to follow all her movements. But when she had finished, the company burst out in a roar, and produced a mirror, in which Lincoln beheld his face streaked in black in most ingenious patterns.

In such games, and now and then in formal dances, Lincoln had come to bear his share. Women liked him, and stood a little in awe of him. He liked women, but he stood in fear of them, and in greater fear of himself. But he was approaching the time when he would marry, and Mary Todd came in sight at a time when he was ready to consider matrimony.

Mary Todd, who later became the wife of Abraham Lincoln, was born in Lexington, Kentucky, December 13, 1818, and died at the residence of her sister, Mrs. Ninian W. Edwards, in Springfield, July 16, 1882. She was the daughter of Honorable Robert S. Todd of Kentucky, and granddaughter of Levi Todd, the only field officer at the battle of Blue Licks who was not killed. Her great-uncle, John Todd, was the first governor of what later became Illinois. He organized civil government under the authority of Virginia. He had previously accompanied George Rogers Clark to Illinois, and was present in 1778 at the capture of Kaskaskia and Vincennes. Of him Mr. Arnold says, "He may be justly regarded as the founder of the state, a pioneer of progress, education, and liberty."*

*Arnold: *Life of Lincoln*, p. 68.

MARY TODD LINCOLN
From photograph in Springfield about 1858

Levi Todd, grandfather of Mary Todd, was born in 1756, educated in Virginia, and studied law in that state in the office of General Lewis. He emigrated to Kentucky, and with his brother John, served as an officer under George Rogers Clark, and commanded a battalion in the battle of Blue Licks. He succeeded Daniel Boone in command of the militia, ranking as major general. He married, February 25, 1779, Miss Jane Briggs. The seventh child of this union was Robert S. Todd, born February 25, 1791. He served in both houses of the Kentucky Legislature, and for over twenty years was president of the Bank of Kentucky at Lexington. He died July 16, 1849.

On her mother's side the ancestry of Mary Todd was hardly less distinguished. Anne Eliza Parker was a cousin of her husband, Robert S. Todd. She traced her descent from General Andrew Porter of the Revolution. Her great uncles, George B. Porter, Governor of Michigan, James Madison Porter, Secretary of the Navy under President Tyler, and David R. Porter, governor of Pennsylvania, were all men of note. She was able to trace her lineage for many generations, and she had occasion for just pride in her family traditions.

Mary Todd first visited Springfield in 1837, and remained three months. She returned to Kentucky, but was unhappy there. Her mother died when she was still young, and like Mary Owens, she had a stepmother with whom she was not entirely happy.* In each of Lincoln's two most serious love-affairs after the death of Ann Rutledge, a stepmother and a married sister were important factors in his matrimonial prospects. In each of these two cases the young woman came from Kentucky, visited her sister, went back to Kentucky and came on again to Illinois with little intention of returning to Kentucky to live. There was this difference, however, Mary Owens had only one young man in mind when she returned from Kentucky to

---

*It appears in evidence in a suit among heirs that Mary was not the only child by the first wife of Robert S. Todd who left home to avoid the stepmother.

10

New Salem. Mary Todd returned to Springfield heart-whole and fancy free. She knew that she could have her pick. Springfield was moderately full of ambitious young men, and she was well aware of her power.

Mrs. Lincoln furnished to Herndon in 1865 this short autobiographical statement:

My mother died when I was still young. I was educated by Madame Mantelli, a lady who lived opposite Mr. Clay, and who was an accomplished French scholar. Our conversation at school was carried on entirely in French—in fact we were allowed to speak nothing else. I finished my education at Mrs. Ward's Academy, an institution to which many people from the North sent their daughters. In 1837 I visited Springfield, Illinois, remaining three months. I returned to Kentucky, remaining until 1839, when I again set out for Illinois, which state finally became my home.

Her sister Elizabeth, Mrs. Ninian W. Edwards, supplemented the above statement with the detail that Mary "left her home in Kentucky to avoid living under the same roof with a stepmother." She had two other sisters, Frances, who was married to Doctor William Wallace, and Anne, who subsequently married C. M. Smith, a merchant. All these sisters lived in Springfield. When Mary Todd came to live with her sister Elizabeth she was not quite twenty-one years old. She was a young woman of unusual ability, quick wit and brilliant repartee. She was of less than medium height, and when she stood beside Abraham Lincoln, she seemed very short. In 1861, when she and Abraham Lincoln stood at a reception in Washington, he spoke jokingly of "the long and short of the presidency." Among other women, however, she seemed of average height. She was compactly built, and while she did not tend to such stoutness as came to Mary Owens, she grew more plump as she advanced in years. When Mary Todd arrived in Springfield she weighed about one hundred and thirty pounds. She was a brunette with rosy cheeks. She had rich, dark brown hair, and her eyes were a bluish gray.

She was handsome and vivacious and had a proud bearing. Herndon says of her as he first knew her:

She was a good conversationalist, using with equal fluency the French and English languages. When she used the pen, its point was sure to be sharp, and she wrote with wit and ability. She not only had a quick intellect, but an intuitive judgment of men and their motives. Ordinarily she was affable and even charming in her manner; but when offended or antagonized, her agreeable qualities instantly disappeared beneath a wave of stinging satire or sarcastic bitterness, and her entire better nature was submerged. In her figure and physical proportions, in education, bearing, history—in everything, she was the exact reverse of Lincoln. On her return to Springfield she immediately entered society, and soon became one of the belles, leading the young men of the town a merry dance. She was a very shrewd observer, and discreetly and without apparent effort kept back all the unattractive elements in her organization. Her trenchant wit, affability, and candor pleased the young men not less than her culture and varied accomplishments impressed the older ones with whom she came in contact.

Herndon relates an incident which appears to indicate that he offended her on the occasion of their first meeting, and it is certain that they cordially disliked each other. She found repeated occasion to be rude to Herndon after he became her husband's partner, and he had his cruel revenge in what he told about her in his *Life of Lincoln* and his lecture on Ann Rutledge.

If there are any people who suppose that the advent of women into American politics began with their recent successful struggle for the ballot and the adoption of an amendment to the Constitution permitting them to vote, those people know little about life in Springfield in the early days after it had become the capital of the state. In those days nearly all the ambitious young men in Springfield were seeking distinction at the bar and in politics. Young women, in considering the availability of young men as possible husbands, rated prominently among their assets their chances of political preferment. There is nothing strange about the statement credited to Mary Todd that she intended that the man she married should be president of the United States. Forty other girls in Springfield probably said the same thing; but Mary Todd had greater reason than most of them to indulge that ambitious hope and expectation. Illinois was emerging into national politics. The campaign of 1840, having for its leading and successful candidate a man whose friends boasted proudly concerning him that he had once lived in a log cabin and that his drink was hard cider, brought the presidency easily above the horizon of the Springfield imagination. Mary Todd arrived to make her home in Springfield in 1839. Three married sisters lived there; and they, especially Mrs. Ninian W. Edwards in whose home she lived, were in position to pave her way to a brilliant social career. She soon had all the prominent young men of Springfield on tiptoe. It was not by any means impossible that some one of these might yet be president of the United States. Nor was it even then impossible that Abraham Lincoln would be the man.

Mary, Mary, quite contrary, how did the fashions go? Piled up hair, and shoulders bare, and vertebrae all in a row. No girl in Springfield had a more attractive pile of hair upon her well poised head, or a prettier pair of shoulders, or a better knowledge of all the arts of coquetry. She led Abraham Lincoln a merry dance that had its periods of anger and of tears. I should like to tell the truth about Mary Todd and Abraham Lincoln, and that is not wholly a simple matter. For there are those who ought to know who assure you that from beginning to end they fought each other, and married without love, and others equally in position to know who assure you that the course of true love never flowed so smoothly as with them. And I do not believe either of these stories.

But consider for a moment Mary herself. Let me relate one little incident which can not be all gossip because it has perpetuated itself in poetry. Poetry is the oldest form of history. The most ancient volumes of historical writing have embedded in them scraps of poetry and song still earlier; and this sober piece of historical writing shall be no exception.

The state capitol in Lincoln's day was in the very heart of Springfield, being, indeed, the present Sangamon county court-house with one additional story built under the original structure. The land where the present capitol building stands was vacant and almost suburban; but just beyond it, where the new Centennial Building now is erected, stood the two fine houses of Ninian W. Edwards and Lawson Levering. In 1840, Mercy Levering, of Georgetown, in the District of Columbia, was visiting her brother, the visit resulting in her marriage, September 11, 1841, to James Conkling. At the same time, as we know, Mary Todd was visiting her sister, Mrs. Edwards. A very gay time these two maidens had while next-door neighbors.

There came a period of three weeks in which these girls were hardly able to step out-of-doors on account of the incessant rains. When at length the sun broke through the clouds, Springfield was one vast mud-hole. There were sidewalks on Monroe Street, and around the Square, but none on Fifth Street. But the two girls resolved to go to the Square, and look in at the stores and hear the gossip of the town. A bundle of shingles was in the yard of the Edwards home, and the young ladies each took an armful of them. Carefully picking their way, they laid shingles over the mud-holes which they could not step across, and so made their way to the nearer end of the sidewalks, and accomplished the purpose of their pilgrimage. But how were they to return? For the shingles which had been none too secure a foundation when first laid, would have been submerged by other feet, and the mud was deep.

Springfield had a drayman named Hart, who drove his two-wheeled sloping-bedded vehicle about town, backing it up at the doors where he had freight to deliver. The rear-end of his dray possessed no tail-board, but had an iron rod which fitted into a socket and was a convenient standard to which a rope might be tied on occasion. The rod could be pulled out for convenience in loading and unloading. As the girls were considering how to get home, Hart's dray came by, and Mary Todd called to Hart, and asked him to convey her and Mercy to their homes. He backed up his dray to the curb and Mary climbed aboard. Mercy was too horrified to follow her example, though greatly wishing that she dared. Mary stood erect, holding tight to the iron stake, and the dray splashed and plowed its way to the Edwards home, and then backed up and let her dismount.

If Springfield had been New York, and Fifth Street had been Fifth Avenue, and the time had been the present, the daughter of any of New York's Four Hundred might have ridden home on a dray, wearing a dunce-cap and tooting a striped horn, and few pedestrians would so much as have turned their heads; but Springfield was much more conventional than New York.

Perhaps there was not another girl in Springfield who would have dared to do what Mary did; but people said, "That's just like Mary Todd," and laughed merrily about it. "There is a great deal of flourishing about in carriages," wrote Abraham Lincoln to Mary Owens. And Mary Todd was flourishing about in Hart's dray!

Doctor E. H. Merriman, who was Lincoln's second in the "duel" with Shields, was of those who saw Mary Todd riding home on a dray; and for that matter, who did not see her? He wrote a poem about it, not for publication, but to be passed around among their discreet mutual friends. Mercy Levering became the final owner of the manuscript, which only lately has been given by Mercy's daughter to the Illinois State Historical Society. Not wholly for the beauty of its lines, nor yet for the historical value of the event, but as affording a side light on the vivacity and daring of Mary Todd, this literary gem is here enshrined :*

Journal of the Illinois State Historical Society, April, 1923, p. 146. I have smoothed the meter in two or three places.

RIDING ON A DRAY

By Doctor E. H. Merriman

As I walked out on Monday last,
    A wet and muddy day,
'Twas there I saw a pretty lass,
    A-riding on a dray,
    A-riding on a dray!

Quoth I, "Sweet lass, what do you there?"
    Saith she, "Good lack-a-day,
I had no coach to take me home,
    So I'm riding on a dray;
    I'm riding on a dray!

"At Lowry's house I got aboard
    Next door to Mr. Hay,
By yellow Poll and Spottswood then
    A-riding on a dray,
    A-riding on a dray."

The ragged boys threw up their caps,
    And poor folks ran away
As by James Lamb's and o'er the bridge
    She plodded on her way,
    She plodded on her way.

Then up flew windows, out popped heads,
    To see this lady gay
In silken cloak and feathers white
    A-riding on a dray,
    A-riding on a dray.

At length arrived at Edwards' house,
    Hart backed the usual way,
And taking out the iron pin
    He rolled her off the dray,
    He rolled her off the dray.

When safely landed on her feet,
    Said she, "What is to pay?"
Quoth Hart, "I can not charge you aught

For riding on my dray,
For riding on my dray.

"Fair maid, an honor such as this
    I meet not every day;
For surely I'm the happiest man
    That ever drove a dray,
    That ever drove a dray."

And now a moral I'll append
    To this my humble lay:
When you are sticking in the mud,
    Why, call out for a dray;
    Just call out for a dray!

It is not easy for one who has not lived in such a community, to form an adequate or even just idea of social usages as they existed in Springfield during Lincoln's residence there. The town was small, unkempt and unattractive. The streets were unpaved, and there were no sewers. Livestock ran at large, and public sentiment was on the side of the owners of the hogs rather than with the owners of the gardens. A resident of Springfield in that early day has said that a man and a hog had equal right upon a sidewalk. The street crossings after a rain were places of deep mud with here and there a slab or a scrap of plank laid treacherously across some of the deeper mud-holes. A large proportion of the people still dressed in frontier style. In political life nothing was so damaging to a man as the charge that he was an aristocrat. Candidates who had fine clothes were careful to conceal the fact.

On the other hand the advertisements of the merchants showed increasingly the importation of textures of finer grade. Silks were a marketable commodity in Springfield. Some of the Springfield women boasted of silk gowns that would stand alone. There was a certain formality of address which was the more rigid because social life was so near the boundary of frontier living. Springfield ladies did not address their husbands by their first names, but habitually spoke of them by their title. Men in professional life would sit and joke with the utmost informality, but there were certain lines that were rigidly drawn. Stephen A. Douglas, who was born in New England, was much more familiar in his bearing toward his equals than was Abraham Lincoln of the western backwoods. Douglas, in walking with a friend, would throw an arm around him, or slap him on the back, or even now and then sit upon his knee. There was in Lincoln something which forbade this kind of familiarity, and Lincoln did not himself indulge in it.

Consider for a moment the glory of Springfield's elite society at the time when Mary Todd entered it. In 1809, Ninian Edwards was territorial governor of Illinois; and in 1826 he became the third governor of the state. He was inaugurated in a gold-laced cloak over a fine broadcloth suit, and wore knee-breeches and top-boots. He was driven from place to place in a magnificent carriage drawn by a pair of spirited horses, and on the box were a colored coachman and footman. Illinois governors did not maintain in perpetuity that degree of pomp and circumstance, but the governor of Illinois was still a great man when Abraham Lincoln removed to Springfield and Mary Todd came to live with her sister, Mrs. Ninian W. Edwards. Much of the old dignity still hedged the governor about, and made the state social functions of Springfield glorious. The Edwards home stood in the most aristocratic part of Springfield—where now the State Centennial building lifts its stately façade to greet the dome of the capitol. Its owner was the son of old Governor Edwards; its hostess was the great-niece of old Governor Todd. If this free democracy of ours had an aristocracy anywhere, it was in Springfield, and of it Mary Todd was an important part.

After Governor Matteson's time, the governors gave receptions—he was the first Illinois governor to use the word; prior to that time these affairs were called *levees*. Mary Todd liked the word *levee*. Her farewell social function in Springfield was a levee. Springfield's high society did not give "dances." They

had dances, to be sure; when a few loads of young people drove
over to Rochester or Jacksonville and had a "dance" in one of the
taverns and got home about daylight. Springfield had "hops,"
which were more or less informal; and "cotillions" which were
subscription affairs; and "balls" which were great events. A
new governor was inaugurated with a ball, unless he was a
Methodist or very strict Presbyterian, in which case he gave a
promenade party. At a promenade party the guests gossiped and
ate and flirted instead of dancing, eating and flirting. When
Lyman Trumbull married Julia Jayne, he, being a staid Presbyterian, gave a promenade party. The Edwardses were Episco-
palians; they gave balls. The Episcopal church in Springfield
was said to have been erected out of Elizabeth Edwards's pound
cakes.

Behold now a levee, or a ball, or a promenade party of about
1840, with Springfield's high society present in a body. One-
half the pretty girls from all over Illinois are in attendance in
their best frocks as house guests of relatives actually or officially
resident of Springfield. And behold Mary Todd as she enters;
for all eyes are turned toward her. She is dressed in "change-
able silk, shot with blue and flame color," or perhaps on this occasion she wears "four illusion skirts over white satin," the over-
skirt "looped with dew-gemmed Stars of Bethlehem." The waist
of her dress is not much to speak of, being cut very low, and
revealing plump arms and attractive neck and shoulders; but the
skirt has twelve breadths of silk, and stands out over from eight
to twelve starched petticoats. She has tugged hard at her corset-
stays and has a relatively slender waist; but still she is a good
armful, plump, and pulsating with vitality. When she came in at
the front door, she wore a flowered bonnet tied with a great
double bow-knot under her pretty chin. Now, having removed
her bonnet, she wears a flower, or perhaps an ostrich-plume in
her hair. You need not try to keep your eyes off her; it will be
of no use, and furthermore she is quite willing to be seen. In
the language of the period, she is "dressed to kill," and she

knows the fatality of her attire. She moves down the hall, to quote the late Colonel Ingersoll, "like an armed warrior; like a plumed knight," or, if you prefer to take a figure of speech from the Bible, you will discover it in that simile said to have been formulated by a gentleman who was something of a connoisseur in the matter of pretty women,—"fair as the moon, clear as the sun, and terrible as an army with banners."

Entering the lists against the most eligible men in Springfield, men of wealth, men of education, men of culture, men who knew how to flirt and dance and indulge in pretty compliments to women, Abraham Lincoln set out to win the heart of Mary Todd, and to the amazement of all Springfield he succeeded.

Elizabeth Edwards and her two sisters intended to make a brilliant match for Mary. She had no lack of suitors. Stephen A. Douglas was among the men whose hearts were laid at her feet. After all possible allowance is made for exaggeration, hers must have been a brilliant social career in Springfield. With practically all the young men of Springfield to choose among, she accepted Abraham Lincoln, and they became engaged sometime in 1840, and it is said that they were to have been married on the first day of January, 1841.

What followed has been told by Herndon in words that have become the occasion of fierce controversy:

The time fixed for the marriage was the first day of January, 1841. Careful preparations for the happy occasion were made at the Edwards mansion. The house underwent the customary renovation; the furniture was properly arranged, the rooms neatly decorated, the supper prepared, and the guests invited. The latter assembled on the evening in question, and awaited in expectant pleasure the interesting ceremony of marriage. The bride, bedecked in veil and silken gown, and nervously toying with the flowers in her hair, sat in the adjoining room. Nothing was lacking but the groom. For some strange reason he had been delayed. An hour passed, and the guests, as well as the bride, were becoming restless. But they were all doomed to disappointment. Another hour passed; messengers were sent

out over town, and each returning with the same report, it became apparent that Lincoln, the principal in this little drama,
had purposely failed to appear. The bride, in grief, disappeared
to her room; the wedding supper was left untouched; the guests
quietly and wonderingly withdrew; the lights in the Edwards
mansion were blown out, and darkness settled over all for the
night. What the feelings of a lady as sensitive, passionate, and
proud as Miss Todd were, we can only imagine; no one can ever
describe them. By day-break, after persistent search, Lincoln's
friends found him. Restless, gloomy, miserable, desperate, he
seemed an object of pity. His friends, Speed among the number,
fearing a tragic termination, watched him closely in their rooms
day and night. "Knives and razors, and every instrument that
could be used for self-destruction, were removed from his reach."
Mrs. Edwards did not hesitate to regard him as insane, and of
course her sister Mary shared in that view.

Such an event, if thus advertised in advance, could hardly
have failed to be a feature in the season's social life, but the
newspapers of Springfield make no announcement of it. The
records of Sangamon County have been diligently searched, and
no license appears to have been issued.

Lamon tells us of an estrangement between Lincoln and Miss
Todd on account of Miss Matilda Edwards, a sister of Ninian
W. Edwards, but we have that young lady's declaration that Lincoln never so much as paid her a compliment. Herndon intimates that Miss Todd's admiration for Stephen A. Douglas became a factor in the problem; but there seems to be good reason
for the opinion that Mary Todd had chosen deliberately and
finally between the two men.

Lamon informs us, on the authority of Herndon, that Mrs.
Edwards stated that Lincoln went "crazy as a loon"; and Herndon says that on account of this trouble Lincoln absented himself from the Legislature then in session. No known evidence
confirms the report of his insanity. As for his absence from the
Legislature, Lincoln was present on the second day of January,
the day after the "fatal first of January, 1841." The third was
Sunday. Lincoln was not present on Monday, but he was

present and answered to roll-call on Tuesday and in every legislative day thereafter until the thirteenth. He was absent from
the thirteenth to the eighteenth inclusive. Herndon says that on
the nineteenth John J. Hardin announced his illness, but no such
announcement appears on the record. On the contrary, Lincoln was present on the nineteenth. He was absent again on
the twentieth, but was present again on the twenty-first, and on
every day thereafter until the end of the session, March first.*

As for the fear of his committing suicide, this is not confirmed
by those who were of the Butler household where he then
boarded. He seems to have taken about his usual part in legislative business. On February eighth he joined in preparing,
signing and sending out the Whig Circular. On February twenty-sixth he signed with others a protest against the reorganization of the judiciary. On January twenty-third, which was the
day of his desperately sad letter to John T. Stuart, he made a
speech in the Legislature.

Nor did he flee from Springfield as soon as the Legislature
adjourned to recover his reason on the Speed farm. During the
remainder of the spring and early summer he was in Springfield,
attending to business. He was certainly there on June nineteenth
and June twenty-fifth and apparently later. The visit to the Speed
home near Louisville occurred late in the summer; his letter of
acknowledgment was dated September 27, 1841.

Nevertheless, Lincoln was under great mental strain. On
January 23, 1841, he wrote to Stuart: "I am now the most miserable man living. If what I feel were equally distributed to the
whole human family, there would not be one cheerful face on the
earth. Whether I shall ever be better I can not tell; I awfully
forebode I shall not. To remain as I am is impossible. I must
die, or be better, it appears to me. The matter you speak of on
my account you may attend to as you say, unless you shall hear
of my condition forbidding it. I say this because I fear I shall

* *Life of Lincoln*, I:194-195. See also Weik's *The Real Lincoln*, pp. 60-
63.

be unable to attend to any business here, and a change of scene might help me."

Nicolay and Hay thus account for Lincoln's strange conduct in those days of Lincoln's depression:

It has been the cause of much profane and idle discussion among those who were constitutionally incapacitated from appreciating ideal sufferings, and we would be tempted to refrain from adding a word to what has already been said if it were possible to omit all reference to an experience so important in the development of his character.

In the year 1840 he became engaged to be married to Miss Mary Todd, of Lexington, Kentucky, a young lady of good education and excellent connections, who was visiting her sister, Mrs. Ninian W. Edwards, at Springfield. The engagement was not in all respects a happy one, as both parties doubted their mutual compatibility, and a heart so affectionate and a conscience so sensitive as Lincoln's found material for exquisite self-torment in these conditions. His affection for his betrothed, which he thought was not strong enough to make happiness with her secure; his doubts, which yet were not convincing enough to induce him to break off all relations with her; his sense of honor, which was wounded in his own eyes by his own act; his sense of duty, which condemned him in one course and did not sustain him in the opposite one—all combined to make him profoundly and passionately miserable. To his friends and acquaintances, who were unacquainted with such finely wrought and even fantastic sorrows, his trouble seemed so exaggerated that they could only account for it on the ground of insanity. But there is no necessity of accepting this crude hypothesis; the coolest and most judicious of his friends deny that his depression ever went to such an extremity. . . . Orville H. Browning, who was constantly in his company, says that Lincoln's worst attack lasted only about a week; that during this time he was incoherent and distraught; but that in the course of a few days it all passed off, leaving no trace whatever. "I think," says Mr. Browning, "it was only an intensification of his constitutional melancholy; his trials and embarrassments pressed him down to a lower point than usual."

The truth apparently is that the date had not been set for the wedding; that preparations had not gone as far as Herndon describes; that the breaking of the engagement happened as the result of a quarrel which may have occurred on "the fatal first of January," and that the rupture was known only to the intimate friends of Lincoln and Mary Todd.

Two events occurred which had an important bearing upon this matter. The first was that Lincoln's intimate friend, Joshua F. Speed, was also hesitating about getting married. He was haunted by doubts not wholly different from those of Lincoln. He married, and he and Lincoln had a correspondence of the frankest possible nature. The marriage of Speed occurred in February. In March, Speed wrote to Lincoln that he was happier than he had ever expected to be. Lincoln received this letter with genuine rejoicing, and wrote to Speed:

It cannot be told how it now thrills me with joy to hear you say you are far happier than you ever expected to be. I know you too well to suppose your expectations were not, at least, sometimes extravagant, and if the reality exceeds them all, I say, Enough, dear Lord! I am not going beyond the truth when I tell you that the short space it took me to read your last letter gave me more pleasure than the total sum of all I have enjoyed since the fatal 1st of January, 1841. Since then, it seems to me, I should have been entirely happy, but for the never absent idea that there is one still unhappy whom I have contributed to make so. That still kills me. I cannot but reproach myself for even wishing to be happy while she is otherwise. She accompanied a large party on the railroad cars to Jacksonville last Monday, and on her return spoke, so that I heard of it, of having enjoyed the trip exceedingly. God be praised for that.

The other incident was one of which Lincoln was afterward heartily ashamed, but it had a result of incidental value:

General James Shields was a man of ability and a rival of Lincoln. He was born in Ireland in 1810, being thus about a year younger than Lincoln. He served in the Legislature with Lincoln in 1836, and in 1841 was auditor of public accounts. Later he became associate justice of the supreme court, and he served for two years in the Mexican War. His record as a soldier was good, and gave him great prestige. In 1849 he was elected United States senator, but was defeated for reelection in 1855, by Lyman Trumbull. He removed to Minnesota, and in 1858, was elected to the United States Senate. In 1861, Lincoln, his old-time rival, presented him with a commission as brigadier general. In 1879 he served a very brief term as senator from Missouri, and died at Ottumwa, Iowa, June 1, 1879.

General Shields shares the common fate of men opposed to Lincoln of having been needlessly belittled by historians. He had certain vanities and foibles which exposed him to ridicule while he was living, but he was a man of courage and of more than moderate ability.

Lincoln's access to the press offered him a tempting opportunity and he published over an assumed name in the *Journal,* a satirical letter dated from "Lost Townships," and signed "Aunt Rebecca." The wit of this communication was more apparent then than now, but it can plainly be seen why Shields should have been angered by it.

Unfortunately the matter did not end with Lincoln's own satirical composition. Mary Todd and her friend, Miss Julia Jayne, who subsequently became Mrs. Lyman Trumbull, made further contributions to the *Journal,* over the same signature, holding Shields up to ridicule and contempt. Shields was furious. He demanded that Mr. Francis should tell him the name of the author of the articles, and Francis, on Lincoln's instructions, gave him Lincoln's name and concealed the part which the young women had in the performance. Shields challenged Lincoln to a duel, and Lincoln accepted. The duel was to have been fought on the opposite side of the Mississippi from Alton. Fortunately, mutual friends of the two parties interposed their good offices, and there was no bloodshed.

In later years it happened once or twice that people who thought they knew Lincoln well enough to venture some remark about this affair spoke of it to him. He answered them with unexpected severity, indicating that he was thoroughly ashamed of it, and wished it to be forgotten.

This incident brought Lincoln and Mary Todd together in the home of Simeon Francis, editor of the *Journal*. There seems no doubt that their meetings in the Francis home, and the affection of Mrs. Francis for Mary and of Simeon Francis for Lincoln, had the effect of bringing the hesitating Lincoln to a decision. Another favoring circumstance was that Lincoln continued to receive from Speed reports of his matrimonial happiness.

Plans for the wedding of Abraham Lincoln and Mary Todd were finally consummated with great rapidity. Apparently no one knew until the morning of Friday, November 4, 1842, that Lincoln and Mary were to be married. They both were superstitious and had they been choosing their wedding with some deliberation, would certainly have chosen some day other than Friday. They had come to a hasty agreement perhaps only the night before, and they decided to take no chance of any further delay.

When the Long Nine were log-rolling the seat of government away from Vandalia to Springfield in 1837, one of the most potent arguments is alleged to have been that in Vandalia the statesmen of Illinois were compelled to eat venison, wild-duck, quail and prairie chicken; while in Springfield they would get hog-meat.* The promise was abundantly fulfilled. But pork was not the only delicacy Springfield boasted in 1842. The frosting on the Lincoln wedding cake was still too warm to cut well when the time came for it to be served, but there was cake and much besides that was good. Ices they did not have; and the salads had melted butter instead of olive oil; but they had amazingly good things to eat at weddings and other festivals as well.

In 1837, Judge Samuel D. Lockwood, of Jacksonville, wrote to his niece, wife of Major John T. Stuart, Lincoln's first law

---

Springfield Society Before the War, by Mrs. Caroline Owsley Brown; Journal of the *Illinois State Historical Society* XV, 1922, p. 478.

partner: "We are installing a new invention to-day, my dear Mary, called a cooking-stove; it is said to be a panacea for all evils, but in my opinion it will not work."

It worked and still works. Beaten biscuit and pound cake and all the delicacies that formerly were cooked in the old iron oven on the hearth were even better cooked in the new cooking-stoves that were installed in Springfield about the time of the removal of the capital to that city.

After the railway came through, it was customary to hold weddings at five or six o'clock in the morning. That gave just time for a wedding breakfast before the departure of the one train for St. Louis. Springfield society was then accustomed to rising for a five o'clock wedding, to enable the bride and groom —usually if not invariably accompanied by the best man and maid of honor—to spend a honeymoon at the Planter's Hotel or in a voyage upon the Mississippi.

There was no wedding trip when Lincoln married Mary Todd. The arrangements were too hastily made. No invitations were issued.*

A few intimate friends were invited verbally. Lincoln stepped over to the court-house and obtained a license, the original of which, with the minister's return, has recently been found.

THE PEOPLE OF THE STATE OF ILLINOIS.
To any Minister of the Gospel, or other authorised Person—
GREETING

---

*So far as I am aware, there is only one scrap of evidence against the generally accepted belief, which I share, that the final arrangements for the wedding were made on the very day of the wedding. That is the following letter alleged to have been sent by Lincoln to John Hanks, who was then still living at Decatur:

"Dear John:

I am to be married on the 4th of next month to Miss Todd. I hope you will come over. Be sure to be on deck by early candle light.

Yours,

A. Lincoln."

This invitation is given by Mr. Weik in his *The Real Lincoln*, p. 58. Mr. Weik says:

"I did not see this note in the original. A lady living near Decatur, who said she was a granddaughter of John Hanks, furnished me the copy."

Evidently Mr. Weik was not convinced of its genuineness, which I also greatly doubt.

PARLOR IN THE EDWARDS HOUSE
Where Abraham Lincoln married Mary Todd
Photographed for this work by Eugene J. Hall

THESE are to license and permit you to join in the holy bands
of Matrimony   Abraham Lincoln   and
      Mary Todd   of the County of
Sangamon and State of Illinois, and for so doing, this shall be
your sufficient warrant.
                    Given under my hand and seal of office, at
                    Springfield, in said County this 4th
                    day of Novmb   1842
                    N W Matheney, Clerk.
   Solemnised on the same 4th day
of Nov. 1842.   Charles Dresser.*

Reverend Charles Dresser was rector of the Episcopal Church
of which Mrs. Lincoln at that time was a communicànt.
   On the day of the wedding, Lincoln received a letter enclosing a fee of five dollars, a sum just about large enough to pay
his own fee to Mr. Dresser. Judge Logan had carried the letter
for nearly three weeks before he remembered to hand it to Lincoln. Lincoln waited another week before acknowledging the re-
mittance. Just a week after his marriage he wrote† to his friend,
Samuel Marshall, of Shawneetown:

   Friend Sam: Yours of the 10th October enclosing five
dollars was taken from the office in my absence by Judge Logan,
who neglected to hand it to me till about a week ago, and just
an hour before I took a wife. . . . Nothing new here, except my
marrying, which to me is matter of profound wonder.
                       Yours forever,
                              A. Lincoln.

----

*When Nicolay and Hay were compiling their *Abraham Lincoln: A
History,* they obtained what they believed was the original license and printed
it in their work, vol. I, p. 189. The clerk in the office of the county court
at the time of their procuring this copy was a descendant of N. W. Matheney,
and he made the copy on one of the blanks which were in use at a later
date than the original, and with some effort at the use of a handwriting
similar to that of his grandfather, as well as that of the minister. The
publication by Nicolay and Hay was in good faith, but it has given a wrong
impression. Sangamon County had no seal when Lincoln was married, and
the wording of the license was different. The authentic original is in the
Library of the Illinois State Historical Society, and from that original the
copy here given is made.
   †From the original letter in the Chicago Historical Society.

So far as I am aware, this is Lincoln's only contemporary allusion in his correspondence to his marriage, and it is not likely that he talked much about it to his friends. "Profound wonder" at the end of a week of married life was the only emotion of which Lincoln made record.

CHAPTER XIX

IN previous chapters we have considered the career of Abraham Lincoln as a member of the General Assembly of Illinois. He became a candidate for the Legislature in 1832, and was defeated. In 1834 he was elected, and was reelected in 1836, 1838, and 1840. His term of service in the lower House of the Illinois Legislature covers eight consecutive years from 1834 to 1842. These were years of important change in Illinois and in the nation.

They were years notable for their inventions. The steamboat had been invented by Robert Fulton in 1807, and it was an important factor in the life of the communities in which Abraham lived. The Erie Canal, begun on July 4, 1817, was finished in the fall of 1825. By 1830 or 1831 lake navigation had become sufficiently developed to transport goods from New York City by way of the canal and the lakes to Chicago, whence they might be carted overland to points in central Illinois and sold for less money than when brought up the river from New Orleans. In 1819 the first steamship crossed the ocean. In 1828 the first passenger railroad in the United States was begun. In 1836 friction matches began to be used, and about the same time gas pipes and water pipes began to be laid in the streets of the larger towns. The cotton gin had been invented by Eli Whitney in 1793, and this gave a mighty impetus to slavery. Cyrus McCormick invented his reaper in 1834, an invention which had large results in enabling extensive fields to be reaped with great economy of labor. In an important sense the reaper presented to the North by a Virginian, was an offset for the cotton gin, invented for the South by a Connecticut Yankee. It was the age of invention. Abraham Lincoln, who was always interested in mechanical appliances, himself dreamed of inventions of his own, and for one of them he subsequently obtained a patent.

It was a period of intellectual activity. Marked improvements were made in the common school system. In Massachusetts, in 1839, two normal schools were established for the training of teachers, and these became the norm of a new series of institutions established throughout the country. The reading of newspapers became general about this time. The *New York Sun* was founded in 1833, the *Herald* in 1835, and the *Tribune* in 1841. These represented a new type of journalism. They displayed far more energy in the gathering of news than any of their predecessors, and much wider latitude in the discussion of topics.

It was a period of phenomenal activity in the development of American literature. Already the *North American Review*, which was established in 1815, was printing the writings of Washington Irving, William Cullen Bryant, James Fenimore Cooper and Fitz-Greene Halleck. Soon after the close of the first third of the nineteenth century the nation became familiar with the writings of Whittier, Longfellow, Holmes, Hawthorne, Emerson, Poe, Bancroft and Prescott, who began their career as authors about this time.

It was a period in which organized philanthropy had its birth. The first asylum for the blind in America was opened in 1832, and persons deprived of sight were soon taught to read books with raised letters. Asylums for the deaf were opened, and institutions for the treatment of the insane. In 1826 the American Temperance Society was organized in Boston. This was the first society to proclaim the doctrine of total abstinence. Before that time moderate drinking was all that was understood to be included in temperance reform. In 1840 the Washingtonian movement originated in Baltimore. While its primary object was to aid in the reformation of drunkards, it powerfully affected the total abstinence movement. Abraham Lincoln joined the society. In Springfield and elsewhere, the celebration of Washington's birthday was primarily a temperance celebration. One of Lincoln's earliest public addresses was before such an organization. The meetings of the temperance societies did more than inculcate a hatred of strong drink; they were literary societies, and fostered social life in rural communities upon the basis of literary ideals with ethical purposes.

Most significant of the reforms of this period was the anti-slavery reform. The outstanding leaders of the Revolution, including many of the broad-minded men from the South, such as Washington and Lee, were opposed to slavery. Washington's will provided for the liberation of his slaves. Richard Henry Lee, of Virginia, joined with Manasseh Cutler, of Massachusetts, in demanding that the Northwest Territory, out of which five great states have since been made, should be free from the curse of slavery. The Constitution of the United States provided for the termination of the slave trade in 1808. There was general expectation and desire that slavery should also come to an end. The invention of the cotton gin made slavery unexpectedly profitable. The constitutional provision that the slave population of the states where slavery existed should count on a three-fifths basis in congressional representation, gave slavery an unexpected influence in politics.

In 1831 William Lloyd Garrison began, in Boston, the publication of his paper called the *Liberator*. He advocated immediate and unconditional emancipation, and denounced the Constitution of the United States as a "covenant with death and an agreement with hell." In various centers in the North publications opposed to slavery began to be printed. Andrew Jackson in his Message to Congress in 1835, recommended the prohibition, under severe penalties, of circulation through the mails of "incendiary publications intended to instigate the slaves to insurrection." In the same year in which Garrison began the publication of the *Liberator,* an insurrection of the slaves occurred in Virginia. It was led by a negro called Nat Turner. It was soon put down, but it served to alarm the South. In 1837, as we have been reminded, Elijah P. Lovejoy was killed at Alton, Illinois, and his printing-press was destroyed.

Of the original thirteen states, six were slave states and seven were free. In spite of the emancipation movement headed by Thomas Jefferson, the growth of the political power of slavery was marked. The removal of the capital of the nation from New York and Philadelphia to a new city located in slave territory on the line between Maryland and Virginia was important. In order to maintain balance of power, the habit was formed in Congress of admitting new states in pairs. Vermont, admitted February 15, 1791, and Kentucky, February 4, 1792, came in practically simultaneously. Tennessee, January 1, 1796, and Ohio, November 29, 1803, balanced each other; then came Louisiana, April 8, 1812, and Indiana, December 11, 1816, and afterward Mississippi, December 10, 1817, and Illinois, December 3, 1818. In 1819, Alabama, a new slave state, was admitted to the Union, and there was no free state in sight to balance it. This, however, was not regarded as an alarming situation. There were twenty-two states, eleven slave and eleven free. The Senate was thus equally divided. In the House of Representatives, on the other hand, the representation from the free states was larger, owing to the much more rapid growth of population north of the Ohio River. That river up to 1819 had been the dividing line between the free states and the slave states. East of the Ohio the line was projected in the old survey of Mason and Dixon, 39° 45′ north latitude, the dividing line between Pennsylvania and Maryland.

Late in 1818, the territory of Missouri applied for admission into the Union as a state. Nearly the whole state lay north of the line projected westward from the mouth of the Ohio River. On the other hand, most of it lay south of the northern boundaries of Maryland, Virginia and Kentucky. If Missouri was admitted as a free state and the great domain lying west of the Mississippi should come in like fashion into the sisterhood of states, it meant the inevitable doom of the slave power in American politics. For that region was destined to become transformed into great states, each with two senators and an increasing group of representatives, all politically anti-slavery.

Geographically, Missouri was debatable ground. The northern two-thirds of the state was on a line with Illinois, Indiana and Ohio, but its southern boundary was almost exactly the southern boundary of Kentucky.

In 1820, Missouri was proposed as a slave state. The famous Missouri Compromise was suggested by Jesse B. Thomas, of Illinois, and adopted largely through the influence of Henry Clay, then speaker of the House of Representatives. It provided that Maine should be admitted as a free state, and that Missouri was to be a slave state, but that thereafter slavery should be prohibited in all territory of the Louisiana purchase lying north of the line of 36° 30′. This compromise having been arranged, the South permitted Maine to enter the Union as a free state, March 3, 1820, thus preserving the balance of power. But Missouri's actual enrollment in the list of states was delayed until 1821.

For the first time in American legislation the nation recognized by law a line dividing the country into a free North and a slave-holding South. Metes and bounds were set, and it was believed and duly announced that the slavery issue, as a political question, was settled.

James Monroe was the last of the Revolutionary statesmen to be chosen president of the United States. By the end of his second term a new generation of men had come to the front, and new methods of choosing them for office began to come into play. The men who made the Constitution of the United States never expected the people to elect the president. They did all they knew how to prevent it. It was their plan that the people should elect in each state a group of electors, and that these electors should elect the president. It was not intended at the outset that the electors should be pledged in advance to support a particular candidate.

From 1804 to 1820 presidential candidates were nominated by a caucus of the members of Congress. This plan fell out in 1820, because there was no opposition to the nomination of Monroe. In 1824, an attempt was made to nominate a president by the old method. A few members of Congress met and nominated William H. Crawford, of Georgia. But this plan of choosing a president who had been selected by members of his party who were representatives in Congress by Congress had become unpopular. The Legislature of Tennessee placed in nomination Andrew Jackson; Kentucky's Legislature nominated her favorite son, Henry Clay, and that of Massachusetts proposed John Quincy Adams. No candidate received a majority of the electoral votes. Accordingly, the choice of a president fell to the House of Representatives. Jackson was the strongest candidate; the members who were opposed to Jackson united and elected John Quincy Adams as president. John C. Calhoun was elected vice-president by the Electoral College. Adams appointed Henry Clay secretary of state. The friends of Jackson and Crawford denounced this appointment as a corrupt bargain between Adams and Clay. They solidified their opposition into a new party known as the Jacksonians, or Jackson Democrats. Thus new political organizations took their rise.

In 1836, Lincoln was a candidate for the Legislature and announced his principles through the columns of the *Sangamo Journal*. In that letter, which bore the date at New Salem, June 13, 1836, his only reference to national politics was the following sentence:

"If alive on the first Monday in November, I shall vote for Hugh L. White for president."

Hugh L. White was perhaps the least conspicuous of the three Whig candidates. The Jackson Party was sufficiently organized to unite on Martin Van Buren, whom Jackson himself placed in nomination as his own successor. Those opposed to Jackson, who from this time were called Whigs, had no sufficient organization to agree on a candidate, but divided their vote among William Henry Harrison, Daniel Webster and Hugh L. White. White was from Tennessee and presumably had more local backing in the neighborhood of New Salem than either of the other Whig candidates. White was a Whig only as Tyler was later a Whig, being an Anti-Jackson Democrat affiliated with the Whig Party.

In 1840, Lincoln fairly got into national politics. He warmly advocated the election of Harrison against the reelection of Van Buren. Harrison was elected, but Illinois went Democratic, and cast its presidential vote for Van Buren.

In 1844, Henry Clay was the candidate of the Whigs, against James Knox Polk. Lincoln was a candidate for elector. He stumped Illinois and part of Indiana. At this time he returned to his boyhood home and was pleasantly received. Lincoln fully believed that Clay would be elected. But Illinois sent nine Democratic electors to vote for James K. Polk and Polk prevailed in the nation also. Lincoln was grievously disheartened at this result. Later he lost some of his admiration for Henry Clay, but at this time Clay was his idol, and his own hope of political preferment was in the national triumph of the Whig Party.

Herndon accounted for Lincoln's marriage to Mary Todd on the ground of his political ambition. He began his second volume with an account of Lincoln's matrimonial affairs:

The year 1840 finds Mr. Lincoln entering his thirty-second year, and still unmarried. "I have come to the conclusion," he suggests in a facetious letter two years before, "never again to think of marrying." But meanwhile he had seen more of the world. The state capital had been removed to Springfield, and he soon observed the power and influence one can exert with high family and social surroundings to draw upon. The sober truth is that Lincoln was inordinately ambitious. He already had succeeded in obtaining no inconsiderable political recognition, and numbered among his party friends men of wealth and reputation; but he himself was poor, besides lacking the graces and ease of bearing obtained through mingling in polite society—in fact, to use the expressive language of Mary Owens, he was "deficient in those little links which make up the chain of a woman's happiness." Conscious, therefore, of his humble rank in the social scale, how natural that he should seek by marriage in an influential family, to establish strong connections, and at the same time foster his political fortunes! This may seem an audacious thing to insinuate, but on no other basis can we reconcile the strange course of his courtship, and the tempestuous chapters in his married life.*

It is not so easy, however, thus to account for Lincoln's courtships and matrimonial choice on the basis of any such cool and deliberate calculation. Lincoln was well aware of his own social deficiencies, and he knew well the value of such social standing as his marriage to Mary Todd would bring to him; but if he reckoned with so much of deliberation as Herndon surmises, and pursued his lady with so cold a fire, he was doomed to swift disappointment. For some reason, not wholly explained, Lincoln immediately after his marriage seems to have suffered some measure of political eclipse.

Lincoln was now married and living in the Globe Tavern, at a total expense for himself and wife of four dollars a week for room and board. This was not a large sum, but it was more than he had paid to William Butler, and Butler did not send in his bill every week. Lincoln was eager to be earning more money. His "national debt" still hung like a millstone about his neck. He had reduced it a little, but it still seemed large, and since his marriage his payments nearly ceased. He wanted to go to Congress, where he could have a larger income and be advancing in politics.

In the spring of 1843, he thought he saw his opportunity, and he entered into a fierce battle for the nomination on the Whig ticket. The candidates were Edward D. Baker, John J. Hardin and Abraham Lincoln. Lincoln encountered unexpected opposition. Baker was a member of the Church of the Disciples

---

*Herndon's *Lincoln*, ii, pp. 205-6.

of Christ, and on occasion preached, as later Garfield did. Baker was not unaware of the political value of his pulpit ministrations. The Disciples appear to have stood very solidly behind Baker.

Springfield and the region adjacent went for Baker. Lincoln's old friends in Menard, however, were true to Lincoln. The result of the primary convention in Springfield, however, sent Lincoln to the district convention as a delegate pledged to the support of Hardin. At this time he had a letter from one of his friends in Menard, asking whether, under the circumstances, they should vote for him as they had been instructed. He replied telling them to obey their instructions, as he was obeying his instructions. He also added interesting details of his own situation. He was required by his instructions and his sense of honor to vote for his rival, being thus compelled to act as best man at the wedding of his girl to another man; but he was performing his part according to the rules of the game:

It is truly gratifying to me to learn, that, while the people of Sangamon have cast me off, my old friends of Menard, who have known me longest and best, stick to me. It would astonish, if not amuse, the older citizens (a stranger, friendless, uneducated, penniless boy, working on a flat-boat at ten dollars per month) to learn that I have been put down here as the candidate of pride, wealth, and aristocratic family distinction. Yet so, chiefly, it was. There was, too, the strangest combination of church influence against me. Baker is a Campbellite; and therefore, as I suppose, with few exceptions, got that church. My wife has some relations in the Presbyterian Churches, and some with the Episcopal Churches; and therefore, wherever it would tell, I was set down as the one or the other, while it was everywhere contended that no Christian ought to vote for me, because I belonged to no church, was suspected of being a deist, and had talked about fighting a duel.

This letter shows, and we have other sources of information, that Lincoln did not spring into immediate popularity after his marriage. Indeed, when it became evident to the county convention that Lincoln was certain to be defeated, Baker came to him and proposed that Lincoln should transfer his support to

Baker against Hardin before it became evident by a direct vote how small was Lincoln's strength in the convention. This was arranged after a preliminary battle, and Lincoln accepted his election as a delegate pledged for Baker, having also Baker's promise that after Baker should have served one term he would then support Lincoln for the next term.*

So Lincoln attended the district convention, and voted for Baker; but John J. Hardin was nominated and elected.

The Whigs were now in control in Sangamon County and in the congressional district in which it was the largest political unit. There appears to have followed a kind of gentlemen's agreement between Hardin, Baker, Logan and Lincoln, all Whig aspirants for congressional honors, whereby each of them should have one term in Congress. Hardin was the first to succeed, and Lincoln was the next to follow and did so follow. Hardin kept his agreement, but when he got the office he would have been willing to be urged to hold it. Lincoln, however, wanted the place, and said in a letter dated January 7, 1846:

That Hardin is talented, energetic, unusually generous and magnanimous, I have, before this, affirmed to you, and do not now deny. You know that my only argument is that "turn about is fair play."

The time came not long afterward when Lincoln, according to his own statement, would have been quite as willing as Hardin to be urged to serve in Congress for another term. He was not urged.

All through 1845 and 1846, Lincoln was busy endeavoring to secure his own election to Congress. He easily won the Whig nomination after the withdrawal of Hardin in his favor. His opponent on the Democratic ticket was the Reverend Peter Cartwright, the celebrated Methodist preacher.

Peter Cartwright was at that time one of the outstanding

---

*I have the details of this information from Judge E. W. Baker, nephew of Senator E. D. Baker.

figures in Illinois. The son of pioneer parents, he was born in Kentucky in 1785, converted in the great revival of 1799-1802, ordained a deacon at twenty-one, an elder at twenty-three and in 1804 admitted to the Western Conference of the Methodist Church, which then embraced all the territory west of the mountains. In 1824 he moved his family to Illinois, making his home at Pleasant Plains, in Sangamon County. His circuit extended from Kaskaskia River to the northern bounds of settlement in the state, including a mission to the Pottawattomie Indians on Fox River. Through a region destitute of ferries, bridges and roads, he journeyed, preaching, exhorting, arguing, denouncing, singing and shouting. For forty-eight years he lived in Illinois. He preached nearly eighteen thousand sermons, baptized nearly fifteen thousand converts, and received into membership nearly twelve thousand communicants. He was five feet ten in stature, squarely built and in vigorous health. For two generations he was one of the most notable characters in Illinois. He was a man of heroic courage, a Jackson Democrat, a hater of slavery and of whisky. He served two terms in the Illinois Legislature, and in 1846 had his notable campaign against Abraham Lincoln for Congress.

It is related that during this campaign, Lincoln made a speech in a town where Cartwright had an appointment to preach in the evening, and that Lincoln attended the service at night, sitting in the rear of the room. At the close of the sermon, Cartwright called upon all who expected to go to Heaven to rise, and all rose except Lincoln. Then Cartwright, following the well-known evangelistic method of the period, asked all who expected to go to hell to rise. Still Lincoln remained seated. Cartwright never hesitated to be personal in his applications and appeals. He leaned across the pulpit and said, "I have asked all who expect to go to Heaven to rise, and all who expect to go to hell to rise; and now I should like to inquire, where does Mr. Lincoln expect to go?" Lincoln rose, saying that he had not expected to participate in the service otherwise than by his presence, but since

11

278 THE LIFE OF ABRAHAM LINCOLN

Mr. Cartwright insisted on knowing where he expected to go, he would answer; "I expect to go to Congress."

In his old age, Peter Cartwright suffered a great sorrow and humiliation. One of his grandsons was indicted for murder. Lincoln was counsel for the defense. The young man was acquitted.

Cartwright had defeated Lincoln in his first campaign for the Legislature; Lincoln defeated Cartwright in the race for Congress. The congressional election was held in August, 1846, but Lincoln did not take his seat until the assembling of the Thirtieth Congress in December, 1847.

In the interval between his election and his journey to Washington, Lincoln made his first recorded visit to Chicago.

So far as the author is aware, no biographer of Lincoln before the year 1921* had ever heard of the River and Harbor Convention of 1847. It is not mentioned by Herndon, by Nicolay and Hay, by Arnold, by Morse, or in Miss Tarbell's *Life of Lincoln*. But it was that which, so far as we know, first brought Lincoln to Chicago. The Chicago papers, truthful then as always, stated that this was the first visit of the Honorable A. Lincoln to the metropolis of the state.†

He was more welcome than he might have been at some earlier period in his career. In the first place he was the only Whig member of Congress from Illinois; he was just elected and had not yet taken his seat. In the second place, he was thoroughly

*In that year I delivered before the Illinois State Historical Society an address in which I called attention to the importance of this event, and in the following year Mr. James Shaw, of Aurora, treated it at length. Miss Tarbell records this meeting in her *Following the Footsteps of the Lincolns*, published in 1923, and properly credits Mr. Shaw for having called her attention to it as he was the first, also, to suggest to me its significance.

†"Abraham Lincoln, the only Whig representative to Congress from this state, we are happy to see in attendance upon the Convention. This is his first visit to the commercial emporium of the state, and we have no doubt his first visit will impress him more deeply, if possible, with the importance, and inspire a higher zeal for the great interest of River-and-Harbor improvements. We expect much from him as a representative in Congress, and we have no doubt our expectations will be more than realized, for never was reliance placed in a nobler heart and a sounder judgment. We know the banner he bears will never be soiled."—*Chicago Journal*, July 6, 1847.

committed to the policy of developing inland waters and of connecting the lakes with the rivers. It is interesting to consider what the Convention did for Abraham Lincoln. The presiding officer was Edward Bates, of Missouri. Lincoln probably did not know it at the time, but then and there he formed the impression which later made Bates a member of his Cabinet. It was there that Lincoln first heard Horace Greeley, and Greeley heard Lincoln in a short and tactful speech. Greeley did not know it, but he was forming an impression of Lincoln, which thirteen years later was to influence his judgment in accepting Lincoln, though reluctantly, as the compromise candidate who could not only defeat Seward in the Convention, but also defeat the Democratic nominee in the election following. What Lincoln came to learn of the qualities essential to unifying his own state went far toward making him capable of unifying the nation.

The attendance upon the River and Harbor Convention was not limited to residents of lake cities. There were seven delegates from Connecticut, one from Florida, two from Georgia, twelve from Iowa, two from Kentucky, two from Maine, twenty-eight from Massachusetts, forty-five from Missouri, two from New Hampshire, eight from New Jersey, twenty-seven from Pennsylvania, three from Rhode Island, one from South Carolina. There were long lists from New York, Ohio, Indiana, Illinois, Michigan and Wisconsin. These were enrolled by counties and show a wide-spread representation from all parts of these states. The convention was felt to be of vast economic interest and was by no means lacking in political importance. Theoretically it was assembled for the consideration of internal improvements; but in addition to this it was convened for the sake of opposing James K. Polk and all his political associations.

Horace Greeley wrote up the convention for the *New York Tribune,* and ever afterward advised young men to "Go West, and grow up with the country." Thurlow Weed reported it for the *Albany Journal,* and gave an interesting account of his own journey around the lakes on "the magnificient steamer *Empire."*

David Dudley Field was present to speak for the administration. He did it with shrewdness; Greeley gives the gist of his address. The convention did not treat him any too courteously, and Lincoln followed with his one speech, a tactful one, of which we have no report, but one that appears to have stood for fair play while being ardently in favor of the whole plan of internal improvements. The convention at its next session apologized to Mr. Field for the uncivil treatment he had received, but did not alter its program or change its convictions on account of this apology for bad manners.

The River and Harbor Convention of 1847 put Chicago upon the nation's map. It did more than any previous or subsequent assembly to link the fortunes of the great state of Illinois with the North and East.

It must have been a very illuminating event to Lincoln. It was probably* his first view of the Great Lakes. It was his first important reminder that, while he was elected from central Illinois, he, as the only Whig member of Congress from the state, must find his political support thereafter largely in the newer portion of the state where the Whigs were more largely in control. It must have reminded him, and he was soon to be rudely reminded again, that Chicago and northern Illinois with her, was thenceforth to be reckoned with as an important political as well as economic factor.

The Thirtieth Congress convened on December 6, 1847, with Robert C. Winthrop as speaker. A marked change had come over the complexion of the House since its last session. In the preceding Congress the Whigs had had seventy-five members and the Democrats one hundred forty-two. In this the Whigs had one hundred sixteen and the Democrats one hundred eight. Among Lincoln's colleagues from Illinois, all Democrats, were John A. McClernand, whom he knew well, and who was subse-

---

*See an address on *The Influence of Chicago upon the Career of Abraham Lincoln* delivered before the Chicago Historical Society, by William E. Barton, on Lincoln's Birthday, 1922.

quently a general in the Union Army, and John Wentworth, of Chicago. Among his fellow-members on the floor were ex-President John Quincy Adams, George Ashmun, who in 1860 presided over the convention that nominated Lincoln for president, John G. Palfrey, the historian, Andrew Johnson, Alexander H. Stephens, and a group of men who later became prominent as leaders in the Confederacy. In the Senate were Daniel Webster, John C. Calhoun, Jefferson Davis, Thomas H. Benton, Simon Cameron, Lewis Cass, John A. Dix, and other men scarcely less noted. At this time Lincoln and Alexander H. Stephens were on the same side. Stephens several years after Lincoln's death, wrote of him as he knew him in Congress:

I knew Mr. Lincoln well and intimately, and we were both ardent supporters of General Taylor for president in 1848. Mr. Lincoln, Toombs, Preston, myself and others formed the first Congressional Taylor Club, known as "The Young Indians," and organized the Taylor movement, which resulted in his nomination. Mr. Lincoln was careless as to his manners, awkward in his speech, but was possessed of a very strong, clear, vigorous mind. He always attracted and riveted the attention of the House when he spoke. His manner of speech as well as his thought was original. He had no model. He was a man of strong convictions, and what Carlyle would have called an earnest man. He abounded in anecdotes. He illustrated everything he was talking about by an anecdote, always exceedingly apt and pointed, and socially he always kept his company in a roar of laughter.

What Lincoln thought about Stephens may be inferred from the following letter to Herndon:

Washington, Feb. 2, 1848.

Dear William:

I just take up my pen to say that Mr. Stephens, of Georgia, a little, slim, pale-faced, consumptive man, with a voice like Logan's, has just concluded the very best speech of an hour's length I ever heard. My old, withered, dry eyes are full of tears yet. If he writes it out anything like he delivered it our people shall see a good many copies of it.

Yours truly,

A. Lincoln.

The allusion to the voice of Stephen T. Logan is of interest, as his thin, whining tone was a matter of mirthful comment in Springfield.

Little did either Lincoln or Stephens think how they were later to meet as the Civil War was drawing to its close when they were to engage in fruitless negotiations for peace.

Lincoln was ambitious to distinguish himself in Congress. A few days after the House met, he closed a letter to Herndon thus:

By way of experiment, and of getting the hang of the House, I made a little speech two or three days ago on a post-office question of no general interest. I find speaking here and elsewhere almost the same thing. I was about as badly scared and no more than when I speak in court.

Lincoln was on the Committee on Post-Offices and Post Roads. This gave him an excuse for his first address. On December 22, 1847, he introduced a series of resolutions which have become famous as the "Spot Resolutions." He quoted in his preamble, from President Polk's Message of May 11, 1846, in which the president charged that Mexico had invaded our territory and shed the blood of our citizens on our own soil. In these resolutions, Lincoln proposed that Congress should request the president to designate "the spot" where this invasion and bloodshed on the part of Mexico had occurred. On January 12, 1848, he called up the resolutions and made a speech upon them. It was a sensible and very clear speech, and won Lincoln immediate recognition. One paragraph in this speech was often quoted against him in the four years beginning with 1861:

Any people anywhere, being inclined and having the power, have the *right* to rise up and shake off the existing government, and form a new one that suits them better. This is a most valuable, a most sacred right,—a right which, we hope and believe, is to liberate the world. Nor is this right confined to cases in which the whole people of an existing government may choose to exercise it. Any portion of such people, that *can,* may revolutionize, and make their *own* of so much of the territory as they inhabit.

Of Lincoln's brief experience as a "Yearling" in the House of Representatives, we have a brief account by Elihu B. Washburne:*

Mr. Lincoln took his seat in Congress on the first Monday in December, 1847. I was in attendance on the Supreme Court of the United States at Washington that winter, and as he was the only member of Congress from the State who was in harmony with my own political sentiments, I saw much of him and passed a good deal of time in his room. He belonged to a mess that boarded at Mrs. Spriggs, in "Duff Green's Row" on Capitol Hill. At the first session, the mess was composed of John Blanchard, John Dickey, A. R. McIlvaine, James Pollock, John Strohm, of Pennsylvania; Elisha Embree, of Indiana; Joshua R. Giddings, of Ohio; A. Lincoln, of Illinois, and P. W. Tompkins, of Mississippi. The same members composed the mess at Mrs. Spriggs' the short session, with the exception of Judge Embree and Mr. Tompkins. Without exception, these gentlemen are all dead. He sat in the old hall of the House of Representatives, and for the long session was so unfortunate as to draw one of the most undesirable seats in the hall. He participated but little in the active business of the House, and made the personal acquaintance of but few members. He was attentive and conscientious in the discharge of his duties, and followed the course of legislation closely. When he took his seat in the House, the campaign of 1848 for president was just opening. Out of the small number of Whig members of Congress who were favorable to the nomination of General Taylor by the Whig Convention, he was one of the most ardent and outspoken.

Some of Lincoln's messmates at Mrs. Spriggs's table he was to know again in after life. James Pollock, of Pennsylvania, became in 1861, by Lincoln's appointment, director of the mint at

---

Reminiscences of Abraham Lincoln by Distinguished Men of His Times, pp. 17-18.

Philadelphia; it was he who first placed on the coinage of the United States the motto, "In God We Trust." Joshua R. Giddings was already a leader of note and it is believed with some reason that Lincoln's anti-slavery sentiments may have been strengthened by association with him during this period.

As the only Whig congressman from Illinois, Lincoln had more than what might otherwise have been his share of appointments on committees of arrangement for formal functions officially or semi-officially under authority of Congress. He was one of the official managers of the inauguration ball in honor of President Taylor. He and Stephen A. Douglas were the Illinois delegation on the committee in charge of the celebration of Washington's birthday in 1848. A pathetic postponement of this celebration occurred by reason of the impending death of John Quincy Adams, who was stricken with paralysis in the House on February twenty-first, and died two days later. The Washington's birthday celebration was postponed until March first; Lincoln was on the committee in charge of the funeral of ex-President Adams.

Those who remembered in later years the appearance of Lincoln in the House, recalled that the House Post-office was a favorite lounging-place of his, and that there, as at Mrs. Spriggs's table, his stories were highly popular.

Early in July, 1848, Lincoln attended, as a delegate from Illinois, the Whig National Convention in Philadelphia. He was an enthusiastic advocate of General Zachary Taylor, and was happy to have had a share in his nomination. Returning to Congress, he found prompt opportunity to make upon the floor a campaign speech, in favor of Taylor, and against General Cass, the Democratic candidate. It is fair to assume that he had his old constituents in mind rather than members of the House in making this speech. Its humor and sarcasm were of the general type of stump oratory in that period.

Lincoln had opposed the Mexican War, which on July 4, 1848, was officially ended by promulgation of a treaty of peace.

He had voted for supplies for the troops, but he voted against practically everything else that furthered the plans of Polk's administration.

He voted repeatedly for the Wilmot Proviso, an amendment or rider introduced by David Wilmot, from Pennsylvania, declaring that it should be a condition to the acquisition of any territory from Mexico, "that neither slavery nor involuntary servitude should ever exist in any part thereof, except for crime, whereof the party should be duly convicted." This proviso was adopted in the House but died in the Senate.

Lincoln's most important and significant act while in Congress was his introduction into the House of a bill providing for the abolition of slavery in the District of Columbia. The persons already slaves were to be gradually emancipated with compensation to their owners. No slaves were to be imported into the district, and all children born to slave parents were to be free. Lincoln did not like the Fugitive Slave Law. As he wrote to Speed, he disliked to see the poor creatures hunted down and returned to their unrequited toil. But he was a Whig and remained a Whig until the very end of that party. Not liking the Fugitive Slave Law, he believed that the South was entitled to some such protection; and in the bill which he introduced into Congress, January 10, 1849, providing for the gradual emancipation of slaves within the District of Columbia, was a section which would have enacted a fugitive slave law for that district. The previous Fugitive Slave Law had not applied in the District of Columbia. Southern people brought their slaves with them and took them away again; but a slave escaping from his master and reaching the District of Columbia could not be dragged back to slavery from under the shadow of the Capitol of the Republic. Slaves were, however, bought and sold in the District of Columbia. The fifth section of this bill, enacting a fugitive slave law for the District of Columbia, raised deep indignation on the part of the abolitionists. The bill did not become a law, and so attracted no large immediate attention. But when in 1860,

Abraham Lincoln was nominated as president of the United States, Wendell Phillips denounced Lincoln as "the slave-hound of Illinois." Had Lincoln's bill been only a bill to enable masters to recover their runaway slaves who escaped to Washington, this severe epithet might have been justified; but the fifth section was a concession aimed to assist in securing the passage of a bill whose real purpose was the restriction of slavery. Lincoln was willing to concede the operation of the Fugitive Slave Law in the District of Columbia as it held throughout the North, if thereby he could secure the final abolition of slavery in the capital of the nation. This being Lincoln's manifest intent, the fiery words of Phillips are seen to be unjust.

Mr. Arnold in summing up the record of Lincoln in the Legislature of Illinois says:

If he had died at the close of his service in the General Assembly, neither the nation nor his own state would have known much of Abraham Lincoln. He had not yet developed those great qualities, nor rendered those great services, which have since made him known throughout the world. All who closely studied his history will observe that he continued to grow and expand in intellect and character to the day of his death.*

At the close of Lincoln's single term in Congress not much could have been added to the foregoing statement. Lincoln did not feel that his experience as a member of Congress had been a brilliant one. He hoped that it was the beginning of his career in national politics. Instead, he soon came to believe that it was the end.

*Arnold, *Life of Lincoln,* p. 60.

LINCOLN completed his one term in Congress with the unhappy realization that he must not permit his name to be used
as a candidate to succeed himself, and that even if he were at
liberty to do so, he could not be reelected. He and Logan and
Hardin and Baker had agreed that the Whig nomination for
representative in Congress from the district to which Springfield belonged, should be passed around among them. There
was always, of course, a possibility that a man once in Congress
might establish such a record that the people would rise up and
demand his renomination and election. Hardin hoped that
he had done his work so creditably that the people would demand
his return. They did not demand it and Lincoln was unwilling
that they should demand it. Lincoln secured his nomination by
the withdrawal of Hardin on a general understanding which
Lincoln expressed that "turn about was fair play." When Lincoln saw his term nearing its end, he himself began to seek for
some indication that the people would demand his reelection.
In this he was disappointed. Not many people in Springfield
were interested in his support of the Wilmot Proviso, or in his
bill to abolish slavery in the District of Columbia; but many
were offended because he did not more ardently support the administration during the War with Mexico. Viewed from this
distance, Lincoln's course in these matters appears to have been
decidedly to his credit. We can say that his career in Congress,
while not brilliant, was distinctly creditable. The system whereby the office of representative in Congress was handed around,

287

was a bad system; and the period of Lincoln's service would have been a good time to break it. But Lincoln's constituents were otherwise minded, and Lincoln was a man of honor. He had made a bad bargain and he stood by it.

Mrs. Lincoln was in Washington with Lincoln during the major part of his first winter there. The taste which she had of Washington life made her very willing to consider remaining there. During the second winter she was in Springfield attending to her family cares; but she would have looked with favor upon a proposal that would have given herself and her husband a permanent home in the nation's capital.

Lincoln supported Taylor in the Philadelphia convention in 1848. He believed that Taylor could win, and he was sure that Clay could not. Taylor was "a Whig but not an ultra Whig." As a popular soldier in the Mexican War, he could count upon considerable support from those who favored the War with Mexico, while as a Whig he might expect the united support of those who had opposed the War with Mexico. He hardly recognized himself as a Whig; his party platform had to prove it. Any one could qualify as a Whig if he could defeat a Democrat.

In this, Taylor and his supporters were mistaken. James Russell Lowell in the *Biglow Papers* spoke for a large number of influential Whigs in bitter opposition to Taylor and all associated with him. In Massachusetts there was a formidable secession of Whig leaders growing out of Taylor's nomination. This was the historic Free-soil movement which at one time appeared so significant. It was led by Henry Wilson, Charles Francis Adams, Charles Sumner, Anson Burlingame, John A. Andrew, E. Rockwood Hoar, John G. Palfrey, and other men of scarcely less prominence. This secession alarmed the Whig leaders of New England. They invited certain western speakers, including Lincoln, to come to Massachusetts and deliver stump speeches in behalf of Taylor. Lincoln was happy to accept. He wanted to help elect Taylor, and he had no doubt that Taylor would reward him for his assistance.

Congress adjourned August 14, 1848. Lincoln went to New England early in September. The Whig State Convention met in Worcester, September 13, 1848. Nowhere in New England was the Free-soil secession more formidable than in Worcester. Lincoln delivered an address at the City Hall on the evening before the convention. The burden of his address was his opposition to the Free-soil Party, whose leaders, as he alleged, by their withdrawal from the Whig ticket, were helping to elect Cass. In the main, his address appears to have been tactful and cogent; but an allusion which he made to the murder of Lovejoy, with no word of condemnation for those who had committed that atrocity, was deemed by the Free-soilers to be heartless, and Lincoln was careful to omit it from his subsequent speeches. Lincoln's argument in all his New England addresses was that the nation's hope of relief from the iniquity of the Democratic Party lay in the united support of the Whig candidate; and that any votes withdrawn from the Whig Party in support of the Free-soil ticket were half votes for Cass and the Democrats. This line of argument has been employed against all attempts to create new parties and probably will continue to be employed for many generations to come.

On the morning of September fourteenth, Lincoln spoke again in Worcester, this time at an open air meeting. At the convention which was held that day, he heard, among others, a brilliant speech by Rufus Choate, and another from Robert C. Winthrop, Speaker of the House of Representatives.

Lincoln spoke in Boston, in Washington Hall on Bromfield Street, on Friday, September fifteenth. He spoke in Lowell on Saturday, September sixteenth. He delivered an address in Richmond Hall, Lower Mills, Dorchester, on Monday, September eighteenth. On Tuesday, September nineteenth, he spoke in Chelsea. On Wednesday, September twentieth, he spoke in the daytime in Temperance Hall in Dedham, and evoked so much enthusiasm that his audience was unwilling to have him leave for Cambridge, where he spoke that night. On Friday,

September twenty-second, he and William H. Seward spoke in Tremont Temple. This is said to have been the only political speech that Seward ever delivered in Boston. Seward's *Life* records that after this meeting as they sat together in their hotel, Lincoln said:

"Governor Seward, I have been thinking about what you said in your speech. I reckon you are right. We have got to deal with this slavery question and got to give much more attention to it hereafter than we have been doing."*

The Whig newspaper, *The Atlas,* gave more than a column to Seward's speech, but stated that it had no room for the notes which had been taken of Lincoln's. It described Lincoln's speech, however, as "powerful and convincing," and said that it was "cheered to the echo."

None of Lincoln's New England addresses are preserved in full. Herndon thus summarizes the impression which he made:

It is evident from all the contemporary reports that Mr. Lincoln made a marked impression on all his audiences. Their attention was drawn at once to his striking figure; they enjoyed his quaintness and humor; and they recognized his logical power and his novel way of putting things. Still, so far as his points are given in the public journals, he did not rise at any time above partisanship. And he gave no sign of the great future which awaited him as a political antagonist, a master of language, and a leader of men. But it should be noted, in connection with this estimate, that the Whig case, as put in that campaign, was chiefly one of personalities, and was limited to the qualities and career of Taylor as a soldier, and to ridicule of his opponent, General Cass. Mr. Lincoln, like other Whig speakers, labored to prove that Taylor was a Whig.

Many requests came to the Whig Committee for addresses to be delivered by Lincoln, but on the day following the Tremont Temple speech he started for his home in Illinois. On the whole,

*Seward's *Life,* ii, p. 80.

he made a good impression in New England, and he went back to Springfield with renewed conviction that Taylor would win and that Lincoln would not lose his reward.

On his way home from New England, Lincoln stopped at Niagara Falls, and continued his homeward journey by way of Lake Erie. It was on this voyage that this vessel got stranded on a sand-bar and the captain ordered the deck hands to fasten together empty barrels and force them under the water beside the boat. This was what set Lincoln's mind to work on an invention for lifting vessels over shoals by means of expansive buoyant air chambers. Lincoln obtained a patent upon this device. It is the most eagerly sought of the models in the Patent Office in Washington. So far as is known it was never employed by any vessel, but it bears interesting evidence of Lincoln's mechanical genius and his interest in navigation.

On his way back to Springfield, Lincoln stopped in Chicago, and there delivered his first campaign speech in that city. He had spoken there but once, and then briefly, at the River and Harbor Convention in July, 1847. On Friday evening, October 6, 1848, he spoke for two hours in the interests of General Taylor.

It is worth noticing that his next formal address in that city was on Thursday, July 25, 1850, when he delivered, by invitation of the Common Council, and also of a committee of influential Whigs, an address commemorative of President Taylor, who died in office July 9, 1850.*

Lincoln appears not to have realized until his return to Springfield the extent to which sentiment in his own district had changed regarding him. Lincoln wrote to Herndon in January, 1848, in an effort to discover whether his constituents were likely to rise up and demand his reelection. He said:

I made the declaration that I would not be a candidate again,

---

*This address, but recently discovered, has been published in a limited edition, with an introduction by William E. Barton. The publishers are Messrs. Houghton Mifflin Company.

more from a wish to deal fairly with others, to keep peace among our friends, and to keep the district from going to the enemy, than from any cause personal to myself; so that if it should happen that if nobody else wishes to be elected, I could not refuse the people the right of sending me again. But to enter myself as a competitor of others, or to authorize any one so to enter me, is what my word and honor forbid.

Herndon was not entirely unwilling that Lincoln should be disillusioned. He knew how a group of men, who had been for some time prominent in Whig politics, had parceled out all prospective political favors among themselves, leaving, as Herndon believed, no hope for younger men or for the party. He believed that the Whig Party was going on the rocks and he was willing to see it go. He felt strongly resentful of the attitude of the older politicians, and a little later, told Lincoln so. He said in respect to certain letters which Lincoln wrote to him, while Lincoln was still in Washington:

He was endeavoring through me to rouse up all the enthusiasm among the youth of Springfield possible under the circumstances. But I was disposed to take a dispirited view of the situation, and therefore was not easily warmed up. I felt at this time, somewhat in advance of its occurrence, the death-throes of the Whig Party. I did not conceal my suspicions, and one of the Springfield papers gave my sentiments liberal quotation in its columns. I felt gloomy over the prospect, and cut out these newspaper slips and sent them to Lincoln. Accompanying these I wrote him a letter equally melancholy in tone, in which among other things I reflected severely on the stubbornness and bad judgment of the old fossils in the party who were constantly holding the young men back.

This was the communication to which Lincoln replied in his well-known letter of July 10, 1848, in which he advised Herndon to get over his feeling of jealousy, and to depend upon his own exertions, assuring Herndon that he himself had never waited for old men to hunt him up and push him forward. Lincoln wrote as an old man, being at that time thirty-nine years old.

His associations, however, were with the older element of the Whig Party.

When he came to see that he was not going to be asked to run again, he frankly accepted the situation as one in which he was already bound by his word and honor. He made no effort to secure a renomination. He stepped aside for Judge Stephen T. Logan, who was duly nominated and defeated. The defection in the Whig Party in Lincoln's district was more serious than he thought.

Lincoln immediately began to consider what office he could secure for himself by presidential appointment. The best political plum which was likely to fall to an Illinois Whig was that of commissioner of the Land Office in Washington. Other men besides Lincoln had their eyes on this. Lincoln wrote to Speed:

I believe that, so far as the Whigs in Congress are concerned, I could have the General Land Office almost by common consent; but then Sweet and Don Morrison and Cyrus Edwards all want it, and, what is worse, while I think I could easily take it myself, I fear I should have trouble to get it for any other man in Illinois.

Lincoln found that he could not get the Land Office for any of these men, and he set himself industriously to obtain it for himself. He was correct in his judgment that he could more probably secure it for himself than for any of these applicants, and he greatly desired it. Nevertheless, he made no effort to obtain it until it became evident that none of these men could have it; either it would come to Lincoln himself or to Justin Butterfield, of Chicago.

There was more than one reason why Lincoln did not desire that Butterfield should have the position. Butterfield was a Whig who had supported the Mexican War. Butterfield represented the growing Whig interests in the northern end of the state. Whatever hope Lincoln and his friends had of retaining their prestige with the Whig administration depended upon their standing out against the ascendent interests of Chicago in Whig politics. Before Lincoln left Washington in the summer of 1848 he discovered the impossibility of securing the Land Office for Cyrus Edwards. On May 19, 1849, he wrote a letter to Judge Gillespie saying that Butterfield would be commissioner of the General Land Office unless prevented by strong and speedy efforts. He did not suggest to Gillespie who was to be recommended instead of Butterfield, but he declared that Butterfield's appointment would be a fatal blunder to the administration and to the Whigs of Illinois.

When Cyrus Edwards learned that Lincoln had applied for the position himself, he was offended, and accused Lincoln of treachery. There appears no ground for this charge; on the contrary, Lincoln appears to have been loyal to his political friends to his own disadvantage. Had he earlier inaugurated his own campaign, quite possibly he might have received the appointment. But Justin Butterfield* had personal friends in New England who had personal influence with Daniel Webster. Webster had not favored the election of Taylor, but he was too prominent a Whig to be ignored. Moreover, it was evident that the Whig Party must increasingly find its support in northern Illinois. President Taylor appointed Butterfield against Lincoln's strenuous endeavor to secure the position for himself.

Lincoln went back to Springfield and faced a constituency disgruntled by his career in Congress, and he had to meet Judge Logan, who had some reason to feel that he owed his own defeat to Lincoln's opposition to the Mexican War. He had also to meet Cyrus Edwards, who unjustly accused Lincoln of treachery. It was anything but a cheerful experience for Abraham Lincoln. Again he wrote thus to Joseph Gillespie:

---

*Justin Butterfield was born in Keene, N. H., in 1790. He studied at Williams College, and was admitted to the bar at Watertown, N. Y., in 1812. After some years of practise in New York State he removed to New Orleans, and in 1835, to Chicago. He soon attained high rank in his profession. In 1841, he was appointed by President Harrison, United States District Attorney. He was logical and resourceful and many stories are told of his quick wit. He died October 25, 1855.

Springfield, July 13, 1849.

Dear Gillespie:

Mr. Edwards is unquestionably offended with me in connection with the matter of the General Land Office. He wrote a letter against me which was filed at the Department.

The better part of one's life consists of his friendships; and, of them, mine with Mr. Edwards was one of the most cherished. I have not been false to it. At a word I could have had the office any time before the Department was committed to Mr. Butterfield—at least Mr. Ewing and the president say as much. That word I forbore to speak, partly for other reasons, but chiefly for Mr. Edwards' sake—losing the office that he might gain it. I was always for [him]; but to lose his *friendship,* by the effort for him, would oppress me very much, were I not sustained by the utmost consciousness of rectitude. I first determined to be an applicant, unconditionally, on the 2d of June; and I did so then upon being informed by a telegraphic despatch that the question was narrowed down to Mr. B. and myself, and that the Cabinet had postponed the appointment three weeks for my benefit. Not doubting that Mr. Edwards was wholly out of the question, I nevertheless, would not then have become an applicant had I supposed he would thereby be brought to suspect me of treachery to him. Two or three days afterwards a conversation with Levi Davis convinced me Mr. Edwards was dissatisfied; but I was then too far in to get out. His own letter, written on the 25th of April, after I had fully informed him of all that had passed, up to within a few days of that time, gave assurance I had that entire confidence from him which I felt my uniform and strong friendship for him entitled me to. Among other things it says: "Whatever course your judgment may dictate as proper to be pursued shall never be excepted to by me." I also had a letter from Washington, saying Chambers, of the *Republic,* had brought a rumor there, that Mr. E. had declined in my favor, which rumor I judged came from Mr. E. himself, as I had not then breathed of his letter to any living creature. In saying I had never, before the 2d of June, determined to be an applicant, *unconditionally,* I mean to admit that, before then, I had said, substantially, I would take the office rather than it should be lost to the State, or given to one in the State whom the Whigs did not want; but I aver that in every instance in which I spoke of myself I intended to keep, and now believe I did keep, Mr. E. above myself. Mr. Edwards' first suspicion was that I had allowed Baker to overreach me, as his friend, in behalf of Don Morrison. I know this was a mistake; and the result has proved it. I understand his view now is, that if I had gone to open war with Baker I could have ridden him down, and had the thing all my own way. I believe no such thing. With Baker and some strong man from the Military tract and elsewhere for Morrison, and we and some strong men from the Wabash and elsewhere for Mr. E., it was not possible for either to succeed. I believed this in March, and I *know* it now. The only thing which gave either any chance was the very thing Baker and I proposed—an adjustment with themselves.

You may wish to know how Butterfield finally beat me. I cannot tell you particulars now, but will when I see you. In the meantime, let it be understood I am not greatly dissatisfied—I wish the office had been so bestowed as to encourage our friends in future contests, and I regret exceedingly Mr. Edwards' feelings towards me. These two things away, I should have no regrets—at least I think I would not. Write me soon.

Your friend, as ever,
A. Lincoln.

Lincoln returned to Springfield disappointed, humiliated and burdened. He had lost favor with his own constituents, but being a Whig in a Whig administration he had not released himself from the responsibilities of his former position. The defeat of Judge Logan left Lincoln, though without office, responsible for the Whig patronage of his district. He was compelled to take the responsibility and blame of securing offices for other men, and could get nothing that he wanted for himself. The high standing to which he should have been entitled as the only Whig representative from Illinois in the preceding Congress, and as one who had labored effectively to secure Taylor's nomination and election, had not come to him. He was rocked in the trough of the political sea. The Whigs at Springfield blamed him for Judge Logan's defeat, and the administration at Washington gave him no credit for Taylor's victory. His law practise had suffered by his absence. There was only one bright star in his sky. He had lived economically in Washington, and saved up money enough to pay the balance of the debt which he had incurred in New Salem. It had taken him fifteen years to establish himself in business and remove this burdensome obligation. It had been in part a debt of honor and he had honorably discharged it. Whatever his mistakes in the Legislature and in Congress, he had not profited financially by any of the various opportunities which political life had offered to him. By hard toil and painful economy he had paid his debt. Having done this, he was compelled to begin life over again.

The new administration was not totally oblivious of its obligation to Abraham Lincoln. Though President Taylor did not see fit to offer him the Land Office in Washington, his successor, President Fillmore, did offer him the governorship of Oregon. Lincoln was sorely tempted to accept. He anticipated little joy in Springfield. There was much that was irksome to him in the practise of law. He did not care much to be governor of the territory, but he reflected that before long Oregon would be a state, and that the territorial governor would stand a chance of being one of the first senators.

Mrs. Lincoln vetoed this proposition. She had no intention of going to live in Oregon. If she could not live in Washington, Springfield was the next best thing. Her home was there, and her friends were there, and she had more faith than Lincoln had just then in his political future.

In considering Lincoln's political position in 1849, we are impressed by his caution and conservatism. He was not an abolitionist; he was not even a Free-soiler. He had not yet risen to the high vision of his subsequent statesmanship. In his several efforts to limit the power of slavery, notably by his support of the Wilmot Proviso, and his bill for the elimination of slavery in the District of Columbia, he manifested the faith that was surely in him, but he did not carry his convictions beyond the restricted limits of their logical requirement. He did not belong to the more progressive element of the Whig Party. He had

seen Clay defeated in 1844, and he advocated the nomination and
election of Taylor, chiefly because he believed that Taylor was
the Whig candidate who would most certainly be elected.   He
wrote almost exultantly concerning the prospects for the election
of "Old Rough and Ready" because Taylor would gather in
large numbers of the disaffected.   He said:

In my opinion we shall have a most overwhelming triumph.
One unmistakable sign is that all the odds and ends are with us
—Barn-burners, Native Americans, Tyler men, disappointed of-
fice-seeking locofocos, and the Lord knows what not.   Taylor's
nomination takes the locos on the blind side.   It turns the war
thunder against them.   The war is now to them the gallows of
Haman, which they built for us and on which they are doomed
to be hanged themselves.

Lincoln was correct in his prediction concerning the election
of Taylor, but entirely mistaken in supposing that the Whig
Party was to be permanently stronger by the accretion of these
odds and ends.   Not only in Massachusetts, but in his own district, was the Whig Party disintegrated by the loss of some of
its most valuable strength.

It is interesting to recall that Lincoln gained no marked political advantage from his visit to Massachusetts.   The Whig leaders whom he met on that journey did not become his permanent
friends or political supporters.   George Lunt, who presided at
Tremont Temple when Lincoln and Seward gave their addresses
there, was to the end of his life a pro-slavery conservative.   Honorable Benjamin F. Thomas met Lincoln at the Worcester
Convention, and spoke on the same platform at the open air
meeting, but as a member of Congress in the early part of the
Civil War he was obstructive of the president's policy.   Honorable Rufus Choate, whose acquaintance Lincoln formed in New
England, died in 1859, "but judged by his latest utterances, his
marvelous eloquence would have been no patriotic inspiration if
he had outlived the national struggle."   Honorable Robert C.
Winthrop, whom Lincoln had met on the platform in New Eng-

land, presided over the House of Representatives during Lincoln's first term, voted against Lincoln in 1860 and again in 1864. On the other hand, the Free-soilers whom Lincoln went to Massachusetts to discredit, became to a man his supporters. Charles Sumner and Henry Wilson and Charles Francis Adams and John A. Andrew and Anson Burlingame and Charles A. Dana and John G. Palfrey in 1848 were all on the stump against Taylor when Lincoln was speaking for him, but they became during the Civil War Lincoln's stalwart supporters.

We can not help asking, and we need not attempt to answer, whether it would have been better if Lincoln in 1847 had entirely abandoned the Whig Party and gone with the Free-soilers? Would it have been better if he could have discerned that the defeat of Clay in 1844 was really the doom of the Whig Party and of all schemes of compromise? Would he have been a braver, more capable leader, if at that time he had joined the ranks of the ardent young Free-soilers who were demanding release from the footless series of makeshifts which for years had prevented the Whigs from accomplishing their mission?

Abraham Lincoln retired from politics before the Whig Party met its final and utter doom. Wearily and sadly he went back to Springfield, and took up again the practise of law.

CHAPTER XXI

LINCOLN's partnership with Colonel Stuart was dissolved when Stuart became a member of Congress. The partnership with Judge Logan was dissolved because both he and Lincoln desired to be elected to Congress, and Logan, who was an older man of established reputation, did not look with favor upon the aspirations of his junior partner. On the same day on which the firm of Logan and Lincoln dissolved, the firm of Lincoln and Herndon was established in a partnership between Abraham Lincoln and William H. Herndon. This partnership was never dissolved but continued until the death of Lincoln.

During Lincoln's partnership with Stuart, that gentleman was looking after his own political interests, and left Lincoln largely in charge of the office. During Lincoln's short partnership with Judge Logan, Lincoln was forced, against his inclination, to pay attention to the details of legal practise, for Judge Logan was a successful lawyer, and accurate in the drawing of all legal documents.

In each of these two offices Lincoln as the younger man was the one more readily available to send out upon unimportant cases in other county-seats. Lincoln liked this work much better than he liked office work, and continued it during his partnership with Herndon. A part of the time Herndon accompanied him on his travels; but Lincoln established a method of becoming associate counsel with some local lawyer in almost every county-seat in the judicial district, and this obviated the necessity of taking his associate with him, reduced expense of travel, and kept his partner in the office.

These local associations are often spoken of as partnerships; they were not technically so. Lincoln had but three partners, as heretofore indicated. But he had a number of more or less permanent associations, some of them continuing for a number of years and making him a *quasi* member of several different firms. Usually his local associate was a younger lawyer, who found it an advantage to be able to offer the service of Lincoln with his own, and so to increase the number of his clients and his hope of winning his cases.

Milton Hay, who was a law-student when Lincoln was in practise in Springfield, and who at times shared Lincoln's bed, says of the legal practise of those days:

In forming our ideas of Lincoln's growth and development as a lawyer, we must remember that in those early days litigation was very simple as compared with that of modern times. Population was sparse and society scarcely organized, land was plentiful and employment abundant. There was an utter absence of the abstruse questions and complications which now beset the law. There was no need of that close and searching study into principles and precedents which keeps the modern law-student buried in his office. On the contrary, the very character of this simple litigation drew the lawyer into the street and neighborhood, and into close and active intercourse with all classes of his fellow-men. The suits consisted of actions of tort and assumpsit. If a man had an uncollectible debt, the current phrase was, "I'll take it out of his hide." This would bring on an action for assault and battery. The free comments of the neighbors on the fracas or the character of the parties would be productive of slander suits. A man would for his convenience lay down an irascible neighbor's fence, and indolently forget to put it up again, and an action of trespass would grow out of it. The suit would lead to a free fight, and sometimes furnish the bloody incidents for a murder trial.

Occupied with this class of business, the half-legal, half-political lawyers were never found plodding in their offices. In that case they would have waited long for the recognition of their talents or a demand for their services.   Out of this characteristic of the times also grew the street discussions I have adverted to.   There was scarcely a day or hour when a knot of men might not have been seen near the door of some prominent store, or about the steps of the court-house, eagerly discussing a current political topic—not as a question of news, for news was not then received quickly or frequently, as it is now, but rather for the sake of debate; and the men from the country, the pioneers ,and farmers, always gathered eagerly about these groups and listened with open-mouthed interest, and frequently manifested their approval or dissent in strong words, and carried away to their neighbors a report of the debaters' wit and skill.   It was in these street talks that the rising and aspiring young lawyer found his daily and hourly forum.   Often by good luck or prudence he had the field entirely to himself, and so escaped the dangers and discouragements of a decisive conflict with a trained antagonist.

During his term in Congress Lincoln continued as Herndon's partner, but his connection with the firm of Lincoln and Herndon had become merely nominal.   Springfield was still his home, but Lincoln hoped that he was never to return to live in Springfield.   One of the great disappointments of his life rose up and smote him when he went back to his dingy office.   Law offices at the time were seldom orderly places, and that of Lincoln was regarded by other lawyers as the very most disorderly of them all.   A new law student, who once undertook to put things in order, found upon the table a package of congressional garden seeds which had begun to sprout amid the accumulated litter.

Grant Goodrich, a Chicago lawyer, proposed in 1849 to take Lincoln into partnership, and suggested Lincoln's removal to that city.   Lincoln declined the offer, giving as a reason that he tended to consumption, and if he moved to Chicago would have to address himself more diligently to office work than was good for him.   He preferred a more general practise, and one that took him out upon the circuit.

Law practise in Lincoln's day was not specialized.   Each

ABRAHAM LINCOLN
Photograph by Alexander H. Hessler

lawyer took whatever cases came to him. Criminal law, civil practise and equity cases were all included in the routine of every office. The people of central Illinois were litigious, but most of the practise was petty. There were lawsuits over line fences and the sale of livestock; there were criminal prosecutions for assault, and occasional trials for murder or arson. There were no personal-injury cases, but there was much prosecution for slander. Lincoln took his share in whatever cases came. Now and then he refused a case where he strongly believed that justice was on the other side. In a few instances where he felt that right lay wholly with the other party, he left the conduct of the case entirely to his partner. But in the main, Lincoln took whatever practise walked into his office or was secured by his local associate.

Herndon thus describes the return of Lincoln to practise, with some account of the change which at this time came over Lincoln:

While a member of Congress and otherwise immersed in politics Lincoln seemed to lose all interest in the law. Of course, what practise he controlled had passed into other hands. I retained all the business I could, and worked steadily on until, when he returned, our practise was as extensive as that of any other firm at the bar. Lincoln realized that much of this was due to my efforts, and on his return he therefore suggested that he had no right to share in the business and profits which I had made. I responded that as he had aided me and given 'me prominence when I was young and needed it, I could afford now to be grateful if not generous. I therefore recommended a continuation of the partnership, and we went on as before. I could notice a difference in Lincoln's movement as a lawyer from that time forward. He had begun to realize a certain lack of discipline— a want of mental training and method. Ten years had wrought some change in the law, and more in the lawyers, of Illinois. The conviction had settled in the minds of the people that the pyrotechnics of court room and stump oratory did not necessarily imply extensive or profound ability in the lawyer who resorted to it. The courts were becoming graver and more learned, and the lawyer was learning that as a preliminary and indispensible condition to success he must be a close reasoner, besides having at command a broad knowledge of the principles on which the statutory law is constructed.   There was of course the same riding on circuit as before, but the courts had improved in tone and morals, and there was less laxity—at least it appeared so to Lincoln.   Political defeat had wrought a marked effect on him. It went below the skin and made a changed man of him.   He was not soured at his seeming political decline, but still he determined to eschew politics from that time forward and devote himself entirely to the law.   And now he began to make up for time lost in politics by studying law in earnest.   No man had greater powers of application than he.   Once fixing his mind on any subject, nothing could interfere or disturb him.   Frequently I would go out on the circuit with him.   We, usually, at the little country inns, occupied the same bed.   In most cases the beds were too short for him, and his feet would extend over the foot-board, thus exposing a limited expanse of shin bone.   Placing a candle on a chair at the head of the bed, he would read and study for hours.   I have known him to study in this position till two o'clock in the morning.   Meanwhile, I and others who chanced to occupy the same room would be safely and soundly asleep.   On the circuit in this way he studied Euclid until he could with ease demonstrate all the propositions in the six books. How he could maintain his mental equilibrium or concentrate his thoughts on an abstract mathematical proposition while Davis, Logan, Swett, Edwards and I so industriously and volubly filled the air with our interminable snoring was a problem none of us could ever solve.   I was on the circuit with Lincoln probably one-fourth of the time.   The remainder of my time was spent in Springfield looking after the business there, but I know that life on the circuit was a gay one.   It was rich with incidents, and afforded the nomadic lawyers ample relaxation from all irksome toil that fell to their lot.   Lincoln loved it.   I suppose it would be a fair estimate to state that he spent over half the year following Judges Treat and Davis around on the circuit.   On Saturdays the court and attorneys, if within reasonable distance, would usually start for their homes.   Some went for a fresh supply of clothing, but the greater number went simply to spend a day of rest with their families.   The only exception was Lincoln, who usually spent his Sundays with the loungers at the country tavern, and only went home at the end of the circuit or term of court.*

In this fashion Lincoln spent somewhat more than half his time from 1849 until 1860. The taverns were crude enough. In general they were two-story buildings with only a few large rooms. The lawyers were placed two in a bed, and most of the rooms had at least two beds. The food was abundant, but badly cooked. Lincoln was as nearly immune to the discomforts of tavern life as any of his associates. He never seemed to notice whether the food was good or poor, or whether the beds were clean or soiled. None of the beds were long enough for him, and he did not expect that they would be. He accepted the situation, and made the most of it without much conscious discomfort.

Lincoln once attempted some study of algebra, and his textbook on that subject is in the Library of the Chicago Historical Society. Inside the back cover are memoranda which he made in pencil, perhaps for use in an address to young lawyers, or instructions to a law-student: They are mere catch-words:

Your Honor—When in court—Face the Court
(Study) Be prepared to the full extent of the case tried.
Never contradict the court—
    if so be sure you have the law without doubt
    on your side—
Be on time when court is ready to call your case.
Converse with client—consent of court.
Have client appear neat as possible in front of court.

Whatever the purpose for which Lincoln designed these notes, their meagerness is apparent.

He traveled with Judge Davis from one county-seat to another, and if the judge had a bed to himself in the tavern it was not chiefly because his judicial dignity entitled him to it, but be-

---

*Life of Lincoln, i, pp. 307-309.

cause his great bulk left but little room in the bed for a companion. In some of the taverns there was a room with a single
bed for Judge Davis and a double bed occupied by Lincoln and
some other lawyer. Into the judge's room in the evening were
gathered nearly all the members of the bar and the choice spirits
of the local county-seat, and they sat up late at night swapping
stories, Lincoln being the acknowledged leader in the art of
story-telling.

Some of the lawyers rode on horseback from one county-
seat to another. Lincoln more frequently drove his own horse
hitched to a buggy. He almost invariably had a brother lawyer in the seat with him. Sometimes, however, he depended
upon the stage-coach, especially for reaching the more remote
county-seats.

Only a part of his free time did Lincoln give to story-telling.
He was always inclined to meditation, and the habit grew upon
him. He usually rose earlier in the morning than his associates,
and sometimes sat before the fire moodily meditating, and at
other times reading in desultory fashion a volume which he had
brought with him. Herndon, who was with him perhaps a
fourth of the time, says:

During the six years following his retirement from Congress,
Lincoln, realizing in a marked degree his want of literary knowledge, extended somewhat his research in that direction. He was
naturally indisposed to undertake anything that savored of exertion, but his brief public career had exposed the limited area
of his literary attainments. Along with his Euclid, therefore, he
carried a well worn copy of Shakespeare.

Lincoln had always had an ear for poetry, though not for
music. He committed stanzas of poetry, and sometimes entire
poems, including Poe's *Raven* and other compositions generally
of a mournful nature. In New Salem he had learned the poem,
"Oh, why should the spirit of mortal be proud?" He may have
learned this from Ann Rutledge, though her sister did not know

it, and could not remember that Ann knew it. It was Lincoln's favorite, and he often asked and probably never learned who was its author.*

Of the new vigor which Lincoln brought to the practise of the law in 1849, there can be no doubt. In his autobiographical sketch written for Jesse W. Fell he says:

In 1846 I was once elected to the lower House of Congress. Was not a candidate for reelection. From 1849 to 1854, both inclusive, practised law more assiduously than ever before.

In his short autobiography written for Scripps, in June, 1860, he says, speaking throughout of himself in the third person:

Upon his return from Congress he went to the practise of law with greater earnestness than ever before.

The Eighth Judicial District comprised thirteen counties.† There was one judge for the entire circuit. Honorable David Davis presided over this court during nearly the whole period of Lincoln's life as a lawyer after his return from Congress and until his inauguration as president. Lincoln had a growing practise outside this district, but the greater number of his cases were in these thirteen counties.

Lincoln's law cases were not all jury trials. He appeared as counsel in the Supreme Court of Illinois in one hundred seventy-five cases—a record equaled by very few lawyers in the history of the state. The greater number of these cases occurred after his return from Congress. In addition he appeared in two cases before the Supreme Court of the United States, to which he was admitted to practise March 7, 1849.

Before the Supreme Court of Illinois, he appeared alone as counsel in fifty-one cases, and thirty-one were decided in his

---

*The author was William Knox, an English poet. Lincoln and those who learned the poem from him called it "Immortality"—a most inappropriate title; the real title, given it by Knox, was "Mortality."

†For a description of the Eighth Judicial Circuit, see the Appendix.

12

favor. Of the whole number of cases in which he was associate counsel, one hundred twenty-four, the parties in whose behalf he appeared were successful in sixty-five. It would appear that Lincoln did not advise his clients to appeal to the Supreme Court unless there was a strong possibility of success; and that his own judgment in that matter averaged better than the judgment of attorneys with whom from time to time he was associated. Altogether the record is highly to his credit. Out of the whole number of cases, one hundred seventy-five, in which he appeared before the Supreme Court of Illinois, either alone or as associate counsel, he was successful in ninety-six.*

As Lincoln's fame grew, it was associated as attorney in a number of important cases, several of which have become notable. In 1855 occurred his suit as attorney for the Illinois Central Railroad. For this he received the large fee of five thousand dollars, one-half of which went to his partner, Herndon. There has been much dispute about this case. Herndon tells the story in a way that makes the action of the railroad a very ungenerous one and it is certain that Lincoln had to sue the company to secure this fee. The railroad company, however, gives a somewhat different version of the affair. The fee was large, and it was felt that some other authority than the attorney's demand for it should be given the officials of the company before they paid it. A friendly suit was therefore entered, and when Lincoln won, the company paid the amount promptly and cheerfully. This account of the affair might seem to lack probability were it not for the fact that the relations between the company and Lincoln appear to have remained friendly, and he acted as attorney for the Illinois Central Railroad afterward. It is often stated that the lawyer opposed to Lincoln in this case was George B. McClellan. This is not true. McClellan was out of the country at the time. It is true, however, that Lincoln's employment as attorney with the Illinois Central gave him his first acquaintance with McClellan.

---

*Abraham Lincoln—the Lawyer-Statesman, by John T. Richards, pp. 64-70; Lincoln, the Litigant, by William H. Townsend.

Another case is notable for its bringing Lincoln into contact with a man who afterward sustained important relations to Lincoln. This was the well-known Reaper case which was tried in Cincinnati in September, 1855. Lincoln was junior counsel in this case, his associates being George Harding, of Philadelphia, and Edwin M. Stanton. Stanton was unfavorably impressed by Lincoln's appearance, and did not permit Lincoln to make one of the arguments in the case. Lincoln was deeply hurt by Stanton's incivility.

Lincoln's legal business brought him to Chicago occasionally, and there he practised in the District Court of the United States. The Chicago fire in 1871 destroyed the records of all these cases. Only two of them are known. The first of these was the case of *Hurd vs. the Rock Island Railroad Bridge.* It is popularly known as the *"Effie Afton* case." The *Effie Afton* was a steamboat owned in St. Louis. She ran against one of the piers of the Rock Island Railroad Bridge and took fire. The bridge was damaged and the boat was wholly destroyed. The case was considered of great importance, because St. Louis depended for its hope of growth on the commerce of the Mississippi River, and Chicago depended on her railroads and the lakes. It was popularly charged in Chicago that the St. Louis Board of Trade had bribed the steamboat captain to steer his boat against the pier of the bridge. Lincoln appeared for the Railroad Company. His argument is not on record, but it is remembered that he based his claim for the railroad upon the simple proposition that "one man has as good a right to cross the stream as another man had to navigate it."

The other case was that of *Johnson vs. Jones,* and was tried in the United States District Court in Chicago in April, 1860. But little more than a month later Lincoln was nominated to the presidency. This was his last appearance in the city of Chicago before his nomination. The case involved the ownership of certain lands north of the mouth of the Chicago River, formed by

---

*Reported in *McLean's U. S. Reports,* vi, p. 539.

accretion from the lake. It is popularly known as "the Sandbar Case." It had been in litigation for some years before Lincoln became connected with the case, and it subsequently went to the Supreme Court of the United States. Lincoln's connection with it, however, ceased with the trial in Chicago in April, 1860. This trial occupied several days. It was on the occasion of this visit that the Volk life-mask of Lincoln was made. Volk was a cousin by marriage of Stephen A. Douglas, and had already made a bust of Douglas. Lincoln's fame as an opponent of Douglas caused the sculptor to propose that Lincoln should sit for a life-mask. The undertaking was a complete success, and the result is a most perfect record of the living features of Abraham Lincoln.

While Lincoln was not notably a criminal lawyer, his practise was diversified, covering the whole range of civil and criminal law and equity and he appeared as attorney in not a few criminal cases. Most noted of these is the Armstrong case, which was tried in Beardstown, Illinois, May 7, 1858. This case has attained a prominence greater than it deserves, on account of Lincoln's personal relation to the parents of the defendant and a question which has risen concerning Lincoln's ethics in defense of a criminal. The trial arose out of the murder of a man named James Preston Metzker, which occurred near a camp-meeting at Virgin's Grove in Mason County, on Saturday night, August 29, 1857. It was illegal to sell liquor within one mile of a camp-meeting. A bar was established about a mile from the meeting, and a number of rough young men drank heavily. Among those drinking were Preston Metzker, James H. Norris and William Armstrong, popularly known as Duff. Duff Armstrong was the son of Jack Armstrong of the Clary Grove gang. A fight occurred between ten and eleven o'clock on the Saturday night in question, and Metzker was badly beaten by Norris and Armstrong. He rode away to his home, falling from his horse once or more, and on his arrival at home went to bed, having sustained severe injury. Three days later he died.

Both Norris and Armstrong were arrested, charged with the murder of Metzker. Norris already had killed a man named Thornburg, at Havana, about a year before, but had been acquitted on the ground of self-defense. He was tried for the murder of Metzker, was found guilty of manslaughter, and sentenced to the penitentiary for ten years. He served eight years, and then was pardoned by Governor Richard Yates.

The local attorneys for Armstrong secured for him a change of venue, which delayed the trial and caused it to be held in Beardstown some months later. Jack Armstrong, William Armstrong's father, died, and was buried in Concord Cemetery, where Ann Rutledge was first buried. His interment occurred on the very day of his son's arrest. His widow, "Aunt Hannah," drove to Springfield and besought Lincoln to come to Beardstown and defend her son. Lincoln promised to do so, and on the night before the trial he arrived in Beardstown.

The trial of Norris had disclosed the evidence of the prosecution. The local attorneys had doubtless informed Lincoln of its general character. The principal witness for the prosecution was Charles Allen. He had sworn in the trial of Norris that by the aid of the brightly shining moon he had seen the fatal blow inflicted by Armstrong with a slung-shot. Metzker, as the post mortem showed, had two wounds in the head, one in the back of the brain alleged to have been produced by Norris using the neck-yoke of a wagon, and the other in front, said to have been caused by a blow from Armstrong with the slung-shot. Either one of these blows, it was alleged, was sufficient to have caused the death of Metzker.* In the defense of Norris attempt had

---

*A reasonably full outline of the evidence in this case is on file in Springfield in the office of the governor. It was submitted July 10, 1863, by William W. Allen, who had been one of the attorneys for Norris. This evidence with all the documents accompanying was unearthed for me by Honorable Frank O. Lowden, at that time governor of Illinois. I was particularly desirous of learning whether in the appeal for a pardon for Norris it was alleged that Armstrong was really the guilty man. No such affirmation was made in the papers on file in Springfield. Rather, it was assumed that both men were falsely accused. The fight was not denied, but it was denied that Allen could have been a witness to the killing or either of the

been made to prove that Allen could not have witnessed the killing, as he was declared by certain witnesses to have been in another part of the grounds at that time; but no one in the first
trial appears to have challenged the moonlight. Lincoln, however, produced an almanac showing that on the night in question
the moon did not give sufficient light at the time the murder
took place.

When Edward Eggleston published his story, *The Graysons,*
he caused the issue of the trial to hinge upon this question of the
position of the moon. He also represented the case of the crime
as having occurred while Lincoln was still a young and obscure
lawyer. Eggleston wrote this story while he was in Europe, and
he took pains to state that he did not attempt to follow accurately
the historic detail. The prominence which he gave to the almanac centered upon that pamphlet an attention far greater than
it had received in the trial.

It has often been declared that Lincoln produced an almanac
showing that there was no moon on the night of the murder. If
such an almanac was produced, it was not a genuine almanac
for the year and date in question. Professor Edwin B. Frost,
of the Yerkes Observatory of the University of Chicago, Professor Joel Stebbins, Director of the Observatory of the University of Illinois, and Professor W. S. Eichelberger, of the United
States Naval Observatory at Washington, have separately computed the position of the moon on the night in question and
agree that it set in Cass County, Illinois, on Saturday night,
August 29, 1857, at five minutes after midnight, that is, at five
minutes after the beginning of Sunday.*

An almanac is in existence which claims to be the one which
Lincoln used. It is an almanac ingeniously made over from one

---

two men accused struck the fatal blow. The Armstrong evidence is not reviewed in the plea to the governor. But the evidence against Norris shows
the essential character of the charge against Armstrong.

*I acknowledge the courtesy of these distinguished astronomers in mak-
ing this computation for me. The point assumed by them was the center of
Cass County and they all agreed precisely in their answer to my question.

of the year 1853.* If that almanac was the one really used, a fraud was perpetrated upon the court.

I have examined this almanac with great care, and compared the stories about its preparation. These stories for the most part agree that Lincoln himself, aided by some local penman, prepared the almanac on the night before the trial. It could not have been so prepared, nor does any story account for it as it is. I do not believe, however, that Abraham Lincoln used this fraudulent almanac. The reasons are these:

1. No fraud was necessary. The truth was all that Lincoln needed. There was a moon on the night in question, but it was too low down and too dim to have permitted Allen to see what he declared that he saw.

2. Lincoln could not have afforded such a fraud. He was at that time not an obscure lawyer in whom the ruse if discovered would have been pardoned as a clever trick, but was, next to Stephen A. Douglas, the most prominent man in Illinois politics. He had come within measurable distance of being chosen as his party's candidate for vice-president in 1856, was

---

*This almanac was in the Gunther collection. Mr. Gunther was an enthusiastic but not always a discriminating collector. His collection was sold to the Chicago Historical Society, which does not, however, profess any confidence in its genuineness. Gunther paid fifty dollars for it, and received with it a certificate from the man who sold the books of J. Henry Shaw, that this almanac was among those books. I have a signed statement from Mr. T. L. Mathews, formerly of Beardstown, but now of Fremont, Nebraska, a banker and a man of standing in that town, concerning the man who furnished this almanac:

"I knew him very well. He was not considered a very amicable man. He was a bitter Democrat, and was said to have been a member of the 'Knights of the Golden Circle.' He was arrested for disloyalty during the war, and taken to Jacksonville, and held there in custody for some time. Many years later, he produced this almanac, professing to have discovered it among the effects of J. Henry Shaw. I consider his claim without foundation. After Shaw died, his books and papers were placed in my charge, and I had an inventory made of them, and employed this man, who was an auctioneer, to sell them at public vendue. If he found such an almanac, he did not inform me, and retained it without my knowledge and without right to do so. When I read in the papers, some years after the sale, the story of the alleged discovery, I went to see him, and asked him to show me the almanac. In a hesitating way he answered that he had found the almanac, and had sold it to some person in New York, but could not give me the purchaser's name."

certain to be a candidate for senator, and was already mentioned as a candidate for the presidency in 1860.

Lincoln was not given to careful preparation of his criminal cases. He took them as they came, and depended far more upon his ability to influence a jury with the story of the kindness of Duff Armstrong's parents to him, when a poor boy, than he did upon astronomical evidence. Lincoln was well known in Beardstown. He spoke there against Douglas in the following year, not on the same day, for Beardstown was not one of the seven appointed places for joint debate, but on the day following the speech of Douglas. His returning to Beardstown for this trial was something of an event, for Lincoln was now at the head of the Illinois bar, and had been associated more or less intimately with Beardstown ever since his coming to Illinois.

Abraham Lincoln was a man of extreme caution. He was not reasonably, but unreasonably cautious. If he had been a man bad enough to perpetrate the fraud described, he had far too much at stake; and he did not need to do it. He knew how to make an appeal to a Beardstown jury that would clear Duff Armstrong, and he did it.

3. The fraud, if Lincoln had attempted it, would certainly have been discovered. The evidence had emphasized the fact that the murder occurred on Saturday night, the twenty-ninth of August, 1857. In the 1853 almanac, which was alleged to have been used, it was plainly shown that the twenty-ninth of August occurred on Monday. No juror looking down the column to find the figures "29" could have failed to note that the day shown in the next column was not Saturday but Monday. Neither the judge nor the opposing counsel would have permitted so palpable a fraud to have gone to the jury. Fourteen men at the very least inspected the almanac, the judge, the prosecuting attorney and the jury. It is barely possible that some one man out of the fourteen might have been stupid enough to be imposed upon, but certainly not the whole fourteen.

4. The almanac shown is one issued by the American Tract

Society. Several persons who were present at the trial have told me that Lincoln sent out to the drug store and obtained a patent medicine almanac which he used.* Lincoln knew that the moonlight would enter into the case, and doubtless had consulted the almanac and knew what it would show, and at the proper time he sent Jacob Jones, a cousin of Armstrong, across the corner to the drug store. Jones brought back the almanac, and Lincoln found the place, passed it to the judge, who gave it to the opposing counsel and it was then handed to the jury.

I am devoting more space to this incident than it deserves, because I have been told by so many and such respectable people about this fraud, which Lincoln is alleged to have perpetrated, that I have gone to unusual lengths to ascertain the facts. I do not wish to leave in the mind of the reader any doubt as to my own conviction of the matter. I think I have followed this question to the limit of possibility of learning further truth concerning it, and I believe that the almanac used by Lincoln was one obtained from the local drug store, and that it showed that there was a moon, but too low and dim to have enabled Allen to see what he declared that he had seen.

I regret to state that since I made my last examination of this almanac, in 1922, it has disappeared from the library of the Chicago Historical Society. At the present writing it is not known whether, being a small item, in an envelope, which came in with the Gunther Collection, it has been mislaid in the mass of that material, or whether it has been stolen. I do not think that those who profess to have examined this almanac gave it very careful attention, for their published accounts are not accurate; and I am glad to have examined it minutely, at different times, and with use of a microscope.

---

*The almanac which local tradition declares to have been used was *Ayer's American Almanac*. The general manager of the Ayer's Company informs me that their firm has always understood that their almanac was so employed and has sent me photographs of the title page and the page for August for 1857 made from the only copy of the almanac which the firm has. These photographs show plainly that the almanac as then issued showed the time of the sunrise and sunset and also the phases of the moon and time of its setting. That almanac, therefore, would have served his purpose.

I am able to state definitely that this almanac could not possibly have been produced in the hasty manner described by those who have undertaken to account for it. The changes required the use both of pen and type, and skill in the use of both. My own judgment is that it was made to sell.

The trial of Duff Armstrong attracted little attention at the time. In Springfield, all that was said was that Mr. Lincoln was out of town, trying a case in Beardstown. In Beardstown there was interest in his coming, but not much in the trial; the case had been brought over from another county, and no one in Beardstown was particularly concerned with it. Lincoln had no occasion to give the case more than usual attention. The trial of Norris had made him aware just what evidence would be introduced, and Lincoln knew its weak points. One man was in jail already for the murder, and popular demand for justice was fairly well satisfied.

That Lincoln was sure of securing an acquittal was shown on the night of his arrival in Beardstown, for the relatives of Duff came to him and told him that Allen, the principal witness against Armstrong, was not at all anxious to testify; that they had slipped him out of town; that he was staying in the hotel at Virginia, and the prosecution would fail without him. Lincoln insisted that they drive over to Virginia and produce Allen and have him in court in the morning. Lincoln knew that Allen would be compelled to say what he had said at the trial of Norris, but that he would not add to the story to the needless harm of Armstrong.

The trial was not nearly so dramatic as has been represented. The almanac was a mere incident. The real feature of the trial, and one that brought tears to the eyes of the jury, was Lincoln's story of how he came, a poor boy, to the home of Duff's father and mother, and how good they had been to him.

The prosecuting attorney, J. Henry Shaw, remembered what it was that impressed the jury:

He told the jury of his once being a poor, friendless boy; that Armstrong's parents took him into their home, fed and clothed him and gave him a home. There were tears in his eyes as he spoke. The sight of his tall, quivering frame, and the particulars of the story he so pathetically told, moved the jury to tears, and they forgot the guilt of the defendant in their admiration of the advocate. It was the most touching scene I ever witnessed.*

The prosecuting attorney believed Armstrong guilty, but he knew that his evidence was of little value against such a story. The almanac was chiefly useful as throwing additional doubt on the question whether Allen could have seen as much as he professed to see. Lincoln would have won easily without the almanac, but the almanac helped. And its use was legitimate.

5. Abraham Lincoln was too honest a man to have perpetrated a fraud of this character. In all the years of his practise no similar case is charged against him. His whole career at the bar proves him to have been morally incapable of such a deception.

Lincoln's argument sought first to break down the testimony of Allen by showing that he was not near enough to have seen what he professed to see, and that it was not light enough for him to have witnessed what he described so accurately. Lincoln's instructions to the jury which the judge accepted and which are preserved in his handwriting show plainly that he did not rely upon the moon incident, but endeavored to shift the blame upon Norris, who already had been convicted and was serving his sentence. Lincoln's strongest plea, however, was his narration of the kindness of Jack and Hannah Armstrong in the days when he was poor and friendless. Lincoln by this time was a great man. Every one knew that he had come to Beardstown to plead for this young man because of his own gratitude to Armstrong's father and mother. Lincoln knew that that kind of plea meant more to the jury than any display of almanac.

---

*J. Henry Shaw, Letter to Herndon, August 22, 1866.

Armstrong was acquitted, as every one in Beardstown was willing he should be; and that night Lincoln delivered a political speech, which was listened to with interest by judge, jurors and the parties to the trial. For Beardstown had known Lincoln since his flat-boating days, and he had now become famous, and was the predestined rival of Stephen A. Douglas, whom also Beardstown hoped soon to hear.

It should be said in conclusion that William Armstrong gave up drink and became a good citizen.* He and three of his brothers served in the Union Army. Armstrong became rather prominent as a member and an officer in the Disciples' Church. He maintained to the end of his life that he did not strike Metzker with anything harder than his fist. The jury appears to have had no doubt of the soundness of Lincoln's plea. Lincoln seldom had an easier legal victory.

---

*William or Duff Armstrong himself told the story of the trial to J. McCann Davis in 1896. I have a signed statement prepared for me by Armstrong's brother John and a detailed statement by Honorable Thomas P. Reep, of Petersburg, a prominent attorney and a nephew by marriage of Jack Armstrong. I also have interviewed many people present at the trial or resident in the neighborhood at the time or in the years immediately succeeding. Duff Armstrong's life subsequent to the trial was respectable, and his good conduct did much to temper the judgment even of those who believed that Lincoln, as a reward for Hannah Armstrong's kindness to him when he was a poor boy, had cleared a guilty man. I am quoting the substance of his own statement in the Appendix.

CHAPTER XXII

HOME LIFE IN SPRINGFIELD
1842-1860

AFTER their marriage Lincoln and his wife established themselves in the Globe Tavern, which was situated about two hundred yards southwest of the old state-house. Arnold, in his *Life of Lincoln,* testifies that it was a very comfortable hotel.

After the birth of Robert, August 1, 1843, the Lincolns were esteemed less desirable boarders than they had previously been. Robert cried and annoyed some of the other boarders, and Mrs. Lincoln found the situation inconvenient. In the autumn the family moved to a small house at 214 South Fourth Street, where the Argus Hotel now stands. There they lived in a small rented cottage until the purchase of their permanent home.

In 1844 Mr. Lincoln purchased from Reverend Charles Dresser* a house at that time a story and a half in height, and which Mrs. Lincoln, during one of Lincoln's absences on the circuit, raised to be two stories high. This was their home until he left Springfield to be inaugurated president of the United States.

The yard was bare. Lincoln was no gardener. One year only he cultivated a garden, then gave it up. He planted no shade or fruit trees, no vines or shrubbery, except a few roses, and these died of neglect. His wife's sister, Mrs. Wallace, tried to remove the nakedness of the house by planting a few flowers, but these were uncared for and perished.

---

*Reverend Charles Dresser was the Episcopal minister who married Abraham Lincoln to Mary Todd. The contract for the sale of the house, dated January 16, 1844, is in Lincoln's handwriting. The consideration was $1,200. The deed is dated May 2, 1844. The house, still standing, and the property of the state of Illinois, was then in the outskirts of Springfield.

Lincoln had a horse and cow. He curried and fed his own horse, and milked his own cow. He did the family marketing, carrying a basket on one arm and leading one of his boys with the other hand. The boy chatted, and sometimes Lincoln heard, and sometimes he was deep in his own thoughts.

Lincoln habitually dressed in black, wearing a frock coat and tall hat, neither of them any too well brushed. In winter he wore a gray shawl around his shoulders. This was not uncommon in his day.* He made the daily purchases at the market, walked home with his basket of meat and groceries, and then made his way to his office.

While Springfield's custom as to the dress of men as prominent as Lincoln called for the long coat and the tall hat, and that apparel was a mark of dignity and almost of gentility, it did not require that the owner of the coat should brush it before putting it on, much less that he should brush or blacken his boots. Lincoln was his own bootblack, and is known to have continued so to be while in the White House. "In England, Mr. Lincoln, no gentleman blacks his own boots," is said to have been the surprised remark of an Englishman of rank as he came upon Mr. Lincoln in the act of applying blacking to his own pedal covertures. "Whose boots does he black?" inquired Lincoln as he spat on his brush. It is to be hoped that when he got to the White House he used the brush more frequently than in Springfield. In summer, the long black coat, which was Lincoln's habitual dress, gave place to one of bombazine, not any too well fitted, and sometimes to a linen duster, that was not always immaculately clean. His straw hat is said to have cost twenty-five cents, and to have been just about worth the price.

Lincoln never formed the habit of shaving himself, but pat-

_____

*My own father, physician and druggist in Illinois, wore a shawl as Lincoln did. He had an overcoat, a very heavy one, as I remember it, but this he rarely wore. In all but the most extremely cold weather, if he needed a wrap, he wore his gray shawl. There was a certain art in the wearing of those shawls, and they did not lack dignity. In the days of my travel in the Kentucky mountains, I sometimes carried a "saddle-shawl" of this character. When not in use, it was more conveniently carried than a coat.

ABRAHAM LINCOLN'S SPRINGFIELD HOME
Photograph by Eugene J. Hall

ronized a barber. His son Robert declares that Abraham Lincoln never owned a razor.

Lincoln during nearly the whole of his residence in Springfield wore no beard; but not till he reached the White House did he shave daily. There a colored barber took him in hand, and cared for him every morning; in Springfield two or at most three shaves a week, with an extra one for an important social event, were all that custom required.

Lincoln spent most of his day at his office, and his evening with companions at the store or state-house. But his habits about the house are well defined. He was not quite at home in his own house. His favorite position was lying on the floor, with a chair tilted so as to give a slanting support to his back. There he would lie and read. The habit he had learned in the "blab school" never left him; and it was not easy for him to read or write silently. He read aloud; and when he wrote, he spoke the words as he slowly wrote them, weighing each one as he uttered and recorded it. Lying on the floor, coatless, and with hair awry, he sometimes answered a knock at the door, much to the displeasure of Mrs. Lincoln. She had a maid, and wanted her callers to know that the maid was properly aware of her duties. But Lincoln, if he was lying on the floor of the living-room, would rise, welcome the callers, and excuse himself while he went back to "trot out" Mrs. Lincoln.

Mrs. Lincoln had, indeed, a maid, many maids. She did not find it easy to keep help. She wrote to her Kentucky sisters, congratulating them that they, at least, could keep their help, while she had to wrestle with the "wild Irish." The wild Irish in Mrs. Lincoln's kitchen lost little of their wildness.

Lincoln and his wife were both of a generous nature, but their home was one of somewhat restricted hospitality. Mrs. Lincoln had the problem of limited resources, and in addition the long and frequent absences of her husband, and his lack of social graces. Lincoln was not wholly wrong when he wrote to Mary Owens that if she married him she would see other people enjoying wealth, and be unable to share it.

I have heard it said in Springfield, "Lincoln never felt free to invite a guest to his home; his poverty and Mrs. Lincoln's inability to keep help prevented any hospitality." But this is not true. I find in Senator Browning's *Diary* many such entries as these:

Springfield, Monday, [1852 January]
At night delivered a lecture in 3rd Presbyterian church for the benefit of the poor. After the lecture went to Mr. Lincoln's to supper.

Thursday July 22 [1852]
After tea Mrs B & self called at Mr. Ridgleys, Mr. Edwards, & spent the evening at Lincolns

Thursday Feby 5 [1857]
......At night attended large & pleasant party at Lincolns.

Wednesday Feby 2, 1859.
......At large party at Lincoln's at night.

Thursday June 9, [1859]
......Went to a party at Lincolns at night.

The Lincolns did less entertaining than some of their more prosperous neighbors, but they did their share.

When there was company at the Lincoln home, Mrs. Lincoln had her trials. She was never sure that her husband would use the butter-knife, and not reach for butter with his own knife. He tried to please her, but if he got interested in telling stories, he sometimes forgot and reverted to his early habits. There was no separate knife for the butter in the home of Nancy Hanks, and probably none in the Rutledge tavern, nor was there always one in the "City Hotel" at the county-seat where Lincoln attended court.

Still, Lincoln acquired some measure of what may truly be called culture. One who knew him well said that whatever Mr. Lincoln lacked of social grace was made up by his kindness of heart; he was so inherently kind that he could not help being a gentleman.

I have witnessed with genuine satisfaction, and more than once, a play entitled *Abraham Lincoln* written by a talented Englishman, John Drinkwater. It is wrong in all its details and right in its essential message. It opens with a scene in Lincoln's home in Springfield just before the arrival of the committee sent down from the Chicago Convention to inform Lincoln of his nomination. That scene depicts a small group of Lincoln's neighbors, sitting in Mrs. Lincoln's parlor, smoking and talking about Lincoln. They refer to him as "Abraham." They use that name in speaking to Mrs. Lincoln, when she enters and finds them smoking before her open fire. But in Lincoln's parlor there was no open fire. The parlor had been modernized with a hot-air stove. Those men would never have thought of smoking in that parlor or any other; they might have chewed tobacco and spat into the open fire. if there had been one, but they would not have smoked. And they would not have called Mr. Lincoln "Abraham" to his wife. Nor would she have called him "Abraham" to them. She would have spoken of him as "Mr. Lincoln."

Springfield had its social laws and requirements. Mary Todd was a born aristocrat, and her marriage to a man socially her inferior did not demote her socially. Her husband was not of prominent family as she was, but he was an increasingly popular politician, and from the beginning he stood well in the capital city of Illinois. The social set in which they both moved prior to their marriage was the best in Springfield, and that is saying much; and during their married life they maintained their position.

Springfield was a town with a fashionable life of its own; and Lincoln and his wife were not outside the fashionable group. Lincoln's little eccentricities did not make him unwelcome in even the best homes in Springfield; indeed, he had a kind of adaptation which made him feel at home even when he did not know all the details of what might be required of him socially.

The Lincoln's had visiting cards. Those of Mrs. Lincoln were neat and of the proper size and style; Lincoln's were written, and neatly written; and that, also, was good form. He did not make many social calls with her, but she left his card with her own, and it was a proper card.

While Mr. Lincoln in his personal appearance and attire was not all that a vain and society-loving woman might have desired, he and Mrs. Lincoln had their full share in the best social life of Springfield, and she had far more frequent occasion to be pleased with him than to be ashamed of him. Indeed, she was inordinately proud of him; nor did she ever see any other man whose social graces made sufficient compensation for Lincoln's more important qualifications to cause her to regret having married him. And Lincoln was proud of his plump little wife, and was happy when his increasing prosperity enabled her to dress as became her station. Not that she ever had dressed shabbily; Mary Todd always made a good appearance in society; but there came a time when Lincoln could afford to provide her money to buy for herself some things which he could not have afforded when they were first married.

They had as much social life as she cared for, and perhaps rather more than Lincoln cared for, and it was of the best.

Springfield was not without intellectual stimulus in those days. It was the period of the Lyceum lecture; and this gave Springfield and the Lincolns contact with the larger interests of the time.

Ralph Waldo Emerson used to lecture in Springfield on his western trips; and distinguished men from different parts of the nation came thither and talked on a multitude of topics, educational, philanthropic and entertaining.

The time of Lincoln's return from Washington was a time of importance in his family life and in the life of the country. He came back to Springfield with his debts paid. From that time on, the family had a little more freedom in matters financial.

It was the time of discovery of gold in California; and that event was giving to America a new frontier on the Pacific coast, and compelling vast changes looking toward its future development.

It was a time of significance in the world. It was the time when Cavour and Victor Immanuel were coming to the front, as well as Louis Napoleon and Bismarck. In England it was a time of labor agitation, of Chartism, of effort to lift the intolerable burdens of child labor and the dehumanization of woman under the weight of grinding toil. It was the period of Christian Socialism, with Kingsley and Maurice and Ruskin and Carlyle writing and preaching their reforms.

In America it was the dawn of the golden age in literature, with Emerson and Lowell and Longfellow and Bryant and Whittier and Poe and Hawthorne and Irving and Prescott and Motley and Bancroft and Parkman dipping their pens deep into the warm life of the time; while Britain had its Wordsworth and Coleridge, its Tennyson, Macaulay, Thackeray, Dickens, George Eliot, Bulwer and the Brownings.

It was a time when men were interested in making the world better. There was real hope of universal peace. There was new vigor in the temperance movement. There was new interest in the welfare of prisoners and the insane. Boards of education and of health were organized. It was an age of steam, just coming to its own; an age of invention and discovery. Springfield was not too remote from the course of the world's progress to feel the effect of all of these developments.

It was a period of new life for women. Beside the rugged pioneer had journeyed a "gaunt and sad-faced woman, sitting on the front seat of the wagon, following her lord where he might lead, her face hidden in the same ragged sunbonnet which had crossed the Appalachians." That woman had been succeeded by another, to whom life was not so strenuous; she had a home with several rooms, one of them, shut up most of the time except for funerals, a parlor with a store carpet and horse-hair furniture. She had a silk dress, and a bonnet very unlike the old sunbonnet; and in time she discarded half of her white petticoats and wore hoop-skirts.

About 1851, there came a period of dress reform. Women

were no longer to submit to the restrictions of their prescribed dress. Mrs. Amelia Bloomer taught them the new freedom. The period of sex-emancipation had come, and women were no longer to be "street-sweepers." Not only in Springfield and Chicago, but in Bloomington and Aurora and as far south as Cairo there was evidence of the new day for woman.

What matter that we know now that the wave of reform receded, and that hoop-skirts and bustles and trails and all the other follies came back, as they will come back again? Those days of which we are writing were great days for women as well as for men; and Springfield felt its share in the movements of the time.

But Springfield was conservative. It had to set a standard for less favored communities. It was not a city set on a hill, but it could not be hid; and to it the tribes went up, to court, to the Legislature, and to great political conventions, which were then becoming popular; though conservative men like Lincoln did not like them.

Children came to Abraham and Mary Lincoln with becoming regularity. They had no daughters, but four sons. Robert Todd Lincoln was born August 1, 1843, and is living as this book is written; Edward Baker Lincoln was born March 10, 1846, and died in Springfield February 1, 1850; William Wallace Lincoln was born December 21, 1850, and died in the White House, February 20, 1862; and Thomas, or "Tad" Lincoln was born April 4, 1853, and died in Chicago, July 15, 1871. The care of these children restricted Mrs. Lincoln's social activities. She was not a model mother; she was too nervous, too impetuous; her chidings and her caresses depended too much upon her own moods. In time of sickness, she was too anxious and too excitable to be a good nurse. But she loved her children passionately.

She was a good housekeeper, but she did not get on well with her help. Her own correspondence tells this, and gives her long list of reasons why her "hired girls" were unsatisfactory;

the neighbors gave some reasons why Mrs. Lincoln was not always satisfactory to the hired girls.*

As for Lincoln, he was not easily disturbed by the hired girl or by the misdemeanors of the children or by the changing moods of his wife. Little annoyances did not greatly irritate him, and he bore the larger ones, for the most part, philosophically.

In their early years of married life, Mrs. Lincoln was a member of the Episcopal Church, and when she attended, attended there. Lincoln rarely went with her. A sermon interested him, but not a liturgy.

But an important change in the family's habit came in 1850. Little Edward died, and Mr. Dresser was out of town. The family called in Reverend James Smith, pastor of the First Presbyterian Church, who conducted the funeral service. He became a warm friend of the Lincoln family. Mrs. Lincoln joined the Presbyterian Church, and Lincoln took a pew, and paid his pew-rent regularly till his departure for Washington. He became a somewhat regular attendant, and his views of Christian truth were definitely modified by his contact with Doctor Smith.† Doctor Smith declared that Lincoln's views of doctrine were changed by the reading of Doctor Smith's book, *The Christian's Defense*, and by conferences with Doctor Smith, and Lincoln did not deny that this was the case. Lincoln never united with any church, but his attitude toward Christian doctrine underwent a marked change under the instruction of James Smith.

---

*Mrs. Harriet Chapman, daughter of Dennis Hanks, who spent some months in the Lincoln home, told partly in words and partly in discreet silence the story of her trials. See Weik, *The Real Lincoln*, p. 55.

†This subject is fully treated in my book, *The Soul of Abraham Lincoln*.

CHAPTER XXIII

LINCOLN AND SLAVERY
1848-1854

ABRAHAM LINCOLN kept rather well out of politics from 1849 to 1854. In 1852 he made a few political speeches in favor of General Scott who was running for president on the Whig ticket. Lincoln was one of the Whig nominees for presidential elector, but he had no great enthusiasm for the cause, and no clear conviction that his work was of any value. In the sketch which he furnished to Scripps he said of himself:

In 1852 he was upon the Scott electoral ticket, and did something in the way of canvassing, but owing to the hopelessness of the cause in Illinois, he did less than in previous presidential campaigns.

While Lincoln was keeping out of politics, slavery was getting deeper into politics.

John C. Calhoun died in 1850. Henry Clay and Daniel Webster both died in 1852. Thus simultaneously passed from the stage the men of the great triumvirate who so long had held the political leadership of the country. The foremost men in the Democratic Party now were Stephen A. Douglas, of Illinois, and Jefferson Davis, of Mississippi. Among the Whigs, Alexander H. Stephens, of Georgia, still held the South, but there was lack of a great national leader as well as of a clear conviction of issue. Daniel Webster had died in 1852, but his political death occurred when he delivered his seventh of March speech in 1850, defending the Compromise, a part of which was the

Fugitive Slave Law. California, one of the first fruits of the Mexican War, had entered the Union as a free state September 9, 1850. The slavery issue was destined to be the rock on which the nation was to split.

The Mexican War was waged by a Democratic president, but both its leading generals, Scott and Taylor, were Whigs. The Whig Party had won the election of 1848 by nominating one of the heroes of the Mexican War, Zachary Taylor, who was popularly known as "Old Rough and Ready." He acknowledged himself to be a Whig, "but not an ultra-Whig." President Taylor died in office, July 9, 1850.* The Whig Party thought it had learned how to win an election, and put up as his successor, in 1852, the other famous Mexican War hero, General Winfield Scott, whom the soldiers called "Old Fuss and Feathers." The Free-soil Party was again in the field, this time with John P. Hale, of New Hampshire, as its candidate. The Free-soilers polled an ominously smaller vote than they had registered four years previously. The Whigs carried only four states, two northern and two southern, Massachusetts, Vermont, Tennessee and Kentucky. The Democrats carried the country overwhelmingly in the election of Franklin Pierce. It seemed as though the slavery issue had been side-tracked, if not permanently removed from American politics.

In that year, 1850, Harriet Beecher Stowe published *Uncle Tom's Cabin*. Within twelve months from the day of its publication, three hundred thousand copies had been sold.

What did Abraham Lincoln think about the various efforts to create a new party based on the slavery issue? The answer is that Lincoln did not sympathize with any of these attempts. He was a very conservative Whig. In 1844, he opposed the Liberty

*Both Whig presidents, Harrison and Taylor, died soon after their inauguration. It was freely charged that both were murdered in order to throw the government into the hands of the vice-presidents alleged to have been in secret sympathy with the opposition. See, for instance, *History of the Plots and Crimes of the Great Conspiracy to Overthrow Liberty in America*, by John Smith Dye—New York, 1866.

Party, which was organized in that year with James G. Birney as its candidate. He charged that party with responsibility for the defeat of Henry Clay. In 1848, he opposed the Free-soilers in New England and elsewhere, and again was strongly opposed to them in Illinois in 1852. His letter to Williamson and Madison Durley, of Hennepin, Illinois, written October 3, 1845, sets forth his view upon the slavery question as it belonged to politics at this time:

When I saw you at home it was agreed that I should write to you and your brother Madison. Until I then saw you I was not aware of your being what is generally called an abolitionist, or, as you call yourself, a Liberty man, though I well knew there were many such in your county.

I was glad to hear that you intended to attempt to bring about, at the next election in Putnam, a union of the Whigs proper and such of the Liberty men as are Whigs in principle on all questions save only that of slavery. So far as I can perceive, by such union neither party need yield anything on *the* point in difference between them. If the Whig abolitionists of New York had voted with us last fall, Mr. Clay would now be president, Whig principles in the ascendant, and Texas not annexed; whereas, by the division, all that either had at stake in the contest was lost. And, indeed, it was extremely probable, beforehand, that such would be the result. As I always understood, the Liberty men deprecated the annexation of Texas extremely; and this being so, why they should refuse to cast their votes [so] as to prevent it, even to me seemed wonderful. What was their process of reasoning, I can only judge from what a single one of them told me. It was this: "We are not to do *evil* that *good* may come." This general proposition is doubtless correct; but did it apply? If by your votes you could have prevented the *extension*, etc., of slavery, would it not have been *good,* and not *evil,* so to have used your votes, even though it involved the casting of them for a slave-holder? By the *fruit* the tree is to be known. An *evil* tree can not bring forth *good* fruit. If the fruit of electing Mr. Clay would have been to prevent the extension of slavery, could the act of electing have been evil?

But I will not argue further. I perhaps ought to say that individually I was never much interested in the Texas question. I never could see much good to come of annexation, inasmuch as they were already a free republican people on our own model. On the other hand, I never could very clearly see how the annexation would augment the evil of slavery. It always seemed to me that slaves would be taken there in about equal numbers, with or without annexation. And if more *were* taken because of annexation still there would be just so many the fewer left where they were taken from. It is possibly true, to some extent, that, with annexation, some slaves may be sent to Texas and continued in slavery that otherwise might have been liberated. To whatever extent this may be true, I think annexation an evil. I hold it to be a paramount duty of us in the free States, due to the Union of the States, and perhaps to liberty itself (paradox though it may seem), to let the slavery of the other States alone; while, on the other hand, I hold it to be equally clear that we should never knowingly lend ourselves, directly or indirectly, to prevent that slavery from dying a natural death—to find new places for it to live in, when it can no longer exist in the old. Of course I am not now considering what would be our duty in cases of insurrection among the slaves. To recur to the Texas question, I understand the Liberty men to have viewed annexation as a much greater evil than ever I did; and I would like to convince you, if I could, that they could have prevented it, without violation of principle, if they had chosen.

I intend this letter for you and Madison together; and if you and he or either shall think fit to drop me a line, I shall be pleased.

Yours with respect,

A. Lincoln.

When Lincoln delivered his State Fair speech in reply to Douglas, in October, 1854, he had a narrow escape from being committed in advance to the policy of abolition. Among those who heard him was Owen Lovejoy, who felt that a new champion had risen for the abolition cause. As soon as Lincoln had finished his speech in the House of Representatives, Lovejoy moved forward, and announced that there would be a meeting of all the friends of freedom, in that place in the evening. Herndon, who was a radical abolitionist, has told the story of Lincoln's action following that announcement:

Among those who mingled in the crowd and listened to them was Owen Lovejoy, a radical, fiery, brave, fanatical man, it may be, but one full of the virus of Abolitionism. I had been thoroughly inoculated with the latter myself, and so had many others, who helped to swell the throng. The Nebraska movement had kindled anew the old zeal, and inspired us with renewed confidence to begin the crusade. As many of us as could assembled together to organize for the campaign before us. As soon, therefore, as Lincoln finished his speech in the hall of the House of Representatives, Lovejoy, moving forward from the crowd, announced a meeting in the same place that evening of all the friends of freedom. That, of course, meant the Abolitionists with whom I had been in conference all the day. Their plan had been to induce Mr. Lincoln to speak for them at their meeting. Strong as I was in the faith, yet I doubted the propriety of Lincoln's taking any stand yet. As I viewed it, he was ambitious to climb to the United States Senate, and on grounds of policy it would not do for him to occupy at that time such advanced ground as we were taking. On the other hand, it was equally as dangerous to refuse a speech for the Abolitionists. I did not know how he felt on the subject, but on learning that Lovejoy intended to approach him with an invitation, I hunted up Lincoln and urged him to avoid meeting the enthusiastic champion of Abolitionism. "Go home at once," I said. "Take Bob with you and drive somewhere into the country and stay until this thing is over." Whether my admonition and reasoning moved him or not I do not know, but it only remains to state that under the pretense of having business in Tazewell County he drove out of town in his buggy, and did not return until the apostles of Abolitionism had separated and gone to their homes. I have always believed that this little arrangement —it would dignify it too much to call it a plan—saved Lincoln. If he had endorsed the resolutions passed at that meeting, or spoken simply in favor of freedom that night, he would have been identified with all the rancor and extremes of Abolitionism. If, on the contrary, he had been invited to join them, and then had refused to take a position as advanced as theirs, he would have lost their support.*

There was real danger to Lincoln's career of his being identi-

---

*Herndon's *Lincoln,* ii, pp. 40-41.

fied, at this state of his experience, with the extreme positions of abolitionism. Four years later, in the first debate between Lincoln and Douglas, the latter accused Lincoln of having participated in that abolition meeting, and quoted against him the resolutions alleged to have been adopted that night. Lincoln was glad to be able to reply that not only were the resolutions which had been furnished to Douglas as those of that meeting not the ones which the meeting actually adopted, but that Lincoln himself was not present at the meeting. Due to Herndon's advice or his own caution, he had a convincing alibi; he was present at the meeting in Representatives' Hall in the morning, but in the afternoon he left Springfield on important business in another county-seat, and was not in town when the abolitionists held their meeting.

Even the murder of Lovejoy did not draw from Lincoln the swift and indignant condemnation which might have been expected. Lincoln was as much opposed to radical abolitionism as he was to slavery; and Lincoln did not sympathize with Lovejoy's persistent refusal to cease an agitation whose inevitable result he felt to be mob violence.

Lincoln refused to identify himself with the Free-soil movement as a national political party, but in 1855 he joined an association of that name which was organized in Illinois on behalf of freedom in Kansas. In those meetings the abolitionists took the more prominent part. Lincoln spoke at one of the meetings. He opposed radical demonstrations, declaring that forcible defiance of the laws of Kansas would be criminal, and would jeopardize the cause of freedom there. He did not sympathize with John Brown. He, however, joined the Kansas Free-soil movement and contributed to the fund.

Soon after the election of Trumbull to the Senate, Lincoln went with Herndon to the governor of Illinois to intercede on behalf of a free negro, who hired out as a laborer in some capacity on a Mississippi steamboat, and was seized in Louisiana and held in prison in New Orleans. The mother of this young man lived in Springfield, and came to Lincoln and Herndon to prevent her son being sold into slavery to defray the expense of his arrest and imprisonment. The governor of Illinois examined the law and decided that he had no right to interfere. The governor of Indiana was appealed to with like result. Lincoln and Herndon came again to the Illinois governor, Garner, and as he still found no legal way of interfering, Lincoln drew up a subscription list which Herndon circulated, and procured money enough with which to procure the young man's liberty. They sent the money to a friend in New Orleans, and in due time the young man was restored to his overjoyed mother. This incident is significant chiefly as showing the resolution to which Lincoln was coming with regard to slavery. At the close of his second interview with the governor he rose from his chair, hat in hand, and exclaimed with emphasis:

"Garner, I'll make the ground in this country too hot for the foot of a slave!"

About this time Lincoln wrote to his friend Speed in Kentucky under date of August 24, 1855, as follows:

I confess I hate to see the poor creatures hunted down and caught and carried back to their unrequited toil; but I bite my lips and keep quiet. In 1841, you and I had a rather tedious low-water trip on the steamboat from Louisville to St. Louis.* You may remember, as well as I do, that from Louisville to the mouth of the Ohio, there were on board ten or a dozen slaves shackled together with irons. That sight was a continual torment to me; and I see something like it every time I touch the Ohio or any slave border. It is not fair for you to assume that I have no interest in a thing which has, and continually exerts, the power of making me miserable. You ought rather to appreciate how much the great body of the Northern people do crucify their feelings in order to maintain their loyalty to the Con-

---

*It is noteworthy that in Lincoln's letter to Miss Mary Speed, written shortly after the event, Lincoln refers to these same enchained negroes as happy and even joyous. But if the slaves did not suffer, Lincoln suffered; and the more he considered the matter the more it was "a continual torment" to him.

stitution and the Union. I do oppose the extension of slavery, because my judgment and feeling so prompt me; and I am under no obligations to the contrary. If for this you and I must differ, differ we must.

Abraham Lincoln had never remembered the time when he did not believe slavery to be wrong. From the time that he saw slaves chained and sold in the New Orleans market, he had felt some measure of moral accountability for a system which prevailed in his country and which his conscience condemned. His protest and that of Dan Stone in the Illinois Legislature on March 3, 1837, professed the belief of the signers "that the institution of slavery is founded both on injustice and bad policy." While this protest also declared that the dissemination of abolition doctrines increased rather than decreased the evil, it was nevertheless an outspoken declaration against an otherwise proslavery utterance of the Legislature.

Lincoln's opposition to slavery did not prevent his accepting a fee from a slave-holder, any more than his opposition to murder kept him from accepting a fee from a murderer. In the Matson Slave Trial in Charleston, in 1847, Lincoln represented a slave-holder in an effort to send a mother and her children back into slavery. All was grist that came to the mill of the practising lawyer in those days, and Lincoln seldom declined a case. It is quite certain that William H. Seward or Salmon P. Chase would have declined this one, and it is good to know that Lincoln lost it.

One of Lincoln's important cases was one that caused him to study those aspects of slavery which were legal and constitutional. In Tazewell County, Illinois, lived one Nathan Cromwell, who had in his service a negro girl named Nance. Cromwell sold the girl to a neighbor named Bailey, the purchase being conditional upon the delivery of papers proving that Cromwell had legal right to sell the woman under the laws of the state. These papers Cromwell failed to produce, and before the money was paid, Cromwell died. His heirs sued Bailey for the purchase price of the negress. Bailey employed Lincoln as his attor-

ney. On the first trial, in September, 1839, the case was decided against Bailey. Lincoln appealed, and the case was tried
before the Supreme Court of the State of Illinois. It was one of
Lincoln's first appearances before the Supreme Court, and he
made more than his usual preparation for the trial. Under the
Ordinance of 1787, slavery was prohibited in Illinois; but public
sentiment in southern and central Illinois was essentially that of
Kentucky and Missouri. Slavery in those states existed in its
mildest form, and did not greatly outrage the conscience of good
people. Though prohibited by law in Illinois, it was permitted
by public sentiment, and continued under the form of indenture.
Lincoln came to the clear conviction that this was both illegal
and unrighteous. Later, in his Peoria speech, he traced the attitude of the government toward slavery in the Declaration of Independence, and in the Ordinance of 1787. He said:

Thus with the author of the Declaration of Independence, the
policy of prohibiting slavery in the new territory originated.
Thus, away back of the Constitution, in the pure, fresh, free
breath of the Revolution, the State of Virginia and the National
Congress put that policy into practice. Thus, through sixty odd
of the best years of the republic did that policy steadily work to
its great and beneficent end. And thus in those five states, Ohio,
Indiana, Illinois, Michigan and Wisconsin, with its five millions
of free, enterprising people, we have before us the rich fruits of
this policy. . . .
Slavery is founded in the selfishness of man's nature, opposition to it in his love of justice. These principles are in eternal
antagonism; and when wrought into collision so fiercely as slavery extension brings them, shocks and throes and convulsions
must ceaselessly follow. Repeal the Missouri Compromise—repeal all compromise—repeal the Declaration of Independence—
repeal all past history, you still cannot repeal human nature. It
still will be out of the abundance of man's heart that he will declare slavery is wrong; and out of the abundance of his mouth
he will continue to speak.

There was a time when Abraham Lincoln would not have felt
warranted in making affirmations so uncompromising as these.

There was a time when, holding as he did to the inherent immorality of slavery, he also believed in the compromises of Henry Clay, and in the efforts of the Whig Party to deal with the slavery issue by palliative methods. But the time came when Lincoln was compelled to contemplate the career of Henry Clay with grave misgivings as to that statesman's adequate vision. Doctor Holland says that Lincoln made a visit to Henry Clay and was disillusioned. No other authority has been found for that visit,* but we know that Lincoln's ardor for Clay measurably cooled. On July 16, 1852, Lincoln delivered in Springfield a funeral oration on the great Kentuckian. He praised Clay for framing the Missouri Compromise by which, in 1820, Missouri was admitted to the Union as a slave state, with the provision that beyond the western boundary of Missouri there should be no slavery north of 36° 30′. In this eulogy on Clay, Lincoln quoted from an address of Clay in 1827, in which slavery was spoken of as a detestable crime and as the product of fraud and violence. Then Mr. Lincoln said:

Pharaoh's country was cursed with plagues, and his hosts were lost in the Red Sea, for striving to retain a captive people who had already served them for more than four hundred years. May like disasters never befall us.

In 1808, one year before the birth of Lincoln, the slave trade ceased by constitutional limitation. If slavery itself could have gone out with the importation of slaves, the history of Lincoln and our nation had been quite otherwise. It was not so, and in 1820 came the Missouri Compromise. For thirty-four years that Compromise stood; but thirty-four years is a long time, and slavery had been gaining ground. The Louisiana Purchase had brought in material for a number of new slave states, and the Mexican War had brought in others. California had, indeed,

---

*The visit, however, is not inherently improbable. Mr. and Mrs. Lincoln visited her relatives in Lexington, and Lincoln would have been likely to call upon Clay.

13

entered the Union as a free state, but that was not the fault of the slave-holding element in Congress, or even of the then occupant of the White House.

The removal of the Capitol of the United States from New York and Philadelphia to a small district taken from and bounded by the two slave states of Maryland and Virginia did much to strengthen slavery socially and politically. In 1854, the Kansas-Nebraska Bill repealed the Missouri Compromise, started Kansas to bleeding, set John Brown's soul and body marching in the path that led to the gallows, and called Abraham Lincoln back into politics.

CHAPTER XXIV

THE REPEAL OF THE MISSOURI COMPROMISE
1854

THE year 1854 opened with no indication that it would recall Abraham Lincoln to political life. Franklin Pierce on March fourth preceding had begun his administration with a profound conviction that no serious and disturbing issue was likely to arise in his administration. His chief opponents, the Whigs, had carried only four states, and the Free-soil Party, which in 1848 had polled nearly 300,000 votes for Martin Van Buren, had been able in 1852 to muster only about half that number for John P. Hale. The new compromise of 1850, which included the Fugitive Slave Law, seemed likely to settle the most disturbing aspects of the slavery question. But the calm was that which preceded the storm. If, on the first day of January, 1854, Mrs. Lincoln's New Year's callers congratulated her upon the fact that her husband was making better progress in the law than he had ever made in politics, and if Lincoln shared her satisfaction, that feeling had but three days of grace before it was to encounter a rude shock.

On January 4, 1854, Senator Stephen A. Douglas reported from the Committee on Territories, of which committee he was chairman, a bill to organize the territory of Nebraska, embracing all the country west of the state of Missouri and north of 36° 30′ north latitude. The bill further provided that said territory or any portion of it, when admitted as a state or states, should be received into the Union with or without slavery, as the people of that territory, by the constitution of their own adoption, might prescribe at the time of their admission.

Three days later Douglas inserted a further provision that all questions pertaining to slavery in the territories and in the new states to be formed therefrom, should be left to be determined by the people residing therein.

Twelve days after the Nebraska Bill was first reported, Senator Dickson, of Kentucky, offered an amendment repealing the Missouri Compromise outright. Douglas at first objected to and then accepted this amendment. A few days later he brought in a new bill, dividing the new territory into two parts, Kansas and Nebraska. The clear object of this division was to give to the slave-holding people of Missouri opportunity to make a slave state of the southern portion, named Kansas. That they would succeed in this endeavor seemed practically certain.*

The principle enunciated in this scheme of Douglas was called by him "popular sovereignty." It was declared to be the principle of the right of the people to govern themselves. It was popularly known as "Squatter Sovereignty."

The Illinois Legislature was in session when Douglas introduced the Nebraska Bill. Lincoln wrote to Joshua Speed, saying that of the one hundred members of the two Houses, seventy were Democrats, and that they held a party caucus to consider the measure. It appeared that only three of the seventy were in favor of it. Lincoln said that a few days later orders came from Douglas that the Illinois Legislature should pass a resolution favoring the bill. Party discipline prevailed, and the resolution passed by a large majority.

The Kansas-Nebraska Bill passed both Houses of Congress and became a law on May 30, 1854. The repeal of the Missouri Compromise was the recall of Abraham Lincoln to political life.

---

*I am following popular and, as I suppose, well understood phraseology in speaking of the repeal of the Missouri Compromise. Only that part of the "compromise" was repealed which related to the extension of slavery. Douglas expressly proposed that his principle of "popular sovereignty" should apply to the territories as well as to the states. But the opponents of the extension of slavery held that the people of Maine, for instance, had a legitimate interest in the question whether Kansas, or any other territory, was used for the extension and perpetuation of the system of slavery.

The repeal of the Missouri Compromise grew primarily out of factional strife in Missouri between Thomas Hart Benton and David R. Atchison. Atchison was the real author of the measure; but the leader of the movement in the Senate was Stephen A. Douglas.* Much that has been written about the part which Douglas took, and of his motive in the matter, is not sustained by adequate evidence, and some things which Douglas claimed, as, for instance, that for eight years prior to the repeal he had steadily advocated it, appear to be unreliable. But conceding, as we may well concede, the authorship of the repeal to David R. Atchison, and perhaps also in part to Judge William C. Price, it is Douglas with whom we have to reckon as the man responsible for the form of the presentation to Congress of the plan for the admission of Kansas, for its report from the committee, and for its adoption by Congress and discussion by the country.

Whatever Douglas' motive at the outset, or even if he had then no motive except that of averting the possibility of being removed from the chairmanship of the Committee on Territories to make way for Atchison who introduced the bill, he must ultimately have seen that he was certain to be held responsible for it; and it seemed well for him, if he expected to be a candidate for the presidency, to use to his advantage in the southern states what was certain to be used to his disadvantage in the states where a strong anti-slavery sentiment existed.

Senator Douglas did not return to Illinois after the passage of his bill until September 1, 1854. On that date he spoke in Chicago, and attempted to defend his course in the repeal of the Missouri Compromise. He met a very cold reception and much pronounced opposition.

He spoke again in Springfield in the Representatives' Hall of the state-house on October 3, 1854. As soon as the announcement of Douglas' speech was made, Lincoln determined to reply to him on the following day and from the same platform.

---

*P. Orman Ray, *The Repeal of the Missouri Compromise.*

Horace White, who was then a young reporter, thus described the address with which Lincoln reentered the political arena:

I heard the whole of that speech. It was a warmish day in early October, and Mr. Lincoln was in his shirt-sleeves when he stepped on the platform. I observed that, although awkward, he was not in the least embarrassed. He began in a slow, hesitating manner, but without any mistake of language, dates or facts. It was evident that he had mastered his subject, that he knew what he was going to say, and that he knew that he was right. He had a thin, high-pitched falsetto voice, of much varying power, that could be heard at a long distance in spite of the bustling tumult of the crowd. He had the accent and pronunciation peculiar to his native state, Kentucky. Gradually he warmed up to his subject, his angularity disappeared and he passed into that attitude of unconscious majesty that is so conspicuous in St. Gaudens' Statue at the entrance of Lincoln Park in Chicago. I have often wondered how this artist, who never saw the subject of his work, could have divined his presence and dignity as a public speaker so perfectly.

Progressing with his theme, his words began to come faster, and his face to light up with the rays of genius, and his body to move in unison with his thoughts. His gestures were made with his body and his head rather than with his arms. They were the natural expression of the man, and so perfectly adapted to what he was saying that anything different from it would have been quite inconceivable. Sometimes his manner was very impassioned, and he seemed transfigured with his subject. Perspiration would stream from his face, and each particular hair would stand on end. Then the inspiration that possessed him took possession of his hearers also. His speaking went to the heart because it came from the heart. I have heard celebrated orators who could start thunders of applause without changing any man's opinion. Mr. Lincoln's eloquence was of the higher type, which produced conviction in others because of the conviction of the speaker himself. His listeners felt that he believed every word he said, and that, like Martin Luther, he would go to the stake rather than abate one jot or tittle of it. In such transfigured moments as these he was the type of the ancient Hebrew prophet as I learned that character at Sunday School in my childhood.

Lincoln would willingly have debated with Douglas in 1854. Honorable Lawrence Weldon wrote of his first meeting with Lincoln:

The first time I met him was in September, 1854, at Bloomington; and I was introduced to him by Judge Douglas, who was then making a campaign in defense of the Kansas-Nebraska bill. Mr. Lincoln was attending court, and called to see the Judge. They talked very pleasantly about old times and things, and during the conversation the Judge broadened the hospitalities of the occasion by asking him to drink something. Mr. Lincoln declined very politely, when the Judge said: "Why, do you belong to the temperance society?" He said:

"I do *not* in theory, but I do in fact, belong to the temperance society, in this, to wit, that I do not drink anything, and have not done so for very many years."

Shortly after he retired, Mr. J. W. Fell, then and now a leading citizen of Illinois, came into the room, with a proposition that Mr. Lincoln and Mr. Douglas have a discussion, remarking that there were a great many people in the city, that the question was of great public importance, and that it would afford the crowd the luxury of listening to the acknowledged champions of both sides. As soon as the proposition was made it could be seen that the Judge was irritated. He inquired of Mr. Fell, with some majesty of manner: "Whom does Mr. Lincoln represent in this campaign—is he an Abolitionist or an Old Line Whig?"

Mr. Fell replied that he was an Old Line Whig.

"Yes," said Douglas, "I am now in the region of the Old Line Whig. When I am in Northern Illinois I am assailed by an Abolitionist, when I get to the center I am attacked by an Old Line Whig, and when I go to Southern Illinois I am beset by an Anti-Nebraska Democrat. I can't hold the Whig responsible for anything the Abolitionist says, and can't hold the Anti-Nebraska Democrat responsible for the positions of either. It looks to me like dogging a man all over the State. If Mr. Lincoln wants to make a speech he had better get a crowd of his own; for I most respectfully decline to hold a discussion with him."

Mr. Lincoln had nothing to do with the challenge except perhaps to say he would discuss the question with Judge Douglas. He was not aggressive in the defense of his doctrines or enunciation of his opinions, but he was brave and fearless in the protection of what he believed to be the right. The impression he made when I was introduced was as to his unaffected and sincere manner, and the precise, cautious, and accurate mode in which he stated his thoughts even when talking about commonplace things.*

Abraham Lincoln reentered politics in 1854 in response to a mighty impulse of his own conscience. It was impossible to resist the conviction that that which brought him from his place of growing leadership at the bar, with its increasing emoluments and widening distinction, into the uncertainties of the political arena, was a profound conviction of duty. It is not, however, to be understood that Lincoln was completely disinterested. He saw in the changed situation an opportunity which he thought might make him United States senator.† In the latter part of 1854, he began writing to his friends, both Whigs and Democrats, whom he believed to be offended by the Kansas-Nebraska Bill, asking for their influence and support in electing him United States senator. He marked these letters "Confidential." He received sufficient encouragement to make him believe that he was likely to be chosen.

At this time Lincoln had no thought of running against Douglas. The senatorial term which was then expiring was that of General James Shields, Lincoln's old opponent and a man with whom Lincoln had once almost fought a duel. Shields was a Democrat. Lincoln had the impression that Lyman Trumbull would be a Democratic candidate against Shields. Trumbull was

---

Reminiscences of Abraham Lincoln by Distinguished Men of His Time, pp. 198-199.

†So little was Lincoln thinking of becoming a candidate for the United States Senate until this crisis arose, that he had consented against the excellent advice of his wife to accept a nomination and election as a member of the Illinois House of Representatives. Lincoln was well past the stage in his career when such election could be counted a high honor; still as his home was in Springfield, it was an honor which he thought he could afford to accept, as it then seemed to him, without any very serious disadvantage; and he permitted himself to be elected. Very soon he discovered his mistake. There was more than a possibility that he could defeat Shields and become a United States senator. He quickly resigned his seat in the Illinois Legislature and essayed to secure election to the Senate of the United States.

a Democrat, but an Anti-Nebraska man. The repeal of the Missouri Compromise had cut across the old party lines. Among the state senators in Illinois were three Democrats who were opposed to the repeal of the Missouri Compromise. These were Norman B. Judd, of Chicago, Burton C. Cook, of Ottawa, and John M. Palmer, of Carlinville. All these had refused to follow Douglas. Both the old parties were threatened with disintegration. The Democrats stood more solidly than the Whigs, but neither party could carry its full strength in support of the Kansas-Nebraska Bill. If the opponents of Douglas could have coalesced at once they could have elected any man upon whom they agreed; but there still was a line between the Whigs and the Anti-Douglas Democrats. The Whig Party cherished the fatuous hope that it was to profit by the split in the Democratic Party. The sequel proved that the rift in the Whig Party was deeper than that in the Democratic Party. The Democrats could not elect Shields, but it did not follow that the man who succeeded him would be a Whig.

The two Houses of the Illinois General Assembly met in the hall of the House of Representatives on February 8, 1855, to choose a senator. The floor and the lobby were crowded by members and their political friends. The gallery was filled with women, including Mrs. Lincoln and other distinguished ladies of Springfield and other parts of Illinois. Lincoln had already been named as candidate for senator by a caucus of forty-five members, including all the Whigs but one, and most of the Free-soilers.

General James Shields was nominated by State Senator Graham; Abraham Lincoln was nominated by Representative Stephen T. Logan. Lyman Trumbull was nominated by Senator John M. Palmer.

On the first roll-call, Lincoln had forty-five votes, Shields forty-one, Trumbull five, and there were eight scattering votes, a total of ninety-nine. On the second and third ballots, Lincoln had forty-three, and Trumbull six. On the fourth, Lincoln had thirty-eight and Trumbull had eleven. On the sixth, Lincoln had thirty-six, and Trumbull eight. The seventh ballot startled the Assembly. The Democratic vote was transferred bodily from Shields to Governor Joel A. Matteson. On that vote, Matteson had forty-four, Lincoln thirty-eight and Trumbull nine votes. On the eighth ballot Matteson gained two votes, and Trumbull rose from nine to eighteen, while Lincoln fell to twenty-seven. On the ninth ballot Lincoln dropped to fifteen, and Trumbull rose to thirty-five, while Matteson had forty-seven, lacking only three of a majority.

Intense excitement followed, for it was confidently expected that the tenth ballot would see an election. As both Matteson and Trumbull were Democrats, and Matteson had almost a majority, with Lincoln running as a very lonely third, it seemed that in the next ballot Matteson would be elected.

Then Lincoln did a brave thing. He had reason to believe that some of his own supporters had betrayed him, and gone over to Matteson. As between Matteson and Trumbull, he strongly preferred Trumbull. He conferred with Judge Logan, and asked that his own votes be transferred to Trumbull. This request was a grief to Logan, but he saw the wisdom of it. On the last ballot fifteen of Lincoln's votes went to Trumbull, who was elected by a vote of fifty-one to Matteson's forty-seven.*

This result amazed the Democrats. They regarded Trumbull as a traitor to their cause. That party in the State Legislature had endorsed the position of Douglas. Trumbull had opposed it, and still opposed it. Palmer, Judd and Cook were also regarded as traitors. Their three votes and two Democratic votes from the House of Representatives were all that prevented Shields from having a plurality over Lincoln on the first ballot. Many of the Democrats would rather have seen Lincoln elected than Trumbull. Trumbull went to the United States Senate, where he at once took his position as an Anti-Nebraska Democrat.

---

*On this final ballot, one member cast a wild vote and another did not vote at all.

Mrs. Ninian W. Edwards had planned a great reception in honor of Senator-elect Abraham Lincoln and his lady. When Trumbull was elected she changed the form of the invitation and made it a reception in honor of Senator-elect Lyman Trumbull and lady. Mr. and Mrs. Lincoln stood in the receiving line, and the funereal baked meats of Lincoln's political ambition did freshly furnish forth the festive refreshments for Trumbull.

On the following day Lincoln wrote Elihu B. Washburne, telling the whole story of the election and his defeat. He said:

I regret my defeat moderately, but am not nervous about it. I could have headed off every combination, and been elected had it not been for Matteson's double game—and his defeat gives me more pleasure than my own gives me pain. On the whole it is perhaps well for our general cause that Trumbull is elected.

Lincoln accepted the election of Trumbull so cheerfully as to give some color to the charge that he and Trumbull had entered into a corrupt bargain with respect to the senatorship. Douglas in his first speech against Lincoln in the joint debate at Ottawa on August 21, 1858, said:

In 1854, Mr. Lincoln and Mr. Trumbull entered into an arrangement, one with the other, and each with his respective friends, to dissolve the old Whig Party on the one hand, and to dissolve the old Democratic Party on the other, and to connect the members of both into an Abolition party, under the name and disguise of a Republican Party. The terms of that arrangement between Mr. Lincoln and Mr. Trumbull have been published to the world by Mr. Lincoln's special friend, James H. Matheny, Esq., and they were, that Lincoln should have Shields' place in the United States Senate, which was then about to become vacant, and that Trumbull should have my seat when my term expired. Lincoln went to work to abolitionize the old Whig Party all over the state, pretending that he was then as good Whig as ever; and Trumbull went to work in his part of the state preaching abolitionism in its milder and lighter form, and trying to abolitionize the Democratic Party, and bring old Democrats handcuffed and bound hand and foot into the abolition camp. In pursuance of the arrangement, the parties met at Springfield in October, 1854, and proclaimed their new platform. Lincoln was to bring into the abolition camp the old-line Whigs, and transfer them over to Giddings, Chase, Fred Douglass, and Parson Lovejoy, who were ready to receive them and christen them in their new faith. . . .

These two men having formed this combination to abolitionize the old Whig Party and the old Democratic Party, and put themselves into the Senate of the United States, in pursuance of their bargain, are now carrying out that arrangement. Matheny states that Trumbull broke faith; that the bargain was that Lincoln should be the Senator in Shields' place, and Trumbull was to wait for mine; and the story goes, that Trumbull cheated Lincoln, having control of four or five abolitionized Democrats who were holding over in the Senate; he would not let them vote for Lincoln, which obliged the rest of the Abolitionists to support him in order to secure an abolition senator. There are a number of authorities for the truth of this besides Matheny, and I suppose that even Mr. Lincoln will not deny it.

Mr. Lincoln demands that he shall have the place intended for Trumbull, as Trumbull cheated him and got his, and Trumbull is stumping the State traducing me for the purpose of securing the position for Lincoln, in order to quiet him. It was in consequence of this arrangement that the Republican Convention was empanelled to instruct for Lincoln and nobody else, and it was on this account that they passed resolutions that he was their first, their last, and their only choice.

Douglas probably believed this to be true, but he was mistaken. No such corrupt bargain existed between Lincoln and Trumbull, and Lincoln never believed that Trumbull was untrue to him. He did believe, however, that some of his own professed followers failed him, and the Matteson movement appears to have been the result of a coalition not wholly honorable Neither Lincoln nor Trumbull, however, had any share in this. That coalition represented opposition to both Trumbull and Lincoln. Looking back from this distance, we may well be grateful that Abraham Lincoln was not elected senator to succeed James Shields. If he had been comfortably seated in the United States

Senate, in 1855, and Lyman Trumbull had been the opponent of Stephen A. Douglas in 1858, some important chapters in the history of the United States would have had to be rewritten.

A series of Lincoln and Douglas debates was threatened in 1854, but was called off by a truce between Lincoln and Douglas. The account of this truce is given by Herndon and is not wholly satisfactory:

By request of party friends, Lincoln was induced to follow after Douglas, and, at the various places where the latter had appointments, to speak in reply to him. On the 16th of October they met at Peoria, where Douglas enjoyed the advantages of an "open and close." Lincoln made an effective speech, which he wrote out and furnished to the Sangamon *Journal* for publication, and which can be found among his public utterances. His party friends, in Springfield and elsewhere, who had urged him to push after Douglas until he cried "enough," were surprised a few days after the Peoria debate to find him at home, with the information that by agreement with the latter they were both to return home and speak no more during the campaign. Judge of his astonishment a few days later to find that his rival, instead of going direct to his home in Chicago, had stopped at Princeton and violated his express agreement by making a speech there! Lincoln was much displeased at this action of Douglas, which tended to convince him that the latter was really a man devoid of fixed political morals. I remember his explanation in our office made to me, William Butler, William Jayne, Ben F. Irwin, and other friends, to account for his early withdrawal from the stump. After the Peoria debate Douglas approached him and flattered him by saying that he was giving him more trouble on the territorial and slavery questions than all the United States Senate, and he therefore proposed to him that both should abandon the field and return to their homes. Now Lincoln could never refuse a polite request—one in which no principle was involved. I have heard him say, "It's a fortunate thing I wasn't born a woman, for I cannot refuse anything, it seems." He therefore consented to the cessation of debate proposed by Douglas, and the next day both went to the town of Lacon, where they had been billed for speeches. Their agreement was kept from their friends, and both declined to speak—Douglas on the ground of hoarseness, and Lincoln gallantly refusing to take advantage of "Judge Douglas's indisposition." Here they separated, Lincoln going directly home, and Douglas, as before related, stopping at Princeton and colliding in debate with Owen Lovejoy. Upon being charged afterwards with his breach of agreement Douglas responded that Lovejoy "bantered and badgered" him so persistently that he could not gracefully resist the encounter. The whole thing thoroughly displeased Lincoln.*

Apparently we do not yet know, and perhaps never shall know, the precise nature of Lincoln's truce with Douglas. Their failure to speak at Lacon, where they had been advertised, can not be attributed to the hoarseness of Douglas, for Douglas repeatedly spoke when he was hoarse, and Lincoln did not on those occasions refrain from using his own voice to its utmost. Apparently something was involved in the arrangement which has not fully been disclosed.

The address of Douglas at Princeton occurred on Wednesday, October 18, 1854. John H. Bryant, who was present, said that Douglas spoke a half-hour and was answered by Lovejoy in another half-hour, and that Douglas then talked until dark.

Whatever the nature of the agreement, we have reason to be glad that the real debate was reserved until the campaign of 1858.

The repeal of the Missouri Compromise opened to the possibility of slave occupation an area equal to that of the original thirteen states. Kansas lay directly west of Missouri, and could only be reached from the east by the crossing of Missouri. Senator David Atchison, who had been president of the United States Senate, and who disputed with Douglas the honor of having been the author of the repeal of the Missouri Compromise, began the organization of so called "Blue Lodges" whose purpose was to make Kansas a slave state. Bands of border ruffians set out to terrorize those settlements in Kansas that were known to be anti-slavery.

---

*Herndon's *Lincoln,* ii, pp. 42-43.

Anti-slavery New England took up the challenge. Eli Thayer, of Worcester, began the movement to beard the principle of Squatter Sovereignty in its den by providing a majority of anti-slavery squatters. Colonies moved westward from New England, taking their household goods, and some of them also, their rifles.

Then rose Old John Brown, of Ossawatomie. He had no theory that slavery was to be dealt with tenderly. Much that he did is open to debate, and has been and will be hotly debated; but this he did that needed to be done, he made the doctrine of Squatter Sovereignty a two-edged sword, whose keener edge was turned to the throat of the slave-holding power. For a time there was civil war in Kansas. The term "Bleeding Kansas" was used in Congress and throughout the nation. Not all the blood was shed on one side. The "Emigrant Aid Societies" organized in New England were as determined as were the "Border Ruffians" from Missouri.

Left to itself, Kansas would have received a large proportion of its immigration from Missouri and the South, while Nebraska would have been populated largely from New England and the other northern states. But the Emigrant Aid Societies made it an object for northern immigrants to go to Kansas, furnishing the provisions, building materials, Bibles and Sharp's rifles. Squatter sovereignty was to settle the question whether Kansas was to be a free state or a slave state; but the slave-holders were not doing all the squatting. Eli Thayer and the abolition press were taking a hand in the settlement of Kansas, and so was John Brown, of Ossawatomie.

CHAPTER XXV

THE REPUBLICAN PARTY
1856

WHEN, in 1854, Abraham Lincoln reentered politics, he supposed that he was still a Whig; but the Whig Party was already dead, and neither Lincoln nor the party knew it. He had been a Whig ever since he first defined his political principles. But the Whig Party had sinned away its day of grace. It was scarcely less culpable than the Democratic Party for the condition of slavery in the country. Lincoln and the men who joined with him in opposition to the further extension of slavery were a voice crying in the wilderness.

It might have been expected that Lincoln would have been among the first to discover that the old parties were both on the verge or disruption, and that his future lay with the new party which even in 1854 was coming to the birth; but such was not the case.

On November 17, 1854, a group of men who called themselves the Republican State Central Committee met in Chicago, and Lincoln's name was on the list of those invited to membership. He was out of Springfield when the letter of invitation reached his home, and he may not have been sorry. He wrote a courteous letter,* explaining his failure to reply before the date of the meeting, and added:

I have been perplexed some to understand why my name was placed upon that committee. I was not consulted on the subject,

---

*Letter to Icobod Codding. Nicolay and Hay, *Works of Lincoln, Gettysburg Edition*, i, p. 264.

nor was I apprised of the appointment until I discovered it by accident two or three weeks afterward. I suppose my opposition to the principle of slavery is as strong as that of any member of the Republican Party; but I have also supposed that the extent to which I feel authorized to carry that opposition, practically, was not at all satisfactory to that party. The leading men who organized that party were present on the 4th of October at the discussion between Douglas and myself in Springfield, and had full opportunity to not misunderstand my position. Do I misunderstand them?

Apparently they did not as yet fully understand each other, and Lincoln went on thinking himself a Whig. As for the Republican Party in Illinois, in 1854, the children came to the birth, and there was not strength to bring them forth. The Whig Party had but a name to live, and the Republican Party did not know that it was yet alive. The hope of freedom lay between two worlds, one dead, the other powerless to be born.

The Whig Party was never really an anti-slavery party. In its organization it included all elements opposed to Jacksonianism. Horace Greeley, in 1838, gave this account of its origin and spirit:

The American Whig Party was formed in the spring of 1834 by a union, so far as their common objects and views seemed to dictate, of all those who condemned the most arbitrary and unconstitutional removal of the deposits of the public treasure by General Jackson, from the one safe, advantageous and proper depository designated by law, into forty or fifty State banks. That reckless and most indefensible measure—which lies at the foundation of all our subsequent commercial, financial and general calamities, necessarily gave rise to an intense political excitement, and to a new organization of parties, in which was partially merged all former distinction.

Greeley then gave five classes of those who made up the Whig Party in 1834,—those who had supported Adams and Clay as National Republicans; "most of those who, acting in defense of what they deemed the assailed or threatened rights of the states, had been stigmatized as *Nullifiers;*" the Anti-Masons; the Democrats who had revolted against the tyranny of Jackson; and those who had taken no part in politics, but now entered as a protest against the high-handed acts of the administration of Jackson.*

The old political parties were disrupted. A portion of the Whig Party, fearing the influence of foreign domination in American political affairs, formed the "American" or "Know-Nothing" Party. Its principles were the opposition of the party to the influence of men of foreign birth in American affairs. Its motto was "America for Americans." With this party Lincoln had no sympathy. We shall discover later how highly he valued the foreign vote, especially the German vote. Moreover, Lincoln did not feel that the danger to American politics from the naturalized foreigners was nearly so great as it was from the presence of slavery as a controlling issue in the politics of America.

A portion of the Whig Party greater in number than that which went toward the organization of the Know-Nothings, began the organization of what was to be the Republican Party. This, also, for a time, Lincoln regarded with little favor. In general, the older and more conservative Whigs became Know-Nothings, and the younger and more radical became Republicans. For a time Lincoln did neither. He remained an Anti-Nebraska Whig.

But the new Republican Party was not composed wholly of men who had seceded from the Whigs. With them were associated the abolitionists, the Free-soilers, and such as remained from the old Liberty Party. There was also a considerable group of intelligent Germans, Swedes and Norwegians, whose principles were anti-slavery.

In addition to all these, however, there was a large secession from the Democratic Party. David Wilmot, author of the Wil-

---

*Horace Greeley in *The Whig Almanac* for 1838, quoted in Gorham's *Life of Edwin M. Stanton*, page 23. For a severe condemnation of the heterogeneous combination in the Whig Party, see Bowers' *Party Battles of the Jackson Period*.

mot Proviso, John C. Frémont, William Cullen Bryant, Francis
D. and Montgomery Blair, Lyman Trumbull, and other men who
believed in what they thought the Democracy of Jefferson, left
this party and became members of the new Republican Party.

Lincoln's most intimate Whig associates in and about Springfield were not ahead of him in their advocacy of the new experiment. They still hoped, as Lincoln hoped, for the rejuvenation
of the Whig Party. It was a vain hope.

Of the doom of the Whig Party, and of Lincoln's gradual
readjustment to that fact, Herndon wrote:

The Whig Party having accomplished its mission in the political world, was now on the eve of a great break-up. Lincoln
realized this, and, though proverbially slow in his movements,
prepared to find a firm footing when the great rush of waters
should come and the maddening freshet sweep former landmarks
out of sight....

Finding himself drifting about with the disorganized elements
that floated together after the angry political waters had subsided, it became apparent to Lincoln that if he expected to figure
as a leader he must take a stand himself. Mere hatred of slavery
and opposition to the injustice of the Kansas-Nebraska legislation were not all that was required of him. He must be a Democrat, Abolitionist, Know-Nothing or Republican, or float forever about in the great political sea without compass, rudder or
sail. At length he declared himself. Believing the times were
ripe for more advanced movements, in the Spring of 1856 I drew
up a paper for friends of freedom to sign, calling a county convention in Springfield to select delegates for the forthcoming Republican State Convention in Bloomington. The paper was
freely circulated, and generously signed. Lincoln was absent at
the time; and, believing I knew what his feelings and judgment
on the vital questions of the hour were, I took the liberty to sign
his name to the call. The whole was then published in the
Springfield *Journal*. No sooner had it appeared than John T.
Stuart, who, with others, was endeavoring to retard Lincoln in
his advanced movements, rushed into our office, and excitedly
asked "if Lincoln had signed that Abolition call in the *Journal?*"
I answered in the negative, adding that I had signed his name

myself. To the question, "Did Lincoln authorize you to sign it?" I returned an emphatic "No." "Then," exclaimed the startled and indignant Stuart, "you have ruined him." But I was by no means alarmed at what others deemed hasty and inconsiderate action. I thought I understood Lincoln thoroughly, but in order to vindicate myself if assailed, I immediately sat down, after Stuart had rushed out of the office, and wrote Lincoln, who was then in Tazewell County, attending court, a brief account of what I had done and how much stir it was creating in the ranks of his conservative friends. If he approved or disapproved my course, I asked him to write or telegraph me at once. In a brief time came his answer: "All right. Go ahead. Will meet you, radicals and all." Stuart subsided, and the conservative spirits who hovered around Springfield no longer held control of the political fortunes of Abraham Lincoln.*

It is possible that Herndon exaggerated somewhat his own part in this proceeding, but his statements can not be wholly wrong. Lincoln emerged at last from the chaos of the collapse of the Whig Party and became a Republican. He was nearly two years in making the decision, and then was in advance of some of his associates; but when he made the choice he made it irrevocably.

The first national convention of the new Republican Party was preliminary and tentative, and was held in Pittsburgh, on Washington's birthday. It paved the way for the formal nominating convention which was held in Philadelphia in June of 1856. It nominated John C. Frémont as president and William L. Dayton as vice-president. It is remarkable that Abraham Lincoln was recognized from the outset as leader of the new party in the Northwest. On the informal ballot for vice-president he received one hundred ten votes.

The Democratic National Convention was held in Cincinnati, June 2, 1856, and nominated James Buchanan for president and John C. Breckenridge, for vice-president. Pierce was not renominated, largely because he had become unpopular on account of the outrages in Kansas. Douglas, who, on the sixteenth ballot,

*Herndon's *Lincoln,* ii, pp. 381-383.

received 121 votes to Buchanan's 168, probably owed his defeat to his responsibility for the Kansas-Nebraska Bill.

Shortly before the National Republican Convention of 1856, a call was issued for a state convention of all who were opposed to the extension of slavery. Lincoln's name, signed by Herndon, as already related, had appeared in the call for a county convention in Springfield to elect delegates from Sangamon to this convention. This convention, at which the Republican Party of Illinois was organized, was held in Bloomington, May 29, 1856.

John M. Palmer, who had been a Democrat, and afterward reverted to his former party relationship, presided. Lyman Trumbull, who had been a Whig and then a Democrat, and who later returned to the Democratic Party, assisted at the birth of the Republican Party of his state. Owen Lovejoy, afterward a member of Congress, was leader of the radicals. Orville H. Browning, afterward senator, led the conservatives.

The convention was made up of men who had come out of different parties, including some who were not more than half-way out. It was made up of men who had never worked together before, and some who could not work together long, unless they were fused into unity by the flame of some guiding purpose, and the leadership of a strong personality.

This convention is notable as the scene of delivery of Lincoln's "Lost Speech." There had been a sharp contest between Browning of the conservatives and Lovejoy of the radicals, and Lincoln had acted as peacemaker. He was chosen at the head of the state electoral ticket, and was from the first recognized as the outstanding leader of the assembly. The speech of Lincoln was described by Joseph Medill, of the *Chicago Tribune*:

Mr. Emery, a "free-state" man just from "bleeding Kansas," told of the "border ruffian" raids from Missouri upon the free-state settlers in Kansas: the burnings, robberies, and murders they were then committing; and asked for help to repel them. When he finished, Lincoln was vociferously called for from all parts of Major's large hall. He came forward and took the platform beside the presiding officer. At first his voice was shrill and hesitating. There was a curious introspective look in his eyes, which lasted for a few moments. Then his voice began to move steadily and smoothly forward, and the modulations were under perfect control from thenceforward to the finish. He warmed up as he went on, and spoke more rapidly; he looked a foot taller as he straightened himself to his full height, and his eyes flashed fire; his countenance became wrapped in intense emotion; he rushed along like a thunderstorm. He prophesied war as the outcome of these aggressions, and poured forth hot denunciations upon the slave power. The convention was kept in an uproar, applauding and cheering and stamping; and this reacted on the speaker, and gave him a tongue of fire. The thrilling scene in that old Bloomington hall forty years ago arises in my mind as vividly as the day after its enactment.

There stood Lincoln in the forefront, erect, tall, and majestic in appearance, hurling thunderbolts at the foes of freedom, while the great convention roared its endorsement! I never witnessed such a scene before or since. As he described the aims and aggressions of the unappeasable slaveholders and the servility of their Northern allies as illustrated by the perfidious repeal of the Missouri Compromise two years previously, and their grasping after the rich prairies of Kansas and Nebraska, to blight them with slavery and to deprive free labor of this rich inheritance, and exhorted the friends of freedom to resist them to the death, the convention went fairly wild. It paralleled or exceeded the scene in the Revolutionary Virginia convention of eighty-one years before, when Patrick Henry invoked death if liberty could not be preserved, and said, "After all we must fight." Strange, too, that this same man received death a few years afterwards while conferring freedom on the slave race and preserving the American Union from dismemberment.

Just what Lincoln said in that speech no one knows. He had not written it out, but he had thought much about it. The reporters were too much interested to take even the most fragmentary notes. Henry C. Whitney, an attorney, who had been at Danville where Lincoln had been attending court for about three weeks, wrote out many years afterward what he believed to be the substance of this speech. Medill, who heard the speech itself, thought that Whitney had fairly reproduced the thought, and in some instances the very phraseology, of the address. The concluding paragraphs,* as Whitney recalled them, were:

The Union is undergoing a fearful strain; but it is a stout old ship, and has weathered many a hard blow, and "the stars in their courses," aye, an invisible power, greater than the puny efforts of men, will fight for us. But we ourselves must not decline the burden of responsibility, nor take counsel of unworthy passions. Whatever duty urges us to do or to omit, must be done or omitted; and the recklessness with which our adversaries break the laws, or counsel their violation, should afford no example for us. Therefore, let us revere the Declaration of Independence; let us continue to obey the Constitution and the laws; let us keep step to the music of the Union. Let us draw a cordon, so to speak, around the slave States, and the hateful institution, like a reptile poisoning itself, will perish by its own infamy. [Applause.]

But we cannot be free men if this is, by our national choice, to be a land of slavery. Those who deny freedom to others, deserve it not for themselves; and, under the rule of a just God, cannot long retain it. [Loud applause.]

Did you ever, my friends, seriously reflect upon the speed with which we are tending downwards? Within the memory of men now present the leading statesmen of Virginia could make genuine, red-hot abolitionist speeches in old Virginia; and, as I have said, now even in "free Kansas" it is a crime to declare that it is "free Kansas." The very sentiments that I and others have just uttered, would entitle us, and each of us, to the ignominy and seclusion of a dungeon! and yet I suppose that like Paul, we were "free born." But if this thing is allowed to continue, it will be but one step further to impress the same rule in Illinois. [Sensation.]

The conclusion of all is, that we must restore the Missouri Compromise. We must highly resolve that *Kansas must be free!* [Great applause.] We must reinstate the birthday promise of the Republic; we must reaffirm the Declaration of Independence; we must make good in essence as well as in form Madison's avowal that "the word *slave* ought not to appear in the

---

*From Tarbell's *Life of Lincoln,* ii, 306-321.

Constitution"; and we must even go further, and decree that only local law, and not that time-honored instrument, shall shelter a slave-holder. We must make this a land of liberty in fact, as it is in name. But in seeking to attain these results—so indispensable if the liberty which is our pride and boast shall endure—we will be loyal to the Constitution and to the "flag of our Union," and no matter what our grievance—even though Kansas shall come in as a slave State; and no matter what theirs—even if we shall restore the Compromise—WE WILL SAY TO THE SOUTHERN DISUNIONISTS, WE WON'T GET OUT OF THE UNION AND YOU SHAN'T!!! [This was the climax; the audience rose to its feet *en masse*, applauded, stamped, waved handkerchiefs, threw hats in the air, and ran riot for several minutes. The arch-enchanter who wrought this transformation looked, meanwhile, like the personification of political justice.]

But let us, meanwhile, appeal to the sense and patriotism of the people, and not to their prejudices; let us spread the floods of enthusiasm here aroused all over these vast prairies, so suggestive of freedom. Let us commence by electing the gallant soldier Governor (Colonel) Bissell who stood for the honor of our State alike on the plains and amidst the chaparral of Mexico and on the floor of Congress, while he defied the Southern Hotspur; and that will have a greater moral effect than all the border ruffians can accomplish in all their raids on Kansas. There is both a power and a magic in popular opinion. To that let us now appeal; and while, in all probability, no resort to force will be needed, our moderation and forbearance will stand us in good stead when if ever, WE MUST MAKE AN APPEAL TO BATTLE AND TO THE GOD OF HOSTS!! [Immense applause and a rush for the orator.]

Opinions differ widely as to the accuracy of Whitney's report. A considerable number of those who had attended the convention in 1856 assembled in Bloomington fifty years later for a semi-centennial celebration, and united in the expression of the judgment "that Lincoln's lost speech is still lost."*

Horace White believed that the "lost speech" was not lost;

---

*I have talked with every known survivor of those who heard the "lost speech." Without exception these men deny the reliability of Whitney's report.

that Lincoln repeated the substance of it again and again as he was constantly speaking throughout the campaign of 1856, and that virtually the whole speech was preserved. Lincoln when invited to write out this address said that he was unable to do so. It is altogether likely that he was not unwilling to let the speech be lost. He had met the situation with a strong forceful utterance that went far enough to please the radicals, and which did not offend the conservatives, and he probably did not care to have the address, just as he delivered it, used in other situations for which it might have been less fitted. Mr. Medill wrote:

My belief is that, after Mr. Lincoln cooled down, he was rather pleased that his speech had not been reported, as it was too radical in expression on the slavery question for the digestion of central and southern Illinois at that time, and that he preferred to let it stand as a remembrance in the minds of his audience. But be that as it may, the effect of it was such on his hearers that he bounded to the leadership of the new Republican party of Illinois, and no man afterwards ever thought of disputing that position with him. On that occasion he planted the seed which germinated into a Presidential candidacy and that gave him the nomination over Seward at the Chicago convention of 1860, which placed him in the Presidential chair, there to complete his predestined work of destroying slavery and making freedom universal, but yielding his life as a sacrifice for the glorious deeds.

It is interesting to know that not all who heard Lincoln's "lost speech" were profoundly impressed by it. Senator O. H. Browning, who as chairman of the Committee on Resolutions, had no doubt that his was the most important contribution to the work of the Convention. As for the oratory of the occasion, he wrote only this in his Diary:

I was called out and made two speeches in the afternoon Convention also addressed by Lovejoy, Lincoln, Cook & others—.

The "lost speech" was lost on Senator Browning.
Whether the speech was lost or not, its influence was not lost.

Not only did it commit Lincoln uncompromisingly to the whole program of the new Republican Party, but it committed that party in Illinois to Lincoln. Not that the party thought unitedly of him as president; but he was thenceforth the unchallenged leader of the party in his own state. The "lost speech" furnished the party its working basis. It unified the discordant elements within the party. Whatever the Committee on Resolutions reported, the real platform of the Republican Party in Illinois was from the hour of its birth the character and personality of Abraham Lincoln.

The young Republican Party, born of discordant elements, leaped into the arena of national politics with a vigor that put to shame the dignified procedure of the old Whig organization.

Frémont was the popular hero of the westward-moving frontier, the explorer of the Rocky Mountain region—"the pathfinder of the West." If his judgment was unstable and erratic, what of it? He was a hero to inspire the people's imagination, and he was opposed to the extension of slavery. They did not talk of "slogans" in those days. That word, taken over from "The Relief of Lucknow"—

> "The Campbells are coming! Dinna ye hear the slogan
>   far awa?
>   The McGreggors—ah, I ken it weel—
>   It's the grandest of them a'!"

was pressed into service when James G. Blaine and John A. Logan almost won an election:—

> "Dinna ye hear the slogan?
>   It's all for Blaine and Logan!"

Slogans by any other name are effective; and our free and intelligent country is largely ruled by them. This was the Republican slogan in 1856; and no party ever had a better one:

> "Free land; free speech, free men, Frémont!"

John C. Frémont had done other brave deeds than the opening
of a path to the Pacific.   He had made love to Jessie Benton, the
delicately reared daughter of Thomas Hart Benton, senator from
Missouri.   As a girl she had not been permitted to turn a door-
knob lest it spread her dainty hand; and the sun had been carefully veiled away from her cream-white complexion.   This
tanned, blustering explorer sought her hand—her delicate hand
—and his was as calloused and brown as his saddle!   The old
Roman father snorted and thundered his refusal.   Whereupon,
Frémont and she ran away and were married.   Oh, young Loch-
invar had come out from the West; in all the wide border his
steed was the best!   How could such a lover fail to ride away
with the presidential election!   What exploit had James Buchanan ever performed to compare with that?   He never ran away
with any one's daughter!   He was a hopeless old bachelor!   With
John and Jessie in the White House there would be most interesting possibilities: the American Eagle might divide honors
with the stork; but "Old Buck"—They sang in contempt of him
to the old English melody of *Vilikins and his Dinah:*

> "Here come Johnnie and Jessie
>   Get out of the way;
> It's too late in the season
>   For you to make hay!"

But the Democratic organization was strongly entrenched; the
Republican Party was new and made up of many and heterogeneous elements.   If all the Whigs had become Republicans,
they, with the anti-slavery Democrats who entered the Republican Party in 1856, could easily have elected Frémont.   The scale
was turned by appeals to conservative Whigs not to vote for a
sectional candidate and thus disrupt the Union.   This plea for
the union turned enough conservative Whigs to the Democratic
Party to insure the success of its ticket.   Spite of all good
reasons in favor of Frémont and his Jessie, the elected president
in 1856 was James Buchanan.

CHAPTER XXVI

THE LINCOLN-DOUGLAS DEBATES
1858

MEANTIME, an event had occurred which both strengthened and weakened Douglas. There had been held at Lecompton, Kansas, a Constitutional Convention, presided over by John Calhoun, Lincoln's old friend, the Illinois surveyor. This convention provided a constitution which practically nullified the doctrine of "popular sovereignty" by making it impossible for the people of Kansas in adopting it to vote separately on the question whether the new state should be admitted as a slave state or a free state. President Buchanan, in his address to Congress, December 9, 1857, urged the admission of Kansas as a slave state under the Lecompton Constitution. This proposition Douglas strongly opposed. He declared that his opposition was not based on his approval or disapproval of slavery, but on his consistent regard for the principle of popular sovereignty. He even went to far as to say that if this principle was adhered to, he did not care whether slavery was voted up or voted down; but he did care that the people of Kansas should have a fair opportunity to decide the slavery matter for themselves.

This opposition of Douglas to the plan of the administration exasperated the slave leaders, who proposed as a punishment that Douglas should be deposed from his position as chairman of the Senate Committee on Territories.

He called at the White House on official business. Mr. Buchanan expostulated with him for opposing the administration in its Kansas policy. At length he went so far as to warn Douglas of the personal consequences. Recalling the fact that Doug-

364

las had always been a great admirer of General Jackson, the president said:

"You are an ambitious man, Mr. Douglas, and there is a brilliant future for you, if you retain the confidence of the Democrat Party; if you oppose it, let me remind you of the fate of those who in former times rebelled against it. Remember the fate of Senators Rives and Talmadge who opposed General Jackson, when he removed the government deposits from the United States Bank. Beware of their fate, Mr. Douglas."

"Mr. President," replied Douglas, "General Jackson is dead. Good morning, sir!"

Thus Douglas, by an attitude wholly consistent with his past record, and much to his credit, incurred the disfavor of the president and the unqualified opposition of the pro-slavery leaders of his party. But what he lost in the support of the leaders in his own party, he gained in whole or in part in the favor with which his courageous stand was received by many of the leaders among the old-time Whigs. Several of them believed that the duty of the Republicans of Illinois was not to nominate a candidate of their own for senator, but to endorse Douglas. Horace Greeley held this view; in a letter to Lincoln he plainly implied his belief that it was unwise for Lincoln to aspire to the place. He told Lincoln that so far as any help from the *Tribune* was concerned, he must "paddle his own dug-out." These letters profoundly depressed Lincoln.*

Greeley wrote to Joseph Medill, of the *Chicago Tribune,* that the Republicans of Illinois by supporting Lincoln were repelling Douglas, who might have been conciliated and attached to their side.† He apparently saw no danger to the cause in repelling and repudiating Lincoln!

Thus it seemed to some of the foremost Republican leaders in the East that the wisest policy was to reelect Stephen A.

---

*"Lincoln was gloomy and restless the entire day. Greeley's letters were driving the enthusiasm out of him." *Herndon,* ii, p. 391.

†*Abraham Lincoln: A History,* Nicolay and Hay, ii, p. 140.

Douglas to the United States Senate in 1858, as the most available opponent of a pro-slavery administration, and perhaps make him the Republican candidate for president in 1860.*

Lincoln was compelled to face Douglas, therefore, at a moment when Douglas stood not only as a notable leader of his own party, but as one who had so far incurred the animosity of the leaders of that party that he appeared to some to have become almost a champion of the principles for which the Republican Party stood. Lincoln knew that for himself the future lay in a more uncompromising attitude toward slavery than Douglas could ever assume, and than Lincoln himself had previously felt justified in advocating as the basis of a national political organization.

It is declared by some who heard Lincoln in his "lost speech" at Bloomington in 1856, that he there gave expression to the dictum that the government could not permanently endure half slave and half free. It is said that he eliminated the sentence from his subsequent campaign speeches of that year, in obedience to the emphatic protest of Judge T. Lyle Dickey and others, who believed that its delivery would solidify not only the abolition sentiment of the North but also intensify the slavery sentiment of the South. Judge Dickey himself affirmed this in a letter written in 1866.

Lincoln knew that he would be nominated as the Republican candidate for senator by the Springfield Convention in 1858, and he worked with great care on the address which he was there to deliver. The opening paragraph he committed to memory, and delivered it word for word as he wrote it. It contained the kernel of the issue which he was to contest in the succeeding months with Stephen A. Douglas. This paragraph was modeled upon the opening paragraph of Webster's reply to Hayne:

---

*As Douglas came so near to being forced into the Republican Party in 1856, it is interesting to inquire whether he himself would have become a Republican if he had lived to the end of the war. The answer, of course, is a matter of conjecture, but in view of the position he took after the war broke out we can hardly believe that he would have supported McClellan in 1864.

STEPHEN A. DOUGLAS
From a contemporary steel engraving

Mr. President and gentlemen of the convention: If we could first know where we are, and whither we are tending, we could better judge what to do, and how to do it. We are now far into the fifth year since a policy was initiated with the avowed object and confident promise of putting an end to slavery agitation. Under the operation of that policy, that agitation has not only not ceased, but has constantly augmented. In my opinion, it will not cease until a crisis shall have been reached and passed. "A house divided against itself cannot stand." I believe this government cannot endure permanently half slave and half free. I do not expect the Union to be dissolved; I do not expect the house to fall; but I do expect it will cease to be divided. It will become all one thing, or all the other. Either the opponents of slavery will arrest the further spread of it, and place it where the public mind shall rest in the belief that it is in the course of ultimate extinction, or its advocates will push it forward till it shall become alike lawful in all the States, old as well as new, North as well as South.

Lincoln prepared this speech by writing its paragraphs on stray envelopes and scraps of paper as ideas suggested themselves, and dropping them into that miscellaneous receptacle, his hat. As the convention drew near he copied the whole on connected sheets. On the night before the convention, he invited a dozen or so of his friends into the library of the state-house and read it to them. All but one condemned it. Herndon rejoiced to the day of his death in his own recollection that he encouraged Lincoln to deliver the speech just as he had read it. He said to Lincoln, as he afterward recalled it, "Deliver that speech as read, and it will make you president."

Apparently the full significance of this paragraph was not grasped by all who were present. O. H. Browning wrote in his Diary:

Fine warm day—Attending court—Republican Convention to meet tomorrow & delegates arriving—At night had a small caucus for consultation at the Library, and directed me to draft resolutions.

14

On the following day, Wednesday, June 16, 1858, Browning wrote:

Lovely day—Republican convention in session. Koerner president—Immense gathering—over a thousand delegates in attendance, and great harmony and enthusiasm. Nominated Miller for Treasurer, & Bateman for superintendent of public instruction. I drafted the platform which was adopted without dissent.

Browning forgot to record the two really significant incidents of the convention, the nomination of Abraham Lincoln as Republican candidate for senator, and the delivery of Lincoln's "house-divided-against-itself" speech.

Browning, like Lincoln, was a Kentuckian, and his wife also was from Kentucky. He was an able and a conscientious man, and one who deplored the evils of slavery, but was far from being an abolitionist. Absorbed as he was in his own work for the convention, and it was not light or unimportant, and fully appreciative of his own share of what was said and done there, he still was amazingly oblivious of the most significant facts which occurred on this occasion directly under his observation. Fortunately, he usually was more observant.

Lincoln's address was not received by the convention in 1858 with the united enthusiasm of the Bloomington speech of two years before, but it represented his deliberate and unalterable conviction, and his party accepted it. On that issue and as thus defined, Abraham Lincoln entered the arena against Stephen A. Douglas.

Lincoln delivered his "house-divided-against-itself" speech four months before William H. Seward delivered his famous "irrepressible conflict" address. The famous sentence in Seward's Rochester speech read thus:

It is an irrepressible conflict between opposing and enduring forces, and it means that the United States must and will, sooner or later, become either entirely a slave holding nation, or entirely a free labor nation.

Whether Seward had seen Lincoln's speech or not we do not know. In his debate upon the repeal of the Missouri Compromise in March, 1854, he had said:

"Slavery is an eternal struggle between truth and error, right and wrong."

This was a significant utterance, but it did not include the further declaration which both Lincoln and Seward expressed so uncompromisingly in 1858 that the government must ultimately become either wholly free or slavery become national.

Lincoln was a proverbially cautious man. He preferred to fight on the defensive. He moved slowly toward any new position. His "house-divided-against-itself" speech astonished his opponents and dismayed his friends. Under existing circumstances it might have seemed wise on the part of Lincoln to have let his moderation be known by all men, by forcing Douglas to take an extreme position. Douglas himself had some right to claim that he had been a mediator and the author of successful and peacemaking compromise. He could and did defend the Nebraska Bill as a thoroughgoing expression of the American principle of self-determination. He could point with just pride to his opposition to the Lecompton Constitution. He could and did declare that the position which he had taken in Congress had been approved by resolution of the Legislature in his own state.

In these conditions it was a courageous act on the part of Abraham Lincoln to throw to the winds his habitual caution, and against the advice of most of his political friends and supporters, go forth to battle upon the platform of his declaration that the United States could not permanently remain half free and half slave. His political supporters knew what kind of answer Douglas would make to that speech, and they had reason to fear that upon that platform Lincoln would be defeated. Douglas rejoiced when he read Lincoln's "house-divided-against-itself" speech. It gave him an opportunity which he fully appreciated and skilfully used.

When Douglas made his first appearance in Chicago after his

vote in favor of the repeal of the Missouri Compromise, church bells tolled in Chicago as if for a funeral; and flags floated at half-mast on vessels in the harbor. He was received with such manifestations of popular disapproval that when he spoke in Chicago on September 3, 1854, it was with no little difficulty he was permitted to deliver his address. Very different was his reception in 1858. No man ever received a more brilliant welcome to the city of Chicago. The streets were decorated, and thronged with people. He was met at the train by an enthusiastic crowd, who escorted him to the Tremont House, where, amid illuminations and decorations such as Chicago had never witnessed, he addressed a crowd that packed Lake Street solidly with eager and enthusiastic citizens. This was the opening speech of his campaign, and was delivered from the balcony on the second floor of the Tremont House, on Friday evening, July 9, 1858.

Douglas had just reached the city, and had been, as he said, two nights without having gone to bed. But he spoke with great vigor. Lincoln knew that this address was coming, and being in Chicago in attendance upon the United States Court, he went to hear it.

Lincoln was received courteously, and he occupied a seat upon the platform. Douglas referred to him more than once, and courteously, in his address. Douglas had committed to memory the opening paragraph of Lincoln's "house-divided-against-itself" speech, and quoted it that night, and in all his speeches throughout the campaign.

Speaking in front of the Tremont House and with Lincoln on the platform behind him, Douglas thus ably defended his own position and accepted the challenge of Lincoln's Springfield speech:

A few days ago the Republican Party of the state of Illinois assembled in convention at Springfield, and not only laid down their platform, but nominated a candidate for the United States Senate, as my successor. I take great pleasure in saying that I have known, personally and intimately, for about a quarter of a century, the worthy gentleman who has been nominated for my place, and I will say that I regard him as a kind, amiable and intelligent gentleman, a good citizen and an honorable opponent; and whatever issue I may have with him will be of principle, and not involving personalities. Mr. Lincoln made a speech before that Republican Convention which unanimously nominated him for the Senate,—a speech evidently well prepared and carefully written,—in which he states the basis upon which he proposes to carry on the campaign during this summer. In it he lays down two distinct propositions which I shall notice, and upon which I shall take a direct and bold issue with him.

His first and main proposition I will give in his own language, scripture quotations and all [laughter]; I give his exact language: "A house divided against itself cannot stand. I believe this government cannot endure, permanently, half *slave* and half *free*. I do not expect the Union to be *dissolved*; I do not expect the house to *fall;* but I do expect it to cease to be divided It will become *all* one thing or *all* the other."

In other words, Mr. Lincoln asserts, as a fundamental principle of this government, that there must be uniformity in the local laws and domestic institutions of each and all the States of the Union; and he therefore invites all the non-slaveholding States to band together, organize as one body, and make war upon slavery in Kentucky, upon slavery in Virginia, upon the Carolinas, upon slavery in all of the slaveholding States in this Union, and to persevere in that war until it shall be exterminated. He then notifies the slaveholding States to stand together as a unit and make an aggressive war upon the free states of this Union with a view of establishing slavery in them all; of forcing it upon Illinois, of forcing it upon New York, upon New England, and upon every other free state, and that they shall keep up the warfare until it has been formally established in them all. In other words, Mr. Lincoln advocates boldly and clearly a war of sections, a war of the North against the South, of the free states against the slave states,—a war of extermination,—to be continued relentlessly until the one or the other shall be subdued, and all the States shall become either free or become slave.

Now, my friends, I must say to you frankly that I take bold, unqualified issue with him upon that principle. I assert that it is neither desirable nor possible that there should be uniformity in the local institutions and domestic regulations of the different States of this Union. The framers of our government never contemplated uniformity in its internal concerns. The fathers of the Revolution and the sages who made the Constitution well understood that the laws and domestic institutions which would suit the granite hills of New Hampshire would be totally unfit for the rice plantations of South Carolina; they well understood that the laws which would suit the agricultural districts of Pennsylvania and New York would be totally unfit for the large mining regions of the Pacific, or the lumber regions of Maine.

Douglas shrewdly reminded his constituents that Maine had adopted a law prohibiting the sale of liquor, a law which Maine had a right to adopt if she chose, but no right to impose upon Chicago. Our system of government was intentionally elastic so as to permit such diversity of legislation. Maine had a right to take such steps as she chose to control the liquor-traffic within her own borders, and Illinois had the same right and might choose a very different method. Could not the house of the Federal Union stand, though thus divided?

From this view of the case, my friends, I am driven irresistibly to the conclusion that diversity, dissimilarity, variety, in all our local and domestic institutions, is the great safeguard of our liberties, and that the framers of our institutions were wise, sagacious, and patriotic, when they made this government a confederation of sovereign states, with a Legislature for each, and conferred upon each Legislature the power to make all local and domestic institutions to suit the people it represented, without interference from any other State or from the general Congress of the Union. If we expect to maintain our liberties, we must preserve the rights and sovereignty of the states; we must maintain and carry out that great principle of self-government incorporated in the Compromise measures of 1850, indorsed by the Illinois Legislature in 1851, emphatically embodied and carried out in the Kansas-Nebraska bill, and vindicated this year by the refusal to bring Kansas into the Union with a Constitution distasteful to her people.

Douglas took pains to disclaim any leanings toward abolition as the ground of his opposition to the Lecompton Constitution.

He opposed that constitution, as he declared, solely because it was imposed upon the people of Kansas in violation of the principle of self-government. If the people of Kansas had themselves framed and adopted that constitution, he would have made no objection to it:

I will be entirely frank with you. My object was to secure the right of the people of each state and of each territory, North or South, to decide the question for themselves, to have slavery or not, just as they chose; and my opposition to the Lecompton Constitution was not predicated upon the ground that it was a pro-slavery Constitution, nor would my action have been different had it been a Free-soil Constitution. My speech against the Lecompton fraud was made on the ninth of December, while the vote on the slavery clause in that Constitution was not taken until the twenty-first of the same month, nearly two weeks after. I made my speech against the Lecompton monstrosity solely on the ground that it was a violation of the fundamental principles of free government; on the ground that it was not the act and deed of the people of Kansas; that it did not embody their will; that they were averse to it; and hence I denied the right of Congress to force it upon them, either as a free state or a slave state. I deny the right of Congress to force a slaveholding State upon an unwilling people. I deny their right to force a free state upon an unwilling people. I deny their right to force a good thing upon a people who are unwilling to receive it. The great principle is the right of every community to judge and decide for itself whether a thing is right or wrong, whether it would be good or evil for them to adopt it; and the right of free action, the right of free thought, the right of free judgment upon the question is dearer to every true American than any other under a free government. My objection to the Lecompton contrivance was, that it undertook to put a Constitution on the people of Kansas against their will, in opposition to their wishes, and thus violated the great principle upon which all our institutions rest. It is no answer to this argument to say that slavery is an evil, and hence should not be tolerated. You must allow the people to decide for themselves whether it is a good or an evil.

The next night, Lincoln replied to Douglas, speaking from the same balcony of the Tremont Houe. The crowd was smaller

than that which had greeted Douglas, but still was large.   Douglas did not attend Lincoln's meeting.   He went to the theater
with a group of political friends.   Lincoln was probably disappointed that Douglas did not pay him the compliment, if it would
have been a compliment, of hearing him.   Whitney expressed
the opinion that Lincoln felt ill at ease "in having intruded upon
what was properly Douglas's occasion, and felt that it was not
quite the proper thing to be right at his heels at the first moment
of his constituents' welcome."*   He also thought Lincoln's
speech a poor and inadequate reply to Douglas.   But not every
one shared that opinion.

It would be difficult to say that Lincoln delivered a more able
address than Douglas, or as able an address as the one which Lincoln had delivered in Springfield.   But he met squarely the charge
of Senator Douglas, or "Judge Douglas" as he habitually called
him, that Lincoln favored a policy that was sure to result in
civil war.   He defended frankly and with marked ability the
position he had chosen in the Springfield speech.   He gave
Douglas credit for opposing the Lecompton Constitution, but
said that he himself and other Republicans had opposed it before Douglas did, and that Douglas could not claim any virtue
above or beyond theirs for taking that position, meritorious
though it was.

The Tremont House speech of Lincoln is notable because in
it Lincoln uncompromisingly stood by his position with respect
to the country's ultimately either becoming wholly slave or wholly free, and because he declared perhaps more emphatically than
he ever had before, his own personal hatred of slavery.

Lincoln said in part:

I am not, in the first place, unaware that this government has
endured eighty-two years, half slave and half free.   I know that.
I am tolerably well acquainted with the history of the country,
and I know that it has endured eighty-two years, half slave and
half free. I *believe*—and that is what I meant to allude to there—

---

*Life on the Circuit with Lincoln, p. 462.

I *believe* it has endured, because during all that time, until the introduction of the Nebraska bill, the public mind did rest all the time in the belief that slavery was in course of ultimate extinction. That was what gave us the rest that we had through that period of eighty-two years,—at least, so I believe. I have always hated slavery, I think, as much as any Abolitionist—I have been an Old Line Whig—I have always hated it, but I have always been quiet about it until this new era of the introduction of the Nebraska bill began. I always believed that everybody was against it, and that it was in course of ultimate extinction. [Pointing to Mr. Browning, who stood near by.] Browning thought so; the great mass of the nation have rested in the belief that slavery was in course of ultimate extinction. They had reason so to believe.

The adoption of the Constitution and its attendant history led the people to believe so; and that such was the belief of the framers of the Constitution itself, why did those old men, about the time of the adoption of the Constitution, decree that slavery should not go into the new territory, where it had not already gone? Why declare that within twenty years the African Slave Trade, by which slaves are supplied, might be cut off by Congress? Why were all these acts? I might enumerate more of these acts; but enough. What were they but a clear indication that the framers of the Constitution intended and expected the ultimate extinction of that institution? And now, when I say, as I said in my speech that Judge Douglas has quoted from, when I say that I think the opponents of slavery will resist the farther spread of it, and place it where the public mind shall rest with the belief that it is in course of ultimate extinction, I only mean to say that they will place it where the founders of this government originally placed it.

Douglas had excited a laugh by his reference to Lincoln's use of the Scripture in his "house-divided-against-itself" speech. Lincoln in his peroration referred to Douglas's reference to Lincoln's use of the Bible. Lincoln's answer to Douglas at this point is a fine expression of his own practical statesmanship and his ethical idealism. If perfect conformity to the ideal was impossible, Lincoln would accept the best that was available, but he would not forget nor hold in scorn the ultimate ideal, however presently unattainable:

My friend has said to me that I am a poor hand to quote Scripture. I will try it again, however. It is said in one of the admonitions of our Lord, "As your Father in Heaven is perfect, be ye also perfect." The Saviour, I suppose, did not expect that any human creature could be perfect as the Father in Heaven; but He said, "As your Father in Heaven is perfect, be ye also perfect." He set that up as a standard; and he who did most toward reaching that standard, attained the highest degree of moral perfection. So I say in relation to the principle that all men are created equal, let it be as nearly reached as we can. If we can not give freedom to every creature, let us do nothing that will impose slavery upon any other creature. Let us then turn this government back into the channel in which the framers of the Constitution originally placed it. Let us stand firmly by each other. If we do not do so we are turning in the contrary direction, that our friend Judge Douglas proposes—not intentionally —as working in the traces tend to make this one universal slave nation. He is one that runs in that direction, and as such I resist him.

In this address Lincoln met the scornful declaration of Douglas that the freedom of the slaves would result in social equality and in intermarriage of the races. This was the most clever of all of Lincoln's rejoinders:

We were often—more than once at least—in the course of Judge Douglas's speech last night, reminded that this government was made for white men; that he believed it was made for white men. Well, that is putting it into a shape in which no one wants to deny it; but the Judge then goes into his passion for drawing inferences that are not warranted. I protest, now and for ever, against that counterfeit logic which presumes that because I did not want a negro woman for a slave, I do necessarily want her for a wife. My understanding is that I need not have her for either, but, as God made us separate, we can leave one another alone, and do one another much good thereby. There are white men enough to marry all the white women, and enough black men to marry all the black women; and in God's name let them be so married. The judge regales us with the terrible enormities that take place by the mixture of races; that the inferior race bears the superior down. Why, Judge, if we do not let them get together in the territories they won't mix there.

Lincoln did not stand wholly on the defensive in this Chicago speech. Without claiming to be more altruistic than a politician might reasonably claim to be, he advanced to a position where he could demand that this slavery issue be met, not as something morally indifferent, but as a question profoundly ethical. He said:

I do not claim, gentlemen, to be unselfish; I do not pretend that I would not like to go to the United States Senate,—I make no such hypocritical pretense; but I do say to you that in this mighty issue, it is nothing to you—nothing to the mass of the people of the nation, whether or not Judge Douglas or myself shall ever be heard of after this night; it may be a trifle to either of us, but in connection with this mighty question, upon which hang the destinies of the nation, perhaps, it is absolutely nothing; but where will you be placed if you re-indorse Judge Douglas? Don't you know how apt he is, how exceedingly anxious he is at all times, to seize upon anything and everything to persuade you that something *he* has done *you* did yourselves? Why, he tried to persuade you last night that our Illinois Legislature instructed him to introduce the Nebraska bill. There was nobody in that Legislature ever thought of such a thing; and when he first introduced the bill, he never thought of it; but still he fights furiously for the proposition, and that he did it because there was a standing instruction to our Senators to be always introducing Nebraska bills. He tells you he is for the Cincinnati platform, he tells you he is for the Dred Scott decision. He tells you, not in his speech last night, but substantially in a former speech, that he cares not if slavery is voted up or down— he tells you the struggle on Lecompton is past—it may come up again or not, and if it does he stands where he stood when in spite of him and his opposition, you built up the Republican party. If you endorse him, you tell him you do not care whether slavery be voted up or down.

Lincoln's address was received with an enthusiasm almost equal to that which had greeted Douglas. The campaign of 1858 was fairly opened.

Then Douglas began his triumphal tour of Illinois, making between July ninth and November seventh almost if not quite a

hundred political addresses in various parts of the state. He
waited just a week in Chicago and then set forth on a special
train with much waving of banners and with many cheers.

On the following Friday, July sixteenth, Douglas spoke at
Bloomington. Lincoln went over from Springfield to hear him.
Again Douglas quoted Lincoln's Springfield speech. With great
ability Douglas set forth the inevitable disaster which would
follow the acceptance of Lincoln's announced position. The nation always had been half slave and half free. The government
at the outset had recognized that situation. It was a condition
which could not be changed without violence on the part of one
section against the other, and the ultimate disruption of the
Union itself:

The Republican Convention, when it assembled at Springfield,
did me and the country the honor of indicating the man who was
to be their standard-bearer, and the embodiment of their principles, in this state. I owe them my gratitude for thus making
up a direct issue between Mr. Lincoln and myself. I shall have
no controversies of a personal character with Mr. Lincoln. I
have known him well for a quarter of a century. I have known
him, as you all know him, a kind-hearted, amiable gentleman, a
right good fellow, a worthy citizen, of eminent ability as a lawyer, and I have no doubt, sufficient ability to make a good Senator. The question, then, for you to decide is, whether his
principles are more in accordance with the genius of our free
institutions, the peace and harmony of the Republic, than those
which I advocate. He tells you, in his speech made at Springfield, before the Convention which gave him his unanimous nomination, that

"A house divided against itself can not stand."

"I believe this Government can not endure permanently, half
slave and half free."

"I do not expect the Union to be dissolved—I don't expect the
house to fall—but I do expect it will cease to be divided."

"It will become all one thing or all the other."

That is the fundamental principle upon which he sets out in
this campaign. Well, I do not suppose you will believe one
word of it when you come to examine it carefully, and see its

consequences. Although the Republic has existed from 1789 to this day, divided into free states and slave states, yet we are told that in the future it can not endure unless they shall become all free or all slave. For that reason he says, as the gentleman in the crowd says, that they must be all free. He wishes to go to the Senate of the United States in order to carry out that line of public policy which will compel all the States in the South to become free. How is he going to do it? Has Congress any power over the subject of slavery in Kentucky, or Virginia, or any other state of this Union? How, then, is Mr. Lincoln going to carry out that principle which he says is essential to the existence of this Union, to-wit: That slavery must be abolished in all the states of the Union, or must be established in them all? You convince the South that they must either establish slavery in Illinois, and in every other free state, or submit to its abolition in every southern state, and you invite them to make a warfare upon the northern states in order to establish slavery, for the sake of perpetuating it at home.

Douglas demanded to know how Lincoln proposed to accomplish the result which he desired, the making of a nation wholly free, and declared that Lincoln as a lawyer knew there was only one way by which he could do it, which would be by constitutional amendment, and that way would lead to violence. But he maintained that the only way in which slavery had been eliminated from any portion of the United States, had been by the recognition of the principle of popular sovereignty:

How is he to accomplish what he professes must be done in order to save the Union? Mr. Lincoln is a lawyer, sagacious and able enough to tell you how he proposes to do it. I ask Mr. Lincoln how it is that he proposes ultimately to bring about this uniformity in each and all of the states of the Union. There is but one possible mode which I can see, and perhaps Mr. Lincoln intends to pursue it; that is, to introduce a proposition into the Senate to change the Constitution of the United States, in order that all the State Legislatures may be abolished, state sovereignty blotted out, and the power conferred upon Congress to make local laws and establish the domestic institutions and police regulations uniformly throughout the United States. Are you prepared for such a change in the institutions of your country?

There is but one possible way in which slavery can be abolished, and that is by leaving a state, according to the principle of the Kansas-Nebraska Bill, perfectly free to form and regulate its institutions in its own way. That was the principle upon which this Republic was founded, and it is under the operation of that principle that we have been able to preserve the Union thus far. Under its operations, slavery disappeared from New Hampshire, from Rhode Island, from Connecticut, from New York, from New Jersey, from Pennsylvania, from six of the twelve original slaveholding states; and this gradual system of emancipation went on quietly, peacefully and steadily, so long as we in the free states minded our own business, and left our neighbors alone. But the moment the abolition societies were organized throughout the North, preaching a violent crusade against slavery in the southern states, this combination necessarily caused a counter-combination in the South, and a sectional line was drawn which was a barrier to any further emancipation.

On the following day Saturday, July 17, 1858, Senator Douglas spoke in Springfield. He was warmly received, but he knew that he had strong enemies as well as warm friends in his audience. Lincoln was not present, but many of his friends were there, and they heard Douglas tear to tatters the speech to which they had listened with such trepidation when Lincoln delivered it. Douglas repeated the opening paragraph of Lincoln's "house-divided-against-itself" speech, and told the Springfield voters what would follow if that principle were accepted:

Now, Mr. Lincoln says that he will not enter into Kentucky to abolish slavery there, but that all he will do is to fight slavery in Kentucky from Illinois. He will not go over there to set fire to the match. I do not think he would. Mr. Lincoln is a very prudent man. He would not deem it wise to go over into Kentucky to stir up this strife, but he would do it from this side of the river. Permit me to inquire whether the wrong, the outrage of interference by one state with the local concerns of another, is worse when you actually invade them than it would be if you carried on the warfare from another state? . . . . But yet, he says he is going to persevere in this system of sectional warfare, and I have no doubt he is sincere in what he says. He says that the existence of the Union depends upon his success in firing into these slave States until he exterminates them. He says that unless he shall play his batteries successfully, so as to abolish slavery in every one of the States, that the Union shall be dissolved; and he says that a dissolution of the Union would be a terrible calamity. Of course it would. We are all friends of the Union. We all believe—I do—that our lives, our liberties, our hopes in the future depend upon the preservation and perpetuity of this glorious Union. I believe that the hopes of the friends of liberty throughout the world depend upon the perpetuity of the American Union. But while I believe that my mode of preserving the Union is a very different one from that of Mr. Lincoln, I believe that the Union can only be preserved by maintaining inviolate the Constitution of the United States as our fathers have made it. That Constitution guarantees to the people of every state the right to have slavery or not have it; to have negroes or not have them; to have Maine liquor laws or not have them; to have just such institutions as they choose, each state being left free to decide for itself. The framers of that Constitution never conceived the idea that uniformity in the domestic institutions of the different States was either desirable or possible.

An important part of the campaign issue gathered about the Dred Scott decision. A slave by that name had been taken by his master from a slave state into a state where slavery was prohibited. Action was brought in the Federal Court on the ground that Scott, not being an escaped fugitive, but having been voluntarily taken by his master into territory where slavery was prohibited, had by that act of the master become free. The case was argued before the Supreme Court in May, 1854. The decision was postponed until after the presidential election of 1856. It is quite possible that had the decision been announced before the election, the result of the election would have been changed. The decision was handed down by Chief Justice Roger B. Taney. The court held that Dred Scott, being descended from an African slave, was not and could not be a citizen of the United States, and could not come into court. This decision disposed of the case itself, and became the basis for the declaration that the Supreme Court had held that "the negro had no rights which the white man is bound to respect." But as the point had been made in the argument that by the repeal of the Missouri Compromise, Scott was free because he had been taken into a free territory, the court proceeded to say in an *obiter dictum* that Congress had no power to prohibit slavery in the territories, since by the Constitution slavery was legal in all the territories.

This decision virtually nationalized slavery. Furthermore, as both Congress and the president were already committed to the slavery program, this decision seemed to the friends of freedom to deliver the third and last department of the Federal government to the slave holding interests. The whole government, executive, legislative, judicial had become the instrument of slavery.

Douglas did not avoid a discussion of the Dred Scott case. He did not himself defend in its entirety the utterance of Judge Taney in handing down the Dred Scott decision, but he did maintain that the constitutionality of the fugitive slave law had been tested in the legal and proper way, namely, by the orderly and lawful decision of the Supreme Court of the United States. He might have his own opinion, and so might Mr. Lincoln, as to some of the things involved in that decision, but the decision itself had been reached in constitutional fashion. Incidentally, he ventured to forecast the results of a Republican victory if one should occur two years later, and he thought of Mr. Seward as a possible president, and Abraham Lincoln as a judge on the Supreme bench, wrestling with the problem of reversing the Dred Scott decision:

The Constitution says that the judicial power of the United States shall be vested in the Supreme Court, and such inferior courts as Congress shall, from time to time, ordain and establish. Hence it is the province and duty of the Supreme Court to pronounce judgment on the validity and constitutionality of an Act of Congress. In this case they have done so, and Mr. Lincoln will not submit to it, and he is going to reverse it by another Act of Congress of the same tenor. My opinion is that Mr. Lincoln ought to be on the Supreme Bench himself, when the Republicans get into power, if that kind of law knowledge qualifies a man for the bench. But Mr. Lincoln intimates that there is another mode by which he can reverse the Dred Scott decision. How is that? Why, he is going to appeal to the people to elect a president who will appoint judges who will reverse the Dred Scott decision. Well, let us see how that is going to be done. First, he has to carry on his sectional organization, a party confined to the free states, making war upon the slaveholding states until he gets a Republican president elected. ["He never will, sir."] I do not believe he ever will. But suppose he should; when that Republican president shall have taken his seat (Mr. Seward, for instance), will he then proceed to appoint judges? No! he will have to wait until the present judges die before he can do that, and perhaps his four years would be out before a majority of these judges found it agreeable to die; and it is very possible, too, that Mr. Lincoln's senatorial term would expire before these judges would be accommodating enough to die. If it should so happen I do not see a very great prospect for Mr. Lincoln to reverse the Dred Scott decision. But suppose they should die, then how are the new judges to be appointed? Why, the Republican president is to call upon the candidates and catechise them, and ask them, "How will you decide this case if I appoint you judge?" Suppose, for instance, Mr. Lincoln to be a candidate for a vacancy on the Supreme Bench to fill Chief Justice Taney's place and when he applied to Seward, the latter would say, "Mr. Lincoln, I can not appoint you until I know how you will decide the Dred Scott case?" Mr. Lincoln tells him, and Seward then asks him how he will decide Tom Jones's case, and Bill Wilson's case, and thus catechises the judge as to how he will decide any case which may arise before him. Suppose you get a Supreme Court composed of such judges, who have been appointed by a partisan President upon their giving pledges how they would decide a case before it arose,—what confidence would you have in such a court?

Would not your court be prostituted beneath the contempt of all mankind? What man would feel that his liberties were safe, his right of person or property was secure, if the Supreme Bench, that august tribunal, the highest on earth, was brought down to that low, dirty pool wherein the judges are to give pledges in advance how they will decide all the questions which may be brought before them? It is a proposition to make that court the corrupt, unscrupulous tool of a political party. But Mr. Lincoln can not conscientiously submit, he thinks, to the decision of a court composed of a majority of Democrats. If he cannot, how can he expect us to have confidence in a court composed of a majority of Republicans, selected for the purpose of deciding against the Democracy, and in favor of the Republicans? The very proposition carries with it the demoralization and degradation destructive of the judicial department of the Federal government.

I say to you, fellow-citizens, that I have no warfare to make upon the Supreme Court because of the Dred Scott decision. I have no complaints to make against that court, because of that decision. My private opinions on some points of the case may have been one way and on other points of the case another; in some things concurring with the court and in others dissenting; but what have my private opinions in a question of law to do with the decision after it has been pronounced by the highest judicial tribunal known to the Constitution?

Douglas did not fail to employ his best popular argument by reminding the people of the direful consequences of Mr. Lincoln's alleged position that the negro was the white man's equal. If Mr. Lincoln wanted to claim kinship with the negro, Senator Douglas had no objection, but Douglas refused to accept the negro as a relative of his own. He said:

In his Chicago speech he says, in so many words, that it includes the negroes, that they were endowed by the Almighty with the right of equality with the white man, and therefore that that right is divine—a right under the higher law; that the law of God makes them equal to the white man, and therefore that the law of the white man cannot deprive them of that right. This is Mr. Lincoln's argument. He is conscientious in his belief. I do not question his sincerity; I do not doubt that he, in his conscience, believes that the Almighty made the negro equal to the white man. He thinks that the negro is his brother. I do not think that the negro is any kin of mine at all. And here is the difference between us. I believe that the Declaration of Independence, in the words "all men are created equal," was intended to allude only to the people of the United States, to men of European birth or descent, being white men. . . . The Declaration of Independence only included the white people of the United States. The Constitution of the United States was framed by the white people, it ought to be administered by them, leaving each State to make such regulations concerning the negro as it chooses.

On the evening of the same day, Mr. Lincoln replied to Senator Douglas. He spoke of his own humble station and of the high position of Senator Douglas. He said:

Senator Douglas is of world-wide renown. All the anxious politicians of his party, or who have been of his party for years past, have been looking upon him as certainly, at no distant day, to be the president of the United States. They have seen in his round, jolly, fruitful face, post-offices, land-offices, marshalships and cabinet appointments, chargeships and foreign missions, bursting and sprouting out in wonderful exuberance, ready to be laid hold of by their greedy hands. And as they have been gazing upon this attractive picture so long, they can not, in the little distraction that has taken place in the party, bring themselves to give up the charming hope; but with greedier anxiety they rush about him, sustain him, and give him marches, triumphal entries, and receptions beyond what even in the days of his highest prosperity they could have brought about in his favor. On the contrary, nobody has ever expected me to be president. In my poor, lean, lank face, nobody has ever seen that any cabbages were sprouting out. These are disadvantages, all taken together, that the Republicans labor under. *We* have to fight this battle upon principle, and upon principle alone. I am, in a certain sense, made the standard-bearer in behalf of the Republicans. I was made so merely because there had to be some one so placed,—I being in no wise preferable to any other one of the twenty-five, perhaps a hundred, we have in the Republican ranks. Then I say I wish it to be distinctly understood and borne in mind, that we have to fight this battle without many—perhaps without any—of the external aids which are brought to bear against us. So I hope those with whom I am surrounded have principle enough to nerve themselves for the task, and leave nothing undone that can be fairly done to bring about the right result.

Lincoln's position, chosen by himself, had now been challenged. He was now compelled to defend his "house-divided-against-itself" speech in the place where he had made it, and he accepted that challenge. He repeated the declaration of that belief, which he carefully differentiated from any desire on his part of provoking a civil war. He reaffirmed that the government of the United States could not permanently endure if part of the states were to accept slavery as a permanent institution, and the others were to stand in permanent antagonism to it. He said:

When he [Douglas] was preparing his plan of campaign, Napoleon-like, in New York, as appears by two speeches I have heard him deliver since his arrival in Illinois, he gave special attention to a speech of mine, delivered here on the 16th of June last. He says that he carefully read that speech. He told us that at Chicago a week ago last night, and he repeated it at Bloomington last night. Doubtless, he repeated it again to-day, though I did not hear him. In the two first places—Chicago and Bloomington—I heard him; to-day I did not. He said he had carefully examined that speech,—*when,* he did not say; but there is no reasonable doubt it was when he was in New York preparing his plan of campaign. I am glad he did read it carefully. He says it was evidently prepared with great care. I freely admit it was prepared with care. I claim not to be more free from errors than others,—perhaps scarcely so much; but I was very careful not to put anything in that speech as a matter of fact, or make any inferences which did not appear to me to be true and fully warrantable. If I made any mistake I was willing to be corrected; if I had drawn any inference in regard to Judge Douglas, or any one else, which was not warranted, I was fully prepared to modify it as soon as discovered. I planted myself upon the truth and the truth only, so far as I knew it, or could be brought to know it.
    Although I have ever been opposed to slavery, so far I rested in the hope and belief that it was in the course of ultimate

extinction. For that reason, it had been a minor question with me. I might have been mistaken; but I had believed, and now believe, that the whole public mind, that is, the mind of the great majority, had rested in that belief up to the repeal of the Missouri Compromise. But upon that event, I became convinced that either I had been resting in a delusion, or the institution was being placed on a new basis,—a basis for making it perpetual, national and universal. Subsequent events have greatly confirmed me in that belief. I believe that bill to be the beginning of a conspiracy for that purpose. So believing, I have since then considered that question a paramount one. So believing, I thought the public mind will never rest till the power of Congress to restrict the spread of it shall again be acknowledged and exercised on the one hand, or, on the other, all resistance be entirely crushed out. I have expressed that opinion, and I entertain it to-night.

Both in Chicago and in Springfield Lincoln followed Douglas, and answered him on the same or the following day. For this program Lincoln was much criticized. He was declared to be taking advantage of the reputation of Senator Douglas to secure crowds which his own reputation would not have sufficed to assemble; and, of course, in each such case, Lincoln had the advantage, highly prized by lawyers, of the closing argument. Again, after an interval of two weeks, the two men were in Chicago, and both at the Tremont House. Although they met personally, and on friendly terms, the formalities of their arrangement were conducted through seconds. Lincoln sent to Douglas, under date of July twenty-fourth, a formal challenge to stump the state together in a joint debate. Douglas replied that his dates were already fixed, and that Democratic candidates, congressional and local, were expecting to be present and speak at his several appointments, thus occupying all the time. But he accepted the challenge to the extent of seven joint debates, one in each congressional district except the two containing the cities of Chicago and Springfield, in which they had already spoken. Lincoln thereafter absented himself from Douglas's exclusive meetings, and informed Douglas of his purpose so to do. The corre-

spondence involved some sparring, and concluded with the selection by Douglas, as the challenged party, of the dates and
places indicated in the final letters of this correspondence:

Mr. Douglas to Mr. Lincoln

Bement, Piatt Co., Ill., July 30, 1858.

Dear Sir:—Your letter dated yesterday, accepting my proposition for a joint discussion at one prominent point in each Congressional District, as stated by my previous letter, was received
this morning.
The times and places designated are as follows:—

Ottawa, La Salle County.....August	21st,	1858.
Freeport, Stephenson County..	"	27th,	"
Jonesboro, Union County . ....September	15th,	"
Charleston, Coles County	"	18th,	"
Galesburg, Knox County ....October	7th,	"
Quincy, Adams County	"	13th,	"
Alton, Madison County	"	15th,	"

I agree to your suggestion that we shall alternately open and
close the discussion. I will speak at Ottawa one hour, you can
reply, occupying an hour and a half, and I will follow for half
an hour. At Freeport, you shall open the discussion and speak
one hour, I will follow for an hour and a half, and you can then
reply for half an hour. We will alternate in like manner in each
successive place.
Very respectfully, your obedient servant,
S. A. Douglas.
Hon. A. Lincoln, Springfield, Ill.

Mr. Lincoln to Mr. Douglas

Springfield, July 31, 1858.
Hon. S. A. Douglas: Dear Sir,—Yours of yesterday, naming
places, times and terms, for joint discussion between us, was received this morning. Although, by the terms, as you propose,
you take *four* openings and closes, to my *three,* I accede, and
thus close the arrangement. I direct this to you at Hillsboro,

and shall try to have both your letter and this appear in the
Journal and *Register* of Monday morning.

Your obedient servant,
A. Lincoln.

The political newspapers of Chicago made elaborate preparations for the reporting and printing of the speeches. The *Press
and Tribune,* now the *Tribune,* employed Horace White and
Robert R. Hitt as its reporters, and the *Times* employed Henry
Binmore and James B. Sheridan. These were four competent
reporters. There was a considerable variation in the reports.
The outdoor surroundings, the variable winds, the jostling
crowds, the noise and inadequate facilities in the way of tables,
made accurate reports difficult; and it must be acknowledged
that each side reported its own candidate more carefully than the
other. The charges of misquoting lessened as the campaign
proceeded. The speeches were not telegraphed to Chicago. The
reporters transcribed their notes, taking them personally from
the nearer places, and mailing them or sending them by messengers from the more distant cities. In the printed volumes,
Lincoln's speeches are quoted from the *Press and Tribune,* and
those of Douglas from the *Times.*

The first joint debate was held in Ottawa, Saturday, August
21, 1858. Douglas had the opening hour and closing half-hour,
and Lincoln spoke one and one-half hours between. In this debate there was free interchange of personalities, courteous according to the standards of the time, but with a free and rough
humor much appreciated by the audience. Each speaker told
how successful the other man had been, and how unsuccessful he
himself was, and neither deceived any one by his mock humility.

Douglas led off in this play to the galleries:

In the remarks I have made on this platform, and the position
of Mr. Lincoln upon it, I mean nothing personally disrespectful
or unkind to that gentleman. I have known him for nearly
twenty-five years. There were many points of sympathy between us when we first got acquainted. We were both com-

paratively boys, and both struggling with poverty in a strange land. I was a school-teacher in the town of Winchester, and he a flourishing grocery-keeper in the town of Salem. He was more successful in his occupation than I was in mine, and hence more fortunate in this world's goods. Lincoln is one of those peculiar men who perform with admirable skill everything which they undertake. I made as good a school-teacher as I could, and when a cabinet maker I made a good bedstead and tables, although my old boss said I succeeded better with bureaus and secretaries than with anything else; but I believe that Lincoln was always more successful in business than I, for his business enabled him to get into the Legislature. I met him there, however, and had a sympathy with him, because of the up-hill struggle we both had in life. He was then just as good at telling an anecdote as now. He could beat any of the boys wrestling, or running a foot-race, in pitching quoits or tossing a copper; could ruin more liquor than all of the boys of the town together; and the dignity and impartiality with which he presided at a horse-race or fist-fight excited the admiration and won the praise of everybody that was present and participated. I sympathized with him because he was struggling with difficulties, and so was I. Mr. Lincoln served with me in the Legislature in 1836, when we both retired, and he subsided, or became submerged, and he was lost sight of as a public man for some years. In 1846, when Wilmot introduced his celebrated proviso, and the Abolition tornado swept over the country, Lincoln again turned up as a member of Congress from the Sangamon district. I was then in the Senate of the United States, and was glad to welcome my old friend and companion. Whilst in Congress, he distinguished himself by his opposition to the Mexican War, taking the side of the common enemy against his own country; and when he returned home he found that the indignation of the people followed him everywhere, and he was again submerged or obliged to retire into private life, forgotten by his former friends. He came up again in 1854, just in time to make this abolition or Black Republican platform, in company with Giddings, Lovejoy, Chase, and Fred Douglass, for the Republican party to stand upon.

Lincoln had, indeed, kept a country store; but a "grocery" as then understood, was a place principally for the sale of liquor.

Lincoln took pains to have it understood that he had never kept that kind of establishment, and he also took pains to refute the charge that he had shown lack of loyalty to his country or her soldiers, in his opposition to the Mexican War:

Now I pass on to consider one or two more of these little follies. The judge is woefully at fault about his early friend Lincoln being a "grocery-keeper." I don't know as it would be a great sin, if I had been; but he is mistaken. Lincoln never kept a grocery anywhere in the world. It is true that Lincoln did work the latter part of one winter in a little still-house, up at the head of a hollow. And so I think my friend the Judge is equally at fault when he charges me at the time when I was in Congress of having opposed our soldiers who were fighting in the Mexican War. The judge did not make his charge very distinctly, but I can tell you what he can prove, by referring to the record. You remember I was an old Whig, and whenever the Democratic party tried to get me to vote that the war had been righteously begun by the president, I would not do it. But whenever they asked for any money, or land-warrants, or anything to pay the soldiers there, during all that time, I gave the same vote that Judge Douglas did. You can think as you please as to whether that was consistent. Such is the truth; and the Judge has the right to make all he can out of it. But when he, by a general charge, conveys the idea that I withheld supplies from the soldiers who were fighting in the Mexican War, or did anything else to hinder the soldiers, he is, to say the least, grossly and altogether mistaken, as a consultation of the records will prove to him.

As I have not used up so much of my time as I had supposed, I will dwell a little longer upon one or two of these minor topics upon which the Judge has spoken. He has read from my speech in Springfield, in which I say that "a house divided against itself cannot stand." Does the judge say it *can* stand? I don't know whether he does or not. The judge does not seem to be attending to me just now, but I would like to know, if it is his opinion that a house divided against itself *can stand*. If he does, then there is a question of veracity, not between him and me, but between the judge and an authority of a somewhat higher character.

The second of the joint debates occurred at Freeport, Friday, August twenty-seventh. This was the northernmost point in which a debate occurred, and Lincoln took advantage of this fact to propound to Douglas a series of interrogatories whose answers by Douglas are known as the "Freeport heresy." The crucial question which he propounded to Douglas was, "Can the people of a United States territory in any lawful way, against the wish of any citizen of the United States, exclude slavery from its limits prior to the formation of a state constitution?"

This was no new question to Douglas, for Lyman Trumbull had propounded it to him more than two years earlier on June 9, 1856. At that time, however, the Dred Scott decision had not been rendered, and Douglas was able to say that this was a judicial question and that a good Democrat would stand by the decision of the court. Now that decision had been rendered, and Douglas made the best of a painful necessity, and declared that the people of a state could attain that result by virtue of the police power which they might exercise through unfriendly legislation. Lincoln knew that this answer would gain Douglas some immediate support, but ultimately would lose him many votes in the South, and very possibly would defeat his hopes for the presidency. This is the answer of Douglas:

The next question propounded to me by Mr. Lincoln is, Can the people of a Territory in any lawful way, against the wishes of any citizen of the United States, exclude slavery from their limits prior to the formation of a state constitution? I answer emphatically, as Mr. Lincoln has heard me answer a hundred times from every stump in Illinois, that in my opinion the people of a territory can, by lawful means, exclude slavery from their limits prior to the formation of a state constitution. Mr. Lincoln knew that I had answered that question over and over again. He heard me argue the Nebraska bill on that principle all over the state in 1854, in 1855, and in 1856, and he has no excuse for pretending to be in doubt as to my position on that question. It matters not what way the Supreme Court may hereafter decide as to the abstract question whether slavery may or may not go into a territory under the Constitution, the people have the lawful means to introduce it or exclude it as they please, for the reason that slavery cannot exist a day or an hour anywhere, unless it is supported by local police regulations. Those police regulations can only be established by the local legislature; and if the people are opposed to slavery, they will elect representatives to that body who will by unfriendly legislation effectually prevent the introduction of it into their midst. If, on the contrary, they are for it, their legislation will favor its extension. Hence, no matter what the decision of the Supreme Court may be on that abstract question, still the right of the people to make a slave territory or a free territory is perfect and complete under the Nebraska bill. I hope Mr. Lincoln deems my answer satisfactory on that point.

Lincoln can not have been very well satisfied with the immediate effect of this answer; and some of his friends regretted his having asked it. Lincoln knew, however, that whatever Douglas gained in the North by this declaration, he would lose in the South. It is claimed that by this question Lincoln deliberately gave Douglas the senatorship, that later he might defeat Douglas for the presidency; but this is too much to claim in the way of political sagacity and foresight. Few if any politicians, with a high office within their grasp, deliberately sacrifice it for the sake of a larger possibility two years remote. The contingencies of political life are too many and too uncertain for such a gamble against the fates. Lincoln knew what Douglas would answer, and knew that Douglas would lose quite as much as he would gain by it.

The discussions at Jonesboro and Charleston followed on Wednesday and Saturday, September fifteenth and eighteenth respectively, and then occurred the memorable debate at Galesburg, Thursday, October seventh. Knox College, on whose campus this discussion occurred, believed in Lincoln, and when he was elected president, conferred on him the degree Doctor of Laws.*

*The motion to confer this degree on Lincoln was made by O. H. Browning, a member of the Knox College Board of Trustees.

Lincoln was among his friends at Galesburg. Above the stand where he and Douglas spoke was a great banner bearing the legend, "Knox College for Lincoln." There Lincoln set forth more strongly than he had done elsewhere, not simply his own conviction that the nation must become either wholly slave or wholly free, but his belief that the position taken by Douglas with reference to the Dred Scott decision was preparing inevitably to make slavery national. If property in slaves was the same morally as property in horses or other chattels, then Douglas was right, and his position was entirely logical in profession not to care whether slavery was voted up or down. But Lincoln contended that between slavery and all other forms of property was a high moral distinction which Douglas with his great skill and ability was steadfastly endeavoring to obliterate. Commenting on Douglas's statement that he did not care whether slavery was voted up or down, he said:

This is perfectly logical, if you do not admit that slavery is wrong. If you do admit that it is wrong, Judge Douglas cannot logically say he don't care whether a wrong is voted up or voted down. Judge Douglas declares that if any community wants slavery they have a right to have it. He can say that logically, if he says that there is no wrong in slavery; but if you admit that there is a wrong in it, he cannot logically say that anybody has a right to do wrong. He insists that, upon the score of equality, the owners of slaves and owners of property—of horses and every other sort of property—should be alike, and hold them alike in a new Territory. That is perfectly logical if the two species of property are alike and are equally founded in right. But if you admit that one of them is wrong, you can not institute any equality between right and wrong. And from this difference of sentiment,—the belief on the part of one that the institution is wrong, and a policy springing from that belief which looks to the arrest of the enlargement of that wrong; and this other sentiment, that it is no wrong, and a policy sprung from that sentiment, which will tolerate no idea of preventing the wrong from growing larger, and looks to there never being an end to it through all the existence of things,—arises the real difference between Judge Douglas and his friends on the one hand, and the Republicans on the other.   Now, I confess myself as belonging to that class in the country who contemplate slavery as a moral, social, and political evil, having due regard for its actual existence amongst us and the difficulties of getting rid of it in any satisfactory way, and to all the constitutional obligations which have been thrown about it; but, nevertheless, desire a policy that looks to the prevention of it as a wrong, and looks hopefully to the time when as a wrong it may come to an end.

Webster, Calhoun and Clay were dead.   Douglas was probably the ablest man in the United States Senate in the year 1858.   His success as a compromiser had caused him frequently to be alluded to as a successor of Henry Clay.   One of the ablest paragraphs in Lincoln's address at Galesburg was that in which he quoted Clay himself on the slavery question, contrasting his position with that of Douglas, and planted himself irrevocably on the moral aspects of the issue.   The Republican Party had been charged by Douglas with being a sectional and divisive party. Lincoln declared that it was the friends of slavery who were sectional and divisive.   Freedom was national; slavery was sectional, and the issue between those who favored freedom and those who favored slavery was incontestably a moral issue. Here Lincoln made a frank avowal of the doctrine of the Liberty Party of 1840 and 1844.   But Lincoln cited as his authority, not that party but Henry Clay.   This is the fine paragraph in which Lincoln quoted Clay against Douglas and reaffirmed the unalterable quality of the slavery issue:

I have said once before, and I will repeat it now, that Mr. Clay, when he was once answering an objection to the Colonization Society, that it had a tendency to the ultimate emancipation of the slaves, said that "those who would repress all tendencies to liberty and ultimate emancipation must do more than put down the benevolent efforts of the Colonization Society—they must go back to the era of our liberty and independence, and muzzle the cannon that thunders its annual joyous return; they must blot out the moral lights around us; they must penetrate

the human soul, and eradicate the light of reason and the love of
liberty!" And I do think—I repeat, though I said it on a former
occasion—that Judge Douglas and whoever, like him, teaches
that the negro has no share, humble though it may be, in the
Declaration of Independence, is going back to the era of our
liberty and independence, and, so far as in him lies, muzzling the
cannon that thunders its annual joyous return; that he is blowing out the moral lights around us, when he contends that whoever wants slaves has a right to hold them; that he is penetrat-
ing, so far as lies in his power, the human soul, and eradicating
the light of reason and the love of liberty, when he is in every
possible way preparing the public mind, by his vast influence,
for making the institution of slavery perpetual and national.

The Galesburg meeting was the high-water mark of the debates. Both men had thoroughly learned each other's method
and material, and each was certain of his own resources. The
two discussions at Quincy and Alton, on Wednesday and Friday, October thirteenth and fifteenth, closed what proved to be
an epoch-making campaign such as America never has witnessed
before or since.

At every one of the places appointed, excepting only Jonesboro and Alton, the two southernmost points on the circuit, the
crowds were vast. The largest, according to Horace White
who reported the addresses, was at Galesburg. When Douglas
began this campaign, his rich smooth voice was clear. In the
closing addresses he was so hoarse that it was difficult for him
to be heard. His flow of words was so continuous and unhesi-
tating, his method of approach was so direct, and his personality was so pleasing, he was listened to with great satisfaction.
Lincoln had a thin tenor voice that was almost a falsetto. It had
good carrying power, and better wearing qualities than the rich
baritone of Douglas, but it was not so pleasing or impressive.
Audiences were uniformly impressed with the fact that the little
man had the big voice, and the big man had the little voice. The
grace and self-confidence of Douglas made all the more apparent the awkwardness of Lincoln, and the difficulty which he

sometimes encountered of getting his address under way. But when he had fairly got into his subject, Lincoln was no longer constrained or awkward. Not only was his great stature impressive, but there was a certain fine dignity in his vast proportions and a convincing quality in his method of argument.

In this campaign, the apathy, if not hostility, of Horace Greeley was a continued sorrow to Lincoln. His sorrow was increased as election approached, by tidings which reached Lincoln to the effect that John J. Crittenden, the venerable Kentucky Whig senator, was giving aid and comfort to Douglas. Lincoln could hardly credit this information. He wrote to Senator Crittenden and his worst fears were confirmed. Crittenden believed that Douglas had manifested in the Senate such an attitude of heroism in the matter of the Lecompton Constitution, that he ought to be reelected regardless of the effect of his election on the new Republican Party of Illinois. This was bad enough, but as yet it had not been made public. About a week before the election, T. Lyle Dickey, one of Lincoln's long-time friends, who, however, sympathized with the view of Greeley regarding Douglas, published a letter from Crittenden which he had been keeping for some time as an eleventh-hour document. This letter, frankly supporting Douglas, amazed Lincoln's friends. The *Journal* tried to explain it away, but some one telegraphed to Crittenden and he repudiated the *Journal's* explanation. He was frankly opposed to Lincoln. This was a last straw, and more than a straw. Lincoln believed that it was the determining factor in his defeat.*

Besides his several discussions with Douglas, Lincoln filled thirty-one appointments made for him by the State Committee; and he spoke at several other places not arranged for by the party managers. A few days before the end of the campaign, he returned to Springfield and was at home over the last week-

---

*Lincoln's letters to Crittenden are to be found in the various editions of Lincoln's writings; and those of Crittenden to Lincoln are in the *Life of John J. Crittenden,* by Mrs. Coleman, his daughter.

end. On the last Saturday before the election, Herndon wrote
to Theodore Parker:

Springfield, Ill., October 30, 1858.

Friend:—To-day is Saturday and in a little while Mr. Lincoln
opens on our square, close to the state-house, on the great, vital,
and dominant issues of the day and age. We feel, as usual, full
of enthusiasm and of hope, and there is nothing which can well
defeat us but the elements, and the wandering, roving, robbing
Irish, who have flooded over the State. This charge is no humbug cry: it is a real and solid and terrible reality, looking us
right in the face, *with its thumb on its nose.* We, throughout
the States have this question before us: "What shall we do?
Shall we tamely submit to the Irish, or shall we rise and cut
their throats?" If blood is shed in Illinois to maintain the purity of the ballot-box, and the rights of the popular will, do not be
at all surprised. We are roused and fired to fury. My feelings
are ideas to some extent and therefore cool—I try to persuade
both parties to keep calm and cool, if possible; but let me say to
you, that there is great and imminent danger of a general and
terrible row, and if it commences woe be to the Irish—poor
fellows!

You know my position now, and let me state to you that I
am amidst the knowing ones, clubs, county committees, State
committees, leaders, sagacious men, etc., and from all places
and persons comes up this intelligence, "All is well." I, myself,
fear and am scolded because I cannot feel as I should—as others
do. My intuition—brute forecast, if you will—my bones, tell
me that *all* is not safe; yet I hope for the best. How are you—
are you up and walking about? Quit reading and writing, if you
can, and go off on a spree.

Your friend,
W. H. Herndon.

Lincoln was one of several speakers at this Saturday meeting.
He had been accustomed to speak without notes, or with very
few notes, in the seven great joint meetings, but on this occasion
he wrote carefully his brief address.* He must have known that

---

*It is probable that he spoke in part extemporaneously, but he wrote the
portion that he considered of supreme importance.

in all probability the following Tuesday would see the election of representatives and state senators who would make certain the choice of Douglas as senator to succeed himself. Reviewing the campaign from the experience available at its close, Lincoln reaffirmed in the strongest possible terms his unalterable opposition to the extension of slavery. He said that he had prayed earnestly to God, and had chosen his position in a clear conviction of duty. He said that he had not intended in that campaign to speak harshly of any one, and if he had done so inadvertently or without being conscious of doing so, he was truly sorry. He said that he had been charged with being ambitious, and he did not deny the charge. But he affirmed that if he could be assured that the Missouri restriction would be re-enacted, and slavery put back into its historic position as an acknowledged evil, to be presently tolerated within its then present limits as a necessity, but to be opposed in confident hope of its ultimate extinction, he would gladly, in consideration, agree never to be a candidate for any office, nor to oppose the candidacy of Judge Douglas for any office, so long as either of them should live.

This last speech of Lincoln was never printed. It is in reality his "lost speech." Delivered on Saturday, it found no place in the *Journal* of Monday, for that paper was already well set with the last campaign material that could be printed before election.

In considering the words which Lincoln spoke on that occasion, we are to remember how bitter had been some of the charges against him, and how cruelly he believed himself to have been wounded in the house of his friends. T. Lyle Dickey, who procured the Crittenden letter and held it until just before election, was a personal and political friend. As for Senator Crittenden, Lincoln, speaking a year later in Cincinnati, told of Crittenden's letters written in the interest of Douglas, and which Lincoln believed defeated him, called him "a senator from Kentucky whom I have always loved with an affection as tender and

15

enduring as I have ever loved any man." Under these conditions, Lincoln's short address reveals a noble and lofty spirit. It is our privilege after sixty-five years to read the words which Lincoln spoke on that memorable day :*

My friends, to-day closes the discussions of this canvass. The planting and the culture are over ; and there remains but the preparation, and the harvest.

I stand here surrounded by friends—some *political, all personal* friends, I trust. May I be indulged, in this closing scene, to say a few words of myself. I have borne a laborious, and, in some respects to myself, a painful part in the contest. Through all, I have neither assailed, nor wrestled with any part of the constitution. The legal right of the Southern people to reclaim their fugitives I have constantly admitted. The legal right of Congress to interfere with their institutions in the States, I have constantly denied. In resisting the spread of slavery to new territory, and with that, what appears to me to be a tendency to subvert the first principle of free government itself my whole effort has consisted. To the best of my judgment I have labored *for,* and not *against,* the Union. As I have not felt, so I have not expressed any harsh sentiment towards our Southern brethren. I have constantly declared, as I have really believed, the only difference between them and us, is the difference of circumstances.

I have meant to assail the motives of no party, or individual ; and if I have, in any instance (of which I am not conscious) departed from my purpose, I regret it.

I have said that in some respects the contest has been painful to me. Myself, and those with whom I act, have been constantly accused of a purpose to destroy the Union ; and bespattered with every imaginable odious epithet ; and some who were friends, as it were but yesterday have made themselves most active in this. I have cultivated patience, and made no attempt at a retort.

Ambition has been ascribed to me. God knows how sincerely I prayed from the first that this field of ambition might not be opened. I claim no insensibility to political honors ; but to-day could the Missouri restriction be restored, and the whole slavery

---

*For the courtesy of using this hitherto unknown but highly important address, I am indebted to the owner of the manuscript, my friend, Mr. Oliver R. Barrett, whose collection of Lincoln manuscripts, the most valuable in any private ownership, has been placed at my service.

question replaced on the old ground of "toleration" by *necessity* where it exists, with unyielding hostility to the spread of it, on principle, I would, in consideration, gladly agree, that Judge Douglas should never be *out,* and I never *in,* an office, so long as we both, or either, live.

These are not the words of a politician whose ethics are those of opportunism. They are the words of a noble statesman and an honest man. They are words that deserve to become as well known and as immortal as the best known and most cherished of the utterances of Lincoln.

Lincoln was defeated, but not badly so. The Legislature elected on Tuesday, November 2, 1858, gave Douglas fifty-four votes, to Lincoln's forty-six. A change of five legislative votes would have elected Lincoln. Indeed, he had a popular majority of over four thousand, and but for the bad apportionment law which then existed, would have defeated Douglas.

As Herndon had written to Theodore Parker just before the election, so he wrote again a few days after that event. The letter gives an analysis of the political situation as it then appeared to this hot-headed abolitionist friend of Lincoln:

Springfield, Ill., Nov. 8, 1858.

Friend Parker.

Dear Sir:—We are beaten in Illinois, as you are aware; but you may want to know the causes of our defeat. Firstly, then, I have more than once said our State presents three distinct phases of human development: the extreme north, the middle, and the extreme south. The first is intelligence, the second timidity, and the third ignorance on the special issue, but goodness and bravery. If a man spoke to suit the north—for freedom, justice—this killed him in the center and in the south. So in the center, it killed him north and south. So in the south, it surely killed him north. Lincoln tried to stand high and elevated, so he fell deep.

Secondly, Greeley never gave us one single, solitary, manly lift. On the contrary, his silence was his opposition. This our people felt. We never got a smile or a word of encouragement outside of Illinois from any quarter during all this great canvass.

The East was for Douglas *by silence*. This silence was terrible to us. Seward was against us too. Thirdly, Crittenden wrote letters to Illinois urging the Americans and Old Line Whigs to go for Douglas, and so they went "helter-skelter." Thousands of Whigs dropped us just on the eve of the election, through the influence of Crittenden.

Fourthly, all the pro-slavery men, north as well as south, went to a man for Douglas. They threw into this State money and men, and speakers. These forces and powers we were wholly denied by our Northern and Eastern friends. This cowed us somewhat, but let it go. Do you know what Byron says about revenge? He goes off in this wise: "There never was yet human power," etc. I shall make no hasty pledges, notwithstanding. I am bent on acting practically, so that I can help choke down slavery, and so I shall say nothing—not a word.

Fifthly, thousands of roving, robbing, bloated, pock-marked Catholic Irish were imported upon us from Philadelphia, New York, St. Louis, and other cities. I myself know of such, by their own confession. Some have been arrested, and are now in jail awaiting trial.

I want distinctly to say to *you* that no one of all of these causes defeated Lincoln; but I do want to say that it was the combination, with the power and influence of each, that "cleaned us out." Do you not *now* see that there is a conspiracy afloat which threatens the disorganization of the Republican party? Do you not see that Seward, Greeley, and Crittenden, etc., are at this moment in a joint common understanding to lower our platform?

In such conclusion let me say that as Douglas has got all classes to "boil his pot," with antagonistic materials and forces, that there is bound, by the laws of nature, to be an explosion—namely, somebody will be fooled. Look out! Greeley is a natural fool, I think, in this matter—his hearty Douglas position. So with Seward, Crittenden, with South and North. Douglas cannot hold all these places and men. Mark that! I am busy at Court and have no time to cut down or amplify—hope you can understand.   Your friend,

W. H. Herndon.

Lincoln was not greatly surprised when Douglas was elected. He had foreseen the result, but he had a kind of abiding faith that his own defeat brought ultimate success nearer, and he was right. The debates were printed in full, and eagerly read throughout the country. They served as the best popular interpretation of the issue between the two parties. They made it more certain than the wisest man could have understood in 1858, that Douglas and his party could not forever stand on the platform which he had laid down in that campaign. Lincoln wrote a few days after his defeat:

Douglas had the ingenuity to be supported in the late contest both as the best means to break down and uphold the slave interest. No ingenuity can keep these antagonistic elements in harmony long. Another explosion will soon occur.

Election day was dark and rainy. That night Lincoln remained in the telegraph office with a group of friends until the returns came in that indicated his defeat. Then he walked home alone in the dark and rain. November 7, 1864, was another such a day; and in the evening a small group gathered in the White House and listened to the returns that told of Lincoln's triumphant reelection to the presidency. The company was small, for Washington had been depopulated by those who had gone home to vote. Recalling that former election night in 1858, with the weather similar but other conditions quite different, Lincoln told his friends his recollections of that evening, and John Hay recorded it in his diary:

"For such an awkward fellow," said Lincoln, "I am pretty sure-footed. It used to take a pretty dexterous man to throw me. I remember the evening of the day in 1858 that decided the contest for the Senate between Mr. Douglas and myself, was something like this, dark, rainy and gloomy. I had been reading the returns, and had ascertained that we had lost the Legislature, and I started to go home. The path had been worn pig-backed and was slippery. My foot slipped from under me, knocking the other out of the way; but I recovered and said to myself, *'It's a slip and not a fall!'*"

CHAPTER XXVII

LINCOLN THE RAILSPLITTER
1860

Little did Abraham Lincoln realize when he was splitting rails to fence his father's first farm in Illinois, or to pay for a pair of homespun trousers, or to earn a few dollars from Major Warnick with the possible added advantage of seeing the major's daughter Polly, that he would see those same rails or any of them thirty years afterward, borne in triumphal procession as evidence of his fitness for the presidency of the United States.

Lincoln returned to Springfield after his defeat at the hands of Douglas, disappointed but not completely discouraged. If anything could have disheartened him, it would not have been the defeat, but the fact that the campaign had been a severe strain upon him financially. At that time he owned a house and lot, a small and unremunerative tract of land in Iowa acquired by him from the government in recognition of his military service in the Black Hawk War, and a law practise from which his annual income did not exceed three thousand dollars. For six months he had earned practically nothing while he was giving his time to the campaign against Douglas. The total value of his property as estimated by Mr. Arnold may have been ten or twelve thousand dollars. When he returned to Springfield he received a request from the Republican State Committee that he make a personal contribution toward the expense of the campaign. Lincoln wrote to his friend Norman B. Judd:

I have been on expenses so long, without earning anything, that I am absolutely without money now even for household expenses. Still, if you can put in $250 for me towards discharging the debt of the committee, I will allow it when you and I settle the private matter between us. This, with what I have already paid, with an outstanding note of mine, will exceed my subscription of $500. This, too, exclusive of my ordinary expenses during the campaign, all of which, being added to my loss of time and business, bears pretty heavily upon one no better off in this world's goods than I. But as I had the post of honor, it is not for me to be over nice.

Lincoln paid his share of the campaign expense, and went back to his law practise; but he was now a national figure, and one certain to play an important part in the political life of the country.

Lincoln then had some thought of entering the lecture field. He prepared a lecture on "Discoveries and Inventions," and delivered it in a few towns in Illinois, but it won him no great renown, and he soon gave up the lecture field. During the autumn of 1859, Douglas was delivering political addresses in Ohio, and Lincoln accepted an invitation to speak in Cincinnati and Columbus, in each place following Douglas. This short tour added to his fame. It also brought to him a gratifying offer from a Columbus firm to print his speeches with those of Douglas, delivered in the memorable debate. This was the more gratifying to Lincoln because he himself had made some effort to get those speeches published in Springfield, and had not been able to secure a publisher.

On Sunday night, October 16, 1859, John Brown, who had stood resolutely for freedom in Kansas, endeavored to bring in the kingdom of Heaven by violence. With a small body of armed men he seized the United States arsenal at Harper's Ferry, on the Potomac River, in Virginia. He believed that if the slaves were given a leader and an opportunity of freedom, they would rise and throw off the yoke of oppression. The slaves exhibited no favorable response to John Brown's attempt to free them. Brown's insurrection was speedily put down by United States troops. Several of his followers, including two of his sons, were killed. Brown himself was severely wounded and captured. He was tried by the Virginia courts, condemned and on December 2, 1859, was hanged. The slave-holding South was terribly agitated by his insurrection, believing that virtually the whole North was endeavoring to incite the slaves to bloody insurrection. In the North, Brown's futile effort was regarded for the most part with disapproval for its unwisdom and its violation of law; but it stirred the admiration of many thousands who honored the heroism of a deed they could not wholly approve; and it quite certainly brought nearer the day when the whole country would have to face the irrepressible conflict between slavery and freedom.

In the winter of 1859 Lincoln visited Kansas. There he was received with marked evidence of popular favor. The free state of Kansas realized that it owed to Lincoln not a little for its freedom. He spoke at Atchison, Troy, Leavenworth and other towns. His speeches were essentially a repetition of the arguments which he had used in his debate with Douglas, and he could not have found better material for his speeches in Kansas, nor audiences more in sympathy.

Lincoln was careful not to take the side of John Brown in his armed attack upon the government; but he warned the men upon the other side, who had hanged Brown, that if they made violent attack upon the nation, as a protest against the election of a candidate whom they did not like, they might expect a like result.

What Lincoln thought about Brown was carefully written and stated in his Cooper-Union address a few weeks later:

John Brown's effort was peculiar. It was not a slave insurrection. It was an attempt by white men to get up a revolt among slaves, in which the slaves refused to participate. In fact, it was so absurd that the slaves, with all their ignorance, saw plainly enough it could not succeed. That affair, in its philosophy, corresponds with the many attempts related in history, at the assassination of kings and emperors. An enthusiast broods over the oppression of the people till he fancies himself commissioned by Heaven to liberate them. He ventures the attempt, which ends in little else than his own execution. Orsini's attempt on Louis Napoleon and John Brown's attempt at Harper's Ferry were, in their philosophy, precisely the same. The eagerness to cast blame on old England in the one case, and on New England in the other, does not disprove the sameness of the two things.

Just after the John Brown raid another event occurred which had wide influence, the publication of *The Impending Crisis*, by Hinton Rowan Helper, of North Carolina. Helper was a southern man in his birth and sympathy, but he was opposed to slavery. His book was a forceful declaration that slavery was a bad thing for the white man. Especially did he make his argument on the basis of the welfare of the non-slaveholding whites in the South, whose labor was degraded by competition with slave labor. This was a thrust between the joints of the armor. The slaveholders had no answer to it. They could hang John Brown, and exclude Garrison's *Liberator* from the mails, and denounce *Uncle Tom's Cabin,* but there was no like way of disposing of the *Impending Crisis*. It was easy to raise the cry of "social equality" and to pour contempt upon the northern abolitionist "who thought that the chief end of man was nigger," but when a southern man advanced the argument that slavery degraded the white man, no such reply was possible. Attempts were made to prevent the sale of the book in the South, but there was no very good ground on which this could be done. No one could claim that it incited the slaves to insurrection; it did not profess greatly to care for the slaves. No one could pretend that it was a morbid attempt to make the black man the white man's equal: it was simply an endeavor to remove an artificial and corrupting inequality between white men. The book was denounced, but it was read, and next to *Uncle Tom's Cabin,* it helped to bring an end to slavery in the United States.

In the latter part of 1859 the name of Lincoln came to be prominently mentioned as that of an available candidate for the presidency of the United States. Lincoln met the first suggestions of this character with deprecation. He said that he did not think he was fit for the presidency, or that there was any possibility of his being nominated. Still the idea was pleasing to him. When in December, 1859, Mr. Jesse W. Fell, Secretary of the Republican Central Committee, asked Lincoln for a brief biographical sketch which might be used to further his interests, Lincoln demurred, but furnished the sketch written on three pages of paper. Quietly but steadily his reputation grew, and as the year 1860 brought the presidential election nearer, there was more frequent mention of Abraham Lincoln as a candidate.

Plymouth Church, Brooklyn, conducted a lecture course. In the autumn of 1859 Lincoln was invited to deliver a lecture there. He had tried out his *Discoveries and Inventions* on Illinois audiences, and was not satisfied with it. He replied accepting the invitation, provided he might be at liberty to deliver a political address, if he could not find time to prepare another. This condition was accepted; but in negotiations between the Plymouth Church lecture committee and The Young Men's Central Republican Union of New York City, the place and management were changed. Lincoln did not clearly understand the change, but went east still expecting to speak in Plymouth Church. A larger opportunity even than that which Henry Ward Beecher could have given him in Brooklyn, awaited the arrival of Lincoln in New York. He attended Plymouth Church on Sunday, heard Beecher preach, and learned the details of the modified plan.

On Monday evening, February 27, 1860, Mr. Lincoln delivered what was in some respects the greatest of his political orations. He spoke at Cooper Institute, in the City of New York. Horace Greeley, who in 1858 had advised the Illinois Republicans not to oppose Douglas in his canvass for reelection to the Senate, heard Lincoln's address, and said, "No man has been welcomed by such an audience of the intellect and mental culture of our city since the days of Clay and Webster."

William Cullen Bryant presided. With him on the platform

were some of the foremost men of New York. Lincoln delivered an address devoid of all the characteristics of stump oratory. It was a carefully reasoned, thoughtful discourse, addressed to the intelligence and conscience of his hearers. He surprised his audience by his knowledge of American political history and the principles underlying our national legislation. Lincoln obtained most of the facts of his Cooper Institute speech from Elliot's *Debates on the Federal Constitution*. It is said that when the speech was edited in New York for publication, those who prepared the address for printing spent three weeks in verifying its historical statements, and that they found no important errors. This may be an exaggeration as to the length of time expended, but it clearly indicates that Lincoln had prepared his address with great deliberation and care. He never had given to any other discourse so much of thoughtful preparation as he gave to this one.

The Cooper Institute address was printed in the papers the next day,* and afterward issued in pamphlet form and read throughout the country. It had much to do with Lincoln's nomination for the presidency.

Robert T. Lincoln is a very reticent man, and for the most part declines to speak for publication concerning his father; but one thing he modestly affirms, which is that he made his father president. In the autumn of 1859, Robert went to Cambridge expecting to enter Harvard. He was required to submit to an entrance examination covering sixteen subjects, and he failed in fifteen of them. The Lincoln family wrote him not to return home, but to enter Phillips Academy at Exeter, New Hampshire, and complete his preparation. This he did, and at the end of a year was able to enter Harvard and complete a regular course. But Mr. Lincoln was somewhat anxious about Robert's studies, and one of his reasons for being ready to visit New York and

---

*It was not telegraphed to Chicago, but was reprinted in the Chicago papers three days later as set from the copy furnished by the columns of the New York papers.

speak at Cooper Institute was to visit Robert and see how he was getting on at Exeter. Robert T. Lincoln believes that if he had failed in less than fifteen studies his father might have been less solicitous, and might not have delivered the Cooper Union speech, or having delivered it, might have returned from New York direct to Springfield. As it was, he determined to visit Robert and make a few speeches in New England.

Only once, and then a dozen years before, had Lincoln visited New England. Then he was speaking for Zachary Taylor, and exhorting Whig voters to stand by the old party. Now he was an earnest advocate of the new party.

Lincoln's address at Cooper Union was delivered on Monday evening, February 27, 1860. On Tuesday evening, February twenty-eighth, he spoke before a large audience in Railroad Hall, Providence, Rhode Island. On the following day, Wednesday, February twenty-ninth, he was on his way to New Hampshire, and did not speak. On Thursday, March first, he spoke at Concord, New Hampshire, in the afternoon, and at Manchester in the evening. At Concord he was introduced by Governor Frederick Smith, who referred to him as "the next president of the United States." Such an introduction was exceptional. At Norwich, Connecticut, where he spoke later, Honorable Daniel P. Tyler, who spoke before Lincoln, went the full length of the general imagination and suggested that Lincoln might be the next vice-president; beyond doubt, he had Seward in mind as the head of the ticket. On Friday, March second, Lincoln spoke at Dover, New Hampshire. On Saturday he spoke at Exeter, and spent Sunday with Robert.

Biographers of Lincoln have not considered adequately the effect of these New England speeches. Several of these authors, beginning with Lamon, state that Robert was in Harvard at that time; he did not enter Harvard until seven months later, and if he had been safe in Harvard, the tour might not have been made.

On Monday, March fifth, Lincoln spoke at Hartford, Connecticut; on Tuesday he spoke in New Haven, on Wednesday at

ABRAHAM LINCOLN IN 1860

Photograph by Brady at the time of the Cooper Union Address

Meriden, Connecticut; on Thursday at Woonsocket, Rhode Island; on Friday at Norwich, Connecticut; on Saturday at Bridgeport, Connecticut. In all, he delivered eleven speeches. He had large audiences everywhere. The spring elections were just at hand, and it is certain that his addresses had value, especially in Connecticut, where Governor Buckingham, the Republican candidate and a firm friend of Lincoln, was elected by a plurality of only 451. If Lincoln's addresses changed as many as 220 votes, his work was not in vain.

It was on this trip that he was interviewed by Reverend J. P. Gulliver, to whom Lincoln told of his learning to "demonstrate" his propositions. It was at Hartford, that Lincoln first met the "Wide-Awake" organization, with torchlights and oilcloth capes. The name originated in that city, though it is popularly believed to have been of western origin. In months that followed, Lincoln was to hear processions singing, to an old camp-meeting air that the Confederates later confiscated to celebrate the joys of those who "jine the cavalry":

"Old Abe Lincoln came out of the wilderness,
Out of the wilderness, out of the wilderness,
Old Abe Lincoln came out of the wilderness,
    Down in Illinois."

"Ain't I glad I jined the Wide-Awakes,
Jined the Wide-Awakes, jined the Wide-Awakes,
Ain't I glad I jined the Wide-Awakes,
    Down in Illinois!"*

These New England addresses did much for Lincoln. They helped to give voice to a more conservative type of Republican

*A few months before America entered the World War, there was a Preparedness Parade in Chicago, with a large reviewing stand on Michigan Boulevard in front of the Art Institute. As I was on my way to the reviewing stand, I encountered an old man with an oilcloth cap and cape "the same that I wore in 1860, sir, when I marched for Abe Lincoln!" In an interval between the noise of passing brass bands, he lifted his cracked old voice, and sang, "Ain't I glad I jined the Wide-Awakes?" Perhaps this was the last appearance of a representative of that body on any important occasion in any American city.

doctrine than that associated with the thought of John Brown and Helper of the *Impending Crisis* while standing squarely for a nation that was not to be permanently divided by slavery.

When Lincoln returned to Springfield after the Cooper Institute speech and the New England town he knew that there was a possibility of his nomination as president. Seward was the most likely nominee; Chase was next; but strange things happen in politics, and Lincoln knew that Seward and Chase and the other leading candidates might kill each other off and leave him as the most available candidate. Herndon wrote:

It was apparent now to Lincoln that the presidential nomination was within his reach. He began gradually to lose his interest in the law and to trim his political sails at the same time. His recent success had stimulated his self-confidence to unwonted proportions. He wrote to influential party workers everywhere. I know the idea prevails that Lincoln sat still in his chair in Springfield, and that one of those unlooked-for tides in human affairs came along and cast the nomination into his lap; but any man who has had experience in such things knows that great political prizes are not obtained in that way. The truth is, Lincoln was as vigilant as he was ambitious, and there is no denying the fact that he understood the situation perfectly from the start. In the management of his own interests he was obliged to rely almost entirely on his own resources. He had no money with which to maintain a political bureau and he lacked any kind of personal organization whatever. Seward had all these things, and, behind them all, a brilliant record in the United States Senate with which to dazzle his followers. But with all his prestige and experience the latter was no more adroit and no more untiring in pursuit of his ambition than the man who had just delivered the Cooper Institute speech.

The Republican State Convention was held at Decatur May 9 and 10, 1860. Lincoln as a Whig politician had been very reluctant to accept the method of a nominating convention. He preferred the popular scramble. But he learned, what the Whig Party learned too late, that if they were to succeed against the

Democrats they must iron out their differences in conventions of their own, and not go to the polls with a divided vote. Long before 1860 Lincoln was thoroughly committed to the principle of the party convention, and he looked forward to his own state convention with no little solicitude and hope. He wrote to Norman B. Judd:

I am not in a position where it would hurt much for me to not be nominated on the national ticket, but I am where it would hurt some for me to not get the Illinois delegates. Can you help me a little in your end of the vineyard?

It was in Judd's end of the vineyard that Lincoln needed help, for the northern end of Illinois was the old Whig end of the state, and was strong for Seward. But Judd did something very much more important than that of swinging a few delegates in northern Illinois from Seward to Lincoln. He so managed, as a member of the Republican National Committee, as to secure the Republican Convention for the City of Chicago.

When, therefore, the State Convention was held in Decatur on May ninth and tenth, it was with the knowledge that the National Convention would be held in the same state less than a week later.

Lincoln was not without influential friends in the northern end of Illinois. On February 6, 1860, the *Chicago Tribune* came out editorially for Lincoln. A number of other Illinois papers beginning with one in Rock Island, and largely representative of the northern end of Illinois, had already endorsed Lincoln, or soon did so. The campaign of publicity was well planned and actively pursued.

Lincoln attended the Republican Convention at Decatur. Some of his friends questioned the wisdom of his going there. Lincoln himself said that he felt that he was "too much of a candidate to go and not quite enough of a candidate to stay away."

Lincoln's friends were confident of securing his nomination in Illinois. But they wanted to do more than this. They desired to stage for him a great demonstration. Lincoln's friend, Richard J. Oglesby, afterward governor of the state, was a resident of Decatur. A brilliant idea occurred to him. He had heard that only a little distance from Decatur Abraham Lincoln had split fence rails in the early days of his residence in Illinois. Old John Hanks, who had worked with Lincoln, still lived in that vicinity. Oglesby himself interviewed John and later told the story, and it is the best account we have of the introduction into the Decatur convention and into national politics of the rails that Abraham Lincoln split.

Oglesby took John Hanks in his buggy ten miles west of Decatur to the site of Abraham Lincoln's first Illinois farm. They found what appeared to be the old fence still in service after thirty years. John said that the rails were principally locust and black walnut and testing some of them with his pocket-knife, he assured Oglesby and himself of their genuineness. Two of these rails they carried away with them, fastening them to the axles of the buggy and carrying them back to Decatur where for several days they were hidden in Oglesby's barn.

At an important moment in the convention, Oglesby rose and announced that an old Democrat desired to make a contribution to the convention. The proceedings stopped, and in came John Hanks, who, with such assistance as was required, brought in two rails from the lot which he and Lincoln split together in 1830. They bore a legend:

> Abraham Lincoln
> The Rail Candidate
> For President in 1860.

The convention went wild. No delegate could doubt after that exhibition that Lincoln was the best man in the United States for president. The Illinois State Republican Convention went on record for Abraham Lincoln.   Seward no longer had standing with the state delegates of Illinois.

The effect upon the country was hardly less picturesque than that upon the Decatur Convention.   The name and fame of Abraham Lincoln were borne aloft on the rails which he had split while a laborer in the Prairie State.   John Hanks became notable in Illinois political gatherings.   He accompanied Oglesby on various expeditions.   The bringing in of the rail was a feature in several ratification meetings; John C. Frémont rode a considerable distance toward the White House on his sobriquet of "Pathfinder."   Abraham Lincoln was destined to go down to fame as "Railsplitter."

CHAPTER XXVIII

LINCOLN AS A NEWSPAPER OWNER

LINCOLN's intimate association with Simeon Francis had given him constant reminder of the power of the press. Lincoln wrote many of the editorials on political subjects. Lincoln knew that the organization of the Republican Party in Illinois was virtually the work of twenty-five editors. As Lincoln grew in political power his appreciation of the press increased. Herndon assures us that Lincoln never overlooked a newspaper man who could say a good or bad word about him. He was very eager to see his speeches in print, and he read newspapers with sedulous attention to their value for his uses.*

As the campaign of 1860 approached, Lincoln became very desirous of holding to the Republican Party every considerable block of votes which might be held or attracted to it. He was especially solicitous concerning the foreign vote.

In the later 'forties and early 'fifties there was a large increase in immigration. Political revolutions on the Continent, economic distress in Ireland, and other untoward conditions abroad constituted a strong push, and the discovery of gold in California, together with unprecedented activity on the part of emigrant agents in Europe resulted in the coming of vast numbers of Europeans, especially Germans and Irish. The immigration from 1851 to 1854 more than trebled the numbers who had come to this country in the entire preceding decade.

These immigrants caused congestion in the cities, where they greatly complicated the labor problem, and roused much resent-

---

*Herndon's *Lincoln,* ii, pp. 309, 363, 367.

ment. Some firms were constrained to hang out the sign, "No Irish need apply." There were unfriendly demonstrations toward "the Dutch" in the industrial world.

In politics they occasioned another problem. The laws of many of the states were framed so as to permit voting by immigrants at a very early period of residence and before naturalization. These immigrants were to be reckoned with in politics almost as soon as they arrived. They voted "early and often." They voted in solid blocks. Both parties bid for their vote, but the Democratic Party went farther after this vote than the Whig, and got more of it.

The era was one of religious unrest, and there was strong belief that the Roman Catholic Church aspired to gain political control in the United States.

In 1850 Illinois contained about 30,000 Germans. Of these Governor Reynolds estimated that fully 18,000 had settled in St. Clair County. At the outset, most of the Germans were Democrats; but on the organization of the Republican Party, many of them united with that party on account of its opposition to slavery. Gustav Koerner and other Democrats of German birth but anti-slavery principles came over in large numbers to the Republican Party.*

Gustav Koerner had appeared with Lyman Trumbull in 1843 before the Supreme Court of Illinois in an argument in the case of a negro woman, Sarah Borders and her three children, held under the indenture act, and had claimed that slavery in Illinois

---

*Gustav Koerner was born in Germany in 1809, and received a university education. He emigrated to Illinois in 1833, and settled at Belleville, where he became an intimate friend of Lyman Trumbull. He became a prominent Democratic politician. He was elected to the General Assembly in 1842, and three years later, in 1845, was appointed to the Illinois Supreme Bench. In 1852 he was elected lieutenant governor on the Democratic ticket with Governor Matteson. At the close of his term he became a Republican. He was a member of the convention that nominated Lincoln, and became a colonel in the Civil War. In 1862, President Lincoln appointed him minister to Spain, a post which he resigned in 1865. He held various offices, and wrote several works. He died at Belleville, April 9, 1896.

was illegal under the Ordinance of 1787.* The court ruled against them. Trumbull, later, in the case of *Jarrot vs. Jarrot,* appeared before the Supreme Court with the same plea, and his success virtually ended negro slavery in Illinois.

In 1854, when party cohesion had been weakened by the slavery agitation, and the Whig Party was disintegrating, there rose to national proportions a political party whose name was "the American Party," but which was organized in a group of lodges, and was known popularly as the "Know-Nothing Party."†

Many of Lincoln's Whig friends joined this party, among them his former partner, Judge Stephen T. Logan, and his friend, Doctor William Jayne.‡ Many reputable men who did not join its lodges believed in its principle of "America for the Americans." In 1854 it became a power in politics, and in 1856 it held a national convention in Philadelphia, Washington's birthday, February twenty-second, and nominated Millard Fillmore and Andrew Jackson Donelson as its candidates.†† The remnants of the Whig Party, meeting in national convention in Baltimore, September 12, 1856, endorsed the nomination.

But the Northern Whigs, for the most part, in 1856 joined the new Republican Party and voted for John C. Frémont; and Fillmore did not return to the White House.‡‡ The Whig Party went down and completely disappeared. Of it and the American Party which for a time appeared as its successor, Griffis says:

---

*Harris, *Negro Servitude in Illinois,* p. 108; White, *Life of Lyman Trumbull,* pp. 28-29.

†See *The Know-Nothing Movement in Illinois,* by John P. Henning. *Journal of the Illinois Historical Society,* April, 1914.

‡In the courthouse at Dixon is a life-sized oil painting of "Father" John Dixon. He stands in the portrait with his right hand partly within his coat; the index and little fingers on the outside of the flap, the two middle fingers inside. This is explained as being the hailing sign of the Know-Nothings, with which body Father Dixon was affiliated.

††See *Life of Millard Fillmore,* by William Elliot Griffis, Andrus and Church, Ithaca, N. Y., 1915.

‡‡Fillmore received 874,534 votes, or 21.57%; Fremont, 1,342,264, or 33.09%; and Buchanan 1,838,169 votes or 45.34%.

The Whig Party, now dead for ever, had done its work. It had had its own office to perform. In its members, rather than in its leaders, was preserved most of the nationalizing spirit of the United States. In a word, while the people of the various states were not yet ready for true nationality, the preparatory work in behalf of the final consummation was crudely but effectively done for the making of the United States of our day. . . . Know-nothingism, as described by its critics and opponents, with its "riotous career," was a sudden tornado of opinion, blowing from an independent quarter across the field of the regular parties and for a little while confusing their lines. When civil war was impending in 1860, it was as the flicker of a dying flame, that under the name of the Constitutional Union Party, some ex-members of the old Whig Party, in the border states, nominated John Bell and Edward Everett for president and vice-president.*

In Massachusetts a constitutional amendment was proposed, requiring of foreign-born citizens a residence of seven years in the United States before they were permitted to vote. They might be naturalized at the end of five years, but were not to be permitted to vote for two years after naturalization. This amendment was submitted to popular referendum May 9, 1859. The vote was light, 21,119 for and 15,398 against the amendment. The total vote was only about one-fourth that cast in the presidential election of 1856, but the majority was decisive. The Republicans of Massachusetts in general supported the amendment. Among those who opposed it was S. G. Bowles, of the *Springfield Republican,* of which paper Doctor J. G. Holland was at that time an associate editor. Among all of Lincoln's biographers he is the only one who appears to have appreciated the difficulty which this action involved for Mr. Lincoln. He says:

It is to be remembered in this connection that Massachusetts was a representative Republican state, and regarding the ignorant foreign population, particularly of the eastern states as hold-

*Life of Millard Fillmore, p. 137.

ing the balance of power between the Democratic and Republican parties, which it never failed to exercise in the interest of the former and in support of African slavery, had instituted measures which rendered naturalization a more difficult process. This embarrassed the Republicans of the west, who were associated with a large and generally intelligent German population with leanings toward the Republican Party rather than to the Democratic.*

The Germans of Iowa and Illinois were loud in their denunciation of the "Two-Year Amendment" and promptly demanded of all prominent Republicans whether this represented their sentiments. It threw the Republican candidates in states having foreign populations into something approaching a panic.†

Prominent Republican leaders in Illinois were quick to make it known that they did not share the views of the Republicans of Massachusetts. In open letters addressed to different leading Germans, Elihu B. Washburne, Lyman Trumbull, Norman B. Judd and other Republican leaders promptly sent in their letters of disavowal. Abraham Lincoln furnished his letter to Doctor Theodore Canisius, of Springfield, and it was published at once in the *Illinois State Journal,* a paper devoted to Lincoln's interests.‡

Lincoln's letter was carefully written. It refrained from any criticism of the Republicans of Massachusetts. It said that Massachusetts was a sovereign state, and he did not regard it as his privilege to scold her, but he did feel free to state how he stood with reference to such action as that of Massachusetts in any state where he had the right to vote:

As I understand the Massachusetts provision, I am against its adoption in Illinois, or in any other place where I have the

---

*Life of Lincoln, p. 197.

†See a very interesting monograph on The Premises and Significance of Abraham Lincoln's Letter to Theodore Canisius, by Professor F. I. Herriott of Drake University. Reprinted from Deutsch-Amerikanische Geschitsblatter Jahrbuch der Deutsch-Amerikanische Historischen Gesellschaft von Illinois-Jahrgang, 1915 (Vol. XV).

‡The original manuscript of Lincoln's letter is in the library of the Chicago Historical Society.

right to oppose it.   Understanding the spirit of our institutions to aim at the elevation of men, I am opposed to whatever tends to degrade them.   I have some little notoriety for commiserating the oppressed condition of the negro; and I should be strangely inconsistent if I should favor any project for curtailing the existing rights of white men, even though born in different lands and speaking different languages from myself.*

This letter was dated May 17, 1859, and on the same date was furnished by Canisius for publication in the *Journal* with a letter which stated that:

This letter of one of the gallant champions of our state is in accordance with the views of the whole German population, supporting the Republican Party, and also with the views of the entire German-Republican press.

The *Journal* published these on the following day, incorporating them in a leading editorial, declaring that Mr. Lincoln's views were the views of the Republican Party.

So far as the general public knew, or has since been informed, that was all that there was of the story of Lincoln's attitude toward the German vote.   It was not unknown, however, that Doctor Theodore Canisius became a very ardent supporter of the Republican Party and later of Mr. Lincoln.   Canisius was editor of a then recently established paper, *The Illinois*

---

*Honorable Joseph Gillespie is authority for the statement that Lincoln was surprisingly popular among the Germans:

"In 1858 Mr. Lincoln delivered a political address in Edwardsville.   In the afternoon he said to me quite excitedly that he was to speak next day in Greenville and had forgotten to mention it sooner.   I told him I would take him over to Greenville, but that he could go only as far as Highland that night.   He seemed delighted with the idea of stopping in Highland, as he understood the place was a little Germany.   We stopped there and had a good time.   It was soon noised around that Lincoln was in the place and the house where we were stopping was crowded and jammed.   The people were perfectly enraptured; the bare sight of the man threw them into ecstasies.   I here got the first inkling of the amazing popularity of Mr. Lincoln among the Germans.   I could see that there was some magnetic influence at work that was perfectly inexplicable, which brought him and the masses into a mysterious correspondence with each other.   This relation increased and was intensified to such an extent that afterward at Springfield I witnessed a manifestation of regard for Mr. Lincoln such as I did not believe possible." *Transactions of Illinois State Historical Society for 1912*, p. 108.

Staats-Anzeiger. That paper began immediately a vigorous campaign for the support of the Republican Party, and in due season came out strongly for Lincoln as the Republican nominee.

The following facts, however, the public did not know and they are of interest and importance. Doctor Canisius was in financial straits. He owed his landlord, John Burkhardt for rent and perhaps also for money advanced. Burkhardt had acquired, under chattel mortgage or otherwise, a title to the property of the newspaper. Lincoln through Canisius purchased Burkhardt's title and became the owner of the *Staats-Anzeiger.* The transaction occurred immediately after the incident of Lincoln's letter to Canisius, which letter was evoked by an inquiry from a Committee of German citizens in Springfield.

Lincoln had learned the value of the press. He was a constant contributor to the columns of the *Journal,* many of his contributions appearing as editorials. The plan for the propagation of his nomination was in a large sense a plan to use the newspapers of Illinois. Lincoln knew that while the *Chicago Tribune* and many of the down-state papers were committed to him, the chief German paper in Illinois, the *Chicago Staats-Zeitung,* was for Seward. He knew that it would advance his interests if a well-edited German newspaper could be depended upon to stand for the Republican Party first, and in due time to announce itself for Lincoln.

On May 30, 1859, a contract wholly in Lincoln's handwriting, was drawn up by Lincoln and signed by himself and Theodore Canisius. In the agreement it was stated that the type and other equipment were the property of Lincoln, by virtue of Lincoln's purchase of the same from Burkhardt. Canisius was granted the free use of this property for the publication of a German newspaper, which was strongly to support the Republican Party. If the paper failed thus to support the Republican Party, Lincoln, as owner, was authorized to take possession and dispossess Canisius. It was stipulated also that the paper, while published in German, should carry occasional articles in English.

The contract was written on the two sides of a single sheet of legal cap, and the second page was only partly filled. On December 6, 1860, a month after Lincoln's election as president, he wrote a supplementary endorsement, filling the blank space. Therein he certified that Doctor Theodore Canisius had faithfully fulfilled the obligations of the contract and satisfied all financial claims of Lincoln, who therefore, for a valid consideration, conveyed the type, paper and good will to Canisius.

Canisius had to borrow his four hundred dollars with which to repay Lincoln. He obtained it from Charles F. Herman, a prominent German in Springfield, who at that time was freight agent of the Wabash Railroad and a somewhat near neighbor of Lincoln. Canisius gave Herman his note for four hundred dollars, with this contract as collateral. The daughters of Mr. Herman* state that the note remained and still remains unpaid.

This ended Abraham Lincoln's ownership of a German newspaper. It was his property for eighteen months from May 30, 1859, to December 6, 1860. It did not continue long after his election. Lincoln speedily gave Doctor Canisius a consulate in Samoa, and Canisius continued in the consular service of the United States at various posts from 1861 to 1885.

The relation between Lincoln and Canisius was not, however, wholly commercial. Lincoln knew Canisius and held him in high regard and Canisius was a warm admirer of Lincoln. His paper adopted no change in principle when Lincoln became its owner. The principles of its editor were in full accord with those of Lincoln.

Arnold relates an incident concerning a German editor whom Lincoln caused to be appointed to a diplomatic position. He said:

In the early part of Lincoln's administration, a prominent editor of a German newspaper published in the West, came to Washington to seek an appointment abroad. With the member

---

*I am indebted to these ladies for this first publication of the facts concerning Lincoln's one investment in a newspaper.

of Congress from his district, he visited the "Executive Mansion," and his wishes were stated.   The editor had supported Mr. Seward for nomination as president.   Mr. Lincoln immediately sent a messenger to the secretary of state, asking him to come to the White House.   Mr. Seward soon arrived, and Lincoln, after a cordial greeting, said: "Seward, here is a gentleman (introducing the editor) who had the good sense to prefer you to me for president.   He wants to go abroad, and I want you to find a good place for him."   This Mr. Seward did, and the president immediately appointed him.*

This may refer to Doctor Theodore Canisius,† of Springfield. If this be true, it is interesting to learn from this authoritative source that Canisius had at first preferred Seward to Lincoln as a presidential candidate and this is wholly probable.   Presumably Lincoln had not at that time emerged into sufficient prominence to be regarded by Canisius as a candidate who could command the German vote throughout the nation.   The files of the paper edited by Doctor Canisius are not known to be in existence, and it would not be wise to dogmatize concerning the editorial policy of the paper after Lincoln became its owner.   It would not be unreasonable to infer, however, that Doctor Canisius and his paper did not from that time forth press Seward's claim to the extent of violent opposition to Lincoln; and certainly after Lincoln's nomination the paper gave him undivided support.

The admiration of Canisius for Lincoln continued through his life.   He wrote a biography of Lincoln in German and it ran through several editions, which were published in different cities of Europe.   It was based upon his personal knowledge of Lincoln and was a sincere and worthy tribute by one of Lincoln's own neighbors, and expressed the sentiments of that large body of citizens of foreign birth who held Lincoln in high regard.

_____

*Arnold: *Life of Lincoln*, pp. 194-195.
†It is barely possible that the editor mentioned was Colonel Schneider, of the *Staats-Zeitung*.

CHAPTER XXIX

THE NOMINATION OF LINCOLN
May, 1860

THE convention that nominated Lincoln was the first to meet in a building erected especially for its own requirements. No American city at that time had a permanent structure known as a convention hall, or one intended for the particular use of great national gatherings. Up to that time in every city entertaining a national convention a theater or other hall, erected for local purposes, had been found sufficiently large to house any convention that was held within that municipality. When Chicago invited the Republican convention of 1860, it was with the knowledge that it would be necessary for the city to erect a building adequately to care for the gathering.

If we were to depend entirely upon the press reports concerning "this gigantic structure, the largest audience-room in the United States," as the newspapers of the time truthfully described it, we might possibly exaggerate in our own minds the largeness of the building. If, for instance, it were to be compared with the Coliseum in which the Chicago conventions of recent years have been held, we should discover that the old Wigwam could have been lost almost anywhere inside of the Coliseum. It was just about the size of the Coliseum Annex which now serves for offices, restaurant and other adjunct uses of national conventions. The Wigwam stood at the corner of Lake and Market Streets near the fork of Chicago River. It had a frontage of one hundred eighty feet on Market Street and a depth of one hundred feet on Lake. Four hundred and sixty-six delegates and about sixty newspaper correspondents were seated upon an elevated platform, which, with a committee room at either end, occupied one entire side of the building. The rest of the structure was open to the public, the ladies and some delegations provided with tickets being seated in the gallery. Chicago announced that the building and the hospitality of the city were equal to taking care of all creation.

Chicago at this time had forty-two hotels, all operated on the American plan. Their rates were from one dollar and a half to two dollars and a half per day for board and room, and the hotel proprietors then and ever since were accused of extortion. The number of visitors who came, however, was far beyond the ability of hotels to accommodate; private houses opened their doors, some for pay and others out of hospitality. The eastern railroads granted a special round-trip rate of fifteen dollars from Buffalo, and the western roads somewhat reluctantly followed their example.

The railroad trains approaching Chicago took what now are known as straw-votes among their passengers bound for Chicago. On a Michigan Central train of twelve coaches, Seward had 210 votes against 30 for all other candidates. On a Chicago and Northwestern train Seward had 127 and all others 44. On a Chicago and Rock Island train Seward had 112 and the others totaled 41. On these three trains there appeared not to have been a single vote for Lincoln; but on a Chicago and Milwaukee train Seward had 368, Lincoln 93 and all others 46; while on a New Albany and Salem, Indiana, train Lincoln had 51, Seward 43, and the other candidates totaled 131.*

Within the Wigwam on the morning of May sixteenth were crowded fully ten thousand persons. Four years before when the Republican National Convention met in Philadelphia, a hall

---

*These figures are given by Professor P. Orman Ray, in an address before the Chicago Historical Society, from which I have obtained much valuable information. Professor Ray says of this vote on the Indiana train that it is the only one which he found mentioned in the newspaper reports or elsewhere in which Lincoln had more votes than Seward.

seating two thousand people had been ample for both delegates and spectators. At this convention ten thousand people jammed the Wigwam, and twenty thousand stood with hardly less enthusiasm outside.

The convention assembled at noon on Wednesday, May 16, 1860, Seward's fifty-ninth birthday. It was confidently expected that he would receive the nomination as a birthday present.

Governor Morgan, of New York, Chairman of the National Committee, called the convention to order. David Wilmot, of Pennsylvania, author of the famous Wilmot Proviso, was made temporary chairman and delivered the "key-note" speech. He was not a success as a presiding officer. A good deal of time was consumed discussing the question whether the convention would accept the invitation of the Chicago Board of Trade to take a short excursion on the lake at five o'clock in the afternoon. At two o'clock the convention took recess for three hours and reconvened at five to effect its permanent organization. At the five o'clock session Honorable George Ashmun, of Massachusetts, was elected permanent chairman. He had a good voice, and his rulings were clear and just. His election was a relief after the indecision and feeble presiding of Wilmot. A committee on resolutions was appointed to draft a platform. The convention adjourned until ten o'clock next morning. The evening appears to have been spent by a considerable number of the delegates in a sail on Lake Michigan, but the politicians were otherwise engaged.

On Thursday morning, the Seward men, all wearing badges, formed a large and picturesque procession in front of the Richmond House, and marched to the Wigwam preceded by a finely uniformed band playing in honor of Seward one of the popular airs of the day, entitled *Oh, Isn't He a Darling*. The forenoon of Thursday passed with no very exciting incidents.

On Thursday afternoon the first excitement occurred. The Committee on Platform earnestly desired to present a safe and

THE LIFE OF ABRAHAM LINCOLN

sane doctrine which would solidify all forces opposed to the Democratic administration. It therefore omitted from the first draft some of the more pronounced utterances of the Platform of 1856. Perhaps the most radical of the omitted affirmations was one quoted from the Declaration of Independence declaring that all men were endowed by their Creator with certain inalienable rights, among which were life, liberty and the pursuit of happiness. When the committee presented a Platform from which that affirmation had been omitted, Joshua R. Giddings, of Ohio, a white haired, battle-scarred veteran of the anti-slavery warfare, arose and moved its reinsertion. The convention voted his amendment down, and Giddings rose and indignantly started to walk out of the Wigwam, but was detained and took a seat in the rear of the room, refraining from participation in the proceedings until the vote was rescinded. A little later George William Curtis, one of the youngest of New York's delegates, rose, and in an earnest and tactful speech renewed Giddings' motion. His amendment prevailed, and Giddings returned placated, and the Platform was adopted amid tremendous enthusiasm. Thus the first threatened split was averted.

This result was achieved with a suddenness that surprised the Convention, and brought it at an earlier hour than had been expected to the time for nominations.

If printers invariably kept their promises, Abraham Lincoln would not have been president of the United States. If the convention could have got to balloting on Thursday night, William H. Seward would have been nominated. But the secretary was compelled to announce that the papers necessary for the keeping of the tally were not at hand, but would arrive in a few minutes. The convention was impatient at the delay, and a motion was made by some unknown delegate "that this convention adjourn until ten o'clock to-morrow morning." The motion to adjourn prevailed. If the unnamed delegate who made the motion to adjourn could be identified, he, perhaps animated by no higher motive than restlessness or the desire for a drink,

THE REPUBLICAN CONVENTION OF 1860
From a contemporary drawing

would be entitled to mention as one of the otherwise nameless voices that have uttered the messages of destiny.

The New York delegation was the largest and best organized of the state delegations. It was headed by Thurlow Weed, and had as one of its next most important attractions, a distinguished prize-fighter who served as bartender for the Seward interests at the Richmond House. Between these two notable men, the delegates had very nearly all the Republican leadership of New York, except Horace Greeley.

Horace Greeley did not come to the Convention of 1860 as a member of the New York delegation. That body was controlled by the Seward interests. Greeley sat in the convention as the substitute for a delegate from Oregon, the state over which as a territory Lincoln had been offered the office of governor.

Greeley came to the Chicago Convention as the avowed opponent of Thurlow Weed and William H. Seward. Thurlow Weed was a politician as adroit as America has ever seen. Desiring no office for himself, he greatly desired to say what men should occupy office. He was editor of the *Albany Journal*, and the ablest paragrapher of his generation. During the period when the Whig Party was coming to its end and the Republican Party was in process of formation, Weed and Seward had no more earnest or effective assistant than Horace Greeley, a younger man, who had come into great power as editor of the *New York Tribune*. The *Tribune* had begun with many difficulties attending it; but it grew to be one of the strongest papers in the nation. It was read as few papers are read in rural communities, and it influenced the thought of its readers as few papers then or since have done.

On Saturday evening, November 11, 1854, Greeley wrote to Governor Seward a notable letter, beginning as follows:

Governor Seward:

The election is over, and its results sufficiently ascertained. It seems to me a fitting time to announce to you the dissolution of the political firm of Seward, Weed and Greeley by the withdrawal of the junior partner—said withdrawal to take effect on the morning after the first Thursday in February next.*

When Horace Greeley mailed that letter, he made it possible for Abraham Linclon to be chosen president six years later.

So Greeley came to the Chicago Convention, unrecognized by the New York state delegation, but entitled to a seat, a voice and a vote. He came to defeat Seward. He did not favor Lincoln, though he had heard Lincoln in Chicago in 1847, and met him in Washington in 1848, where his impression was that Lincoln was "a genial, cheerful rather homely man, noticeably tall, and the only Whig from Illinois, not remarkable otherwise."†

Greeley came to Chicago with strong expectation of uniting the votes opposed to Seward in support of Edward Bates.‡ But Bates had no possible hope of winning, and Greeley, after midnight of Thursday, sadly faced the fact that if Seward was defeated it must be by another man than Bates. Reluctantly he came to believe that the man who could defeat Seward in the convention without losing the election at the polls was Lincoln.

It was possible for Lincoln to be chosen as the nominee of the Republican Convention not because he was believed to be an abler man than Seward, but because Seward by his greater prominence had awakened certain antagonisms which Lincoln by his obscurity had avoided. It must be admitted as we view the matter from its present point of vantage that the hostilities which Seward had aroused were mostly to his credit.

Nevertheless, it was then clearly discerned that Pennsylvania would be hopelessly lost to the Republican Party if Seward were nominated, and Indiana also was more than doubtful. Some of the states which would probably vote against Seward were "October" states, whose national elections were held a month earlier than those of the majority of the states, and whose influence was

---

*The letter, together with a long account of the circumstances inspiring it, is given in full in Greeley's *Recollections of a Busy Life*, pp. 315-320.
†*Greeley's Estimate of Lincoln: An Unpublished Address.* The Century, July, 1891.
‡See *Recollections of a Busy Life*, by Horace Greeley, pp. 389 seq.

therefore accounted greater as foreshadowing the probable result of the general election. Seward was defeated because it was so well known just where he stood on the great national issues.

Lincoln was keeping in close touch with the situation. Several men in the convention were keeping him informed. Among them was Mark W. Delahay, of Kansas. Delahay was a Marylander by birth, who had come to Illinois and moved on to Kansas, where he was first a Douglas Democrat, and afterward became a Republican. He is the man who wrote to Lincoln that he thought he could be elected a member of the Kansas delegation, and do something to swing it for Lincoln, but that he could not afford to pay his own expenses to Chicago and back, and to whom Lincoln wrote saying that Lincoln would send him a hundred dollars toward his expenses. But Delahay did not suc-ceed in getting on the delegation, and the delegates from Kansas were instructed for Seward. Lincoln wrote to Delahay saying to come with the delegation; "not to stir them up to anger" by too great insistence upon Lincoln, but to come, and Lincoln still would pay the hundred dollars.* Delahay came to Chicago, and was in frequent communication with Lincoln during the Convention. On Thursday afternoon Delahay wired Lincoln that his nomination appeared hopeless, and asked if Lincoln would accept a nomination as vice-president if Seward was chosen as nominee for president. Lincoln replied confidentially that he would accept, provided his friends thought it wise for him to do so.†

At eleven-forty Thursday night, Horace Greeley, who had been earnestly endeavoring to defeat Seward, telegraphed the *New York Tribune,* "My conclusion from all that I can gather

---

*Herndon quotes these letters without naming Delahay. (Vol. iii, pp. 457-459). Delahay continued to exercise more influence over Lincoln than was good for Lincoln, and Lincoln appointed him to a judgeship, from which President Grant was forced to remove him. A sketch of the life of Delahay, by his daughter, is in the *Reports of the Kansas Historical Society,* Vol. X, pp. 638-641. Delahay was a distant relative of Lincoln, his mother's father being Joshua Hanks.

†This statement I have from Honorable Addison G. Procter of the Kansas delegation, to whom Delahay showed the telegram.

to-night is that the opposition to Governor Seward can not concentrate on any candidate, and that he will be nominated."

Many accounts have been given of what followed. It is certain that William H. Seward would have been nominated if Horace Greeley had not quarreled with Seward and his manager, Thurlow Weed. It is quite certain that Greeley on Thursday night gave up all hope of defeating Seward, but that before morning he had changed his judgment by reason of his faith that Abraham Lincoln not only could defeat Seward in the convention, but also could defeat the Democratic candidate at the polls. Honorable Addison G. Procter, the sole surviving delegate to the convention, attributes the determining influence to the border-state leaders, notably Cassius M. Clay.*

On Friday morning the Seward forces gathered behind their magnificent brass band, and paraded through the streets of Chicago in triumphal procession to the Wigwam. The Lincoln forces, with much less of display, packed the Wigwam with shouters. There were so many Lincoln shouters in the Wigwam that a considerable part of the Seward crowd that had followed the band could not obtain entrance. The story of the disappointment of the Seward men when they returned from their procession and found themselves excluded from the seats for which they held tickets in the galleries of the Wigwam, has been told often, and appears entirely reliable. One incident hitherto unpublished may shed light on the way in which the Lincoln shouters were able to get into the Wigwam ahead of the Seward men, and occupy the seats. There were no reserved and numbered seats, but it was not expected that tickets would be issued in excess of the capacity of the building. On the evening before the nomination, however, Ward Hill Lamon obtained from the printers of the seat-tickets a large supply of extra tickets. He set certain young men at work signing these tickets with the

---

*Mr. Procter's interesting and valuable reminiscences are published by the Chicago Historical Society, in a booklet issued by the University of Chicago Press.

names of the officers of the Convention.*   These young men
did their part right merrily, and signed tickets nearly all
night.   In the morning, these tickets were furnished in liberal
number to friends of Lincoln, who were clamoring for tickets
for their friends.   The tickets were given out with the suggestion that it would be well to get in early.   Of course, neither
Lincoln nor any of his responsible managers knew of this piece
of work, which had the effect of crowding out a large fraction
of Seward's shouting strength, and giving the space over to the
shouters for Lincoln.   A brass band upon the street may be considerably less effective than a well placed company of leather-
lunged shouters.   But neither they who followed the band nor
they who packed the Wigwam knew that already the nomination
had very nearly been settled.   It had come to be believed by a
considerable number of wavering delegates that if Seward
should be nominated, he would be defeated; for he could not
carry Pennsylvania, Indiana, or perhaps Illinois.   Illinois and
Indiana were for Lincoln, and the delegates had been hearing
more and more about him, and coming to think more and more
favorably for him.   When the Pennsylvania delegation came
over to Lincoln, the matter was practically settled.

A pamphlet had been circulated among the Pennsylvania men,
ostensibly favorable to Cameron as president, but in reality
planned to produce a sentiment favorable to his election as vice-
president on a ticket with Edward Bates, of Missouri, who was
Greeley's candidate.   Cameron was certain to be named as the
"favorite son" of Pennsylvania, but it was certain that he could
not be nominated as president and not likely that he could
win the nomination as vice-president.   The enthusiastic friends
of Lincoln did not hesitate to declare to leading Pennsylvania
delegates that if they would be content with a seat in the Cabinet
for Cameron, there would be no trouble about arranging the

---

*Honorable John H. Marshall, for many years circuit judge, residing, as
did his father who was state senator and Lincoln's friend, at Charleston, Illinois, informs me that his brother, Senator Marshall's oldest son, was one
of these young men.

matter, provided Pennsylvania would go for Lincoln. That was welcome news to Pennsylvania. Lincoln had no share in the making of this bargain, but he kept it.

At ten o'clock on Friday morning the Wigwam was jammed, and the crowd outside is said to have reached two blocks away. The New Yorkers prepared to do all necessary cheering for Seward. But the Illinois attendants at the convention were far more numerous. In the matter of lung power the men of the prairies were far and away superior to the New York delegation, because there were more of them.

Nominations began almost immediately. There were then no nominating speeches, such as later have come to thrill and sometimes to weary conventions. Honorable William H. Evarts first obtained the floor, and presented the name of Seward in these words:

"I take the liberty to name as a candidate to be nominated by this convention for the office of president of the United States, William H. Seward."

He was immediately followed by Norman D. Judd, of Illinois, with these words:

"I desire, on behalf of the delegation from Illinois, to put in nomination as a candidate for president of the United States, Abraham Lincoln, of Illinois."

There were other nominations equally brief, and a few seconds. The only one of these that contained any attempt at oratory was that of Mr. Delano, of Ohio, seconding the nomination of Abraham Lincoln as "a man who can split rails and maul Democrats." That little speech set the convention on fire.

In the balloting now, the roll-call of the states is in alphabetical order. It is an impressive sound, the musical names beginning with Alabama, Arkansas, and so on down the alphabet. But in 1860 a geographical order prevailed, beginning with New England and moving westward. There were four hundred and sixty-five votes; two hundred and thirty-three necessary to choice. On the first ballot Seward had one hundred seventy-three and one-half, Lincoln one hundred and two, with Cameron, of Pennsylvania, third with fifty and one-half. On the second ballot the name of Cameron was withdrawn, and the vote stood, Seward one hundred eighty-four and one-half, a gain of eleven votes, and Lincoln one hundred eighty-one, a gain of seventy-nine. Chase, of Ohio, now stood third with forty-two and one-half votes. On the third ballot, Seward had one hundred eighty, a loss of four and one-half, while Lincoln had two hundred thirty-one and one-half, lacking only one and one-half of receiving the number necessary to nominate. Hundreds of people were keeping tally-sheets, and it was plainly seen how nearly the third ballot had come to nominating Lincoln. Before the vote was announced, Mr. Carter, of Ohio, sprang upon his chair and announced a change of five votes from Chase to Lincoln. A cannon had been placed on the roof, but the confusion was such that for a moment or two the man in charge could not be made to understand what had happened. When he understood and fired the gun, it could hardly be heard in the Wigwam. The *Chicago Tribune* declared that earth had heard no such tumult since the walls of Jericho fell down.

Other states then hurried to change their votes. There was the familiar "rush to get into the band-wagon." When the vote was finally announced, out of four hundred sixty-six votes cast, with two hundred thirty-four necessary to choice, Abraham Lincoln, of Illinois, had three hundred sixty-four.

The nomination of Lincoln occurred about half-past twelve, and was followed by a number of speeches endorsing the nomination. At about half past one the convention adjourned until five o'clock, at which time it reconvened and nominated Hannibal Hamlin, of Maine, for vice-president. Then the convention gave cheers for the nominees, the platform, and the ladies of Chicago, and adjourned to "meet at the White House on the fourth of March next."

CHAPTER XXX

THE ELECTION OF LINCOLN

WITH the keenest possible interest Abraham Lincoln awaited in Springfield the news of the convention. On Thursday he accepted his probable defeat but he did not give up hope. On Friday morning he went early to his office. The convention did not assemble until ten o'clock, and Lincoln dropped in at the office of James C. Conkling, who had been attending the convention and returned unexpectedly to Springfield. Mr. Conkling brought Lincoln more favorable news than he had ventured to believe. Conkling told him that he was to be nominated that day. Lincoln had sent a message to his friends the day before, by the hand of one of the editors of the *Journal,* making his comment in pencil on the margin of a copy of the *Missouri Democrat,* which contained some passages with regard to Seward's stand on the slavery issue. Accepting this article as a correct statement of Seward's position, he had written:

"I agree with Seward in his 'irrepressible conflict,' but I do not endorse his 'Higher Law' doctrine. Make no contracts that will bind me." Thus, and by telegraph, had Lincoln had meager communication with the managers of his campaign in Chicago; it was heartening to get news direct from Conkling that his chance for the nomination was good.

Lincoln returned from Conkling's office to the office of Lincoln and Herndon.* Herndon was in Chicago. Lincoln was

*Many accounts are current in Springfield of the place and manner of Lincoln's receiving news of his nomination. No less than three men, all honest and highly esteemed, have told me in detail of having been the first to inform him of his nomination. I give what I think to be the correct account.

too nervous to sit down alone. He went out and played a few games of hand-ball in an open court on North Sixth Street between John Carmody's store and a brick building owned by Judge Logan. The *Journal* office was just across the alley from the Carmody store. He was in his office when the news of the first ballot reached him. The second ballot he appears to have received in the telegraph office, and the news of the third and final ballot in the *Journal* office shortly before one o'clock.

It is a matter of some importance that, when the final news came, Lincoln did not wait long to receive the congratulations of his friends, and said:

"There is a little woman over on Eighth Street that will be glad to hear the news; if you'll excuse me, I'll go and tell her."

The next day, Saturday, a special train left Chicago, bearing to Springfield the committee appointed to inform Lincoln of his nomination.* Willie and Tad Lincoln were the first members of the family to greet the delegation, which they did with a shout of "Hooray."

Inside the door Mr. Lincoln received them. Mr. Ashmun, President of the Convention, made the announcement briefly, and Lincoln accepted in an address of like brevity. There was a moment of silence, and Mr. Lincoln addressed Honorable William D. Kelley, of Pennsylvania:

"Judge Kelley, you are a tall man; what is your height?"

"I am six feet three, Mr. Lincoln."

"I beat you," said Lincoln, "I am six feet four."

These formalities and informalities being over, Mr. Lincoln said:

"Mrs. Lincoln will be pleased to see you in the other room, gentlemen. You must be thirsty after your journey."

They passed into the library and met Mrs. Lincoln, and had light refreshments; but the drink consisted wholly of water.

---

*This occasion has often been described in my hearing by Charles Carleton Coffin, who was present representing the *Boston Journal*.

Some of Lincoln's friends had offered to provide wine, but Lincoln declined.

Lincoln's letter of acceptance is as follows:

Springfield, Illinois, June 3, 1860.

Sir: I accept the nomination tendered me by the Convention over which you presided, of which I am formally apprised in a letter of yourself and others, acting as a Committee of the Convention for the purpose. The declaration of principles which accompanies your letter meets my approval and it shall be my care not to violate it or disregard it in any part. Imploring the assistance of Divine Providence, and with due regard to the views and feelings of all who were represented in the Convention, to the rights of all the states and territories and people of the nation, to the inviolability of the Constitution, and the perpetual union, prosperity and harmony of all, I am most happy to cooperate for the practical success of the principles declared by the Convention.

Your obliged friend and fellow citizen,
Abraham Lincoln.

Hon. George Ashmun.

The Democratic Convention of 1860 was held at Charleston, South Carolina. Practically the whole mass of the northern Democrats were for Douglas and the South was against him. Douglas and his managers offered as their platform the Cincinnati platform of 1856, with the addition of the demand for the annexation of Cuba, and an endorsement of the Dred Scott decision and of any future decisions of the Supreme Court, recognizing slavery in the territories. But the southern delegates would not accept this platform nor the man who stood upon it. A two-thirds vote was required to nominate, and many ballots were taken with Douglas in the lead, but not with a sufficient majority to give him the necessary two-thirds.

The convention adjourned to Baltimore. In the interval between the two meetings Douglas continued in the Senate an acrimonious debate against Jefferson Davis.

The Baltimore Convention split. One division nominated

Stephen A. Douglas, of Illinois, for president, and Hershel B. Johnson, of Georgia, for vice-president. Their platform was popular sovereignty. The pro-slavery wing of the Democratic party nominated John C. Breckenridge, of Kentucky, for president, and Joseph Lane, of Oregon, for vice-president. To increase the hopelessness of the Douglas campaign, the American Party, containing a forlorn remnant of old Whigs and some Democrats, renamed themselves the Constitutional Union Party, with John Bell, of Tennessee, for president, and Edward Everett, of Massachusetts, for vice-president. Lincoln and Douglas were opposed to each other again, but on most unequal terms. Every day it grew increasingly plain to Lincoln and his friends that he was certain to be elected in November. The cleavage in the Democratic ranks went to the very bottom. Two years previous Lincoln had mirthfully taken note of the hostility between Douglas and Buchanan, and had spoken of it in terms of that cheerful neutrality of the woman in the frontier story: "Go it, husband! Go it, bear!" Even more gleefully could he now enjoy that fight.

The Democrats, in that hour when union was an absolute necessity, if any hope of success was to be cherished, divided hopelessly. There was a conundrum current in that day, the answer to which was that Stephen A. Douglas was a greater man than Abraham Lincoln, for Lincoln split rails and Douglas split the Democratic Party.

The Republican Party needed every omen of good cheer to encourage it after the nomination of Lincoln. There came a swift reaction. Delegates from the east returned to their homes to meet the question, "Why did you pass by the great statesmen of the Republican Party and give us a railsplitter?" Even Illinois felt a kind of awestricken reaction. It had gone for Lincoln as a "favorite son," hardly more than half believing it possible that he could be nominated; and now the Illinois Republicans had an awful fear that the really great leaders of the party would leave them and their candidate to get out of the situation as best they could.

Honorable O. H. Browning was a friend of Lincoln, and of course as a delegate voted for him as president. We may profitably read a few pages from his diary at this point. He had been in frequent consultation with Lincoln; and, being in Springfield, Wednesday, February 8, he wrote:

At night Lincoln came to my room, and we had a free talk about the Presidency. He thinks I may be right in supposing Mr. Bates to be the strongest and best man we can run—that he can get votes even in this county that he cannot get—and that there is a large class of voters in all the free States that would go for Mr. Bates, and for no other man. He says it is not improbable that by the time the National convention meets in Chicago he may be of opinion that the very best thing that can be done will be to nominate Mr. Bates. Dick Yates and Philips also think Mr. Bates stronger in this State than any other man who has been named. I hope to start home at 6 o'clock in the morning.

Of the convention he wrote:

My first choice for the Presidency was Mr. Bates of Missouri, but under instructions our whole delegation voted for Mr. Lincoln. Many reasons influenced to support Mr. Bates, the chief of which, next to his eminent fitness, were to strengthen our organization in the South, and remove apprehension in the South of any hostile purpose on the part of Republicans to the institutions of the South—to restore fraternal regard among the different sections of the Union—to bring to our support the old whigs in the free States, who have not yet fraternized with us, and to give some check to the ultra tendencies of the Republican party. Mr. Bates received 48 votes on the first ballot, and would probably have been nominated if the struggle had been prolonged.

After the convention he was sure that the election was lost unless Bates would take the stump for Lincoln. On Tuesday, May 22, he wrote:

Fine day. At work in office. Mrs. B. and I out at Cox's to tea. "Help me Cassius or I sink." This P. M. I received a long letter from Hon. David Davis, Thos. A. Marshall, N. B. Judd, E. Peck & O. M. Hatch, entreating me in the most earnest terms to go, without delay, to St. Louis, and see Judge Bates, and try and prevail upon him to come into Illinois, and assist us in the campaign. They want his influence to carry the old whig element for Lincoln. Some of these same men had blamed me for supporting Judge Bates for the Presidency and had asserted, in the most emphatic terms, that he could not carry Illinois. I believed before the convention, and believe now, that he would have carried the entire Republican party, and the old whig party beside, and I think others are beginning to suspect the same thing, and that we have made a mistake in the selection of candidates.

I immediately wrote a long and urgent letter to Judge Bates, and follow it in person tomorrow—for in my opinion, the existence of the party and the highest good of the country, are alike dependent on our success, and I am willing to forego all personal preferences, and make any reasonable sacrifice to secure a triumph.

Judge Bates at first was non-committal; he was not sure it would be dignified for a man who had been a candidate before the convention to go on the stump. Browning was overjoyed when Bates, a week later, in an open letter committed himself to the Lincoln cause.

If Orville H. Browning, of Illinois, felt thus, how did such men as Charles Francis Adams, of Massachusetts, feel? He delivered an able speech in the House of Representatives on May 31, 1860, two weeks after the convention, on *The Republican Party a Necessity*. In carefully formulated logic he delivered that address, which the Republican National Committee reprinted as a campaign document. It was a strong plea for the Republican Party, but it did not contain the name of Abraham Lincoln!

To their lasting honor let it be recorded that Lincoln's rivals before the convention, Seward and Chase and Cameron and Bates, supported him loyally.

In time the enthusiasm which at first was lacking, rose; for it became evident that, owing to the divisions in the Democratic Party, Lincoln had more than an even chance of winning.

There was much that was picturesque in the campaign of 1860. There was oratory and martial music; there were torch-light processions and long parades. There was much singing. Some very reputable poets wrote campaign songs for the marching clubs. William Cullen Bryant wrote one. Edmund Clarence Stedman rewrote *The Star Spangled Banner* in praise of Honest Abe of the West:

> He's the Chief in whose rule all the land shall be blest,
> Is our noble Old Abe, Honest Abe of the West!

Even Horace Greeley dropped into poetry in a very good song, written for *The Bobolink Minstrel*:

> As trembles the earth to its mighty emotion,
>   More firm grows each patriot knee,
> While people and States from the lakes to the ocean,
>   Proudly join in the march of the free!

It must be admitted that these well-wrought poems did not attain to popularity. Richard Grant White, at the close of the Civil War, compiled a book of war poetry, and went out of his way, both in the text of the book and in the Introduction to record his scorn of "that senseless farago," *John Brown's Body Lies a-Mould'ring in the Grave*. He lamented the fact that they had begun to sing it in England, but predicted that it would soon die there as already, in 1866, it was alleged to be dying in this country.

The songs that were popular in 1860, on Lincoln's side (and I forbear to quote those that were sung in derision of him), were not composed by well-known poets. They were jingles set to such tunes as *Rosin the Bow* and *Old Uncle Ned*. They were songs that informed *Old Buck* of his ultimate destination, and the route, namely, Salt River.

There were songs in recognition of the predestined fate of *Little Doug,* as this, which was sung to the tune of *Uncle Ned*:

There was a little man and his name was Stevy Doug,
  To the White House he longed for to go;
But he hadn't any votes in the whole of the South,
  In the place where his votes ought to grow.

His legs were short, but his speeches they were long,
  And nothing but himself he could see;
His principles were weak, but his spirits they were strong,
  For a thirsty little soul was he.

As for songs about "Old Abe," they were abundant. Even Willie and Tad Lincoln sang in the house in Springfield, and later in the White House how—

> Old Abe Lincoln came out of the wilderness,
>   Down in Illinois.

Arnold, who participated in this campaign, tells its story as the culmination of long deferred hope:

This Presidential campaign has had no parallel. The enthusiasm of the people was like a great conflagration, like a prairie fire before a wild tornado. A little more than twenty years had passed since Owen Lovejoy, brother of Elijah Lovejoy, on the bank of the Mississippi, kneeling on the turf not then green over the grave of the brother who had been killed for his fidelity to freedom, had sworn eternal war against slavery. From that time on, he and his associate abolitionists had gone forth preaching their crusade against oppression, with hearts of fire and tongues of lightning, and now the consummation was to be realized of a President elected on the distinct ground of opposition to the extension of slavery. For years the hatred of that institution had been growing and gathering force. Whittier, Bryant, Lowell, Longfellow, and others, had written the lyrics of liberty; the graphic pen of Mrs. Stowe, in "Uncle Tom's Cabin," had painted the cruelties of the overseer and the slaveholder, but the acts of slaveholders themselves did more to promote the growth of anti-slavery than all other causes. The per-secutions of abolitionists in the South; the harshness and cruelty attending the execution of the fugitive slave laws; the brutality of Brooks in knocking down, on the floor of the Senate, Charles Sumner, for words spoken in debate; these and many other out-rages had fired the hearts of the people of the free states against this barbarous institution. Beecher, Phillips, Channing, Sum-ner, and Seward, with their eloquence; Chase, with his logic; Lincoln, with his appeals to the principles of the Declaration of Independence, and to the opinions of the founders of the re-public, his clear statements, his apt illustrations, above all, his wise moderation—all had swelled the voice of the people, which found expression through the ballot-box, and which declared that slavery should go no further. It was now proclaimed that "the further spread of slavery should be arrested, and it should be placed where the public mind should rest in the belief of its ultimate extinction."*

At that time Ohio, Pennsylvania and Indiana all held their elections in October. These all voted for Lincoln. The result was now as certain as any future event could be and Lincoln and his wife anticipated the happy day when he was to be elected president.

. After his nomination, Lincoln moved his headquarters from his law office to a room in the state-house building. He left virtually all his law business to Herndon and spent his days receiving delegations and individuals who came to consult him. His secretary, John G. Nicolay, was with him in the office, and before he departed for Washington he engaged another secre-tary, John Hay.

It was commonly supposed in Springfield that Lincoln would not vote. Lincoln himself had thought that he would not vote for his own electors and he adhered to this plan. He decided to cast a vote for the state ticket, but not to vote for himself. He went to the polls accompanied by his law partner, William H. Herndon, his Danville associate, Ward Hill Lamon, and a young

---

Life of Lincoln, pp. 170-171.

law student, Elmer Ellsworth, at that time a member of his household.

The election of November sixth showed the following results: Lincoln received 180 electoral votes, and a popular vote of 1,866,452. Douglas received 12 electoral votes and a popular vote of 1,375,157. Breckenridge received 72 electoral votes and a popular vote of 847,953. Bell received 39 electoral votes and a popular vote of 570,631. Douglas carried but one state outright, but had some scattering votes. Breckenridge swept the South, and Bell the border states, but Lincoln had the solid North. But though Douglas had only twelve votes in the electoral college, he had a popular vote of more than one and a third millions, and stood as a dangerous second to Lincoln in popular regard. He had fought the campaign to its finish, stumping the country on his own behalf as presidential candidates at that time had rarely done, and he went down with his colors flying.

After the election, Lincoln's days were increasingly full. Photographers came to photograph him and artists to paint him. The Representatives' Hall was not then occupied, and the painters set up their easels there. Lincoln posed for the artists a little while each morning as he looked over his mail.

He greeted all who came to see him cordially. Even Hannah Armstrong, widow of his Clary Grove friend, made a pilgrimage to Springfield, and was entertained at the Lincoln home, but she was not very sure that Mrs. Lincoln enjoyed having her there.

The period that followed Lincoln's election was one of growing perplexity. He was beset by office holders and distressed by the demands of different factions that he should commit himself to one policy or another. He had no peace by day, and none too much rest at night.

Lincoln remained in Springfield after his nomination for the presidency. Except for one journey to Chicago, and one which he made to visit his aged stepmother, he hardly left Springfield. He made no speeches. Neither did he make or permit to be made on his behalf any other formal declaration than the party platform. Honorable Lawrence Weldon wrote:—

Mr. Lincoln took no public part in the campaign of 1860. He attended one political meeting, but declined to speak. On the day appointed by law the Republican electors met at Springfield and were entertained at dinner by Mr. J. C. Conkling, the elector for the district. Mr. Lincoln was there as one of the guests, and talked freely but sadly as to the condition of things incident to his election. Governor Yates, who had been elected governor, was of the party, and expressed to him the necessity of being firm and determined. Lincoln replied that he hoped he would be adequate to the responsibility of the situation; and that in his hands, as president, the Republic of Washington would not perish.*

Among the various things that Lincoln did between his nomination and his departure for Washington was this, that he decided to grow a beard. This gave much concern to the artists who were thronging Springfield at the time, and resulted in two sets of pictures, one set made in the spring and summer of 1860, showing Lincoln without a beard, and the other made later with a set of whiskers that covered his face except his upper lip. Artists generally have deplored the change; for the beard did not hide the lower lip which was the least attractive feature, and it hid the finely modeled chin. But after the beard had passed its experimental stages, and had found its metes and bounds, it became a decorative feature which can not be spared from the countenance of Lincoln.

A few days after the election, Lincoln arranged for a visit to Chicago, where, by appointment, he met the vice-presidential candidate, Honorable Hannibal Hamlin, who journeyed from Maine to meet him. For several days there were conferences in the city, which became the center of political interest of the nation. Chicago had never seen a president elect nor a vice-president elect nor the wife of a president elect, and it was determined to miss none of them. After various private conferences and visits and some shopping, there was a notable reception in

*Reminiscences of Abraham Lincoln by Distinguished Men of His Time, p. 209.

the Tremont House on Friday, November twenty-second. Lincoln stood first in line; Mrs. Lincoln stood next to him on his right; Mr. Hamlin stood next. All three shook hands with all comers. Lincoln received them all graciously, now holding to the hand of a particularly tall man, and now and then greeting with special cordiality an old friend. A small boy who shouted for the Republican candidates was caught up by Mr. Lincoln and tossed almost to the ceiling, to the mutual delight of the lad and the future president. Eight little girls halted the procession while Mr. Lincoln painstakingly wrote his autograph for each of them. The next day, Saturday, Mr. Hamlin returned east, and the Lincolns went back to Springfield, where they remained, with the exception of one visit of his, until they left for Washington.

On this visit Mr. and Mrs. Lincoln met in Chicago by appointment, Joshua F. Speed and his wife. The two men had a good visit and a happy recalling of old times. The two women were equally happy shopping; Mrs. Lincoln intended to go to Washington wearing good clothes.

Thomas Lincoln, Abraham's father, had died, January 17, 1851. Shortly before Abraham Lincoln left Springfield. he made a journey to Coles County where his stepmother was still living, and bade her an affectionate farewell. The relations which existed between this good woman and her stepson were ideal, and the meeting was one which left her with the tenderest memories. But she had a deep foreboding with respect to their parting. Some shadow, it seemed to her, hung over this beloved son of hers. She felt that even if she should live to the time of the completion of his presidential term, she should never see him again.

CHAPTER XXXI

BETWEEN the presidential election in November and the inauguration on March fourth, is a space of approximately four months.* In some instances it has proved none too long an interval. When a new man is elevated to an office as important as the presidency, four months is a period well suited to his education. He has a Cabinet to select, an inaugural address to prepare, and a multitude of matters to learn and prepare to do. Grover Cleveland may be instanced as a president to whom the interval of four months was invaluable. So might it have been for Lincoln. He needed the time. But it was a period of peril in 1860-1, and it has often proved too long an interval for the best interests of the country. While Lincoln was in Springfield, preparing his inaugural address, much water flowed down the Potomac, as well as the Sangamon. Of matters as they were moving in Washington, three may be mentioned, the disruption and reorganization of Buchanan's Cabinet, the Crittenden Compromise, and the Peace Conference. All these were in the background of Lincoln's thinking as he wrote out his address, and these influenced the character of his utterance and the definition of his policies.

Within a month after the election of Lincoln, the Congress convened. President Buchanan was in the unhappy situation of having to present a message after the nation had repudiated his

---

*The date of the election in 1860 was November sixth.

policy and party. A fragmentary diary kept by John B. Floyd,* Buchanan's Secretary of War, shows that from the very week of Lincoln's election Buchanan's Cabinet was split. According to this document, Buchanan's first impulse was to accept the result of the election, and to resist attempts at secession, but to call a convention to compromise, if possible, the controversy that threatened to disrupt the Union. The Cabinet at this time consisted of General Lewis Cass, of Michigan, Secretary of State; Howell Cobb, of Georgia, Secretary of the Treasury; John B. Floyd, of Virginia, Secretary of War; Isaac Toucey, of Connecticut, Secretary of the Navy; Jacob Thompson, of Mississippi, Secretary of the Interior; Joseph Holt, of Kentucky, Postmaster-General; and Jeremiah S. Black, of Pennsylvania, Attorney General.

On December 3, 1860, President Buchanan presented his message to Congress, knowing that his Cabinet was split in twain on the matters contained in that document. Cass, Black, Holt and Toucey were on one side, and Floyd, Thompson and Cobb on the other. There was some shifting of positions among the Cabinet members, but practically the line of division followed that between the seceding and the loyal states.

President Buchanan's policy was the preservation of the Union at all hazards.† But his attempts to preserve it were feeble and pathetic. His Message to Congress displayed an

---

*Published entire in *The Early Life, Campaigns and Public Services of Robert E. Lee*. Alleged to have been written by "a distinguished Southern Journalist" and published in 1871 by E. B. Treat, New York. Cited by Nicolay and Hay, *Century*, October, 1887.

†For a defense of Buchanan and his administration, see *Mr. Buchanan's Administration on the Eve of the Rebellion*. This book, at first issued anonymously, was later acknowledged as the work of ex-President Buchanan himself. It was published by Appleton, New York, in 1866. The Manuscript Division of the Library of Congress has an able monograph by Honorable Jeremiah S. Black, and also an article on the same subject and using much of the material, by his son, Chauncey F. Black, intended as a concluding chapter to the first volume of Lamon's *Life of Lincoln*. So far as I am aware, or the records of the Manuscript Division show, these papers have not been examined by any one except the author of this work since they were deposited with the Library of Congress. They appear, among other things, to settle the question of the real authorship of Lamon's book.

earnest hope that the Union might be preserved, and a declaration that no state had a right to secede, while disclaiming all authority on the part of the administration to make that hope effective, or to prevent the illegal act.

On December twentieth, at 1 :15 P. M. a convention convened in Charleston, South Carolina, passed an ordinance of secession; and Mr. Buchanan did not know of any way in which he could prevent it. On December twenty-sixth, South Carolina sent a Commission to Washington to treat with Mr. Buchanan concerning the peaceable departure of South Carolina from the Union, and the president received and conferred with them on the next day. The point just then immediately at issue was the question whether the forts in Charleston harbor were to be defended against the government of South Carolina which considered itself an independent state, no longer in the Union. The president vacillated; but the demands of the commissioners were at length refused by him through the opposition of the reorganized Cabinet.

While the last months of Buchanan's administration displayed an appalling impotence upon his part, there was an element of saving vigor in the loyalty of a portion of his Cabinet. There was full need of all the loyalty that existed, for within the Cabinet as originally constituted was quite sufficient material for the nucleus of a Cabinet for the Confederacy. Of the seven men whom Buchanan had chosen as his official advisers were three secessionists of the most radical type. Howell Cobb was considered by the Confederate States as a possible president instead of Jefferson Davis. Jacob Thompson, in December, 1860, while still a member of the Cabinet, left Washington, and visited North Carolina seeking to encourage that state to secede. This mission did not induce him to resign his place in the Cabinet, and he even claimed, what it would seem could not possibly have been true, that Buchanan knew and approved his mission. John B. Floyd, while still in the Cabinet, delivered over to the Confederate States, organized as an independent and hostile government, everything within them belonging to the government which he as Secretary of War could control.

Jeremiah S. Black was a northern man, from Pennsylvania, the president's own state. He furnished to Buchanan an elaborate opinion, which Buchanan used as the basis of his last message to Congress, to the effect that no state had a right to secede, but affirming that the president had no power under the Constitution to use the resources of his office for the preservation of the Union.

Early in December, Howell Cobb resigned from the Treasury and left it conveniently empty. Philip F. Thomas, of Maryland, a Secessionist, succeeded Cobb. He had nothing to spend and a short time in which to have expended it. His appointment was unimportant. General Cass, a Jackson Democrat of the old school, resigned from the State Department, December thirteenth. In his place Buchanan appointed Judge Black, and brought into the Cabinet as attorney general, Edwin M. Stanton. This was a change of very great importance. On December twenty-ninth Mr. Floyd resigned, and went where he belonged. He was succeeded by Joseph Holt, a staunch, loyal Democrat, who had been serving as postmaster general. On January eighth Jacob Thompson resigned his position as secretary of the interior, and the vacancy was unfilled. On the following day Philip F. Thomas, who had succeeded Howell Cobb as secretary of the treasury, resigned. The New York bankers forced Buchanan to appoint as his successor General John A. Dix, an old time Democrat, but a strong Union man. His telegram on January twenty-ninth was the first cheering and virile word representing the administration: "If any man attempts to haul down the American flag, shoot him on the spot."

On Sunday morning, December thirtieth, the South Carolina commissioners who had arrived in Washington, demanded recognition and the right to treat with the government as though they represented a foreign power. Buchanan declined to receive them in that capacity, but was not unwilling to treat with them as intermediary between those commissioners and Congress. He found, however, that he must reckon with the loyal members of his Cabinet. As he could come to no terms with Black, Stanton and Holt consistent with his giving aid and comfort to these enemies of his country, he accepted a reply to them drafted by Black and approved by Stanton and Holt. This was so unsatisfactory to the Confederate commissioners that they returned to South Carolina. Thenceforth the South covered Buchanan with abuse, perhaps greater even than that of the North. That poor unfortunate man in his senile indecision waited helplessly for the end of his troubled administration.

The loyal members of Buchanan's Cabinet, however, engaged in secret counsel seeking the preservation of the Union. As these four members of Buchanan's Cabinet, including Dix, represented the hope of the united nation in the dying administration, so in a very real sense did William H. Seward at this time emerge in Congress as the representative of the incoming administration.

To all intents and purposes Buchanan abdicated on Sunday morning, December 30, 1860. From that time until the end of his administration the Cabinet virtually governed whatever was left of the Union. Stanton and Holt, and subsequently Dix, made a strong trio of uncompromising Union men, and Black swung around first to a degree of partial cooperation with them, and later to essential leadership of their earnest efforts to save the Union.

While President Buchanan and his Cabinet were thus working at cross purposes, and unable to arrive at any result, the Senate undertook the consideration of a possible preventive of war and disruption of the Union. The venerable John J. Crittenden, of Kentucky, then seventy-three years of age, had for many years been a leader of the Whig Party. He had served long in the Senate and was about to retire, the then vice-president of the United States, Honorable J. C. Breckenridge, having been chosen as his successor, to take his seat with the new administration, March 4, 1861. Senator Crittenden earnestly desired to crown his service in the Senate with a compromise which should weld the Union together. Of his loyalty and good faith there can be no question. His resolutions introduced December 18, 1860, proposed, in his own words:

. . . The restoration of the Missouri Compromise, extending the line throughout the Territories of the United States to the eastern border of California, recognizing slavery in all the territory south of that line, and prohibiting slavery in all the territory north of it; with a provision, however, that when any of those Territories, north or south, are formed into States, they shall then be at liberty to exclude or admit slavery as they please; and that, in the one case or the other, it shall be no objection to their admission into the Union. "In this way, sir," he said, "I propose to settle the question, both as to territory and slavery, so far as regards the Territories of the United States.

"I propose, sir, also, that the Constitution shall be so amended as to declare that Congress shall have no power to abolish slavery in the District of Columbia so long as slavery exists in the States of Maryland and Virginia; and that they shall have no power to abolish slavery in any of the places within their special jurisdiction within the Southern States."*

Further provisions of the Crittenden Compromise were to prevent an apprehended prohibition of inter-state traffic in slaves; to provide that if in any state or locality local sentiment or popular uprising should prevent the enforcement of the Fugitive Slave Law, the owners of the slaves should be compensated; and that the foregoing constitutional amendments should be made absolutely irrepealable.

The imminent danger to the Union and the utter failure of the Buchanan administration to prevent its disruption, gave to these proposals remarkable popularity. They appeared to be the only effective proposal for the salvation of the Union.

Mention has been made of the reaction that followed Lincoln's nomination. It must be remembered that a mightier reaction

---

*Life of John J. Crittenden, by his daughter, Mrs. Chapman Coleman, Philadelphia, 1871; ii, pp. 224-225.

followed his election.   Noted abolitionists were denied the use
of public halls.   The entire North seemed to have been seized
with a determination to disavow any sentiments which could
be considered as bordering upon abolition.   Timidity and reaction became general.   Republican leaders made haste to explain
that they were not in sympathy with any measures which could
offend the South.

On February 6, 1861, an all-day meeting was held in Faneuil
Hall, in Boston, in favor of the Crittenden Compromise.   The
Mayor, Honorable Joseph M. Wightman, presided.   Reverend
Doctor Blagden offered prayer.   Repeated references were made
to Faneuil Hall as a place appropriate for such a meeting. A petition was read which, it was stated, had been signed by 22,000
citizens of Massachusetts, favorable to such a compromise.   Horace Greeley believed that if the Crittenden Compromise had been
submitted to popular vote, it would have prevailed by an overwhelming majority.

Greeley himself, however, did not favor the compromise.
Writing of it later, he said:

The Republican Party, which had been called into existence by
the opening of free soil to slavery, seemed in positive danger
of signaling its advent to power by giving its direct assent to the
practical extension of slavery over a region far larger and more
important than that theoretically surrendered by the Kansas-
Nebraska bill.*

So astute a politician as Thurlow Weed believed that this compromise ought to be adopted, and Seward, he of the "irrepressible conflict," probably agreed with him.   Weed went to Springfield about the time that Crittenden introduced his Resolutions,
and is believed to have advised Lincoln to accept this compromise.

Lincoln declined.†

---

*Recollections of a Busy Life, pp. 396-7.
†Professor Nathaniel Wright Stephenson makes this decision "the crisis"
in Lincoln's career, and thinks that Weed went to Springfield as Seward's
henchman to induce Lincoln to accept the compromise.   He even thinks that

Why did Lincoln refuse the Crittenden Compromise? One reason may have been that he already had some occasion to distrust Crittenden as a compromiser. One of Crittenden's compromises had cut Lincoln deeply. Lincoln believed that he might have been elected Senator if Crittenden had kept out of Illinois politics, or had stood by a long-time Whig in his contest with a Democrat. Lincoln wrote to Crittenden after the election of 1858:

The emotions of defeat at the close of a struggle in which I felt more than a merely selfish interest, and to which defeat the use of your name contributed largely, are fresh upon me; but even in this mood I cannot for a moment suspect you of anything dishonorable.

No one who knew Senator Crittenden could suspect him of anything dishonorable; but Lincoln, when urged to follow Crittenden in a compromise at the end of 1860, could not have failed to remember the advice of Crittenden at the time of the Lincoln-Douglas debates. Lincoln was too great and magnanimous a

---

Lincoln's decision was announced on December twentieth, "the very day South Carolina adopted its Ordinance of Secession," and that this coincidence, "one of the great events in American history," occurred on this day "by a rare propriety of dramatic effect." But this seems to me an overstraining of the situation. Crittenden introduced his Compromise Resolutions on December eighteenth; there was not time for Weed and Seward to have come to such deliberate judgment and for Weed to have made the journey and had his long conference by December twentieth. Further, Lincoln had already declined this proposal in a letter to Washburne. Moreover, in Weed's own account of this, his second visit to Springfield since Lincoln's nomination, he makes no mention of the compromise as a topic of conversation. Still further, Lincoln had already told Weed, in his letter of December seventeenth, in answer to Weed's inquiry of the eleventh, that Weed might say that he judged from Lincoln's speeches that Lincoln would be "inflexible on the territorial question," and that he would not accept the plan of extending the Missouri line. Lincoln further added, that, as Weed would find very little in Lincoln's speeches about secession, and these published speeches were to be the assumed basis of his information of Lincoln's position, Lincoln was willing to have this said to a possible conference of governors about which Weed had written:

"My opinion is that no state can in any way lawfully get out of the Union without the consent of the others; and that it is the duty of the president and other government functionaries to run the machine as it is."

This was, of course, decisive as to the Crittenden Compromise, which appears to have been hardly mentioned when Weed and Lincoln met later in December.

man to have carried his resentment against Crittenden, even if
he felt such resentment, to the point of opposing through revenge the policy of a man whom he believed to have injured
him; still, Lincoln could not forget how wrong, as it seemed
to him, had been the judgment of Senator Crittenden two
years before, and he did not follow that judgment in December, 1860.

But there was a further reason why Lincoln did not accept
the Crittenden Compromise. Lincoln did not believe in December, 1860, that the South would really go the length of declaring war. Serious as the situation was, he believed that the
South would yield before it would resort to actual bloodshed.
And he fully expected that when he showed a kindly firmness,
the effect would be a reuniting of the Union, even after South
Carolina had passed her Ordinance of Secession.

A further and appreciative word is due the memory of Senator
Crittenden. In the closing hours of Congress, just before he
was to leave the Senate for ever, he took the floor, not on behalf
of his compromise, but in favor of an amended measure, which,
it was believed, might possibly unite the Union. When certain
of the senators urged the original Crittenden measure, he said
that while he personally would have preferred his own, he would
vote against his own and in favor of the measure which presented the larger hope of effecting an agreement capable of
saving the Union. With that measure we shall presently deal.
Senator Crittenden, old and feeble, returned to Kentucky, and
there addressed the Legislature in a strong speech in favor of
the Union. His own son, a West Point graduate, and a colonel
in the United States Army, resigned and became a major general
in the Confederate Army, but the father stood firm for the
Union. He no longer had a seat in the Senate, but he was
elected to the House, and there served with conspicuous loyalty
until his death, July 26, 1863. He hoped to live to see the
Union restored by the complete defeat of the Confederate
Army, and he prepared a resolution which he hoped to present

to Congress, providing for a restored Union on a basis of mag-
nanimity and good will.*

The Peace Convention, which related itself somewhat intimately to the Crittenden Compromise, was called by resolution
of the Legislature of Virginia, and met in Washington, at noon,
on Monday, February 4, 1861, exactly a month before the inauguration of Abraham Lincoln. At the outset the following
states were represented by commissioners:

New Hampshire, Rhode Island, New Jersey, Pennsylvania,
Delaware, Maryland, Virginia, North Carolina, Kentucky, Ohio
and Indiana.

Before the close, the roll showed representatives present from
Maine, New Hampshire, Vermont, Massachusetts, Rhode Island, Connecticut, New York, New Jersey, Pennsylvania, Delaware, Maryland, Virginia, North Carolina, Tennessee, Kentucky, Missouri, Ohio, Indiana, Illinois, Iowa and Kansas.

The venerable John Tyler, ex-President of the United States,
was chairman, and the representatives of the several states were
men of high standing. The convention continued its sessions
until Wednesday, February twenty-seventh, Mr. Lincoln having
arrived in Washington on the Saturday previous.

This convention practically accepted the Crittenden Resolutions as the basis of its discussions, and at length, but by a
divided vote, approved a modification of the Crittenden Resolutions as a proposed Amendment to the Constitution of the
United States, and sent ex-President Tyler to the Congress to
present the results of the deliberations.†

It ought to be remembered that there were those who doubted,
up to the very hour of the inaugural, whether Lincoln would
have opportunity to read his address. The Constitution of the
United States reads:

---

*This resolution, found among his papers after his death, is in his *Life*,
by his daughter, ii, p. 369.

†The discussions were held in secret, but full notes were preserved, and
just before adjournment the ban of secrecy was removed. The *Proceedings*
were published in 1865, having been edited by L. E. Chittenden, one of the
delegates from New York, and later auditor of the Treasury.

The President of the Senate shall, in the presence of the Senate and House of Representatives, open all the certificates, and the votes shall then be counted.

By whom were the votes to be counted? It was the duty of the president of the Senate to open the certificates, but whose duty was it to count the votes? What power was there to compel any one to count them? What could be done to punish any one who should refuse to count the votes?

The president of the Senate was John C. Breckenridge, an unsuccessful candidate for the presidency; suppose he should "open all the certificates" as the Constitution required, and entertain a motion to refer to a special committee the question whether there was authority for any counting of the votes, and if so, what the authority was, and whose the duty was? There were members of Congress who held that, as the counting of the votes which, as was known, would declare Abraham Lincoln president, would wreck the nation, any tactics of delay or obstruction that might avert that calamity, no matter what the alternative, would be meritorious.

Lincoln himself was somewhat worried over this possibility. The pro-slavery element still in Congress was strong; what if it should show its strength by making the election of Lincoln a nullity by preventing the counting of the vote?

Happily, no such condition arose. On the second Wednesday in February, 1861, the two Houses of Congress met in joint session, and the vice-president opened the certificates of election. Stephen A. Douglas, also a defeated candidate for the presidency, led in a movement to simplify the procedure. The vote was counted without incident, and Vice-President Breckenridge declared that Abraham Lincoln, of Illinois, had been duly elected president of the United States, for a term of four years beginning at noon on March 4, 1861.

The South had hardly expected that Lincoln could be elected. In December, 1856, a meeting of governors of slave states was held, and Governor Wise, of Virginia, declared that if Frémont had been elected he would have marched to Washington at the head of twenty thousand men, and prevented his inauguration.

The dreaded event which had seemed impossible had finally occurred. An anti-slavery president had been elected. Although the new Congress did not have a Republican majority in either House, the southern leaders were thoroughly aroused and alarmed.

As soon as the results of the election were assured, the South Carolina Legislature called a convention and adjourned. The convention assembled, and on December 20, 1860, passed an ordinance declaring "that the Union now subsisting between South Carolina and other states under the name 'United States of America' is hereby dissolved." Within about six weeks Mississippi, Florida, Alabama, Georgia and Louisiana held conventions and passed secession ordinances. On February 23, 1861, Texas joined the list of seceding states. The other slave states did not immediately follow.

On February 4, 1861, just four weeks before the inauguration of the new president, delegates from the seceded states met at Montgomery, Alabama, and organized a government under the name of the "Confederate States of America." A constitution was promptly adopted by a newly elected southern Congress, and was soon ratified by the states to which it was referred. Jefferson Davis, of Mississippi, was elected president, and Alexander H. Stephens, of Georgia, was elected vice-president.

These preparations in the South produced what was very nearly a moral panic in the North. War, it was felt, must be averted at whatever cost. In Boston twenty-two thousand citizens signed a petition to Congress to make such concessions as should avert war. A meeting held in that city to commemorate the anniversary of the hanging of John Brown was broken up by a mob. The *New York Tribune* came out with an editorial on November sixteenth advising that the "erring sisters," the Southern States, be permitted to "depart in peace." Thurlow Weed's paper, the *Albany Journal,* took essentially the same po-

17

sition, and so did two other prominent New York Free-soil papers, the *Times,* and the *Courier and Inquirer.* The *Indianapolis Journal* advocated compromise and concession. The *Detroit Free Press* declared editorially that if an army was sent south to subdue the seceding states, it would encounter a fire in the rear.

Through all this and much more, Mr. Lincoln remained silent. But he did much thinking, and some confidential writing. On December eleventh, he wrote to Mr. Kellogg, the Illinois member of the Committee of Thirty-three appointed by the lower House of Congress to consider the emergency:

Entertain no proposition for a compromise in regard to the extension of slavery. The instant you do this, they have us under again; all our labor is lost, and sooner or later must be done over again. The tug has to come, and better now than later.

To Elihu B. Washburne, Member of Congress from the Galena district, he wrote December thirteenth:

Prevent as far as possible any of our friends from demoralizing themselves or their cause by entertaining propositions of any sort on slavery extension. . . On that point hold firm as a chain of steel.

But on almost any other point Lincoln was more than ready to make concessions. He was himself in a state of great anxiety over the situation. Yet he did not really believe that the southern states would leave the Union, or that they would resort to war.

On December twenty-second, the *New York Tribune* announced editorially:

We are enabled to say in the most positive terms that Mr. Lincoln is utterly opposed to any concession or compromise that shall yield one iota of the position occupied by the Republican party on the subject of slavery in the territories, and that he

stands now as he stood in May last, when he accepted the nomination, square upon the Republican platform.

Beyond this, Lincoln was ready to make concessions; but not
on the extension of slavery.

But what about the man Abraham Lincoln, all this time?
How did he feel and what did he think during those anxious
months?

Lincoln entered upon his presidential campaign with something almost like elation. Herndon tells us that Lincoln's success
at Cooper Union strengthened his already large estimate of his
own powers. It "stimulated his self-confidence to unwonted
proportions."* To be sure, he realized that only a series of most
favorable conditions could make him president, but he also realized that none of those conditions were impossible. As the Chicago Convention approached, he was alternately in hope and
fear; and there were days when he would willingly have exchanged his uncertain hope for the certainty of a nomination as
vice-president with Seward at the head of the ticket.

After the nomination, his mood was prevailingly a happy one.
Practically every day he met enthusiastic delegations who gave
him renewed assurance of the success of his campaign. Lincoln had little fear of defeat at the polls.

From the time of the Democratic split in the Baltimore Convention, Mr. Lincoln, as well as every other politician of the
smallest sagacity, knew that his success was as certain as any
future event could be.†

It has been alleged that the period between Lincoln's election
and his departure for Washington was one of deep gloom. Certain of his friends, calling on him and finding him oppressed
with a sense of the responsibilities which had come upon him,
and wearied by the persistence of the office-seekers, and worried further by the fact that nearly all his neighbors appeared

*Herndon's *Lincoln,* iii, p. 457.
†Lamon, *Life of Lincoln,* p. 500.

suddenly to have become active in efforts to obtain positions for themselves or their relatives, near and remote, have given some ground for this impression, but that is not the impression which one receives who talks with the people who knew Lincoln best in those days. On the whole, he was cheerful, and at times even merry. A few evenings, after the visitors of the day had gone, he met with his old friends, and they exchanged jokes in all the freedom of the old days, and remembered him in the happy good humor of what must have been at that time his prevailing mood.*

Lincoln was a man of moods, and he went from gaiety to depression without warning and with little apparent occasion. It is not likely that he spent four months in Springfield after his election without some bad quarter-hours. But his prevailing mood was happy at this time. Lamon says that at this time "ambition charmed his whole heart" and that "hope elevated and joy brightened his crest."

Thurlow Weed, who was a most astute judge of men, after his second visit to Lincoln, said:

While Mr. Lincoln never underestimated the difficulties which surrounded him, his nature was so elastic, and his temperament so cheerful, that he always seemed at ease and undisturbed.†

All in all, the president-elect at this time was a happy man. No one at this date will grudge to Abraham Lincoln the happiness of those days.

---

*Professor Stephenson thinks that Lincoln was "firm as steel" until the day he refused to accept the Crittenden Compromise, but that that momentous decision brought its swift reaction, and that he became melancholy and irresolute, and lived his last months in Springfield in mingled gloom, desperation and a vain attempt to recover hope. I can find no evidence in support of this view.

†For this entire incident, see Weed's *Autobiography*.

CHAPTER XXXII

Most of the time of the president-elect after his election and before his removal to Washington, was taken up with people from out of town. Mrs. Lincoln accepted invitations to dine with her friends, and Lincoln now and then stole away for an evening with his old associates; but the days were mostly filled with other matters. As the time of their departure approached, Mrs. Lincoln endeavored to pay her social obligations. There was a children's party in the Lincoln home a few weeks before the departure of the family; some people now in Springfield cherish the invitations which they received as boys or girls, written in Mrs. Lincoln's own hand. And once, at least, and probably more than once, small groups of friends gathered in response to a neatly written invitation:

> Mr. and Mrs. Lincoln
> will be pleased to see you
> Thursday evening
> at 8 o'clock

A week before they left Springfield Mr. and Mrs. Lincoln gave a general reception to their old friends and neighbors. The Springfield papers, filled with national matters, do not give the affair adequate space; probably the Lincolns preferred that it be a sort of home affair; but the *Missouri Democrat,* of St. Louis, had a somewhat full account of what is called Mr. Lincoln's first levee after his election. It occurred on Wednesday evening,

February sixth, and the account was written on the following day.*

The first levee given by the President-elect, took place last evening, [Wednesday, February sixth] at his own residence, in this city, and it was a grand outpouring of citizens and strangers, together with the members of the legislature. Your humble servant was invited to attend. Mr. Lincoln threw open his house for a general reception of all the people who felt disposed to give him and his lady a parting call. The levee lasted from seven to twelve o'clock in the evening, and the house thronged by thousands up to a late hour. Mr. Lincoln received the guests as they entered and were made known. They then passed on, and were introduced to Mrs. Lincoln, who stood near the center of the parlors, and who, I must say, acquitted herself most gracefully and admirably—She was dressed plainly, but richly. She wore a beautiful, full trail, white moire antique silk, with a small French lace collar. Her neck was ornamented with a string of pearls. Her head dress was a simple and delicate vine, arranged with much taste. She displayed but little jewelry, and this was well and appropriately adjusted. She is a lady of fine figure and accomplished address, and is well calculated to grace and to do honors at the White House.

Mr. Lincoln rented his house to Mr. Tilton, Superintendent of the Wabash Railway, and spent the last week of his life in Springfield in the Chenery House. A change had become necessary, also, in Lincoln's office arrangements. The Legislature met early in December, and it was no longer convenient for Lincoln or the governor for him to occupy an office in the capitol building. Joel Johnson, an old friend, had recently erected some brick buildings on the northwest corner opposite the Chenery House, and he offered Lincoln the double parlors on the second floor as a reception-room. Lincoln gratefully accepted, and it was there that he received his guests from the first of December until the early part of February. Mr. Johnson's buildings later became the Revere House. The weeks flew by swiftly

*Illinois State Historical Society Journal, ii, 1918-19, p. 386.

enough for the Lincoln family, but far too slowly for the welfare of the nation. Increasingly Lincoln felt the weight of his new responsibility; yet to some who saw him he seemed to realize it all too inadequately.

On the night before the departure from Springfield, Sunday, February tenth, Mr. Lincoln roped the family trunks with his own hands, took some of the hotel cards, and turning them over wrote upon them, "LINCOLN, EXECUTIVE MANSION, WASHINGTON." These cards he tacked to the trunks and had them ready for transportation to the station early in the morning. Monday, February 11, 1861, dawned dark, cold and drizzly. Lincoln's friends and neighbors to a number which the reporters estimated at a thousand, gathered in and about the Wabash station. A special train stood waiting. At half past seven Lincoln and his family entered the dilapidated hotel bus and rode down to the station. There was a short farewell reception in the waiting-room. Lincoln stood silent for the most part, and shook hands with his neighbors and friends. Time did not permit his taking the hand of each. The ringing of the engine bell warned him and his family to go on board the train where the other members of the party awaited him. The press reports state that Lincoln was pale and seemed to be bearing up under deep emotion. The somberness of the weather was reflected in the demeanor of the assembled company. Gloom and depression of spirit were manifest on the faces of the whole company. The leave-taking was solemn. In after years, it seemed as though some premonition had been in everybody's mind, by no means excepting that of Mr. Lincoln. Mr. Lincoln disappeared, entering the front end of the rear car, but in a moment reappeared on the rear platform. In a voice that choked with emotion, and with tears filling his eyes, he delivered this last address to his old neighbors:

My friends: No one, not in my situation, can appreciate my feeling of sadness at this parting. To this place, and the kindness of these people, I owe everything. Here I have lived a quarter of a century, and have passed from a young to an old man. Here my children have been born, and one is buried. I now leave, not knowing when or whether ever I may return, with a task before me greater than that which rested upon Washington. Without the assistance of that Divine Being who ever attended him, I cannot succeed. With that assistance, I cannot fail. Trusting in Him, who can go with me, and remain with you, and be everywhere for good, let us confidently hope that all will yet be well. To His care commending you as I hope in your prayers you will commend me, I bid you an affectionate farewell.*

The presidential party which made the whole journey, consisted of Mr. and Mrs. Lincoln, their three sons, Robert, William and Thomas, their brother-in-law, Doctor W. S. Wallace, the two secretaries, John G. Nicolay and John Hay, Lockwood Todd, Honorable Norman B. Judd, Honorable David Davis, J. M. Burgess, George C. Latham, W. S. Wood, B. Forbes, Colonel E. V. Sumner, Major David Hunter, Captain George W. Hazard, Captain John Pope, Colonel Ward Hill Lamon and Colonel Elmer E. Ellsworth. A considerable number of other men, including Senator O. H. Browning and Governor Richard Yates, accompanied the train when it left Springfield, and dropped off at Indianapolis or other places along the route. Personal friends and local committees joined the party from time to time, so that a considerable number of people first and last, were members of the presidential party. At all the important points along the road the train was scheduled to stop for a longer or shorter time to enable people to see and hear Lincoln.

Besides the advertised stops, the train was occasionally halted at a junction or to take water, and there, also, Lincoln had to appear and speak to the people who assembled about the station.

---

*The text of the address as here quoted is that which was prepared by Mr. Lincoln with the assistance of his secretary immediately after the train left Springfield. It differs slightly from the forms printed at the time, and is that which has been accepted by the Illinois State Historical Society for the Lincoln monument on the grounds of the capitol at Springfield. This form was first published by Nicolay and Hay in 1886, from the original manuscript and is the form which Lincoln approved, and is graven on the base of the statue in front of the Illinois State Capitol building.

If he had grown somewhat rumpled and untidy in appearance since the last stop, Mrs. Lincoln "fixed him up" before he went upon the platform, he lifting her to the car-seat to adjust his cravat and brush his hair a little. One of these unscheduled stops was at a railway junction near Lafayette, Indiana, six hours from Springfield, and Lincoln spoke of the contrast in speed between the time when he left Indiana in 1830 and that which his train was making. That can not have been the only contrast of which he was thinking. By day as he traveled and by night as he lay in luxurious quarters in hotels provided in the several cities where he spent the night, he must have thought much of the strange way by which he had come and of that which was now taking him to the White House.*

The journey of Lincoln to Washington occupied almost two weeks. There were scheduled stops in a number of important cities, including five state capitals where the Legislatures were in session. All these stops were in response to official invitations. Beside these, there were frequent wayside stops where Lincoln made brief addresses.

The first halt was at Indianapolis, on Monday afternoon, February eleventh. The Lincoln family was entertained at the Bates House, and Lincoln spoke from the balcony to a large assembly.

Next morning, Tuesday, February twelfth, was Lincoln's fifty-second birthday. His special train left Indianapolis at eleven o'clock in the morning and accomplished the run to Cincinnati in five hours and fifteen minutes. The weather was excellent, and there was a procession along decorated streets leading ultimately to the Burnett House, where the Lincoln family spent the night.

Lincoln **in his address** recalled the fact that he had spoken just once before in Cincinnati, and that in the year 1859, after his debates with Stephen A. Douglas. On that previous occasion he had addressed no small portion of his remarks to the people of Kentucky; and being now at the southernmost point in his

---

*This little address is in *The Soul of Abraham Lincoln,* p. 385.

journey, he spoke again quite as much to the people south of the river as he did to those of Cincinnati.

On the morning of Wednesday, February thirteenth, he left Cincinnati, and arrived at Columbus where the Legislature was in session. He addressed the General Assembly and held a packed reception in which he attempted to shake hands with every one, but had to give it up, so great was the crowd. Here as everywhere he was met by a committee composed of leading citizens and officials. He spent that night in the governor's residence.

On Thursday, February fourteenth, he left Columbus at eight o'clock in the morning and reached Pittsburgh in a pouring rain which interfered much with the program. It was announced, however, that he would speak next morning at eight o'clock, and leave at eleven.

On Friday, February fifteenth, Lincoln delivered an address in Pittsburgh and left for Cleveland, where the night was spent in the Weddell House. What Lincoln said in Cleveland is typical of his addresses on this tour. He avoided a technical discussion of national issues and endeavored to allay excitement. He said:

I am convinced that the cause of Liberty and the Union can never be in danger. Frequent allusion is made to the excitement at present existing in our national politics. It is well that I should also allude to it here. I think there is no occasion for any excitement. The crisis, as it is called, is altogether an artificial crisis. In all parts of the nation there are differences of opinion on politics. There are differences of opinion even here. You did not all vote for the person who now addresses you. A large number of you did—enough for all practical purposes—but not all of you. Farther away there were fewer who voted for me, and their numbers decreased as they got farther away. What is happening now will not hurt those who are farther away from here. Have they not all the rights now that they ever had? Do they not have their fugitive slaves returned as ever? Have they not the same Constitution that they have lived under for the last seventy-odd years? Have they not a position as citizens of this common country, and have we any power to change that position? What then is the matter with them? Why all this excitement? Why all these complaints? As I said before, this crisis is all artificial. It has no foundation in facts. It was not argued up, as the saying is, and cannot therefore be argued down. Let it alone, and it will go down of itself.

This speech and others like it must indicate either that Lincoln was deliberately avoiding the facing of the issue, or that he did not realize how serious the situation actually was. The crisis was very much more severe than any word of Lincoln's in the early part of his journey would indicate. It is probable that to some extent he was moved by the great demonstrations in his favor and gave to them a more hopeful interpretation than they deserved.

On Saturday, February sixteenth, Mr. Lincoln left Cleveland and arrived in Buffalo. At a small station an incident occurred which was much commented upon at the time, and is worth recalling as it was reported in the daily press:

At North East station a flag inscribed "Fort Sumter" was carried right up where Mr. Lincoln stood, but he did not seem to take the hint, and made no allusion to it in his few remarks. At the same station Mr. Lincoln took occasion to state that during the campaign he had received a letter from a young girl of this place, in which he was kindly admonished to do certain things, and among others to let his whiskers grow, and that, as he had acted upon that piece of advice, he would now be glad to welcome his fair correspondent, if she was among the crowd. In response to his call, a little lassie made her way through the crowd, was helped to the platform, and kissed by the President.*

In the several capital cities Lincoln was greeted by governors and high officials. In Buffalo the reception committee was headed by ex-President Fillmore. In that city the party spent Sunday, and was glad of a day of rest. Lincoln's addresses had been brief, but there had been many of them, and he was weary and growing hoarse.

*New York Herald, Sunday, February 17, 1861.

By this time Mr. Lincoln had had opportunity to get some reaction from the impression which his speeches were making on the country. Some papers were disposed to speak kindly of his wayside addresses, but few, if any, were enthusiastic. James Gordon Bennett, of the *New York Herald,* was frankly antagonistic, and his criticism of Lincoln's addresses, which the *Herald* denominated "drippings from the inaugural" was on the whole less caustic than might have been expected. It said,

Abraham Lincoln, as President elect of the United States, is in a fair way to lose that high reputation which he gained in his Illinois stumping campaign of 1858 with Judge Douglas, as a candidate for the United States Senate. Since his departure from Springfield, *en route* for the White House, he has made several little speeches, but in none of them has he manifested the disposition or the capacity to grapple manfully with the dangers of this crisis in reference to the restoration of the Union, or the maintenance of the peace of the country. . . . If Mr. Lincoln has nothing better to offer upon this fearful crisis than the foolish consolations of his speech at Columbus, let him say nothing at all.

On Monday, February eighteenth, the party moved on to Albany. Here Lincoln was greeted by Governor Morgan. Here also, he met the most prominent officials of New York State and an important delegation which came from the city of New York. The impression which he appears to have made at Albany was that he was less saintly and more shrewd than had commonly been reported. The impression that he was a good-natured man without force began to yield a little to the conviction that Lincoln possessed some elements of strength of character. The reporter for the *New York Herald* who accompanied the expedition generally reflected in his daily story the known sentiment of the editorial columns, but as the train neared New York, he gave the following impression of the personality of Lincoln:

Towering above all, with his face and forehead furrowed by

a thousand wrinkles, his hair unkempt, his new whiskers looking as if not yet naturalized, his clothing illy arranged, Mr. Lincoln sat near the rear of the saloon car. Putting prejudice aside, no one can see Mr. Lincoln without recognizing in him a man of immense power and force of character and natural talent. He seems so sincere, so conscientious, so simple hearted, that no one can help liking him and esteeming any disparagement of his ability or desire to do right, as a personal insult.

This was a courageous bit of writing on the part of the *Herald* reporter, and, violently opposed to Lincoln as Bennett was, he printed the tribute as it was written.

Lincoln could not fail to realize a difference in the atmosphere in Albany from that which he had experienced in the capitals of Indiana and Ohio. Republican New York had been for Seward, and was not yet reconciled to his defeat; but New York as a whole was not Republican. Governor Morgan was then and for a time continued, one of Lincoln's strongest opponents, and Fernando Wood, Mayor of New York City, was a Democrat of the deepest dye.

Part of the way from Buffalo to Albany "the Prince of Rails" as some of the newspapers now called Mr. Lincoln, rode upon the engine. It is recorded that he expressed himself as highly gratified by the experience.

On Monday, February 18, 1861, while Abraham Lincoln was in Albany, doing his best to make a good impression upon the Legislature of New York State, Jefferson Davis was inaugurated president of the Confederate States of America, at Montgomery, Alabama. Lincoln was aware of this event while he was receiving a measured courtesy in Albany. He had opportunity to read about it next day as he was on his way to New York City.

He also had opportunity to read in the columns of the *Herald* a categorical demand that Mr. Lincoln should devote himself immediately to patching up a peace with the seceded states, calling a special session of Congress to pass an amendment to the

Constitution such as the South would approve, and filling not a single office, except his Cabinet, until such a constitutional amendment was assured of adoption.

The *Herald* further inquired in a leaded editorial,

What will Mr. Lincoln do when he arrives? What will he say to the citizens of this great metropolis? Will he kiss our girls, and give a twirl to the whiskers which he has begun to cultivate? Will he tell our merchants, groaning under the pressure of the greatest political convulsion ever experienced in America that "nobody is hurt" or that "marching troops into South Carolina" and bombarding its fortresses is "no invasion"?

The *Herald* editorial of the following day says:

The masses of the people did not turn out. There was a faint cheer as Mr. Lincoln entered his carriage at the railway station, but none of those spontaneous movements for which our people are noted.

The celebration arranged for Lincoln in New York City was the most imposing anywhere along the route; New York would have been content with nothing less; but in no other city had there been such manifest coldness, and Lincoln must have left it with a distinct chill.

On Wednesday, February twentieth, Lincoln arrived in Trenton. The New Jersey Legislature was in session and he visited both Houses. It was in his address before the New Jersey Legislature that he spoke of the marked influence upon his own boyhood of his reading the story of the battles of the Revolutionary War, and especially, of his early profit in the use of Weems' *Life of Washington*.

On Thursday, February twenty-first, Lincoln arrived in Philadelphia. On the following morning he visited Independence Hall, and raised a flag over the building where the Declaration of Independence was signed. By this time Lincoln had a greatly deepened sense of the solemnity of his undertaking. He had been informed of a plot to assassinate him on the way to Washington. To this plot he made reference in his address that morning:

All the political sentiments I entertain have been drawn, so far as I have been able to draw them, from the sentiments which originated in, and were given to the world from, this hall. I never had a feeling, politically, that did not spring from the sentiments embodied in the Declaration of Independence. . . . It was not the mere matter of the separation of the colonies from the mother-land, but that *sentiment* in the Declaration of Independence, which gave liberty not alone to the people of this country, but I hope to the world, for all future time. It was that which gave promise that, in due time, the weight would be lifted from the shoulders of men. This is the sentiment embodied in the Declaration of Independence. Now, my friends, can this country be saved upon that basis? If it can, I will consider myself one of the happiest men in the world, if I can help to save it. If it cannot be saved upon that principle, it will be truly awful! But if this country cannot be saved without giving up the principle, I was about to say: *"I would rather be assassinated on the spot,* than surrender it." . . . I have said nothing but what I am willing to live by, and if it be the pleasure of Almighty God, to die by.

Before leaving Springfield, Lincoln took the manuscript of his Inaugural Address to the office of the *Journal,* and had it put in type, in order that he might have copies for use in obtaining the advice of friends. So far as known, however, he did not part with more than one copy at a time, nor leave any copy permanently out of his possession. He appears to have carried all his eggs in one basket. He had the address in a satchel, which was mislaid at Harrisburg. When a satchel which Lincoln thought he recognized as his was found his key opened it, but it was found to contain a soiled shirt, some paper collars, a pack of cards and a bottle of whisky nearly full, none of which articles belonged in Lincoln's bag. Finally, his own bag was found, much to Lincoln's relief; for Lamon declares that he never saw Lincoln so annoyed, perplexed and angry as he was when he thought the bag was lost, and that the finding of the bag with the whisky produced a laugh that restored his good humor. The finding of Lincoln's own satchel brought him back his "certificate of moral character, written by himself."

Why did Lincoln, on his way to Washington, content himself with the utterance of platitudes? Why did he not utter some really great message to each assembled crowd? The trip was admirably planned for effective speech-making. In five great states, Indiana, Ohio, New York, New Jersey and Pennsylvania, Legislatures were in session; and from each of these bodies Lincoln received and accepted invitations to address their Houses in joint session. Five short speeches, each uttering some one strong and reassuring paragraph would not have been too much for an orator like Lincoln. The cities of Cleveland, New York and Philadelphia all offered exceptional opportunities to influence the thought of the nation. Judged by the effect, we cannot affirm that in any one of these places Lincoln rose to the full opportunity offered by the occasion. At Cincinnati he spoke to the people across the Ohio River; there more than anywhere else he seemed aware of his opportunity. Why did he not rise to it in other cities?

The answer doubtless is twofold. First, Lincoln did not fully realize the seriousness of the crisis, nor the importance of his wayside utterances. Secondly, Lincoln was reserving his message to be incorporated in his Inaugural Address. Into that address he had put his very best endeavor, and he was yet to change it after consulting Seward and other influential friends. Lincoln's habitual caution prevented his saying anything which he might have occasion to modify, or speaking as president while another man sat in the presidential chair. Hence the newspapers failed to find in his addresses *en route* any great statesmanlike affirmations such as they might have desired to discover in the words of a president-elect.

Lincoln left Philadelphia at half past nine on the morning of Washington's birthday and arrived at Harrisburg, the capital of Pennsylvania, where he was greeted by the Legislature. There he delivered his last address *en route*. There, also, he received what appeared to be confirmation of the rumor that there was a plot to assassinate him as he passed through Baltimore. He left the special train and the presidential party at Harrisburg, and, acting on advice which he believed to be valid, made a night journey to Washington. Concerning this trip, there has been much discussion, and it is claimed by some and denied by others, that Lincoln regretted having entered Washington in the way he did. The reports of his disguise were all fabricated, but the utmost secrecy was maintained concerning his withdrawal from the party and the manner and time of his arrival in Washington. His only companions on this last lap of his journey were Colonel Ward Hill Lamon and Allan Pinkerton. The entire party returned together from Harrisburg to Philadelphia, where at midnight Lincoln and his two associates took their berths in a sleeping-car of the regular train from New York. They arrived in Washington at six o'clock on the morning of Saturday, February twenty-third. They were met in the station by Honorable E. B. Washburne, who conducted them to the Willard Hotel, where a little later they were joined at breakfast by William H. Seward. Late that evening Lincoln's family arrived, having encountered no sign of danger or any incivility as they passed through Baltimore.

There had been no plan for a public entry into Washington. In that city the celebration was to occur more than a week later. It had been planned from the beginning that the arrival of the Lincoln party should be without formality, but no one had contemplated so humiliating an end of a journey that had been on the whole one of such triumph. The comments of the newspapers in many instances were not flattering, and some caricatures held the president-elect up to ridicule as a man of faint heart. For this charge there was no justification. Lincoln accepted the advice of responsible men, who believed the danger to be real. Lincoln was a man of prudence, but he was never a coward.

The journey of the special train upon Saturday was a sad ending of what had been a spectacular journey. From Harrisburg to Baltimore and on to Washington, people continued to gather, curious to see the president-elect. It became necessary to tell the crowds that Mr. Lincoln was not on the train. The crowds could scarcely credit the statement, and those who had to make the announcement from time to time did it with very little joy or pride. They invented the best excuse they could think of; important business had suddenly called Mr. Lincoln to Washington; but the members of the presidential party made this statement with little liking, and when the train arrived in Baltimore and there was no demonstration of an adverse character, the feeling of resentment grew against those who had advised the president to desert the party and slip into Washington in such undignified fashion. However the journey ended and Mrs. Lincoln and the children reached Willard's Hotel that night. The Lincoln family was reunited and glad enough that this part of the performance was well over.

A full week and more intervened between Lincoln's arrival and the service of inauguration. It was a solemn week. If Lincoln left home with something less than a realizing sense of the gravity of the situation, and if the enthusiasm of his greetings along the way did something to encourage in him a false sense of security, a week in Washington left him with no possible illusion as to the gravity of the situation confronting him and the nation. Secession was an accomplished fact, and civil war was about to begin. What qualities, what training had Abraham Lincoln to fit him to cope with so desperate a situation? The nation and the world asked that question, and Lincoln himself must have given it most solemn consideration in that ominous week.

Stephen A. Douglas was in Washington, busy in many matters relating to those perplexing times. He was loyal to Lincoln and the government. But now and then the oddity of the situation came over him, a sense of the absurdity of the election of a man like Lincoln to the presidency which Douglas had himself so long aspired to attain. He, also, took a journey, and then returned to Washington. In the days of his debate with Lincoln, Douglas traveled on a special train with a flat car attached, carrying a brass cannon, while Lincoln rode in the day coach. Now Lincoln was traveling in state, while Douglas was on the regular train. But some luxury was granted to Douglas; he had the comfort of a berth in a sleeping-car, then a relatively new and crude affair; and he had also a bottle of liquor. Lying in his berth, half awake, and less than half sober, he thought over the incongruity of the situation, and burst out at length into uproarious laughter: "Abe Lincoln, President of the United States! Good lord! Abe Lincoln, President of the United States!"

APPENDIX

ABRAHAM LINCOLN lived and died without knowing where the marriage record of his parents could be found.   He had never had occasion to inquire about it while his parents were living, and when he emerged into prominence it was too late.   His mother died in 1818 and his father in 1851.   When, in 1860, he found occasion to inquire about it, the record was not found in Hardin County, Kentucky, where he was born and where he supposed his parents were married.   His inquiries resulted only in starting unpleasant rumors, and these were long in finding disproof.   One important step in the proving of the chastity of Lincoln's mother, though not the only or the final one, was the discovery, in 1878, of a marriage return, in Washington County, Kentucky, certifying that Thomas Lincoln and Nancy Hanks were married, June 12, 1806, by the Reverend Jesse Head, a deacon in the Methodist Episcopal Church.

But who was Jesse Head?   Doctor J. M. Buckley, editor of *The Christian Advocate,* made diligent inquiry thirty years ago and discovered a grandson of Jesse Head, the Reverend E. B. Head, then serving on the Lawrenceburg circuit in Anderson County, Kentucky.   Some information was obtained from him and others, but it left much room for research.

The Christian Advocate on May 25, 1882 (p. 322), presented full proof of the identity of Jesse Head.   Doctor Buckley then wrote: "The following points may be considered as for ever settled: 1. There was such a man as Jesse Head, a local deacon in the Methodist Episcopal Church in 1806.   2. The Reverend Jesse Head was at no time nor in any place a member of an

479

Annual Conference, or duly admitted on trial in any Conference, and therefore, notwithstanding his long and honorable career, he escaped all record in Methodism."

Despite the facts brought out by *The Christian Advocate* there were those who affirmed that there never had been such a man as Jesse Head; that the whole record was a fraud, of modern creation, made seventy years after the events described, and intended to falsify history by fraudulent documentary proof of the legitimacy of Abraham Lincoln. For a good while it seemed unlikely that we should ever learn anything very definite about Jesse Head. It now is possible to write his life history.

Jesse Head was born in Frederick County, Maryland, June 10, 1768, son of William Edward Head, a Revolutionary soldier. He was married, January 9, 1789, to Jane Ramsey, daughter of Robert and Susannah Ramsey, of Bedford County, Pennsylvania. She was born April 10, 1768. The young couple removed to Washington County, Kentucky, and located near Springfield, the county-seat. He was a cabinet-maker by trade. He had a farm of fifty-four acres on Road Run, near to the Berrys and Lincolns. It is probable that his being a neighbor was the occasion of their calling him to solemnize the marriage of Thomas Lincoln and Nancy Hanks, for both the Lincolns and Hankses were Baptists. He probably located in Kentucky about 1796. His name is not in the Washington County tax list for 1795, but is there in 1797, in 1800, 1801, 1803 and 1805. The intermediate lists and many subsequent lists have perished. He was in Washington County until 1810. He became a justice of the peace, his service beginning January 6, 1798. He became a trustee of the town of Springfield, April 3, 1802, and chairman of that board June 10, 1803. His last signed document in Washington County is a court order as justice of the peace, October 10, 1810. His work as a carpenter included the erection of stocks and a whipping-post and pillory at the Washington County court-house.

But what about his ecclesiastical standing? On October 2,

1805, was held at Anthony Houston's in Scott County, Kentucky, a meeting of the Western Conference of the Methodist Episcopal Church. Bishop Asbury presided. A list was reported of the deacons and local preachers of the conference, and among the former was recorded the name of Jesse Head. This is the one known record, and this recently discovered, which shows his ecclesiastical status in the records of any conference. But this was not the beginning of his career as a Methodist deacon. Honorable L. S. Pence, of Lebanon, Kentucky, discovered a book of "court martials" of men reported as delinquent in militia duty, and on May 25, 1798, it was recorded that Jesse Head was cleared of delinquency, "he having a license to preach, according to the rules of the church to which he belongs."

The records of that period are, of course, fragmentary and meager; but these two certify to the standing of Jesse Head from 1798 on.

Among the Draper manuscripts in the library of the University of Wisconsin is a letter of General Robert B. McAfee, of November 25, 1845, in which he states that the famous Harrodsburg Springs were discovered, in 1806, by Reverend Jesse Head, a Methodist minister. This letter was written long before Jesse Head was known in connection with the marriage of the Lincolns. The year 1806, in which this discovery of the Springs is said to have been made, is the same in which Jesse Head married the Lincolns. Four years later, in 1810, Jesse Head moved to Harrodsburg, and there he lived for thirty-two years. He died March 22, 1842; and his wife died August 30, 1851. They were buried in their own yard in Harrodsburg, but after some years their bodies were removed to the Harrodsburg cemetery. Their graves were unmarked, and were in danger of becoming unknown; but recently they have been identified, and on November 2, 1922, a simple and appropriate monument with bronze tablet was erected above their graves.

Jesse Head was an editor, a straight old-fashioned Democrat. The story that he inculcated abolition principles in Thomas and

Nancy Lincoln is without foundation, but he was a friend to colored people and had influence with them.

He did not accumulate money. Twice he would have been sold out at sheriff's sale but for the kindness of his son. Once all his furniture was exposed for sale and the other time his house. They were all bidden in by local parties, for his son, then living in Washington, D. C. This dutiful son provided a home for his parents while they lived.

The Misses Mary A. and Martha Stephenson have dug deep into the dust of ancient records in Harrodsburg to learn for me all that may be found about Jesse Head. Among the rest, they have found the court orders of these sales, made to George M. Head, and they enable us to learn just what were the worldly goods and chattels of Jesse Head.

He owned three beds, one valued at $10, one at $7.50 and one at $7.25. There was a toilet glass at which he shaved, and it was bid in at $1.12½. There was a folding table, of his own workmanship, which brought $2.12½. There was "a lott of cupboardware," $3.25; six plates, 25 cents; tinware and coffee mill, 62½ cents; two small tables, 25 cents; a pair of andirons, 50 cents. There was a bookcase which brought $5, and a small table which brought $1. There were pots and pans and "kittles" and skillets and tongs and spinning wheel which need not here be separately priced. He owned a horse, the value of which was $15.25, as determined by the highest bid, a spotted cow and a red cow and calf, each of which brought $6.25. He had a "waggon" which was found to be worth $11.25.

He had some books, a good many for a man of his station and financial ability. He had seven volumes of the sermons of John Wesley and two volumes of Wesley's Notes. He had Fletcher's Works in three volumes, and several volumes of church history. His library, sold book by book, brought $16.74½. His whole personal property brought $114.30. His son bid all this in. No single item appears to have been sold outside.

There was a sale at the court-house door. The sheriff came to the home of Jesse Head and loaded the $11.25 "waggon," hitched up to it the $15.25 horse, and led the red cow and the spotted cow behind, and took them to the court-house door and sold them under the hammer. But there appears to have been no competition. Every one appears to have understood that Jesse Head's son intended to buy these articles, and to have a bill of sale made out to him, and to send the goods back for the use of his parents so long as they lived. So after a time, they all came back, the red cow and calf, and the spotted cow and the horse and "waggon" and the tongs and "kittles" and spinning wheel and the rest, and the books which were the old man's pride. And I imagine that Jesse Head and his wife knelt down in the midst of their house that had been left to them desolate and thanked God for a faithful son. In like manner the house was kept from being sold above their heads, and they had a home as long as they lived.

So far as any record has been found, Jesse Head was never ordained an elder, but held his deacon's orders through life, and signed his marriage returns, of which there are many, "Jesse Head, D.M.E.C.," which meant "Deacon in the Methodist Episcopal Church." He was never pastor of the Methodist Church in Harrodsburg, nor is there any record of his having founded a Methodist church in any other city, though that claim has been made for him. His grandson thought that he was an intimate friend of Methodist bishops, but if this is the case, no record is found of it. If he ever attended an Annual Conference we do not know it. But he maintained his standing as a deacon, and was proud of his membership in the Methodist Church. He was fond of controversy, was a hard hitter, and made enemies and warm friends. He was a man of courage and fidelity. There is no reason to suppose that concerning slavery he was in advance of his generation; indeed, there is the best of reason to suppose that he was not. He was the owner of a negro woman and her children, the negress being a cook and maid of all work for Mrs. Head, until his poverty compelled him to part with her and with most of his property. He was a good fighter, a courageous pioneer preacher. He was not widely known in his own day, and owes his fame solely to the accident of his having married, among scores of obscure couples, one for whom was reserved the distinction of distinguished parenthood. But he and the men like him deserve high honor for their zeal, their integrity, their contribution to the welfare of a new society. He was one of a considerable number of local preachers and exhorters and deacons who, never attaining to any clerical distinction, do their work faithfully and well. Methodism has a right to claim Jesse Head, and to remember that he was one among many of her faithful preachers in the days of the pioneers. But he belongs in no exclusive sense to any one sect. He is a worthy representative of a goodly group of humble, honest and most useful men, the pioneer preachers.

II.   AN AUTOBIOGRAPHICAL LETTER

This letter, containing important data concerning the Hanks family, was written by Dennis F. Hanks for William H. Herndon, and preserved in the Library of the University of Chicago.

Aprial the 2d 1866

Dennis F Hanks was Born in Hardin County on the tributary branch of the South fork of Nolin on the old Richard Creal farm in the old peach orchard in a Log Cabin 3 miles from Hogins Vill thence we moved to Murcur County and Staid there a Bout 3 years and Moved Back a gain to the same place and there Remained untill we moved to Spencer County Indiana this was I think in the year 1816 if my Memory serves me Rite My mother and Abes mothers mother was sisters My mothers Name was Nancy Hanks Abes Grand Mother was Lucy Hanks which was my mothers Sister the woman that raised me was Elizabeth Sparow the Sister of Lucy and Nancy The other Sister hir Name was polly Friend So you see that there was 4 sisters that was Hankses

I Have No Letter from my friends yet I Dont No the Reason

Bily did you write to William Hall in Misouri Frankford I think he coul tell you sumthing that would Be Rite He is my half Brother try him

William I have seen a Book which states that Lincolns was Quakers I say this is mis take They was Baptist all this talk about their Religious talk is a humbug they try to make them out Puritins This is Not the case

You asked me what sort of songs or Intress Abe tuck part in I will say this anything that was Lively He never would sing any Religious Songs it apered to me that it Did not souit him But for a man to preach a Sermond he would Lissin to with great Atention

Did you find out from Richard Creal if He lived on the place whare A Lincoln was Born or Not I am gowing there in May to Visit my Birth place the 15th of May this is my Birth Day 1799 it has Ben 48 years Sence

Any thing you want to No Let it Cum your friend

D. F. Hanks

My first School Master was By the Name Warden taught School at the old Baptist church on Nolin nere Brunks farm at the Big Spring Down in a Deepe hollow Close By the House

III. NEW SALEM ELECTIONS

The Illinois State Historical Society has the Poll Books of New Salem during the half dozen years when it was a voting precinct. A number of them are in Lincoln's handwriting. The following are the summaries of these elections, with records of the vote and official service of Abraham Lincoln:

A Pole Book of an election held in Clarys Grove Precinct on the first day of August 1831 at the house of John M. Cameron in New Salem to elect one Representative to Congress; two magistrates and two constables in the above mentioned Precinct.

Abraham Lincoln voted for James Turney for congress, Robert Conover for Magistrate, Pollard Simmons for Magistrate, John Armstrong for constable, Henry Sinco for Constable.

At an election held at the house of John McNeil in the New Salem precinct in the county of Sangamon and State of Illinois on the 20th day of September in the year of our Lord one thousand eight hundred and thirty two the following named persons received the number of votes annexed to their respective names for constable.

John Clary had Forty-one votes for constable

John R. Herndon had Twenty-two votes for constable.

William McNeely had Thirteen votes for constable.

Baxter B. Berry had nine votes for constable

Edmund Greer had four votes for constable

Samuel Rutledge }
Hugh Armstrong   } Judges of the election.
James White   }

Attest A. Lincoln }
William Green   } Clerks of the election

I certify that the above Judges and Clerks were qualified according to law, September 20, 1832. Bowling Green J. P.

I certify that the Judges and Clerks this election was duly qualified.

Bowling Green
Nov. 5th 1832.   J. P.

At an election held at the house of Samuel Hill in the New Salem precinct in the county of Sangamon and State of Illinois on the fifth day of November in the year of our Lord one thousand eight hundred and thirty-two the following named persons received the number of votes annexed to their respective names for the following described offices (to wit)

Daniel Stookey had one hundred and eighty-five votes for elector of President and Vice President.

Abner Flack had one hundred and eighty-five votes for elector of President and Vice President.

James Evans had one hundred and eighty-five votes for elector of President and Vice President.

Adam Dunlap had one hundred and eighty-five votes for elector of President and Vice President.

John C. Alexander had one hundred and eighty-five votes for elector of President and Vice President.

William B. Archer had seventy votes for elector of President and Vice President.

Leonard White had seventy votes for elector of President and Vice President.

James B. Moore had Seventy votes for elector of President and Vice President.

Elijah Iles had seventy votes for .elector of President and Vice President.

Pierre Menard had seventy votes for elector of President and Vice President.

James Rutledge
Bowling Green   } Judges of the election
Hugh Armstrong

A. Lincoln   } Clerks of the election
William Green

Lincoln voted for....
William B. Archer
Leonard White
James B. Moore
Elijah Iles
Pierre Menard

At an election held at the house of William F. Berry the New Salem precinct in the county of Sangamon and State of Illinois on the fifth day of May in the year of our Lord one thousand eight hundred and thirty four the following named persons received the number of votes annexed to their respective names for the following described office to wit.

Garrett Elkin had eighty-four votes for Sheriff.
David Dickinson had seventy seven votes for Sheriff
Zachariah Peter had four votes for Sheriff.

Certified by us.

Bowling Green
Hugh Armstrong   } Judges of the election
David Whray

Attest A. Lincoln   } Clerks of the election.
Mentor Graham

I certify that Hugh Armstrong, David Whray, Mentor Graham and A. Lincoln were qualified by me according to law as Judges and Clerks of the election.   Bowling Green J. P.

I certify that Bowling Green was qualified by me according to law as Judge of the election.

Mentor Graham.

Abraham Lincoln voted for David Dickson for Sheriff
New Salem Precinct, Poll list August 4, 1834.

At an election held at the house of William F. Berry in the New Salem precinct in the County of Sangamon and State of Illinois on the twenty-seventh day of October in the year of our Lord one thousand eight hundred and thirty four the following named persons received the number of votes annexed to their respective names for the following described offices (to wit)

William L. May had Seventy two votes for Representative to Congress,

James Turney had one vote for Representative to Congress.

Benjamin Mills had three votes for Representative to Congress.   Certified by us

James Pantier
Pollard Simmons } Judges of the election
William Jones

Attest A. Lincoln } Clerks of the election.
Mentor Graham

I certify that the Judges and Clerks of this election was sworn according to law, New Salem October 27, 1834.

Bowling Green   J. P.

and John Clary served as constable.

Lincoln voted for William L. May.

At an election held at the house of N. Alley in the New Salem Precinct in the county of Sangamon and State of Illinois on the third day of August in the year of our Lord one thousand eight hundred and thirty five, the following named persons received the number of votes annexed to their respective names for the following described offices to wit.

John Calhoun had ninety-eight votes for State Senator in place of E. D. Taylor. Resigned.

A. J. Herndon had seventy-seven votes for State Senator in place of E. D. Taylor. Resigned.

Peter Cartwright had fifty three votes for State Senator in place of George Forquer. Resigned.

Job Fletcher had one hundred and twenty-votes for State Senator in place of George Forquer. Resigned.

Edward Mitchell had twenty-eight votes for County Recorder.

William Herndon had thirty-eight votes for County Recorder.

James Campbell had one vote for County Recorder.

Benjamin Tabott had thirty three votes for County Recorder.

Andy Orr had nine votes for County Recorder.

William L. Fowkes had one vote for County Recorder.

Martin M. Morgan had twenty-one votes for County Recorder.

Thomas M. Neale had one hundred and twenty-nine votes for County Surveyor.

Reuben Harrison had thirty-eight votes for County Surveyor.

Parnell Hamilton had three votes for County Surveyor.

William G. Cantrill had thirty-eight votes for County Commissioner.

William Statts had ninety-four votes for County Commissioner.

Young McLemon had one vote for County Commissioner.

David Newsom had two votes for County Commissioner.

Peter G. Cawardin had thirteen votes for County Commissioner.

I. Langston had thirty-three votes for Coroner.

George W. Dickinson had two votes for Coroner.

Joseph H. Shepherd had fourteen votes for Coroner.

Boracha Dunn had thirteen votes for Coroner.

Bowling Green had one hundred twenty-one votes for Justice of the Peace.

Robert Conover had seventy-five votes for Justice Peace.

Thomas Wynne had one hundred and two votes for Justice Peace.

Samuel Combs had forty-three votes for Justice Peace.

Hugh Armstrong had one hundred and twenty-seven votes for Constable.

Jesse Shirley had seventeen votes for Constable.

Bennett Abell had Seventy-two votes for Constable.

Samuel B. Neely had thirty seven votes for constable.

John Duncan had fifty-three votes for constable.

Asa Combs had thirty-eight votes for Constable.

A. Lincoln voted for John Calhoun for Senator, Voted for Job Fletcher for Senator. Voted for Thomas M. Neale for County Surveyor.

Voted for Edward Mitchell for County Recorder. Voted for William Statts County Commissioner. Voted for I. Langston for Coroner. Voted for Bowling Green for Justice of the Peace. Voted for Robert Conover for Justice of the Peace. Voted for Hugh Armstrong for Constable. Voted for Asa Combs for Constable.

Precinct in the County of Sangamon State of Illinois. At an election held at New Salem on Monday the 1st day of August one thousand and thirty six, the following named persons received the number of votes annexed to their names for the following described offices viz.

John T. Stuart had eighty-six votes for representative to Congress.

William L. May had fifty-nine votes for representative to Congress.

Job Fletcher had seventy-three votes for State Senator.

Moses K. Anderson had sixty-seven votes for State Senator.

Ninian W. Edwards had eighty-four votes for State Representative.

Dan Stove had eighty-one votes for Representative.

A. Lincoln had one hundred and seven votes for representative.

John Dawson had eighty-two votes for representative.

William F. Elkin had eighty-four votes for representative.

R. L. Wilson had sixty-nine votes for representative.

Andrew McCormick had sixty-seven votes for representative.

Aaron Vandever had forty-seven votes for representative.

John L. Thompson had none.

John Clahoun had sixty-two votes for representative.

Jacob M. Early had fifty-nine votes for representative.

Michael Mann had thirty-nine votes for representative.

Richard Quinton had fifty-six votes for representative.

George Power had fifty-four votes for representative.

Thomas Wynne had seventy-one votes for representative.

Thomas Young had three votes for representative.

James Baker had none.

William G. Cantrill had forty-four votes for County Commissioner.

William Hickman had forty-five votes for County Commissioner.

Christopher B. Stafford had sixty votes for County Commissioner.

Thomas J. Nance had one hundred and nine votes for County Commissioner. James Pantier had sixty-two votes for County Commissioner.

Zachariah Peter had seventy-two votes for County Commissioner.

John Kelley had two votes for County Commissioner.
Garrett Elkin had eighty votes for Sheriff.
Edmund Taylor had sixty votes for Sheriff.
Jackson Langston had forty odd votes for Coroner.
S. C. Hampton had none, for Coroner.
David W. Clark had thirty-five votes for Coroner.
Certified by us

James Black ⎫
Jesse Mallby ⎬ Judges of the election
Andrew Beane ⎭

Attest. Mentor Graham ⎫
Charles J. F. Clarke ⎬ Clerks of the election.

I certify that the foregoing Judges and Clerks was Duly
Sworn according to Law. New Salem August 1, 1836.
Bowling Green J. P.

In this election of August 1, 1836, in the list of voters I do
not find that Abraham Lincoln voted. There is a name that
follows that of Bowling Greene, which looks like Abraham
Seward, and I have endeavored to make it read Abraham Lincoln, especially as I find no Abraham Seward in other New
Salem elections, but it does not look like the name Lincoln.

At an election held at the house of Caleb Carman in the New
Salem Precinct on the 7th day of November A. D., one thousand
eight hundred and thirty-six for the purpose of electing electors
to vote for a President and Vice president of the United States
of America; the following named persons received the number
of votes annexed to their respective names.
J. D. Whiteside had for elector thirty-four votes.
Samuel Leach had for elector thirty-four votes.
John Pearson had for elector thirty-four votes.
John Wyate had for elector thirty-four votes.
J. Hackleton had for elector thirty-four votes.
Benjamin Bond had for elector sixty-five votes.
J. A. Whiteside had for elector sixty-five votes.
Levan Lane had for elector sixty-five votes.
A. G. Wight had for elector sixty-five votes.
John Henry had for elector sixty-five votes.

18

Certified to, by us.

Jas Black

Jas Golds by } Judges of the above election.

Elijah Houghton

Attest

Mentor Graham } Clerks of the above election.

Thomas I. Nance

I do certify that the above Judges and Clerks were legally sworn according to law by me.

Bowling Green

November 7, 1836.   J. P.

Lincoln voted for Benjamin Bond, J. A. Whiteside, A. G. Wight, Levan Lane, John Henry.

IV. LINCOLN IN THE LEGISLATURE

The following data, from the *Blue Book of Illinois*, gives the dates on which the General Assembly convened and adjourned during Lincoln's membership in that body:

8th General Assembly 1832-1834, Convened at Vandalia, December 3, 1832. Adjourned March 2, 1833.

9th General Assembly, 1834-1836.

First session convened at Vandalia December 1, 1834; adjourned March 6, 1837. Second session July 10, 1837; adjourned July 22, 1837.

10th General Assembly, 1836-1838.

First Session convened at Vandalia December 5, 1836; adjourned July 22, 1837.

11th General Assembly, 1838-1840.

First session at Vandalia, December 3, 1838; adjourned March 4, 1839. Second session convened at Springfield, December 9, 1839; Adjourned February 3, 1840.

12th General Assembly, 1840-1842.

First session convened at Springfield November 23, 1840; Adjourned December 5, 1840. Second session December 7, 1840; Adjourned March 1, 1841.

V. LINCOLN'S ATTENDANCE IN 1841

The following is compiled for me by Miss Georgia L. Osborne, Assistant Librarian of the Illinois State Historical Society, and shows the attendance of Lincoln at the session of the General Assembly of Illinois for the term of 1840-41, as recorded in the House Journal, from "the fatal first of January" until the adjournment of the session.

Present Jan.   1st, 1841
   "   "   2nd,   "   Jan. 3rd, was Sunday
   "   "   5th,   "   (Tuesday)
   "   "   6th,   "
   "   "   7th,   "
   "   "   8th,   "
   "   "   9th,   "   Jan. 10th, Sunday
   "   "   11th,   "
   "   "   12th,   "   Jan. 17th, Sunday
   "   "   19th,   "   (Present in the morning)
   "   "   21st,   "
   "   "   22nd,   "
   "   "   23rd,   "   Jan. 24th, Sunday
   "   "   25th,   "
   "   "   26th,   "
   "   "   27th,   "
   "   "   28th,   "
   "   "   29th,   "
   "   "   30th,   "   Jan. 31st, Sunday
   "   Feb.   1st,   "
   "   "   2nd,   "
   "   "   3rd,   "
   "   "   4th,   "
   "   "   5th,   "
   "   "   6th,   "   Feb. 7th, Sunday
   "   "   8th,   "
   "   "   9th,   "
   "   "   10th,   "
   "   "   11th,   "
   "   "   12th,   "
   "   "   15th,   "
   "   "   13th,   "   Feb. 14th, Sunday

Present Feb. 16th, 1841
   "   "   17th, "
   "   "   18th, "
   "   "   19th, "
   "   "   20th, "   Feb. 21st, Sunday
   "   "   22nd, "
   "   "   23rd, "
   "   "   24th, "
   "   "   25th, "
   "   "   26th, "
   "   "   27th, "   Feb. 28th, Sunday
   "   March 1st,   "   Adjournment

VI. THE GRAVES OF ANN RUTLEDGE

The following letter from Honorable Thomas P. Reep, of Petersburg, gives the facts concerning the original and present graves of Ann Rutledge:

The Concord Cemetery was set apart by one of the Berrys, who owned the land at the time. It was probably opened as a grave-yard about 1828-9, and was the community burying ground for the Sand Ridge settlement. The marker bears the date 1837, but the cemetery was used many years earlier; Ann Rutledge and her father were buried there in 1835. The marker of David Rutledge bears date of June 7, 1842.

The facts concerning the removal of Ann's body are rather sordid. The Oakland Cemetery at Petersburg was established some thirty-five years ago with Edward Laning as President, and my cousin, Samuel Montgomery, as Secretary. Montgomery was a local undertaker. He conceived the idea that there would be some advertising value, and a consequent increase in the sale of lots, in the removal of the body of Ann Rutledge to Oakland Cemetery, and mentioned the idea to Mr. Laning, who approved. McGrady Rutledge, Ann's cousin, approved the plan, and consented on behalf of the Rutledge family. He had been present at Ann's burial, and said that he could not remember on which side of her brother, David, Ann was buried, but she was buried on one side and a child on the other. The grave of David Rutledge was marked, and the marker is still there. On May 5, 1890, Samuel Montgomery and McGrady Rutledge went to Con-

cord Cemetery, accompanied by two men as diggers. The graves
on each side of that of David Rutledge were opened, and, as
McGrady had predicted, the bones of a child were found upon
one side and those of an adult on the other. Those of the grown
person were removed to Oakland Cemetery at Petersburg as
those of Ann Rutledge. Mr. Montgomery made oath to these
facts in 1922; I prepared the affidavit, and it is among the files
of the Lincoln League at Petersburg, and also on record in the
Recorder's Office, in order that hereafter there may be no dispute about the facts.

VII. SANGAMON, AND THE JOURNAL

The Sangamon Journal was published weekly from November
10, 1831, to June 13, 1848. It appeared first as a daily on Monday, June 13, 1848, and has since been issued both daily and
weekly, under the various titles of *Sangamo Journal, Sangamon
Journal,* and *Illinois State Journal.* The title of *Sangamon
Journal* was retained from the beginning till January 12, 1832,
when, with number 11, it was changed to *Sangamo Journal.* This
paper supported the Whig Party, thus favoring a national bank,
protective tariff, and internal improvements. From the birth of
the Republican Party the *Journal* supported its principles. Published by Simeon and Josiah Francis, 1832-1835; Simeon Francis, 1835-1838; Simeon, Allen and J. Newton Francis, 1838-1843;
Simeon and Allen Francis, 1843-1855; W. H. Bailhache and
Edward L. Baker, 1855-1862. On September 23, 1847, the
name was changed to *Illinois Journal,* and on August 13, 1855,
was changed to that by which it has since been known, namely:
Illinois State Journal.

The name Sangamon, derived from the Pottawatomie
through the French, was pronounced *Sangamaw* in early days,
and in conformity with this pronunciation was often spelled
Sangamo. It is now uniformly spelled and pronounced *Sangamon.*

Of the signification of the name Governor Reynolds says:

The Indians, long before a white man saw the Sangamon
Country, were appraised of its fertility and rich products. In the

Pottawatomie language—"Sangamon" means the country where there is plenty to eat. According to our parlance, it would be termed the land of milk and honey.*

VIII. THE LINCOLN CIRCUIT

The Eighth Judicial District was constituted in 1847, and the courts established under this distribution remained unchanged for more than a decade. The counties included were Sangamon, Tazewell, Woodford, Logan, DeWitt, Piatt, Champaign, Vermilion, Edgar, Shelby, Moultrie, Macon and Christian. Menard, Mason and Livingston were in the Eighth district just previous to the change in the sitting of the courts in 1847.

In traveling the circuit from one county-seat to another, the road crossed Coles, and Lincoln often practised there; but there is no record that Coles was ever officially a part of the circuit.

During all the years after Lincoln's return from his one term in Congress, Judge David Davis was on the bench, and Lincoln accompanied him from one county-seat to another.

Lincoln was the only one of the lawyers who rode the entire circuit. Of his associates on the circuit it is recorded that Logan rarely left Sangamon County; Stuart went only into Tazewell, Logan and McLean Counties; the Macon County lawyers went into Piatt only; Swett and Gridley attended McLean, DeWitt, Champaign and Vermilion Counties, and Moore of DeWitt, and Lodge of Piatt, limited their practise to their own counties and McLean. Joseph Cunningham, the youngest of these associates of Lincoln on the Circuit, practised only in Champaign and Vermilion Counties. Oliver P. Davis, Oscar F. Harmon and E. S. Terry, of Danville, with the Indiana lawyers, Dan Mace and Jim Wilson of Lafayette, Ned Hannegan, Dan Voorhies and Joe Ristine of Covington, made the court at Danville of great interest.

The Lincoln circuit is now marked, the roads being designated, and the county-seats having granite markers with bronze

---

*Reynolds', *My Life and Times*, p. 237.

tablets set in, bearing a head of Lincoln in bas-relief, and this inscription:

```
ABRAHAM LINCOLN
travelled this way as he
Rode the Circuit
of the
Old Eighth Judicial District
1847          1859
Erected 1921
```

(Insignia of D. A. R.)   (Monogram of L. C. M. A.)

IX. THE FIRST LINCOLN-DOUGLAS DEBATE

It is well known that Lincoln and Douglas met in joint debate at Peoria, in October, 1854. Their plan for other joint discussions, and the truce which they made, have been the occasion of much discussion; and I have never felt satisfied with Herndon's explanation, (iii. pp. 373, 374). Several times Lincoln engaged in important joint debates with other political opponents. One such incident occurred in the campaign of 1840, where Lincoln met on the same platform at Albion, Honorable Isaac T. Walker (*Journal of the Illinois Historical Society* for January, 1917, pp. 489-491). A similar discussion with Honorable Anthony Thornton, at Shelbyville, June 15, 1856, has been made the subject of an historical painting (*Journal of the Illinois State Historical Society* for April, 1917, pp. 97-100). Doubtless there were many other joint debates in which Lincoln participated, most of which have left no permanent record. There is, however, a contemporary record of what may have been the first public debate between Abraham Lincoln and Stephen A. Douglas. It is preserved in the *Illinois State Register* of Saturday, November 23, 1839, and it is notable not only as the first joint debate between Lincoln and Douglas, nine years preceding their epoch-making contest, but for the criticism it

makes upon Lincoln's mannerisms as they appeared to an unfriendly critic at that stage of his career, and also because this
may be the first time that Springfield heard Stephen A. Douglas
referred to as "the little giant." This discussion occupied three
evenings, Tuesday, Wednesday and Thursday, October 19-21,
1839. The report in the *Register* is in two editorials and a communication. The leading editorial follows:

THE CAMPAIGN

The Federal Candidates for electors of President and Vice
President are already in the field. Cyrus Walker Esq., one of
them, addressed the citizens of this place in the Court House, on
Tuesday last. He was replied to by Stephen A. Douglas Esq.,
and it was the general opinion of all present that Mr. Douglas
left the Federal Candidate for elector not an inch of ground to
stand upon. Mr. Lincoln, another Federal Candidate for elector,
followed in the evening.

His argument was truly ingenious. He has however, a sort
of assumed clownishness in his manner which does not become
him, and which does not truly belong to him. It is assumed—
assumed for effect. Mr. Lincoln will sometimes make his
language correspond with this clownish manner, and he can thus
frequently raise a loud laugh among his Whig hearers, but this
entire game of buffoonery convinces the mind of no man, and is
utterly lost on the majority of his audience.

We seriously advise Mr. Lincoln to correct this clownish
fault, before it grows upon him.

But we have digressed. The main object of calling in Mr.
Lincoln, was to raise up Mr. Walker, who had been actually
demolished by Mr. Douglas in the afternoon. Lincoln made out
to get Walker rather unsteadily on his legs again, and between
two Whig Speakers our Democratic "little giant," as Walker
called him, had a rough time of it. Lincoln misrepresented
Douglas, as was apparent to every man present.

This brought a warm rejoinder from Mr. Douglas. Mr.
Walker then rose, complained of Mr. D. for his warmth, and
went on for an hour starting new points. Thus a concerted plot
of "two pluck one," began to show itself. But under these disadvantages Mr. Douglas literally swamped his adversaries   His

arguments were not answered; while his opponents were driven from every ground which they assumed.

On Wednesday evening Mr. Douglas took the floor, before a large audience, and delivered one of the most powerful arguments against an United States Bank that we ever listened to. It sunk deep into the hearts of his hearers. There was a profound silence upon his conclusion, and a settled gloom covered the countenances of the Whigs—. They saw how utterly hopeless must be the attempt to answer him. Mr. Lincoln was however again put forward; but he commenced with embarrassment and continued without making the slightest impression. The Mr. Lincoln of Wednesday night was not the Mr. Lincoln of Tuesday. He could only meet the arguments of Mr. Douglas by relating stale anecdotes and old stories, and left the stump literally whipped off of it, even in the estimation of his own friends.

On Thursday evening Mr. Wiley and Mr. Baker spoke. We have not time to do justice to the remarks of the former, who in a modest and quiet speech, threw more light on the subject by the facts which he produced than any speaker who preceded him. He enlightened his audience. His remarks will be "bread cast upon the waters," which will be gathered after many days.

We view the situation of Mr. Walker, Mr. Lincoln, and their Federal colleagues, as peculiarly unfortunate.

If they are asked who they intend to vote for (if elected) for President they cannot answer. If they are asked whether they are in favor of Mr. Clay's project of a U. S. Bank, they are dumb.

When they are called upon for their measure for collecting and disbursing the public money, they have none to give. In short, they have no measures, no principles, to advance. The people are left to grope in the dark, amidst the phantoms raised by these Federal orators.

Their ground is opposition—opposition to the Administration; and when reminded that the great Bank, under whose banner they have been fighting for eight years, is broken down, and utterly insolvent, they seek to disown their great paper champion.

Under such disadvantages, it is not wonderful that Mr. Walker and Mr. Lincoln, two of the Federal Candidates for electors, should have got used up on the occasion alluded to. The men are smart enough, but the cause they have espoused is rotten to the core.

Again Lincoln and Douglas met in joint discussion at the State Fair at Springfield in October, 1854. Douglas spoke on the first day of the fair, Tuesday, October third. "I will mention," said he in his opening remarks, "that it is understood by some gentlemen that Mr. Lincoln of this city is expected to answer me. If this is the understanding, I wish that Mr. Lincoln would step forward and let us arrange some plan upon which to carry out this discussion." Lincoln was not present at the moment in Representatives' Hall, where the crowd had been driven by unfavorable weather, but he soon appeared and heard Douglas in the main part of his address. The next day Lincoln spoke in the same place, the hall being packed on each occasion. Douglas sat directly in front of Lincoln, and said at the beginning, "My friend Mr. Lincoln expressly invited me to stay and hear him to-day, as he heard me yesterday, and to answer and defend myself as best I could. I thank him for his courteous offer." Twelve days afterward, on October sixteenth, they met again in joint debate in Peoria, where Lincoln made one of his most notable addresses, embodying, as Horace White believed, the substance of what two years later he delivered in Bloomington and known as his "lost speech."

X   THE LINCOLN AND DOUGLAS SPEAKING DATES IN 1858

Douglas stated that in the one hundred days, exclusive of Sundays, between his return to Illinois and the November election in 1858, he delivered one hundred thirty political addresses. Lincoln began later, and spoke somewhat less frequently, but after he got well into the campaign, he was speaking almost every day. Not all the speeches are of record. While the method of speaking from the rear platform of a train had not then reached its present recognition, both candidates, in passing through cities not on their official list, made more or less formal addresses. The Democratic campaign committee kept standing at the head of some of the newspapers of that political faith, notably the

Register of Springfield and the *Times* of Chicago, a list of Douglas's advance engagements, keeping the list revised so as to give notice about two weeks ahead. The *Press and Tribune* of Chicago and the *Journal* of Springfield performed a like service for Lincoln. From those newspapers these lists of dates have been compiled. Where blanks occur, the speaker was usually making a rather long journey, or one involving inconvenient train connections, to his next appointment, and sometimes was speaking while on the way.

Thursday, June 17, 1858. Lincoln's speech at the Republican Convention at Springfield.

Friday, July 9. Douglas's speech at Tremont House, Chicago. Lincoln was present.

Saturday, July 10. Lincoln's speech at same place. Douglas was not present.

Friday, July 16. Douglas's speech at Bloomington. Lincoln was present.

Saturday, July 17. Douglas's speech at Springfield in the afternoon; Lincoln's speech at Springfield in the evening. Neither of the candidates was present when the other spoke at Springfield.

Although both candidates were speaking frequently, the formal announcements of Douglas in state-wide publication do not begin until July 27, and those of Lincoln August 12. For convenience in tracing their routes, the two series of dates are arranged in a single table, giving both town and county, and day of week and month. It will be noted that Lincoln was careful, wherever possible, to follow Douglas, and not permit Douglas to follow him.

DOUGLAS		LINCOLN
	JULY	
	Tuesday, 27	
Clinton, Dewitt Co.		
	Thursday, 29	
Monticello, Piatt Co.		

DOUGLAS   LINCOLN

Saturday, 31

Paris, Edgar Co.

AUGUST

Monday, 2

Hillsboro, Montgomery Co.

Wednesday, 4

Greenville, Bond Co.

Friday, 6

Edwardsville, Madison Co.

Saturday, 7

Winchester, Scott Co.

Monday, 9

Pittsfield, Pike Co.

Tuesday, 10
Wednesday, 11

Beardstown, Cass Co.

Thursday, 12

Beardstown, Cass Co.

Friday, 13

Havana, Mason Co.

Saturday, 14

Havana, Mason Co.

Monday, 16

Lewiston, Fulton Co.

Tuesday, 17
Wednesday, 18

Peoria, Peoria Co.

Thursday, 19

Lacon, Marshall Co.   Peoria, Peoria Co.

Friday, 20
Saturday, 21
First Joint Debate

Ottawa, La Salle Co.   Ottawa, La Salle Co.

Monday, 23
Tuesday, 24
Wednesday, 25

Galena, Jo Daviess Co.   Augusta, Hancock Co.

Thursday, 26
Friday, 27

Second Joint Debate

Freeport, Stephenson Co. Freeport, Stephenson Co.

Saturday, 28

Junction, Du Page Co.

Monday, 30
Tuesday, 31

Joliet, Will Co. Carlinville, Macoupin Co.

SEPTEMBER

Wednesday, 1
Thursday, 2

Pontiac, Livingston Co. Clinton, Dewitt Co.

Friday, 3
Saturday, 4

Lincoln, Logan Co. Bloomington, McLean Co.

Monday, 6

Jacksonville, Morgan Co. Monticello, Piatt Co.

Tuesday, 7

Mattoon, Coles Co.

Wednesday, 8

Carlinville, Macoupin Co. Paris, Edgar Co.

Thursday, 9

Hillsboro, Montgomery Co.

Friday, 10

Belleville, St. Clair Co.

Saturday, 11

Waterloo, Monroe Co. Edwardsville, Madison Co.

Monday, 13

Chester, Randolph Co. Greenville, Bond Co.

Tuesday, 14
Wednesday, 15

Third Joint Debate

Jonesboro, Union Co. Jonesboro, Union Co.

Thursday, 16

Benton, Franklin Co.

DOUGLAS   LINCOLN

Friday, 17
Saturday, 18
Fourth Joint Debate
Charleston, Coles Co.   Charleston, Coles Co.
Monday, 20
Sullivan, Moultrie Co.
Tuesday, 21
Danville, Vermilion Co.
Wednesday, 22
Danville, Vermilion Co.
Thursday, 23
Urbana, Champaign Co.
Friday, 24
Urbana, Champaign Co.
Saturday, 25
Kankakee, Kankakee Co.
Monday, 27
Jacksonville, Morgan Co.
Tuesday, 28
Hennepin, Putnam Co.
Wednesday, 29
Henry, Marshall Co.   Winchester, Scott Co.
Thursday, 30
Metamora, Woodford Co.

OCTOBER

Friday, 1
Pittsfield, Pike Co.
Saturday, 2
Pekin, Tazewell Co.
Monday, 4
Oquawka, Henderson Co.   Metamora, Woodford Co.
Tuesday, 5
Monmouth, Warren Co.   Pekin, Tazewell Co.
Wednesday, 6
Thursday, 7
Fifth Joint Debate
Galesburg, Knox Co.   Galesburg, Knox Co.

Friday, 8

Saturday, 9

Macomb, McDonough Co.   Oquawka, Henderson Co.

Monday, 11

Carthage, Hancock Co.   Monmouth, Warren Co.

Tuesday, 12

Wednesday, 13

Sixth Joint Debate

Quincy, Adams Co.   Quincy, Adams Co.

Thursday, 14

Friday, 15

Seventh Joint Debate

Alton, Madison Co.   Alton, Madison Co.

Saturday, 16

Gillespie, Macoupin Co.

Monday, 18

Decatur, Macon Co.   Mt. Sterling, Brown Co.

Tuesday, 19

Wednesday, 20

Springfield, Sangamon Co.   Rushville, Schuyler Co.

Thursday, 21

Atlanta, Logan Co.

Friday, 22

Bloomington, McLean Co.   Carthage, Hancock Co.

Saturday, 23

Monday, 25

Macomb, McDonough Co.

Tuesday, 26

Toulon, Starke Co.

Wednesday, 27

Thursday, 28

Geneseo, Henry Co.

Friday, 29

Rock Island, Rock Island Co.   Petersburg, Menard Co.

Saturday, 30

Lincoln delivered at Springfield his last speech of the campaign. The election occurred on Tuesday, November 2.

XI. THE ARMSTRONG MURDER TRIAL ALMANAC

I have given much space in the text to the almanac alleged to have been used in the Armstrong murder trial, but the disappearance of the pamphlet from the Chicago Historical Library seems to me to make it advisable to publish the notes which I made concerning it. I have no doubt that I examined it more carefully than any other critic; and as, unhappily, the almanac itself is not and may not hereafter be available for the inspection of others, this evidence is pertinent.

The almanac is one published by the American Tract Society, and is entitled,—

Illustrated Family Christian Almanac
for the Year of Our Lord
1857
By David Young,
Hanover Neck, N. J.

Mr. Gunther procured the almanac in 1893 from a lawyer living in Alton, Illinois. Three letters from him to Mr. Gunther accompany the pamphlet, and there is reference to an affidavit by John Huston, of Beardstown, alleged to have been deputy sheriff, and presumably certifying that the almanac was, as he believed, the same used at the trial. In a newspaper clipping from an Alton paper, contemporary with the sale, and based on information furnished by this lawyer, it is stated that he originally paid five dollars for it. The correspondence shows that he sold it to Gunther for fifty dollars. In the second letter, dated July 31, 1893, this lawyer says,—

The almanac I have, and which is unquestionably that used by Mr. Lincoln, was an almanac of 1854 with date changed to '57. This I am able to ascertain only by a brief note in an obscure place and seems to have been overlooked at the time. The almanac was prepared in the hotel of E. C. Foster, an old respected citizen who states that he was cognizant of the work while being done by Mr. L. and the Dr. (Moore,* I believe). . . . There is not a shadow of a doubt in my mind that the facts are as he stated.

The letter which accompanied the book and completed the sale was a month later, August 30, 1893.

The author of the above letters was incorrect as to the year to which the almanac belonged. The obscure note in which he found the year unchanged was this:

Venus will be a morning star till May 13; then an evening star until Feb. 28, 1854.

The year 1853 was understood after the date May thirteenth. That was the year for which the almanac was issued. The back cover shows the church festivals for the year 1853, and is unaltered.

The front cover originally bore its date in comparatively light type, wrought into the scroll work of the cover-design. It has been scratched out with a knife, and the date 1857 printed in bold type. On the title page the character 3 is changed to 7 by scratching and writing in with a pen. I judge that the top bar of the 7 is the original top of the 3.

Twelve pages have the date at their top, one for each month. In every case the date is changed with type, a character 7 being used after a knife had been employed in scratching.

The man who did this work was so desirous of doing it well that he overdid it, and had to change back in one place where it said that "The sixteenth Presidential term of four years began on the fourth day of March 1853 and will expire on the third of March 1857." These figures were scratched, but changed back to allow Millard Fillmore his full four years.

One thing is certain, this work was not done hastily in the Beardstown hotel on the night before the almanac was used.

---

*The name of the physician appears to have been Parker.

Lincoln reached Beardstown that night. If the work was done there under Lincoln's direction that was the time when it was done. But it is too well performed to have been done in that way. Both in the matching of the type and in the work done by the pen there is evidence of more skill than could thus have been extemporized. It called for careful work.

And yet the work does not pass anything like a critical examination. Every page where the changes have been made shows when held to the light that the paper has been scraped, and a very little scrutiny reveals the substitution of the 7 for the erased figure. It is hardly conceivable that some one of the twelve jurors would not have detected the imposture, and quite unlikely that either the judge or the prosecuting attorney would have permitted the exhibit to have gone to the jury with a fraud so readily discernible.

Whoever prepared the almanac did it with reference to this case. Either it is the original almanac, or some one who knew of the case and of the rumor that Lincoln played a trick upon the court thought of it as an interesting experiment and undertook to see how well he could succeed in such a venture as Lincoln was alleged to have undertaken. Did Lincoln do it, or did some clever and curious journeyman printer undertake to see how good an imitation he could make of the almanac which Lincoln was alleged to have used? The man who did the actual work was a printer, and besides that was clever with the use of the knife in erasure and of the pen in the drawing of figures for which he had no font of type, as on the title page where he needed to insert one part of one figure.

It was not a job hastily done in one evening by the light of tallow dips. It called for daylight and time and care. It was not done in Beardstown on the night before the trial.

But among the difficulties of the imposture was this, that by no possibility could the days of the week in 1853 be made to correspond with the days of the week in 1857. The 1853 almanac thus produced showed that August twenty-ninth occurred on Monday. Every member of the jury knew that the murder occurred on Saturday night. Would any lawyer dare to proceed on the assumption that twelve men who could read would fail to see that the important line began "29 Mo" and not "29 Sa"? Was it possible that the prosecuting attorney would not have discovered this the very instant he looked at the page?

Everybody knew that the murder occurred on the last Saturday night before the close of the camp-meeting. That fact had come out strongly not only in the Armstrong trial but in the earlier trial of his associate, Norris. To find on the closely printed page with its abbreviations the date on which the position of the moon was to be learned, it was necessary to run the eye down the margin to find in adjacent columns "29 Sa." It was impossible to leap over the "Sa" from the "29" to the position of the moon and not notice that the day of the week was wrong. If all that had been desired had been to make an 1853 almanac look like one of 1857, the figures at the top of the pages would have passed a superficial examination. But for the purpose which this almanac required to be used, it was necessary that Saturday should fall on August twenty-ninth, and that combination could not have been found in an almanac earlier than 1857 and later than 1846.

A local account preserved in an undated clipping from the period of the Armstrong interview says,—

Duff Armstrong's faith in the genuineness of the almanac is not generally shared by the Petersburg people, who remember the trial. Uncle Johnny Potter, who was an intimate friend of the Armstrongs, laughed and shook his head when he was asked what the real facts were. It seems that after the trial the friends of the Armstrongs talked the matter over. Some of them remembered as positively as the witnesses had done that there was nearly a full moon on the night Pres Metzker was beaten at the camp-meeting. They insisted on their recollections in spite of Mr. Lincoln's documentary evidence. There was an overhauling of old almanacs in various households. Sure enough, they showed a moon nearly in mid-heavens at the hour of the affray. Then there was inquiry for the almanac which had been presented by Mr. Lincoln in court. The little pamphlet could not be found.

The present almanac is alleged to have been preserved by Honorable J. Henry Shaw, and to have been found after his death by John Husted, who is said to have been deputy sheriff at the time of the trial and to have gone to Virginia after Allen. Husted appears to have owned the almanac in 1888 when the Eggleston story appeared.

Those persons who believe this to be the genuine almanac hold two or three different opinions. One is that Mr. Lincoln was himself imposed upon. This is not likely. It would not have been easy to deceive as astute a man as Mr. Lincoln with this almanac. If Mr. Lincoln used this, he may be presumed to have prepared it or at least to have accepted it with full knowledge of the use to which it was adapted.

When Edward Eggleston published his *The Graysons,* popular interest was roused in the Armstrong trial. The Perrysburg of his story is supposed to be Petersburg. In this story Lincoln is represented as a young and almost unknown man, whereas in 1858 Lincoln was already a national figure and was aspiring to be president. He had already received a large vote for the vice-presidency in the Convention of 1856. There are other wide departures from historic accuracy, to which accuracy the story does not pretend.

At that time Duff Armstrong was himself living and he was interviewed by J. McCan Davis, and the interview widely published. Armstrong was at this time a member of the Disciples Church and a respected man in the community. He denied that he was guilty, and declared that Metzker attacked him without provocation and that he acted only in self-defense. As to the almanac, Armstrong said:

It's all foolishness to talk about Lincoln having had that almanac fixed up for the trial. He didn't do anything of the kind. I recollect that after he had been asking the witnesses about the moonlight he suddenly called for an almanac. There wasn't any in the court room of the year he wanted. So he sent my cousin Jake out to find one. Jake went out and after a while he came back with the almanac. Lincoln turned to the night of the fight at the camp-meeting and it showed that there wasn't any moon at all that night. Then he showed it to the jury. That was all there was to the almanac story. That almanac was all right.

All members of the Armstrong family who have been interviewed appear to be united·in this testimony. None of them admit that the almanac was other than a genuine almanac. The people of Beardstown confidently point out the drug-store, still in operation, where the almanac used was obtained.

One thing grows clear as tradition is explored, and that is that the almanac has a far larger place in the story than it had in the trial. The story has been so improved as to make it seem that Mr. Lincoln placed his sole dependence upon this exhibit. It has been told that he introduced no witnesses for the defense: that he did not cross-examine the witnesses; that he appeared to be neglecting the case until the last dramatic moment when he produced his one and unanswerable argument. Lincoln did introduce witnesses, chiefly to show such previous good character as Duff Armstrong could claim; for there was no opportunity for direct evidence against that of the state's principal witness, Allen. He did all that was ordinarily done in such a case, and appears to have left nothing undone that a lawyer might have been expected to do in such a case. Lincoln was at this time a distinguished lawyer, and his presence was a matter of some note. Nevertheless, this was only a case of local interest, and his acceptance of the case was considered chiefly in the light of his friendship for the family. Not that Lincoln had outgrown criminal practise. Lawyers in Illinois in that day did not specialize. They took such cases as came to them, whether civil or criminal.

It was only after Lincoln had become president that Beardstown recalled with pride Mr. Lincoln's relations to the town from

the day when one of its citizens, Denton Offutt, hired him and
John Hanks and John D. Johnston, all living at that time near
Decatur, to build a flat-boat and go with it to New Orleans, till
he returned in 1858 to plead for the life of the son of Hannah
Armstrong. Six visits, all told, Lincoln is known to have made
to Beardstown, but four of them were in 1831 and 1832. He
had not been in Beardstown, so far as is known, from 1832 till
1858, a period of twenty-six years. He returned to defend Duff
Armstrong, May 7, 1858, and in the same summer, August 12,
1858, when he followed Stephen A. Douglas, who had spoken
in the same place on the preceding day.

There were Democrats enough in Beardstown who would
have reminded him of the fraud, if it had occurred, and Stephen
A. Douglas could not have failed to learn of it, or to refer to it
to the discrediting of Lincoln who was to speak in Beardstown
on the following day.

For many years no one was able to get a statement from Duff
Armstrong for publication. J. McCan Davis, of Springfield, Illinois, at length persuaded Armstrong to tell what he remembered of the broil in which he was supposed to have murdered
a companion, and also of the trial in which Lincoln secured his
release. Armstrong was in his sixty-third year when he gave this
interview and had long been a respected citizen of the little village of Ashland. He had been for several years a member of the
Christian or "Disciples" Church. His trial for the murder of
"Pres" Metzker was a subject he seldom talked about; he would
fain forget it, and those about him have not often been inquisitive.

The accounts hitherto printed he pronounces glaringly inaccurate. This is his own story of the alleged murder and of the
trial:

DUFF ARMSTRONG'S OWN STORY

"It was on a Saturday night, and camp-meeting was over for
the day. In the edge of the grove were three bars where liquor

was sold. Here gathered all the men and boys who went to camp-meeting to drink whisky and have a good time—and a great many went for no other purpose. I had been at the meeting two or three days, and had been drinking much, but I was then becoming sober. Up to this time 'Pres' Metzker and I had been good friends; but 'Pres' had been drinking and was in an ugly mood. He had a loaded whip in his hand and was determined to have a fight with me. I hit him a terrible blow, knocking the skin from one of my knuckles. We clinched, and 'Pres' rather got the best of me. I was strong for one of my size, and was able to catch him and throw him back over me. He got up first and came at me again. Then we fought like tigers. At last he got me under him. More than a hundred people stood by watching the fight, and when the boys saw 'Pres' was getting the best of me they pulled him off. We walked up to the bar, and, each taking a drink of whisky, we bumped glasses and were friends again. I saw nothing more of him until the next morning, when he walked to the bar with a stolen quilt around him. His right eye was swollen shut. He bathed it with a glass of whisky, drank another glass, and then mounted his horse and rode away. Several days after that he died. Then the officers came and arrested me and put me in jail.

"I had a preliminary trial at Havana and was held without bail. All the bad luck in the world seemed to come to me now. On this very day my father, 'Jack' Armstrong, died. On his deathbed he said to my mother: 'Hannah, sell everything to clear "Duff."' These were almost his last words.

"After the change of venue to Beardstown Lincoln told my mother he would defend me. At the trial I had about twenty-five witnesses. The strongest witness against me was Charles Allen. He was the witness that swore about the moon; he swore it was a full moon and almost overhead. 'Uncle Abe' asked him over and over about it, but he stuck to it. Then he said he saw me strike Metzker with a slung-shot. 'Uncle Abe' asked him to tell how it was done. He got up and went through the motion, struck an overhand blow, just as he declared he saw me do by the light of the full moon. 'Uncle Abe' had him do it over again. After Allen's testimony everybody thought I would be convicted. After 'Uncle Abe' had talked to the jury a little while, he said: 'Now, I will show you that this man Allen's testimony is a pack of lies; that he never saw Armstrong strike Metzker with a slung-shot; that he did not witness this fight by the light of the full moon, for the moon was not in the heavens that night.' And then 'Uncle Abe' pulled out the almanac and showed the jury the truth about the moon. I do not remember exactly what it was—whether the moon had not risen, or whether it had set; but whatever it was it upset Allen's story completely. He passed the almanac to the jurors and they all inspected it. Then 'Uncle Abe' talked about the fight, and showed that I had acted in self-defense and had used no weapon of any kind. But it seemed to me 'Uncle Abe' did his best talking when he told the jury what true friends my father and mother had been to him in the early days, when he was a poor young man at New Salem. He told how he used to go out to Jack Armstrong's and stay for days; how kind mother was to him, and how, many a time, he had rocked me to sleep in the old cradle. He said he was not there pleading for me because he was paid for it; but he was there to help a good woman who had helped him when he needed help. Lawyer Walker made a good speech for me, too, but 'Uncle Abe's' beat anything I ever heard.

"As 'Uncle Abe' finished his speech, he said: 'I hope this man will be a free man before sundown.' The jury retired and nearly everybody went to supper. As soon as the judge and the lawyers got back from supper the jury was brought in. They had to pass me, and I eyed them closely for some hopeful sign. One of them looked at me and winked. Then I knew it was all right; when the foreman handed up the verdict of 'not guilty' I was the happiest man in the world, I reckon. 'Uncle Abe' would not charge my mother a cent; he said her happiness over my freedom was his sufficient reward.

"When the war broke out the four brothers of us enlisted in the army. Jim was wounded at Belmont; Pleasant died. I served on until the end of the war, when mother took a notion she wanted me. People laughed at her when she said she would write to the President, but she said, 'Please goodness, I am a-going to try it.' She got 'Squire Garber of Petersburg to write to 'Uncle Abe,' and in a few days mother got a telegram signed 'A. Lincoln,' telling her I had been honorably discharged. At that time I was at Elmira, N. Y., helping pick up deserters, and a discharge was the last thing I was dreaming of."

XII.   LINCOLN'S BEARD

Delphos, Kansas.
Mar. 1, 1923.

Rev. Wm. E. Barton,
  Oak Park, Ill.
Dear Sir:
  Yours of recent date at hand and I take pleasure in complying with your request, and will repeat the story of the correspondence and subsequent meeting with Mr. Lincoln.

  I have a very vivid remembrance of those weeks preceding Mr. Lincoln's election, filled with excitement and the turbulent years which followed. My father was an ardent admirer of the great man and the principles for which he stood and, childlike, I followed in his footsteps. I recall my indignation at the unkind comments of my school-mates whose friends were supporting the opposition, and you may be sure that I resented them. I think I did not see his picture until later when my father brot home a poster to us children; it was crude and coarse—Mr. Lincoln and Hamlin occupied the center and their faces were surrounded by a rail fence, by way of frame; the outer edge of the picture was finished with portraits of former presidents. Possibly I was a trifle disappointed with his appearance for I thot to myself that he would look better if he had whiskers and I posted a letter with that advice that very afternoon to Mr. Lincoln. I told him that I had seen his picture and thot that he would be better looking if he wore a beard and told him that if he would, I would try to coax my two brothers, who were Democrats, to vote for him and, if he had not time to reply, would he have his little girl answer my letter. I must have been fearful that his feelings would be hurt for I told him that I thot the rail fence around his picture looked *real* pretty. I do not remember anything more that I wrote him.

In a few days came a letter in reply which follows: (I still have this in my possession).

Private

Springfield, Ill.,
Oct. 19, 1860.

Miss Grace Bedell

My Dear Little Miss.

Your very agreeable letter of the 15*th* is received—

I regret the necessity of saying I have no daughter—I have three sons—one seventeen, one nine and one seven, years of age. They, with their mother constitute my whole family—

As to the whiskers, having never worn any, do you not think people would call it a piece of silly affection if I were to begin it now?

Your very sincere well wisher,
A. Lincoln.

It seems to me that his letter shows the kindly humorous side of his nature and also the public interest shown through these passing years.

In February, 1861, while on his way to Washington to be inaugurated he was accompanied by ex-Governor Patterson and others on that memorable trip. President Lincoln asked ex-Governor Patterson, who was a former resident of our town, if he knew of a family by the name of Bedell living there and received an affirmative reply. After a short speech delivered by Mr. Lincoln from the platform at the rear end of the car he said, "I have a correspondent in this place and, if she is present, I would like to see her." I was with friends in the crowd but I had neither heard nor seen the great man. The people began to shout, "Who is it?—Give us her name." He said, "Her name was Grace Bedell and she wrote me that she thought I would be better looking if I wore whiskers."

I was half led, half carried to the platform, running by the track on which Mr. Lincoln's train stood. He stepped down, took my hand as he said, "You see, I let those whiskers grow for you, Grace." He stooped and kissed me and then resumed his journey, leaving a much-confused child who had but one thought; to get home to her mother. When I reached home and told my story, I found a little bunch of stems which was all that was left of a bouquet of winter-roses, which I had hoped to give the President with some others which were to be presented.

Perhaps I might add one thing which has always lived in my memory. The humiliation which was mine when I was asked how I happened to write to him and how I had addressed my letter. I said, "I addressed it 'Hon. Abraham Lincoln, Esq.' I knew it was right." My mother turned her face aside and smiled and said, "Well, I think the postman had no trouble in delivering to that address."

Very sincerely,
Grace Bedell Billings.

BOOK II

ABRAHAM LINCOLN IN 1861
Photograph by C. S. Germon

THE LIFE OF
ABRAHAM LINCOLN

CHAPTER I

THE FIRST INAUGURAL

In the first weeks following his election, Lincoln lived much as he had lived in the interval between his nomination and election. He had already deserted the office and left his law practise to Herndon, practically from the time of his nomination, and occupied an office temporarily assigned him in the state capitol building, which, it must be remembered, stood in the center of the town, and not as now at one side. About a month after his election, it had become apparent that he must adopt some schedule, or at least an approach to one. The *Journal* each day announced his program for the day following, and the hours at which he would receive callers. That he did not adhere to this plan very rigidly is certainly true; but in the last two months he was compelled to reserve for himself some time to devote to preparation for his impending responsibilities. Every day these grew more serious.

Late in January he began his work on his inaugural address. Across the street from the state-house, in an upper room, dingy, dusty and at the back of the building on whose ground floor was a store, Lincoln hid himself away from intruders and began serious work upon this paper whose content might wreck or reunite the Union.

Lincoln owned very few books. He had a modest law-library,

and there were a few gilded volumes on the center-table in his parlor; but a library he can not be said to have had. Herndon, on the contrary, was a buyer of books and a great reader. When Lincoln was ready to prepare his address, he gave to Herndon a list of the books he wanted to use. Herndon procured them for him. He asked for a copy of the Constitution of the United States, and copies of Clay's speech on the Compromise of 1850, and Jackson's proclamation against Nullification. Later he asked for Webster's reply to Hayne. These, according to Herndon, were the only books which he had with him in the dingy back room where, locked away from the visitors then thronging Springfield, he prepared his address. We know how he wrote, pronouncing each word as he wrote it down, and we can imagine with what painstaking care he did his work. When the address was finished, and just before he left for Washington, he took the manuscript to the office of the *Journal,* had it set in pica type, and a very few copies struck off for his own use. We have already reminded ourselves how nearly he lost his copy at Harrisburg, and it would appear from this fact that his duplicates, if he had any with him, were in the same carpet-bag with the original, on which he had been making, and was still to make, corrections and changes.

Lincoln carefully guarded the text of his inaugural address from any premature publication. At one time he appears to have believed that that message could be made at once so firm and so conciliatory that it would be received alike by North and South, as speaking the final and unifying word. He was not, however, quite as silent as is commonly supposed. There is good reason to believe that some addresses in Congress delivered by Illinois members incorporated ideas of the president-elect. It is practically certain that the *Illinois State Journal* gave forth editorial utterances which had Lincoln's approval, and some of them may have come from his own pen. How firm Lincoln deemed it wise to be is shown in an editorial which appeared in that paper on January 22, 1861, entitled *The Right of Coercion and Mak-*

ing War on the States. This contained four definite propositions:

1. No state has a right to secede.

2. It is the duty of the president to enforce the laws.

3. The first Republican president will discharge that duty
fearlessly and faithfully.

4. He will confine himself to the enforcement of those laws
which affect the interests of the country at large—the collection
of revenue and protection of national property—but will not invade a state to secure a repeal of unconstitutional acts of its
Legislature; he will merely resist encroachments upon federal
authority.

This appeared to some of Lincoln's friends as definite and as
kindly a statement as could have been formulated, but it did not
meet with universal approval. James Gordon Bennett commented upon this utterance in a leading editorial in the *New
York Herald* of Monday, January twenty-eighth:

The great difficulty to any proposition of compromise from
the Republican party is not located at Washington, but at the
little village of Springfield, Illinois. The President-elect is this
difficulty. The magnates, the managers and the Wide-Awakes
of the Republican camp look upon Mr. Lincoln now as their
fountain of authority, power and spoils. . . . The Union is
dissolved. Within a month there will be an organized Southern
Confederacy; and then, as the attempt to enforce the Federal
laws within its boundary will be the inauguration of a general
war, the question recurs, not how to save the Union—for the
Union is gone—but how can we preserve the relations of peace?
We answer, in the recognition of the Southern Confederacy for
the sake of peace.

Just before he left Springfield, Lincoln authorized another utterance in the columns of the *State Journal.* The phraseology is
more rhetorical than Lincoln at this time was accustomed to
employ, and we can hardly assume that it is wholly the product
of his pen; still less can we believe that it was published without his full knowledge and approval:

The seceding states are in rebellion against the Federal Government, and it is the duty of the government to put down the rebellion. Away with compromises. We should not talk of compromise while the flag of the traitors floats over an American fort and the flag of our country trails in the dust. Let us never talk about compromise. Let the stolen forts, arsenals and navy yards be restored to their rightful owners—tear down your rattlesnake and pelican flag and run up the ever glorious Stars and Stripes, disperse your traitorous mobs and let every man return to his duty.*

Except for the heated rhetoric, Lincoln was in this frame of mind when he prepared his inaugural address.

Lincoln had the benefit of much advice from the press of the country while this speech was in preparation. On the Saturday night before the Monday morning of Lincoln's leaving Springfield, Honorable O. H. Browning spent an hour with him, their first long interview since the election. Lincoln two days previously had invited Browning to accompany him to Washington. Browning had declined on account of certain business which he could not well neglect, but did accompany Lincoln as far as Indianapolis, and was, perhaps, the very first man to whom Lincoln submitted his manuscript for criticism. Browning recorded in his diary on that Saturday night that he found Lincoln firmer than he expected, wholly opposed to the Crittenden Compromise, and determined to preserve the Union from disruption. He and Browning were in entire agreement in these matters. It is worth while to remember this, because Lincoln was compelled to change his attitude toward some questions before he delivered the address.

William the Conqueror stumbled and fell as he stepped out of the boat that had conveyed him across the English Channel. His superstitious followers looked on aghast; the accident

---

*My own conjecture is that Herndon wrote this editorial. The style certainly is not that of Lincoln, but Lincoln surely knew of it and approved its sentiments.

seemed to them a portent of disaster. But William rose with a handful of earth in each hand: "Thus do I grasp England," he shouted. His followers were happy; he had changed the omen of defeat to one of victory. No such good fortune came to Abraham Lincoln to retrieve the unhappy impression made by his secret arrival in the city of Washington. His friends regretted what appeared to have been the necessity for it, and his critics made merry over his care to protect himself from danger while leaving his family on the imperiled train. No one could pretend that he had entered the capital with his best foot foremost.

Sunday morning, February 24, 1861, the reunited Lincoln family sat down to breakfast together in the Willard Hotel. It was interesting to look out of the windows of the extemporized presidential suite at Willard's, a suite located on the second floor, on the Pennsylvania Avenue side, immediately above the main entrance, and see the throng that passed and repassed along the main artery of the nation's capital. But Mrs. Lincoln was more than ready to get to housekeeping again, and the whole family felt dislocated and in lack of a habitation.

On Sunday morning, February twenty-fourth, Lincoln walked with Seward to the latter's customary place of worship, Doctor Pyne's Episcopal Church. Doctor Pyne read the usual prayers for the president of the United States, and interpolated a brief but earnest petition for the incoming administration. After the service, Seward introduced Lincoln to a number of persons present at the service, and to others whom he met on the way back to the Willard. Mrs. Lincoln remained in the hotel. Seward spent the rest of the day in a careful reading of Lincoln's proposed inaugural, and that evening he returned the manuscript to Lincoln with a number of suggestions, several of which Lincoln adopted.

On that afternoon Lincoln had some opportunity to look over the newspapers, to consider their comment on the speeches he had made on his way to the inaugural, and in general to review the situation in the light of his increasing experience. He had started out by affirming that as yet "nobody was hurt," and that "the crisis was artificial." It had become apparent that somebody was likely to be hurt before long, and the manner of his entry into Washington had given evidence that he himself might possibly be among those who were injured. It was no longer possible to treat the crisis as artificial; it was real and imminent. In conversation with prominent men in Washington, Lincoln admitted that he was more troubled about the outlook than he thought it was discreet to show.

Lincoln received several calls on Sunday afternoon, but he had time to realize how much his journey had wearied him, and to feel the chagrin of public comment on his manners and his utterances. He was caricatured as a buffoon; he was referred to as the "Illinois ape." The fact that he wore black gloves to the opera in the evening of his sojourn in New York, and hung the enormous pair of kid covertures over the red velvet box front, had not escaped attention.

Even that Sabbath day was not free from the intrusion of office seekers. They had greatly annoyed Lincoln before he left Springfield. Lincoln himself was no stranger to the business of office seeking, and he knew, or thought he knew, something of what was before him when he became president. But the pressure and persistence of those who desired office went beyond all that he could have imagined. It left him no rest that day nor any day for months thereafter.

Eight days elapsed between Lincoln's arrival in Washington and his inaugural. There were certain official duties to be performed. He made a formal visit to the White House, where he was politely received by Mr. Buchanan and his Cabinet. He visited the two Houses of Congress, where friends of the new administration welcomed him heartily, and where his enemies received him with ominous silence. He visited the Supreme Court of the United States, and Chief Justice Taney and his associates accorded him courteous recognition. He received calls from two men who had been candidates against him, Breck-enridge and Douglas.

The mayor of Washington and other officials called upon the president-elect. In some respects the most notable of all these visits was one from a deputation headed by an ex-president of the nation. The Peace Conference completed its work on Wednesday, February twenty-seventh. By formal resolution this body sent a delegation to call upon the president-elect, and placed at its head its chairman and most distinguished member, ex-President John Tyler.

Thus a week went by and another Sunday came. That day brought to Lincoln, not an invitation to walk to church with Seward, but a letter withdrawing Seward's acceptance of Lincoln's invitation to head his Cabinet.

This declination of Seward was doubtless prompted by his jealousy of Chase, and by the hearing of some rumor that led Seward to believe that Chase would have a larger influence in the Cabinet than would be comfortable for Seward:

Washington, March 2, 1861.

My dear Sir:

Circumstances which have occurred since I expressed to you in December last my willingness to accept the office of Secretary of State seem to me to render it my duty to ask leave to withdraw that consent.

Tendering to you my best wishes for the success of your Administration, with my sincere and grateful acknowledgments of all your acts of kindness and confidence toward me, I remain, very respectfully and sincerely,

Your obedient servant,
William H. Seward.

The Hon. Abraham Lincoln, President-elect.

Lincoln was much disturbed, and spent Sunday in thoughtful consideration of the matter. Early in the morning of the inauguration he sent to Seward this note, which was dated, as a matter of form, from the White House, though actually written at Willard's:

Executive Mansion, March 4, 1861.

My dear Sir:

Your note of the 2nd instant, asking to withdraw your acceptance of my invitation to take charge of the State Department, was duly received. It is the subject of the most painful solicitude with me; and I feel constrained to beg that you will countermand the withdrawal. The public interest, I think, demands that you should; and my personal feelings are deeply enlisted in the same direction. Please consider and answer by 9 o'clock A. M. tomorrow.

Your obedient servant,

A. Lincoln.

Hon. William H. Seward.

On Monday night Lincoln and Seward had a long and confidential conference. Lincoln could not afford, as he said to Nicolay, "to let Seward take the first trick." Moreover, Seward had already been, for several months, virtually the spokesman of the administration. This conference brought about an adjustment of the situation; and next morning Seward sent to the president the following short and satisfactory note, and the first internal crisis of the new administration was passed:

March 5, 1861.

My dear Sir:

Deferring to your opinions and wishes as expressed in your letter of yesterday, and in our conversation of last evening, I withdraw my letter to you of the 2d instant, and remain, with great respect and esteem,

Your most obedient servant,

William H. Seward.

The President of the United States.

There was hot debate in both Houses of Congress in its closing hours concerning the Report of the Peace Conference and its recommendations for a constitutional amendment. The hours of that Congress were numbered, but just before its session ended, a proposed constitutional amendment, numbered Thirteen, was agreed to by more than two-thirds of both Houses of Congress. To that proposed Amendment Lincoln made reference in one paragraph of his inaugural address:

I understand a proposed amendment to the Constitution—which amendment, however, I have not seen—has passed Congress, to the effect that the Federal Government shall never interfere with the domestic institutions of the States, including that of persons held to service. To avoid misconstruction of what I have said, I depart from my purpose not to speak of particular amendments so far as to say, that, holding such a provision to now be implied constitutional law, I have no objection to its being made express and irrevocable.

It was well, indeed, if this was what he meant, that he should have said this "to avoid misconstruction" of other portions of the address; for it fitted ill with the remainder of the message. Lincoln, in Springfield, in December, 1860, and again on February 9, 1861, had refused the Crittenden Compromise: Lincoln, on the steps of the capitol, on March 4, 1861, accepted this approach to the essential principle of that compromise! One fact doubtless gave him comfort; the proposed amendment did not touch the question of the extension of slavery.

How can we account for this change in Lincoln?

First, and most evident, Lincoln recognized the proposed amendment as virtually a part of the Constitution, which made it a very different thing from what it was when Crittenden had presented it. Both Houses of Congress had adopted it by the necessary two-thirds vote, and the approval of the states was an apparent certainty. Whether he liked it or not, the thing appeared to have been done.

In the next place, Lincoln had come to a much deeper realization of the gravity of the situation. He could no longer regard the crisis as "artificial" nor comfort himself nor attempt to comfort his countrymen with the information that no one as yet had been hurt. Cautious as he had intended his inaugural address to be, all the important changes which Seward had suggested had been in the line of greater caution, and Seward was the man who had proclaimed the "irrepressible conflict." It was a time for prudent utterance. Lincoln was not responsible for the new so-called Thirteenth Amendment, but if it became a part of the Constitution, that was what he was swearing to support, and he wished no doubt to be entertained that he would keep his word.

It might almost be regarded as a grim joke of providence or fate, that the swift outbreak of war left the proposed Thirteenth Amendment to oblivion. The adoption which Lincoln and the Congress regarded as certain did not occur. Only two of the states took action with regard to it. When, later, a Thirteenth Amendment was really adopted, and that by means which Lincoln himself devised, it was a very different thing from the one Lincoln wrote about in a hastily interpolated paragraph in his inaugural address.*

Washington was filled to overflowing to witness the inauguration of the first Republican president. Every bed in the hotels was filled to its capacity, and hotel beds in those days were elastic, and many people slept upon the floors. Very early in the morning the city began to get itself into condition for the inaugural ceremonies. How anxious General Scott was, and how fearful that some tragedy might interrupt the inaugural proceedings, was shown by the fact that soldiers were stationed along the whole line of march, and riflemen were on the housetops on Pennsylvania Avenue. The president's carriage was surrounded by an armed guard.

Pennsylvania Avenue still lacks the dignity which ought to characterize the most important official thoroughfare in Amer-

*How much the country hoped, and how vainly, from this proposed amendment to the Constitution may be inferred from a cartoon in *Harper's Weekly* for April 13, 1861. It represents Columbia, seated, and wearing the Liberty Cap, handing to Lincoln the amended Constitution. At the feet of the goddess is the American eagle, with the olive branch and no arrows in its claw. Lincoln has on the floor behind him his hat, containing the Chicago platform. With downcast look, and half-extended hand, he accepts the amendment.

ica. But it was far worse then. It was lined on each side by irregular two-story buildings, and the roadway itself was rough. The carriage containing the president and the president-elect made its way down Pennsylvania Avenue, almost hidden from view by the guard. Some observers commended General Scott for his protection of the president-elect, and others sharply criticized him for precautions which they deemed not only wholly unnecessary, but in themselves an incitement to violence.

Shortly before noon, President Buchanan drove from the White House to Willard's Hotel. He was a large, heavy man, rather awkward in his movements. His hair was gray and thin, cut shorter than was the fashion of the time. His face was full, but seamed with wrinkles. His head, which was curiously inclined toward the left shoulder, was surmounted by a low-crowned, broad-brimmed silk hat. He wore an old-fashioned standing collar, forced up to his ears by a white cravat so huge that it resembled a poultice. He was dressed in black throughout, and his swallow-tailed coat was not cut in the latest style.

He dismounted from the open barouche of which, except for the driver, he was the only occupant, entered the front door of the Willard, and soon returned, arm in arm with Mr. Lincoln. A large and curious crowd watched while the two men entered the barouche, sat down side by side, and moved down Pennsylvania Avenue near the head of a rather disorderly and not very impressive procession.

The capitol building was not completed. Work upon it continued practically every day during the Civil War. When Buchanan and Lincoln reached the north side of the capitol, they had to pass through a long board tunnel which had been constructed for the protection of the president-elect.

The crowd was not so large as had usually attended inaugural proceedings, many staying away on account of anticipated disturbance or through lack of sympathy.

A square platform had been built out from the steps of the

eastern portico, with benches on three sides for distinguished spectators.

There was no delay; General Scott had insisted on promptness. The president-elect came forward, dressed in new tall hat, new black clothes, new black boots, and new black whiskers. He carried a new black cane, ebony, surmounted by a gold head of unusually large size. He hardly knew what to do in his painfully new clothes, and was especially troubled as to where to deposit his shiny new hat. As Lincoln rose to deliver his address, Stephen A. Douglas, who occupied a seat at the end of the benches on the right of the president, rose and took the president's hat, and held it until it was time for Lincoln to replace it on his head—an act of courtesy which was much commented on at the time, and which must not be omitted from the picture of the inauguration.

Chief Justice Taney, a cadaverous figure in black robe, stood and administered the oath of office.

No man listened to the address of the president with keener interest, or, on the whole with more complete approval, than Stephen A. Douglas. He leaned forward, taking in every word, and nodding his head in conspicuous approval of the more important passages.

Stephen A. Douglas was a politician, and knew well the tricks of his trade. He was accused of insincerity, and he may have been insincere at times. Ambitious he certainly was, and not always unselfishly so. He has suffered at the hands of those authors who have thought it necessary to disparage him in order to make Lincoln seem the greater. This is as unnecessary as it is unfair. Certainly the conduct of Douglas on the day of the inauguration and in the anxious days that followed it is worthy of all praise. Of it mention will be made again in connection with the death of this notable statesman. Suffice it to say that in the early days of his clouded administration, Abraham Lincoln had no truer friend, and that no voice was raised in more eloquent devotion to the Union than that of Stephen A. Douglas.

In a clear, thin, high voice, that carried to the outskirts of the vast assembly that gathered on the unkempt capitol lawn, the new president read the words of his inaugural address:

Fellow Citizens of the United States: In compliance with a custom as old as the government itself, I appear before you to address you briefly, and to take in your presence the oath prescribed by the Constitution of the United States, to be taken by the President "before he enters upon the execution of his office." . . .

Apprehension seems to exist, among the people of the Southern states, that by the accession of a Republican administration their property and their peace and personal security are to be endangered. There has never been any real cause for such apprehension. Indeed, the most ample evidence to the contrary has all the while existed and been open to their inspection. It is found in nearly all the published speeches of him who now addresses you. I do but quote from one of those speeches when I declare that "I have no purpose, directly or indirectly, to interfere with the institution of slavery, in the States where it now exists. I believe I have no lawful right to do so, and I have no inclination to do so." Those who nominated and elected me did so with a full knowledge that I had made this and many similar declarations, and have never recanted them. . . .

I now reiterate those sentiments, and in doing so I only press upon the public attention the most conclusive evidence of which the case is susceptible, that the property, peace, and security of no section are to be in anywise endangered by the now incoming administration. . . .

I hold that in contemplation of universal law, and of the Constitution, the Union of the States is perpetual. Perpetuity is implied, if not expressed, in the fundamental law of all national governments. . . .

I therefore consider that, in view of the Constitution and the laws, the Union is unbroken, and to the extent of my ability I shall take care, as the Constitution itself expressly enjoins upon me, that the laws of the Union be faithfully executed in all the states. . . .

This clear and emphatic declaration left no doubt of the position of the new president; and it produced a visible sensation;

and Mr. Arnold states that there were "sober but hearty cheers." The president continued:

In doing this there need be no bloodshed nor violence; and there shall be none, unless it is forced upon the national authority. The power confided to me will be used to hold, and occupy, and possess the property and places belonging to the government, and to collect the duties and imposts; but beyond what may be necessary for these objects there will be no invasion, no using of force against or among the people anywhere. . . .

Physically speaking, we cannot separate. We cannot remove our respective sections from each other, nor build an impassable wall between them. A husband and wife may be divorced, and go out of the presence, and beyond the reach of each other, but the different parts of the country cannot do this. . . .

This country with its institutions, belongs to the people who inhabit it. Whenever they shall grow weary of the existing government, they can exercise the constitutional right of amending, or their revolutionary right to dismember or overthrow it. . . .

My countrymen, one and all, think calmly and well upon this whole subject. Nothing valuable can be lost by taking time. If there be an object to hurry any of you in hot haste to a step which you would never take deliberately, that object will not be frustrated by taking time; but no good object can be frustrated by it. Such of you as are now dissatisfied, still have the old Constitution unimpaired, and on the sensitive point, the laws of your own framing under it. The new administration will have no immediate power, if it would, to change either. If it were admitted that you who are dissatisfied hold the right side in dispute, there still is no single good reason for precipitate action. Intelligence, patriotism, Christianity, and a firm reliance on Him, who has never yet forsaken this favored land, are still competent to adjust, in the best way, all our present difficulties. . . .

The day was bleak and windy, and the inaugural service partook of its chill. Chief Justice Taney was old and feeble, and his words were scarcely audible. The retiring President Buchanan was visibly uncomfortable. General Scott was old and anxious. Lincoln was pale and nervous. Every one was glad when the formal service was over and Abraham Lincoln rode back along Pennsylvania Avenue with ex-President Buchanan and arrived at the White House without getting shot.

Lincoln's inaugural was addressed particularly to the South. He had used a similar form of direct address on his visit to Cincinnati in 1856, saying that Kentucky was almost within hearing, and he therefore spoke directly to the Kentuckians reminding them that no act of theirs could move Kentucky away from the borders of Ohio and Illinois. So in his inaugural address he spoke directly to the people of the states that had already withdrawn from the Union, and those that were on the verge of withdrawal.

His address excited less discussion in the South than might have been expected. Secession was then considered an accomplished fact, and the inauguration address containing the flat declaration of the president, that secession ordinances were void, was considered only as emphasizing the hopelessness of the situation. Although the tone of the address was nothing if not pacific, it was accepted in the Cotton States as a certain indication that now there must be war.

Comment in the North was not wholly favorable. The literary form of the address was criticized by many. The *Atlas and Argus* of Albany characterized it as "weak, rambling, loose-jointed, and inviting civil war."

Other northern papers treated it as a commonplace production.

Some newspapers spoke rather well of it, commenting on its directness, its simplicity and its kindliness. Foremost among these was the *New York Tribune*.

It is marked by no feeble expression. "He who runs may read" it; and to twenty millions of people it will carry tidings, good or not, as the case may be, that the federal Government of the United States is still in existence, with a Man at the head of it.

The *Boston Transcript* also gave to the address some guarded words of commendation:

The style of the address is as characteristic as its temper. It has not one fawning expression in the whole course of its firm and explicit statements. The language is level to the popular mind—the plain, homespun language of a man accustomed to talk with "the folks" and "the neighbors"; the language of a man of vital common-sense, whose words exactly fit his facts and thoughts.

The *New York Herald* made the following comment:

It would have been almost as instructive if President Lincoln had contented himself with telling his audience yesterday a funny story and letting them go. . . . The inaugural is not a crude performance; it abounds in traits of craft and cunning. It bears marks of indecision, and yet of strong coercion proclivities, with serious doubt whether the government will be able to gratify them. It is neither candid nor statesmanlike, nor does it possess any essential of dignity or patriotism. It would have caused a Washington to mourn, and would have inspired Jefferson, Madison, or Jackson with contempt. . . . With regard to the ultimate projects of Mr. Lincoln, the public is no wiser than before. It is sincerely to be trusted that he is not ignorant of them himself.

The same newspaper a few days previous had quoted the inaugural of Jefferson Davis with interest and appreciation. It did not in so many words commend the subject-matter of that address, portions of which Davis himself afterward virtually apologized for, but said that it was "an address that indicates the man of experience, and a cultivated mind of high order."

In the evening occurred that dreary event, the inauguration ball. Mr. Lincoln now and then attended a formal ball at Springfield, where he enjoyed sitting with the men and telling stories while other people danced. Mrs. Lincoln enjoyed those occasions, and looked forward to the inauguration ball as a great event in her life. High society in Washington looked in at the ball and reckoned the number of the missing; the tawdry ball-room was not more than half full, and those who constituted the

LINCOLN AND HIS SECRETARIES
John G. Nicolay and John Hay

attendants were many of them of the lesser luminaries of Washington society. But Mrs. Lincoln did not miss anybody. She was attired in a new blue gown, and wore a large blue feather in her hair. It was her coming-out party, and she made the most of her opportunity. If there were those present who thought her dress unbecoming, she happily was unaware of the fact. Whatever joy she had in the occasion she richly deserved, for she had done her full share toward making Abraham Lincoln president of the United States. Sorrows enough were in store for her; it would be gratifying if we could know that that event brought her unclouded joy. As for her husband, he looked tired out and ill at ease. In one respect, however, he was above criticism; he wore a pair of new white kid gloves, and in them his hands seemed larger and more clumsy than ever.

Henry Adams, in pursuit of that education which he was never to acquire, but still in the earlier stages of the discovery that all was vanity, attended the inaugural ball, being then a young man and his father's private secretary. Of Washington in general and of Lincoln in particular he wrote:

The mass of ignorance in Washington was lighted up by no ray of knowledge. Society, from top to bottom, broke down. From this law there was no exception, unless, perhaps that of old General Winfield Scott, who happened to be the only military figure that looked equal to the crisis. No one else either looked it, or was it, or could be it, by nature or training. Had young Adams been told that his life was to hang on the correctness of his estimate of the new President, he would have been lost. He saw Mr. Lincoln but once; at the melancholy function called an Inaugural Ball. Of course he looked anxiously for a sign of character. He saw a long, awkward figure; a plain, plowed face; a mind, absent in part, and in part evidently worried by white kid gloves; features that expressed neither self-satisfaction, nor any other familiar Americanism, but rather the same painful sense of being educated and of needing education that tormented a private secretary; above all a lack of apparent force. Any private secretary in the least fit for his business would have thought, as Adams did, that no man living needed so much education as the new President, but that all the education he could get would not be enough.*

His father, Honorable Charles Francis Adams, would have agreed with this estimate of the character and ability of Lincoln. Speaking in 1873 before the two Houses of the Legislature of New York in honor of William H. Seward, then deceased, Adams said:

Let me not be understood as desiring to say a word in a spirit of derogation from the memory of Abraham Lincoln. He afterward proved himself before the world a pure, brave, capable and honest man, faithful to his arduous task, and laying down his life at the last for his country's safety. At the same time, it is the duty of history, in dealing with all human actions, to do strict justice in discriminating between persons, and by no means to award to one honors that clearly belong to another. I must then affirm, without hesitation that, in the history of our Government down to this hour, no experiment so rash has ever been made as that of elevating to the head of affairs a man with so little previous preparation for his task as Mr. Lincoln.†

Mrs. Lincoln returned from the inauguration ball to the White House, tired but triumphant. If notable people had been absent, she had not known Washington well enough to miss them. Many pleasing attentions had been shown to her, and she enjoyed her social success. No one at this day can wish her other than the full of such satisfaction as the occasion brought to her, or be sorry for even that lack of knowledge which mercifully veiled from her eyes some part of the hollowness of the event. Her husband, relieved that the affair was over, drew off his tight white kid gloves, hung up his new swallow-tail coat, and looked around to discover whether the White House possessed a boot-jack, and a place where a very weary man could secure a few hours of sleep.

---

*The Education of Henry Adams, pp. 106-7.
†The Life and Character of William Henry Seward, pp. 48-9.

CHAPTER II

ON THE night of November 6, 1860, Abraham Lincoln sat up and waited for the election returns. By two o'clock on the following morning it was certain that he was elected. He then went to bed, but did not sleep. He later told Gideon Welles that as he lay awake that night he constructed the framework of his Cabinet. In the days that followed, he asked advice from many people, and he seemed to make many changes; he himself was in some measure of uncertainty concerning a number of the members; but when he announced his nominations on the day following his inauguration, the men he named were the same ones whom he had tentatively selected on that wakeful night.

This was an achievement both more and less difficult than at first it might appear. Lincoln had long known that he was practically certain to be elected, and he must have given much thought to the selection of his ministers. Furthermore, some promises had been made prior to his nomination, and while he had sent word to his friends in the convention that he would not be bound by such promises, he knew that it was altogether expedient for him to make them good. Still further, he knew the incongruous elements which had gone into the making of the Republican Party, and which were expecting representation in the Cabinet. Hence, although some measure of uncertainty existed almost to the hour of the inauguration, and there was danger that the slate would be broken, and perhaps at the top, Lincoln thought through the problem as he lay in his bed in

Springfield, his conclusions of that night were essentially the conclusions that remained after all the uncertainty and questioning.

In no single instance were Lincoln's selections determined by what might have been called his personal preferences. Not one of the seven men chosen could have been called his near friend; nor is there any reason to believe that he ever asked himself who were the men who were likely to be personally congenial. The considerations that appear to have influenced him were, first an honest attempt to secure the best available men; secondly, an effort to harmonize the various and discordant elements in the Republican Party; and thirdly, a desire to see that different sections of the country were represented.

The first conspicuous fact about Lincoln's Cabinet was the number of selections he made from among those men who had been his rivals in the convention. On the first ballot, twelve men received votes for the presidential nomination: William H. Seward, Abraham Lincoln, Simon Cameron, Salmon P. Chase, Edward Bates, William L. Dayton, John McLean, Jacob Collamer, Benjamin F. Wade, Charles Sumner, John C. Frémont and John M. Reed. The votes for Frémont were a sentimental reminder of 1856, and had no real significance. Charles Sumner and Benjamin F. Wade were not candidates, but were outstanding leaders certain to receive recognition before the real voting began. Most of the others were "favorite sons" whose states desired to give them a complimentary vote, but had no expectation of gaining for them any considerable following. Lincoln chose as members of his Cabinet practically all the candidates who were seriously considered in the convention.

Seward and Chase and Bates and Cameron would appear to have been Lincoln's first selections. The mutual hostility of the Seward and Chase elements in the party made Lincoln slow in offering a place to the latter, and Cameron's foes in Pennsylvania so nearly equaled in number those of his friends that Lincoln regretted that he was practically committed to Cameron, but these three men stood foremost in Lincoln's list. As for Edward Bates, he had been Greeley's candidate, and was a competent and reliable man; but the fight in Missouri practically compelled Lincoln to find an additional man from that state, and he was not wholly sorry to select two members from slaveholding soil.

It was no new thing in American politics for a president to head his Cabinet with his principal rival within his own party. Indeed, there was a rather long and interesting line of established precedents for such a course. James Madison had appointed as secretary of state his opponent, James Monroe; Monroe passed on the compliment to his rival, John Quincy Adams, and profited ever afterward by having Adams' policy christened with his own name, the Monroe Doctrine. John Quincy Adams in his turn appointed Henry Clay, and William Henry Harrison would have continued him in that office, but Clay, who is alleged to have said that he would rather be right than be president, could have said with even more of truthfulness that he would rather be president than forever to be secretary of state to the men who defeated him. James K. Polk appointed James Buchanan, and Buchanan appointed General Lewis Cass. But no president had ever made up the bone and sinew of his Cabinet of men each of whom believed that he ought to have been seated in the presidential chair instead of the man who was there. And further, of no previous president had it seemed possible to say with so much of confidence what could be said, and was said, of the superior fitness of these several men to that of the president himself.

Furthermore, of Lincoln's Cabinet, four were chosen from that faction of the new party that either had been Democratic or were supposed to represent that wing of the combination. Whigs, Anti-slavery Democrats, Free-soilers, Know-Nothings and abolitionists, Lincoln had to think of them all in making up his Cabinet. In the judgment of many, he thought too much of the Democrats, for Lincoln himself had been nothing if not a

Whig. Chase, Cameron, Welles and Blair all represented the Democratic wing of the new party—a majority of four against three. To those who reminded him of this fact, Lincoln said, "You seem to forget that I am to be there." They did seem to forget that fact; but it was a fact not to be forgotten.

These were the seven men whom Lincoln nominated, and who constituted his first Cabinet: William H. Seward, of New York, Secretary of State; Salmon P. Chase, of Ohio, Secretary of the Treasury; Simon Cameron, of Pennsylvania, Secretary of War; Gideon Welles, of Connecticut, Secretary of the Navy; Caleb B. Smith, Secretary of the Interior; Edward Bates, of Missouri, Attorney General; and Montgomery Blair, of Missouri, Postmaster-General.

Not a few of Lincoln's advisers were startled by his selections. They believed that such a Cabinet was certain to lack harmony. There was good ground for this fear. More than one of these men accepted Mr. Lincoln as a political accident, and regarded the election as a mistake to be corrected in 1864. At least one of them began immediately to lay his plans to serve the country as its president as soon as Mr. Lincoln should have completed his one and only term.

These facts were not unknown to Lincoln. If ever a president rose above petty fear of suffering by reason of his appearance among strong men, it was Abraham Lincoln. He held that the times were too grave for considerations of personal vanity. He knew that each one of these men enjoyed the confidence of an important element in the party which had elected him, and that each one had important relations to a particular section or group, and that each one strengthened the Cabinet and would strengthen the administration. Moreover, he recognized the ability of these men, and earnestly desired to compensate for his own limitations by the utilization of their strong qualities. Not always has an American president chosen for his Cabinet men whom he knew to be so likely to oppose him. Abraham Lincoln was himself so magnanimous a man that he believed he could trust his associates to be magnanimous. The experiment was a trying one, but it was successful.

LINCOLN AND HIS CABINET
From a contemporary steel engraving

It will be well for the reader to be introduced to the seven men who constituted Lincoln's first Cabinet.

On the day that the Republican Convention assembled in Chicago, William H. Seward was fifty-nine years old. What celebration of the event occurred on that day within his own family is not known; the real celebration was set for the second day thereafter. For Seward had no doubt what was to be his birthday present. Upon his lawn assembled a large company of his neighbors and political friends, awaiting the happy moment when they might congratulate him on his nomination as president. A cannon, loaded, stood at the gate, ready to announce the nomination of William H. Seward.

On that day, William H. Seward mingled with his guests, hospitable, friendly, confident, appreciative. He recognized the honor that was presently to come to him as an honor that was his due. For thirty years he had been in politics, and he was regarded as one of the finest types of American manhood in political life. To be sure, he was short in stature, and his gestures were not graceful, and his scholarship was versatile rather than profound, but he was a man of character, ability, learning and culture. Although he sometimes used an oath in a moment of exasperation, so that Lincoln could ask another man, "Are you an Episcopalian? You swear like Seward," he was a truly religious man, and a man who for righteousness' sake was capable of suffering. He had labored long and arduously for the creation of the Republican Party. He had brought to its organization his prestige as having been twice governor of New York and the still further honor of a distinguished career in the United States Senate. He combined dignity with urbanity, and learning with a practical knowledge of the leadership of men.

As for his nomination, who could doubt that that was to come to him for the asking? His affairs were in the hands of Thurlow Weed, the most adroit politician in New York State, and with an organized force that left little doubt of the result. So the cannon stood, loaded, and ready to fire as soon as the news should come of Seward's nomination.

The first ballot showed him strongly in the lead. The second followed, and Seward was still leading, though he had gained but little and Abraham Lincoln's vote had risen alarmingly. "I shall be nominated on the next ballot," said Mr. Seward smilingly. So it would have appeared; for he had 184½ votes, Lincoln 181, and the 99½ scattering votes would seek a permanent alignment on the third ballot, and who could doubt where the greater half of them would go?

The third ballot came swiftly, and a telegram showing the result was handed to Seward. He turned ashen pale. Abraham Lincoln had been nominated. Seward was, as he said to his wife, "a leader deposed by my own party in the organization for decisive battle."

Alas for the brazen-throated messenger that had been borrowed and brought to the village of Auburn for that day! The load was drawn unfired; and as the cannon was hauled away, it was as if the funeral of a mighty leader were being celebrated, and his body carried to its burial on a gun-carriage.

There was joy that night in Springfield, Illinois; but there was deep sorrow in Auburn, New York.

Seward's disappointment was hardly greater than that of his followers. Returning delegates, filled with enthusiasm which they had gathered in Chicago, found their constituents very glum. "We sent you to Chicago to nominate a statesman," they said, "and you have given us a railsplitter."*

Many years afterward Richard Grant White wrote in the *North American Review:*

Mr. Seward saw the crown of his life petulantly snatched from him and given to—no matter whom, if not to him—but to one who had done nothing to merit it, and who was so unknown to

---

*Honorable Addison G. Procter, a native of Massachusetts but a delegate from Kansas, went east after the convention and made a visit to his old home. He was full of enthusiasm when he left Chicago, but his ardor was much dampened as he went eastward. Arriving at his old home at Gloucester he endeavored to work up a ratification meeting, but found no favorable sentiment. The sentence above is quoted from answers made to him.

a majority of his countryment, that his identity had to be explained to them.*

Charles Francis Adams, in his address on Seward before the New York Legislature, said:

The veteran champion of the reforming policy was set aside in favor of a gentleman as little known by anything he had ever done as the most sanguine friend of such a selection could desire. The fact is beyond contradiction. that no person, ever so nominated with any reasonable probability of success, had had so little of public service to show for his reward.

The Republican Central Committee of New York wrote to Seward on the day following the nomination of Lincoln:

The result of the Chicago Convention has been more than a surprise to the Republicans of New York. That you who have been the earliest defender of Republican principles—the acknowledged head and leader of the party, who have given directions to its movements and form and substance to its acts—that you should have been put aside on the narrow ground of expediency, we can hardly realize or believe. Whatever the decision of this, or a hundred other conventions, we recognize in you the real leader of the Republican party.

Lincoln recognized that Seward had a standing in the party and the nation which he himself did not possess. Lincoln never forgot that he had been nominated by a convention two-thirds of whose members preferred other candidates. Lincoln knew that but for Seward's break with Horace Greeley, and Greeley's quarrel with Thurlow Weed, Lincoln would not have been nominated.

It deserves to be recorded to the everlasting honor of William H. Seward, that his loyalty in that crisis gave to the Lincoln nomination its first assurance of the united support of the whole party. Seward's reply to the letter already quoted from the Re-

*North American Review for 1877, page 226.

publican Central Committee of his own state, contained a hearty
endorsement of the platform and a loyal support to the candidate.
Seward said:

I find in the resolutions of the convention a platform as satisfactory to me as if it had been framed with my own hands; and
in the candidates adopted by it, eminent and able Republicans
with whom I have cordially cooperated in maintaining the principles embodied in that excellent creed.

Seward then took the stump on behalf of Lincoln. His addresses contained no half-hearted platitudes. His support was
unqualified. He did not damn his successful rival with faint
praise. He gave to Lincoln and the party his good faith and his
utmost effort.

After the election, Seward was in Washington and Lincoln
was in Springfield. Lincoln was maintaining his policy of dignified silence. The *Illinois State Journal* expressed his opinions
now and then through an editorial which he had approved or
possibly written. Orville H. Browning or Lyman Trumbull or
Elihu B. Washburne now and then spoke a word which was understood to be authoritative. But William H. Seward was really
the accredited voice of the incoming administration. As one of
the senators from New York, and a man most prominent in the
leadership of the Republican Party and one certain to be the
leading member of the new Cabinet, he spoke for the Republican
Party as no other man could speak. In the whole history of
American political life no other man has occupied a position
quite like that of Seward in the last two months of 1860 and the
first two months of 1861. He was, and he knew himself to be,
the leader in the Senate of those who stood for loyalty and the
hope of a united country. He was not unconscious of his importance. His letters to his wife in this period show how fully
he felt himself to be the sole hope of the new administration and
of the nation. When on December 28, 1860, he wrote to her
telling her that he had accepted Lincoln's invitation to be secre-

tary of state, he added: "It is inevitable. I will try to save freedom in my country."

In other letters he said:

I have assumed a sort of dictatorship for defense, and am laboring day and night with the cities and States.

I am trying to get home; but as yet I see no chance. It seems to me that if I am absent only three days, this administration, the Congress, and the District would fall into consternation and despair. I am the only hopeful, calm, conciliatory person here.

These read like boastful words, but they were very nearly true. There were not many men in Washington at that time who were hopeful, calm and conciliatory, and among those who had that temperament and conviction there was no other who could speak for the administration as Seward was believed to speak. A few days after the inauguration Seward wrote again, giving his wife his feeling in accepting the secretaryship:

The President is determined that he will have a compound Cabinet; and that it shall be peaceful and even permanent. I was at one time on the point of refusing—nay, I did refuse, for a time, to hazard myself in the experiment. But a distracted country appeared before me; and I withdrew from that position. I believe I can endure as much as any one; and it may be that I can endure enough to make the experiment successful.

It is certain that Mr. Seward overrated himself, and yet more certain that he underrated Mr. Lincoln, but it must not be forgotten that at this time Mr. Lincoln was in Springfield and the man in the White House was an impotent and senile temporizer, and it was of incalculable worth to the nation to have a man of Seward's undoubted strength in Washington and in a position where he could speak strong but conciliatory words.

If ever a president had reason to anticipate uncomfortable experiences in choosing as his chief adviser a man who believed himself, and was believed to be superior in education, wisdom,

experience and political sagacity to the president, that president
was Abraham Lincoln. His motive in selecting Seward is deserving of all praise. On the other hand, it should be remembered that Seward in accepting the position understood fully that
he was preparing for himself very much of discomfort and
anxiety. It was not the president alone in association with
whom Seward anticipated unhappiness; he was bitterly opposed
to Salmon P. Chase, and both he and Chase believed that if
either one was selected for a place in the Cabinet, the other
would not be chosen.

The American secretary of state is not an English prime minister. That officer in England forms the Cabinet and defines
the policy of the administration. Seward was compelled to
realize, and that very quickly, that he had no such power. Three
of the Cabinet members were men to whom he was bitterly
hostile. Nevertheless, Seward accepted his uncomfortable
honor.

He began his duties as secretary of state with unabated confidence that the salvation of the nation depended upon his wisdom. He did not fail to let the president know how much
greater man he was than he believed the president to be.
On April 1, 1861, he handed the president a letter whose content
was well in keeping with the character of the author:

SOME THOUGHTS FOR THE PRESIDENT'S CONSIDERATION,
APRIL 1, 1861

First. We are at the end of a month's administration, and yet
without a policy, either domestic or foreign.

Second. This, however, is not culpable, and it has even been
unavoidable. The presence of the Senate, with the need to meet
applications for patronage, have prevented attention to other and
more grave matters.

Third. But further delay to adopt and prosecute our policies
for both domestic and foreign affairs would not only bring
scandal on the administration, but danger upon the country.

Fourth. To do this we must dismiss the applicants for office.
But how? I suggest that we make the local appointments forth-

with, leaving foreign or general ones for ulterior and occasional action.

Fifth. The policy at home. I am aware that my views are singular, and perhaps not sufficiently explained. My system is built upon this idea as a ruling one, namely, that we must

CHANGE THE QUESTION BEFORE THE PUBLIC FROM ONE UPON SLAVERY, OR ABOUT SLAVERY, for a question upon UNION OR DIS-UNION:

In other words, from what would be regarded as a party question, to one of patriotism or union.

The occupation or evacuation of Fort Sumter, although not in fact a slavery or a party question, is so regarded. Witness the temper manifested by the Republicans in the free States, and even by the Union men in the South.

I would therefore terminate it as a safe means for changing the issue. I deem it fortunate that the last administration created the necessity.

For the rest, I would simultaneously defend and re-enforce all the ports in the Gulf, and have the navy recalled from foreign stations to be prepared for a blockade. Put the island of Key West under martial law.

This will raise distinctly the question of union or disunion. I would maintain every fort and possession in the South.

FOR FOREIGN NATIONS

I would demand explanations from Spain and France, categorically, at once.

I would seek explanations from Great Britain and Russia, and send agents into Canada, Mexico, and Central America to rouse a vigorous continental spirit of independence on this continent against European intervention.

And, if satisfactory explanations are not received from Spain and France,

Would convene Congress and declare war against them.

But whatever policy we adopt, there must be an energetic prosecution of it.

For this purpose it must be somebody's business to pursue and direct it incessantly.

Either the President must do it himself, and be all the while active in it, or

Devolve it on some member of his cabinet.   Once adopted,
debates on it must end, and all agree and abide.

It is not in my especial province;

But I neither seek to evade nor assume responsibility.

To this amazing letter, Lincoln replied:

EXECUTIVE MANSION, April 1, 1861
Hon. W. H. Seward.

My dear sir: Since parting with you, I have been considering your paper dated this day, and entitled "Some Thoughts for
the President's Consideration."   The first proposition in it is,
"*First,* We are at the end of a month's administration, and yet
without a policy, either domestic or foreign."

At the beginning of that month, in the inaugural, I said:
"The power confided to me will be used to hold, occupy, and
possess the property and places belonging to the government,
and to collect the duties and imposts."   This had your distinct
approval at the time; and taken in connection with the order I
immediately gave General Scott, directing him to employ every
means in his power to strengthen and hold the forts, comprises
the exact domestic policy you now urge, with the single exception that it does not propose to abandon Fort Sumter.

Again, I do not perceive how the re-enforcement of Fort
Sumter would be done on a slavery or a party issue, while that
of Fort Pickens would be on a more national and patriotic one.

The news received yesterday in regard to St. Domingo certainly brings a new item within the range of our foreign policy;
but up to that time we have been preparing circulars and instructions to ministers and the like, all in perfect harmony,
without even a suggestion that we had no foreign policy.

Upon your closing proposition—that "whatever policy we
adopt, there must be an energetic prosecution of it.

"For this purpose it must be somebody's business to pursue
and direct it incessantly.

"Either the President must do it himself, and be all the while
active in it, or

"Devolve it on some member of his cabinet.   Once adopted.
debates on it must end, and all agree and abide"—I remark that
if this must be done, I must do it.   When a general line of policy
is adopted, I apprehend there is no danger of its being changed

without good reason, or continuing to be a subject of unnecessary debate; still, upon points arising in its progress I wish, and suppose I am entitled to have, the advice of all the cabinet.

Your obedient servant,
A. Lincoln.

Seward's letter was not more remarkable for its incivility to the president than it was for its bad statesmanship. It proposed a course of action on the part of the United States Government which would surely have involved us in war with one or more European nations. After its discourtesy toward President Lincoln, the most notable fact was its calm assumption of superiority. Lincoln showed in this trying situation a promptness of action, a firmness of decision and a fine magnanimity which must ever redound to his honor. He answered the letter on the very day on which it was received. He calmly and definitively informed his subordinate that he himself was, and intended to be, the president; and then he pocketed Mr. Seward's communication and told of it to no one.

The finest traits in Lincoln's character were his integrity and his magnanimity. Not until Lincoln and Seward were both dead, and many years had passed, did the world know of this correspondence.

The other members of the Cabinet criticized Seward's curiosity concerning their departments, and his reticence about his own. Secretary Welles records, about October 1, 1861, an incident in which the president and members of the Cabinet, meeting Generals Scott and McClellan in the office of the general, undertook to learn about forces in and about Washington, but Scott could not, and McClellan did not, tell. But Seward produced a slip of paper from which he read a list of the several commands, and McClellan, in answer to a question, said that the information given by Seward was essentially correct. General Scott was highly displeased. Said he:

This is a remarkable state of things. I am in command of

the armies of the United States, but have been wholly unable to get any reports, any statement of the actual forces; but here is the Secretary of State, a civilian, for whom I have great respect, but who is not a military man, nor conversant with military affairs, and this civilian is possessed of facts which are withheld from me!*

Seward was a thorn in Lincoln's flesh during the early months of his administration. But Lincoln proved to be the master of the situation, and Seward came to recognize that fact. The greatness of Lincoln made a greater man of Seward, and his wisdom became one of the valuable assets of Lincoln's administration. A president less great than Lincoln would have lost the valuable counsel of his able and loyal secretary of state. The relation which began unhappily on both sides, grew into one of intimate and happy companionship.

For secretary of treasury Lincoln chose Salmon P. Chase, of Ohio. Chase, although of Democratic antecedents, was an outstanding abolitionist. His had been the determining influence in the Free-soil convention at Buffalo in 1848, whose platform he wrote. As governor of the state of Ohio he had stood nobly for the furtherence of the cause of freedom. In the United States Senate he and Charles Sumner had opposed Douglas's scheme for the repeal of the Missouri Compromise. He had been attorney for the slave in practically every notable case that was litigated in the Ohio courts, and, like Lincoln, he had argued at least one of his cases on the ground of the Ordinance of 1787.

It has come to be popular to treat Chase as the Judas of Lincoln's administration.† Chase's distrust and ambition during the whole of Lincoln's first term is well known. In John Hay's

---

*Diary of Gideon Welles, i, p. 241.

†It is well known that in John Drinkwater's play, *Abraham Lincoln,* the character Burnet Hook, while not intended literally to follow the course of Chase's opposition to Lincoln's plans, was drawn with Chase rather definitely in mind. I asked Mr. Drinkwater, "In your character of Burnet Hook were you thinking of Salmon P. Chase?" and he answered, "More or less; I think so; yes."

diary, printed but not published, is the following entry which shows how nobly Lincoln met such embarrassment as he suffered at the hands of Chase:

October 18, 1863.

On presenting myself to the President this morning, I gave him my impression of the conduct of Mr. Chase, in trying to get under in the way he was doing, instancing what D— of New York had related. He said, "It was very bad taste, but that he had determined to shut his eyes to all these performances; that Chase made a good Secretary, and that he would keep him where he is:— if he becomes President, all right! I hope we may never have a worse man. I have all along clearly seen his plan of strengthening himself. Whenever he sees that an important matter is troubling me, if I am compelled to decide it any way to give offense to a man of some influence, he always ranges himself in opposition to me, and persuades the victim that he, Chase, would have arranged it very differently. . . . I am entirely indifferent as to his failure or success in these schemes so long as he does his duty as the head of the Treasury Department."*

Lincoln was tall, gaunt and awkward. Seward was short of stature and not graceful in his movements. Salmon P. Chase was tall and of commanding appearance. He had a head almost as massive and imposing as that of Daniel Webster. He was gifted, beyond any leader in the Republican Party, as the authority of party platforms and political proclamations. He was not a popular orator, but had marked gifts as a reasoner. His appeal was to sound judgment and clear thinking. He had a good college education, and was the master of three modern languages. He had excellent legal training, and beside all this he had sacrificial devotion to the cause of freedom. He had been the un-

---

*Copies of this diary are in the Library of Congress and the Library of the Chicago Historical Society, and have been used by me. Proper names are omitted, initials only being used. Henry Adams made a key of which these libraries have copies, and its use is permitted guardedly. The Massachusetts Historical Society has an even more precious document, a photostatic copy of the original of Hay's Diary, which was made for Thayer's *Life of John Hay.* Its use is allowed only by special permission, which permission I gratefully acknowledge.

compromising foe of slavery, long before Lincoln had uttered himself plainly on that subject.

It was inevitable that Chase should believe himself, not only the superior of Lincoln, but also the superior of Seward. He did not covet a place in the Cabinet, but, if he had any place, he never doubted but that he should have been secretary of state. It grieved and humiliated him when Lincoln sent for him and asked if he would accept the position of secretary of the treasury, but added that Lincoln, while making this inquiry, was not yet ready to offer him the position. Chase knew the reason for Lincoln's hesitation. Lincoln told him plainly that he had already offered the position of secretary of state to Seward. Plainly, Lincoln did not intend to make Chase secretary of the treasury if by so doing he was to lose Seward as secretary of state. Chase said frankly that if Lincoln offered him any place in the Cabinet, it should have been the first place, and that if Lincoln offered him any other position, it should, at least, have come as promptly and unreservedly, as Lincoln's offer to Seward. Humiliated, and resentful, Chase accepted the subordinate position. But not for one moment did he suppose that he was other than the chief figure in the administration.

What Chase thought of Lincoln may be inferred from a record which he made in his diary after he had been in the Cabinet for a year and a half. Chase asked Major General David Hunter his opinion of Lincoln. It was something which he ought not to have done, but he did it and he recorded the answer in his diary with manifest marks of approval. This is the description of Lincoln which General Hunter gave, and which Chase recorded with evident agreement:

A man irresolute, but of honest intentions; born a poor white in a slave state, and, of course, among aristocrats; kind in spirit and not envious, and anxious for approval, especially of those to whom he has been accustomed to look up—hence solicitous of support of the slave owners in the border states, and unwilling to offend them; without the large mind necessary to grasp great questions, uncertain of himself, and in many things ready to lean too much on others.

Chase could have forgiven Lincoln for his weakness in leaning on others, if Chase himself had more frequently been the man on whom Lincoln leaned.

While Lincoln's deference to Seward made him cautious about too much reliance upon Chase, and Chase's own temperament offered its further bar to intimacy, there was a very real sense in which Lincoln's reliance upon Chase was great. Chase was not primarily a financier, but he was conscientious and thorough, and he mastered the work of his office in a way that made him indispensable to the country. Any war of considerable length and importance depreciates the currency of a country, and causes the disappearance of silver and gold coin. Gold, which became abundant after the discovery of the rich deposits in California, disappeared from circulation in 1861, and there came a time when it required $2.85½ in paper money to buy one dollar in gold. Silver also went into hiding. The silver quarters, dimes, half-dimes and three cent pieces, which had been abundant, disappeared from circulation. Change had to be made in postage stamps. As these were certain to stick together when carried in the pocket, ungummed stamps were issued to be used as a circulating medium. These in time gave place to the "shin-plasters," paper money on sheets measuring two to three inches, and issued in denominations of five, ten, twenty-five and fifty cents. Later there issued three cent and fifteen cent "shin-plasters." These solved for many years the problem of fractional currency. But there was need for something other than this, that of national bank notes to supply the demand for a medium of exchange in larger units. Salmon P. Chase became "the father of the greenback," a direct promise to pay on the part of the United States, and a legal tender except for duties and taxes to the United States Government, which still had to be paid in coin.

In a very important sense the greenback saved the country.

Although Chase was not primarily a financier, he was a man of recognized ability and of undoubted integrity. The moneyed interests of the country believed in him. While his presence in the Cabinet gave much discomfort to some of his associates and to Abraham Lincoln, Chase grew to be an invaluable man.

Seward and Chase were easily the leaders in Lincoln's Cabinet as it was first organized. Subsequently, they were compelled to share their responsibility with the new secretary of war, Edwin M. Stanton, who comes later into this narrative. The remaining members of the original Cabinet call for less extended consideration.

Simon Cameron, of Pennsylvania, was thrust upon Lincoln's administration by the support of the Pennsylvania delegation which secured Lincoln's nomination in Chicago in 1860. Cameron accepted the position of secretary of war, and his appointment proved acceptable to his political friends. Cameron is believed to have been personally honest, but some of his friends were not so; and he was in bad repute with a large section of his own party in his own state. Lincoln did not retain him long. Cameron was furnished with a post sufficiently far beyond the ocean to remove him from overmastering temptation to serve his friends in the matter of fat army contracts.

Besides Seward, Chase and Cameron, a fourth member of Lincoln's Cabinet had been his opponent in the Chicago convention. Edward Bates, whom Lincoln appointed attorney general, was a fine, dignified, gentlemanly and scholarly lawyer of the old school. In 1847 he had presided over the River and Harbor Convention in Chicago. There Lincoln first met him, and there Greeley also first came to know him. Bates was Greeley's first choice as a compromise candidate for the presidency against Seward, and he believed that Bates' residence in Missouri would make him strong in the border states. Though a former rival of Lincoln, Bates proved a loyal member of the Cabinet and an efficient supporter of Lincoln's administration.

For secretary of the navy, Lincoln appointed Gideon Welles, a leading editor of New England. Though inexperienced in naval matters, he conducted his department with no little ability. He was one of Lincoln's most loyal supporters, as subsequently he was a staunch defender of Andrew Johnson.

The diary of Gideon Welles is the most intimate document we possess in the inner workings of the government in Lincoln's administration, and shows us plainly the antagonisms which existed in the Cabinet and near it. Welles himself had his own very marked prejudices. He was a Democrat, and had no love for Seward. Stephen A. Douglas distrusted Seward, and communicated his added distrust to Welles in the short period in which Douglas was in Washington after the beginning of Lincoln's administration. Welles came to cherish a deep hostility toward Stanton, and he hated General Halleck, but his pet aversion was Senator John P. Hale, of New Hampshire, chairman of the Senate Committee on the Navy. Welles found that the War Department was inclined to think the Navy Department little more than a subordinate branch of its own sphere of influence, and one to be ignored or denounced as occasion might seem to justify.

Caleb B. Smith, whom Lincoln appointed secretary of the interior, was a prominent Indiana politician. Lincoln had known him since they had served together in Congress in 1847 and 1848. He was a fair representative of the sentiment of Indiana, and, while one of the less conspicuous members of the Cabinet, was a faithful one.

Montgomery Blair, who accepted the office of postmaster general, represented a famous Missouri family. His father, Francis P. Blair, Sr., had been a prominent editor during Jackson's administration, and was one of the ablest men associated with Jackson. He was a friend of Martin Van Buren and Thomas Hart Benton. He was a strong opponent of slavery, and a fearless man. His wise counsels and his trenchant pen had done much in building up the party which had now come to power. His two sons, Montgomery and Francis P., Jr., had opposed the Dred Scott decision, and had done much to hold Missouri in the Union. While the Blair family was cordially hated by one faction in Missouri, it had the unfaltering loyalty of another and influential faction. Lincoln strengthened his Cabinet by the inclusion in it of a member of this distinguished family, but did not promote the Cabinet's comfort thereby.

Such was the official family which Abraham Lincoln gathered around him at the beginning of his administration. It is little wonder that his selections caused his friends grave solicitude. If Chase accepted with bad grace a position subordinate to Seward, Seward's friends with equally bad grace insisted that Chase should have had no place whatever in the Cabinet. But Lincoln was able to hold both these men and all the others, through an ability of leadership which, at the outset, few men understood, and which the Cabinet itself came slowly and reluctantly to recognize.

On the night of the inaugural ball, Stephen Fiske, then Washington correspondent of the *New York Herald,* asked Mr. Lincoln if he had any message to send to James Gordon Bennett, editor of that paper. Bennett was frankly antagonistic to Lincoln and his administration. "Yes," answered Lincoln, "you may tell him that Thurlow Weed has found out that Seward was not nominated at Chicago."

Not for some time did the correspondent understand that this was one of Lincoln's jokes. It was a very serious joke; it was Lincoln's declaration that he was master of the situation. Thurlow Weed, who had been endeavoring to crowd Chase out of the Cabinet, and Seward, who had declined a secretaryship on the very eve of the nomination, had both discovered that Weed had not succeeded either in the nomination or in the control of the executive.

While Lincoln suffered from both Seward and Chase, he valued them highly. At one time when they resigned simultaneously, Lincoln very skilfully played each against the other. Remembering his boyhood experiences in carrying loads on horseback, he said, "Now I can ride ahead; I have a pumpkin in each end of my sack."

The late lamented P. T. Barnum had in his menagerie a cage which was the most popular among those who frequented his show, containing a "happy family." It was composed of animals of diverse disposition which had been taught to live together. Lincoln's Cabinet was something after this sort. It was not the ingenuity of the showman that devised Lincoln's "happy family," but the skill of a leader who gathered about him men of ability and character, with little regard for their liking for him or one another, but each of whom he judged to be capable of rendering to the country a service. It was his genius and patience and unselfishness which taught these men to live and work together, not always comfortably, but on the whole effectively.

CHAPTER III

INSIDE THE WHITE HOUSE

It has already been recorded in this narrative that at the close of the inauguration services Mr. Buchanan rode back with the president along Pennsylvania Avenue, saw him safely across the White House threshold, bade him a dignified farewell and took his departure. Other carriages promptly dropped the remaining members of the president's family at the White House door. There stood "Old Edward" who had served as doorkeeper through many administrations. With becoming dignity he opened the door and in walked Abraham Lincoln. Mrs. Lincoln and family followed promptly.

Seventeen persons sat down to dinner in the White House that day, and they were ready for it. An unpublished account of the dinner exists in the handwriting of Mrs. Elizabeth Todd Grimsley, Mrs. Lincoln's cousin. Viewing the arrangements with feminine eye, she pronounced them perfect. Miss Harriet Lane, President Buchanan's niece and housekeeper, had organized a good group of servants, with chef and butler, and the White House was in thorough order. The dinner which Miss Lane had caused to be prepared was all that could have been desired. Mr. and Mrs. Lincoln and the boys and Mrs. Lincoln's relatives and the few personal friends who joined them ate with hearty appetite. Then the party separated, the women scattering to the rooms assigned, and preparing for the inauguration ball. Willie and Tad inspected the house from the top floor to the basement, and within a few hours had interviewed every servant and watchman about the building.

A more careful inspection of the executive mansion by the women of the party revealed the public rooms in good condition, but the family apartments more or less shabby. The furniture was as unattractive as that in the home at Springfield, and lacked the simple comfort which that home had possessed.

It might have been hoped that the few remaining hours of Lincoln's first day in the White House would have been free from the encroachments of office-seekers. But not only the president, but every member of the family, male or female, suffered that intrusion. Every member of the family had visits that afternoon from total strangers, beseeching him or her to use his or her influence with the president on behalf of some applicant for office. Mrs. Grimsley says:

The day was not half spent before the house was full of office-seekers. Halls, corridors, offices and even private apartments were invaded. This throng continued and increased for weeks, intercepting the President on his way to meals; and, strange to say, every tenth man claimed the honor of having raised Mr. Lincoln to the Presidency; until he was fain to exclaim, "Save me from my friends!"

The ladies of the family were not exempt from marked attention and flattery; but they soon had their eyes open to the fact that almost every stranger that approached us "hoped we would use our influence with the President in his behalf." And it was a hard matter to persuade them that they would stand a better chance without interference, we, to quote Mr. Lincoln, having no influence with this administration.*

The family was not long in learning that one of the occupants of the White House was in the employ of the press, and that even their most unguarded actions and utterances were liable to appear in print. What they spoke to each other in the ear was shouted from the housetop; and it was some time before they understood it. A new order of journalism then known as "Jen-

---

*Mr. H. E. Barker, of Springfield, permits me the use of this very interesting manuscript.

kinism" was in vogue. It dealt with kitchen-gossip and back-door rumor; and its representatives were securely berthed in the White House from the day of Lincoln's arrival.

The first Sunday in the White House the family attended the New York Avenue Presbyterian Church, the Reverend Doctor Phineas D. Gurley, pastor, and this continued to be the church home of the president and his family throughout their stay in Washington. Robert returned to Harvard, but Willie and Tad were regular members of the New York Avenue Sunday-school.

Ralph Waldo Emerson believed in the law of compensation as applicable to all human life. "The President pays well for his White House," said the learned sage. Lincoln began to pay high rental from the moment of his occupancy. Brief, indeed, was the period which the Lincoln family and their immediate guests had for the curious and happy inspection of their new home. Andrew Jackson is credited with the doctrine that "to the victors belong the spoils," but it was accepted as a good political doctrine in Lincoln's time. The changes at the beginning of Lincoln's administration were greater than at the beginning of Jackson's régime.*

The first social clash was between Mrs. Lincoln and Mr. Seward. The latter indicated that he thought it proper for the secretary of state to give the first official reception of the new administration. He failed to reckon with the ambition of Mrs. Lincoln. The first official reception was given on Friday evening, March eighth, at the White House. It was a jam. Long before it was over the president and his official family were weary, and it was a relief when the Marine Band played *Yankee Doodle* as a signal that it was to end.

The first state dinner, given March twenty-eighth, was not a very gay affair. Few of the Cabinet ladies were in Washington. Secretary Seward's home was presided over by his daughter-in-

---

*Claude G. Bowers says of Jackson's political changes, "There was no such massacre as followed the election of Lincoln." *Party Battles of the Jackson Period,* p. 72

law; Secretary Chase's brilliant daughter, Kate, afterward the wife of Governor Sprague, of Rhode Island, was not yet in Washington, and some of the other Cabinet members had not yet brought their families. The men were stiff and formal and unused to one another.

The first diplomatic reception was distinctly cold. The foreign legations were not out in full force, nor did they come in a body as their custom had been, nor were they any too cordial. Lord Lyons of England was dignified and distant, and the French minister, Mercier, stayed away altogether.

Washington was in a state of social disintegration. The oldest, proudest families were daily departing; and among those who remained there was an atmosphere of suspicion and uncertainty. No one knew whom to trust. No one knew who next would be missing. Some of Mrs. Lincoln's relatives called for a none too cordial farewell before they left Washington to join the Confederacy. Deserted, misrepresented, and thrust into a situation for which she had no adequate training, it is little wonder that Mrs. Lincoln was not always at her best.

Among the residents of the White House in those early days was John Hay. He kept a diary portions of which have been printed but not published, and in which as printed important names are thinly disguised by the use of initials. His pet names for Lincoln were the "Chief," the "Ancient," the "Tycoon." He describes the president sitting in most undignified attire, loafing and lounging in his hours of ease, and sometimes rising in the night to walk around the offices and hunt up a paper, wearing a costume consisting only of a shirt, or in colder weather of an overcoat slipped on over his shirt. He tells of Lincoln's rising from bed and coming in at night where his secretaries were still sitting up, and reading with great gusto to them an amusing paragraph. His descriptions bear upon their faces the indisputable evidence of accuracy. But while Hay exhibits these intimate snapshots of the president at close range, it is interesting to note how his reverence for Lincoln grew, and his appreciation of Lincoln's real greatness was unmarred by his sense of the ludicrous in much that Lincoln said and did.

In 1866, Mr. Hay, then a member of the United States Legation in Paris, wrote this account of Lincoln's life in the White House:*

Lincoln went to bed ordinarily from ten to eleven o'clock, unless he happened to be kept up by important news, in which case he would frequently remain at the War Department until one or two. He rose early. When he lived in the country at the Soldiers' Home he would be up and dressed, eat his breakfast (which was extremely frugal, an egg, a piece of toast, coffee, etc.), and ride into Washington, all before eight o'clock. In the winter, at the White House, he was not quite so early. He did not sleep well, but spent a good while in bed. Tad usually slept with him. He would lie around the office until he fell asleep, and Lincoln would shoulder him and take him off to bed. He pretended to begin business at ten o'clock in the morning, but in reality the ante-rooms and halls were full long before that hour —people anxious to get the first axe ground. He was extremely unmethodical; it was a four years struggle on Nicolay's part and mine to get him to adopt some systematic rules. He would break through every regulation as fast as it was made. Anything that kept the people away from him he disapproved, although they nearly annoyed the life out of him by unreasonable complaints and requests. He wrote very few letters and did not read one in fifty that he received. At first we tried to bring them to his notice, but at last he gave the whole thing over to me, and signed, without reading them, the letters I wrote in his name. He wrote perhaps half a dozen a week himself—not more.

Nicolay received Members of Congress and other visitors who had business with the Executive Office, communicated to the Senate and House the messages of the President, and exercised a general supervision over the business. I opened and read the letters, answered them, looked over the newspapers, supervised the clerks who kept the records, and in Nicolay's absence did his work also. When the President had any rather delicate matter to manage at a distance from Washington, he rarely wrote, but

*Herndon's *Lincoln,* iii, pp. 514-517.

sent Nicolay or me. The house remained full of people nearly all day. At noon the President took a little lunch, a biscuit, a glass of milk in winter, some fruit or grapes in summer. He dined between five and six, and we went off to our dinner also. Before dinner was over, members and senators would come back and take up the whole evening. Sometimes, though rarely, he shut himself up and would see no one. Sometimes he would run away to a lecture, or concert, or theater for the sake of a little rest. He was very abstemious, ate less than any man I know. He drank nothing but water, not from principle, but because he did not like wine or spirits. Once, in rather dark days early in the war, a temperance committee came to him and said that the reason we did not win was because our army drank so much whiskey as to bring the curse of the Lord upon them. He said it was rather unfair on the part of the aforesaid curse, as the other side drank more and worse whiskey than ours did. He read very little. He scarcely ever looked into a newspaper unless I called his attention to an article on some special subject. He frequently said, "I know more about it than any of them." It is absurd to call him a modest man. No great man was ever modest. It was his intellectual arrogance and unconscious assumption of superiority that men like Chase and Sumner never could forgive. I believe that Lincoln is well understood by the people; but there is a patent-leather, kid-glove set who know no more of him than an owl does of a comet blazing into his blinking eyes. Their estimates of him are in many cases disgraceful exhibitions of ignorance and prejudice. Their effeminate natures shrink instinctively from the contact of a great reality like Lincoln's character. I consider Lincoln republicanism incarnate, with all its faults and all its virtues. As, in spite of some rudeness, republicanism is the sole hope of a sick world, so Lincoln with all his foibles, is the greatest character since Christ.

A feeling of danger was in the air when Lincoln and his family first became the inhabitants of the White House. General Scott insisted on placing guards about the house, much to Lincoln's dissatisfaction. One night soon after their arrival the whole family except the servants was taken ill. Physicians were hastily summoned, and there was for a time a belief that the president and his family had been poisoned. It proved, however, that the family had indulged too freely in a dish which they were enjoying for the first time, "Potomac shad."

On May 26, 1861, a funeral was held in the East Room of the White House. Colonel Elmer Ellsworth, who was virtually a resident of Lincoln's household, a young man whom Lincoln had known and loved in Springfield and who had come east on the same train with Lincoln, had fallen a martyr to his rash zeal in hauling down a Confederate flag in Alexandria.

On June third, the White House was draped in mourning for the second time in three months. This was for the death of Stephen A. Douglas. He had been Lincoln's rival in politics for years, and also in early days his rival in love, but the two men entertained a genuine respect for each other. Douglas was believed to have brought on his last illness by his overwork in his endeavor to hold his former associates in the Democratic Party to loyalty for the Union. He had gone west on a speaking campaign and Lincoln trusted his good faith and regarded him with genuine personal affection. Lincoln had supplanted him in love and in politics, and Douglas had risen above all petty considerations to support Lincoln and the Union. Lincoln regarded his death as a deep personal sorrow, and draped the White House in his memory.

The death of Colonel Edward D. Baker, at the Battle of Ball's Bluff, October twenty-first, was felt at the White House as another intimate and personal sorrow.

Not many days after the Lincoln family had established itself in the White House, Lincoln gathered at breakfast a group of his old Illinois friends, including Judge David Davis, Colonel Lamon, Major Wallace and other friends. Mrs. Grimsley recorded an incident of this breakfast which is worth preserving as a side-light on the relations of Abraham Lincoln and his wife. One of the lawyers told of a hotel at Tremont, in Tazewell County, where the lawyers were accustomed to stop during court week, whose landlady was particularly partial to Lincoln and to Major Stuart. Stuart was a handsome man in comfortable flesh, and Lincoln, then, as always, shrunken and cadaverous. The landlady said, "Mr. Stuart, how fine and pert you do look! But Mr. Lincoln, whatever have you been doing? You do look powerful weak." Lincoln mournfully replied, "Nothing out of the common, ma'am, but did you ever see Stuart's wife, or did you ever see mine? Whoever marries into the Todd family gets the worst of it."

Major Wallace also had married into the Todd family, being a brother-in-law of Lincoln, and was the only portly man at the table. This story, told in the presence of Mr. and Mrs. Lincoln, and of Mrs. Grimsley who was also a Todd, brought on a general and merry discussion of the alleged domestic sorrows of the men who had married into the Todd family, all of whom as it appeared were none the worse but rather the better for it.

The significance of a trivial incident such as this, lies in the fact that such a story could be told at the Lincoln table and be enjoyed by both Mr. and Mrs. Lincoln. Their friends could not have indulged in that degree of familiarity if they had not known that it would not give offense.

The elevation of Lincoln to power did not wean him from his old friendships. During the days when he was bearing heavy burdens in the presidential office, it was a joy to him to welcome some old comrade of former days from Illinois. Honorable Isaac N. Arnold, who was in Washington during this period, and a habitual visitor to the White House, thus speaks of Lincoln's attachment to his old friends:

There was something very beautiful and touching in the attachment and fidelity of these his old Illinois comrades to Lincoln. They had all been pioneers, frontiersmen, circuit-riders together. They were never so happy as when talking over old times, and recalling the rough experiences of their early lives. Had they met in Washington in calm and peaceful weather, on sunny days, they would have kept up their party differences as they did at home, but coming together in the midst of the fierce storms of civil war, and in the hour of supreme peril, they stood together like a band of brothers. Not one of them would see an old comrade in difficulty or danger, and not help him out. The memory of these old Illinois lawyers and statesmen: Baker, McDougall, Trumbull, Lovejoy, Washburne, Browning, and others, recalls a passage in Webster's reply to Hayne. Speaking of Massachusetts and South Carolina, the great New England orator said: "Shoulder to shoulder they went through the Revolution together; hand in hand they stood around the administration of Washington, and felt his own great arm lean on them for support."

So, in the far more difficult administration of Lincoln, these old comrades of his, Baker, McDougall, Trumbull, Browning, Lovejoy, and the others, whatever their former differences, stood shoulder to shoulder, and hand in hand, around the administration of Lincoln; his strong arm leaned on them for support, and that support was given vigorously and with unwavering loyalty.*

The narrative of Mrs. Grimsley records the extreme anxiety of the White House family when battles went against the Union cause. She also states that after the battle of Bull Run General Scott advised the president to take his family to Philadelphia for a few weeks, believing the capital itself to be in danger. Lincoln positively refused to go, but told Mrs. Lincoln of General Scott's advice and suggested that she should go and take the boys. This she emphatically refused to do. If her husband was in peril she would remain with him and share that peril.

The president had occasion to remind his wife's cousin at least once of her need to be cautious on account of her southern relatives. Mrs. Grimsley announced her intention of accompanying a party of friends to Mount Vernon, along the road unguarded against Confederate incursion.

"Mr. Lincoln rose from his chair, looked at me silently an instant, as was his wont, then said gently, as was his habit in speaking to women, 'Cousin Lizzie, have you taken leave of your senses? Can you compute the amount of trouble in which you

*Arnold: *Life of Lincoln*, pp. 240-241.

would involve General Scott and myself if a member of my family should be captured? And the enemy would be only too glad to get you in their clutches, particularly your cousin David Todd, now in charge of the Rebel prison in Richmond.'"

Lincoln's family knew of the burden which he bore in the matter of men condemned to death. Lincoln gave orders to his doorkeeper that no one who came to intercede on behalf of a condemned person should be turned away until the president had given the matter a personal investigation. He said to his family, "It makes me feel rested after a hard day's work, if I can find some good excuse to save a man's life."

Lincoln looked with little favor upon the efforts made by innumerable people to secure office by appealing to Mrs. Lincoln or to other occupants of the White House. Colonel H. C. Huidekoper, who was in Harvard during the early part of the war, and who knew Robert Lincoln while a student there, tells of a fight for the Cambridge post-office in which the friends of a particular candidate succeeded in interesting more or less the president's son Robert. At the earnest solicitation of these friends Robert wrote a letter to his father, who replied:

"If you do not attend to your studies and let matters such as you write about alone, I will take you away from college."

Robert very wisely preserved this letter and made good use of it. When after that any one attempted to secure his influence in favor of any candidate Robert produced the letter and it proved to be an effective protection.

Mrs. Lincoln, also, found occasion to protect herself against the importunity of office-seekers. She instructed the president's secretaries to open her mail as well as that of the president, in order to give her some measure of relief from distressing and often non-meritorious appeals. It is pathetic to remember also another reason why she came to desire her mail to be opened. She wanted the president's secretaries to be able to testify that she had no secret correspondence, through her relatives or otherwise, with any one in rebellion against her country. The president's secretaries, who had thus thrust upon them the duty of reading Mrs. Lincoln's correspondence, were of those who bore strongest testimony to her loyalty to her husband and the Union.

The editors of the country did not leave Mr. Lincoln lacking in instruction. They wrote long editorials for his guidance, and sent marked copies of the papers to the White House. The president, always deeply interested in public opinion, at first endeavored to read all these editorials. Finding this a physical impossibility, he directed that they should be read and briefed and arranged for his perusal. After about two weeks, however, he discovered that even this was impossible. And he gave up all attempt to keep up with the newspapers except a few of the dailies of different political faiths in the more important cities.

One of the president's perplexities grew out of the demand for appointments of chaplains. Not a few ministers, weary of the more or less monotonous and exacting demands of their parishes, and others who had no pulpits and perhaps did not deserve them, were very eager to look after the spiritual welfare of the soldiers, some of them being especially desirous of being attached to the more or less permanent posts and cantonments. Mr. Stoddard says that Lincoln had very little respect for these "loose-footed ministers." He had very little inclination to disturb himself in the effort to provide office or emolument for these men who were "anxious for the rank and pay of religious majors without the toil and exposure and peril of keeping company with a regiment in the field."

Nevertheless, Lincoln sometimes found himself under the pressure of influential friends on behalf of some of these men. In the case of one such man he sent to Stanton the papers of recommendation endorsed, "Appoint this man chaplain." Stanton returned them with the endorsement, "He is not a preacher." A few days later Lincoln returned the papers, with the endorsement, "He is now." Stanton replied, "There is no vacancy."

Lincoln concluded "Appoint him anyway." And so, presumably, he was appointed.

Mrs. Grimsley affirmed that Mrs. Lincoln and the other women of the White House never made but one attempt, and that a successful one, to influence the president concerning a political appointment. Their former pastor, the Reverend James Smith, had grown old and had retired from the active ministry. His son had been United States Consul at Dundee, Scotland, and had died there. Mrs. Lincoln earnestly desired that Doctor Smith be permitted to succeed his son. He was abundantly competent to care for the not very arduous duties of the consulate, and the salary, while small, was enough to assure him of a support. Mrs. Lincoln and her cousins vowed that if Lincoln would grant them this one favor, they would never again ask him to appoint any friend of theirs to any office. It was not very difficult for them to secure the granting of their request. Lincoln honored Doctor Smith, and quite probably would have done the very thing they asked even if they had not requested it. But he received the delegation with all proper dignity, and after having made his protest against being coerced in matters of this character by members of his own household, he very cheerfully made the appointment.

Notwithstanding wars and rumors of wars, there was something of home life in the White House. The Lincoln boys were constantly making new friends and new discoveries, and their daily chatter and gossip kept things alive, and Lincoln was not always sad or cast down. His ability to be natural and even mirthful when things were at their worst was a quality of saving value. Sometimes the boys were sick, and Lincoln was anxious and Mrs. Lincoln almost hysterical. She was too nervous and excitable a mother to be a good nurse, but she loved her children devotedly.

Once, Lincoln was sick. The Lincoln boys, visiting the soldiers, encountered small-pox, and the president himself had a mild attack of it. They called it varioloid, and the White House was not quarantined. If the infectious nature of the president's illness kept any office-seeker away, the fact is not of record. "Come in," said Lincoln cheerfully, "I have something now that I can give everybody."

CHAPTER IV

THE HOUSE DIVIDED

IF WARS must be it ought at least to be clear precisely what the fighting is about. The bewilderment of the little boy in Southey's poem, and the inability of his grandfather to explain the situation intelligibly, has been shared by historians since time began. Little Peterkin asks:

> "Pray tell us all about the war,
> And what they fought each other for?"

The historian is hard put to it to answer this wholly reasonable, but always disconcerting inquiry:

> "It was the English," Caspar cried,
>   "Who put the French to rout,
> But what they fought each other for,
>   I could not well make out.
> But everybody said," quoth he:
> "That 'twas a famous victory."

It is not easy even yet to reach entire agreement concerning the cause of America's Civil War.

A very simple answer from the southern point of view is that the United States was not organized as a nation, but a confederacy; that the states united in creating it by voluntary consent, and that some of them at the time expressly reserved the power and full right of withdrawal. Jefferson Davis, in his *History of the Confederate States,* reminded his readers that not only Virginia, but New York and Rhode Island, in ratifying the Constitution of the United States, expressly reserved the right of secession.*

Alexander H. Stephens, Vice-President of the Confederacy, wrote a history in two volumes of what he called *The War Between the States.* Stephens had been so earnest a defender of the Union that Lincoln at one time had serious thought of inviting him to be a member of his Cabinet, remembering his great admiration for Stephens, when Lincoln himself was a member of Congress.

Stephens, whose book was published in 1868, dedicated it "To all true friends of the Union under the Constitution." He believed, however, that that Constitution provided only for a federation based upon the common consent of the states uniting, and that any state could terminate its own union with the other states whenever it chose.

The doctrine of the right of secession was not confined to the South. Extreme abolitionists, like William Lloyd Garrison and Wendell Phillips, insistently denounced the Union, and believed that the free states had a right to secede from the states that held slaves. It would thus be a grave mistake to assume that all believers in secession were also believers in slavery. This is an assumption upon which many authors have mistakenly insisted.

Andrew Jackson firmly believed that no state had a right to nullify an act of the general government, or to withdraw from the Union. Jackson died regretting that he had never been able to shoot Henry Clay or to hang Calhoun.†

It has been said with good reason that the federal idea, that of the union of sovereign states in the more inclusive unity of a nation is the greatest contribution of the Anglo-Saxon race to

---

*Mr. Davis devotes a short chapter to this subject and earnestly endeavors to refute the application of any such terms as rebellion or treason as applied to the secession of the slave states. See his *History*, pp. 50, 52.

†Claude G. Bowers' *Party Battles of the Jackson Period*, p. 480.

the science and practise of government.* At the time of the signing of the Declaration of Independence the idea of a government in which the powers of a state were to be divided between the component units and the general authority of the nation, was practically unknown. The men who established the American colonies stood in fear of a strong government, and held in general to the theory that that government was best which governed least. The progress of the Revolutionary War demonstrated the necessity for a stronger government than the Articles of Federation provided for. The Constitution of the United States was construed from the beginning as a grant of power to, and not as a limitation upon powers inherent in, a federal state.

After the adoption of the Constitution, proposals of nullification or secession based upon doctrine of States' Rights, were evoked perhaps as frequently in the North as in the South. The Whisky Rebellion in Pennsylvania in 1795, and the Hartford Convention in New England in 1814, were based upon as radical a conception of state sovereignty as the Kentucky Resolutions of 1799, of which Thomas Jefferson subsequently acknowledged himself to be the author. In 1825 the state of Georgia forcibly prevented the execution of federal laws and Alabama pursued a similar course in 1832. In that same year the state of South Carolina, led by John C. Calhoun, set forth in its baldest form the theory of the right of a state to nullify the acts of the general government.

On the other hand fourteen northern states in the decade before the Civil War took action to prevent the enforcement of the Fugitive Slave law in acts known as Personal Liberty laws, which made it a crime to enforce within the state a particular statute of the nation.

The Civil War settled, and we hope forever, the question

---

*See an interesting and valuable article by Honorable Marvin B. Rosenberry, of the Supreme Court of Wisconsin, in the *North American Review* for August, 1923. I summarize here some of the conclusions of that article.

whether the United States was one nation or several nations; but the process by which the federal idea came to national recognition did not end with the surrender of Lee's Army at Appomattox. That process has been continuous and is not yet at an end.

Daniel Webster held to the basic unity of the United States as something in its very nature indissoluble. Lincoln fully accepted Webster's position. He believed that the Union could not be broken up by the act of any single state, nor by any group of states acting without the consent of all the rest.

Thus it might seem that the question concerning the origin of the war was a very easy one to answer. The South believed, and very many men in the North admitted, the right of a state to secede. The South asserted that right; the North opposed it with force and arms. The North won the war, and that settled the question so far as war can ever settle a question of this character.

This, however, is far from being a satisfactory solution of the problem. Admitting that the South believed that individual states had a right to secede, why did they care to exercise that right? Surely, the fact that the political parties then in the majority in those states had been defeated in an honest election was not an adequate reason for the disruption of the Union.

Alexander H. Stephens' love for the Union has already been mentioned. In 1861 he spoke concerning the Constitution of the Confederate States of America, and said:

The new Constitution has put at rest forever all the agitating questions relating to our peculiar institution, African slavery. This was the immediate cause of the late rupture, and present revolution. The prevailing ideas entertained by Jefferson, and most of the leading statesmen at the time of the old constitution were that the enslavement of the African was wrong in principle, socially, morally, and politically. Our new government is founded upon exactly the opposite idea; its foundations are laid, its corner stone rests, upon the great truth that the negro is not

he equal of the white man; that slavery—subordination to the
white man—is his natural and normal condition. This, our new
government, is the first in the history of the world based upon
his great physical, philosophical, and moral truth.

Abraham Lincoln declared at Gettysburg that the nation
which began with the Declaration of Independence was conceived in liberty and dedicated to the proposition that all men
were equal. He and Alexander H. Stephens would have agreed
that the war was fought to determine whether that affirmation
was correct.

For a very long time the leaders who believed in the moral
righteousness and political expediency of slavery had been apprehensive that their power was destined to fail. The westward
expansion of the country, though maintained for a considerable
time with a balance of power secured by the admission of one
free state for each slave state, could not permanently establish
that ratio. The success of the Mexican War in securing new
territory south of Mason and Dixon's line was destined to be
more than offset by the entrance of California and Kansas into
the Union as free states, and the opening of new free territories
in the West and Northwest. How to hold for slavery an adequate part of the new area of the nation, was a perplexing political question. On this the Democratic Party itself was divided.
Stephen A. Douglas was the man who elected Abraham Lincoln president. He who protested against Lincoln's declaration
that a house divided against itself could not stand, was himself
living in a divided house, the Democratic Party, and his foes
were they of his own household.

The census of 1860 showed a total population in the United
States of 31,453,790. Of this the slave states had 12,315,372,
and the free states 19,128,418. A large part of the population
of the slave states, however, was in the border states, some of
which did not secede. The seceded states stretched from the
Atlantic to the extreme western point of Texas, and from the
Gulf of Mexico north nearly to the old dividing line of 36° 30',

21

with Virginia lying north of that line and carrying the north
ern boundary of the Confederacy to the very gates of the capi
tal city. A comparison of the census of 1860 with that o
1850 showed an increase of more than one-third in population
with a growing proportion of that increase in the free states
The United States at that time led all nations in agriculture
the cotton crops being one of the country's most important pro
ducts and one of the leading exports. Manufacturers were in
creasing. Railroads had been extended until there was a tota
mileage of 30,000 in 1860, against 7,500 in 1850.

This increase was very largely in the North. South of th
border states there was no large city except New Orleans
There were hardly any manufacturing establishments of an
importance south of Maryland.

Politically, the North and the anti-slavery cause had mad
large and permanent gain. Minnesota and Oregon had entere
the Union as free states, and Kansas, no longer bleeding an
no longer halting between two opinions, had taken her place i
the sisterhood as a free state. The control of the Senate ha
been hopelessly lost to the slave states before the first of the
seceded.

The two sections seriously misunderstood each other. Th
South believed that the North was so engrossed in money mak
ing that it would not fight, or if it did, would fight ineffectively
There was a popular delusion that one southern man could whi
seven Yankees. In the North it was believed that the South wa
given to bluster, but that the southern states would not fight, o
if they did, would quickly be subdued. Each section had to lear
that the other was fully capable of heroic fighting. When th
two armies met each other in the field, each had to face a brav
antagonist. Both armies were American, and neither coul
count upon the cowardice or irresolution of the other.

For some time it was uncertain just how many states woul
join the Confederacy. The first group of states to secede wa
South Carolina, Mississippi, Florida, Alabama, Georgia an

Louisiana. These were the states represented in the Constitutional Convention at Montgomery, Alabama, on February 4, 1861. On February twenty-third, Texas joined the ranks of seceding states. Arkansas followed May sixth, North Carolina May twentieth, Virginia May twenty-third, and Tennessee June eighth. In no case was this action ratified by a free popular vote. Virginia and Tennessee were in possession of the Confederate troops when the vote was taken in those states, and no vote of the electorate was taken in the others. Kentucky, Maryland and Missouri, important border states containing many secessionists, remained in the Union. The eastern end of Tennessee remained loyal, and the western end of Virginia, denying the right of a state to secede, itself seceded from secession and entered the Union as the state of West Virginia.

Soon after the inauguration of Lincoln, William H. Seward, Secretary of State, refused to recognize a delegation sent from the Confederate Congress to treat with the Federal Government for an amicable separation. Lincoln, whom many believed to be an irresolute man without strength of will, had come to the White House with his mind fully made up on two important matters. One was that there should be no compromise based upon any plan that admitted the further extension of slavery. The other was that no state was to be permitted to take itself out of the Union. In the interregum between his election and inauguration Lincoln had carefully thought this out in all its possible bearings. He was not yet president, and had no right to give any military or political orders, but on both these points he communicated his desires and inflexible purpose in letters whose contents reached both Congress and the army. Two letters, the originals of which are in the Washburne manuscripts of the Chicago Historical Society, show with what convictions and purposes Lincoln came to the presidential chair. On December 13, 1860, he wrote to his confidential friend, Elihu B. Washburne:

Confidential

SPRINGFIELD, ILL., Dec. 13, 1860.

Hon. E. B. Washburne—My Dear Sir: Your long letter received. Prevent as far as possible, any of our friends from demoralizing themselves and our cause, by entertaining propositions for compromise of any sort on the slavery extension. There is no possible compromise upon it, but which puts us under again, and leaves us all our work to do over again. Whether it be a Missouri line, or Eli Thayer's Popular Sovereignty, it is all the same. Let either be done, and immediately filibustering, and extending slavery recommences. On that point hold firm, as with a chain of steel.   Yours as ever,

A. Lincoln.

Again, on the twenty-first of December, he wrote as follows:

Confidential

SPRINGFIELD, ILL., DEC. 21, 1860.

Hon. E. B. Washburne—My Dear Sir: Last night I received your letter, giving an account of your interview with General Scott, and for which I thank you. Please present my respects to the General, and tell him confidentially, I shall be obliged to him to be as well prepared as he can to either *hold,* or retake, the forts, as the case may require, at and after the inauguration.

Yours as ever,

A. Lincoln.

When Lincoln came to the presidency, the government was crippled not only by the impotence of Buchanan, but by participation in the government until the very eve of his inauguration of men already committed to the Confederacy. Honorable Isaac N. Arnold, who spoke out of personal knowledge, says:

There was a meeting held at the capital on the night of January 5th, [1861], at which Jefferson Davis, Senators Toombs, Iverson, Slidell, Benjamin, Wigfall, and other leading conspirators were present. They resolved in secret conclave to precipitate secession and disunion as soon as possible, and at the same time resolved that senators and members of the House should remain in their seats at the Capitol as long as possible, to watch and control the action of the Executive, and thwart and defeat any hostile measures proposed.

In accordance with concerted plans, some of the senators and members, as the states they represented passed ordinances of secession, retired from the Senate and House of Representatives. Some went forth, breathing war and vengeance, others expressing deep feeling and regret. Nearly all were careful to draw their pay, stationery, and documents, and their mileage home from the treasury of the government which they went forth avowedly to overthrow. There were two honorable exceptions among the representatives from the Gulf states—Mr. Bouligny, representative from New Orleans, and Andrew J. Hamilton, from Texas. They remained true to the Union.*

Men like Jefferson Davis, who were already chosen to offices under the Confederate Government, had withdrawn before the inauguration of Lincoln, but not a few of those who later fought against the Federal Government retained their seats in Congress until their terms expired on March 4, 1861. Not only their votes but their active influence in Washington did much to demoralize the government.

Not all of the division was between the North and South. The loyal element in the South was much larger than is commonly known. On the other hand, a very large section of the North was opposed to the employment of forcible measures to retain within the Union any state that desired to go out of it. Even Horace Greeley declared that when any state or group of states desired to go out of the Union he would oppose all coercive measures to keep them in. Greeley changed his mind about this as he did about some other matters. Greeley with all his inconsistencies, was loyal to the government, though sorely perplexed as to the best way for the government to function in that trying emergency.

There was a strong element in the North which sympathized actively with the South. Of its distribution and influence we shall take note hereafter.

---

*Life of Lincoln, p. 177.

Of Lincoln's living predecessors in office, Millard Fillmore, then living at an advanced age in quiet retirement in New York State, was the only one who could be said to sympathize with Lincoln. Buchanan's course has already been noted. John Tyler died January 18, 1862, a member of the Confederate Congress. Franklin Pierce, though a northern man, wrote on January 6, 1860, to Jefferson Davis:

If through the madness of Northern Abolitionists, that dire calamity (disruption of the Union), must come, the fighting will not be along Mason and Dixon's line merely. It will be *within our own borders, in our own streets,* between the two classes of citizens to whom I have referred. Those who defy law and scout constitutional obligation, will, if we ever reach the arbitratement of arms, find occupation enough at home.

But must there be war? Both North and South earnestly hoped that this would not be found necessary; yet steadily and inevitably, day by day, the war drew nearer.

It would seem as if the South would have realized at the outset the hopelessness of a war. It had a much smaller population, and no manufactures. If it went to war, and the war continued until the issue became a question of men and resources, the South was doomed to defeat before a single gun was fired.

On the other hand the South had marked advantages in case of any attempt to maintain the Union by force. As it would presumably act on the defensive, it needed fewer men. Its slave population was available for the support of the army, leaving its white men free for military service. Many of the ablest officers in the United States Army were southern men; indeed, most of the Confederate generals of note had been educated at West Point. But the South had no navy, and as it could not look to the North for manufactured products, it would have to depend for them upon Europe.

Hostilities had really begun before Lincoln was inaugurated. Most of the southern forts and arsenals had been surrendered.

Norfolk with two thousand cannon had been handed over to the Confederates. Harper's Ferry had been menaced and abandoned. Of all the forts in all the seceded states only Key West, at the tip of Florida, Fort Pickens at Pensacola, and Fort Sumter in Charleston Harbor, South Carolina, remained in possession of the Federal Government. Of these the most conspicuous was Fort Sumter, then garrisoned by a small force under Major Robert Anderson. Lincoln came to the presidential chair with the knowledge that he must soon decide whether to permit Fort Sumter to be captured by assault, or to be starved into surrender, or whether he would undertake to relieve its beleaguered garrison. If he did this, he knew that he must assume responsibility for being charged with the outbreak of hostilities.

On the morning following his inauguration, Lincoln went to his office in the White House and found a letter from Mr. Holt, who was still acting as secretary of war, informing him that Fort Sumter must be reenforced or else abandoned. Major Robert Anderson had in the previous week taken stock of his provision and sent a report which arrived on the morning of the inauguration. He had food enough to last him about four weeks, or possibly, by careful conservation of rations, for forty days.

On Saturday night, March ninth, Lincoln held his first Cabinet meeting. On that day Lincoln had submitted to General Scott the question whether Fort Sumter ought to be relieved or abandoned. General Scott advised the evacuation of the fort. On March fifteenth, Lincoln laid the whole question before his Cabinet, and asked for a written answer to the question:

Assuming it to be possible to now provision Fort Sumter, under all the circumstances, is it wise to attempt it?

Five members of the Cabinet voted in the negative; they were Seward, Cameron, Welles, Smith and Bates. Seward argued the question at some length. To attempt to provision Sumter would provoke the beginning of hostilities. The slave states still hesitating between the Union and rebellion would be driven over to the side of the South. Sumter was practically useless; it was important that the Union be saved without bloodshed if possible. The two who voted in favor of the relief of Sumter were Chase and Blair.

The first state dinner at the White House occurred on the evening of March twenty-eighth. Just before the party broke up, Lincoln called the members of his Cabinet into an adjoining room and informed them that General Scott had advised in the interests of conciliation that both Fort Sumter and Fort Pickens be given up.

That night Abraham Lincoln's eyes did not close in sleep.

It was Lincoln himself who finally reached the determination to relieve Fort Sumter in the matter of provisions, but not with arms and ammunition. There was indeed a plan that the unarmed vessel carrying the provisions should be followed at no great distance by a sufficient naval force to effect an entrance if necessary. This plan, through a complication involving cross-purposes between Seward and Welles, did not materialize; but Lincoln determined to "send bread to Anderson." He also caused it to be known that he was sending bread only, and not bullets. On April sixth Lincoln ordered the provisioning of Sumter. Pacific and conciliatory as this announcement was intended to be, it did not satisfy the impatient Confederate authorities. The attempt to carry food to Fort Sumter they chose to regard as an invasion of the South.

CHAPTER V

THE Confederate Government was closely patterned after that of the Government of the United States. This was occasion both of strength and weakness in the new organization. It was a form so familiar that the leaders on the southern side were able to get to work at once under methods of administration with which they were familiar; but it carried over existing rivalries and created offices which it was not always easy to fill. Certain southern writers maintain that the South suffered because it had to have a president and had no available man except Jefferson Davis, while possessing many men who thought themselves superior to him in fitness for the position. Jefferson Davis left the United States Senate nearly two months before Lincoln's inauguration. He was elected provisional president of the Confederacy February 9, 1861, his formal election to the presidency occurring some months later. His inauguration took place February eighteenth, fifteen days before that of Lincoln.

For several weeks after their inauguration both presidents pursued a waiting policy. Neither Abraham Lincoln nor Jefferson Davis wished to take the initiative in what threatened to be a civil war. The Confederate Government appointed three commissioners to go to Washington to inform President Lincoln that seven states had withdrawn from the Union and become an independent nation, and to arrange for an adjustment, on terms of amity and good-will, all questions arising out of the separation. These three commissioners were John Forsythe, André B. Roman and Martin J. Crawford.

Crawford arrived in Washington the day before Lincoln's inauguration, and Forsythe arrived a day or two later. These men, believing Seward to be the real power of the new administration, and feeling assured of Seward's earnest desire that war should be averted, endeavored to come to an understanding with the new secretary of state. In the negotiations between these commissioners and the secretary, the go-between was Judge John A. Campbell, an associate justice of the United States Supreme Court, whose conduct in the matter is not above reproach. To him Seward confided his belief that Fort Sumter would not be reinforced, and that if hostilities were averted, the fort must of necessity be evacuated before many weeks. This opinion, which the president and the Cabinet shared, the commissioners accepted as a pledge of the government. Seward was incautious in making this statement, but there is no ground for the charge that he was disloyal to Lincoln or untrue in his representations to Campbell and through him to the commissioners. As we know, the time came when Lincoln determined to relieve Sumter, sending provisions but not arms. This announcement was heralded by certain Confederate authorities, and is still proclaimed by superficial critics, as a violation of agreement. This became the pretext of the Confederates for firing upon Sumter.

As a matter of fact the tension on both sides had been increasing from the time of Lincoln's inauguration. It would not have been possible much longer to avert some act of hostility. Aristotle taught "The causes of war are profound, but the occasions of war are slight." Any one of several events might have brought on war. The firing upon Sumter, however, was not the act of a mob, it was the authorized act of the Confederate Government.

On April twelfth the batteries which had been erected on the shores of Charleston Harbor opened fire upon Fort Sumter. Major Robert Anderson returned the fire. The fort, after thirty-four hours of bombardment, surrendered, the garrison marching out with the honors of war. It can not quite be said that Sumter was forced to surrender. No one had been hurt, and provisions were not exhausted; but an honorable defense had been made, and no relief was expected.

The fall of Fort Sumter unified the North and also unified the South. It hastened the decision of Virginia to enter the Confederacy, and thus forced the line of the seceded states to the bank of the Potomac opposite Washington. It removed from the South the last vestige of belief that the North was not in deadly earnest.

The effect upon the North was not less significant. To the special session of Congress convened shortly after, Lincoln thus defined the issue:

The assault upon and reduction of Fort Sumter was in no sense a matter of self-defense on the part of the assailants. They well knew that the garrison in the fort could by no possibility commit aggression upon them. They knew—they were expressly notified—that the giving of bread to the few brave and hungry men of the garrison was all which would on that occasion be attempted, unless themselves, by resisting so much, should provoke more. They knew that this government desired to keep the garrison in the fort, not to assail them, but merely to maintain visible possession, and thus to preserve the Union from actual and immediate dissolution—trusting, as hereinbefore stated, to time, discussion, and the ballot-box for final adjustment; and they assailed and reduced the fort for precisely the reverse object—to drive out the visible authority of the Federal Union, and thus force it to immediate dissolution. . . .

And this issue embraces more than the fate of these United States. It presents to the whole family of man the question whether a constitutional republic or democracy—a government of the people by the same people—can or can not maintain its territorial integrity against its own domestic foes. . . .

So viewing the issue, no choice was left but to call out the war power of the government; and so to resist force employed for its destruction, by force for its preservation.

Two days after the fall of Fort Sumter Lincoln issued a call for seventy-five thousand volunteers to serve for three months, "to maintain the honor, the integrity and the existence of our national Union." The response was immediate and hearty. The number of men who volunteered was far in excess of the number called for. The men who responded had no doubt that the ninety days of their enlistment would be more than ample to put down the rebellion.

Jefferson Davis answered Lincoln's call for troops with a desperate effort to build up the southern navy under the offer to issue letters of marque and reprisal against the United States. Lincoln on the nineteenth of April, proclaimed a partial, and on the twenty-third, a general blockade of southern ports. The Confederate States, assuming to be an independent power, formally declared war against the United States.

Meantime, Washington was in peril. Confederate troops mustered and drilled within plain sight of the city. The handful of regular troops in Washington was entirely inadequate for the protection of the nation's capital. The first regiments of those who responded to Lincoln's proclamation were hastened by the shortest route to Washington. The route lay through Baltimore.

Eminent military authorities assert that progress in the manufacture of weapons of war results in relative security of life. If two men fight with knives, one is likely to be killed and the other badly wounded in five minutes; but the same men in rifle-pits a mile apart may shoot at each other from time to time all winter and both emerge safe in the spring. The bombardment of Fort Sumter lasted thirty-four hours, and not a drop of blood was shed on either side. That was something for which both sides were thankful. Both governments resolved to be very careful not to do anything which should cause it to bear the onus of shedding the first blood; and each vainly hoped that if bloodshed could be postponed a little longer, actual war might be averted.

The first bloodshed was not in pitched battle, nor was it

authorized by either government. It was an attack by a mob, on April nineteenth, on the Sixth Massachusetts Regiment passing through Baltimore on its way to Washington. To their credit, it should be recorded that the mayor of the city and the marshal of the police force faithfully endeavored to quell the riot, but were unable to do so. The soldiers were compelled to defend themselves, and they returned the fire of the rioters. Four soldiers were killed and thirty-six were wounded. Of the mob twelve were killed and the number of wounded was not accurately reported. It could not longer be said, however, that the conflict was bloodless. The anniversary of the battle of Lexington had been celebrated by the first shedding of blood between the North and South.

Wild rumors filled Washington and came up to the White House, announcing that the Rebels were marching from Baltimore and about to take Washington. It seemed as though the nation's capital might at any time fall into the hands of the Confederates. It is impossible to exaggerate the consternation felt at Washington after this fatal incident.

On the following day and the next, delegations from Baltimore waited upon Lincoln earnestly beseeching him not to permit any more troops to pass through that city. Although there was only one railroad at that time connecting Washington with the North, and that railroad passed through Baltimore, Lincoln tactfully considered the request. For a few days the troops sailed down Chesapeake Bay to Annapolis, and thus reached Washington without passing through Baltimore. This arrangement, however, was only temporary. In a few days Baltimore was open to the unrestricted passage of Union troops.

The days that followed in the White House were days of extreme depression. Expected reenforcements from Massachusetts and Rhode Island did not arrive. On April twenty-fourth John Hay entered in his diary:

This has been a day of gloom and doubt. Everybody seems

filled with a vague distrust and recklessness. The idea seemed to be reached by Lincoln when chatting with the volunteers this morning, he said, "I don't believe there is any North! The Seventh Regiment is a myth! Rhode Island is not known in our geography any longer. You are the only northern realities." Seward's messengers, sent out by the dozen do not return. The Seventh and Butler's are probably still at Annapolis. A rumor this evening says the railroad is in the hands of the government, and the sappers and miners are at work repairing it.

The Seventh New York Regiment was at Annapolis, having sailed down Chesapeake Bay to avoid Baltimore. But the railroad between Annapolis and Washington had been put out of commission. It is amazing that with Annapolis so near to Washington there should have been any lack of certainty as to the presence there of any body of troops, or of their progress toward Washington. It almost passes belief that Seward's messengers should have brought back no tidings. But the rumors which were current on the twenty-fourth proved to be well founded. The next day brought the first train load of troops of the Seventh New York. The capital began to have some faint measure of faith in its own security. The Seventh New York drew up on the White House lawn, weary and dirty from their labor in repairing the railroad, and Lincoln personally received them. Indeed, it became his custom to receive regiments that came for the relief of Washington. The next day General Benjamin F. Butler arrived with fourteen hundred soldiers, and Rhode Island justified her claim to a place on the map by the arrival of twelve hundred troops. Within a few days the total number of troops in Washington is said to have been seventeen thousand. The capital was defended.

The Confederate Congress held only a brief and preliminary session at Montgomery, Alabama. Three days before the people of Virginia were to vote upon the question of secession, the capital of the Confederates was removed to Richmond. The Confederate Congress meeting in Montgomery, adjourned to meet in Richmond on July 20, 1861. The Federal Congress had been called by Lincoln to meet in Washington on July fourth. Immediately there went up a cry from the North declaring that the Rebel Congress ought not to be permitted to meet. Richmond should be occupied by Federal troops, and the meeting of this disloyal Congress prevented. The demand for an advance on Richmond began even before the fall of Sumter, and grew loud and strong after that event.

The two congresses met, the Federal Congress in Washington and the Confederate in Richmond. These two cities are not far apart. The ninety days of the first troops were approaching the expiration of the period of their enlistment. Unless an advance was made soon, the seventy-five thousand would go back to their homes and leave the country without an army.

Ought Abraham Lincoln soon after the fall of Sumter to have ordered General Scott to occupy Richmond? Ought he, as soon as he was safely seated in the presidential chair, to have sent an armed expedition to the relief of Fort Sumter? These are among the questions concerning which debate will be perpetually permissible. It is possible that the calmer judgment of most men will agree that on the whole the patient policy of Abraham Lincoln was better than would have been a policy more precipitate.

At the time of the fall of Sumter the total strength of the United States Army, officers and men, was 17,113. Fully a third of these were certain to withdraw and go with the South. This little band of perhaps ten thousand men was scattered in distant states, doing police duty on the frontier and keeping up the mere skeleton of army organization. As soon as the first volunteers began to arrive in response to Lincoln's proclamation, the cry for an advance on Richmond became strong throughout the North. General Scott opposed an immediate advance, believing that the troops had as yet no adequate preparation for an active campaign.

History furnishes the forum for a perpetual three-fold debate. First, there is always room for discussion concerning what actually occurred. Secondly, there is always room for difference of opinion concerning the causes of events; assuming that we have established with reasonable certainty the facts as they took place, we are then at liberty to discover if we can, who was responsible. Thirdly, there is always opportunity to discuss what would have happened if something had or had not occurred, and if somebody had done something other than he did or is believed to have done.

There is no room to question the loyalty of General Scott. He was true to his country under very trying conditions. He loved his state, Virginia, and it broke his heart to contemplate the necessity of bearing arms against her. Moreover, he had once been a candidate for president, and he did not wholly forget his political interests. It is much to his credit that he stood unfalteringly for the Union. But General Scott was an old man, and had grown cautious to the point of timidity. What would have happened if General Scott had died about the end of Buchanan's administration, and there had been in Washington a man in middle life with military training and some experience, who could have taken command of Lincoln's 75,000 men enlisted for ninety days, and marched them straight toward Richmond, drilling them as he marched? We can never know the answer to this question, but it is easy to imagine what might have happened had Andrew Jackson been in command of these volunteers when they began to assemble about Washington in April, 1861.

On July 21, 1861, the first important battle in the campaign against Richmond was fought at Bull Run, about thirty miles southwest of Washington. Like many battles that followed, this one has two names. The North called it the Battle of Bull Run, and the South called it the Battle of Manassas. Contrary to popular impression, the battle appears to have been well planned. Reenforcements for the Confederates arrived, however, at an opportune moment, and the Union retreat became a panic-stricken race for the Potomac.

We now know that the Confederates were heavy losers, and that for this reason they did not follow up their advantage. General Albert Sidney Johnston said, "The Confederate Army was more demoralized by victory than the United States Army by defeat." But no one in Washington had the comfort of this knowledge when the panic-stricken troops that had gone forth so confidently, so boastfully, returned over the Long Bridge exhausted and terrified.

Foremost among those who had cried for advance upon Richmond was Horace Greeley. After the battle of Bull Run he came in for severe criticism for having pushed an unprepared army forward to certain defeat. Greeley never admitted that he deserved this criticism. He said:

The war cry, "Forward to Richmond!" did not originate with me; but it is just what should have been uttered, and the words should have been translated into deeds. Instead of energy, vigor, promptness, daring, decision, we had in our councils weakness, irresolution, hesitation, delay; and, when at last our hastily collected forces, after being demoralized by weeks of idleness and dissipation, were sent forward, they advanced on separate lines, under different commanders; this enabling the enemy to concentrate all its forces in Virginia against a single corps of ours, defeating and stampeding it at Bull Run, while other Union volunteers, aggregating nearly twice its strength, lay idle and useless near Harper's Ferry, in and about Washington, and at Fortress Monroe. Thus what should have been a short, sharp struggle, was expanded into a long desultory one; while those whose blundering incapacity or lack of purpose was responsible for those ills, united in throwing the blame on the faithful few who had counseled justly, but whose urgent remonstrances they had never heeded.*

Whatever Greeley could find to say in defense of his "on-to-Richmond" policy before the battle of Bull Run, no possible justification can ever be suggested for his letter to Lincoln following that battle. To Greeley it seemed that the Union cause

*Recollections of a Busy Life, pp. 402-403.

was irretrievably lost, and he was ready to consider an armistice looking to the end of the war. A more hysterical and less comforting letter than the following can hardly be imagined:

New York, Monday, July 29, 1861.
Midnight.

Dear Sir: This is my seventh sleepless night—yours, too, doubtless—yet I think I shall not die, because I have no right to die. I must struggle to live, however bitterly. But to business. You are not considered a great man, and I am a hopelessly broken one. You are now undergoing a terrible ordeal, and God has thrown the greatest responsibilities upon you. Do not fear to meet them. Can the rebels be beaten after all that has occurred, and in view of the actual state of feeling caused by our late, awful disaster? If they can,—and it is your business to ascertain and decide,—write me that such is your judgment, so that I may know and do my duty. And if they *cannot* be beaten,—if our recent disaster is fatal,—do not fear to sacrifice yourself to your country. If the rebels are not to be beaten,— if that is your judgment in view of all the light you can get,— then every drop of blood henceforth shed in this quarrel will be wantonly, wickedly shed, and the guilt will rest heavily on the soul of every promoter of the crime. I pray you to decide quickly and let me know my duty.

If the Union is irrevocably gone, an armistice for 30, 60, 90, 120 days—better still for a year—ought at once to be proposed, with a view to a peaceful adjustment. Then Congress should call a national convention, to meet at the earliest possible day. And there should be an immediate and mutual exchange or release of prisoners and a disbandment of forces. I do not consider myself at present a judge of anything but public sentiment. That seems to me everywhere gathering and deepening against a prosecution of the war. The gloom in this city is funeral.— for our dead at Bull Run were many, and they lie unburied yet. On every brow sits sullen, scorching, black despair. It would have been easy to have Mr. Crittenden move any proposition that ought to be adopted, or to have it come from any proper quarter. The first point is to ascertain what is best that can be done— which is the measure of our duty, and do that very thing at the earliest moment.

This letter is written in the strictest confidence, and is for your eye alone. But you are at liberty to say to members of your cabinet that you *know* I will second any move you may see fit to make. But do nothing timidly nor by halves. Send me word what to do. I will live until I can hear it at all events. If it is best for the country and for mankind that we make peace with the rebels at once and on their own terms, do not shrink even from that. But bear in mind the greatest truth: "Whoso would lose his life for my sake shall save it." Do the thing that is the highest right, and tell me how I am to second you.

Yours, in the depths of bitterness,

Horace Greeley.

Lincoln quickly saw the importance of calling for a much larger number of men and for a longer period of service than his original proclamation contemplated. He soon learned that three months would not be long enough. He therefore urged upon Secretary Cameron the acceptance of a larger number than he originally contemplated. Regiment after regiment was added and provisions were made for their equipment and sustenance. Gradually the nation came to understand, and Lincoln earlier than many of the leaders of public opinion, that the war was to be longer and much more bitter than any one, either North or South, had supposed.

The effect of Bull Run was to convince both North and South that the war was not to be a short and easy one, but perhaps its most important result was its influence on European Governments. They believed quite generally after this battle, that superiority of leadership was with the South. With the exception of Russia, all European Governments, and especially that of England and France, tended to side with the South.

Nevertheless, it is more than possible that it was better for the Union cause that its armies did not win at Bull Run. A cheap and easy victory won at that stage of the war might have proved disastrous in the days that followed.

In the West the situation was more favorable. Under Generals Lyons, Frémont and Halleck, the Confederate forces were gradually driven out of Missouri, and that state was saved to the Union. The citizens of German birth in that state were an important factor in the attainment of this result. Kentucky, which at first officially maintained an armed neutrality, was held in the Union by regiments of her own loyal citizens. Thus was the line of the Confederacy pushed far to the south of the Missouri and Ohio Rivers. In the east, however, the Confederate flag flew within sight of the capitol, and it was considered cheering news when the papers could report that all was "quiet along the Potomac."

This is not a history of the Civil War. Many of its battles will not be mentioned. Many of its leading generals and notable events must go without recognition in these pages. Only so much is to be said about the war and those engaged in it as is necessary to our interpretation of the life of Abraham Lincoln. But the "impending crisis" long foretold by Hinton Rowan Helper, the "irrepressible conflict" of which William H. Seward had spoken, the "house divided against itself" of which Lincoln had talked in his debates with Douglas, came swiftly.

Lincoln had been careful to disclaim responsibility for John Brown, whom he regarded as an unauthorized fanatic. But the war which Lincoln found himself compelled to fight gave him unexpected fellowship with that praying old fighter. Not without reason did Lincoln's seventy-five thousand volunteers rally to the defense of the Union, with a song about "Old John Brown." They were fighting, whether they knew it or not, for something more than a definition of the Constitution. They sang as they marched:

"John Brown's body lies a-mould'ring in the grave,
    But his soul goes marching on."

CHAPTER VI

LINCOLN AND CONGRESS

THE president of the United States is commander-in-chief of the Army and Navy of the United States; but he has no power to declare war, and no power to raise or appropriate money to carry on a war. These functions belong to the Congress. But there are certain powers which the Constitution recognizes but does not definitely locate. Even in times of peace it is not easy to say just where the powers of Congress end and those of the president begin; and the extraordinary necessities of war give opportunity for much misunderstanding and friction. Lincoln had seen little of Congress since his own membership for a single term in 1847-8. He had opportunity to behold Congress in session, and to feel its atmosphere a few days before his inauguration.

Lincoln's reception in that Congress was none too favorable. When he reached Washington, the Congress then sitting was near its end. Some of its most prominent members were concluding their service and were about to depart, some to their districts that had elected as their successors men of the new party, and others to the Confederacy, with which already they were virtually identified. Adam Gurowski, in his entertaining *Diary,* in which he claimed to record events as rapidly as they occurred and impressions while yet they were fresh, began his orderly chronicle with the inauguration, but going back for a few days for an introduction to his narrative, wrote:

Some days previous to the inauguration, Mr. Seward brought Mr. Lincoln on the Senate floor, of course on the Republican side; but soon Mr. Seward was busily running among Demo-

crats, begging them to be introduced to Mr. Lincoln. It was
a saddening, humiliating and revolting sight for the galleries,
where I was. Criminal as is Mason, for a minute I got reconciled to him for the scowl of horror and contempt with which
he shook his head at Seward. Only two or three Democratic
Senators were moved by Seward's humble entreaties.*

Ethan Allen is alleged to have demanded the surrender of
Fort Ticonderoga "in the name of the Great Jehovah and the
Continental Congress." It seems almost a pity to learn that this
story does not rest on secure foundation. We should like to discover the Congress of the United States in more normal alignment with the Divine purpose, and in more frequent appeal to
the heroic. During the Revolution, Congress was small comfort
to Washington, and during the Civil War it was sometimes a
thorn in the flesh of Lincoln.

Lincoln's first message to Congress, when that body assembled on July 4, 1861, was a very different document from his
inaugural address. It recited the events which had occurred during his four months of office. It gave a detailed account of
matters relating to Fort Sumter and the call for volunteers. It
recited that after the first call for troops it had been necessary
to increase the number of volunteers to three hundred thousand
and extend the period of service to three years. These calls for
troops he believed to have been justified by "a popular demand
and a public necessity." He did not discuss whether these measures were strictly legal or not. He believed that Congress
would readily ratify them.

The body of the message was a discussion of the question of
the right of secession. This right he denied in the most explicit
terms and in an extended argument. He declared the theory of
the right of secession to be "an ingenious sophism, which if conceded, might be followed by perfectly logical steps, through all
the incidents, to the complete destruction of the Union." This
"sophism" he defined in terms of this proposition:

*Gurowski's *Diary*, p. 15.

That any State of the Union may consistently with the National Constitution, and therefore lawfully and peacefully, withdraw from the Union without the consent of the Union or of any other State.

He said:

Our popular government has often been called an experiment. Two points in it our people have already settled—the successful establishing and the successful administering of it. One still remains—its successful maintenance against a formidable internal attempt to overthrow it. It is now for them to demonstrate to the world that those who can fairly carry an election can also suppress a rebellion; that ballots are the rightful and peaceful successors of bullets; and that when ballots have fairly and constitutionally decided, there can be no successful appeal back to bullets; that there can be no successful appeal, except to ballots themselves, at succeeding elections. Such will be a great lesson of peace; teaching men that what they cannot take by an election, neither can they take it by a war; teaching all the folly of being the beginners of a war.

He considered the fact that certain of the states, as for instance Florida, had involved the government in large expense, either for their purchase price or for expenses incurred in repelling Indian attacks or in the settlement of the claims of the Indian tribes for compensation for the land. Were these states at liberty to withdraw from the Union and leave the remaining states to discharge these obligations? Suppose all the states should secede but one; would that one remaining state be responsible for the debts incurred by the Federal Government of which it was now the sole remainder? Suppose the one remaining state decided to secede, who then would remain responsible for the obligations incurred by the nation?

Avowedly his inaugural address was an appeal to the plain people. So also was Lincoln's first message to Congress. It was couched in language easily understood; but it was a very statesmanlike document, and one deserving at once the attention not only of Congress but of the people.

Lincoln also had in mind the border states, especially Kentucky. Virginia had gone over to secession, but Kentucky was keeping up the pretense of an armed neutrality. For the sake of the border states and also as an appeal to the loyal element in the seceded states he set forth his own purpose with respect to the southern states after the rebellion should be suppressed:

Lest there be some uneasiness in the minds of candid men as to what is to be the course of the government toward the Southern States after the rebellion shall have been suppressed, the executive deems it proper to say it will be his purpose then, as ever, to be guided by the Constitution and the laws; and that he probably will have no different understanding of the powers and duties of the Federal Government relatively to the rights of the States and the people, under the Constitution, than that expressed in the inaugural address.

He desires to preserve the government, that it may be administered for all as it was administered by the men who made it. Loyal citizens everywhere have the right to claim this of their government, and the government has no right to withhold or neglect it. It is not perceived that in giving it there is any coercion, any conquest or any subjugation, in any just sense of those terms.

The Constitution provides, and all the States have accepted the provision, that 'the United States shall guarantee to every State in this Union a republican form of government.' But if a State may lawfully go out of the Union, having done so, it may also discard the republican form of government; so that to prevent its going out is an indispensable means to the end of maintaining the guarantee mentioned; and when an end is lawful and obligatory, the indispensable means to it are also lawful and obligatory.

It was with the deepest regret that the executive found the duty of employing the war power in defense of the government forced upon him. He could but perform this duty or surrender the existence of the government. No compromise by public servants could, in this case be a cure; not that compromises are not often proper, but that no popular government can long survive a marked precedent that those who carry an election can only save the government from immediate destruction by giving up the main point upon which the people gave the election. The people themselves, and not their servants, can safely reverse their own deliberate decisions.

One important fact about this first message of Lincoln's to Congress must not be overlooked. It had virtually no reference to slavery. In this respect it was a decided contrast to the first inaugural. This fact disturbed the abolitionists, but did not rouse immediate criticism to any marked extent. It is to be noted, however, that from this time forward Lincoln was centering his thought upon his primary duty of saving the Union. How far he seemed to some of his associates to have departed from the principles laid down by him in his debate with Douglas, we shall have occasion later to consider. Whether Lincoln was conscious of it or not, this new emphasis on the Union was exactly in line with the suggestions in Seward's "Thoughts"—"Change the question before the public from one upon slavery, or about slavery, for a question upon Union or Disunion."

Congress assembled in a good temper and with a strong working majority on the side of the president. His appropriation proposals were fully met, and his requirements for troops were authorized. As yet the Republican Party had not seriously broken into factions. At this extraordinary session there was almost no ordinary legislation. Congress was in session twenty-nine working days, from July fourth to August sixth. Seventy-six public acts were passed, of which seventy-two bore directly upon the war.

At the same time, Congress can not be said to have had any adequate appreciation of the situation as it existed prior to the battle of Bull Run. Congress believed that that first battle would settle the whole problem. Not a few members of Congress drove across the Long Bridge and toward the front in their joyous anticipation of seeing the rebellion wiped off the map at a single stroke. These men returned to Washington sadder and wiser.

On the day following the battle of Bull Run, John J. Crittenden, of Kentucky, rose to introduce a resolution in the House, and offered a program very different from the famous Crittenden Compromise. That Compromise had failed. Now he offered:

That the present, deplorable civil war had been forced upon the country by the Disunionists of the Southern States, now in arms against the constitutional government, and in arms around the capital; that in this national emergency, Congress, banishing all feelings of mere passion and resentment, will recollect only its duty to the whole country; that this war is not waged on their part in any spirit of oppression or for any purpose of conquest or subjugation, or purpose of overthrowing or interfering with the rights or established institutions of these States, but to defend and maintain the supremacy of the Constitution, and to preserve the Union, with all the dignity, equality, and rights of the several States unimpaired; and that as soon as these objects are accomplished, the war ought to cease.

The Crittenden Resolution was passed in both Houses; there was no debate, and virtually no opposition. Two members of the House of Representatives, however, refrained from voting. They were Thaddeus Stevens and Owen Lovejoy. In the Senate, five men did not vote for the resolution. One of these was Charles Sumner. The reason for their silence was, of course, that the resolution did not specify the overthrow of slavery as a main objective of the war. Mr. Crittenden still had manifestly in mind an appeal to the sentiment of Kentucky and the other slave states not yet in rebellion. Lincoln was in the fullest sympathy with that attitude of mind. He seemed to the extreme abolitionists to have forgotten entirely the anti-slavery issue.

At this first session, however, Congress began a series of legislative acts unfavorable to slavery. On August 6, 1861, a bill introduced by Senator Lyman Trumbull, became a law giving freedom to all slaves that had been employed by the Confederates in carrying on the war. A little later Owen Lovejoy introduced a resolution declaring that it was no part of the duty of the soldiers of the United States to capture and return fugitive slaves. This passed the House by a large majority; and while it did not repeal the Fugitive Slave Law, it was a triumph for the man who two years before, in February, 1859, during his first term in Congress, had replied to the charge of southern Representatives that he was a "Nigger stealer":

"Yes, I do assist fugitives to escape. Proclaim it upon the housetops; write it upon every leaf that trembles in the forest; make it blaze from the sun at high noon, and shine forth in the radiance of every star that bedecks the firmament of God. Let it echo through all the arches of heaven, and reverberate and bellow through all the deep gorges of hell, where slavecatchers will be very likely to hear it. Owen Lovejoy lives at Princeton, Illinois, and he aids every fugitive that comes to his door and asks it. Thou invisible demon of slavery! Dost thou think to cross my humble threshold, and forbid me to give bread to the hungry and shelter to the homeless? I bid you defiance in the name of God."

Shortly after the assembly of Congress, December 2, 1861, Honorable Zachariah Chandler, of Michigan, introduced a resolution to appoint a committee of three to inquire into the conduct of the battle of Balls Bluff, and the reason for that disaster. He said that the defect had been attributed "to civilians, to politics, to everything but the right cause," and that it was "due to the Senate and the country, that the blame should rest where it belonged."

The motion prevailed, and Senator Chandler declining the chairmanship, Senator Benjamin F. Wade, of Ohio, was made chairman, with Senator Zachariah Chandler, of Michigan, and Senator Andrew Johnson, of Tennessee, as his associates. The House of Representatives appointed as its members of the committee, David W. Gooch, of Massachusetts, John Covode, of Pennsylvania, George W. Julian, of Indiana, and Moses F. Odell, of New York.

This committee, having investigated the defeat of Balls Bluff, and having agreed in its report that the disaster occurred through military incompetence, was not permitted to depart in peace. There was occasion soon to investigate the defeat at Bull Run, and from that time the committee was never without employment. Its membership changed somewhat, but it was dominated throughout by Wade and Chandler, two honest and uncompromising men, whose strong convictions were far from being always in accord with the views of the president. These men hated McClellan, and later came to dislike Meade. They thought Lincoln far too timid and given to compromise. Some authors have represented Lincoln as continually in conflict with the Congressional Committee on the Conduct of the War, and at times it was so; but at other times the committee was of large assistance to him and to Secretary Stanton. This committee was in almost continuous session until March 4, 1865, when it was given ninety days to finish its work, its final report bearing date of May 22, 1865.

The Committee on the Conduct of the War was only one of the president's perplexities. So far as any question remained whether the president or Congress was master, Lincoln abated no jot of his contention. The president, as commander-in-chief of the army and navy, must assume and maintain supreme command. But the press of the country was of many minds regarding Lincoln; and besides the war that he had to fight against the Confederates in front, he had to fight other battles with foes, open and secret, in his rear. Besides these were friends, some of them pretended and some real, and not all of them wise, whose efforts constantly embarrassed him. There were wars and rumors of wars; and Lincoln could have said with St. Paul, that his flesh had no rest; without were fightings and within were fears.

The Constitution recognized that in time of war it might be necessary to suspend the writ of *habeas corpus;* but who had the right to declare a suspension of *habeas corpus,* and to hold suspected men and women in prison without trial? Was this re-

sponsibility vested in the Congress or in the president? Very largely the members of Lincoln's own party in Congress held that
these powers belonged to Congress, but Lincoln assumed that
they belonged to the executive.   As the war proceeded, arrests
grew frequent, and the Federal prisons in Washington and elsewhere filled with men and women who were unable to secure
through the civil courts their constitutional peace-time right of
trial.   Was this arbitrary power one which the constitution intended to lodge with the president?   If so, what was the Government of the United States but a military despotism?   This
question was asked by newspapers and orators in many parts of
the country; and it was asked very insistently by certain members of Congress.

There is no way to wage a war gently.   Washington was full
of Confederate spies, and many of them escaped detection and
arrest in spite of the powers assumed by the president.   But the
president believed that these powers, in time of war, must belong
to the commander-in-chief of the army; that is, to the president.
Congress could not well exercise this function, nor did Lincoln
believe that the Constitution recognized Congress as capable of
its exercise; but this opinion of the president was not popular in
Congress, nor yet among the Copperheads.   President Lincoln
had before him a long and hard fight concerning the areas of
power which the government does not assume in time of peace,
nor definitely locate in time of war.   Lincoln was a cautious
man, but such power as he believed was necessary to the conduct
of the war, he assumed; and in time there was loud wailing in
protest in Congress.

If Lincoln ever replied to these criticisms we do not know it.
Certain distinguished lawyers wrote briefs defending the president's assumption of extraordinary powers in war times, and
some of his strong supporters in Congress gave utterance to
views so fully in accord with the position which Lincoln assumed, that some authors believe their addresses to have been
inspired by Lincoln.   Senator Browning, on March 10, 1862,

delivered an address which one brilliant biographer of Lincoln is confident "Surely was inspired—or if not directly inspired, so close a reflection of the president's thinking that it comes to the same thing in the end."* But the remarkable fact is that neither Browning nor any other of the defenders of Lincoln claimed Lincoln's authority for their utterances. At the time when Browning delivered this address, he was calling at the White House almost daily, but did not record in his *Diary* any intimation that what he said on this subject was suggested by the president or that the president thanked him for it.

Lincoln all this time was keeping in close touch with those members of both Houses who could best interpret his spirit to Congress, but no one of these men had the comfortable feeling that he was the president's spokesman.

On the whole, Congress supported the president, and the legislation of the long session was intended to be in accord with his plans. But still he knew that there was a deep-seated occasion of difference between him and the law-making body, and he intended to retain all his powers under the Constitution, and in addition to hold to those that he deemed necessary to him as commander-in-chief of the army.

Lincoln seldom made a pun, a fact which is mentioned elsewhere in this work. He made one toward the end of the first session of Congress. A member of the opposition called upon him, and somewhat testily commented on the fact that the welfare of the negro had had so large a place in the discussions of that session. He said, "Mr. President, we have had Nigger served to us three times a day regularly, dished up in every possible style." Lincoln had learned a new culinary term. He knew about roast chicken, and boiled chicken, and especially about fried chicken, but he had had occasion to learn a new French way of serving that familiar bird. When he was told of the monotony of a diet of Nigger, and of the styles in which

*Professor N. W. Stephenson, in *Lincoln,* p. 216.

it had been served to Congress, he said, "The principal style, I think, was *free-cuss-ee.*"

When Congress adjourned, and Lincoln saw the members departing, he chuckled, and said:

"In 1831, I went to New Orleans on a flat-boat, and we tied up for a day at Alton. The gate of the State Prison opened, and a group of men came out. I inquired who they were and where they were going, and I was told that they were a lot of thieves, going home. They had served their time!"

THE battle of Bull Run made one fact ominously plain; the army must have a younger commanding officer than General Scott. Able and experienced as he was, he was not in condition to fight in the field; and the army needed a visible head. General Scott remained first in command; but Lincoln must already have convinced himself that a younger man must assume the active leadership; and he thought he knew the man.

On the day after the battle of Bull Run, Lincoln summoned General George B. McClellan to Washington. He arrived on the twenty-eighth of July. On the day before his arrival Lincoln appointed him commander of the Army of the Potomac.

McClellan at this time was thirty-four years old. He was in full physical vigor and of fine appearance and bearing. He was a West Point graduate of the class of 1846. He had distinguished himself under General Scott in the Mexican War. He entered the war at the age of nineteen, with the rank of second lieutenant, having recently graduated from West Point; he emerged with the brevet rank of captain, and had won his promotion by undoubted gallantry on the field of battle. When Jefferson Davis was secretary of war in 1855, he sent Captain McClellan to Europe to study army organization, and McClellan was with the British Army during the siege of Sebastopol. After the war he had a varied and successful career. He was for a time chief engineer of the Illinois Central Railroad Company, and later its vice-president. In that capacity he met Abraham Lincoln in connection with certain litigation of the company. In later years he recalled that acquaintance:

More than once I have been with him in out-of-the-way county-seats where some important case was being tried, and, in the
lack of sleeping accommodations, have spent the night in front
of a stove listening to the unceasing flow of anecdotes from
his lips. He was never at a loss for a story, and I could never
make up my mind how many of them he had really heard before, and how many he invented on the spur of the moment.
His stories were seldom refined, but were always to the point.

McClellan was far from being a partisan of Lincoln in his
campaign against Douglas. On the contrary, Douglas traveled
in McClellan's private car, and Lincoln rode on regular trains.

The early military record of General McClellan was one of
success. At the outbreak of the war he was commissioned a
major general in command of the Department of the Ohio. In
a series of engagements in Western Virginia he was notably
successful. Any Union success at that time was vastly encouraging. McClellan's victories were not large, but they were decisive; and he himself turned them to good account in a series
of well-phrased proclamations which he issued from a portable
printing press.

It is not remarkable that the country made McClellan its first
military idol. No one of the generals who came earlier to public
notice combined in anything like the same degree such elements
for popularity. He was handsome, he was well educated, he
had a record of success. On horseback he appeared to good advantage. His features, his pose, his military bearing all combined to win for him an admiration and affection bordering upon
idolatry.

Furthermore, he was a man of integrity and of deep religious
feeling. In his private life he was as pure as Sir Galahad He
possessed a rare power of inspiring confidence and devotion.
Of all the tragedies of the Civil War, and they were not few,
there is none that fills the student with keener sorrow than that
of this brilliant officer. He seemed not only by far the best
man whom Lincoln could have chosen, but a man especially
raised up to meet the nation's need.

22

If Lincoln remembered having met McClellan in the days of his debates with Douglas—and it would seem that he must have remembered him—he could not have forgotten that, although he was attorney for the railroad of which McClellan was then the managing vice-president, he had ridden over that road throughout the campaign with entire lack of such courtesies as McClellan provided for Douglas. Had Lincoln been a man who cherished resentments, some annoying memories must have occurred to him. Lincoln was not naturally inclined to take notice of slights of this character; they made little impression on him, and to that extent he may deserve less credit than a more sensitive man. But it is equally true, and for this Lincoln deserves the highest credit, that in so far as he noticed personal slights or annoyances, he does not appear ever to have permitted personal resentment to influence his sense of duty to the public good. Had he commented on McClellan's conduct in those days, he probably would have said that the Illinois Central Railway, in permitting him to travel on a pass, was doing its full duty by him as one of the attorneys of the road; and that if Captain McClellan chose, on grounds of personal or political friendship, to do more than that for Douglas, that was his privilege. Lincoln is not known ever to have commented on this discrimination; much less did he permit it to influence him in his selection of a general to command the armies between Washington and Richmond.

What McClellan might have done had he possessed executive ability as well as organizing power, we do not know. At the best his task would not have been an easy one. At this time there were pouring into Washington large numbers of men, but they did not constitute an army. They were raw, undisciplined and unsoldierly. McClellan was well able to drill them, and it was believed that he was capable of commanding them, but the country's faith in his leadership was destined to repeated and heartbreaking disappointments.

When McClellan took command of the Army of the Potomac

there were in and about the city of Washington according to his own reports about "50,000 infantry, less than 1,000 cavalry and 650 artillerymen with nine imperfect field batteries of thirty pieces." On October twenty-seventh, three months after General McClellan took command, he reported for the army under him an aggregate strength of 168,318 men, of whom there were present for duty 147,695. The adjutant general three days later made a report for the Army of the Potomac showing a total army of 198,238, of whom 116,737 were present and available for duty.

For a time McClellan was in high spirits. His indiscreet biographer, endeavoring to show how unjustly McClellan had been treated, gave to the world McClellan's confidential letters to his wife. He arrived in Washington July 26, 1861, and assumed command on the following day. His first letter to his wife says:

I find myself in a new and strange position here; President, cabinet, General Scott and all deferring to me. By some strange operation of magic I seem to have become the power of the land.

On July thirtieth he wrote:

They give me my way in everything, full swing and unbounded confidence. Who would have thought when we were married that I should so soon be called upon to save my country?

A few days later he wrote:

I shall carry this thing on *en grand,* and crush the rebels in one campaign.

On August ninth he wrote:

I would cheerfully take the dictatorship and agree to lay down my life when the country was saved.

To make sure that his wife understood how fully he retained

his modesty in all this recognition of his own importance, he said: "I am not spoiled by my unexpected new position."

McClellan combined in himself a strange admixture of confidence in himself and distrust of his resources. His faith in his own ability and of the importance attaching to his personality was almost pathetic; but with it he cherished an amazing inability to appreciate the strength of the army under him, while invariably multiplying the strength of the army opposed to him.

Lincoln at the beginning appears to have shared fully McClellan's own high estimate of his own ability. "I will hold McClellan's horse for him if he will win victories," said Lincoln. McClellan on his part could find no higher praise for Lincoln than this, "The president is honest and means well."

As for General Scott, McClellan counted him only a stupid old meddler, forgetting that at the time he was General Scott's subordinate. McClellan's habitual reference to him in his letters to his wife is in terms like these: "The old General always comes in the way. He understands nothing, appreciates nothing."

In McClellan's mind, everybody else was in his way; nobody understood anything or appreciated anything. He condemned as stupid meddlers or wilful obstructionists the army officials, the politicians and the president, while always magnifying the force in front of him. At a time when the opposing Confederate force was perhaps one-fourth as large as his own, he wrote to his wife:

I am here in a terrible place. The enemy has from three to four times my force. The President, the old General, cannot or will not see the true state of affairs.

At a time when Lincoln was bending all his energies to help McClellan he could write:

I have a set of men to deal with unscrupulous and false. The people think me all powerful. Never was there a greater mistake. I am thwarted and deceived by these incapables at every turn.

McClellan's enemies have been many; but his worst accusers are his own letters.

It is not surprising that McClellan found no one in Washington sufficiently great to command his respect. He found in the Cabinet "some of the greatest geese I have ever seen—enough to tax the patience of Job." He found it "sickening in the extreme" to "see the weakness and unfitness of the poor beings who control the destinies of this great country."

The president he held in undisguised contempt. He formed the habit of hiding at Stanton's house, "to dodge all enemies in the shape of browsing presidents." Stanton at this time did not conceal his own scorn of the president. McClellan did not long continue to respect Stanton's judgment in anything else, and Stanton before long lost his respect for McClellan, but so long as these two agreed in anything, they were agreed in their hostility to Lincoln.

It was inevitable that before long there would be misunderstandings between General McClellan and his superior officer, General Scott. On August eighth, 1861, McClellan wrote a letter to General Scott in which he stated that he was impelled by a sense of duty to tell General Scott how inadequate were the defenses of Washington. General Scott considered this letter offensive. He wrote to the secretary of war calling attention to the stream of irregulars pouring into the city, and complaining of the insubordination of this young junior officer. For two months the friction between the two generals grew. At length, on October twenty-first, General Scott sent to the secretary of war the following letter of resignation:

For more than three years I have been unable, from a hurt, to mount a horse or to walk more than a few paces at a time, and that with much pain. Other and new infirmities—dropsy and vertigo—admonish me that repose of mind and body, with the appliances of surgery and medicine, are necessary to add a little more to a life already protracted much beyond the usual life of man. It is under such circumstances, made doubly painful by the unnatural and unjust rebellion now raging in the Southern States of our so late prosperous and happy Union, that I am compelled to request that my name be placed on the list of army officers retired from active service. As this request is founded on an absolute right granted by a recent act of Congress, I am entirely at liberty to say that it is with deep regret that I withdraw myself, in these momentous times, from the orders of a President who has treated me with distinguished kindness and courtesy, whom I know among such personal intercourses to be patriotic, without sectional partialities or prejudices, to be highly conscientious in the performance of every duty, and of unrivalled activity and perseverance. And to you, Mr. Secretary, I beg to acknowledge my many obligations for the uniform high consideration I have received at your hands.

General Scott's resignation was accepted. He retired with high honor, the president and Cabinet waiting on him in person to present him the thanks of the country for his long and illustrious service. Immediately Lincoln appointed McClellan commander-in-chief of the Army of the United States. The president called personally at McClellan's headquarters in order to congratulate him. McClellan received him with less condescention than on some other occasions. "I should feel perfectly satisfied," said President Lincoln, "if I thought that this vast increase of responsibility would not embarrass you." He had not long to wait for his satisfaction. McClellan assured him that, far from being embarrassed, he was greatly relieved.

This was on the night of November 1, 1861, and from that time on the president and country waited for McClellan to win the one great victory which he was sure would settle the fate of the Confederacy. McClellan, however, did not move. He was busy shifting to other shoulders than his own the blame for the skirmish at Ball's Bluff which occurred on October twenty-first and ended in a Union loss of 49 men killed, 158 wounded and 694 missing, against a Confederate loss of 36 killed and 117 wounded. This engagement, which appears insignificant in comparison with later battles, was notable at the time. It was another though a smaller Bull Run. It resulted in the retirement in disgrace and imprisonment of General Stone, whose severe punishment is believed to have been unmerited, and it brought again a deep sense of personal sorrow to the White House by reason of the death of Colonel Edward D. Baker, Lincoln's long time personal friend.

John Hay made this entry in his diary on November 13, 1861:

I wish here to record what I regard a portent of evil to come. The President, Governor Seward and I went over to McClellan's house tonight. The servant at the door said the General was at the wedding of Colonel Wheaton at General Buell's and would soon return. We went in and after we had waited about an hour McClellan came in, and without paying any attention to the porter who told him the President was waiting to see him, went up stairs, passing the door where the President and the Secretary of State were seated. They waited about half an hour, and sent once more a servant to tell the General they were there; and the answer came that the General had gone to bed.

I merely record this unparalled insolence of epaulettes without comment. It is the first indication I have seen of the threatened supremacy of the military authorities.

Mr. Hay did not at the time regard this incident of particular significance as manifesting McClellan's own feelings toward the president; to Hay it then seemed a possible portent of evil as showing what the military authorities might, as a group, come to assume. It is safe to say that after all allowances had been made for military arrogance, of which many generals had their full share, there never was another general in the Union Army who could possibly thus have treated the president of the United States.

In January, 1862, Lincoln endeavored to impress McClellan with the importance of a forward movement. The country was growing restive; the president was under severe criticism. His arguments met with no response. On Washington's birthday President Lincoln ordered a general forward movement. This also, McClellan ignored. Lincoln grew almost desperate; he had desired McClellan to advance to Manassas. McClellan did not do so. But when on March ninth it became known that the Confederates had evacuated Manassas, McClellan marched his army there and then back again. This performance brought ridicule upon him and deep disappointment and chagrin to Lincoln.

Let us endeavor to do justice to McClellan. He was placed at the head of a large and increasing body of men, but he did not command an army. The first seventy-five thousand had enlisted impulsively in full confidence that ninety days was more than adequate for the purpose of their soldiering. He knew that the war must be won with men who had some discipline, and very few even of his officers realized what that discipline would involve. McClellan was an effective drill-master. He knew the value of military organization. He did not intend to have any more battles like that of Bull Run. Most well informed officers sympathized with him. But the country was restless and eager for a battle that would bring final victory.

On September ninth, McClellan reckoned his army at 85,000 effective men, and was sure the Confederates had 150,000. Month by month he increased his estimate of the forces opposed to him. Late in the autumn he had "a gross aggregate force of 168,318," with 147,695 present for duty, and he was sure the Confederates greatly outnumbered him. As a matter of fact. the Confederate Army confronting him numbered 41,000.

In December, 1861, the Congress created its Committee on the Conduct of the War. It was a committee of civilians charged with the heavy responsibility of passing judgment on military matters in which none of them were expert. McClellan did not conceal his displeasure, nor can he be blamed for his resentment.

Soon after this, on January 11, 1862, Secretary Cameron resigned his portfolio of the War Department, and was succeeded by Edwin M. Stanton, a warm personal and political friend of McClellan; but he and McClellan soon quarreled, and from that time forth were mutually hostile.

Mr. Lincoln's patience with McClellan in this trying situation can but astonish any thoughtful student. McClellan's letters to his wife display an egotism that is amazing, and a contempt for the president most ill-becoming in a general of the army. Lincoln was cautious. By all his traits of character he was disposed to carry caution to the extreme, but his caution was not to be mentioned beside McClellan's. McClellan was fertile in discovering reasons why he could not do anything. The enemies invariably outnumbered his forces beyond any hope of his winning a victory. His army was never in a condition to move; never strong enough for the work expected of it. Lincoln now and then wished that General McClellan would lend him his army if he had no plan to use it himself. Once when McClellan told him that he could not move because the army was resting, Lincoln indulged in sufficient sarcasm to ask just what he had done that should have tired any of them.

The year went by, and McClellan had done nothing worth speaking about. The spring of 1862 came, and on April third the president ordered the secretary of war to direct General McClellan "to commence his forward movement from his new base at once."

To this McClellan replied two days later, "The enemy are in large force along our front; their works formidable."

He felt sure that he would have to fight the whole Confederate Army. The official reports of General Magruder show that he had only eleven thousand men with which to oppose McClellan's one hundred thousand. And he was surprised that day after day went by and McClellan did not move. McClellan, however, was waiting for reenforcements, and Lincoln answered very kindly but firmly:

I suppose the whole force which has gone forward to you, is with you by this time, and if so, I think that it is the precise time for you to strike a blow. By delay, the enemy will relatively gain upon you—that is, he will gain faster by fortifications and re-enforcements than you can by re-enforcements alone; and

once more let me tell you, it is indispensable to you that you
strike a blow. I am powerless to help this. You will do me the
justice to remember I always insisted that going down the bay
in search of a field, instead of fighting near Manassas, was only
shifting, not surmounting the difficulty. . . . The country will
not fail to note—and it is now noting—that the present hesitation to move upon an intrenched enemy, is but the story of
Manassas repeated. I beg to assure you I have never written
. . . in greater kindness, nor with a fuller purpose to sustain
you, so far as in my most anxious judgment I consistently can.
But you must act.

April and May went by and nothing was done. On June 21,
1862, McClellan desired to leave the army and come to Washington and lay before the president his views "as to the present
state of military affairs throughout the whole country." Under
other circumstances Lincoln might have been interested in Mc-
Clellan's views, but he replied good-naturedly and with a little
sting of irony, "If it would not divert your time and attention
from the army under your command, I should be glad to hear
your views on the present state of military affairs throughout
the whole country."

On June twenty-seventh, after some minor and unsuccessful
engagements, McClellan announced his intention to move, but
not to move forward. He ordered a retreat to the James River,
and he sent to the secretary of war an insulting letter saying,
"If I save this army, I tell you plainly, I owe no thanks to you,
nor to any one at Washington. You have done your best to destroy this army."

Not content with this astounding letter, McClellan a few days
later wrote a long communication to the president giving him
paternal advice on matters relating to the government, civil no
less than military.

Thus one opportunity after another was neglected by McClellan, and the army under his command marched and counter-
marched and arrived nowhere, fought skirmishes and retreated,
when it should have fought battles and advanced. He waited

for reenforcements while losing men through inaction, and suffering constantly through loss of courage and loss of what we have learned to call morale.

Early in July, 1862, Lincoln reached the conclusion that the command of the armies defending Washington and organized for an attack on Richmond must devolve on some commander capable of action. General Henry W. Halleck was in the West, and in spite of a cantankerous disposition had proved a successful organizer, and either he or men under him, including one man named Grant, whom Halleck greatly disliked, had been winning victories. Lincoln, on July 11, 1862, issued an order:

That Major-General Henry W. Halleck be assigned to command the whole land forces of the United States as general-in-chief, and that he repair to this capital as soon as he can with safety to the positions and operations within the department under his charge.

McClellan still commanded the Army of the Potomac, but Halleck was above him in authority, a fact little to McClellan's liking.

On July 14, 1862, General John Pope, son of Judge Nathaniel Pope, of Illinois, was placed in charge of the Army of Virginia, consisting of three army corps. Pope came from a successful career in the West, and had the bad taste to tell of it when assuming command. He said:

I have come to you from the West, where we have always seen the backs of our enemies; from an army whose business it has been to seek an adversary, and beat him when found; whose policy has been attack and not defense. In but one instance has the enemy been able to place our Western armies in a defensive attitude. I presume I have been called here to pursue the same system, and to lead you against the enemy. It is my purpose to do so, and that speedily. I am sure you long for an opportunity to win the distinction you are capable of achieving; that opportunity I shall endeavor to give you. In the meantime, I desire you to dismiss certain phrases I am sorry to find in vogue amongst you.

I hear constantly of taking strong positions and holding them —of lines of retreat and bases of supplies. Let us discard such ideas. The strongest position a soldier should desire to occupy is one from which he can most easily advance against the enemy. Let us study the probable line of retreat of our opponents, and leave our own to take care of itself. Let us look before us and not behind. Success and glory are in the advance—disaster and shame lurk in the rear. Let us act on this understanding, and it is safe to predict that your banners shall be inscribed with many a glorious deed, and that your names will be dear to your countrymen forever.

Pope quickly incurred the ill will of McClellan, and when, in August, Pope joined battle with the enemy, McClellan did not send FitzJohn Porter to support his advance or cover his retreat. On August ninth General Halleck telegraphed McClellan:

I am of the opinion that the enemy is massing his forces in front of Generals Pope and Burnside, and that he expects to crush them, and move forward to the Potomac. You must send re-enforcements instantly to Acquia Creek. Considering the amount of transportation at your disposal, your delay is not satisfactory. You must move with all possible celerity!

McClellan did not move. On the following day Halleck telegraphed that General Pope was fighting and needed help, and said:

There *must be* no *further delay* in your movements. That which has already occurred was entirely unexpected and must be satisfactorily explained.

On the twenty-first of August Halleck again telegraphed McClellan that the forces of Burnside and Pope were being hard pushed and needed immediate aid. McClellan on the evening of the twenty-third started in leisurely fashion, and four days later, when it was far too late, reached Alexandria. McClellan might have saved Pope's crushing defeat. One of his generals, Fitz-John Porter, was court-martialed and dismissed for not coming to Pope's rescue.

After the defeat of General Pope, Lincoln and Halleck personally called on McClellan, and placed him in complete command of the forces about Washington. If we judge from McClellan's letter to his wife written that very day, the interview contained no intimation that the president was in a panic. Writing on the day of his interview, September 2, 1862, he said:

I was surprised this morning, when at breakfast, by a visit from the President and Halleck, in which the former expressed the opinion that the troubles now impending could be overcome better by me than by any one else. Pope is ordered to fall back upon Washington, and as he reenters everything is to come into my command again.

In his home letters McClellan never missed an opportunity to tell his wife how great a man he was and how superior to all other men in the situation. We may be sure that this letter told essentially what occurred and there is no evidence whatever, apart from his own long subsequent testimony, that would lead us to suppose that the president was in mortal fear that Washington was lost.

Many years afterward, when McClellan wrote his book, his memory of the incident was that the president and Halleck had both believed that Washington was doomed to capture, and that McClellan was the one calm and unterrified man in Washington :

He (the president) then said that he regarded Washington as lost, and asked me if I would, under the circumstances, as a favor to him, resume command and do the best that could be done. Without one moment's hesitation, and without making any conditions whatever, I at once said that I would accept the command and would stake my life that I would save the city. Both the President and Halleck again asserted that it was impossible to save the city, and I repeated my firm conviction that I could and would save it. They then left, the President verbally placing me in entire command of the city and of the troops falling back upon it from the front.

This story, which McClellan did not relate until years afterward, undergoes still greater expansion in the account written, on McClellan's authority, by George Ticknor Curtis:

"Will you," asked Mr. Lincoln, in his distress, "Will you, dare you, take command in this dangerous crisis?" The peril was instantly assumed by McClellan, without a thought concerning himself. That he did not stipulate for a written order shows how little he was considering his own safety.

Possibly so; and it is equally possible that there is no written order because the thing did not happen in that fashion. Lincoln had been dead a long time before McClellan told the world how all Washington was in terror and Lincoln in hysterics and McClellan the only calm and brave man in Washington. At least four men who were then seeing Lincoln almost daily were keeping diaries, and neither John Hay nor O. H. Browning nor Salmon P. Chase nor Gideon Welles represents the president in any such state of terror.

We know that Lincoln's appointment of McClellan at that crisis was strongly opposed by a majority of the Cabinet, who had no assurance that McClellan was the only man who could save the capital from the Confederates. Doubtless Lincoln was troubled, but we are quite sure we know his reasons for giving the command to the more than willing McClellan. First was the fact that he believed McClellan was capable, and he hoped had learned his lesson. Second was the fact that the soldiers still believed in him. And third was the fact that Lincoln was afraid McClellan would not support any other leader.

It is not strange that in after years McClellan saw himself in that dark hour the one supremely brave and confident man, calmly assuring the terrified president that he, McClellan, would stake his own head on his ability to save the capital. But we know that there were men in and about Washington in those days as timid as McClellan charged the president with having been. One man, an officer in the army, wrote to his wife:

I do not regard Washington as safe against the rebels. If I can quietly slip over there I will send your silver off.

It will certainly interest the reader to know that the brave man who wrote and signed this letter was Major General George B. McClellan.

For a considerable time Lincoln bore, without appearing to notice it, McClellan's discourtesy and thinly veiled scorn. At no time does Lincoln appear to have taken into account McClellan's personal incivility. But Lincoln was losing patience with McClellan's failures to achieve a victory. Especially did Lincoln resent McClellan's failure to cooperate with Pope. General Halleck took command of all the armies on July 23, 1862. He and McClellan utterly failed to agree. When Pope started forth on his campaign from which so much was hoped, he warned the president, according to Chase, that he could not safely command the Army of Virginia if his success was to depend on the cooperation of McClellan. When Pope made his humiliating mistake, and McClellan left him "to get out of his own scrape," the president lost very nearly all the patience he had left.

McClellan was not tried as Porter was, for deliberately failing to support Pope. But on August twenty-ninth, when General Pope was being driven, McClellan, still inactive, telegraphed the president:

I am clear that one of two courses should be adopted: First, to concentrate all our available forces to open communication with Pope. Second, to leave Pope to get out of his scrape and at once use all means to make the capital perfectly safe. No middle course will now answer. Tell me what you wish me to do, and I will do all in my power to accomplish it. I wish to know what my orders and authority are. I ask for nothing, but will obey whatever order you give. I only ask a prompt decision, that I may at once give the necessary orders. It will not do to delay longer.

This was an astonishing message to have followed such a

series of imperative orders as McClellan had been receiving for weeks. Manifestly, his inclination now was to leave Pope to get out of his scrape if he could. Indeed, by that time it was almost necessary thus to leave him, for Pope's broken army was no longer in condition to protect the capital.

Thus was Pope's army crushed, Porter disgraced and the country disheartened. And still McClellan did not move.

By this time, Stanton, who had been McClellan's warm friend, had become his most pronounced critic and relentless enemy. After the defeat of Pope, Stanton was furious. John Hay's diary says:

Stanton was loud about the McClellan business. Was unqualifiedly severe on McClellan. He said that after these battles there should be one court martial if never any more. He said that nothing but foul play could lose us this battle, and that it rested with McClellan and his friends. Stanton seemed to believe very strongly in Pope. So did the President, for that matter.

Seward, also, according to Hay, was bitterly sad about McClellan's apparent betrayal of Pope. Seward met Hay, and spoke of himself as old, and much saddened that he should have lived to discover the rancor of military jealousy. Hay records:

I said it never should have seemed possible to me that one American General should write of another to the President, suggesting that Pope be allowed to get out of his own scrape in his own way. He answered, "I don't see why you should have expected it. You are not old. I should have known it." He said this slowly and sadly.

In John Hay's diary is recorded a conversation which occurred between the president and his secretary on their morning ride from the Soldiers' Home to the White House on Saturday August 30, 1862:

The President is very outspoken in regard to McClellan's

present conduct. He said it really seemed to him that McClellan wanted Pope defeated. He mentioned to me a dispatch of McClellan's in which he proposed as our plan of action "to leave Pope to get out of his own scrape, and devote ourselves to securing Washington." He spoke also of McClellan's dreadful panic in the matter of the Chain Bridge which he had ordered blown up the night before; and also his incomprehensible interference with Franklin's corps which he recalled when they had been sent ahead by Halleck's order, begged permission to recall them again, and only persisted after Halleck's sharp injunction to push them ahead until they whipped something or got whipped themselves. The President seemed to think him a little crazy. Envy, jealousy and spite are probably a better explanation of his present conduct.

It was charged against Lincoln afterward that by this time he had become intent upon making the war the occasion of the removal of slavery, that he did not wish the Confederates defeated at this time; and that the Federal losses, not only under Pope but later at Fredericksburg under Burnside and at Chancellorsville under Hooker, and even those under Meade at Gettysburg, were fairly to be charged to this policy. This is the theory suggested and virtually avowed by George Ticknor Curtis, the biographer of Buchanan, and eulogist of McClellan.* But this charge is not only not supported by the facts, but is squarely opposed to what, on indubitable evidence, we now know to have been Lincoln's attitude toward McClellan, toward slavery and toward the saving of the Union.

If the Confederate Army had appreciated the full value to them of their victory at Bull Run and of their subsequent gains, they might have pressed on and captured Washington. Fortunately for the Union cause then and later, the Confederates were nearly as much demoralized as were the Union troops, and felt themselves in no condition to follow up their advantage. Washington, however, continued in a state of perpetual alarm.

---

*See his scarce pamphlet, *McClellan's Last Service to the Public,* together with a *Tribute to His Memory,* published by Appleton in 1886.

It was filled with Confederate spies and was at times within cannon shot of the Confederate outposts. General Halleck was not unmindful of the value to the Union which the capture of Richmond would involve; but he knew well that the Confederates could well afford at any moment to exchange Richmond for Washington. The seat of the Confederate Government was of no long standing, and having once been removed from Montgomery to Richmond, might be removed from Richmond to some other city, not indeed without loss but without irreparable loss. The capture of Washington, however, would have been a disaster beyond all computation. Its capture would almost certainly have been followed promptly by the recognition of the Confederacy by both England and France. It is quite possible that the Confederate Government itself would have been transferred from Richmond to Washington. The capture of Washington was a possibility so appalling that neither Halleck nor Lincoln could contemplate it with any degree of comfort. McClellan rested in his fatuous conviction that one successful battle fought by him would destroy the Confederate Army and end the Confederate Government. He is not to be blamed for desiring to be fully prepared for that battle. He demanded that all other interests be subordinated to the building up of his one great army. There was no disposition on Lincoln's part to deny to McClellan any reenforcements which the government could possibly spare to him; but it was felt most earnestly that a sufficient body of troops should be held in reserve for the protection of Washington.

We shall have occasion to consider McClellan's character and conduct again when we come to the battle of Antietam, and again when we come to the presidential campaign of 1864. For the present it is enough to remember that after the failure of Pope, McClellan resumed command, and that he fought and won at Antietam his first and only notable victory after his first successes in western Virginia.

CHAPTER VIII

LINCOLN AND STANTON

LINCOLN had accepted, with such grace as he could, Simon Cameron as secretary of war. On January 14, 1862, Cameron resigned this position. Lincoln made no pretense of regret when he accepted Cameron's resignation. He appointed Cameron Minister to Russia. The reason that was permitted to be given to the public was a difference of opinion which existed between the president and secretary of war concerning the arming of men who had been slaves. Cameron's report at the end of 1861 virtually committed the War Department to that policy, and Lincoln, so it was said, "was not prepared to permit a member of his Cabinet, without his consent, to commit the administration to so radical a policy at so early a date." This is the explanation given by John G. Nicolay. But a much more serious reason might have been given, which was that personal friends and political associates of the secretary of war were charged with profiting through dishonorable contracts, by means of which the government was robbed for their financial profit. Whatever the truth of the matter, the resignation of Cameron was very willingly accepted. He continued, however, a warm friend and supporter of Lincoln.

When Cameron resigned there was a strong demand upon Lincoln that others of his Cabinet be dismissed. It was felt that, as Lincoln had asserted himself in that one instance, the time was favorable for his removing some other members who were more or less unpopular. There were even those who advocated an entire new Cabinet. Certain Republican senators earnestly advised him to make a clean sweep, and select seven new men, and so restore the waning confidence of the country.

The president listened with patient courtesy, and when the senators had concluded, he said, with a characteristic gleam of humor in his eye:

"Gentlemen, your request for a change of the whole Cabinet because I have made one change reminds me of a story I once heard in Illinois, of a farmer who was much troubled with skunks. His wife insisted on his trying to get rid of them.

"He loaded his shotgun one moonlight night and awaited developments. After some time the wife heard the shotgun go off, and in a few minutes the farmer entered the house.

" 'What luck have you?' asked she.

" 'I hid myself behind the wood-pile,' said the old man, 'with the shotgun pointed toward the hen-roost, and before long there appeared not one skunk, but seven. I took aim, blazed away, killed one, and he raised such a fearful smell that I concluded it was best to let the other six go.' "

The senators laughed and departed, not questioning the president's logic.

At this time Lincoln called to the position made vacant by the resignation of Cameron, Edwin M. Stanton, a man of great industry and energy. He was no stranger to Lincoln. In 1855 they had met in Cincinnati in the McCormick Reaper case. Stanton is said to have described Lincoln as "a long lank creature from Illinois, wearing a dirty linen duster for a coat, on the back of which the perspiration had splotched wide stains that resembled a map of the continent." He did not permit Lincoln to plead in that case. Lincoln was humiliated and indignant. He said that no man had ever treated him as rudely as Stanton did.

Nothing can more finely illustrate Lincoln's lack of vindictiveness than his choice of Stanton as a member of his Cabinet. He knew that Stanton held him in contempt; that he was profane, abusive and a member of the Democratic Party. He had every reason to believe that Stanton was a man in whose association he would have occasion to anticipate unhappy experiences; but Lincoln believed that Stanton was a man of courage, a man of integrity, a man of large organizing ability, and a man thoroughly loyal to his country. If it ever cost Lincoln a struggle to invite Stanton to this position, he never told of it.

Edwin M. Stanton was born at Steubenville, Ohio, December 19, 1814. He studied at Kenyon College, but did not graduate. He was admitted to the bar, and by industry and integrity he rose to a foremost position among the lawyers of his own state. In the Wheeling Bridge Case he established the principle of national sovereignty over all internal navigable waters, and by the Pennsylvania State Canal and Railway cases he settled the right of the people to control all methods of public transportation. He was sent to California to protect the interests of the Federal Government against an army of fraudulent claimants. An ardent Democrat, he accepted a position in Buchanan's Cabinet as attorney general when Jeremiah S. Black vacated that position to become secretary of state; and when John B. Floyd resigned his position as secretary of war to go with the South, Stanton succeeded him.

While secretary of war under Buchanan, Stanton entered into negotiations with the friends of the Union, and in the months that preceded the inauguration he may be said to have done more than any other one man in Washington, except Seward, to prevent a peaceable disruption of the Union. This loyalty to the Union did not, however, enhance his regard for Lincoln. He wrote to General John A. Dix concerning what he called "the imbecility of Lincoln." He habitually referred to Lincoln as a "gorilla." His criticism of Lincoln's first months as president was incessant and unsparing. He was McClellan's adviser and host at the time when McClellan was in virtual rebellion against Lincoln and General Scott. Several of McClellan's least admirable letters were written from Stanton's house.

Stanton entered the War Department with the declaration that he would "make Abe Lincoln president." There is an impression that he undertook rather to make Edwin M. Stanton president. Yet it really was Stanton who induced Lincoln to assert the supremacy which the Constitution gave him as commander-in-chief of the Army and Navy of the United States. In a very real sense it was Stanton who stood for the authority of the president as over against the ambitions of Seward and Chase, each of whom was disposed to believe himself the president de facto. Of Stanton in his relations to the president might be said what was affirmed concerning the wife of the Reverend Doctor Syntax:

> No tongue she suffered to dethrone
> His reverent greatness but her own.

And, while Lincoln and Stanton can never be said to have been congenial friends, the relations of the same interesting couple might again be cited:

> But they retained with all their pother
> A sneaking fondness for each other.

There was that about Stanton which Lincoln unfeignedly liked, and there was that in Lincoln which Stanton was more and more compelled to admire.

Lincoln did more than tolerate Stanton, he profited largely by Stanton's presence in the Cabinet. It is difficult to see how Lincoln could possibly have spared him. Stanton was a terror to evil-doers. Corrupt contractors could neither bribe nor bully him. If Stanton now and then overruled Lincoln's judgment, the chances are fully even that in those particulars the judgment of Lincoln needed to be overruled; for there were times when Lincoln's judgment warped under pressure.

On one occasion a deputation waited on Stanton with an official order from the president, and Stanton flatly refused to obey the order.

"But we have the president's order," said the spokesman of the deputation.

"The president is a fool," blurted out Stanton.

Forthwith the delegation returned to the White House and gave to Lincoln a report of the conversation.

"Did Stanton say I was a fool?" inquired the president.

"He used that very word."

"Stanton is usually right," said Lincoln. "I will slip over and see him."

He did so, and Stanton convinced the president that the course he had intended to follow was inadvisable. The president accepted the judgment of his secretary.

On the other hand, there were times when Lincoln stood his ground and compelled Stanton to do the thing which he believed was right.

One thing Stanton did, which was to introduce another strong personality into the Cabinet—one who could hold his own against either Seward or Chase.

Cabinet meetings now are formal affairs, and each member has his assigned seat, its distance from the president being dependent on the time when that particular department first came to be represented in the Cabinet. But in Lincoln's day, meetings were very informal. Seward assumed his right to sit next the president, and that is where he would now be expected to sit; but sometimes the president thought Seward's assumption of authority did not seem to leave much responsibility for any one else. On September 16, 1862, Secretary Welles wrote:

At the Executive Mansion the Secretary of State informed me that there was to be no Cabinet meeting. He was authorized by the President to communicate the fact. Smith said it would be as well, perhaps, to postpone the Cabinet meetings altogether and indefinitely—there seemed no use latterly for our coming together. Others expressed corresponding opinions. Seward turned off, a little annoyed. An unfavorable impression is getting abroad in regard to the President and the administration, not without reason, perhaps, which prompted Smith and others to express their minds freely. There is really very little of a Government here at this time, so far as the most of the Cabinet are concerned. Seward, when in Washington, spends more or less of each day with the President, absorbs his attention, and I fear to an extent influences his action, not always wisely. The President has good sense, intelligence, and an excellent heart, but he is sadly perplexed and distressed by events. . . . Seward seeks, and at times has, influence which is sometimes harmful. He is anxious to direct, to be Premier, the real executive.*

Welles came also to resent the usurpation of Stanton. On June 3, 1863, he wrote:

Stanton does not attend one half of the Cabinet meetings. When he comes he communicates little of importance. Not infrequently he has a private conference with the President in one corner of the room, or with Seward in the library. Chase, Blair and Bates have expressed their mortification and chagrin that things were so conducted.†

It is not certain that the world understands Stanton. His rough speeches and hot temper have been made a foil for Lincoln's considerate utterance and calm demeanor. There is good reason to believe that Stanton was a kinder and nobler man than has sometimes been represented. It is true that Stanton treated Lincoln with discourtesy at Cincinnati, and that Stanton is alleged to have said among other harsh things, that he had "met Lincoln at the bar, and found him a low, cunning clown.‡ It is true that Stanton sometimes refused to obey the president's orders; though there is some reason to believe that in these matters Lincoln and Stanton understood each other better than other men understood either of them.†† But it does not appear to be

---

*Diary, i, pp. 131-3.

†Diary, i, p. 320.

‡Ben Perley Poore in *Reminiscences of Abraham Lincoln by Distinguished Men of His Time,* p. 223.

††See J. P. Usher in *Reminiscences of Abraham Lincoln,* etc., p. 100.

true that Stanton was cruel or wilfully unjust. Henry Ward Beecher, who knew him well, said:

"Stanton was as tender as a woman—he was tender as a lover."*

The candid student is forced to the conviction that more than once Stanton's sound judgment and unflinching courage saved the country from disaster. But Stanton is not to be reckoned among those who habitually opposed the president. There is good reason to believe that an understanding existed between them whereby Stanton had authority now and then to do what appeared like an overruling of the president's policies. In the Cabinet Stanton was one of Lincoln's habitual and emphatic supporters. He was from the beginning one of the two members of the Cabinet who believed in the emancipation of the slaves, and his pressure upon Lincoln was not without influence in inducing him to take that step.

Stanton filled the military prisons in and about Washington with men and women accused of disloyalty. It is more than possible that some men were imprisoned who did not deserve that fate; but broadly speaking no very large proportion of the population of the military prisons was sent to jail for being loyal or good.

Lincoln himself was accustomed to tell a story illustrative of the high virtue claimed by practically all people in prison. The governor of a certain state was visiting the state prison, and stopped to talk with a number of prisoners. They told him their story, and in every instance it was one of wrong suffered by an innocent person. The real criminal had always escaped, and the imprisoned man was the unfortunate victim of appearances or of conspiracy or perjury. There was one man, however, who admitted his crime and the justice of his sentence. "I must pardon you," said the governor, "I can't have you in here corrupting all these good men."

---

*See Henry Ward Beecher in *Reminiscences of Abraham Lincoln*, etc., p. 252.

Stanton wore himself out in the service of his country. It was a service as unsparing of himself as it had been uncompromising of its demands upon others. Finally when the war was over and the great president had crowned his sacrifice with his own blood, it was Stanton who assumed the responsibility of the government during the hours before Andrew Johnson was in condition to be inaugurated. A few years later, Edwin M. Stanton, exhausted in body and mind and purse, having given to his country all he had of strength and wealth, and even of honor justly due him, lay down and died.

CHAPTER IX

IT HAS never been easy for Americans to forgive official Great Britain for her attitude toward the United States in the early days of the Civil War. The haste with which Great Britain and France recognized the Confederates as belligerents was in itself a disappointment, and this recognition, itself an unneighborly act on the part of both these nations, was followed by acts of aid and comfort to the Confederate forces which no pretense of neutrality, much less of friendship, could disguise. The readiness of Great Britain to give offense was equaled by her readiness to take offense. The delicacy of the relations between the two countries became painfully apparent in the Trent affair.

On November 8, 1861, Captain Charles Wilkes, commanding the United States steamer *San Jacinto,* halted the British royal mail steamship *Trent,* and removed from her James M. Mason and John Slidell, with their two secretaries, and took them to Boston where they were imprisoned in Fort Warren in Boston Harbor. Mason and Slidell were the accredited envoys of the Confederacy to England and France. They ran the blockade at Charleston in the autumn of 1861, and arrived at Havana. They announced their purpose to sail from there for Great Britain on the Steamer *Trent* on November seventh. On the following day Captain Wilkes compelled the *Trent* to halt as she was sailing through the Bahama Channel, and sent a force of marines on board to take off the emissaries of the Confederate Government. The *Trent* then proceeded upon her voyage.

This act on the part of Captain Wilkes was hailed with great

joy throughout the North.   Secretary Welles wrote to Captain
Wilkes a letter of congratulation, declaring that his conduct was
marked by intelligence, ability, decision and firmness, and that
it "had the emphatic approval of this department."   Secretary
Stanton also applauded the act.

Congress convened just at the time the interest in this matter
was at its height.   One of its first acts on the opening day of the
session was to pass by unanimous consent a vote of thanks to
Captain Wilkes.   This resolution was introduced by Owen Lovejoy, and the House lost no time in placing the hot-headed resolution on its record.

Chittenden in his book of *Recollections,* asserts that Secretary
Seward from the first disapproved the action; but Chittenden's
recollections were sometimes very wide of the facts; Gideon
Welles declares that Seward at the beginning was opposed to
giving up the emissaries, but yielded when the demand of Great
Britain became peremptory.   Considering the attitude of Seward toward Great Britain as shown by his *Thoughts for the
President's Consideration,* on April 1, 1861, in which he was
then ready to go to war with Great Britain, Welles is more likely
to be correct in this matter than Chittenden.

Whatever the attitude of others, there appears to be no doubt
of Lincoln's view of the case.   He had grave misgivings from
the start concerning the right of Captain Wilkes to stop and
search a British vessel on the high seas.

"I fear the traitors will prove to be white elephants," he said.
"We must stick to American principles concerning the rights of
neutrals.   We fought Great Britain for insisting by theory and
practice on the right to do exactly what Captain Wilkes has done.
If Great Britain shall now protest against the act and demand
their release, we must give them up, apologize for the act as a
violation of our doctrines, and thus forever bind her over to keep
the peace in relation to neutrals, and so acknowledge that she
has been wrong for sixty years."

Meantime, Great Britain was working her navy yards night

and day in open and visible preparation for war against the United States. The British press flamed with denunciations of the American insult to the British Navy. At one time war seemed inevitable.

Mr. Frederick Seward, who was assistant to his father, maintained that it was Secretary Seward who at this juncture saved the country from a calamitous and unjustifiable war with Great Britain. Charles Francis Adams, the American Ambassador at the Court of St. James, agreed with him. But while high honor is due to Adams at this juncture, and some also to Seward, it appears to have been Lincoln's common sense and sound judgment which saved the day. All through the excitement he was calmly considering America's historic attitude toward the question of the right of search, and the practical way of saving America the necessity of a war with Great Britain. On Lincoln's advice and practically upon his decision that it must be done, the prisoners were returned to Great Britain. This act greatly strengthened America before the public sentiment of England.

"If reparation were made at all, of which few of us felt more than a hope," wrote John Stuart Mill, "we thought that it would be made obviously as a concession to prudence, not to principle. We thought that there would have been truckling to the newspaper editors and supposed fire-eaters who were crying out for retaining the prisoners at all hazards. . . . We expected everything, in short, which would have been weak, and timid, and paltry. The only thing which no one seemed to expect is what has actually happened. Mr. Lincoln's government have done none of these things. Like honest men they have said in direct terms that our demand was right; that they yielded to it because it was just; that if they themselves had received the same treatment, they would have demanded the same reparation; and if what seemed to be the American side of the question was not the just side, they would be on the side of justice, happy as they were to find after their resolution had been taken, that it was also the side which America had formerly defended. Is there any one capable of a moral judgment or feeling, who will say that his opinion of America and American statesmen is not raised by such an act, done on such grounds?"

In the United States, however, there was no such unanimity of sentiment. The return of Mason and Slidell was denounced by many as an act of weakness on the part of the administration; and some who conceded the practical necessity of the act were grief stricken at the humiliation of it. Owen Lovejoy, who had always refused to be silent in his denunciation of the crime of slavery, spoke out hot words which many men deemed unwise, but whose sentiments very many people shared. He said:

"Every time this Trent affair comes up; every time that an allusion is made to it . . . I am made to renew the horrible grief which I suffered when the news of the surrender of Mason and Slidell came. I acknowledge it, I literally wept tears of vexation. I hate it; and I hate the British government. I have never shared in the traditionary hostility of many of my countrymen against England. But I now here publicly avow and record my inextinguishable hatred of that government. I mean to cherish it while I live, and to bequeath it as a legacy to my children when I die. And if I am alive when war with England comes, as sooner or later it must, for we shall never forget this humiliation, and if I can carry a musket in that war, I will carry it. I have three sons, and I mean to charge them, and I do now publicly and solemnly charge them, that if they shall have, at that time, reached the years of manhood and strength, they shall enter into that war."*

Senator Hale, of New Hampshire, went so far as to threaten the administration of Mr. Lincoln.

"If," said he, "this administration will not listen to the voice of the people, they will find themselves engulfed in a fire that will consume them like stubble: they will be helpless before a power that will hurl them from their places."*

Before many months, however, an event occurred which did

Congressional Globe, 2d Session 37th Congress, january 7, 1862, p. 177.
†*Congressional Globe,* 2d Session 37th Congress, p. 333.

much to strengthen the cause of the North in the sight of Great Britain, particularly with respect to the conflict to be waged on the ocean.

The navy yard at Norfolk, Virginia, had been captured by the Confederates. Among the other vessels which then fell into the hands of the enemy, was a war-ship named the *Merrimac*. The Confederates sheathed her sides with iron, and changed her name to the *Virginia*. She was finished in the spring of 1862, and on March seventh she sailed out of Norfolk Harbor. On the following day she sailed down the James River and attacked and destroyed two United States frigates, the *Cumberland* and the *Congress*. A third vessel, the *Minnesota*, was coming to the aid of the *Cumberland*, but ran aground and lay at the mercy of the destroyer.

The cannon balls fired by these three vessels fell as harmlessly as peas upon the iron armor of the *Merrimac*. The only harm she suffered in this attack which lost the Union Navy two ships, and seemed to doom a third, was the damage done to her own prow when she rammed the *Cumberland*. She withdrew to her anchorage, and waited for another day on which she expected easily to finish the *Minnesota*.

On Sunday morning, March ninth, the *Virginia*, which is still known in literature as the *Merrimac*, moved triumphantly toward the *Minnesota*, never questioning that her wooden walls would be crushed by the first impact. Suddenly, from under the stern of the *Minnesota*, sailed a small nondescript craft and advanced to meet the *Merrimac*.

The *Monitor*, which was the name of this vessel, had been built in a Connecticut shipyard by an ingenious Swedish engineer, John Ericsson. She mounted two eleven-inch Dahlgren guns, each carrying a solid shot weighing one hundred and sixty-eight pounds. These guns were mounted in a revolving turret which stood upon the low deck only a few inches above the water line.

This absurd-looking craft emerged and interposed its ridiculous bulk between the *Merrimac* and the *Minnesota*. Then ensued a battle the like of which had never been witnessed on the high seas. Close against each other the two ships exchanged their heaviest volleys, their iron rasping against iron. The battle between David and Goliath was enacted again between this mighty iron clad behemoth and the little "Yankee Cheesebox" floating upon its raft.

The *Merrimac* was not destroyed, but was so severely injured that she was compelled to withdraw to the shelter of the Norfolk navy yard, and there she lay, a useless and battered hulk, until the Confederates surrendered the yard, when she was destroyed.

The effect upon the country was marvelous. The news of the destruction of the *Cumberland* and the *Congress,* and of the certain doom of the *Minnesota,* had stricken the country with terror. It seemed as though every vessel in the Union Navy was doomed, and that Washington itself would soon be lying helpless under the guns of this invincible iron ship. The *Monitor* had been so hurriedly finished that the mechanics remained on board when she left New England for the Chesapeake. Her arrival was in the nick of time. She actually entered the harbor on the night before her battle by the light of the burning ship *Congress.* The country could hardly believe the glorious news which followed the Sunday battle. In a single day the whole aspect of the war upon the ocean was changed. No longer did Washington fear attack by water. No ship in the Confederate, or any other navy, could stand the shock of the *Monitor's* heavy guns. By the method of their mounting they could be quickly brought to bear upon any point of the compass; and the revolution of the turret permitted them to be loaded without exposing any open port to the fire of the enemy. The mourning of the nation over the loss of the *Cumberland* and *Congress* was changed in a single night to rejoicing.

If there was in Washington one man more happy than any other on the night when the *Monitor* had put the *Merrimac* out of commission, it was Gideon Welles, Secretary of the Navy. He had believed in the *Monitor* when no one else, or few, thought her of much account. When the *Merrimac* had sunk the *Cumberland* and the *Congress,* the Cabinet feared she would steam straight up to Washington, and to New York. Welles assured them that she would not steam in both directions at once, and his calm, as he tells the story, did little to pacify them. They were inclined to hold him responsible for the disaster. He says:

The President himself ever after gave me the credit of being the most calm and self-possessed of any member of the Government. The President himself was so excited that he could not deliberate. . . . But the most frightened man on that gloomy day—the most so, I think, of any during the Rebellion—was the Secretary of War. He was at times almost frantic, and as he walked the room with his eyes fixed on me, I saw well the estimation in which he held me with unmoved and unexcited manner and conversation. . . . Stanton made some sneering inquiry about this new vessel, the Monitor, of which he admitted he knew little or nothing. I described her. . . . Stanton asked about her armament, and when I mentioned she had two guns, his mingled look of incredulity and contempt cannot be described. . . . I was not appalled by his terror or bluster. I more correctly read and understood his character in that crisis than he mine.*

With great satisfaction Welles records that this victory gave him new standing in the Cabinet, and that even Stanton treated him with less roughness than he habitually extended toward his other colleagues.

We recall the effect of the *Monitor's* victory on our relations with England and France, because it is necessary to remember them in this connection. France has been America's traditional friend from the beginning of our history. Whether she has ever been our friend, except when she had something to gain by the friendship, need not here be discussed. Certainly her friendship in the Revolution proves no more than that she thought the best way to harm England was to help free England's colonies,

---

Diary, i, pp. 63-4.

but she did not officially offer that help until she herself, and for quite other reasons, was at war with England. England is our friend, and increasingly so. The ties that bind together the English speaking races must be strengthened in every legitimate way. For that matter, all ties that unite all nations in friendship need to be strengthened. But it deserves also to be remembered, that, while the Union had many warm friends in France and especially in England during the Civil War, the official basis of that friendship was immensely strengthened by the new respect for the American Navy which both nations learned after the defeat of the *Merrimac*. The *Alabama* was still sailing the high seas, firing British-made shot from British-made guns into unarmed American vessels; but the victory of the *Monitor* was a mailed hand stretched across the sea for the grasp of a new friendship.

Russia was the Union's best friend during the Civil War. In 1867 William H. Seward negotiated a treaty with Russia by the terms of which the United States acquired the Territory of Alaska. For it the United States paid the sum of $7,200,000, a sum that now seems very small. But it was then so large that it still remains a question how much of that sum was intended to pay for the territory and how much was to cover the expense of Russia's sending a fleet into New York harbor on a friendly visit, just at a time when the European nations that should have been our friends needed to be reminded that America, fighting for her national integrity and for human freedom, could find a friend, if not in England or France, then in despotic Russia. America still owes Russia something for friendship at a time when friends were fewer than America deserved.

CHAPTER X

By THE end of 1861, it had become evident, both in the North and the South, that the struggle would be severe and long. In most of the actual battles the Confederates had had the advantage. The cheerful confidence of the Northern Army that it could subdue the South in ninety days was entirely gone. But the South itself had had time for very serious thought. Although the Confederates had been recognized as a belligerent, their government had not been acknowledged by any European nation. They had failed to hold Maryland, Kentucky or Missouri. In the West they had lost ground, and in the East they were on the defensive.

The first fighting of 1862 was in the West. General Ulysses S. Grant, who had already done some inconspicuous but successful campaigning, began that year with an advance, and captured Fort Henry on the Tennessee, and Fort Donelson on the Cumberland. In this he was materially aided by a fleet of gunboats under the command of Commodore A. H. Foote. This was the first important victory on the Union side. Very soon, General George H. Thomas won a victory at Mill Springs, which with the victories of Grant, compelled the evacuation by the Confederate Armies of Kentucky and a considerable part of Tennessee. On April 6, 1862, Grant was attacked at Pittsburg Landing, or Shiloh, on the Tennessee River, by General Albert Sidney Johnston. On the first day the Union Army was severely beaten, but on the second day the tide turned, and in the hour of victory reenforcements came under Buell, rendering the Confederate defeat impossible to retrieve. Although the Union losses were larger than the Confederate, and Grant did not pursue the army which he had repulsed, the Confederates were compelled to withdraw, leaving the river in the hands of the Union Army. Soon after, Corinth, an important railroad center near by, was abandoned by the Confederates. Just as Grant was driving back the Confederate forces at Shiloh on April seventh, Commodore Foote captured Island No. 10 on the Mississippi. The Confederate front was thus pushed a considerable distance farther south along the whole western border.

But while these victories in the West were cheering the heart of the North, there was nothing but discouragement in the East. McClellan had failed to capture Richmond; Pope had fought and lost the second battle of Bull Run on August 29 and 30, 1862. The Confederates, swollen with the pride of victory, prepared to move on Baltimore and Philadelphia. They crossed into Maryland, captured Harper's Ferry, and met McClellan's army at Antietam.

The majority of Lincoln's Cabinet were opposed to the reappointment of McClellan. Stanton and Chase, on August twenty-ninth, drew up a formal protest, which was signed by both of them and also by the attorney general and the secretary of the interior. The secretary of the navy agreed with them, but declined to sign the paper lest his doing so should embarrass Lincoln. The appointment, however, stood, and McClellan set himself to work in a manner that appeared to justify Lincoln's partly restored confidence. Fortunately, he found his army in not so deplorable a condition as appeared after the defeat of Pope. All told, he had a hundred thousand men, and he himself reported eighty-seven thousand under his command at the time of the battle of Antietam. Lee had forty thousand. At the outset McClellan felt sure that Lee's army was nearly twice as large as it actually was.

General Lee's invasion of Maryland was his own undertaking. He believed that his invasion of that state would bring to his army a large number of men resident in that state and in sympathy with the South, and also that he would be able to draw McClellan's army away from Washington to a position where Lee could fight it on ground of his own selection.   McClellan had worked industriously in getting his army into shape for fighting.   He now approached Lee with very great deliberation and on September seventeenth fought a bloody battle at Antietam.   McClellan was favored by a fortunate accident through which he captured papers disclosing the entire plan of Lee.   If McClellan had moved more promptly he might have come upon Lee's army divided, and almost have wiped it out of existence. McClellan knew Lee's plan : he could no longer deceive himself with his habitual delusion that the enemy was stronger than he, for he had learned authoritatively that Lee's army was less than half as large as his own.

It was a battle which McClellan could not wholly lose, but which his delays and indecisions brought to a close in a meager victory, of which he took no advantage.

The losses on both sides were heavy.   On the Union side 12,-410 were lost in the battle of Antietam, and the whole campaign involved a loss of 15,203.   This does not include the Union loss of 12,737 involved in Lee's capture of Harper's Ferry.   The Confederate loss as nearly as can be ascertained, was 11,172 at Antietam and their whole loss in this campaign of 13,964.   Nevertheless, it was a Union victory.   Lee suffered a loss which he could not afford, and he saw before him no possible success resulting from further penetration of the North.   He withdrew his army across the Potomac.

If McClellan had only renewed the battle on the morning of the eighteenth, he might materially have shortened the war; but he was inordinately gratified by his success on the preceding day, and quite unwilling to risk his laurels by any further immediate venture.   His corps commanders, according to their own testimony, earnestly advised him to renew the battle on the following morning and McClellan said he would consider it. The next morning he wrote :

Those in whose judgment I rely tell me that I fought the battle splendidly, and that it was a masterpiece of art.

Two days later he wrote:

I feel that I have done all that can be asked in twice saving the country.

Lincoln rejoiced in McClellan's success, but was profoundly saddened when McClellan permitted Lee to return across the Potomac. He himself paid a visit to McClellan's army. Apparently he could discover no hope that McClellan had any plans for aggressive action. Lincoln now removed McClellan from command, and that general ceased to be a figure of military importance from that time forward. But as he disappeared from the military horizon, his star rose as a political rival of Lincoln.

Lincoln had not consulted his Cabinet about the appointment of McClellan to the chief command after the disaster of Pope. There was a Cabinet meeting that afternoon, and, the members assembling before Lincoln came, Stanton in a voice that trembled with anger and excitement told the others what Lincoln had done. When Lincoln arrived, their attitude was one of accusation. Lincoln admitted that he had done it against their judgment, but thought it justified on two grounds, McClellan's organizing ability and the confidence of the army in him. They certainly did not think that McClellan was the only man who could save Washington. Glad enough were they when McClellan after the battle of Antietam was finally removed. But it is not certain that they were better judges of the situation than Lincoln. McClellan had accomplished the thing for which Lincoln had recalled him. He had organized the Army of the Potomac as it had not been organized before, and he had won a victory, though not a brilliant one.

The significance of the battle of Antietam, for the purpose of this biography of Lincoln, is, first, in its bearing upon Lincoln's relations with the general from whom so much had been expected and who had accomplished so little. It is even more notable in its relation to Lincoln's long deferred Proclamation of Emancipation.

CHAPTER XI

EMANCIPATION

LINCOLN'S personal convictions concerning the sin of slavery, and the duty of the United States to eliminate that evil from its moral and political and economic life were pealed forth in trumpet tones in his Peoria speech of October 16, 1854. Never did he recede from the position there taken. But the practical difficulties that might attend the elimination of slavery either in peace or war were never underestimated by him. Because of what seemed to many his wavering policy with respect to that question, let us remind ourselves of what he said in that memorable address, for here, if anywhere, Lincoln spoke his deepest convictions concerning slavery:

This declared indifference, but, as I must think, covert zeal for the spread of slavery, I cannot but hate. I hate it because of the monstrous injustice of slavery itself. I hate it because it deprives our republican example of its just influence in the world; enables the enemies of free institutions with plausibility to taunt us as hypocrites; causes the real friends of freedom to doubt our sincerity; and especially because it forces so many really good men among ourselves into an open war with the very fundamental principles of civil liberty, criticising the Declaration of Independence and insisting that there is no right principle of action but self-interest.

. . . .

The doctrine of self-government is right,—absolutely and eternally right,—but it has no just application as here attempted. Or perhaps I should rather say that whether it has such just application, depends upon whether a negro is not, or is, a man. If he is not a man, in that case he who is a man may as a matter of self-government do just what he pleases with him. But if the negro is a man, is it not to that extent a total destruction of self-government to say that he too shall not govern himself? When the white man governs himself, that is self-government; but when he governs himself and also governs another man, that is more than self-government—that is despotism.

What I do say is, that no man is good enough to govern another man without that other's consent.

The master not only governs the slave without his consent, but he governs him by a set of rules altogether different from those which he prescribes for himself. Allow all the governed an equal voice in the government; that, and that only, is self-government.

Slavery is founded in the selfishness of man's nature—opposition to it in his love of justice. These principles are an eternal antagonism; and when brought into collision so fiercely as slavery extension brings them, shocks and throes and convulsions must ceaselessly follow. Repeal the Missouri Compromise— repeal all compromise—repeal the Declaration of Independence —repeal all past history—still you cannot repeal human nature.

I particularly object to the new position which the avowed principle of this Nebraska law gives to slavery in the body politic. I object to it because it assumes that there can be moral right in the enslaving of one man by another. I object to it as a dangerous dalliance for a free people,—a sad evidence that feeling prosperity, we forget right,—that liberty as a principle we have ceased to revere.

Little by little, but steadily as man's march to the grave, we have been giving up the old for the new faith. Near eighty years ago we began by declaring that all men are created equal; but now from that beginning we have run down to the other declaration that for some men to enslave others is a "sacred right of self-government." These principles cannot stand together. They are as opposite as God and mammon.

Our Republican robe is soiled and trailed in the dust. Let us repurify it. Let us turn and wash it white, in the spirit if not the blood of the Revolution. Let us turn slavery from its claims of "moral right" back upon its existing legal rights, and its arguments of "necessity." Let us return it to the position our fathers gave it, and there let it rest in peace. Let us readopt the Declaration of Independence, and the practices and policy which harmonize with it. Let North and South—let all Americans— let all lovers of liberty everywhere—join in the great and good work. If we do this, we shall not only have saved the Union, but we shall have so saved it, as to make and to keep it forever worthy of the saving. We shall have so saved it that the succeeding millions of free, happy people, the world over, shall rise up and call us blessed to the latest generation.

At the beginning of his administration Lincoln was far from being ready to give immediate freedom to all the slaves. But he hoped to increase the area of freedom by inducing some of the border states to free their slaves. He went further. By the end of 1861, many slaves had been freed by the war itself; as early as May 27, 1861, General Benjamin F. Butler had ingeniously and unanswerably, from the standpoint of a recognition of the slaves as property, declared them to be "contraband of war." Lincoln knew that, by certain processes of law, certain states had acquired title to negroes, and he held it to the lasting honor of Kentucky that that state had never put such negroes on the auction-block. Whose were the negroes whom the war had freed? If not the property, they were morally the wards of the nation. Why not accept them as such, and, under the law of confiscation, take such others as might properly be taken, and colonize them? And why not colonize, also, such free negroes as desired it? This is the portion of his message to Congress, December 3, 1861, which gave rise to the Compensation Bill:

The war continues. In considering the policy to be adopted for suppressing the insurrection, I have been anxious and careful that the inevitable conflict for this purpose shall not degenerate into a violent and remorseless revolutionary struggle. I have, therefore, in every case, thought it proper to keep the integrity of the Union prominent as the primary object of the contest on our part, leaving all questions which are not of vital military importance to the more deliberate action of the legislature.

In the exercise of my best discretion I have adhered to the blockade of the ports held by the insurgents, instead of putting in force, by proclamation, the law of Congress enacted at the late session for closing those ports. So, also, obeying the dictates of prudence, as well as the obligations of law, instead of transcending, I have adhered to the act of Congress to confiscate property used for insurrectionary purposes. If a new law upon the same subject shall be proposed, its propriety will be duly considered. The Union must be preserved; and hence, *all indispensable means must be employed.* We should not be in haste to determine that radical and extreme measures, which may reach the loyal as well as the disloyal, are indispensable.

This was the method which Lincoln favored in liberating the slaves. Senator Browning spent the Sunday afternoon with him before his sending to Congress his message including the Compensation Provision, and wrote:

He is very hopeful of ultimate success. He suggested to me the policy of paying Delaware, Maryland, Kentucky and Missouri $500 apiece for all the negroes they had according to the census of 1860, provided they would adopt a system of gradual emancipation which should work the extinction of slavery in twenty years, and said it would require only about one-third of what was necessary to support the war for one year; and agreed with me that there should be connected with it a scheme for colonizing the blacks somewhere in the American continent. There was no disagreement in our view upon any subject we discussed.

In April, 1862, Congress passed a bill to abolish slavery in the District of Columbia. Lincoln signed it, but not with full approval. Senator Browning wrote in his *Diary,* April 14, 1862, this rather astounding entry:

At night went to the President's to lay before him the bill to abolish slavery in the District of Columbia. Had a talk with him. He told me he would sign the bill—but he regretted the bill had been passed in its present form—that it should have been for gradual emancipation—that now families should at once be deprived of cooks, stable boys, &c., and they of their protectors, without any provision for them. He further told me that he would not sign the bill before Wednesday. That old Governor Wickliff had two family servants with him who were sickly, and who would not be benefited by freedom, and wanted time to remove them but could not get them out of the city until Wednesday, and that the Governor had come frankly to him and asked for time. He added to me that this was told me in the strictest confidence.

For two days Abraham Lincoln pocketed the bill to abolish slavery in the District of Columbia, in order to give Ex-Governor Wickliff time to send two old slaves back to Kentucky before the bill became a law.

When Lincoln became president he cherished and expressed deep concern for the support of the border states. Kentucky, Missouri and Maryland were all slave states. Lincoln feared to alienate them by too pronounced a policy in favor of emancipation. It was said of Lincoln in that day, "Abraham Lincoln hopes that he has God on his side, but thinks he must have Kentucky."

Lincoln was himself a border state man. Not until he had given up hope of winning the border states to a policy of compensated emancipation, did he commit himself in his own mind to the plan of freeing the slaves by executive proclamation. He believed that he had the power to do this as a war measure, but he did not believe that he was justified in doing it, if in so doing he would weaken the cause of the Union by the alienation of the border states, and without material gain for the preservation of the republic.

From the date of his election Lincoln was deluged with advice from both sides. Loyal men from the border states told him that a policy of emancipation would drive those states into the confederacy. On the other hand, the friends of freedom were

UNION GENERALS PROMINENT IN FIRST HALF OF THE WAR
From First Volume of Greeley's *American Conflict*

confidently demanding that he should immediately liberate all slaves.

The sharp antithesis between Lincoln's advisers is well illustrated in two speeches that were delivered on succeeding days, one in the Senate and the other in the House of Representatives. On April 23, 1862, Senator John J. Crittenden, of Kentucky, speaking on the Confiscation Bill, said:

There is a niche in the temple of fame, a niche near to Washington, which should be occupied by the statue of him who shall save this country. Mr. Lincoln has a mighty destiny. It is for him, if he will, to step into that niche. It is for him to be but a President of the people of the United States, and there will his statue be. But if he choose to be, in these times, a mere sectarian and a party man, that niche will be reserved for some future and better patriot. It is in his power to occupy a place next to Washington, the Founder and Preserver, side by side.

On the next day in the House of Representatives in a speech for the same bill, Owen Lovejoy said:

I, too, have a niche for Abraham Lincoln; but it is in Freedom's holy fane, and not in the blood-besmeared temple of human bondage; not surrounded by slave-fetters and chains, but with the symbols of freedom; not dark with bondage, but radiant with the light of Liberty. In that niche he shall stand proudly, nobly, gloriously, with shattered fetters and broken chains, and slave-whips beneath his feet. If Abraham Lincoln pursues the path evidently pointed out for him in the Providence of God, as I believe he will, then he will occupy the proud position I have indicated. That is a fame worth living for; aye, more: that is a fame worth dying for, though that death led through the blood of Gethsemane and the agony of the accursed tree. . . . Let Abraham Lincoln make himself . . . the emancipator, the liberator . . . and his name shall not only be enrolled in this earthly temple, but it will be traced on the living stones of that temple which rears itself amid the thrones and hierarchies of Heaven.

In the early part of the war Lincoln took very conservative ground concerning attempts to force emancipation. He rebuked Frémont and restrained Hunter, and said in his special message to Congress on March 6, 1862, "In my judgment, gradual, and not sudden emancipation is better for all." In this message he proposed to Congress that the United States should give pecuniary aid to any state that would provide for a gradual emancipation of its slaves, with full compensation to the owners. It was this policy that Ralph Waldo Emerson condemned:

> Pay ransom to the owner,
> And fill up the bag to the brim;
> But who is owner? The slave is owner
> And ever was; pay him!

On March 10, 1862, the president held a conference with representatives of the border states, and earnestly urged this plan for their consideration. It brought no practical result.

On May 19, 1862, in a communication called forth by the proclamation of General Hunter, declaring slaves in the states of Georgia, Florida and South Carolina free, the president again alluded to this effort by which he hoped to retain the loyalty of the border states to the Union, while providing for gradual emancipation. He said:

To the people of those states I now earnestly appeal. I do not argue—I beseech you to make the argument for yourselves—you cannot if you would, be blind to the signs of the times. I beg of you a calm and enlarged consideration of them, ranging, if it may be, far above personal and partisan politics. This proposal makes a common cause for a common object, casting no reproach upon any. It acts not the Pharisee. The change it contemplates would come as gently as the dews of heaven, not rending or wrecking anything. Will you not embrace it? So much good has not been done by one effort in all past time, as, in the Providence of God, it is now your high privilege to do. May the vast future not have to lament that you have neglected it.

On July 12, 1862, Lincoln invited all the members of Con

gress of the border states to meet him at the White House. In the address made on that occasion he said:

I intend no reproach or complaint when I assure you that in my opinion, if you all had voted for the resolution in the gradual emancipation message of last March, the war would now be substantially ended. And the plan therein proposed is yet one of the most potent and swift means of ending it. Let the states which are in rebellion see definitely and certainly that in no event will the states you represent ever join their proposed confederacy, and they cannot much longer maintain the contest. . . .

If the war continues long, as it must, if the object be not sooner attained, the institution in your states will be extinguished by mere friction and abrasion, by the mere incidents of the war. It will be gone, and you will have nothing valuable in lieu of it. Much of its value is gone already. How much better for you and for your people to take the step which at once shortens the war and secures substantial compensation for that which is sure to be wholly lost in any other event! How much better to thus save the money which else we sink forever in the war! How much better to do it while we can, lest the war ere long render us pecuniarily unable to do it! How much better for you as seller, and the nation as buyer, to sell out and buy out that without which the war could never have been, than to sink both the thing to be sold and the price of it in cutting one another's throats!

I do not speak of emancipation *at once,* but of a *decision* to emancipate *gradually.* . . .

Upon these considerations I have again begged your attention to the message of March last. Before leaving the Capitol, consider and discuss it among yourselves. You are patriots and statesmen, and as such I pray you consider this proposition and at the least commend it to the consideration of your states and people. As you would perpetuate popular government for the best people in the world, I beseech you that you do in nowise omit this. Our common country is in great peril, demanding the loftiest views and boldest action to bring a speedy relief. Once relieved, its form of government is saved to the world, its beloved history and cherished memories are vindicated, and its happy future fully assured and rendered inconceivably grand. To you, more than to any others, the privilege is given to assure that happiness and swell that grandeur, and to link your own names therewith forever.

To the president's bitter disappointment the border state representatives did not accept his suggestion. He believed then, and said later, that their refusal to follow his advice in this matter brought nearer the necessity for emancipation.

Lincoln had believed that he understood the border states, and that they understood him. Perhaps he was never more bitterly disappointed than in their refusal to accept his plan.

"Oh, how I wish the Border States would accept my proposition," he said to Isaac N. Arnold and Owen Lovejoy one day; "then you, Lovejoy, and you, Arnold, and all of us would not have lived in vain. The labor of your life, Lovejoy, would be crowned with success. You would live to see the end of slavery."

"Could you have seen the President," wrote Sumner once to a friend, "as it was my privilege often—while he was considering the great questions on which he has already acted—the invitation to emancipation in the States, emancipation in the District of Columbia, and the acknowledgment of the independence of Haiti and Liberia, even your zeal would have been satisfied.

"His whole soul was occupied, especially by the first proposition, which was peculiarly his own. In familiar intercourse with him, I remember nothing more touching than the earnestness and completeness with which he embraces this idea. To his mind it was just and beneficent, while it promised the sure end of slavery."

All these efforts failed. To Lincoln it then seemed clear that the alternative was a proclamation of emancipation. He himself has fixed the time of this decision in his letter to A. G. Hodges, of Kentucky, written April 4, 1864:

When in March. May and July, 1862, I made earnest and successive appeals to the border States in favor of compensated emancipation, I believed the indispensable necessity for military emancipation and arming of blacks would come, unless arrested by that measure. They declined the proposition, and I was, in my best judgment, driven to the alternative of either surrendering the Union, or issuing the emancipation proclamation.

On July 22, 1862, just ten days after his futile meeting with the representatives of the border states, Mr. Lincoln called together his Cabinet and read to them a proclamation of emancipation. He proposed to free all slaves that were held in the states then in rebellion, the proclamation to become effective on January 1, 1863.

An excellent account of this Cabinet meeting was preserved by Frank B. Carpenter, the artist who painted the life-size picture commemorative of the event, and who recorded the story while all members of the Cabinet were living. He related that Lincoln read his proposed proclamation and that after some suggestions from others, Secretary Seward said in substance:

"Mr. President, I approve of the proclamation, but I question the expediency of its issue at this juncture. The depression of the public mind, consequent upon our repeated reverses, is so great that I fear the effect of so important a step. It may be viewed as the last measure of an exhausted government, a cry for help; the government stretching forth its hands to Ethiopia, instead of Ethiopia stretching forth her hands to the government." His idea was that it would be considered our last *shriek,* on the retreat. "Now," continued Mr. Seward, "while I approve the measure, I suggest, sir, that you postpone its issue, until you can give it to the country, supported by military success, instead of issuing it, as would be the case now, upon the greatest disasters of the war!" The wisdom of the view of the Secretary of State struck me with very great force. It was an aspect of the case that, in all my thoughts upon the subject, I had entirely overlooked. The result was that I put the draft of the proclamation aside, as you do your sketch for a picture, waiting for a victory. From time to time I added or changed a line, touching it up here and there, anxiously waiting the progress of events.*

---

*Carpenter, *Six Months in the White House,* p. 21.

Seward's suggestion that the time was inopportune had weight with Lincoln. He felt the force of the proposal to delay it until there was a decisive Union victory. On this account he waited, hoping more earnestly than ever for some turn in the military situation to indicate to him and his Cabinet that a fit time for issuing the proclamation had come.

Lincoln never contemplated with satisfaction the prospect of a liberated negro race living side by side with the white race. Emancipation in his mind was logically joined to colonization. Soon after the beginning of the war, it became evident that the progress of that struggle would free many slaves, perhaps all of them. He earnestly desired Congress to appropriate money for the colonization of such slaves as should be freed, and who might willingly accept colonization with their freedom. He carefully considered whether it might be wise to make it a condition of emancipation that the liberated slaves should leave America. At his earnest solicitation Congress in 1862 appropriated six hundred thousand dollars and left it to be expended by the president in removing, with their own consent, free persons of African descent to some country which they might select as adapted to their condition and necessities. He appointed a negro commissioner of emigration, Reverend O. J. Mitchell, to promote the object of this appropriation. We are familiar with the office of commissioner of immigration, but Mr. Mitchell's office was of quite another sort. To Mr. Mitchell we owe the report of an extended conference which the president held on Thursday, August 14, 1862, with a group of free colored men who were believed to be leaders of their race. The president did most of the talking. He admitted at the outset the great wrongs which the negro race in America had endured at the hands of white men, but said that the presence of the negro in America had been the occasion of much injury to the other race. "But for your race among us, there could be no war," he said. There was a war, and white men were cutting each other's throats and no one knew where it would end. The negroes in America suffered inevitable disadvantages, whether free or slave, and the white men suffered on their account. He said to them that it would be far better for both races if the two were separated, and that he had available a large sum of money to assist in the separation. He said it was important that the newly emancipated slaves, with minds clouded by slavery, should have the leadership of men of their own race who had enjoyed the advantages of freedom. He recognized that those who were already free might prefer not to leave America. "This is (I speak in no unkind sense) an extremely selfish view of the case. You ought to do something to help those who are not so fortunate as yourselves." He said that if the white people could know that emancipated slaves were to leave America, one chief objection to emancipation would be removed. Free negroes, therefore, who refused to be leaders in a movement for colonization, obstructed the freedom of their own people. Those colored people whom the war had freed, had gained their liberty at the cost of white men's blood: were they to do nothing themselves by way of sacrifice for their own people? If they remained in this country when they might honorably go elsewhere, they purchased physical comfort at the cost of self-respect.

But where were they to go? The first answer was, to Liberia. The president had been in conference with "the old president" of Liberia, Roberts. There was much to be said for Liberia as the ultimate home of the American negro. But he was favorable to a nearer situation on this side of the ocean. He recommended the purchase of a tract in Central America, within the republic of New Granada. It was well adapted in climate to the constitution of the American negro, and favorable to the growing of cotton and other crops to which the negro was accustomed.

The president appears to have made an impression on some of the colored leaders. An agreement was entered into between the president and A. W. Thompson for the settlement of a tract in New Granada, and Senator S. E. Pomeroy, of Kansas, proposed to accompany and oversee the establishment of the colonists. But the government of New Granada objected to the settlement of a large colony of negroes in that republic and this plan had to be abandoned.

Then the president turned to Hayti, whose government was found to be willing to receive the colonists. In April, 1863, a group of honest contractors began the export of negroes, receiving fifty dollars for each American negro deported, on official certificate of his having been landed in Hayti. After about eighty thousand dollars had been expended, it was found that the region set apart for this colony was wholly unsuitable, and the negroes were brought back at the expense of the original agents who had given a fraudulent description of the country.*

Reluctantly, and with deep sorrow, Lincoln faced the problem of emancipation without the correlative plan of the removal of the free negroes from America.

On August 20, 1862, Horace Greeley addressed a long open letter to Mr. Lincoln through the *Tribune,* complaining "That a large proportion of our regular army officers, with many of the volunteers, evinced far more solicitude to uphold slavery than to put down the rebellion." He accused Lincoln of undue tenderness toward southern slaveholders, and demanded from him a statement of his own policy and purpose. Lincoln answered in a memorable letter which was given to the public:

EXECUTIVE MANSION,
WASHINGTON, August 22, 1862.

Hon. Horace Greeley.

Dear Sir: I have just read yours of the 19th addressed to myself through the "New York Tribune." If there be in it any statements, or assumptions of fact, which I may know to be erroneous, I do not, now and here, controvert them. If there be in it any inferences which I may believe to be falsely drawn, I

---

*The report of the commissioner of emigration in the Department of the Interior for 1863 records these attempts of the president to provide for the emigration of free negroes. The report of the conference of August 14, 1862, presumably written for the *New York Times,* is in Raymond's *Life of Lincoln,* pp. 505-508.

do not, now and here, argue against them. If there be percep-
tible in it an impatient and dictatorial tone, I waive it in deference to an old friend, whose heart I have always supposed to be
right. As to the policy I "seem to be pursuing," as you say, I
have not meant to leave any one in doubt. I would save the
Union. I would save it the shortest way under the Constitution.
The sooner the national authority can be restored, the nearer
the Union will be—"the Union as it was." If there be those who
would not save the Union unless they could at the same time
destroy slavery, I do not agree with them. My paramount object in this struggle is to save the Union, and is not either to
save or to destroy slavery. If I could save the Union without
freeing any slave, I would do it; and if I could save it by freeing
all the slaves, I would do it; and if I could save it by freeing
some and leaving others alone, I would also do that. What I do
about slavery, and the colored race, I do because I believe it
helps to save the Union; and what I forbear, I forbear because I
do not believe it would help to save the Union. I shall do less
whenever I shall believe what I am doing hurts the cause, and I
shall do more whenever I shall believe doing more will help the
cause. I shall try to correct errors when shown to be errors,
and I shall adopt new views so fast as they shall appear to be
true views. I have here stated my purpose according to my view
of official duty; and I intend no modification of my oft-ex-
pressed personal wish that all men everywhere could be free.

Yours,   A. Lincoln.

If any present-day reader thinks that this letter to Greeley
satisfied either Greeley or those for whom Greeley spoke, he is
mistaken. On the contrary, it seemed to very many that Lincoln had utterly abandoned his own principles with respect to
slavery. He had entered his campaign against Douglas with the
determination to force the slavery issue as a moral question on
which no man had a right to be neutral. He had mercilessly
hammered Douglas for his incautious declaration that if the
principle of popular sovereignty were preserved he cared not
whether slavery was voted up or voted down. To very many it
seemed that in this letter to Horace Greeley, Lincoln had gone
squarely over to the position which he had so vigorously con-

demned in Douglas. What did Lincoln mean if not this, that if the Union was preserved, he cared not whether slavery was voted up or voted down? It is little wonder that Greeley was not satisfied with Lincoln's answer, and that many others were disquieted.

On September thirteenth, a deputation of ministers from Chicago called on Lincoln to urge on him the duty of immediate emancipation. Lincoln did not inform them that such a proclamation was already written and awaiting a suitable opportunity to promulgate it. He set forth to them the practical difficulties in the way of an immediate movement of this sort:

What good would a proclamation of emancipation from me do, especially as we are now situated? I do not want to issue a document that the whole world will see must necessarily be inoperative, like the Pope's bull against the comet. Would my word free the slaves, when I cannot even enforce the Constitution in the rebel States? Is there a single court, or magistrate, or individual that would be influenced by it there? And what reason is there to think it would have any greater effect upon the slaves than the late law of Congress, which I approved, and which offers protection and freedom to the slaves of rebel masters who come within our lines? Yet I cannot learn that the law has caused a single slave to come over to us. And suppose they could be induced by a single proclamation of freedom from me to throw themselves upon us, what should we do with them? How can we feed and care for such a multitude? . . . If we were to arm them, I fear that in a few weeks the arms would be in the hands of the rebels; and, indeed, thus far we have not had arms enough to equip our white troops. I will mention another thing, though it meets only your scorn and contempt. There are fifty thousand bayonets in the Union armies from the border slave States. It would be a serious matter if, in consequence of a proclamation such as you desire, they should go over to the rebels.

Then came the battle of Antietam, which was fought September 17, 1862. It was far from being as decisive a victory as Lincoln had hoped for, but it was a victory. Lee was driven out of Maryland. Lincoln hesitated no longer. Indeed, Stanton is authority for the statement that, after the visit of the Chicago ministers, Lincoln moved with a stronger assurance of certainty. He summoned the Cabinet, not to discuss the proclamation on its merits, for this he quietly told them, was a matter he had already settled; he had promised his God that if General Lee was driven out of Maryland he would free the slaves.

The account of Secretary Chase was recorded in his diary on the night of September 22, 1862, the day on which the meeting had been told. He recorded the president as saying in substance:

I have, as you are aware, thought a great deal about the relation of this war to slavery; and you all remember that, several weeks ago, I read to you an order I had prepared on this subject, which, on account of objections made by some of you, was not issued. Ever since then my mind has been much occupied with this subject, and I have thought, all along, that the time for acting on it might probably come. I think the time has come now. I wish it was a better time. I wish that we were in a better condition. The action of the army against the rebels has not been quite what I should have best liked. But they have been driven out of Maryland, and Pennsylvania is no longer in danger of invasion. When the rebel army was at Frederick, I determined, as soon as it should be driven out of Maryland, to issue a proclamation of emancipation, such as I thought most likely to be useful. I said nothing to any one, but I made the promise to myself and [hesitating a little] to my Maker. The rebel army is now driven out, and I am going to fulfill that promise. I have got you together to hear what I have written down. I do not wish your advice about the main matter, for that I have determined for myself. This, I say without intending anything but respect for any one of you. But I already know the views of each on this question. They have been heretofore expressed, and I have considered them as thoroughly and carefully as I can. What I have written is that which my reflections have determined me to say. If there is anything in the expressions I use, or in any minor matter, which any of you thinks had best be changed, I shall be glad to receive the suggestions. One other observation I will make. I know very well that many others might, in this matter as in others, do better than I can; and if I was satisfied that the public confidence was more fully possessed by any one of them than by me, and knew of any constitutional way in which he could be put in my place, he should have it. I would gladly yield it to him. But, though I believe that I have not so much of the confidence of the people as I had some time since, I do not know that, all things considered, any other person has more; and, however this may be, there is no way in which I can have any other man put where I am. I am here; I must do the best I can, and bear the responsibility of taking the course which I feel I ought to take.

An independent account was preserved in the diary of the Secretary of the Navy, Honorable Gideon Welles:

SEPTEMBER 22.

A special Cabinet meeting. The subject was the proclamation for emancipating the slaves, after a certain date, in States that shall then be in rebellion. For several weeks the subject has been suspended, but the President says never lost sight of. When it was submitted, and now in taking up the proclamation, the President stated that the question was finally decided,—the act and the consequences were his,—but that he felt it due to us to make us acquainted with the fact and to invite criticisms on the paper which he had prepared. There were, he had found, not unexpectedly, some differences in the Cabinet; but he had, after ascertaining in his own way the views of each and all, individually and collectively, formed his own conclusions and made his own decisions. In the course of the discussion on this paper, which was long, earnest, and, on the general principle involved, harmonious, he remarked that he had made a vow—a covenant—that if God gave us the victory in the approaching battle he would consider it an indication of Divine will, and that it was duty to move forward in the cause of emancipation. It might be thought strange, he said, that he had in this way submitted the disposal of matters when the way was not clear to his mind what he should do. God had decided this question in favor of the slaves. He was satisfied it was right—was confirmed and strengthened in his action by the vow and results. His mind was fixed, his decision made, but he wished his paper

announcing his course as correct in terms as it could be made
without any change in his determination.

Mr. Chase also summarized the discussion which followed the
presentation of the document:

The President then proceeded to read his Emancipation Proclamation, making remarks on the several parts as he went on,
and showing that he had fully considered the whole subject, in
all the lights under which it had been presented to him. After he
had closed, Governor Seward said: "The general question having been decided, nothing can be said farther about that. Would
it not, however, make the proclamation more clear and decided
to leave out all reference to the act being sustained during the
incumbency of the present President; and not merely say that
the Government 'recognizes,' but that it will maintain, the freedom it proclaims?" I followed, saying: "What you have said,
Mr. President, fully satisfies me that you have given to every
proposition which has been made a kind and candid consideration. And you have now expressed the conclusion to which you
have arrived clearly and distinctly. This it was your right, and,
under your oath of office, your duty, to do. The proclamation,
does not, indeed, mark out exactly the course I would myself
prefer. But I am ready to take it just as it is written, and to
stand by it with all my heart. I think, however, the suggestions
of Governor Seward very judicious, and shall be glad to have
them adopted." The President then asked us severally our opinions as to the modification proposed, saying that he did not care
much about the phrases he had used. Every one favored the
modification, and it was adopted. Governor Seward then proposed that in the passage relating to colonization some language
should be introduced to show that the colonization proposed was
to be only with the consent of the colonists and the consent of
the States in which colonies might be attempted. This, too, was
agreed to, and no other modification was proposed. Mr. Blair
then said that, the question having been decided, he would make
no objection to issuing the proclamation; but he would ask to
have his paper, presented some days since, against the policy,
filed with the proclamation. The President consented to this
readily. And then Mr. Blair went on to say that he was afraid
of the influence of the proclamation on the border States and on

the army, and stated, at some length, the grounds of his apprehensions.   He disclaimed most expressly, however, all objection to emancipation *per se,* saying he had always been personally in favor of it—always ready for immediate emancipation in the midst of slave States, rather than submit to the perpetuation of the system.

The statement of Mr. Welles which relates the Cabinet proceedings is as follows:

All listened with profound attention to the reading, and it was, I believe, assented to by every member.   Mr. Bates repeated the opinions he had previously expressed in regard to the deportation of the colored race.   Mr. Seward proposed two slight verbal alterations, which were adopted.   A general discussion then took place, covering the whole ground—the constitutional question, the war power, the expediency and the effect of the movement.   After the matter had been very fully debated, Mr. Stanton made a very emphatic speech sustaining the measure, and in closing said the act was so important, and involved consequences so vast, that he hoped each member would give distinctly and unequivocally his own individual opinion, whatever that opinion might be.   Two gentlemen, he thought, had not been sufficiently explicit, although they had discussed the question freely, and it was understood that they concurred in the measure.   He referred, he said, to the Secretary of the Treasury and (hesitating a moment) the Secretary of the Navy.   It was understood, I believe, by all present that he had allusion to another member, with whom he was not in full accord.   Mr. Chase admitted that the subject had come upon him unexpectedly and with some surprise.   It was going a step further than he had ever proposed, but he was prepared to accept and support it. He was glad the President had made this advance, which he should sustain from his heart, and he proceeded to make an able impromptu argument in its favor.   I stated that the President did not misunderstand my position, nor any other member; that I assented most unequivocally to the measure as a war necessity, and had acted upon it.   Mr. Blair took occasion to say that he was an emancipationist from principle; that he had for years, here and in Missouri, where he formerly resided, openly advocated it; but he had doubts of the expediency of this executive action at this particular juncture. We ought not, he thought, to put in jeopardy the patriotic element in the border States, already severely tried. This proclamation would, as soon as it reached them, be likely to carry over those States to the secessionists. There were also party men in the free states who were striving to revive old party lines and distinctions, into whose hand we were putting a club to be used against us. The measure he approved, but the time was inopportune. He should wish, therefore, to file his objections. This, the President said, Mr. Blair could do. He had, however, considered the danger to be apprehended from the first objection mentioned, which was undoubtedly serious, but the difficulty was as great not to act as to act. There were two sides to that question. For months he had labored to get those States to move in this matter, convinced in his own mind that it was their true interest to do so, but his labors were vain. We must make the forward movement. They would acquiesce, if not immediately, soon; for they must be satisfied that slavery had received its death-blow from slave-owners—it could not survive the rebellion. As regarded the other objection, it had not much weight with him; their clubs would be used against us take what course we might.

When Congress convened in December, 1862, Lincoln communicated the proclamation to that body in a message reaffirming in the strongest possible terms, his faith in the indivisibility of the Union, and of the righteousness of his proclamation as a means of saving the Union. He said:

I do not forget the gravity which should characterize a paper addressed to the Congress of the nation by the Chief Magistrate of the nation. Nor do I forget that some of you are my seniors, nor that many of you have more experience than I in the conduct of public affairs. Yet I trust that in view of the great responsibility resting upon me, you will perceive no want of respect to yourselves in any undue earnestness I may seem to display. . . . The dogmas of the quiet past are inadequate to the stormy present. The occasion is piled high with difficulty, and we must rise with the occasion. As our case is new, so we must think anew and act anew. We must disenthrall ourselves, and then we shall save our country.

Fellow citizens, we cannot escape history. We, of this Congress and this administration, will be remembered in spite of ourselves. No personal significance, or insignificance, can spare one or another of us. The fiery trial through which we pass will light us down, in honor or dishonor, to the latest generation. We say we are for the Union. The world will not forget that we say this. We know how to save the Union. The world knows we do know how to save it. We—even *we here*—hold the power and bear the responsibility. In *giving* freedom to the *slave* we *assure* freedom to the *free*—honorable alike in what we give and what we preserve. We shall nobly save, or meanly lose, the last, best hope of earth. Other means may succeed, this could not fail. The way is plain, peaceful, generous, just—a way which, if followed, the world will forever applaud, and God must forever bless.

The question of the employment of negro troops gave concern to both armies. General Lee favored enlisting negroes in the Southern Army, and so did Jefferson Davis, but the South had reason to pause before putting uniforms on the backs of slaves and giving them guns with which to fight against soldiers of the white race. Negroes thus fighting in the Confederate Army would, of course, receive their freedom as a reward, and they would thereafter live in the South, after having been taught to shoot white men. In the North there was much disinclination to employ negroes as soldiers, but a growing conviction that there was no good reason why white men should die to make black men free and the black men be sheltered from the perils of the war. Soon after the Emancipation Proclamation went into effect, the enlistment of negro soldiers began. On January 20, 1863, twenty days after the proclamation became effective, Governor John A. Andrew, of Massachusetts, was authorized to enlist negro soldiers, to be formed into a separate corps. How well he did his work, and how well he was aided by George L. Stearns and others, the monument to Colonel Robert Gould Shaw, which stands on Boston Common, fronting the state-house, attests. In August of that year, Honorable Joseph Holt, Judge Advocate

General, sent to the president an official opinion that the president was authorized to enlist slaves as soldiers, remunerating such masters as were loyal for property thus taken from them for the uses of the government in time of war.

Lincoln's desire to provide if possible a gradual method of emancipation with compensation would naturally have restrained him even longer from issuing the Proclamation of Emancipation had not existing conditions made any such provisions impossible. But Lincoln had to deal not only with conservative but with very radical elements in his own party. Through all the months of his administration he had been careful in testing out the sentiments of the country, to determine whether it would bear such a proclamation. The time had come when in some respects it was safer to issue the proclamation than not to do so. There was a growing conviction that Webster was right in his declaration that liberty and Union were one and inseparable. The divided house had not stood. Could it be reunited and rebuilt upon the foundation of liberty? This was the stone which the builders had rejected: Lincoln made it the headstone of the corner.

CHAPTER XII

"HE SAID HE WAS MASTER"

IF LINCOLN supposed that his Emancipation Proclamation would be a popular political move, he was doomed to cruel disappointment. The proclamation succeeded in rousing the most bitter hostility of the pro-slavery element of the North, and by a singular inconsistency it seemed to give some of the extreme anti-slavery advocates a new ground for their attacks upon Lincoln.

The North contained a very strong element which had little or no sympathy with the conduct of the war. The so-called "Copperhead" movement, which later manifested itself in deliberate plans for the overthrow of the government, was in 1862 a strongly entrenched political power opposed to the president. The friends of McClellan turned against Lincoln, alleging that he had first failed to cooperate with this brilliant general, and then ruthlessly removed him from command for reasons of political jealousy. Haters of the negro professed to see in the Emancipation Proclamation the menace of negro equality and of social demoralization. Extremes met. There was a considerable element in the North composed of those who were bitterly opposed to slavery, and who blamed Lincoln severely for not freeing the slaves earlier. Indeed, there were not a few who declared that the president, with what they called his customary vacillation, would find a pretext for recalling his proclamation before January 1, 1863. These people found common ground with those who blamed him for freeing the slaves at all.

The Democratic Party declared that the Emancipation Proclamation had now made abolition the actual purpose of the war. No longer, they affirmed, was the preservation of the Union the paramount object; the real purpose for which white men were expected to lay down their lives was to give freedom and social equality to the black man. This distinctly was not what they had undertaken to do, nor did they propose to do it.

The congressional election in Maine occurred early in September, 1862. Then, as in subsequent elections, the results of that state were closely watched. "As goes Maine, so goes the Union," had already become a proverb. Maine usually elected a Republican governor by a majority of from 10,000 to 19,000. In 1862, Maine chose a Republican governor by a majority of only 4,000, and, for the first time since there had been a Republican Party, Maine sent one Democrat to Congress.

Ohio voted in October, and sent to the National House of Representatives fourteen Democrats and only five Republicans. The Democratic vote in that state exceeded the Republican by a majority of 7,000. In Pennsylvania, where two years before Lincoln had had a majority of 60,000, the Democratic vote exceeded the Republican by about 4,000, and the congressional delegation was divided. Indiana sent to Congress only three Republican representatives and eight Democrats. New York went Democratic by a majority of nearly 10,000, electing Horatio Seymour as governor. New Jersey, which had voted Republican in 1860, went Democratic in 1862. Michigan remained Republican, but its majority was reduced from 20,000 to 6,000. Wisconsin divided its delegation evenly. Illinois, Lincoln's own state, went Democratic by a majority of 17,000, and her congressional delegation was eleven Democrats to three Republicans. New York, New Jersey, Pennsylvania, Ohio, Indiana and Illinois all failed to support Lincoln in 1862.

To their everlasting honor the New England States, and Iowa, Kansas, Minnesota, California and Oregon, stood better in their support of the president. But when the returns were all in, the Democrats, who had only forty-four votes in the

24

House in the Thirty-seventh Congress, had seventy-five in the Thirty-eighth.

In that crisis the border states stood by the president. He had not underestimated the importance of holding them loyally within the Union, and true in their support of the administration. They in 1862 furnished a sufficient number of pro-administration members to save Congress from going over to the opposition.

But among the Republicans were not a few members so bitterly hostile to Lincoln for his cautious policy that it could hardly be said that the president had in Congress any more than a bare working majority.

The elections of 1862 were "off-year" elections. Off-years are often fatal years. The elections of 1862 were not fatal to Lincoln's hopes, but they weakened his support, and prepared the way for a bitter and painful campaign in 1864.

The Emancipation Proclamation went into effect on January 1, 1863. There was a great celebration in Music Hall in Boston, and Ralph Waldo Emerson read his *Boston Hymn* on that occasion. In many other places there were enthusiastic meetings and warm expressions of approval. But that is not the whole story. There was much emphatic disapproval, also. On the day following the proclamation's taking effect, Senator O. H. Browning recorded:

Friday, Jany. 2, 1863. At Mr. Seward's for dinner at 6. No one else there. I asked him why the Cabinet did so useless and so mischievous a thing as to issue the proclamation which had been issued, the only effect of which was to unite and exasperate them in the South and divide and distract us in the North. He replied by telling me an anecdote of a man who after the termination of the Revolutionary War could not rest till he had a liberty pole erected in his village; when asked by his neighbors what he wanted with a pole, and whether he was not as free without it as with it, he would always answer, "What is liberty without a pole?" And what is war without a proclamation? We played whist with Mrs. Seward and Miss Fanny till 9 o'clock, and then

Seward and I went over to the President's. We found General Butler there who had just arrived from New Orleans. He read to us his parting address to the people of New Orleans, and General Banks' proclamation upon assuming command. His conversation indicated that he was a very ultra abolitionist. He gave it as his opinion that the only way to put down the rebellion was to destroy slavery. This class of people do not seem to know that armed rebellion stands between us and slavery, and that to get at the latter we must first crush the former.

There had been a time when the president and Browning seemed to be of one accord in this matter, but that time was past, and it never came back. Browning still supported the president, but confessed this sharp dissent from his view of the way to deal with slavery. And Browning was one of many scores of thousands. Browning hated slavery, as Lincoln did, but wholly disapproved of Lincoln's way of getting rid of it.

If Lincoln was at first disposed to attribute his rebuke at the polls to any other cause than the unpopularity of his methods, he was not lacking in friends who told him with entire and almost brutal frankness their view of the case. We are making considerable use of the *Diary* of Senator Browning. It is our latest and in some respects most intimate authority upon the life of the president in those days. Browning was at the White House almost daily. When the Lincoln family was in trouble, as it was when Willie died, Senator and Mrs. Browning spent not only their days but their nights at the White House. Perhaps Lincoln never had any intimate friends, but if he had any in this period, Browning was one of the closest. Shortly after the November elections in 1862, Browning had a long visit with the president:

He was apparently very glad to see me, and received me with much cordiality. We had a long familiar talk. When speaking of the results of the recent elections I told him that his proclamations had been disastrous to us. That prior to issuing them, all loyal people were united in support of the war and the administration. That the masses of the Democratic Party were satisfied with him, and warmly supporting him, and that their disloyal leaders could not rally them in opposition. They had no issue without taking ground against the war, and that we would annihilate them. But the proclamations had revived old party issues, given them a rallying cry, capital to operate upon, and that we had the results in our defeat. To this he made no reply. I added that the Republican Party could not put down the rebellion—that no party could do it—that it required a union of all loyal men in the free states to give us success, and without that union we must disastrously fail. To all this he fully assented.

About this time the president's support in Congress seemed almost totally to disappear. A visitor to the capitol called upon Thaddeus Stevens and asked to be introduced to some of the president's adherents. Stevens led him over to the desk of Isaac N. Arnold, saying that this man wanted to meet the members of Congress who were in sympathy with the president, and that so far as Stevens knew, Arnold was the only man in the lower House who belonged in that group. This, of course, was putting the matter too strongly, but it was uncomfortably near the truth.

Misfortunes never come singly. Soon after the elections of November, 1862, came the appalling news of the battle of Fredericksburg. On December 13, 1862, General Burnside, with 125,000 men, crossed the Rappahannock on three pontoon bridges and made a frontal attack on Lee, who had 80,000 men well entrenched on the opposite side of the river, his right commanded by Stonewall Jackson and his left by Longstreet. If geography has anything to say about battles, that was a foolhardy proceeding on Burnside's part, and bitterly did his army pay for his folly. The Federal loss was 12,800 against Lee's loss of 4,300. The Federal Army retreated north of the Rappahannock, and the country was compelled to be thankful that the army was able to get back without being captured or destroyed.

The country was well-nigh desperate. On the afternoon of Tuesday, December 16, 1862, the Senate adjourned about half-

past one, and the Republican members held a caucus. We have
an account of it in Browning's *Diary*. Lyman Trumbull bitterly
assailed the administration, denouncing the president and Seward. Ben Wade declared that the Senate ought to go in a body
to the White House and demand the resignation of Seward. He
favored the creation of a lieutenant general, "with absolute and
despotic powers," and he must be a Republican in politics. "He
said a member of the Cabinet* informed him that there was a
backstairs and malign influence which controlled the President,
and overruled all the decisions of the Cabinet, and he understood
Mr. Seward to be meant. He was for demanding his removal."
    Browning and others spoke in defense of Lincoln, if not of
Seward. A motion to adjourn was offered, and was opposed
by Trumbull and others, but prevailed. The caucus took recess
for a day without violent action. Browning's comment on the
speeches of Trumbull, Wade, Grimes, Fessenden and the others
who had attacked Seward, and with him the president, is interesting:

These ultra-radical, unreasoning men, who raised the insane
cry of "On to Richmond" in July, 1861, and have kept up a war
on our generals ever since, who forced through the confiscation
bills, and extorted from the President the Proclamations and lost
him the support of the country, are now his bitterest enemies,
and doing all in their power to break him down.

The next day, the caucus assembled again. "Many speeches
were made," says Browning, "all expressive of a want of confidence in the President and his Cabinet. Some of them denouncing the President and expressing a willingness to vote for
a resolution asking him to resign. Most of those who spoke
were the partisans of Mr. Chase, and excepted him from the
censure they bestowed upon the Cabinet."
    Browning wrote:

---

*It is apparent from subsequent speeches in the caucus that the member
of the Cabinet who furnished Wade his information was Chase.

In my remarks on yesterday I said I knew there was no more honest, upright, conscientious man than the President, and that I knew him to be in favor of the most vigorous prosecution of the war, and that he intended to prosecute until every state was restored to the Union and every rebel compelled to submit to the authority of the government.

Apparently Browning did not speak on the second day. Charles Sumner moved that a committee be appointed "to wait on the President and represent to him the necessity for a change in men and measures." This motion prevailed almost without dissent. The committee was composed of Senators Jacob Collamer, of Vermont, B. F. Wade, of Ohio, William Pitt Fessenden, of Maine, Ira Harris, of New York, James W. Grimes, of New Hampshire, Charles Sumner, of Massachusetts, Lyman Trumbull, of Illinois, Jacob M. Howard, of Michigan, and Samuel C. Pomeroy, of Kansas. It was not a committee whose composition could afford much comfort to the president.

That Lincoln was heart-broken over this revolt of the Senate, and for a time almost in despair, we might assure ourselves if we had no record of the fact; but we have a record again in Browning's *Diary* of Thursday, December 18, 1862:

In the evening went with Mr. D. W. Wise of Boston to the President's. The servant at the door reported that he was not in his office—was in the house, but had directed them to say that he would not be seen to-night. I told the boy to tell him I wished to see him a moment and went up into his room. He soon came in. I saw in a moment that he was in distress—that more than usual trouble was pressing upon him. I introduced Mr. Wise who wished to get some items for the preparation of a biography, but soon discovered that the President was in no mood to talk upon the subject. We took our leave. When we got to the door the President called to me saying he wished to speak to me a moment. He asked me if I was at the caucus yesterday. I told him I was, and the day before also. Said he, "What do those men want?" I answered, "I hardly know, Mr. President, but they are exceedingly violent against the administration, and what we did yesterday was the gentlest thing that could be done. It had to be that or worse." Said he, "They wish to get rid of me, and I am sometimes half disposed to gratify them." I replied, "Some of them do wish to get rid of you, but the fortunes of the country are bound up with your fortunes; and you must stand firmly at your post with a steady hand. To relinquish it now would bring upon us certain and inevitable ruin." Said he, "We are now on the brink of destruction. It appears to me the Almighty is against us, and I can hardly see a ray of hope." . . . He added, "The committee is to be up and see me at 7 o'clock. Since I heard last night of the proceedings of the caucus, I have been more distressed than by any event of my life." I bade him good-night and left him.

The days that followed were no better. On the very next day "old Francis P. Blair came into the marble room" and sent for Browning. The country was very nearly ruined, he told Browning, and advised Browning to go to the president and tell him to get rid of Stanton and Halleck. A little later Reverdy Johnson came to Browning's seat in the Senate and told him the country was going to the devil, and that there must be a new Cabinet.

Browning recorded that he did not wish to thrust his advice upon the president, but he met the president that afternoon and the president told him he was trying "to keep things along." But Browning declared in his *Diary* that things could not be kept along much longer at this rate.

Lincoln met the committee first alone, and then invited them to come again and meet in person the members of the Cabinet and tell them frankly what they were saying to him. They came again, and the entire Cabinet was present except Seward. Senator Collamer presented to the president in writing the view of the Republican caucus. The president invited the members of the Cabinet to reply. Their answer took the wind out of the sails of the report:

Chase, Blair and Bates made speeches—the others said nothing. The purport of the speeches was to prove that the Cabinet did hold meetings, and that there were no dissensions among them—Mr. Chase among others stating that they were all harmonious.

That must have been a surprising statement for Chase to make in the presence of Wade! The committee could not say very much after that, nor does it appear that Lincoln said much of anything. He had no need to say much.

If the committee was astonished at this information, so was the caucus when the committee made its report. "I asked Judge Collamer," wrote Browning, "how Mr. Chase could venture to make such a statement in the presence of senators to whom he had said that Seward exercised a backstairs and malign influence upon the president and thwarted all the measures of the Cabinet." Collamer could only growl out an angry answer concerning Chase. That answer was in two words—"He lied."

With such a report before it, what could the Republican caucus do? It did not see that it could do anything. It heard the report of the committee, learned that it could not depend on Chase to repeat in the presence of the president and the rest of the Cabinet what he had said to Wade, and the caucus ingloriously adjourned.

That night Browning called again at the White House. He was ready with suggestions for the new Cabinet which he hoped Lincoln would appoint. He suggested as secretary of state, first Collamer, of New York, and then Ewing, of Ohio. For secretary of war he would have General Banks. If Lincoln took Collamer as secretary of state, then Ewing would be a good man for secretary of the treasury. For one of the other places he suggested Guthrie, of Kentucky. He did not propose himself as a member, but it is scarcely possible that he thought of a new Cabinet with himself out of it.

Lincoln told him frankly that he did not propose to have any new Cabinet. He said that if he got a new one, the same men would attack it who were now opposing the old one. He said he would rather get along with the one he had than try a new one.

By this time, he had Browning half convinced. And then Browning recalled, and mentioned to the president, that the men who had instigated this revolt were partisans of Chase:

I told him that their game was to drive all the Cabinet out, then force upon him the recall of Mr. Chase as premier, and form a Cabinet of ultra men around him.

Lincoln understood this quite as well as Browning did, and assured Browning that the Senate would not be allowed to compel him to adopt any such measure. When Browning went to the White House that night, December 22, 1862, he told the president "that this was a time of more peril than any we had encountered" and wanted him to make up a new slate for a Cabinet. He left convinced that the president was right in his determination to keep the old Cabinet, and let his opponents howl.

"He said with a good deal of emphasis that he was master," wrote Browning.

He said the truth. He was master, and he knew it, and those who opposed him were to learn it.

Let us pause for a moment to consider this emergence and ascent of Lincoln from out of the depths. Perhaps in no other crisis of his presidency is there a more complete and significant example.

He had promised God that if General Lee was driven out of Maryland, he would issue the proclamation of emancipation. He issued that proclamation against the judgment of several members of his Cabinet, believing that it would commend itself to the favor of the people and to the blessing of God. Apparently it did neither. Lincoln never felt more completely God-forsaken than in the weeks after that proclamation bore its fruit. It seemed to him, as he told Browning, that God was against him, and it seemed also that the people, whom he trusted next to God, had also cast him adrift. Repudiated at the polls, he was deserted by Congress and betrayed by members of his Cabinet.

The ballot failed him; the army failed him; the heavens above him were brass. Never was he nearer despair than on the night when the committee from the Republican senatorial caucus was on its way to the White House.

He met that committee courteously, and received their report requesting him to dismiss his Cabinet and change his entire policy. He dismissed them with a request that they leave their report with him for consideration, and come again. When they came he had his Cabinet there, save only Seward, whose presence might have provoked them and led Seward to indiscretions. He shrewdly kept still and let Chase speak for himself, following the wisdom of the Arab proverb, "When the wind blows your fire, save your breath." He sent the committee back, discomfited, but with no occasion for anger against any one but Chase. Again he could chuckle, as he did when Buchanan and Douglas were fighting each other—"Go it, husband, go it, bear!"

Then, when the committee had gone back to the caucus, and the caucus, having exhausted its oratory and accomplished nothing, adjourned, Browning, thinking the president would now gladly do voluntarily what he could not with good grace have done under compulsion, went over to assist Lincoln with the new Cabinet, and found Lincoln adamantine, and went away more than half believing that Lincoln was right. That lonely man, no longer despairing, no longer forsaken of his God, no longer hesitating between opposing counsels, calmly declared that he was master of the situation. Though his army was defeated and without a general, his Cabinet divided and without heart, his Congress rebellious and his friends in despair, Abraham Lincoln stood calmly, with a new faith in God and the cause for which he was fighting.

That faith was justified. The proclamation of emancipation raised up new friends in Great Britain, and drove the last nail in the coffin of Europe's recognition of the Confederate Government. It gave a new moral definition to the conflict. Again the armies prepared for battle, singing as they marched:

We will rally round the flag, boys,
    We'll rally once again,
Shouting the battle-cry of freedom.

The fortunes of the administration were at a low ebb. One thing, however, was becoming apparent; so far as any one in Washington was in control of the situation, it was not Congress, nor the Committee on the Conduct of the War, nor the Cabinet, nor the army, nor even, as Chief Justice Taney was to learn, the Supreme Court; it was the president. They who had thought him a weak man, easily controlled by stronger natures, were learning that Abraham Lincoln could be almost despotic. They did not hesitate to say this of him, and to declare that under his administration the United States had become a military despotism. The country was beginning to learn who was at the head of the administration. There was one man who never had any doubt who was master. That was the man who was accustomed to receive stacks of letters and telegrams and editorials requesting or demanding that he do this or refrain from doing that, and to stuff them all into a pigeonhole, saying, "I know more about it than any of them." That was the man whom some people thought self-distrustful and many now call modest, Abraham Lincoln.

"He said with a good deal of emphasis that he was master."

CHAPTER XIII

"ABRAHAM LINCOLN, GIVE US A MAN!"

MILITARY success is much more promptly won than is political success. As it is swiftly won, so is it easily lost. Before the close of the Civil War, Horace Greeley published the first volume of his *American Conflict*. It was illustrated with steel engravings, each of them a group picture containing a number of portraits. One of these showed the faces of twelve Union generals who had won fame before the middle of 1863. These were, General Scott, who had the central place, and Generals Wool, McClellan, Butler, Fremont, McDowell, Halleck, Hooker, Burnside, Hunter, Anderson and Buell. The second volume, published shortly after the close of the war, had as its frontispiece a companion group. Not one portrait from the first volume appeared in the second. This was not wholly because the publishers and engravers desired a new group; no general who had made his reputation in the first half of the war retained it to the end. Aspirants for military glory could find few more thought-provoking or profitable lessons than those suggested by a prolonged study of these two groups of pictures. With a few possible exceptions, almost any one could at a guess recall the names that of necessity must have appeared in the second list. General Grant, of course, had the central place. Around him were the portraits of Sherman, Sheridan, Thomas, Meade, Hancock, Blair, Howard, Terry, Curtis, Gilmore and Banks. One can not study this list long without the reflection that not all these names would have survived to appear in a third volume.

A large proportion of the nation's trained soldiers had gone

with the South. It was a fair question whether, after the withdrawal of the southern generals, the North had left a competent military leader.

General Emory Upton, in his *Military Policy of the United
States,** says:

On the thirty-first of March, 1862, the Government had in
service an army of 637,126 men, nearly all of whom were enlisted for the term of three years.

The Confederate Army, composed largely of one-year volunteers, whose enlistments were on the eve of expiring, scarcely
exceeded 200,000 men.

The failure to subdue the Rebellion in 1861 has already been
explained by our total want of military organization and preparation. The failure to subdue it in 1862, with the amazing advantages possessed by the Union, proceeded from a cause entirely different—the mismanagement of our armies.

Humiliated and made wiser by the defeat at Bull Run, the
President, the Cabinet, and the people, were at first disposed to
give the new commander all the time necessary to organize and
discipline his troops; but when several months had passed with
no indication of an advance, the army in the meantime having
increased to above 200,000 men, impatience for action returned
with accumulated force.

When Gen. McClellan assumed command, he found his army
"cowering on the banks of the Potomac," the troops and the
people alike demoralized by the defeat and panic at Bull Run.
He knew that but two things, men, and the time to make them
soldiers, were necessary to restore the ascendency of the Government. The men were given liberally, but time to drill them
could not be accorded. When the armies throughout the country, with scarcely a shadow of discipline, had swelled to the aggregate of 600,000, the expense of supporting them was so great
that the President was forced to declare if something was not
soon done "the bottom would be out of the whole affair."

At the time of the appointment of Gen. McClellan the fate
of the nation seemed to depend upon this single individual. In

*This remarkable book which for years lay pigeonholed in Washington,
is now published, in full and in abbreviated form, by the United States Government for use as a text-book.

the organization of his army he stood alone. None of his brigade, division, or corps commanders had ever seen service as such. None of them, as in Europe, had exercised command at maneuvers or had been practiced in handling large bodies of troops. The colonels, from whom the future brigadiers were mostly to come, were nearly all from civil life, with but little knowledge of tactics or standard of discipline, by which to gauge the proficiency of their troops. A difficulty of nearly equal magnitude confronted him in the staff. The Adjutant General's Department for want of interchangeability with the line could not, as in European services, furnish competent chiefs of staff to him or to any of his corps and division commanders.

It was during the month lost by the delay at Yorktown, that the Confederate Congress abandoned voluntary enlistments, adopted conscription, and took away from the governors the power to commission Confederate officers; it was during this month, when the Army of the Potomac should have been at the doors of Richmond, that almost every regiment of the Confederate Army was reorganized; it was during this month that Confederate conscripts began to pour into the old regiments instead of being formed into new organizations; it was during this and the two succeeding months, while McDowell was held back, that these conscripts, associated with veteran comrades, acquired courage and discipline, and it was by concentration during the last month that the Confederate Army was made to equal its opponent. The loss of battles was but a trifle compared with the other consequences of this one month's delay. It arrayed against us a military system, which enabled the Confederate Government to call out the last man and the last dollar, as against a system based on voluntary enlistment and the consent of the States. It was no longer a question of dealing a dissolving army its deathblow. We had permitted a rival government to reorganize its forces, which we now were compelled to destroy by the slow process of attrition.

One thing the nation learned, or should have learned, out of the tragic experiences of the first years of the war, and that was that the question of winning battles was largely a question of trained leadership. We have tried our best not to learn this lesson. The volunteer soldier despised, or affected to despise.

UNION GENERALS PROMINENT IN LAST HALF OF THE WAR
From Second Volume of Greeley's *American Conflict*

leaders who had had military training. In the Mexican War, General Taylor, as "Old Rough and Ready," achieved a popularity which General Scott, "Old Fuss and Feathers," coveted but never attained. So, in the Civil War, the sympathy and enthusiasm of the volunteer soldier were for the volunteer officer, and the volunteer officer held the West Point graduate in open scorn. But it was the West Point graduates on both sides who proved themselves capable of sustained leadership. Sending soldiers to the front is a hazardous thing at best, but sending them to the front under undisciplined officers is manslaughter, and sometimes murder. The men who won the war were the men trained at West Point. The war did not produce its leaders out of raw material. All soldiers need disciplined leaders, but undisciplined soldiers especially need trained officers, or an army becomes a panic-stricken mob.

But where was the general to lead the Union Armies to victory? There was no lack of men or money, but where was the leader? The Greeks, having two words to our one for "man" have a proverb which we are incapable of translating literally, but the spirit of it might be suggested by the words, "We have plenty of men, but where is the man?"

On September 8, 1862, a week after the appointment of McClellan and shortly before Antietam, Edmund Clarence Stedman published his poem which echoed the pathetic cry of the North, "Abraham Lincoln, give us a man!" We must quote it in full:

WANTED A MAN

Back from the trebly crimsoned field
   Terrible words are thunder-tost;
Full of the wrath that will not yield,
   Full of revenge for battles lost!
   Hark to their echo, as it crost
The Capitol, making faces wan:
   "End this murderous holocaust;
Abraham Lincoln, give us a Man!

"Give us a man of God's own mould,
　　Born to marshal his fellow-men;
One whose fame is not bought and sold
　　At the stroke of a politician's pen;
　　Give us the man of thousands ten,
Fit to do as well as to plan;
　　Give us a rallying-cry, and then,
Abraham Lincoln, give us a Man!

"No leader to shirk the boasting foe,
　　And to march and countermarch our brave,
Till they fall like ghosts in the marshes low,
　　And swamp-grass covers each nameless grave;
　　Nor another whose fatal banners wave.
Aye in Disaster's shameful van;
　　Nor another, to bluster, and lie, and rave;—
Abraham Lincoln, give us a Man!

"Hearts are mourning in the North,
　　While the sister rivers seek the main,
Red with life-blood flowing forth,—
　　Who shall gather it up again?
　　Though we march to the battle-plain
Firmly as when the strife began,
　　Shall all our offering be in vain?—
Abraham Lincoln, give us a Man!

"Is there never one in all the land,
　　One on whose might the Cause may lean?
Are all the common ones so grand,
　　And all the titled ones so mean?
　　What if your failure may have been
In trying to make good bread from bran,
　　From worthless metal a weapon keen?—
Abraham Lincoln, find us a Man!

"O, we will follow him to the death,
　　Where the foeman's fiercest columns are!
O, we will use our latest breath,
　　Cheering for every sacred star!
　　His to marshall us high and far;

Ours to battle, as patriots can
    When a Hero leads to the Holy War!—
Abraham Lincoln, give us a Man!"

September 8, 1862.

The date of this poem is significant. It was written and published just after the reappointment of McClellan.

It would not be difficult to distinguish the principal characters referred to in the leaders so bitterly pilloried in this poem. No one could doubt whom Stedman meant by the leader who shirked the boasting foe, and there had been generals enough whose banners flew in the shameful van of retreat, or who blustered and lied and raved. He who will may try his hand in deciding just what officers the poet had in mind. But the poem went to the heart of Abraham Lincoln. He read it, and as he bent over, between the knotted fingers in which he buried his face, the tears dropped on the poem. Where was he to find that man?

He still hoped against hope that he had already found him. He was trying once more to have faith in McClellan. This general had been recalled against the protests of a portion of the Cabinet, and an influential portion of the Congressional Committee on the Conduct of the War. Indeed, this very poem was part of that protest. How the general had come to impress certain members of that committee, including Zachariah Chandler and Benjamin F. Wade, the biographers of Chandler have set forth, and Chandler himself told on the floor of the Senate:

Originally Mr. Chandler believed that McClellan's selection as the practical successor of General Scott was a wise one, and hoped to see his organizing capacity in camp supplemented by enterprise and courage in the field. Distrust first sprang up with the persistent effort of the Army of the Potomac throughout the last months of 1861, and it was strengthened by contact with the man himself and the study of his character and his plans. An illustration of how this change of opinion was brought about is given in an incident which occurred in the room of the Committee on the Conduct of the War. That committee sent for General McClellan as soon as they took up matters relating to his command, in order to consult with him informally as to the situation. This was in January, 1862, while he was in Washington "organizing" his army, and while there was no little impatience felt because he did not move. He was not formally called before the committee then, but simply called in for general consultation. After the regular business was finished, Mr. Chandler asked him bluntly why he did not attack the rebels. General McClellan replied that it was because there were not sufficient means of communication with Washington; he then called attention to the fact that there were only two bridges and other means of transportation across the Potomac.

Mr. Chandler asked what the number of bridges had to do with an advance movement, and McClellan explained with much detail that it was one of the most important features of skillful strategy that a commander should have plenty of room to retreat before making an attack. To this Mr. Chandler's response was:

"General McClellan, if I understand you correctly, before you strike at the rebels you want to be sure of plenty of room so that you can run in case they strike back!"

"Or in case you get scared," added Senator Wade.

The commander of the Army of the Potomac manifested indignation at this blunt way of putting the case, and then proceeded at length to explain the art of war and the science of generalship, laying special stress upon the necessity of having lines of retreat, as well as lines of communication and supply, always open. He labored hard to make clear all the methods and counter-methods upon which campaigns are managed and battles fought, and, as he was an accomplished master of the theory of war, succeeded in rendering himself at least interesting. After he had concluded, Mr. Wade said:

"General, you have all the troops you have called for, and if you haven't enough, you shall have more. They were well organized and equipped, and the loyal people of this country expect that you will make a short and decisive campaign. Is it really necessary for you to have more bridges over the Potomac before you move?"

"Not that," was the answer, "not that exactly, but we must bear in mind the necessity of having everything ready in case of a defeat, and keep our lines of retreat open."

With this remark General McClellan left the room, whereupon Mr. Wade asked:

"Chandler, what do you think of the science of generalship?"

"I don't know much about war," was the reply, "but it seems to me that this is infernal, unmitigated cowardice."

When it was proposed to reinstate McClellan as commander of the armies around Washington, four members of the Cabinet protested, among them Stanton, who wrote for their signatures this dignified protest, and unofficially expressed his dissent in far stronger language:

The undersigned, who have been honored with your selection as part of your confidential advisers, deeply impressed with our great responsibility in the present crisis, do but perform a painful duty in declaring to you our deliberate opinion that at this time it is not safe to intrust to Major-General McClellan the command of any army of the United States. And we hold ourselves ready at any time to explain to you in detail the reasons upon which this opinion is based.

But on September 2, 1862, Lincoln had reappointed McClellan, and accepted with gratitude for small mercies the meager victory of Antietam. After that, Lincoln could not coax, command or threaten McClellan with sufficient earnestness to force that general to move. Patience ceased to be a virtue, and Lincoln removed McClellan from his command.

It would be good to know that in the appointment of generals and the winning of victories no political consideration had any weight either in the army, in the Congress, in the Cabinet or in the White House. Unfortunately, this was not the case. If any general in command of the Army of the Potomac had been able to win decisive victories against forces of equal or nearly equal strength, he could have held his military position, and gone forward to victory upon the battle-field, and more than possibly have gone from there into the White House. Lincoln was far from being too popular to need to fear the rivalry of a successful

winner of battles, and it is to his immortal honor that, desirous
as he was of succeeding himself, he would willingly have been
defeated by a general who could have saved the country in a decisive victory and carried his success into politics. But no such
general was in sight. McClellan had failed. Pope had failed.
McClellan had failed again. Burnside had failed, and the cry
was loud and long for still another restoration of "Little Mac."
But the Cabinet was united against him. His known idea of a
"military dictatorship," together with his record in battle or the
avoiding of it, made certain that if McClellan achieved any further success he must do it at the polls, and he was not unwilling
to undertake that adventure. If McClellan had been selected as
the successor to Burnside and had won the battle of Gettysburg,
he would have been elected president in 1864.

There was a prominent member of Lincoln's Cabinet who was
very desirous that Hooker should be appointed, and that he
should win. That was Salmon P. Chase, who sincerely believed
that he himself ought to be elected president in 1864. If Hooker
won, he would keep his ambitions within the bounds of military
advancement, and Chase might expect to reap the political benefits of Hooker's military success. In an important and apparently reliable paper by Charles F. Benjamin, published in the
Century War Book,* it is confidently affirmed that Hooker was
appointed because Lincoln was compelled to recognize the power
of the Chase interests. The effort to secure the appointment of
Hooker against the distrust of Lincoln and the open hostility of
Stanton was impossible, he affirms, until connection was made
with a powerful faction which had for its object the elevation of
Mr. Chase to the presidency at the end of Mr. Lincoln's term.

Making every allowance for the strength and availability of
Mr. Chase as against Mr. Lincoln or any other civilian candidate, his friends did not conceal from themselves that the general who should conquer the rebellion would have the disposal of

*Hooker's Appointment and Removal, by Charles F. Benjamin; Battles
and Leaders of the Civil War, iii, 239-243.

the next presidency, and they were on the lookout for the right military alliance, when they came into communication with Hooker's friends, and received their assurances that, if it should be his good fortune to bring the war to a successful close, nothing could possibly induce him to accept other than military honors in recognition of his services. General Hooker thereupon became the candidate of Mr. Chase's friends. Hooker probably knew of these dickerings. Certainly Stanton did, through a friend in Chase's own circle. . . . At this critical moment the needed impulse in the direction of Hooker was supplied by a person of commanding influence in the counsels of the administration, and Mr. Lincoln directed the appointment to be made.

Who this person was, whose influence overbore the caution of Lincoln and the determined opposition of Stanton, and caused Lincoln to make an appointment which he knew to be dictated by the men who were opposing his own reelection, is a matter of conjecture. Certainly it was not a selfish action of Lincoln's part that made Hooker commander of the Army of the Potomac.

Lincoln's letter to Hooker, appointing him commander-in-chief of the Army of the Potomac is one of the classics of the war. Was ever another such letter written by a president to a man appointed to an important position? It is a marvel of kindness mingled with blunt and stern reproof :*

EXECUTIVE MANSION, WASHINGTON, D. C.,
January 26, 1863.

Major General Hooker.—General: I have placed you at the head of the army of the Potomac. Of course I have done this upon what appear to me to be sufficient reasons; and yet I think it best for you to know that there are some things in regard to which I am not satisfied with you. I believe you to be a brave and skillful soldier, which of course I like. I also believe that you do not mix politics with your profession, in which you are right. You have confidence in yourself, which is a valuable if not indispensable quality. You are ambitious, which, within reasonable bounds, does good rather than harm; but I think that,

*The original of this letter was sold at auction in the autumn of 1924. The Library of Congress sent in a bid of $1,000; the letter sold for $10,000.

during General Burnside's command of the army, you have
taken counsel of your ambition, and thwarted him as much as
you could, in which you did a great wrong to the country, and
to a most meritorious and honorable brother officer. I have
heard, in such a way as to believe it, of your recently saying that
both the army and the government needed a dictator. Of course,
it was not for this, but in spite of it, that I have given you the
command. Only those generals who gain success can be dicta-
tors. What I now ask of you is military success, and I will risk
the dictatorship. The government will support you to the utmost of its ability, which is neither more nor less than it has
done and will do for all commanders. I much fear that the
spirit which you have aided to infuse into the army, of criti-
cizing their commander and withholding confidence from him,
will now turn upon you. I shall assist you as far as I can to put
it down. Neither you nor Napoleon, if he were alive again,
could get any good out of an army while such a spirit prevails
in it. And now, beware of rashness. Beware of rashness, but,
with energy and sleepless vigilance, go forward and give us
victories.

             Yours, very truly,   A. Lincoln.

   Hooker spent three months in organizing his army, and then
advanced toward Richmond. He met Lee at a small place called
Chancellorsville, and a terrific battle was fought on May 2 and
3, 1863, with a loss of about 17,000 men. In this battle Stonewall Jackson was killed by the mistaken fire of his own men.
   Hooker was so severely criticized for this defeat and so annoyed by the orders which he received from Washington, that he
asked to be relieved of his command.
   Hooker was succeeded by General George G. Meade, of Pennsylvania. Meade was a graduate of West Point, and had served
in the Mexican War. He came to the command of the Army of
the Potomac just in time to have the honor of winning the battle
of Gettysburg. That victory kept this cautious officer in his
position as commander of the Army of the Potomac until the
end of the war; but his failure to follow Lee was a bitter disappointment to Lincoln, who could not relieve himself from the im-

pression that Meade had been willing that Lee should escape rather than that Meade then should risk a second battle. Meade's fame is secure in the winning of one superb victory, but he did not justify the faith that would have been involved in delegating to him any larger responsibility.

The man whom the nation needed and whom Lincoln was seeking, was even then merging into view. The very day on which Meade won his victory at Gettysburg, and in the very winning of it displayed a lack of those qualities which made it sure that he could win another one, another general came into public notice, and from that time on until the end of the war was seldom out of the public mind, though seldom visible to public view. It is not necessary at this time to name him. In time the nation found the man who could lead its armies to victory.

CHAPTER XIV

GETTYSBURG: WHAT THEY DID THERE

An INCIDENT occurred in the autumn of 1863 which seemed at the time to be of little importance, but which has become one of the outstanding events of Lincoln's public career. The battle of Gettysburg was the one important battle fought on northern soil. The field lay within a state wholly outside of the borders of Confederacy. The system of national cemeteries controlled by the Federal Government had not as yet been devised. A portion of the battle-field at Gettysburg was purchased and held by a commission in which the several northern states that had participated in the battle were represented. This cemetery was set apart with solemn services on November 19, 1863. There President Lincoln delivered an address whose words have become immortal. The importance of the battle, and the world's interest in the address, require some description of the conflict. Before we consider what Lincoln said there, let us visit Gettysburg and remind ourselves as we travel over the field, what they did there.

One's first surprise on reaching Gettysburg is the discovery that it is not a hill town. The visitor has at least two reasons to expect to find it in the heart of the mountains. One is that the battle is described in terms of elevations—Seminary Ridge, Cemetery Ridge, Culp's Hill, Round Top and Little Round Top. The other is that he travels through hills to reach Gettysburg. When the train leaves Highfield, the junction point for the main line of the Western Maryland Railroad, he knows that he is on top of the mountain. The train moves slowly around horseshoe curves among cement-factories and saw-mills. After a few miles, the farms, which have been discovered in the bottoms of the valleys, appear more nearly on the level of the track. Before the train reaches Gettysburg, the hills have been left behind and above. The distance is only twenty-two miles from Highfield to Gettysburg, but the last seven or eight miles find the train upon the floor of a wide valley. The hills have stepped back. The land rises and falls in graceful undulations. The railroad plows through the famous ridges described in the battle, and the cuts are only ten to twenty feet deep. Cemetery Ridge and Seminary Ridge are native to the locality. Culp's Hill, the Round Tops and the Devil's Den are intruders: they are formed of trap rock, thrust up through the floor of the valley. These are real hills, but they are not very high. The public square at Gettysburg—the people of the town call it "the Diamond,"—is only four hundred and twelve feet above sea level. Seminary Ridge is a gentle rise of ground, about forty feet higher, and Cemetery Ridge at its highest point is some fifty feet higher than the Seminary Ridge. Culp's Hill is five hundred eight feet above sea level; Little Round Top is five hundred forty-eight, and Round Top—the highest elevation in the battle—is six hundred sixty-four feet. The highest land that figured in the battle is only two hundred and fifty feet above the plain. The hill up which Pickett's Brigade charged is a very gentle slope. Missionary Ridge and Lookout Mountain are real mountains, but the fighting at Gettysburg had to do with very modest, though very important, elevations.

It is not easy to understand a battle, and still less easy to describe it so that others can understand the description. But it is important to gain an intelligent idea of this one.

In the summer of 1863, General Lee undertook an invasion of the North. It was a desperate and mistaken undertaking. But it did not seem so at the time. There appeared to be opportunity for a bold, successful strike. The war had been going on for two years, and in the main the advantage in the east was on the side of the South. In the West it was not so. Vicksburg was about to fall, and the army of General Grant would be released for service east or south. It was desirable to accomplish something significant in the East as early as possible. The southern boast, that one Confederate could whip three or more northern soldiers, did not seem extravagant after Fredericksburg and Chancellorsville. And Lee had to do something. Either he must continue on the defensive and see his army gradually worn down, or he must make a courageous advance. He decided on the latter policy. The southern armies were nearly destitute of shoes and clothing, and in sore need of medicine. But the men were hardy and seasoned. If Lee could make a successful invasion of the North, he might penetrate the rich state of Pennsylvania, obtain clothing and food, and replenish his supplies. If such a venture succeeded, he might capture Harrisburg, and quite possibly Baltimore and Philadelphia. He could threaten Washington and New York. And, if he could reach Lake Erie, he could control the lines of communication east and west, and profoundly influence European favor. It was a gambler's chance, and it was worth trying.

Lee crossed the Potomac and moved north rapidly. Hooker was in command of the Army of the Potomac, but since his defeat at Chancellorsville the basket had been waiting for his head. The Union Army, which within a few months had been commanded by McClellan, Burnside and Hooker successively, was awaiting another change. McClellan had been timid, Burnside rash, and Hooker boastful and intemperate. Politics and military mismanagement had done their work, and the army had experienced McClellan's indecisive victory at Antietam, Burnside's futile slaughter at Fredericksburg and Hooker's defeat at Chancellorsville. The spirit of the Army of the Potomac was crushed: and now, another experiment in leadership was impending.

To Hooker's lasting credit let it be remarked that he followed Lee promptly, and, marching by parallel roads, managed to keep his own army between that of Lee and the capital at Washington. Just on the eve of battle, Hooker was removed, and Meade

ABRAHAM LINCOLN
Photograph by Gardner, November 8, 1863

reluctantly took his place.   Whatever Meade's deficiencies as a general, he was a gentleman, and a man of strength of character. The responsibility of command in that crisis was one which he had not sought, and if he was so overwhelmed by his new and heavy responsibilities as to show too great caution, there was much to excuse him.   Continuing the movement of Hooker, he pursued Lee, intending to overtake Lee's rear, compel him to fall back, and fight a decisive battle.   The field for this battle Meade selected at Pipe Creek in Maryland.

Neither Meade nor Lee expected or desired to fight a battle at Gettysburg.   As Meade was selecting a favorable spot for the battle at Pipe Creek, Lee was preparing for a fight near Cash-town, toward Harrisburg.   It was the fate of these two skilled officers each to propose a trap so inviting that he was confident the other would step into it, and then to leave both traps baited and unsprung.   The battle occurred where neither general desired it; and each one was so sure that Gettysburg was no place for a battle that neither general arrived on the field until after the first day's fight.

The two armies moved with singularly little knowledge of each other's exact movements.   Lee was worried because Stuart's Cavalry, on which he depended for information, was roving about, swapping sore-backed horses for fresh ones, and trading wornout shoes for new ones, so that Lee could not keep track of their movements.*   To this day it is easily possible to stir the blood of a white-haired member of Jeb Stuart's merry company of horse-thieves, by whistling or fiddling a few bars from that old rebel song—the very melody which Lincoln's marching-clubs had used in honor of the Wide-awakes:

If you want to have a good time, jine the cavalry,
Jine the cavalry, jine the cavalry.

---

*It is not meant to imply that the cavalry rendered no effective service, but only that Lee did not know what it was doing. See *Stuart's Cavalry in the Gettysburg Campaign,* by General John S. Mosby, New York, 1908.

Major General J. E. B. Stuart's cavalry were having their promised good time. They were moving rapidly, here and there, and

Though they had a tolerable notion of aiming at progressive
    motion,
'Twasn't direct; 'twas serpentine.
Like Monsieur's corkscrew, worming through a cork,
Not like corkscrew's proxy—stiff, down-pronged fork.

They were certain to reach Harrisburg by the time Lee did, and would be freshly mounted and in fine fettle for a fight. It is hard to make an infantryman, who carried his gun and thirty pounds of baggage, believe that a cavalry soldier was ever anything more than a jolly raider of stables and hen-roosts. To the men who plodded through the mud, it seemed that he whose happy fate permitted him to "join the cavalry" had few cares. But if the infantry bugle in the early dawn blew the confession:

I can't get 'em up,
I can't get 'em up,
I can't get 'em up in the morning—

the cavalry bugle trumpeted the stern command:—

Get up and water your horses,
You dirty beggars, get up out of bed.

Stuart, a young and brilliant officer, had succeeded to the command of Stonewall Jackson on the death of the latter. Where was Stuart with his cavalry? For eight days, Lee did not know.
And what was Hooker doing all this time? Still on the south side of the Potomac, no doubt, answering the criticisms of the Committee on the Conduct of the War. So Lee hoped.
At the end of June, when Lee was about to descend upon Harrisburg, and capture the capital of Pennsylvania, he heard alarming news. Hooker's whole army was across the Potomac, and

was so placed as to cut off all hope that Lee could damage Washington, and was also where it might easily cut off Lee's line of communication with the South. Greatly disturbed, Lee decided to stop and meet Hooker, to invite him into the pleasant trap he had set for him, and by the defeat of Hooker's army to clear his way for advance and at the same time keep his lines of communication open. It seemed a wise plan. So he moved his army toward the south; his returning advance and the Federal advance meeting at Gettysburg, and each presenting to the other a courteous invitation to fight somewhere else.

And that was how it came to pass that the Southern Army entered Gettysburg from the north, and the Union Army entered it from the south, and Lee encountered not Hooker but Meade, and each general fought when and where he did not intend to fight.

Perhaps it would have worked out otherwise if General Reynolds, who commanded the Federal advance, had not been killed at the very beginning of the battle, north of Gettysburg on the morning of July 1, 1863. But the Federal command shifted more than once that day, and meantime, the Confederates, pushing south, were crowding hard on the Federal lines, and driving them back through and beyond the town. General Lee, arriving after the day's fighting was done, gave up all thought of battle at Cashtown. And General Meade, arriving at about one o'clock the next morning, still hoped that the real battle might be fought at Pipe Creek, but prepared for the bloody engagement which was soon to come that day.

There still is dispute as to who selected the permanent position of the Union Army. It was well selected. Its line was a fishhook. The ring was at Round Top far south and east; the shank extended north through Little Round Top and on to the Cemetery Hill, which curved south of the village; the point was Culp's Hill. Meade found his forces in possession of this favorable ground, and he proceeded to strengthen his position. A mile away, the Confederates posted themselves on a larger and parallel curve, their main positions being on a hill where stood and still stands, the Lutheran Theological Seminary for which it is named. The Confederates had the seminary and the town.

The fighting on the second day began after noon. General Sickles, who ought to have had his soldiers on the ring and shank of the fish-hook, placed them in an exposed position in a peach-orchard and wheat-field, nearer the Confederate lines. The story of that day's fight is a sad one; the most fortunate thing that ever happened to General Sickles was that he got shot. His loss of a leg saved him from a court-martial, and enabled him ever afterward to revisit Gettysburg as a hero. The peach-orchard and the wheat-field bore a sad crop that day. But the ground lost was recovered, though dearly bought, and the two Round Tops were carried by the Union troops, and the line of the fish-hook was preserved intact.

It had been Lee's plan that a simultaneous attack should be made on both flanks, that is to say, at the peach-orchard toward the ring of the fish-hook, and at Culp's Hill, at the point. But simultaneous attacks are seldom simultaneous. Something almost invariably occurs to slow up one or the other movement. So the attack on Culp's Hill came later than was intended, and while it met with immediate success, it came too late for permanent advantage. Night fell, and while the day's fighting had been to the advantage of the Confederates, the Union lines held the ridge. Meade, still sorrowing over the waste of his excellent unused battle-field at Pipe's Creek, found that he had a fairly good position where he was. He could send messages or troops from any part of his fish-hook to any other part, out of sight and gun-fire of the Confederates, while all the movements of the Confederates had to be conducted in the rear of a much larger curve, and there were fewer of the Confederates than of the Union soldiers. So the two armies waited for the next day. But if the two attacks of the Confederates had been simultaneous as was planned, the shank of the fish-hook would have been cut off, its point broken and the Union Army divided and defeated.

"Cave Tertium," the old Romans said. "Beware the third." The third day at Gettysburg was the decisive day. General Lee inspected the whole line, and decided that the weakest point held by the Union Army was just west of the cemetery, where the low ridge sloped down and offered the invitation of an easy ascent. General Lee knew that after two days of hard fighting and heavy losses there was an advantage to the side that would take the initiative. Thoughtfully he laid his plans for the third day. It was possible so to group his cannon along Seminary Ridge as to focus their fire upon that one weakest spot. He would open with a heavy cannon fire, and would follow with a charge. He had an entirely fresh division of infantry. No army ever had a finer body of troops than Pickett commanded. They had seen service on many battle-fields, but had not fired a shot at Gettysburg. That division was to be posted behind the guns, and as soon as the fire of the cannon ceased, they would move across the plain and capture and hold that almost central position in the Union lines. Meantime, he would send a force of cavalry around the point of the fish-hook to make a simultaneous attack in the rear.

Some of General Lee's division commanders protested against this plan. It was impossible, they declared, to capture and hold this place at the curve of the fish-hook, when it was so strongly guarded not only at the ring and point, but by the heavy guns along the curve at the cemetery. General Lee believed his plan a wise one. So far as the cannonade of the charge was concerned, his orders were carried out to the letter. But he was disappointed again in the matter of simultaneous movement. The cavalry did not arrive in time to do what he expected them to do. It is doubtful if, even with their help, he could have carried out so bold an undertaking.

General Lee massed one hundred forty cannon along Seminary Ridge and they are there to-day. They are placed as they were placed at the time of the battle and each battery is plainly designated. At one o'clock on the third day they laid down a barrage, as we now have learned to call it. Such a roar of cannon had never at that time been heard on earth. The point at which he directed his fire was well chosen. The Union soldiers lay behind a low stone wall. They never turned a sod by way of fortification, for it never occurred to them that a charge would be made against that point. After a little more than an hour of heavy cannonading, the Confederate guns being answered by a nearly equal number on the Union side, the firing ceased. For a few moments it was uncertain whether the Confederates had stopped to cool their guns or because their ammunition was exhausted or because this was the prelude of something yet to occur. Not long was any one left in doubt. General Pickett's division of Longstreet's corps had arrived the night before and borne no share in the battle. For this division was reserved what might have been under other conditions the glory of achieving the final victory. These men, numbering in all about fourteen thousand, experienced, seasoned and disciplined, had lain concealed behind the Confederate batteries. When the firing ceased, they formed in double line of battle and charged the Union left center, their objective being a clump of trees which stood and still stands prominently behind the low stone wall which formed the Federal front. They did not run. They moved at a quick walk, or easy trot, their guns at right shoulder shift. They reserved their breath and their fire for the hand to hand struggle which they knew was coming. A braver charge has never been seen on any battle-field. For three-quarters of a mile across an open field, with very little to give them protection, these men moved. The Federal cannon opened upon them and tore gaps in their ranks. They went on until they came within musket range and were shot down by the men behind the wall. How any man among them lived to reach the wall is a mystery. They not only reached it, but fought with clubbed muskets across the wall, and many of them leaped the wall and fought on the other side. There the Confederacy reached its high water mark. The wave which dashed to that height did not roll back; it broke and fell, and the waters flowed again into their place.

General Lee assumed sole responsibility for this charge. "It is all my fault," he said. He believed, and with reason, that the point he attacked was the weakest point in the Union position and that by assaulting the tired Federal troops with fresh and vigorous ones he could cut entirely through. He also depended upon the cooperating movement of cavalry which was to have swung around the Union right and attacked simultaneously from the rear. If only the cavalry had done its duty, Lee still believed that the movement might have succeeded. As it was, the judgment of Longstreet was vindicated. He had refused to speak the word of command to Pickett, but silently bowed his head and turned away. Like the charge of the six hundred at Balaklava, Pickett's men went to their death although their immediate commander, Pickett, and his commander, Longstreet, firmly believed that "some one had blundered."

These American officers were not the only ones who blundered. Colonel Freemantle of Queen Victoria's Coldstream Guards was visiting General Lee's army, and was near General Longstreet when Pickett's charge was made. Standing with his back to the sun and thrilled with admiration as he viewed that heroic charge, he saw, or thought he saw, the attacking column completely victorious. The men moved across the open space unterrified by cannon and musketry. They reached the wall and crossed it. Only a few of them straggled back. Colonel Freemantle rushed up to Longstreet and heartily congratulated him on his glorious victory. Longstreet knew better. Those men were remaining on the other side of the wall, not because they had captured the position, but because they were either killed or prisoners.

General Meade is hardly to be blamed for the fact that he could not at once comprehend or believe the magnitude of his victory. He had been compelled against his will to assume the command of an army to which he was practically a stranger, at a time when it was divided by heated discussion concerning past commanders and had lost faith in all commanding generals. To him it hardly seemed credible that the repulse of Pickett's division was the great victory for which the Army of the Potomac had been praying for more than two bloody and disastrous years. If General Meade be blamed for excessive caution in not following Lee, it is at least to be remembered to his credit that under him for the first time Lee met an army capable of inflicting upon him an incurable loss. Meade did not know how great a victory he had won. But General Lee knew.

CHAPTER XV

GETTYSBURG: WHAT HE SAID THERE

IT IS impossible to study the career of Abraham Lincoln during the Civil War and avoid the conviction that during those anxious months when the president was bearing a burden of responsibility and grief such as few men have ever borne, Abraham Lincoln grew largely in his own spiritual nature.

On the fourth of July, 1863, the president issued an announcement of the success of Gettysburg in the following words:

The President of the United States announces to the country, that the news from the army of the Potomac, up to 10 o'clock P. M. of the 3d, is such as to cover the army with the highest honor—to promise great success to the cause of the Union—and to claim the condolence of all for the many gallant fallen; and that for this, he especially desires that on this day, "He whose will, not ours, should ever be done," be everywhere remembered and reverenced with the profoundest gratitude.

On that evening the president was serenaded at the White House, and said: "I do most sincerely thank Almighty God for the occasion of this call."

Remembering that it was the fourth of July, and the president not then having precisely in mind the exact number of years since the Declaration of Independence, he asked:

How long ago is it? Eighty-odd years since, on the fourth of July, for the first time in the history of the world, a nation by its representatives assembled, declared as a self-evident truth that all men are created equal.

It will be noted that he recurred to this same thought in the following November when he delivered the address at Gettysburg, but that in the meantime he had looked up the exact number of years between 1776 and 1863, and found it "four-score and seven years." On this night of the fourth of July, he went on to allude to other extraordinary events in American history which had occurred on that same month and day, notably the death of Jefferson and Adams in 1826, and then said:

And now on this last fourth of July just past, we have a gigantic rebellion, at the bottom of which is an effort to overthrow the principle that all men are created equal. We have the surrender of a most important position and an army on that very day.

He was speaking of the fall of Vicksburg; and he then alluded gratefully and with expressions of joy to the battle in Pennsylvania as a victory over the cohorts of those who opposed the Declaration of Independence.

The president did not stop with expressions of congratulation. A few days afterward he called for a national day of thanksgiving and praise, appointing the fourth of August as the day for the expression of gratitude to God for these victories, and invited them to call upon God by his Holy Spirit to subdue the anger which had produced and too long sustained a cruel rebellion; to guide the councils of the government; to visit with tender care and consolation those who had been brought to suffer, and finally, to lead the whole nation through paths of repentance and submission to the Divine will, to unity and fraternal peace. A portion of this proclamation read:

It has pleased Almighty God to hearken to the supplications and prayers of an afflicted people, and to vouchsafe to the army and the navy of the United States, victories on the land and on the sea, so signal and so effective, as to furnish reasonable ground for augmented confidence that the Union of these States will be maintained, their Constitution preserved, and their peace

THE GETTYSBURG SPEECH MONUMENT

THE CEMETERY AT GETTYSBURG

and prosperity permanently restored.   But these victories have been accorded not without sacrifice of life, limb, health, and liberty, incurred by brave, loyal, and patriotic citizens.   Domestic affliction, in every part of the country, follows in the train of these fearful bereavements.   It is meet and right to recognize and confess the presence of the Almighty Father, and the power of His hand, equally in these triumphs and these sorrows.

These are the words of a man who, already a man of deep religious sensibility, had passed through experiences that baptized his soul in solemnity and attained a new sense of reliance upon the help of God.

I   THE CEMETERY

When General Lee withdrew from Gettysburg on July 4, 1863, he left behind him at least twenty-five hundred Confederate dead, and the Union Army had lost more than as many men killed in battle.   Besides these some twenty thousand men, Confederate and Union, were in hospitals.   The churches, the theological seminary, and many houses and barns were utilized for the care of the wounded.   Many of the men brought in had received no attention since they were first injured three or four days previously.   Lee endeavored to take with him those of his own wounded who were likely to recover, leaving behind him those who were judged to be mortally wounded.   In many cases, those fared better who were left behind.   In the days following the battle hundreds died.   These and those already lying dead on the battle-field were hastily buried.   In many cases there was no attempt at the digging of a grave.   Sufficient earth to cover the body was hastily scooped and thrown over it.   In a short time portions of these bodies were exposed.   Honorable David Wills, who had been acting by appointment for Governor Andrew G. Curtin, as representative of the state of Pennsylvania, in the care of the wounded, proposed that all the Union bodies should be gathered and buried in one place.   He secured an option at two hundred dollars an acre on the seventeen acres of land immediately adjacent to the village cemetery, being the angle which had resisted the attack of the Louisiana Tigers and the spot where some of the heaviest Union batteries had been posted. This land was purchased by the state of Pennsylvania, acting as trustee for the eighteen states that had Union soldiers buried there. The cost of the purchase and improvement of the grounds and of the burial of the soldiers was apportioned to the several states, not on the basis of the number of their soldiers engaged or buried there, but in the ratio of their representation in Congress. Thus Illinois, that had few soldiers in the battle and only six burials in the cemetery, paid nearly twelve thousand dollars, while other states with a smaller population but more soldiers in that army paid much smaller sums. The Cemetery Association which held the ground, was incorporated after the general plan of cemetery corporations. Up to that time the Federal Government had not inaugurated the policy of maintaining soldiers' cemeteries. When that plan developed, Gettysburg Cemetery was passed over to the government, and is now owned and operated by it.

The cemetery was laid out in a half-circle with a center reserved for an imposing monument, since built by the United States Government at a cost of $50,000.

The work of removing the bodies of dead Union soldiers from their temporary graves was begun at once, but sickness developed in Gettysburg and was attributed to this cause. The work of removal ceased, therefore, until November. A limited number of bodies was in the new and permanent location at the time of the dedication.

II   THE PLAN FOR DEDICATION

It occurred to the commission that it was desirable to arrange for a formal dedication of this ground. Edward Everett, who was believed to be the foremost orator of America, was invited tc deliver the oration. The date named in his invitation was October 23, 1863, and Mr. Everett replied that it would be impossible for him to prepare adequately for such an address in the limited time available. He proposed as a date at which he could come Thursday, November nineteenth. To meet his convenience the dedication was postponed nearly a month.

The date being now fixed, formal invitations were sent to the president and Cabinet, to General Meade and the venerable General Winfield Scott, to the diplomatic corps, to all members of both Houses of Congress and to many other distinguished citizens, requesting them to attend. Few comparatively of those invited accepted the invitation. It was hardly expected that any large portion of them could attend. General Scott declined on account of his age and infirmities. General Meade, smarting under the rebuke of President Lincoln for not following Lee after the battle of Gettysburg, declined to attend, giving as his reason his duties to the army. It was a surprise when the president accepted. The invitation first sent to him was not an invitation to speak, but only such an invitation as went to other prominent men requesting attendance at the dedication.

III LINCOLN'S INVITATION

Colonel Clark E. Carr, who represented Illinois in the membership of the commission, and at whose suggestion the invitation to Mr. Lincoln to speak was subsequently sent, says:

The proposition to ask Mr. Lincoln *to speak* at the Gettysburg ceremonies was an afterthought. The President of the United States had, like the other distinguished personages, been invited to be present, but Mr. Lincoln was not, at that time, invited to speak. In fact, it did not seem to occur to any one that he could speak on such an occasion.

Scarcely any member of the Board, excepting the member representing Illinois, had ever heard him speak at all, and no other member had ever heard, or read from him, anything except political discussions. When the suggestion was made that he be invited to speak, while all expressed high appreciation of his great abilities as a political speaker, as shown in his debate with Stephen A. Douglas, and in his Cooper Institute address, the question was raised as to his ability to speak upon such a grave and solemn occasion as that of the memorial services. Besides, it was said that, with his important duties and responsibilities, he could not possibly have the leisure to prepare an address for such an occasion. In answer to this, it was urged that he himself, better than anyone else, could determine as to these questions, and that, if he were invited to speak, he was sure to do what under the circumstances, would be right and proper.

It must be remembered that Mr. Lincoln had not proved to the world his ability to speak upon such an occasion. He had not yet made a Gettysburg address, and he had not then made that other great address, which for sublimity and pathos ranks next to it, his second inaugural.

It was finally decided to ask President Lincoln "after the oration" (that is to say, after Mr. Everett's oration) as chief executive of the nation, "to set apart formally these grounds to their sacred use by a few appropriate remarks." This was done in the name of the Governors of the States, as was the case with others, by Mr. Wills; but the invitation was not settled upon and sent to Mr. Lincoln until the second of November, more than six weeks after Mr. Everett had been invited to speak, and but a little more than two weeks before the exercises were held.—*Lincoln at Gettysburg,* by Clark E. Carr, pp. 21-25.

Colonel Carr does not distinctly affirm, in this account, that it was he who, representing Mr. Lincoln's own state upon the board, suggested that the president be invited; but it appears that this was the case. He had heard Lincoln and Douglas at Galesburg, had been present and heard Lincoln at his first inaugural, and it was he who insisted, against the misgivings of some of the other commissions, that Lincoln be requested to make "a few appropriate remarks," following the oration by Governor Everett.

There was one other possible reason why the invitation was not given earlier. A year previous, on October 1, 1862, President Lincoln had visited the battle-field of Antietam. The battle had been fought just two weeks earlier, on September seventeenth. The story soon after became current, and was widely circulated in the campaign of 1864, that when the ambulance in which the president was riding with General McClellan and others "reached the neighborhood of the old stone bridge, where the dead were piled highest, Mr. Lincoln suddenly slapped Marshall Lamon on the knee, and called on Lamon to sing a comic song." The following bit of doggerel found a place in the *New York World:*

> Abe may crack his jolly jokes
> O'er bloody fields of stricken battle,
> While yet the ebbing life-tide smokes
> From men that die like butchered cattle.

There were many who were not reluctant to believe this libel; and, indeed, it contained just enough of truth to make it difficult to deny. General McClellan certainly owed it to Lincoln that he should have denied it, but McClellan did not do so. Lincoln himself wrote out an account of the incident as it actually occurred, but decided not to publish it.* The story was believed by many people at the time of Lincoln's visit to Gettysburg.

Certain newspapers of the opposition believed, or professed to believe, that Lincoln's desire to attend the celebration grew out of his wish to use the event in the interests of the approaching presidential campaign. There were thousands of people, and not all of them south of Mason and Dixon's line, who held Lincoln personally responsible for the death of the men who died at Gettysburg.

IV   THE JOURNEY TO GETTYSBURG

The railway authorities of the Baltimore and Ohio, who furnished the special train, planned at first that the president should leave Washington early in the morning of the day of

---

*Lamon, in his *Recollections of Abraham Lincoln,* gives Lincoln's version of this incident in *facsimile.* Lincoln wrote it in his own hand, in the third person, intending that Lamon should copy it and give it to the press as his own. Later he decided that it was better to say nothing about it.

dedication, and return that night. Lincoln himself, with characteristic caution, informed the secretary of war that he did not
like this arrangement. At Lincoln's suggestion, Secretary Stanton procured a change of schedule. Instead of leaving Washington at six o'clock on Thursday morning, the presidential train
left at noon on Wednesday, November eighteenth. The train
contained four coaches. The fourth coach, in which the president
rode, was a directors' car, the rear portion of which was par-
titioned off into a separate compartment with seats. around the
walls. In this car rode with the president, his secretary, John
G. Nicolay, his assistant secretary, John Hay, the three members of his Cabinet who accompanied him, Messrs. Seward,
Usher and Blair, several foreign officials and others. The train
reached Gettysburg at dusk. Lincoln went, according to the invitation previously received, to the home of Mr. Wills, which
faced the public square.

V   THE NIGHT AT GETTYSBURG

The authorities in charge of the dedication assumed a perilous
risk of bad weather when, to give Mr. Everett time for preparation of his oration, they postponed the date from October
twenty-third to November nineteenth. But the weather was pro-
pitious. The night preceding the celebration was clear and
warm, and the moon shone brightly. Gettysburg's usual population of about 1,300 was multiplied manyfold. Never, except
during the battle, had so many people gathered there. Estimates of the crowd vary all the way from fifteen thousand to
one hundred thousand. The former figure is probably nearer
correct than the latter, and is large enough to suggest a crowd
of embarrassing proportions. Several military bands had come
with the different delegations, and they proceeded to give outdoor concerts in the evening. The diary of John Hay tells how
he found congenial spirits who made up a musical party, singing
John Brown and other songs.

Lincoln was serenaded, and spoke a few words which clearly and perhaps not very tactfully showed that he was unwilling to be tormented before the time. It was late that night when quiet resumed its wonted reign in Gettysburg.

VI THE PROCESSION

The event of the day was to have been introduced by a formal procession; and there was a procession of a sort. The United States Marine Band, of Washington, the second United States Artillery Band of Baltimore, the Birgfield Band of Philadelphia, and the band of the Fifth New York Heavy Artillery, were in line and furnished music, and certain military organizations took their assigned places in line; the Cemetery Commissions from the several states were in their places; and the president and the three members of his Cabinet present appeared on horseback. But the vast concourse of people did not join the procession. They were too much interested in seeing the procession to become a part of it. They either stood on the sidewalks or hastened to the cemetery to secure advantageous positions there.

The procession was to have started at ten o'clock. At that hour, Mr. Lincoln, dressed in black, and wearing a tall hat and white gauntlets, emerged from the home of Mr. Wills and mounted a waiting horse. The crowd pressed in upon him and he was compelled to hold an informal reception on horseback. It was eleven o'clock before the procession got under way. The president's horse was too small, and the president did not appear to good advantage.

When the president reached the cemetery, there was another delay. Mr. Everett had not arrived. He did not arrive for half an hour. The exercises began at noon, an hour late.

Colonel Carr, who rode just behind the president, stated that when the procession started, the president sat erect on his horse, and looked the part of commander-in-chief of the army; but as the procession moved on, his body leaned forward, his arms hung limp, and his head was bowed. He seemed absorbed in thought. The route of the procession was only three-quarters of a mile, and the march was over in little more than a quarter of an hour. The tedium of the wait for Mr. Everett was partly relieved by the music of the band. Noon arrived, and with it Governor Everett; and the formal proceedings began. There was more music; a prayer described as eloquent; and then Edward Everett delivered his masterly oration.

VII   EDWARD EVERETT'S ORATION

Edward Everett was in his day America's foremost orator. He had been a noted Boston minister; had followed his work in the pulpit with ten years as a professor of Greek; had then been successively president of Harvard, governor of Massachusetts, United States senator, minister to England and secretary of state. He was a cultured scholar, and an orator whose productions, based on the best Greek models, displayed American scholarship at its best upon the platform. He had delivered memorable orations at historic spots in New England, notably in connection with semi-centennial celebrations of battles in the Revolutionary War. His oration on Washington, a hundred times repeated in many parts of the country, had brought in the money that purchased and saved Mount Vernon. He had been a candidate for vice-president on one of the tickets opposed to Lincoln; but was a hearty supporter of Lincoln's administration. America had no orator in his generation, and has produced none since, who could more worthily represent the nation in a classic oration on such an occasion as that which he met at Gettysburg.

Very properly, he had insisted upon sufficient time to prepare his address. Having carefully written it, he committed it to memory, and doubtless carefully rehearsed it. Every sentence was thoroughly wrought out and balanced. Even the gestures seemed to have been arranged in advance. Leaving nothing to chance, he had spent three days at Gettysburg before the dedication, the guest of Mr. Wills, and had thoroughly studied the field. Every local and topographical allusion was accurate; every reference to the battle was historically correct. He spoke without manuscript or notes. His voice was clear, resonant and musical.

The speakers' platform was approximately where the central monument now stands. The people stood where the graves now are but not many graves were then filled.

Mr. Everett spoke for an hour and fifty-seven minutes, or as some hearers affirm, a trifle over two hours. From the beginning to the end he held the attention of the thoughtful among his hearers. His white hair, his erect form, his graceful pose, his faultless gesticulation, his becoming attire, his poise, his self-control, his clear rich voice, his knowledge, precision and oratorical power, held his audience for two hours after he began, which was three hours after most of the people had taken their places before the platform. The idle and the restless moved away, but the more thoughtful ones in the assembly heard him with interest unabated until the very end of his eloquent peroration.

At length the peerless orator took his seat. A dirge, composed by B. B. French, was sung. Then Ward Hill Lamon introduced the president of the United States, who proceeded to make the "few remarks" suggested in his belated invitation. And the world that thought it would little note has long remembered what he said.

VIII   LINCOLN'S PREPARATION

When and where did Lincoln make his preparation for the Gettysburg Address? The answers to this question, given by men who heard the address, number not less than five or six.

The first answer is that the address was wholly extempore. I have been assured in Gettysburg itself that Lincoln said, "I shall have to trust to the inspiration of the occasion," and that he made no other preparation. Professor Draper, in his *History of the American Civil War,* says that when Lincoln rose to speak, "he unpremeditatedly and solemnly said, 'It is intimated to me that this assemblage expects me to say something on this occasion.' "

Honorable Cornelius Cole, ex-Senator from California, in an address at Wesleyan University, Middletown, Connecticut, in June, 1922, said :*

It has been stated that Mr. Lincoln had prepared his speech in writing, that he had done so on the way from Washington. There is no foundation for a statement of that kind. Mr. Lincoln probably made not a word or note in preparation for that address. I have no doubt whatever that it was wholly extempore and called forth by the circumstances of the occasion.

Senator Cole heard the address and he is a reputable man.

The second answer is that Lincoln wrote the address on the cars, on his way to Gettysburg. Honorable Wayne MacVeagh declared that he saw Lincoln write it then. Honorable Isaac N. Arnold should have known whereof he wrote, and he said:

Edward Everett, late Secretary of State, and Senator from Massachusetts, an orator and scholar whose renown had extended over the world, was selected to pronounce the oration. He was a polished and graceful speaker, and worthy of the theme and the occasion. President Lincoln, while in the cars on his way from the White House to the battlefield, was notified that he would be expected to make some remarks also. Asking for some paper, a rough sheet of foolscap was handed to him, and, retiring to a seat by himself, with a pencil, he wrote the address which has become so celebrated; an address which for appropriateness and eloquence, for pathos and beauty, for sublimity in sentiment and expression, has hardly its equal in English or American literature. Everett's oration was a polished specimen of consummate oratorical skill. It was memorized, and recited without recurring to a note. It was perhaps too artistic; so

---

*Senator Cole died in November, 1924, while the proof-sheets of this book were undergoing revision.

much so, that the audience sometimes during its delivery forgot the heroic dead to admire the skill of the speaker before them. When at length the New England orator closed, and the cheers in his honor had subsided, an earnest call for Lincoln was heard through the vast crowd in attendance. Slowly, and very deliberately, the tall, homely form of the President arose; simple, rude, his careworn face now lighted and glowing with intense feeling. All unconscious of himself, absorbed with recollections of the heroic dead, he adjusted his spectacles, and read with the most profound feeling the address.*

Ben Perley Poore, whose experiences as a shorthand reporter should have made him exceedingly careful to be accurate, wrote in his *Reminiscences* that President Lincoln's "remarks at Gettysburg were written in the car on the way from Washington to the battlefield, upon a piece of pasteboard held on his knee."

It is unfortunate that so much of what is accepted as history is given to the world by writers of fiction, not all of whom admit that it is fiction they are writing. Mrs. Mary Shipman Andrews has made no pretense that the story she gave in her *The Perfect Tribute* was meticulously accurate in its historical portions. It is unfortunate that it is not accurate, for it is accepted by many as being so. She related that on the train the president looked across the car at Edward Everett, and asked Secretary Seward for the brown paper which he had just removed from a package of books. "May I have this to do a little writing?" the president is alleged to have said; and on that paper, with a stump of a pencil, he wrote the Gettysburg Address.

We know that Edward Everett was not on that train, having already been for several days in Gettysburg, and the address was certainly not written on wrapping paper.

The third answer is that Lincoln wrote the address in Gettysburg. Judge Wills, who was Lincoln's host at Gettysburg, believed that Lincoln wrote the entire address in his house. In a

---

* *Life of Lincoln,* p. 328.

letter written for a Lincoln celebration in Philadelphia on the centenary of Lincoln's birth, Judge Wills wrote:

It was on my official invitation that the President came to Gettysburg. Between 9 and 10 o'clock of the evening of the 18th of November, 1863, Mr. Lincoln sent for me to come to his room, he being my guest. I went and found him writing, and he said he had just sat down to put upon paper a few thoughts for the next day's exercises, and wanted to know of me what part he was to take in it, and what was expected of him. We talked over it all very fully. About 11 o'clock he sent for me again, and when I went into his room he had the same paper in his hand and asked me whether he could see Mr. Seward. I told him Mr. Seward was staying with my neighbor next door, and I would go and bring him over. He said, "No, I'll go and see him." I went with him, and Mr. Lincoln carried the paper on which he had written his speech with him, and we found Mr. Seward, and I left him with him. In less than half an hour Mr. Lincoln returned. The next day I sat by him when he delivered his immortal address, and he read it from the same paper on which I had seen him write it the night before.

Honorable Edward McPherson, whose home was in Gettysburg, and who was for many years clerk of the House of Representatives in Washington, and who compiled an excellent documentary history of the Civil War, in a newspaper communication in 1875 declared that on the night when the president was a guest in the home of Mr. Wills, he sent for his host, "and inquired the order of exercises for the next day and began to put in writing what he called some stray thoughts to utter on the morrow."

Honorable Horatio King, in his volume, *Turning on the Light,* stated that in 1885, Governor Andrew Curtin said to him at Gettysburg:

"I saw Mr. Lincoln writing this address in Mr. Wills' house on a long yellow envelope. He may have written some of it before. He said, 'I will go and show it to Seward,' who stopped at another house, which he did and then returned and copied his speech on a foolscap sheet."

Governor Curtin's account is amplified in Mowry's *History of the United States for Schools*. It states that the president, sitting with the members of his Cabinet who were present, Edward Everett, Governor Curtin and others, in "the hotel" but presumably in the Wills house, remarked that he understood he was expected to say something on the following day, and that if they would excuse him he would withdraw and prepare his remarks. He withdrew to an adjacent room, and soon returned with a large-sized yellow government envelope. He sat down, and remarked that he had written something, and with their permission would like to read it to them and invite them to criticize it. He read to them from the envelope what he had written there. Secretary Seward offered one or two suggestions, which Lincoln accepted. Then he said, "Now, gentlemen, if you will excuse me again, I will copy this off." He then retired to his room, and made a fair copy on foolscap paper, from which next day he read the address.

The fourth answer is that it was written in Washington before the president left for Gettysburg. Senator Cameron, in a newspaper item which had wide currency, was declared to have said that he himself saw the address in Washington a day or two prior to the president's departure for the celebration.

Major William H. Lambert, in what is in some respects the most carefully wrought out account of the address, says:

Whatever revision may have been given to the address *en route* or at Gettysburg, whatever changes or additions may have been made in its delivery, the Address existed in substantially completed form before the president left Washington. There can be no doubt that he had given prolonged and earnest thought to the preparation of this Address; he had had more than two weeks' notice that he was desired to speak; and although the demands upon his time and attention were such as to allow him little opportunity for uninterrupted thought, he appreciated the momentousness of the occasion, he knew how much was expected of him, and what was due to the honored dead, and he did not trust to the inspiration of the moment or rely upon his readiness as an impromptu speaker when he dedicated the Soldiers' Cemetery at Gettysburg, for he had wrought and re-wrought until there came there into perfect form the noblest tribute to a cause and its heroes ever rendered by human lips.*

Major Lambert believed that both the two manuscripts in the Library of Congress which came from the president's secretaries were written before the president left Washington, but that the fair copy was inadvertently left in Washington.

Not one of the authorities cited in this list, or of the large number of others that might be quoted, is to be treated with disrespect. If we had any one of these accounts, and no other, we should be disposed to accept it as correct. The conflict of testimony on the part of honest men who had opportunity to know is one of the sobering facts which an author must face who undertakes to tell the true story of the Gettysburg Address, or of the life of Lincoln either in part or in whole.

The fifth answer is that the major part of the address was written in Washington, and that the president may have made a few notes on the train, but that he completed the address in the Wills house in Gettysburg.

Edward Everett sent to Lincoln in advance a copy of his address. Lincoln read and admired it. Noah Brooks, in his *Washington in Lincoln's Time* states that six days before his visit to Gettysburg the president took Everett's address with him on a visit to a photographer's, and read it between the sittings. Isaac Markens in his *Lincoln's Masterpiece* adduces a number of interesting parallels between Everett's address and Lincoln's. That Lincoln was impressed by Everett's oration is attested by his letter a year later, when, acknowledging a gift of flowers from the Gettysburg battle-field, he made a reference which was virtually a quotation. It appears possible that Everett's manuscript was one of the sources of Lincoln's inspiration.

Pennsylvania Magazine of History and Biography, October, 1909, pp. 385-408.

Honorable James Speed, in an interview in the *Louisville Commercial,* in November, 1870, stated that Lincoln told him that, on the day before his departure for Gettysburg, he found time to write about half of it. This probably is true. The first sheet is carefully written with a pen, on ordinary executive mansion stationery, and ends with an incomplete sentence. The original second sheet, in which the sentence was presumably completed, was not used. Lincoln erased the last three words on the first page,—the only erasure in the address,—and completed the sentence, and finished the address in pencil on a half-sheet of pale blue wide-lined legal cap, such as Lincoln was accustomed to use, and such as he employed in writing the second inaugural. John G. Nicolay declares that he was present, after breakfast, on the morning of the nineteenth, when Lincoln completed the writing of his address.

It was after the breakfast hour on the morning of the 19th that the writer, Mr. Lincoln's private secretary, went to the upper room in the house of Mr. Wills which Mr Lincoln occupied, to report for duty, and remained with the President while he finished writing the Gettysburg address, during the short leisure he could utilize for this purpose before being called to take his place in the procession, which was announced on the program to move promptly at ten o'clock.

There is neither record, evidence, nor well-founded tradition that Mr. Lincoln did any writing, or made any notes, on the journey between Washington and Gettysburg. The train consisted of four passenger-coaches, and either composition or writing would have been extremely troublesome amid all the movement, the noise, the conversation, the greetings, and the questionings which ordinary courtesy required him to undergo in these surroundings; but still worse would have been the rockings and joltings of the train, rendering writing virtually impossible. Mr. Lincoln carried in his pocket the autograph manuscript of so much of his address as he had written at Washington the day before. Precisely what that was the reader can now see by turning to the facsimile reproduction of the original draft, which is for the first time printed and made public in this article. It fills one page of the letter-paper at that time habitually used in the Executive Mansion, containing the plainly printed blank heading; both paper and print giving convincing testimony to the simple and economic business methods then prevailing in the White House.

This portion of the manuscript begins with the line "Four score and seven years ago," and ends "it is rather for us the living," etc. The whole of this first page—nineteen lines—is written in ink in the President's strong, clear hand, without blot or erasure; and the last line is in the following form: "It is rather for us the living to stand here," the last three words being, like the rest, in ink. From the fact that this sentence is incomplete, we may infer that at the time of writing it in Washington the remainder of the sentence was also written in ink on another piece of paper. But when, at Gettysburg on the morning of the ceremonies, Mr. Lincoln finished his manuscript, he used a lead pencil with which he crossed out the last three words of the page, and wrote above them in pencil, "we here be dedica," at which point he took up a new half-sheet of paper—not white letter paper as before, but a bluish gray foolscap of large size with wide lines, habitually used by him for long or formal documents, and on this he wrote, all in pencil, the remainder of the word, and of the first draft of the address, comprising a total of nine lines and a half.

The time occupied in this final writing was probably about an hour, for it is not likely he left the breakfast table before nine o'clock, and the formation of the procession began at ten.*

IX   THE DELIVERY OF LINCOLN'S ADDRESS

As to the manner of Lincoln's delivery, we have further conflict of testimony. Those who think that his remarks were purely extempore maintain that he used no notes. Others say that he held his manuscript in his left hand but did not read from it. Others say that he read every word as it was in the manuscript before him. Others say, and these I think are correct, that he held his manuscript in both hands, his glasses adjusted as for reading, and that he did in part read his address;

*John G. Nicolay in *Century Magazine* for February, 1894, pp. 601-602 but that he was so familiar with the greater part of it that he did not need to confine himself to his notes, and that he did, in fact, depart from the language of the written text. On one point there is no important dissent. He did not gesticulate with his hands. He gave emphasis with a motion of his head and shoulders, but his hands were not uplifted.

As Everett approached his peroration, Lincoln grew visibly nervous, as he always did when another man was speaking and he was to follow. He took his manuscript from his pocket, adjusted his spectacles, and, during the closing portion of Everett's oration, refreshed his memory as to the content of his own speech. Either then, or while he was actually speaking, he made a few slight alterations.

The statement in Morse's *Life of Lincoln,* that, having finished the manuscript, he added a quotation from Webster's Reply to Hayne, is inexcusably incorrect. He did nothing of the kind.

X FORMS OF THE ADDRESS

Nicolay and Hay state that there are three sources of knowledge of the Gettysburg Address, Lincoln's original manuscript, the Associated Press report, and Lincoln's final revision, which he made with both the earlier versions before him. Major Lambert made some more extended comparisons. It would appear, however, that we might well place first among our sources of knowledge of what Lincoln actually said, the report made by Charles Hale of the *Boston Advertiser*. He was one of the three Massachusetts commissioners present at Gettysburg, and the three joined in the report to Governor John A. Andrew. In this document they stated positively that the versions of the address then current were all inaccurate, but that the form in which they gave it was "as the words actually spoken by the president, with great deliberation, were taken down by one of the undersigned."

Six times President Lincoln is known to have written the Gettysburg Address in full, and five of these copies are preserved. The first of these is the manuscript in which the major part of the address is written on the printed stationery of the executive mansion and the remainder, being a portion of the last sentence, in pencil on another sheet. There is reason to believe that he originally wrote something in ink on a second sheet, which, however, did not satisfy him, and which probably he never completed on that sheet, but finished on a new sheet after arrival in Gettysburg. The second text is little more than a fair copy of the first, and was quite certainly made before the delivery of the address. Both these are in the Library of Congress, and the paper on which the second part of the first version is written, and the two sheets of the second part, are both the wide-ruled paper which Lincoln was accustomed to use in the White House and on which he later wrote the second inaugural.

Nicolay's is by far the most direct testimony we have concerning the composition of the address. Lincoln, pressed by the heavy responsibilities of his position, and with scant time in which to prepare, did not, however, neglect his preparation. He had and read Mr. Everett's address some six days before the exercises— a courtesy on Mr. Everett's part which Lincoln must have appreciated and by which he profited—and while he felt the disparity between Everett's finished production and his necessarily crowded opportunity, he carefully used such time as he was able to command, and he came to the platform at Gettysburg with his brief address carefully thought out and painstakingly written. Each sentence had been framed in his mind before it was reduced to writing. The part written in ink in the White House contains no erasure in ink. The part written in pencil at Gettysburg shows no erasure. The only change is where the two join, at which point Lincoln modified his original intent and erased with his pencil three words which he had previously written in ink. After this, as I believe, Lincoln copied the entire address before delivering it and held the corrected copy in his hand during the delivery.

Lincoln made a third copy which is not known to be in existence. A few days after the Gettysburg dedication, Mr. Wills wrote to him and asked for the address to be preserved with the report of the proceedings. It was then that the president, noting the differences in form between his versions and those in the press reports, compared the several forms and made a more satisfactory text; but what became of this copy is not known.

The fourth, which is the third extant copy, was made in February, 1864, at the request of Mr. Everett, to be bound with the manuscript of his oration and Mr. Lincoln's letter to him dated November 20, 1863, in a volume to be sold for the United States Sanitary Commission.

The fifth was made at the request of Honorable George Bancroft who desired it for the benefit of the Soldiers and Sailors Fair in Baltimore. Lincoln wrote it on both sides of a sheet of paper.

As the copy made for Mr. Bancroft was unsuitable for reproduction, on account of its use of both sides of the sheet, the President made a sixth and final copy, in March, 1864, and this was used for the purposes of lithographic reproduction in facsimile in a book published for the benefit of the Fair, entitled *Autograph Leaves of Our Country's Authors*. This version embodies the results of Lincoln's mature thought, and may be accepted as the final form.

Not many of the changes made in these revisions were important, but one calls for comment. It is the insertion of the words "under God." This change occurred, I am confident, on the platform. In the first copy, Lincoln wrote the first page in ink, beginning the last paragraph in the last line of that page: "It is rather for us, the living, to stand here," but when he came to the completion of that sentence in pencil, he crossed out the last three words, and, in pencil on that page, wrote, "we here be dedicated." The remainder of that closing paragraph, comprised in one long sentence, is in pencil on the second page, a ruled sheet. The words "under God" are not in it. The fair copy from which he read, and which he probably made in the Wills' house on the morning of the dedication, does not contain those words. My judgment is that under the solemn spell of the occasion, he determined to use those words, for they are in the Hale report and the Associated Press report, and Lincoln himself included those words in each revision of the address subsequent to its delivery.

Joseph L. Gilbert, the reporter for the Associated Press, telling the story in after years, stated that he did not take down the whole of Lincoln's address. Seeing that Lincoln was reading it from manuscript, he "unconsciously stopped taking notes" but obtained the manuscript from Lincoln before he left the stand and copied from the manuscript itself. The variations in the address as thus given to the world from the form shown in Lincoln's original manuscript are partly due, probably, to hasty copying, and partly to faulty telegraphic transmission. *Frank Leslie's* of New York, and the *Philadelphia Inquirer* appear to have had a report of their own, which varies still further, but that form need not be given here. For purposes of study and comparison, we may take, first, Charles Hale's report as giving us the best approach to an accurate transcript of what Lincoln actually said: secondly, Lincoln's original manuscript; thirdly, the Associated Press report, with its liberal intermixture of applause, not taken down at the time but inserted in the revision by the reporter; and finally, Lincoln's last revision of the address.

(Charles Hale's Report.)—Four score and seven years ago, our fathers brought forth
(Autograph Original Draft.)—Four score and seven years ago our fathers brought forth,
(Associated Press Report.)—Four score and seven years ago our fathers brought forth
(Revised Autograph Copy.)—Four score and seven years ago our fathers brought forth

upon this continent a new nation, conceived in liberty and dedicated to the proposition that
upon this continent, a new nation, conceived in liberty, and dedicated to the proposition that
upon this continent a new Nation, conceived in Liberty, and dedicated to the proposition that
on this continent, a new nation, conceived in Liberty, and dedicated to the proposition that

all men are created equal.
"all men are created equal."
all men are created equal. [Applause.]
all men are created equal.

Now we are engaged in a great civil war, testing whether that nation—or any nation so
Now we are engaged in a great civil war, testing whether that nation, or any nation so
Now we are engaged in a great civil war, testing whether that Nation or any Nation so
Now we are engaged in a great civil war; testing whether that nation, or any nation so

onceived and so dedicated—can long endure.   We are met on a great battle-field of that war.
onceived, and so dedicated, can long endure.   We are met on a great battle-field of that war.
onceived and so dedicated can long endure.   We are met on a great battle-field of that war.
onceived and so dedicated, can long endure.   We are met on a great battle-field of that war.

We are met to dedicate a portion of it as the final resting-place of those who
We have come to dedicate a portion of it, as the final resting place for those who died
We are met to dedicate a portion of it as the final resting-place of those who
We have come to dedicate a portion of that field, as a final resting place for those who

ave given their lives that that nation might live. It is altogether fitting and proper that we
ere, that the nation might live. This we may in all propriety do.
ere gave their lives that that nation might live. It is altogether fitting and proper that we
ere gave their lives that that nation might live. It is altogether fitting and proper that we

hould do this.
hould do this.
hould do this.

But in a larger sense, we cannot dedicate, we cannot consecrate, we cannot hallow,
But, in a larger sense, we can not dedicate—we can not consecrate—we can not hallow—
But in a larger sense we cannot dedicate, we cannot consecrate, we cannot hallow
But, in a larger sense, we can not dedicate—we can not consecrate—we can not hallow—

his ground. The brave men, living and dead, who struggled here, have consecrated it
his ground. The brave men, living and dead, who struggled here, have hallowed it
his ground. The brave men living and dead who struggled here have consecrated it
his ground. The brave men, living and dead, who struggled here have consecrated it

ar above our   power to add or detract.   The world will very little note nor long
ar above our poor power to add or detract.   The world will little note, nor long
ar above our   power to add or detract. [Applause.] The world will little note nor long
ar above our poor power to add or detract.   The world will little note, nor long

remember what we say here; but it can never forget what they did here.   It is
remember what we say here; while it can never forget what they did here.   It is
remember what we say here, but it can never forget what they did here. [Applause] It is
remember what we say here, but it can never forget what they did here.   It is

    for us, the living, rather to be dedicated, here, to the unfinished work that they
rather, for us, the living,
        for us, the living, rather to be dedicated here to the unfinished work that they
for us the living, rather, to be dedicated here to the unfinished work which they who

have thus far so nobly carried on. It is rather for us to be here dedicated to the great
                                      we here be dedicated to the great
have thus far so nobly carried on. [Applause.] It is rather for us to be here dedi-
fought here have thus far so nobly advanced.   It is rather for us to be here dedi-

task remaining before us; that from these honored dead we take increased devotion to
task remaining before us—that, from these honored dead we take increased devotion to
cated to the great task remaining before us, that from these honored dead we take increased
cated to the great task remaining before us—that from these honored dead we take increased

that cause for which they here gave the last full measure of devotion; that we here
that cause for which they here gave the last full measure of devotion; that we here
devotion to that cause for which they here gave the last full measure of devotion; that
devotion to that cause for which they   gave the last full measure of devotion—that

    highly resolve that these dead shall not have died in vain;   that the
    highly resolve these   dead shall not have died in vain;   that the
we here highly resolve that the dead shall not have died in vain [applause]; that the
we here highly resolve that these dead shall not have died in vain—   that this

nation shall under God,   have a new birth of freedom, and that government of the
nation, shall   have a new birth of freedom, and that government of the
nation shall,   under God, have a new birth of freedom; and that governments of the
nation, under God,   shall have a new birth of freedom—and that government of the

people, by the people, for the people, shall not perish from the earth.
people, by the people, for the people, shall not perish from the earth.
people, by the people, for the people, shall not perish from the earth. [Long continued
people by the people and for the people, shall not perish from the earth.   applause.]

XI   THE SOURCES OF THE ADDRESS

What were the sources of this notable address?

The first source was Lincoln's own little speech in response to a serenade on the night of July 4, 1863. On that occasion he thought first of the anniversary, and did not have in mind precisely how many years it had been since the Declaration of Independence, but knew that it was "eighty odd years since, on the fourth of July." On that day, as he then declared, "for the first time in the history of the world, a nation by its representatives assembled, declared as a self-evident truth that all men are created equal." This was the very thought with which he began at Gettysburg. The thought was not so precisely apposite, for the Declaration of Independence was not signed in November, but the idea still was pertinent. Meantime, he had looked up the date and computed the interval. It was eighty-seven years. It was more sonorous and metrical to say "four-score and seven years ago."

In that same little fourth of July speech he made the statement which he repeated at Gettysburg, that the purpose of the war was to determine whether that principle could survive as the basis of human government.

Especial interest attaches to the question, Where did Lincoln get the expression "government of the people, by the people, for the people"? It is frequently claimed that these words are found in the prologue of Wycliff's Bible; but they are not in any version of that Bible which I have been able to consult. Expressions similar in form and sentiment are found in a number of books that might or might not have been familiar to Lincoln; but the probable origin of the phrase as used by him was a sermon by Theodore Parker, *The Effect of Slavery on the American People,* delivered at Music Hall, Boston, July 4, 1858. He said:

Democracy is direct self-government, over all the people, for all the people, and by all the people.

Herndon declares that Lincoln was much impressed by these words and underlined them.

Hearers differed in their memory as to whether Lincoln emphasized the prepositions or the thrice repeated noun. Some thought he said,

"Government *of* the people, *by* the people, *for* the people."

Others remember him as having said:

"Government of the *people,* by the *people,* for the *people.*"

Whatever the source from which Lincoln obtained the language, he had already made one important use of it. In his proclamation immediately following the fall of Fort Sumter, Lincoln said:

And this issue embraces more than the fate of these United States. It presents to the whole family of man the question whether a constitutional republic or democracy—a government of the people by the same people—can or can not maintain its territorial integrity against its own domestic foes.

It is remarkably interesting to note that thus early the question had defined itself in Lincoln's mind as a question whether any government established as the American Government was established could long endure; and that his determination from the hour of his first call for troops was to establish the result that government of the people by the same people, and for the common welfare of all the people, should not perish from the earth.

An interesting question relates to the words "under God." It has been conjectured that Lincoln inserted these at the suggestion of Seward, with whom he is said on good authority to have had some conference at Gettysburg on the night before the dedication. But the documentary evidence is against this conjecture. Those two words do not appear in either of the two Library of Congress versions, which were written before the delivery of the address, and they do appear in all the press reports, however defective otherwise, and in all three of Lincoln's sub-

26

sequent revisions. My own belief is that Lincoln interpolated them under the deep feeling of the occasion, and in his revisions was very glad to have them appear as a part of the address, as in very deed they were.

XII   HOW THE ADDRESS WAS RECEIVED

How was the Gettysburg Address received? The Associated Press report indicates that it evoked applause three times during its delivery and at the close was greeted with "long continued applause." However, the Associated Press reporter, while remembering that there was applause, declared that the word was inserted where it was thought it belonged; the report sent out over the wire was not a verbatim report.

Reverend Doctor Henry Eyster Jacobs, of Gettysburg, says:

The fact of the applause we well remember, although we could not, without the memoranda there [i.e. the Associated Press report] venture to locate it.

Reverend Doctor H. C. Holloway, who heard the address, says concerning it:

I am well aware that a difference of opinion has been expressed in regard to the reception given by the people on the occasion of Mr. Lincoln's immortal speech. One writer in his little book, entitled, "The Perfect Tribute,"* which purported to give the story of Lincoln's Gettysburg speech, speaks of how the President for weeks was under a cloud of remorse over his address, believing it to have been a failure, etc. This is totally at variance with the facts in the case as we saw them. It is an unnatural interpretation of the occasion and does not comport with what actually occurred. The address was received with remarkable enthusiasm and in a manner becoming the great occasion.

There was one disappointing feature about it—its marked brevity. The speaker had, as we thought, but barely commenced

---

*Dr. Holloway apparently did not know the author was a woman.

when he stopped. That clear, ringing voice ceased before we were ready for it. There was a pause between the closing of the address and the applause because the people expected more; but when it was apparent that the address was really concluded, the applause was most hearty, rising like the sound of many waters.

Honorable Wayne MacVeagh, later Attorney General of the United States, heard the address and years afterward told of it as he thought he remembered it:

As he came forward he seemed to me, and I was sitting near to him, visibly to dominate the scene, and while over his plain and rugged countenance appeared to settle a great melancholy, it was somehow lightened by a great hope. As he began to speak I instinctively felt that the occasion was taking on a new grandeur, as of a great moment in history, and then there followed, in a slow and very impressive and far-reaching utterance, the words with which the whole world has long been familiar. As each word was spoken it appeared to me so clearly fraught with a message not only for us of his day, but for the untold generations of men, that before he concluded I found myself possessed of a reverential awe for its complete justification of the great war he was conducting, as if conducted, as in truth it was, in the interest of mankind. Surely at that moment he justified the inspired portraiture of Lowell in the "Commemoration Ode."

Arnold obtained a part of his information from Governor Dennison, Postmaster General, who was present and heard the address, and thus reports the effect of it:

Before the first sentence was completed, a thrill of feeling, like an electric shock, pervaded the crowd. That mysterious influence called magnetism, which sometimes so affects a popular assembly, spread to every heart. The vast audience was instantly hushed, and hung upon his every word and syllable. When he uttered the sentence: "the world will little *note* nor long remember what we *say* here, but it can never forget what they *did* here," every one felt that it was not the "honored dead" only, but the living actor and speaker, that the world for all time to come would note and remember, and that he, the speaker, in the thrilling words he was uttering, was linking his name forever with the glory of the dead. He seemed so absorbed in honoring the "heroic sacrifices" of the soldiers, as utterly to forget himself, but all his hearers realized that the great actor in the drama stood before them, and that the words he was speaking would live as long as the language; that they were words which would be recalled in all future ages, among all peoples; as often as men should be called upon to die for liberty and country.*

Among those who listened to the Gettysburg Address and recorded at the time a favorable impression, was Benjamin Brown French, who on Sunday morning, November twenty-second, wrote an account of the exercises at Gettysburg which had occurred on the preceding Thursday. Mr. French wrote a hymn for the occasion and it was sung after Everett's address and before that of the president. Mr. French records:

"Mr. Everett was listened to with breathless silence by all that immense crowd, and he had his audience in tears many times during his masterly effort."

He then quotes his own hymn which was sung, and says:

"I was never so much flattered at any production of my own."

Mr. French was in a frame of mind to write his appreciation concerning anything that occurred that day. Concerning Lincoln's address he said:

"As soon as the hymn was sung, Marshal Lamon introduced the President of the United States, who in a few brief words dedicated the cemetery."

He then quotes the Gettysburg Address, as it appeared in the daily papers, and adds:

Abraham Lincoln was the idol of the American people at this moment. Any one who saw and heard the hurricane of applause that met his every word at Gettysburg, would know that he lived in every heart. It was no cold shadow of a kind reception. It

---

*Arnold, *Life of Lincoln,* p. 329.

was a tumultuous outpouring of exaltation from true and loving hearts at the sight of a man whom everyone knew to be honest and sincere in every act of his life and every pulsation of his heart.   It was the spontaneous outburst of heartfelt confidence in *their own President*.*

Two facts must be noted concerning this account.   One is that it was written under the influence of very marked enthusiasm and is manifestly an exaggeration. The other is that Mr. French gives no indication that this hurricane of applause was produced by the address, but by the appearance of Lincoln himself.

Joseph L. Gilbert, of Philadelphia, the Associated Press reporter who first gave to the world the Gettysburg Address, told the story of it at the National Shorthand Reporters' Association in August, 1917:

President Lincoln then came forward.   I stood immediately in front of him and was impressed by his apparent excellent physical condition.   His face, fringed by a newly grown beard, was more rounded and less care worn and haggard looking than formerly.   He stood for a moment with hands clasped and head bowed in an attitude of mourning—a personification of the sorrow and sympathy of the nation.   Adjusting his old-fashioned spectacles, a pair with arms reaching to his temples, he produced from the pocket of his Prince Albert coat several sheets of paper from which he read slowly and feelingly.   His marvelous voice, careering in fullness of utterance and clearness of tone, was perfectly audible on the outskirts of the crowd.   He made no gestures nor attempts at display, and none were needed.   Fascinated by his intense earnestness and depth of feeling, I unconsciously stopped taking notes and looked up at him just as he glanced from his manuscript with a far away look in his eyes as if appealing from the few thousands before him to the invisible audience of countless millions whom his words were to reach.   No one of the many orators whom, in after years, I heard repeat the

---

Diary and Correspondence of Benjamin Brown French, edited by his grandson, Amos Tuck French.   A few copies printed for private circulation only.   New York, 1904.

address ever made it sparkle with light and meaning as its great author did.

When he began speaking the President had comparatively few hearers, as hundreds who had come to hear him, wearied by Everett's two-hour oration, had wandered away. But his powerful voice speedily recalled the wanderers. Spell-bound with the majestic personality of the great man of whom they had heard so much and now saw for the first time, the multitude stood mute—many with uncovered heads—listening reverently as to an inspired oracle but seemingly unconscious of the spiritual excellence and moral grandeur of the great patriot's imperishable words. It was not a demonstrative nor even an appreciative audience. Narratives of the scene have described the tumultuous outbursts of enthusiasm accompanying the President's utterances. I heard none. There were no outward manifestations of feeling. His theme did not invite holiday applause, a cemetery was not the place for it, and he did not pause to receive it.

Lincoln wrote the address in Gettysburg at the residence of Judge David Wills, where he was a guest for a few hours. None of his attendants, not even his Secretary (Hay), knew of its preparation in advance of its delivery. At the Wills' mansion the President asked for the use of a private room and some writing material, remarking, "I suppose I will be expected to make some remarks out at the Cemetery this afternoon." His request was complied with, and in less than an hour he completed the address from rough notes made by him while on the train from Washington and others he had made, several weeks earlier, when a request from the Dedication Committee "to say a few words" was transmitted to him by Governor Curtin. The letter sheets from which he read were from Judge Wills' office. Before the dedication ceremonies closed, the President's manuscript was copied with his permission; and as the press report was made from a copy no transcript from shorthand notes was necessary.

It will be noted that Gilbert disclaims having made notes with sufficient accuracy to reproduce the speech from his shorthand report. Seeing that Lincoln was reading the address, or at least that he had the manuscript in his hands, he depended upon the use of the manuscript, which later in the day he was permitted to consult. He inserted "Applause" from memory, or from his idea of the proper place for it.   Fortunately, another reporter took down *verbatim* the words as Lincoln uttered them, slowly and deliberately.   Through him we may have the precise words of Lincoln's address.

Lest the reader be too much disconcerted by these contradictions, let him read the varying newspaper accounts of the delivery of, let us say, President Harding's inaugural address, March 4, 1921.   There was applause, of course.   Was it hearty or perfunctory?   Was there much of it or little?   If all the people who clapped their hands had been gathered into a room of moderate size, there would have been no question that the applause was loud and strong.   But in proportion to so great a company, out-of-doors, and most of the people standing too far back to feel any responsibility for expressions of approbation, was the hand-clapping loud or faint, enthusiastic or mildly complimentary?   The answer depends upon the judgment, and somewhat upon the prejudice and the location of the reporter.   It was even so at Gettysburg.   At the time no one, not even the Associated Press reporter, was thinking about the precise places where some manifestation of approval occurred, and after that it was a matter of memory and judgment.

Among those who were in the best position to judge of the effect of Lincoln's address upon the audience that listened to it, was Ward Hill Lamon.   He had entire charge of the special train that conveyed Lincoln and his party to Gettysburg, and the essential truth of his statement is confirmed by many who heard Lincoln's few remarks:

A day or two before the dedication of the National Cemetery at Gettysburg, Mr. Lincoln told me that he would be expected to make a speech on that occasion; that he was extremely busy and had no time for preparation; that he greatly feared he would not be able to acquit himself with credit, much less to fill the measure of public expectation.   From his hat—the usual receptacle for his private notes and memoranda—he drew a sheet of foolscap, one side of which was closely written with what he informed me was a memorandum of his intended address. This he read to me, first remarking that it was not at all satisfactory to him. It proved to be in substance, if not in exact words, what was afterwards printed as his famous Gettysburg speech.

After its delivery on the day of the commemoration, he expressed deep regret that he had not prepared it with greater care. He said to me on the stand, immediately after concluding the speech: "Lamon, that speech won't *scour!* It is a flat failure, and the people are disappointed." (The word *"scour"* he often used in expressing his positive conviction that a thing lacked merit, or would not stand the test of close criticism or the wear of time.) He seemed deeply concerned about what the people might think of his address; more deeply, in fact, than I had ever seen him on any public occasion. His frank and regretful condemnation of his effort, and more especially his manner of expressing that regret, struck me as somewhat remarkable; and my own impression was deepened by the fact that the orator of the day, Mr. Everett, and Secretary Seward both coincided in his unfavorable view of its merits.

The occasion was solemn, impressive, and grandly historic. The people, it is true, stood apparently spellbound; and the vast throng was hushed and awed into profound silence while Mr. Lincoln delivered his brief speech. But it seemed to him that this silence and attention to his words arose more from the solemnity of the ceremonies and the awful scenes which gave rise to them, than from anything he had said. He believed that the speech was a failure. He thought so at the time, and he never referred to it afterwards, in conversation with me, without some expression of unqualified regret that he had not made the speech better in every way.

On the platform from which Mr. Lincoln delivered his address, and only a moment after it was concluded, Mr. Seward turned to Mr. Everett and asked him what he thought of the President's speech. Mr. Everett replied, "It is not what I expected of him. I am disappointed." Then in his turn Mr. Everett asked, "What do you think of it, Mr. Seward?" The response was, "He has made a failure, and I am sorry for it. His speech was not equal to him." Mr. Seward then turned to me and asked, "Mr. Marshal, what do you think of it?" I answered, "I am sorry to say that it does not impress me as one of his great speeches."

In the face of these facts it has been repeatedly published that
this speech was received by the audience with loud demonstrations of approval; that "amid the tears, sobs, and cheers it produced in the excited throng, the orator of the day, Mr. Everett,
turned to Mr. Lincoln, grasped his hand and exclaimed, 'I congratulate you on your success!' adding in a transport of heated
enthusiasm, 'Ah, Mr. President, how gladly would I give my
hundred pages to be the author of your twenty lines!'" Nothing
of the kind occurred. It is a slander on Mr. Everett, an injustice
to Mr. Lincoln, and a falsification of history. Mr. Everett could
not have used the words attributed to him, in the face of his own
condemnation of the speech uttered a moment before, without
subjecting himself to the charge of being a toady and a hypo-
crite; and he was neither the one nor the other.

As a matter of fact, the silence during the delivery of the
speech, and the lack of hearty demonstration of approval immediately afterward, were taken by Mr. Lincoln as certain proof
that it was not well received. In that opinion we all shared. If
any person then present saw, or thought he saw, the marvelous
beauties of that wonderful speech, as intelligent men in all lands
now see and acknowledge them, his superabundant caution closed
his lips and stayed his pen. Mr. Lincoln said to me after our return to Washington, "I tell you, Hill, that speech fell on the audience like a wet blanket. I am distressed about it. I ought to
have prepared it with more care." Such continued to be his
opinion of all his platform addresses up to the time of his death.

I state it as a fact, and without fear of contradiction, that this
famous Gettysburg speech was not regarded by the audience to
whom it was addressed, or by the press and people of the United
States, as a production of extraordinary merit, nor·was it commented on as such until after the death of its author.*

Colonel Carr says:

I am aware, because I noted it at the time, that in the Associated Press report, which appeared in the morning papers, there
were punctuations "Applause" and "Long continued applause,"
according to the invariable custom in those times. Except as he
concluded, I did not observe it, and at the close the applause was

---

Recollections of Lincoln, pp. 170-174.

not especially marked. The occasion was too solemn for any kind of boisterous demonstration.

Having conversed and corresponded with many men who heard Lincoln at Gettysburg, all of them truthful, as I believe, and most of them far above ordinary intelligence, I am prepared to produce material to prove the following statements:

Lincoln made no preparation for the address, but trusted to the inspiration of the occasion; he made no preparation until he reached Gettysburg, and wrote the address the night before its delivery, or on the morning of its delivery; he wrote it on the train; he wrote it in full in Washington and took it with him; he wrote it in full in Washington and inadvertently left it there; he wrote it partly in Washington, partly on the train, partly the night before delivery, and revised it on the morning of the delivery. He delivered the address without notes; he held his notes in his left hand but did not refer to them; he held his notes in his left hand and read them in part and in part spoke without them; he held the manuscript firmly in both hands, and did not read from it, or read from it in part, or read from it word for word as it was therein written. The address was received without enthusiasm and left the audience cold and disappointed; it was received in a reverent silence too deep for applause; it was received with feeble and perfunctory applause at the end, but it was the man and not the address that was applauded; it was received with applause in several places and followed by prolonged applause.

My own opinion is that he began it in Washington and finished it in Gettysburg on the morning of the delivery; that he held it in both hands but was not closely confined to it and that he made verbal departures from the manuscript, and that the applause was not loud or long, and that the general impression upon the audience and upon the men on the platform, including the president himself, was one of disappointment.

How was the Gettysburg Address actually received?

The first impression of the people who heard was one of frank curiosity. Few of them had ever heard or seen Lincoln before. There was a craning of necks and shifting of positions to get a good look at him.

The next impression was one of the disparity between the tall man and the thin high voice. Almost invariably this was the effect when Lincoln began to speak, especially when he spoke out-of-doors. The Gettysburg gathering was the first large outdoor assembly which he had formally addressed since his inaugural, two and a half years before, and Lincoln pitched his voice in a conscious effort to make the people hear. They heard and were surprised and almost amused at so large a man and so thin and high a voice.

The next impression was a realization that Lincoln was a southerner. He was addressing a northern audience which had largely forgotten that he was a Kentuckian. They now heard with a feeling of surprise, his southern intonation and one or two oddities of pronunciation. He pronounced the preposition "to" as if it were spelled "toe." The effect of this was heightened by his deliberate effort to speak distinctly.

In so far as his audience got an impression of the subject-matter of his address, it was that of the propositional and commonplace character of his affirmations. He was telling what everybody knew, and telling it in the simplest and most direct manner possible.

The next and final impression was one of astonishment. Lincoln stopped just when he seemed to have begun. No one expected him to end when he did. He appeared to have been called on to do a matter-of-fact and commonplace thing, and to have done it in a surprisingly matter-of-fact and commonplace way.

The earliest biographies of Lincoln after his address dismiss it with very brief mention. It remained for others than those who first heard and read this remarkable oration to discover within it the essential elements of the noblest oratory.

When the hour came for his "few remarks," he knew that he

had established no point of contact with his audience. At no time had they risen above superficial curiosity concerning him, into an atmosphere of sympathetic interest. They heard his commonplace introduction and the little homily that followed it, and just when they might have begun to be interested, he stopped. Lincoln knew that he had not succeeded.

In the days of his agricultural life he had had experience with rusty plows to whose mold-board the soil stuck instead of turning a clean-cut furrow. Such an effort seemed to him his speech at Gettysburg. It stuck to the mold-board. It did not "scour."

If Everett said to Lincoln that he would be glad to feel that he had said as much in two hours as Lincoln said in two minutes, that fact only shows that Everett knew how to pay a gracious compliment. It does not prove that Everett believed that Lincoln had delivered a real great address. Lincoln believed that he failed; Everett shared his opinion, and so with very few exceptions and none of them well established, did those who heard him speak.

Certain Democratic papers spoke slurringly of "the president's silly little speech," or criticized him for using soldiers' "graves as a stump for political oratory," or took issue with him in his affirmation of the basic principle of the American Government and the purpose of the Civil War. In the president's own home town, the *Register* quoted the first two sentences from his address, and said:

If the above extract means anything at all, it is that this Nation was created to secure the liberty of the negro as well as of the white race, and dedicated to the proposition that all men, white and black, were placed, or to be placed, upon terms of equality. That is what Mr. Lincoln means to say, and nothing else, and when he uttered the words he knew that he was falsifying history, and enunciating an exploded political humbug.

It is of interest to inquire what reference was made to the Gettysburg Address in the sermons preached throughout the

country on the Sunday immediately following the death of Lincoln, or on one of the Sundays immediately succeeding.   Reverend E. T. Carnahan, of Gettysburg, preached an excellent discourse, which is preserved in print.   The sermon was prepared
with care, not being delivered on the day following Lincoln's
death, but on that proclaimed by President Johnson as a day of
public mourning, June 1, 1865.   The sermon is full of praise for
Lincoln, and shows the result of mature thought; but it contains
no suggestion that Lincoln had ever been in Gettysburg, no allusion to the address as something which the people of the congregation had heard and remembered.   That church had been
used as a hospital during and after the battle.   Down its aisle
Abraham Lincoln had walked with John Burns and sat in a pew
still proudly shown.   There he had attended a service on the afternoon of the dedication.   But the sermon contained no allusion
to the fact, no reminder that the dead president had once been a
worshiper with that congregation in a service so solemn that the
one commemorative of his death must have seemed a reminder
of it.

A number of ministers, however, did make reference to this
address.   They did not refer to it as "the Gettysburg Address,"
nor assume that the congregations had it in mind.   They spoke
of it as "the few remarks" with which the president followed the
"eloquent address" of Edward Everett.   They all spoke of it in
terms of appreciation, and at least one of them, Reverend John
McClintock, cited it as evidence of Lincoln's intellectual power.
Almost if not quite invariably the use they made of it was to
urge upon their congregations a dedication of themselves to the
uncompleted task for which Lincoln had given his life.*

XIII   THE RECOGNITION OF MERIT

If the audience that listened to the Gettysburg speech did not

---

*Among them were Reverend Doctors A. N. Littlejohn, James Eells and
John McClintock, of New York, and Henry Wilder Foote, Warren H. Cuds-
worth, W. S. Studley, James Reed and R. H. Neale, of Boston.

discover that it was a great address, who did discover it? Not
the leading editors of the United States. Horace Greeley made
no editorial comment in the *Tribune,* and neither did James Gordon Bennett nor Thurlow Weed nor Joseph Medill. J. G. Holland, in the *Springfield* (Massachusetts) *Republican,* on the day
following the address made this editorial comment:

Surpassingly fine as Mr. Everett's oration was in the Gettysburg consecration, the rhetorical honors of the occasion were
won by President Lincoln. His little speech is a perfect gem;
deep in feeling, compact in thought and expression, and tasteful
and elegant in every word and comma. Then it has the merit
of unexpectedness in its verbal perfection and beauty. We had
grown so accustomed to homely and imperfect phrase in his productions that we had come to think it was the law of his utterance. But this shows he can talk handsomely as well as act sensi-
bly. Turn back and read it over, it will well repay study as a
model speech. Strong feelings and a large brain were its parents
—a little painstaking its accoucher.

The *Providence Journal,* also, was one of the few newspapers
to make immediate and favorable comment:

We know not where to look for a more admirable speech than
the brief one which the President made at the close of Mr.
Everett's oration. It is often said that the hardest thing in the
world is to make a five-minutes' speech. But could the most
elaborate and splendid oration be more beautiful, more touching,
more inspiring, than those thrilling words of the President?
They had in our humble judgment the charm and power of the
very highest eloquence.

The *Evening Bulletin* of Philadelphia, said:

The President's brief speech of dedication is most happily expressed. It is warm, earnest, unaffected, and touching. Thousands who would not read the long, elaborate oration of Mr.
Everett will read the President's few words, and not many will
do it without a moistening of the eye and a swelling of the heart.

The statement often made that English editors were first to recognize the beauty of this production is without foundation.* No one man or group of men discovered the Gettysburg Address. Its worth dawned gradually on the mind of the American people, and a little later on the people of England. Credit must be given to Goldwin Smith for the following brilliant encomium in *MacMillan's Magazine* of February, 1865:

That Lincoln is something more than a boor his address at Gettysburg will in itself suffice to prove. There are one or two phrases here, such as "dedicated to the proposition," which betray a hand untrained in fine writing, and are proofs that the composition is Lincoln's own. But looking at the substance it may be doubted whether any king in Europe would have expressed himself more royally than the peasant's son. And even as to form we cannot help remarking that simplicity of structure and pregnancy of meaning are the true characteristics of the classical style. Is it easy to believe that the man who had the native good taste to produce this address would be capable of committing gross indecencies, that he would call for comic songs to be sung over soldiers' graves?

XIV   THE ADDRESS AS LITERATURE

As a literary production the Gettysburg Address is not wholly beyond criticism. Lincoln himself felt that it was too propositional, too didactic. It seemed to be lacking in emotional appeal. The extreme brevity of the production, however, made this almost inevitable. The phrase "dedicated to the proposition," has been very generally criticized. It is said that Matthew Arnold stopped there and was never able to finish the reading of the address. It shows some limitation in the use of adjectives—"a *great* civil war," "a *great* battlefield of that war." The word *"that"* is used twelve times, six of them in the final sentence. That sentence is too long and too much involved. It

---

*Mr. Isaac Markens and other careful students have searched earnestly, and in vain, for proof of this affirmation, and not only have not found it but have discovered enough to prove that it is not true.

is difficult to remember at the end what was the subject with which it was started; Lincoln himself apparently was not quite clear on this point. These are the criticisms which a pedant might discover and which pedants have discovered in the Gettysburg Address. They are, however, but spots upon the sun. Spite of these trivial rhetorical infelicities the Gettysburg Address is what it is. It rises superior to all such criticisms.

Colonel Carr has pointed out that short as it is, it includes all the essential parts of a formal oration. There is an *exordium* of five short and clear sentences introducing the theme and defining clearly the approach to the discussion. There is an *argument* of four sentences and the climax is reached in the last of these. Then there is the dignified *peroration* in one long sentence. He counts the Gettysburg Address as containing two hundred and sixty-seven words. Thirty-two of them are of Latin origin and with repetitions make a total of forty-six. The other two hundred and thirty-one words are Anglo-Saxon. Four-fifths of the address is in its origin old English.

One of the most discriminating and just of all tributes to the Gettysburg Address, including as it should a tribute also to the second inaugural, is to be found in the Rede Lecture, by Earl Curzon, of Kedleston, Chancellor of the University of Oxford, delivered before the University of Cambridge on November 6, 1913, on "Modern Parliamentary Eloquence." Speaking of the decline of eloquence of modern parliamentary bodies, and raising the question whether that decline was to be regarded as temporary or permanent, he assured his hearers that eloquence could not possibly have taken its final leave of parliamentary bodies. He said:

Just as the oratory of the Georgian era was attuned to an aristocratic age, and that of the Victorian epoch to the middle-class ascendancy, so does it seem to me likely that democracy will produce an eloquence, even an oratory of its own. Should a man arise from the ranks of the people, as Abraham Lincoln from the back-woods of America, a man gifted with real ora-

torical power, and with commanding genius, I can see no reason
why he should not revive in England the glories of a Chatham
or a Gratton. His triumphs might be less in the Senate than in
the arena: his style might not be that of the classics of the past.
But he might by reason of his gifts climb to the topmost place,
where he would sway the destinies of the State, and affect the
fortunes of an empire.

Earl Curzon's closing paragraphs contain even a finer tribute
to Lincoln. He felt that the character of his own address had
been such, surveying as he did in outline the history of British
parliamentary oratory, that he might be expected to designate
what he regarded "as the supreme masterpiece." He found three
of which he said that they "emerge with a superiority which, if
not disputable, will perhaps not be seriously disputed—much in
the same way as the 'Funeral Oration' of Pericles was generally
allowed to be the masterpiece of the ancient world." These three
"supreme masterpieces" of English eloquence he said were, the
toast of William Pitt after the victory at Trafalgar, and Lincoln's two speeches, the Gettysburg Address and the second
inaugural.

That Lord Curzon should have come to America for two of
these three masterpieces was highly complimentary to the oratory of this country. But it was even more significant that both
of these addresses should have been by Abraham Lincoln. Of
them he said:

They were uttered by a man who had been a country farmer
and a district lawyer before he became a statesman. But they
are among the glories and treasures of mankind. I escape the
task of deciding which is the masterpiece of modern English
eloquence by awarding the prize to an American.

The Gettysburg Address is far more than a pleasing piece of
occasional oratory. It is a marvelous piece of English composition. It is a pure well of English undefiled. It sets one to in-
quiring with nothing short of wonder "How knoweth this man

letters, having never learned?" The more closely the address is analyzed the more one must confess astonishment at its choice of words, the precision of its thought, its simplicity, directness and effectiveness.

But it is more than an admirable piece of English composition, it is an amazingly comprehensive and forceful presentation of the principles for which the war then was waging. It was a truthful recital of the events which lay behind the gathering at Gettysburg, and an interpretation of the spirit of the occasion. It joined the local to the national, the occasional to the permanent; it went straight at a declaration of the purpose which animated the soul of Abraham Lincoln, and for which the men buried at Gettysburg had given their lives. Above all it was a declaration of America's fundamental principles. It truthfully represented the spirit of that for which men fought, not only at Gettysburg but at Runnymede, at Bunker Hill, and on the plains of Flanders. The long, hard fought battle for the liberation of humanity has been a struggle for the rights and welfare of humanity.

There is no indication in Lincoln's address that he or any of his hearers appreciated the full significance of the Gettysburg victory. Lincoln said no word to indicate that he believed that Pickett would never lead another brigade against the fatal stone wall, or that that charge and its repulse would justify the erection of a high-water mark monument where such a monument now stands. It was reserved for those who could see that battle in perspective to discover and declare that what the men who fought at Gettysburg did was to settle the question whether a government like that of the United States could long endure. Lincoln referred to it merely as "a great battle-field of that war." He did not know it, but it was that battle-field which decided the answer to the question which his address proposed. Very near to the spot where Lincoln stood when he uttered those words, the thunders of war uttered the decree of Providence that government of the people, by the people and for the people should not perish from the earth.

CHAPTER XVI

THE TURN OF THE TIDE

IT IS now plain that when General Lee was defeated at Gettysburg the South lost its last reasonable hope of successful invasion of the North. It is equally clear that the capture of Vicksburg by General Grant, permitting the Mississippi, in the felicitous phrase of Abraham Lincoln, "to flow unvexed to the sea," effected a hopeless division of Confederate territory and established a base line from which the Confederacy of the East was certain to be pushed ever inward upon Richmond. The fate of the *Merrimac* destroyed any hope of the Confederates that they might dictate terms of peace by the capture of Washington, and it also served notice on foreign nations that the blockade of the Confederate ports would be made increasingly effective. Sherman's march to the sea cut another swath through the heart of the Confederacy. Before his advancing hosts was terror, and behind it were ashes. Apart from any discussion of the military value of his exploit, he showed that the Confederate defenses were a hollow shell and that the South was strained to the utmost to keep up her resistance. His path of devastation, three hundred miles long and sixty miles wide, divided again the Confederacy, which the gunboats of Commodore Foote had cut in twain along the Mississippi's length.

It is very easy now for us to see these facts and appreciate their true significance, but it was not easy nor even possible for the nation, or even its leaders, to understand them at that time. A fierce controversy waged for years, and is still unsettled. as to how far the victory at Gettysburg is one for which the commander of the army deserves credit. There were those, even among his own generals, who questioned whether General

Meade recognized his victory after he had won it. General Doubleday, in his history of the battles of Chancellorsville and Gettysburg, affirms that:

After the battle Meade had not the slightest desire to recommence the struggle. . . . It was hard to convince him that Lee was actually gone.

He also declared that on the morning of July fourth, after the defeat of Pickett's charge, and with Lee's army in full retreat, Meade said he thought he could hold out against Lee for part of another day.* Meade, however, in later years did not admit that he thus misunderstood his own victory.

Lincoln was sadly disappointed that Lee was not pursued, and his army captured or annihilated, after his defeat at Gettysburg. He said that he would give much to be free from the impression that Meade was willing to have him get away. He did not doubt Meade's loyalty, but gravely questioned his power of initiative. He sat down and wrote a letter to Meade containing the following rebuke:

My dear General, I do not believe you appreciate the magnitude of the misfortune involved in Lee's escape. He was within your easy grasp, and to have closed upon him would, in connection with our other late successes, have ended the war. As it is, the war will be prolonged indefinitely. If you could not safely attack Lee last Monday, how can you possibly do so south of the river, when you can take with you very few more than two-thirds of the force you then had in hand? It would be unreasonable to expect and I do not expect that you can now effect much. Your golden opportunity is gone, and I am distressed immeasurably because of it.

I beg you will not consider this a prosecution or persecution of yourself. As you had learned that I was dissatisfied, I have thought it best to kindly tell you why.

---

*Chancellorsville and Gettysburg, by Abner Doubleday, in Campaigns of the Civil War, Series VI, pp. 208, 209.

After he had written it he thought the matter over and decided not to send it, so it remained among his papers unpublished until years afterward.

This is not the only time Lincoln relieved his feelings by writing a letter and then deciding not to send it. Once hearing a man speak very abusively of another, Lincoln advised him to put all his invective into a letter addressed to the man in question. The letter was written and read to Lincoln, who commended it for its severity. The writer was pleased and asked him, "How would you advise me to send it?" "Send it," said Lincoln. "Oh, I wouldn't send it. I sometimes write a letter like that and it does me good, but I never send it."

At this time, however, Lincoln wrote another letter and did send it. If Meade had pursued Lee, it might have been mailed to him, but it was addressed to General Grant. The letter was as follows:

Washington, July 13, 1863.

Major-General Grant.

My Dear General: I do not remember that you and I ever met personally. I write this now as a grateful acknowledgment for the almost inestimable service you have done the country. I wish to say a word further. When you first reached the vicinity of Vicksburg, I thought you should do what you finally did —march the troops across the neck, run the batteries with the transports, and thus go below; and I never had any faith, except a general hope that you knew better than I, that the Yazoo Pass expedition and the like could succeed. When you got below and took Port Gibson, Grand Gulf, and vicinity, I thought you should go down the river and join General Banks, and when you turned northward, east of the Big Black, I feared it was a mistake. I now wish to make the personal acknowledgment that you were right and I was wrong. Yours very truly,

A. Lincoln.

Ulysses S. Grant was a graduate of West Point, where his record as a student was only moderately good. Among his associates while there in school and in subsequent service in the

Mexican War, were a number of brilliant leaders of the Confederate Army, most of whom could remember that their record in the class-room had been better than that of Grant. In the beginning of the Civil War he had been assigned a commonplace task of inspecting army equipments, but was called to more active service through the influence of his friend and townsman, Elihu B. Washburne, Representative in Congress from Galena, Illinois.

General Grant's first services were inconspicuous but successful. He emerged into prominence by his capture of Fort Donelson, where he demanded and secured unconditional surrender. His firmness in demanding and his success in securing this result, while McClellan in the Army of the Potomac was timidly waiting for the enemy to come and offer to be captured, put great heart into the faltering hope of the Union. His initials came to be accepted as applicable to another name than that which at West Point had displaced the name of his baptism, and he was called "Unconditional Surrender" Grant. The laurels which he won at Donelson he almost lost at Shiloh. On the first day of that battle his army was defeated. Grant was criticized for having placed his army on the side of the Tennessee next to the enemy, and leaving it thus exposed to surprise and successful onslaught. He was criticized for being some miles from the front when the battle began. He was declared to have been intoxicated on the first day of the battle. It was still further alleged that if Buell had not arrived when he did, the success of the second day would have been in doubt. How keenly Grant felt these strictures is known to every reader of the Century War Book, *Battles and Leaders of the Civil War*, and of Grant's *Memoirs*. General Halleck disliked Grant, and virtually put him under arrest after the battle of Shiloh. The partisans of Buell loudly proclaimed that but for his timely arrival and superior generalship, Grant and his army would either have been captured or crowded into the Tennessee River. Men in high places declared him to be a man of very mediocre military ability.

But Lincoln had growing faith in the taciturn, bullet-headed soldier from Illinois. It gratified him that Grant took the command that was given to him and went ahead with it, not teasing for impossibilities. The memory of McClellan's perpetual wail for more men and munitions found a pleasant contrast in the silence and pertinacity of Grant. When people asked Lincoln what Grant was doing, Lincoln said frankly that he did not know. Said he, "General Grant is a very meager letter-writer and telegrapher, but a very copious fighter." He said, "I don't know General Grant's plans, and I do not care to know them; I know he has plans, and is at work carrying them out."

When he was told that General Grant drank, he is said to have asked, "Can you tell me the brand of liquor? I should like to send some of it to my other generals."

Thus Grant continued as a major general in spite of all efforts to discredit him.

Abraham Lincoln never considered himself an authority in military matters. He never used his own early title of captain.* His references to his own experiences in the Black Hawk War were generally humorous, and in his one speech in Congress where he made reference to it, that reference was almost in burlesque. He was disposed to trust his general and his secretary of war.

Nevertheless, Abraham Lincoln was not without practical wisdom in military matters. It was his daily custom to go over to the War Department and read the despatches from beginning to end. He studied the maps of the various war fronts. The few suggestions that he made to army officers about plans of the campaign were intelligent suggestions and showed a certain native shrewdness and practical sagacity which had in them the essentials of true military judgment.

---

*Mr. David Davis, of Bloomington, Illinois, has shown me his father's papers on Abraham Lincoln, which, unfortunately, are few in number. I find, however, a statement by Judge David Davis that when Lincoln first came upon the circuit he was sometimes called captain, and did not resent it; but neither did he welcome it; and the title though evidently his, fell rather soon into disuse.

His first letter to Grant congratulating him upon the capture of Vicksburg showed how intelligently Lincoln had been following Grant's movements in the siege of that city. The capture of Vicksburg had involved very severe tactical problems. Vicksburg was on a bluff, and the land occupied by the Union Armies was largely swamp land. Grant endeavored to transport a portion of his fleet below the city, and to this end labored long in the digging of a canal which did not prove a success. At length the hazardous expedition was attempted of running the batteries. A large fleet of gunboats and transports was prepared, and, on the night of the sixteenth of April, 1863, these vessels made a successful passage down the river. The expedition was considered so hazardous that men were not commanded to undertake it, but volunteers were called for. So many men volunteered that selections had to be made. Although some of the boats were damaged and one set on fire, the vessels made the dangerous run in an hour and a quarter and without the loss of a single life.

Grant had done this work so silently, so methodically, so determinedly and in the end so successfully, as to take the nation by surprise. It was almost incredible that simultaneously two such victories should have been won as were won at Gettysburg and at Vicksburg.

But there was this difference in the sequel. Meade having defeated Lee, permitted Lee and his army to escape, so that Lee's army had to be fought again and again for almost two years. Meade rested on his laurels. Grant not only captured Pemberton and his army, but quietly went to work making other plans and saying very little about them. Lincoln did not fail to note the contrast, not only between Grant and Meade, but between Grant and every other general whom up to that time he had known.

At the beginning of 1864 General Grant was still personally unknown to the president, the secretary of war, and very nearly all of official Washington. The Thirty-eighth Congress had recently convened, and Elihu B. Washburne introduced a bill creating the office of lieutenant general. The bill became a law, and on February 22, 1864, Lincoln appointed Ulysses S. Grant to this office, making him commander-in-chief under the president, of all the armies in the United States.

For the first time during the war, Grant visited the capital. He arrived on the eighth of March, and that evening called at the White House. A levee was in progress. Grant entered unannounced, and virtually unknown. Lincoln recognized him, and Grant was immediately hailed as a hero. This experience greatly embarrassed Grant.

On the following day, in the presence of a few friends gathered in the White House, the president presented General Grant his commission in as simple a fashion as perhaps ever accompanied an incident conferring power of this character and extent. The two speeches made on that occasion have been preserved.

President Lincoln said:

"General Grant: The nation's appreciation of what you have done, and its reliance upon you for what remains to be done in the existing great struggle, are now presented with this commission, constituting you Lieutenant General in the army of the United States. With this high honor devolves upon you also a corresponding responsibility. As the country herein trusts you, so, under God, it will sustain you. I scarcely need to add, that with what I here speak for the nation, goes my own hearty personal concurrence."

To this General Grant made the following reply:

"Mr. President: I accept the commission with gratitude for the high honor conferred. With the aid of the noble armies that have fought on so many fields for our common country, it will be my earnest endeavor not to disappoint your expectations. I feel the full weight of the responsibilities now devolving on me, and I know that if they are met, it will be due to those armies, and above all to the favor of that Providence which leads both nations and men."

Honorable John P. Usher, Secretary of the Interior, in an address delivered a quarter-century later,* related his memories of the scene when Lincoln assembled the Cabinet to meet General Grant, and receive his commission. Not one member of the Cabinet, as Usher recalled, had seen Grant. Lincoln did not remember having met him, and said so to Grant, but Grant told Lincoln that he had gone over from Galena to Freeport and had listened to Lincoln and Douglas there in 1858 and shaken hands in the crowd with Lincoln afterward. Mr. Usher said that President Lincoln did not inform the Cabinet in advance of the reason for their having been called together, and while they were assembling, and all of them present except Stanton, he was at work at his disordered desk. General Grant entered the room with Secretary Stanton and General Halleck, and without speaking to any one as they entered, the three walked quickly to the desk and stood before it. The president rose, and standing across the desk from the three, read his short address. General Grant then produced what Usher thought hardly more than a quarter sheet of paper and read his acceptance. He said that Grant stood, as one or more of his photographs show him, in the awkward position known as "hip-shot," and that when he began to read his acceptance, he was so embarrassed that he did not inflate his lungs, and his voice failed him. Grant had been holding the paper in his right hand. When he found that even so simple an effort at oratory required more breath than he had supposed, he changed his position, stood erect with shoulders back, took the paper in both hands, and inhaling a deep breath, began again and quietly read the paper through. It is a detail of no great historic value, but it has the life-like touch that belongs to authentic memory. Usher further relates that it was Lincoln's friend, Judge T. Lyle Dickey, who after the battle of

---

*This incident was narrated by Mr. Usher in an address which he delivered at a banquet in Wyandotte, Kansas, June 20, 1887. It was delivered impromptu, but on the following day was dictated to Mr. Nelson H. Loomis, who subsequently became General Solicitor for the Union Pacific Railroad Company. A few copies were printed for private distribution. It deserves a wider publication.

Corinth, brought to Lincoln so favorable a report of Grant that Lincoln entertained a sincere regard for him before they met, and never afterward doubted Grant's ability to command the nation's armies.

It will be noted that the phrase *"under God"* which the president had interpolated at Gettysburg was not permitted to drop out of his vocabulary, but was used on the presentation of the commission to General Grant and on other occasions. General Grant, also, in his acceptance used similar language.

The president and the new lieutenant general stepped into a photograph gallery and had their pictures taken, and both proceeded to forget the matter, and neither ever saw the photographs that were made. The unretouched negatives were discovered after many years.*

Mrs. Lincoln desired to make the most socially of General Grant's visit to Washington. When the general came to the White House to receive his commission, he found awaiting him an invitation from the mistress of the White House to dine at the executive mansion that evening and attend afterward a party to be given in his honor. General Grant declined with thanks. "Mrs. Lincoln must excuse me," he said. "I must be in Tennessee at a given time." "But we can't excuse you," said President Lincoln, "Mrs. Lincoln's dinner without you would be the play of Hamlet with Hamlet left out." "I appreciate the honor Mrs. Lincoln would do me," replied General Grant, "but time is very important now; and really, Mr. Lincoln, I have had enough of this show business."

So just as Washington was getting on its best clothes and

---

*On the centenary of Lincoln's birth in 1909, it was my privilege to address a celebration in Chicago, the other speaker being General Frederick D. Grant. I informed him that I was in Washington soon after the discovery of these now famous negatives, and had secured an early print of each. He had never seen either of them. A few days later I showed them both to him. He was present with his father on the occasion when these sittings occurred, and it was his first visit to Washington. He was greatly pleased with the photographs, which he pronounced to be excellent representations of his father and of President Lincoln on the day when he first met the latter.

ready to entertain in proper form the new lieutenant general in command of all the armies of the United States, General Grant slipped out of Washington as quietly as he had slipped in, and went back to the army.

Grant said to Lincoln that he wished to return to Nashville and put his command into Sherman's hands, and that it would take him nine days to do that and other necessary things in the West. At the end of nine days he was back in Washington, but as reluctant as ever to participate in any display. After a short interview with Lincoln, he went to the front with the Army of the Potomac.

The appointment of Grant lifted a great load from the shoulders of Lincoln. He had a strong conviction that Grant would evolve a comprehensive plan of campaign, and would hold to it persistently and carry it to a successful issue. He gave to Grant that confidence and support which he had freely given to the successive commanders of the Army of the Potomac. He had now elevated Grant above Meade without displacing Meade. He had also promoted Grant above Sherman and all the other major generals. Grant said he believed that Sherman was an abler general than himself, and more deserving of the honor. But that did not prevent Grant from taking hold of the situation and seeing the matter through.

As Lincoln did not hear from Grant, he thought well to write to him, and on April thirtieth, sent him a letter containing the following as its most significant word:

You are vigilant and self-reliant, and pleased with this I wish not to obtrude any restraints or constraints upon you. . . . I there be anything wanting in my power to give, do not fail to let me know. And now, with a brave army and a just cause may God sustain you.

Grant subsequently wrote the analysis of the situation as he found it when he became lieutenant general:

The armies in the East and West acted independently and without concert, like a balky team, no two ever pulling together; enabling the enemy to use to a great advantage his interior lines of communication for transporting troops from East to West, re-enforcing the army most vigorously pressed, and to furlough large numbers, during seasons of inactivity on our part, to go to their homes and do the work of producing for the support of their armies. It was a question whether our numerical strength and resources were not more than balanced by these disadvantages and the enemy's superior position.

From the first I was firm in the conviction that no peace could be had that would be stable and conducive to the happiness of the people, both North and South, until the military power of the rebellion was entirely broken. I therefore determined; *first,* to use the greatest number of troops practicable against the armed force of the enemy; preventing him from using the same force at different seasons against first one and then another of our armies, and the possibility of repose for refitting and producing necessary supplies for carrying on resistance. *Second,* to hammer continuously against the armed force of the enemy and his resources, until by mere attrition, if in no other way, there should be nothing left to him but an equal submission with the loyal section of our common country to the Constitution and laws of the land.

Whether Grant was a truly great general or not is a question which may be discussed by those who care to discuss it. For the purpose of this biography of Lincoln it is sufficient to record that from the day of Grant's appointment the president experienced a sense of relief. Grant's plan of campaign was simple. He made no claim to being a brilliant strategist. He determined to employ all the armies east and west, to one common closing in upon the armed forces of the Confederacy, and forcing them into closer and closer quarters until they should be compelled to give up the struggle.* Grant knew this plan would involve heavy losses to the Union forces. They must operate upon a longer front and on the offensive. Any success

---

*General Grant's plan was not unlike the "Anaconda" which General Scott recommended to McClellan, and that general cavalierly rejected.

they won would commonly be with loss heavier than that which
they were able to inflict.   To gain a given end, they must ex
pect to lose men, and must reckon that they could afford to lose
more men than the Confederates, but they could not afford to le
the war go on as a series of disconnected skirmishes.

Lincoln had enough military wisdom to understand and ap
prove this plan.   He said that he made no pretense of being
either a military leader or a financier; but he was enough of botl
to know that when a nation got into war it must push the war
with some vigor or the nation would be demoralized and bank
rupt.

General Grant set to work upon this plan.   He fought bloody
battles and sustained heavy losses.   The losses did not daun
him.   He announced his intention to fight it out on that line if i
took all summer.   It took all summer and all winter and part o
the spring, but Grant fought it out on that line just as Lincoln
believed that he would do.

CHAPTER XVII

THE DRAFT RIOTS

ABRAHAM LINCOLN believed with good reason in the loyalty
of the people of East Tennessee, and maintained that by permit-
ing the Confederate Armies to operate in that region, the Union
was in danger of losing a most valuable stake. In Knoxville,
Parson Brownlow had edited the *Knoxville Whig,* to which title
he later added the name "and *Rebel Ventilator."* Brownlow had
been driven out. The mountain region of Kentucky, Tennessee
and West Virginia had furnished large numbers of men for the
Union Army, but Lincoln felt that his generals did not value
highly enough the adherence of the people of that region to the
Union. Burnside after his defeat at Fredericksburg, December
13, 1862, was sent west. Lincoln desired that he should move
through East Tennessee and unite with Rosecrans at Chattanooga. Burnside reached Knoxville, and there encountered
Longstreet, and for a considerable time got no farther. Lincoln, eagerly waiting for news from him, came almost to welcome bad news. On November 24, 1863, there were tidings of
firing at Knoxville. It was the first word from Knoxville for
several days. John Hay's diary quotes Lincoln as saying that
any news that showed Burnside was not overwhelmed was cheering:

"Like Sally Carter, when she heard one of her children squall,
would say, 'There goes one of my young ones! Not dead yet,
bless the Lord!'"

Rosecrans too, delayed his campaign at Chattanooga until he
was out-generaled by Bragg and in danger of losing his whole
army.

This was before Grant had been made commander-in-chie
and Lincoln himself was virtually assuming the responsibility o
that position. He removed Rosecrans after his defeat at Chicka
mauga, and placed Thomas in his stead. He sent Sherman from
the west and Hooker from the east with reenforcements, and he
appointed Grant to the command of the Military Division of the
Mississippi, which included the three departments of the Ohio
Cumberland and the Tennessee. Grant disliked Rosecrans, and
greatly liked Thomas. Sherman, also, Grant trusted fully. As
for Hooker, Grant believed in him as a general capable of a bril
liant dash, but not capable of managing a sustained campaign
He says in his *Memoirs* concerning him, that Hooker was bril
liant but unreliable, and given to the habit of gathering abou
him a group of younger officers and fighting a spectacular bat
tle of his own, regardless of the particular thing he was set to do

Grant took command at Chattanooga in the autumn of 1863
He found Rosecrans still there, and generously ready to com
municate his plans. "They were good plans," said Genera
Grant, "I only wondered why he had not carried them out.'
Grant, however, did not carry out the plans of Rosecrans. Chat
tanooga was so well surrounded by the Confederates fortified or
high elevations, that nothing but a determined and courageou
battle would save it. On November 24 and 25, 1863, that bat
tle occurred. General Hooker, who had almost lost his sou
briquet of "Fighting Joe" at Chancellorsville, regained it a
Chattanooga. Phil Sheridan, also, led in a brilliant and success
ful charge. The Union flag was planted on the summit of Look
out Mountain. The charge upon Missionary Ridge succeeded
beyond the hope of the commanding general. The soldiers had
been ordered to take the rifle pits at the foot of the mountain
and then halt and re-form; but in the ardor of their success the
moved on up the slope, captured the cannon at the top, and
turned them upon the retreating foe.

This victory, when it occurred, did much to establish confi
dence in the ultimate success of the Union cause; but success wa

ABRAHAM LINCOLN
Photograph by Brady, February 9, 1864

long in coming.   Meantime, sentiment in the North against the
war was not diminishing.

On March 3, 1863, a bill was passed for the enrollment of the
entire military force of the United States.   The passage of this
law was promptly followed by a draft of three hundred thousand
men.   There had been a time earlier in the war when such a call
was answered with enthusiasm.   Quotas had been filled rather
promptly.   Volunteers had offered themselves, singing as they
came, "We are coming, Father Abraham, three hundred thousand strong."   That time had passed.   Three hundred thousand
more men could be obtained only by desperate exertion.   The
several northern states paid high bounties to secure their quota,
preferring this to the unpopular method of draft.   The bounty
system was a necessary evil.   And so, also, was the provision
that a man who was drafted might hire a substitute.*

----

*It became more or less popular for men who were not personally liable
to military service to hire substitutes.   The men thus hired were men who
had not been drawn in the draft-lottery, and who were ready, for a sum of
money, to take the place of some one drafted, but who preferred not to go.
In this way, Grover Cleveland, later president, provided a substitute when
he was drafted; and Abraham Lincoln, himself exempt, hired a substitute,
to be credited to the lagging quota of the District of Columbia.   Whether
Lincoln's substitute was paid or whether he offered himself in love for the
president, is not of record.   Probably, however, Lincoln paid him the current
honorarium, if it may be so called, for this service.   The grave of Lincoln's
substitute is at Shroudsburg, Pennsylvania.
   The man who represented Lincoln in person was John Summerfield Staples,
a young volunteer from Pennsylvania, aged about twenty-one years.   Having
been introduced to the president, this young man signified a desire to fill the
honorable position as his substitute and Lincoln gladly accepted him.   The
evidence of the employment of a substitute by Lincoln, is contained in the
following official statement of the commissioner of pensions:
                                      Washington, D. C., May 11, 1910.
   "John Summerfield Staples, residing at Stroudsburg, Pa., filed an application for pension in 1882, stating that in the Civil War he had served in
Company C, One Hundred and Seventy-Sixth Pennsylvania Militia, and
afterwards in Company H, Second District of Columbia Infantry, and that
in his second enlistment he was a substitute for Abraham Lincoln.
   "The records show that said soldier enlisted November 2, in Company C,
One Hundred and Seventy-Sixth Pennsylvania drafted militia, that he was
honorably discharged, May 5, 1863, and that he afterwards enlisted April 3,
1864, in Company H, Second District of Columbia Volunteers, from which
he was honorably discharged at Alexandria, Va., September 12, 1865, and the
record also shows that in this last service he was enrolled as a representative
of Abraham Lincoln, who was not liable to draft.
   "It is shown by the papers on file in this case that during the war, the

The United States learned better at the time of the World War. No man called by the draft could buy a substitute with money.

In New York City in the summer of 1863 a riot occurred. On July thirteenth, attempts to enforce the draft were opposed by a mob. The office of the marshal having charge of the draft was broken into and set on fire. The mob prevented the fire department from extinguishing the flame. A negro orphan asylum was burned, and negroes were hung from lamp posts.

In the New York riots the conspicuous leaders of the mob were Irishmen, and men of southern birth. Lincoln was compelled to send troops to New York to quell the draft riot, and chose General Kilpatrick, whose name, he believed, would have influence with the Irish. The mob was quelled, and order was restored, but not until many outrages had been perpetrated. Nor were the Irish and the southerners of New York the only ones who gave to this disturbance their moral support, if not their active participation. Opposition to the draft was widely prevalent and very powerful.

At this juncture, even the friends of the administration were greatly distressed. A large meeting was called in Illinois for September 3, 1863. All friends of the Union of all parties were invited to meet at the capital and consider the grave situation. A communication was sent to Lincoln from his old neighbors inviting him to attend in person and address the meeting. Lincoln could not go, but sent a letter to his old neighbor, Honorable James C. Conkling, to be read at the meeting.

This letter has not always been understood. Its tone was so earnest, so almost severe, it has been thought that Lincoln in-

---

President decided that he would place in the army a substitute to the credit of the District of Columbia, and that he communicated his desire to do so to the provost marshal of the district, with a request that he select the person who should be placed in the service, and that the provost marshal then sent for Noble D. Larner, then a prominent citizen of this city, and stated to him the President's wishes, and Mr. Larner afterwards succeeded in getting the substitute in the person of Mr. Staples, and he was afterwards mustered into the service.   (Signed)
                              "J. L. Davenport, Commissioner."

tended to censure those who had invited him to be present, and that he possibly meant to rebuke the man to whom the letter was addressed. There is no ground for this opinion, nor does the letter itself give color to it. The meeting gave Lincoln the opportunity of addressing the entire country, and especially those who at heart believed in the Union but were perplexed by the trend of events.

When he employs the second person and says, "You say that you will not fight to free negroes; some of them seem willing to fight for you," he was not addressing Conkling or his own neighbors. He was continuing, after a digression, his address to those who were dissatisfied with him. The letter is a manly and straightforward document, and shows how the president whom some people supposed to be a weak and pliable man, could be and was inflexible in a cause which he believed to be right.

Lincoln's personal letter to Conkling, which accompanied this official communication, contained this single instruction, "Read it very slowly."

Executive Mansion
Washington, August 26, 1863.

Hon. James C. Conkling.

My Dear Sir: Your letter inviting me to attend a mass meeting of unconditional Union men, to be held at the capital of Illinois, on the 3d day of September, has been received. It would be very agreeable for me thus to meet my old friends at my own home; but I cannot just now be absent from here so long as a visit there would require.

The meeting is to be of all those who maintain unconditional devotion to the Union; and I am sure that my old political friends will thank me for tendering, as I do, the nation's gratitude to those other noble men whom no partisan malice or partisan hope can make false to the nation's life.

There are those who are dissatisfied with me. To such I would say: You desire peace, and you blame me that we do not have it. But how can we attain it? There are but three conceivable ways: First—to suppress the rebellion by force of arms. This I am trying to do. Are you for it? If you are, so far we are agreed. If you are not for it, a *second* way is to give up the Union. I am against this. Are you for it? If you are, you should say so plainly. If you are not for *force,* nor yet for *dissolution,* there only remains some imaginable *compromise.*

I do not believe that any compromise embracing the maintenance of the Union is now possible. All that I learn leads to a directly opposite belief. The strength of the rebellion is its military, its army. That army dominates all the country, and all the people within its range. Any offer of terms made by any man or men within that range, in opposition to that army, is simply nothing for the present; because such man or men have no power whatever to enforce their side of a compromise if one were made with them.

To illustrate: Suppose refugees from the South and peace men of the North get together in convention, and frame and proclaim a compromise embracing a restoration of the Union. In what way can that compromise be used to keep Lee's army out of Pennsylvania? Meade's army can keep Lee's army out of Pennsylvania, and, I think, can ultimately drive it out of existence. But no paper compromise to which the controllers of Lee's army are not agreed, can at all affect that army. In an effort at such compromise we would waste time, which the enemy would improve to our disadvantage; and that would be all.

A compromise, to be effective, must be made either with those who control the rebel army, or with the people, first liberated from the domination of that army by the success of our own army. Now, allow me to assure you that no word or intimation from that rebel army, or from any of the men controlling it, in relation of any peace compromise, has ever come to my knowledge or belief. All charges and insinuations to the contrary are deceptive and groundless. And I promise you that if any such proposition shall hereafter come, it shall not be rejected and kept a secret from you. I freely acknowledge myself to be the servant of the people, according to the bond of service, the United States Constitution; and that, as such, I am responsible to them.

But, to be plain. You are dissatisfied with me about the negro. Quite likely there is a difference of opinion between you and myself upon that subject. I certainly wish that all men could be free, while you, I suppose, do not. Yet, I have neither adopted nor proposed any measure which is not consistent with even your view, provided that you are for the Union. I suggested compensated emancipation; to which you replied you wished not to be taxed to buy negroes. But I had not asked you to be taxed to buy negroes, except in such a way as to save you from greater taxation to save the Union exclusively by other means.

You dislike the emancipation proclamation, and perhaps would have it retracted. You say it is unconstitutional. I think differently. I think the Constitution invests its Commander-in-Chief with the law of war in time of war. The most that can be said, if so much, is, that slaves are property. Is there, has there ever been, any question that by the law of war, property, both of enemies and friends, may be taken when needed? And is it not needed whenever it helps us and hurts the enemy? Armies, the world over, destroy enemies' property when they cannot use it; and even destroy their own to keep it from the enemy. Civilized belligerents do all in their power to help themselves or hurt the enemy, except a few things regarded as barbarous or cruel. Among the exceptions are the massacre of vanquished foes and non-combatants, male and female.

But the proclamation, as law, either is valid or is not valid. If it is not valid, it needs no retraction. If it is valid, it cannot be retracted, any more than the dead can be brought to life. Some of you profess to think its retraction would operate favorably for the Union. Why better *after* the retraction than *before* the issue? There was more than a year and a half of trial to suppress the rebellion before the proclamation was issued, the last one hundred days of which passed under an explicit notice that it was coming, unless averted by those in revolt returning to their allegiance. The war has certainly progressed as favorably for us since the issue of the proclamation as before.

I know as fully as one can know the opinion of others, that some of the commanders of our armies in the field, who have given us our most important victories, believe the emancipation policy and the use of colored troops constitute the heaviest blows yet dealt to the rebellion, and that at least one of those important successes could not have been achieved when it was, but for the aid of the black soldiers.

Among the commanders who hold these views are some who have never had an affinity with what is called "abolitionism," or with "republican party politics," but who hold them purely as military opinions. I submit their opinions as entitled to some weight against the objections often urged that emancipation and arming the blacks are unwise as military measures, and were not adopted as such in good faith.

You say that you will not fight to free negroes. Some of them seem willing to fight for you; but no matter. Fight you, then, exclusively to save the Union. I issued the proclamation on purpose to aid you in saving the Union. Whenever you shall have conquered all resistance to the Union, if I shall urge you to continue fighting, it will be an apt time then for you to declare you will not fight to free negroes. I thought that in your struggle for the Union, to whatever extent the negroes shall cease helping the enemy, to that extent it weakened the enemy in his resistance to you. Do you think differently? I thought whatever negroes can be got to do as soldiers, leaves just so much less for white soldiers to do in saving the Union. Does it appear otherwise to you? But negroes, like other people, act upon motives. Why should they do anything for us if we will do nothing for them? If they stake their lives for us, they must be prompted by the strongest motives, even the promise of freedom. And the promise, being made, must be kept.

The signs look better. The Father of Waters again goes unvexed to the sea. Thanks to the great Northwest for it; nor yet wholly to them. Three hundred miles up they met New England, Empire, Keystone, and Jersey, hewing their way right and left. The sunny South, too, in more colors than one, also lent a helping hand. On the spot, their part of the history was jotted down in black and white. The job was a great national one, and let none be slighted who bore an honorable part in it. And while those who have cleared the great river may well be proud, even that is not all. It is hard to say that anything has been more bravely and well done than at Antietam, Murfreesboro, Gettysburg, and on many fields of less note. Nor must Uncle Sam's web feet be forgotten. At all the watery margins they have been present, not only on the deep sea, the broad bay, and the rapid river, but also up the narrow, muddy bayou, and wherever the ground was a little damp, they have been and made their tracks. Thanks to all. For the great Republic—for the principle it lives by and keeps alive—for man's vast future— thanks to all.

Peace does not appear so distant as it did. I hope it will come soon and come to stay; and so come as to be worth the keeping in all future time. It will then have been proved that among freemen there can be no successful appeal from the ballot to the bullet, and that they who take such appeal are sure to lose their case and pay the cost. And there will be some black men who can remember that with silent tongue, and clenched teeth, and steady eye, and well-poised bayonet, they have helped mankind on to this great consummation, while I fear there will be some white ones unable to forget that with malignant heart and deceitful speech they have striven to hinder it.

Still, let us not be over-sanguine of a speedy, final triumph. Let us be quite sober. Let us diligently apply the means, never doubting that a just God, in his own good time, will give us the rightful result.

Yours, very **truly**,   A. Lincoln.

It will be remembered that in the congressional and gubernatorial election of 1862, a strong reaction against Lincoln had been manifest throughout the North. In the autumn of 1863 several states elected governors. Greatly to Lincoln's satisfaction these elections showed a trend of sentiment favorable to the administration. Every state in which elections were held, except New Jersey, gave large majorities for the administration. The result was peculiarly gratifying in Ohio. There the Democratic Party had nominated for governor Clement L. Vallandigham. His disloyalty made him a national figure and of him the nation had heard and yet was to hear much. Ohio in 1863 sustained the president and defeated Vallandigham by a majority of almost one hundred thousand.

This election and the victories around Chattanooga were bright spots in a sky greatly darkened. Lincoln still had much to perplex and dishearten him.

CHAPTER XVIII

JUSTICE AND MERCY

ROBERT G. INGERSOLL characterized Abraham Lincoln as "a man clothed with almost absolute power, who never abused it except on the side of mercy." That mercy, Lincoln had abundant occasion to exercise.

As the war went on, it became necessary for the army to enforce its discipline by punishments against its own soldiers who were guilty of crimes or misdemeanors. Not all soldiers were patriots. Many a man reached the recruiting officer about two leaps ahead of the sheriff. Not a few men in jail for misdemeanors and even for criminal offenses were pardoned on condition that they enter the army. War itself produces criminals. It teaches men to disregard their own word and other men's property and life. There is no crime in the calendar which is not committed by soldiers in every war.

In general these crimes were punished with no more than necessary severity; and, when there were mitigating circumstances, officers well below the president were willing and competent to consider them. Only a very small fraction of the cases of punishment came to his desk. It was only when, all other appeals having been found futile, and usually for just cause, a sentence was to be carried into effect, the friends of guilty men appealed to the president for pardon. The very fact that appeal was taken to him is proof presumptive that the accused had exhausted all ordinary, and probably reasonable, efforts to secure pardon. It is little wonder that when Lincoln interfered in these usually flagrant cases, generals in command protested, and

248

Stanton stormed. The president was breaking down the discipline of the army.

"I know it, but I don't see that shooting him would do any good," Lincoln would say.

He sincerely pitied the man who was found guilty of cowardice. Lincoln was accustomed to say that he was not sure but that he himself would run if he were placed in the front in battle.

It is but fair to say concerning some of the stories of Lincoln's alleged clemency, that so far as is known they are not true.

The attitude of Abraham Lincoln toward the undeserving is entitled to more careful and discriminating treatment than it usually receives. Two natures strove within him. On the one hand, he had a keen sense of justice, and a high regard for law and order. The deliberate violator of law deserved punishment, and society required for its protection that he be punished. So Abraham Lincoln believed; but he also had high regard for the welfare of the man who had broken the law. When he became president, no burden rested more heavily upon him than the fact that in certain cases he had either to accept the judgment of courts sentencing soldiers to be shot, or to interfere in their behalf.

Lincoln was a man of deep sympathy, but his sympathy had a certain well-defined limitation. He felt sympathy where he could see or visualize the personal sorrow that was caused by an act or condition. What was out of sight was more or less out of mind. Lincoln was always able to visualize the case of the individual soldier and of his family. He could see the woman in black before him, declaring that her husband or elder son had lost his life on the battle-field, and that now her youngest son, her baby, was sentenced to be shot for some wholly technical offense. Lincoln had little time to investigate and it is to be feared that in some cases the alleged widow had rented the black clothes for the occasion, and had help in inventing the fiction about her family.

In cases of this character Lincoln was very easily imposed

upon, and the imposture was to the great detriment of the service. In the long run it had been better for the discipline of the army if he had kept his hands off except in cases where the mitigating circumstances were more pronounced than was usually the case.

Literature since the war has been rather full of stories of the pardons issued by Lincoln. One of them, particularly, the case of William Scott, of Vermont, has become the occasion of much oratory and literature. It comes to us on the authority of Honorable L. E. Chittenden, who was register of the treasury from 1861 till 1865. According to this story, Scott, a private in a Vermont regiment, volunteered to act as sentinel in place of a friend who was sick, and so was awake all night, the first time in his life. On the very next night he himself was called out to act as sentinel. On this second night he went to sleep at his post. His commanding officer, General W. F. Smith, known to the soldiers as "Baldy" felt that the sentence of the court-martial must be inflicted, and that sentence was death. Some of his comrades went to Chittenden, who was a Vermonter, and offered to hire him as an attorney to plead the case of Scott in an appeal to the president. Chittenden refused their money, but went with them to Lincoln, who pardoned the boy. Scott became a more than ordinarily faithful and brave soldier and died nobly in battle.

Mr. Chittenden, while in ordinary matters a truthful man, was a very unreliable historian. Charles Francis Adams had occasion to review one incident recorded by Mr. Chittenden, to discover the "residuum" of truth in it. When Mr. Adams had done with it, the "residuum" was about as great as the speck of soapy water that remains after the pricking of a soap bubble.* Not that Mr. Chittenden was the greatest liar in Washington; he was not. But he was one of many men who colored their

---

*See Mr. Adams' paper on *The Laird Rams* in *Proceedings of the Massachusetts Historical Society,* October, 1899; reprinted with changes in his *Studies Military and Diplomatic,* MacMillan, 1911.

memories with their imagination until their accounts became wholly unsafe as historical data.

It would be interesting to know whether any soldier was actually shot to death during the Civil War for going to sleep on guard duty. Thus far the War Department has not found any such case. During the World War, though there were convictions, no soldier was actually shot for this offense. The Military Law of the United States does not permit the extreme penalty for this offense in time of peace, though at any time it is a grave offense; but it is a penalty permitted, though rarely imposed, in time of war.* It would appear quite improbable that a capital sentence should have been imposed where there were so many and such mitigating circumstances as are assembled in the popular story of William Scott. The record does not show that Scott offered in his own defense any such evidence. Apparently he was not required to stay awake all night, much less two successive nights. He was one of three men stationed at a given point, dividing the night into three watches. Between three and four o'clock in the morning the officer of the guard found all three asleep. There was no dispute as to the facts. Scott, having had two-thirds of a night's sleep, and being charged with responsibility for an important post, went to sleep on duty. His two companions had a right to sleep. He was the guilty man. The prisoner, though he pleaded "Not guilty," offered no defense and produced no witnesses. Apparently there were no mitigating circumstances. The rules of war provide that "The fact that the accused had been previously overtaxed by excessive guard duty is not a defense, although evidence to that effect may be received in extenuation of the offense." Apparently there was no such evidence, except such as was later manufactured by sentimental authors for the benefit of posterity.

Who pardoned the prisoner or mitigated the sentence does not appear of record. There is no evidence that Lincoln ever knew

---

*See the Eighty-Sixth Article of the *Manual for Courts Martial,* p. 242. Government Printing Office.

of the case, though he may have done so. If any such case came to his knowledge, with such mitigating circumstances, it is easy to guess what he would have done.

What we know is that Scott did not die. The sentence of death was pronounced, and may have had its salutary effect upon sleepy young Vermonters; but he did not die. A petition was signed by officers and privates of his regiment, this petition being addressed to General Smith. Whether he or some superior officer or the president pardoned Scott, or whether the sentence was mitigated, is not of record. The fact we know is that whoever exercised mercy in this case appears to have been justified. William Scott, a native of Groton, Vermont, enrolled as a private in Company K, Third Vermont Regiment, was shot in the chest in the battle at Lee's Mills, in the vicinity of Yorktown, Virginia, April 16, 1862, and died on the following day. Perhaps Lincoln pardoned him; he pardoned many men less worthy. It is much more likely that it was not necessary to appeal to Lincoln; if his pardon had been by the president, some record should be available. We do not know. Mr. Chittenden was a truthful man and a lawyer of experience, but he was a very inaccurate historian.

The adjutant general of the army writes:

Nothing has been found of record to show that President Lincoln pardoned a Vermont soldier named William Scott sentenced to die for the offense of sleeping on post.

It is possible that a pardon for such an offense may have been granted by President Lincoln in one or more cases, [of sleeping on duty] but in the absence of the name of the soldier it would probably be impracticable to identify the record thereof.

A record has been found of the pardon by President Lincoln of a private of Company E, 3rd Regiment New York Infantry Volunteers, who had been found guilty by a general court martial, sitting at Fort Monroe, Virginia, in October, 1862, of sleeping on post, and sentenced to forfeiture of pay and allowances and confinement at hard labor for the term of one year. The President, on January 3, 1863, ordered the case examined for mitigating circumstances, and on February 28, 1863, ordered that the part of the sentence remaining unexecuted be remitted. The directions issued in the case by President Lincoln are in his handwriting.

It is shown that this soldier was subsequently honorably discharged. Nothing is found to show that he was afterwards killed.

Usually, a soldier sentenced to be shot, had against him some charge more serious than going to sleep on sentry duty. Perhaps the most frequent charge was desertion. Bounty jumping became a very profitable vocation, and was indulged in by literally thousands of men, who accepted pay for enlisting, and on the first convenient occasion deserted, and promptly accepted pay for enlisting again under some other name in some other regiment, and then deserting again. Not many men were shot for merely getting homesick and running away; they were punished by imprisonment or loss of pay, and given hard and perhaps perilous duty. Now and then a deserter was sentenced to be shot, and in some extreme cases, deserters were shot.

Now and then a deserter, facing the practical certainty of arrest for his offense, hastened to the White House and was fortunate if he got there ahead of the officers of justice. The following letter* is not known to have been published:

EXECUTIVE MANSION

Washington, Feb. 24, 1865.

To-day H— H— voluntarily calls under apprehension of being punished as a deserter. Now on condition that he serves out his term Co. A in 50th New York Engineers, he is fully pardoned for any supposed desertion.

A. Lincoln.

Romancers are under strong temptation to invent a sequel to such stories and to show how the men pardoned died bravely on the field of battle. To the right of the main corridor, just in front of the entrance of the National Museum in Washington is

*From the original in the collection of Oliver R. Barrett, Chicago.

a *facsimile* of a letter from Lincoln pardoning a deserter. Th
letter is genuine; not so the appended note which tells that thi
letter was found on the body of the soldier to whom Lincoln
gave it. That letter follows:

EXECUTIVE MANSION

Washington, Oct. 4, 1864.

Upon condition that Roswell McIntyre of Co. E. 6th Regt. o
New York Cavalry returns to his Regiment and faithfully serve
out his term, making up for lost time, or until otherwise lawfully
discharged, he is fully pardoned for any supposed desertion here
tofore committed; and this paper is his pass to go to his regiment

Abraham Lincoln.

This note accompanies the letter:

Taken from the body of R. McIntyre at the battle of Five
Forks, Va., 1865.

That appended note is untrue. Roswell McIntyre was no
killed in the battle of Five Forks, or in any other battle of the
Civil War.

How seriously the army was suffering on account of desertions, Lincoln perhaps realized better after a visit to McClellan's
army in June of 1862, for on his return to Washington, he
wrote to McClellan under date of July 13, 1862:

My dear sir: I am told that over 160,000 men have gone
into your army on the Peninsula. When I was with you the
other day, we made out 86,500 remaining, leaving 73,500 to be
accounted for. I believe 23,500 will cover all the killed,
wounded, and missing in all your battles and skirmishes, leaving 50,000 who have left otherwise. Not more than 5,000 of
these have died, leaving 45,000 of your army alive and not with
it. I believe half or two-thirds of them are fit for duty to-day.
Have you any more perfect knowledge of this than I have? If I
am right, and you had these men with you, you could go into
Richmond in the next three days. How can they be got to you,
and how can they be prevented from getting away in such numbers for the future?

A. Lincoln.

Lincoln pardoned some guilty soldiers just because they were young. "His mother says he is but seventeen," was his reason in one case. "I am unwilling for any boy under eighteen to be shot," he telegraphed in another case.

He found it very difficult to resist the appeal of women. If there were no places in Washington where they rented widow's clothes and attractive babies to women who wanted to make appeals to the president, an abundant supply was obtainable and was used persistently. Lincoln was not unaware of his weakness when women made their appeal to him.

Donn Piatt, one of the brightest newspaper writers in the country, told a good story in regard to the president's refusal to sanction the death penalty in cases of desertion from the Union Army.

"There was far more policy in this course," said Piatt, "than kind feeling. To assert the contrary is to detract from Lincoln's force of character, as well as intellect. Our war-president was not lost in his high admiration of brigadiers and major generals, and had a positive dislike for their methods and the despotism upon which an army is based. He knew that he was dependent upon volunteers for soldiers, and to force upon such men as those the stern discipline of the Regular Army was to render the service unpopular. And it pleased him to be the source of mercy, as well as the fountain of honor, in this direction.

"I was sitting with General Dan Tyler, of Connecticut, in the ante-chamber of the War Department, shortly after the adjournment of the Buell Court of Inquiry, of which we had been members, when President Lincoln came in from the room of Secretary Stanton. Seeing us, he said: 'Well, gentlemen, have you any matter worth reporting?'

" 'I think so, Mr. President,' replied General Tyler. 'We had it proven that Bragg, with less than ten thousand men, drove your eighty-three thousand men under Buell back from before Chattanooga, down to the Ohio at Louisville, marched around us twice, then doubled us up at Perryville, and finally got out of the state of Kentucky with all his plunder.'

" 'Now, Tyler,' returned the president, 'what is the meaning of all this; what is the lesson? Don't our men march as well, and fight as well, as these rebels? If not, there is a fault somewhere. We are all of the same family—same sort.'

" 'Yes, there is a lesson,' replied General Tyler; 'we are of the same sort, but subject to different handling. Bragg's little force was superior to our larger number because he had it under control. If a man left his ranks, he was punished; if he deserted, he was shot. We had nothing of that sort. If we attempt to shoot a deserter you pardon him, and our army is without discipline.'

"The president looked perplexed. 'Why do you interfere?' continued General Tyler. 'Congress has taken from you all responsibility.'

" 'Yes,' answered the president impatiently, 'Congress has taken the responsibility and left the women to howl all about me,' and so he strode away."

Lincoln had sympathy for the deserter, when his offense was induced by homesickness; and he pardoned every man for whom he could find an excuse, and some for whom there was no excuse. How many such men he pardoned, the War Department does not know; but the number was large. Was it too large? For the sake of military discipline, it was far too large; but Lincoln's heart told him there were other and valid considerations. Perhaps, under the circumstances, it was better that Lincoln should have abused his great power on the side of mercy.

The actual number of desertions from the United States Army during the Civil War is unknown, but it has been estimated, from the best data obtainable, that the number of actual deserters at large at the close of that war (making due allowance for those incorrectly reported as deserters) was 117,247, and that the total number of desertions during the war was not less than 200,000.

Many cases of desertion have been removed by the War Department under the acts of July 5, 1884, May 17, 1886, and March 2, 1889, and the acts amendatory thereof on the ground of error in the record. No record has been kept showing the number of cases in which the charges of desertion have been removed by the War Department, and it would be impossible to determine the number, even approximately, without examining in detail the records of the Department from the war period to the present time.

According to the most recently compiled official statistics on deaths in the United States Army during the Civil War, a total of 267 soldiers was executed by the United States military authorities. How many of those 267 men were sentenced to death as the result of their conviction under a charge of desertion is not known, no attempt having ever been made by the Department to classify those cases according to the nature of the charges preferred.

The War Department is unable to state to what extent President Lincoln intervened to save the lives of convicted deserters who had been sentenced to die, no data having ever been gathered by the Department bearing upon the subject. His proclamation of March 10, 1863, respecting soldiers absent without leave must have saved thousands of men from the stigma of being classed as deserters, some of them, doubtless, also from conviction and execution. In that proclamation, after commanding all soldiers then absent from their regiments without leave to return to their commands, he continued as follows:

And I do hereby declare and proclaim, that all soldiers now absent from their respective regiments without leave, who shall, on or before the first day of April, 1863, report themselves at any rendezvous designated by the General Orders of the War Department number fifty-eight, hereto annexed, may be restored to their respective regiments without punishment, except the forfeiture of pay and allowances during their absence; and all who do not return within the time above specified shall be arrested as deserters, and punished as the law provides.

In the matter of Lincoln's sympathy for women and of his sometimes making mistakes, the famous letter to Mrs. Lydia Bixby is an illustration, though in that case the prime responsibility for the mistake rested not upon Lincoln but upon Governor John A. Andrew, of Massachusetts. Mrs. Bixby had, indeed, five sons, but not all of them were in the army, and not all of those that were in the army were killed; it is just possible that one or more of them deserved to be killed. The letter grew out of a mistaken knowledge of the facts. But the mistake concerning the facts, while it diminishes the honor of some members of the Bixby family, detracts nothing from the noble and sympathetic spirit of Abraham Lincoln:

EXECUTIVE MANSION,
Washington, November 21, 1864.

Mrs. Bixby, Boston, Massachusetts.

Dear Madam: I have been shown in the files of the War Department a statement of the Adjutant-General of Massachusetts that you are the mother of five sons who have died gloriously on the field of battle. I feel how weak and fruitless must be any words of mine which should attempt to beguile you from the grief of a loss so overwhelming. But I cannot refrain from tendering to you the consolation that may be found in the thanks of the Republic they died to save. I pray that our heavenly Father may assuage the anguish of your bereavement, and leave you only the cherished memory of the loved and lost, and the solemn pride that must be yours to have laid so costly a sacrifice on the altar of freedom.

Yours very sincerely and respectfully,
Abraham Lincoln.

Lincoln was not the only tender-hearted man in Washington, and some men who came to know of cases that appealed to their sympathies conspired to help women in their approach to Lincoln. One of the stories told, it is said by John Sherman, may indicate that General Sherman's brother had as tender a heart toward women as Lincoln had, or for that matter, General Sherman himself:

Senator Sherman had an appointment with President Lincoln

at six o'clock one afternoon, and as he entered the vestibule of the White House his attention was attracted toward a poorly clad young woman, who was violently sobbing. He asked her the cause of her distress. She said she had been ordered away by the servants, after vainly waiting many hours to see the president about her only brother, who had been condemned to death. Her story was this:

She and her brother were foreigners, and orphans. They had been in this country several years. Her brother enlisted in the army, but, through bad influences, was induced to desert. He was captured, tried and sentenced to be shot—the old story.

The poor girl had obtained the signatures of some persons who had formerly known him, to a petition for a pardon, and alone had come to Washington to lay the case before the president. Thronged as the waiting-rooms always were, she had passed the long hours of two days trying in vain to get an audience, and had at length been ordered away.

Senator Sherman's feelings were touched. He said to her that he had come to see the president, but did not know if he would succeed. He told her, however, to follow him up-stairs, and he would see what could be done for her.

Just before reaching the door, Mr. Lincoln came out, and, meeting the senator, said good-humoredly, "Are you not ahead of time?" Sherman showed him his watch, with the hand upon the hour of six.

"Well," returned Mr. Lincoln, "I have been so busy to-day that I have not had time to get a lunch. Go in and sit down; I will be back directly."

Senator Sherman made the young woman accompany him into the office, and when they were seated, said to her: "Now, my good girl, I want you to muster all the courage you have in the world. When the president comes back, he will sit down in that armchair. I shall get up to speak to him, and as I do so you must force yourself between us, and insist upon his examination of your papers, telling him it is a case of life and death, and admits of no delay."

These instructions were carried out to the letter. Mr. Lincoln was at first somewhat surprised at the apparent forwardness of the young woman, but observing her distressed appearance, he ceased conversation with Senator Sherman, and commenced an examination of the document she had placed in his hands.

Glancing from it to the face of the petitioner, whose tears had broken forth afresh, he studied its expression for a moment, and then his eye fell upon her scanty but neat dress. Instantly his face lighted up.

"My poor girl," said he, "you have come here with no governor, or senator, or member of Congress to plead your cause. You seem honest and truthful; and you don't wear hoopskirts—and I will be whipped, but I will pardon your brother." And he did.

It was never easy for Lincoln to refuse the requests of his friends. When political appointments were desired, and the applicants brought or caused to be sent great numbers of letters of endorsement, some of them signed by Lincoln's personal friends, he found it hard to be as inflexible as in loyalty to conscience he sometimes was. It is recorded that, on one occasion, being confronted by two piles of letters written by friends of two different applicants, he simplified his problem by tossing both bundles unopened into a scale and appointing the man that had presented the heavier package. On one occasion, the sole recommendation received by him on behalf of a second lieutenant who desired promotion was from that officer's wife. This rather pleased Lincoln, who thought that it was much to a man's credit that his wife believed in him, and he wrote to Stanton:

EXECUTIVE MANSION,
Nov. 13, 1861.

Hon. Sec. of War.
   My dear sir
      Please have the Adjutant General ascertain whether 2nd. Lieut of Co. D. 2nd. Infantry—Alexander E. Drake, is not en-

titled to promotion—His wife thinks he is. Please have this
looked into.

Yours truly
A. Lincoln

My honored and lamented friend, Honorable Daniel Fish, of
Minneapolis, compiler of the well-known Lincoln *Bibliography*,
owned the original letter of a young woman in Pennsylvania
who wrote to Lincoln asking a furlough for her lover. The
pathetic story is told in the following missive, and its effect on
Lincoln is plainly indicated by his autograph endorsement:

April 5, 1864

Washington Co., Pa.

To the Honorable
      Abraham Lincoln
President of U. S. A.
    Hon. Sir
After long hesitation through dread and fear I have at last
concluded to inform you of my troubles. In order to make the
case clear it is necessary to give you a brief history connected
with myself and would be husband. We have been engaged for
some years. In August 1862 he enlisted to serve his country
for a term of three years. In July 1863 he was taken to Baltimore to a Hospital sick and on or about the first of October
1863 he had recovered and while waiting to be sent to his regiment he had a chance with his fellow Key Stone soldiers to attend the election. Here allow me to state that he did not forget
our Curtin.
    It was our design to marry while he was at home and under
those determinations we very foolishly indulged too freely in
matrimonial affairs and at last our union was defeated by my
Father. In consequence of him he was forced to return to the
army a single man. The result of our indulgences are going to
bring upon us both an unlawful family providing you do not
take mercy upon us and grant him a leave of absence in order to
ratify past events. I am Honored Sir one that circumstances
must apologize for the boldness to ask of you this favor under
these agravating circumstances. I hope and pray to God that
you will not cast me aside in scorn and dismay. Remember that

I have a Father and mother and a wide circle of friends and if we cannot remedy past events I only pray that Death may come to me at an early period of time.

Allow him time if it is thy will to remove me to Philadelphia, Pa. to reside during his stay in the army. Dear Sir I can only ask and it lies in your power to grant my request. May God soften your heart if need be. May you view this subject as a serious one connected with me.

The Soldier I speak of is A—— L—— G—— private Company —— of the 140th Reg. P. Vol. The said regiment is in the 1st Brigade 1st Division 2nd Army Corps Army of the Potomac.

It may seem strange to you that I have taken this correspondence to you upon myself as it would seem more reasonable for him to perform that duty. In answer to this he says they have orders prohibiting any correspondence with those in authority at the seat of Government for furloughs. I will close leaving all to your decision and remaining your obedient servant,

Miss C—— N——.

(Indorsed)
Hon. Sec. of War
    Send him
to her by all
means.
        A. Lincoln
April 14, 1864
Furlough granted
        File A. G.

The War Department records have been searched at my request in an effort to identify this soldier and verify the incident, but without success.

It has often been alleged that Lincoln's assassination was the result of his refusal to pardon John Yates Beall who was hanged at Governor's Island in New York Harbor, February 24, 1864. He was convicted of conspiracy to blow up bridges and assist Confederate prisoners to escape. It is alleged, though without adequate proof, that his fate determined Booth to take revenge on Lincoln. Beall was a superior man and a brave man, whose acts, like those of Nathan Hale and André in the Revolution, and the men in Andrews' railway raid in the Civil War, bring deserved applause for their courage, but are clearly liable to the death penalty. There was much to admire in Beall, but Lincoln was unmoved by the appeals in his behalf, and Beall was hanged.

Lincoln's refusal to pardon a slave-trader under sentence of hanging shows how little he was prepared to tolerate that crime:

Whereas it appears that at a term of the Circuit Court of the United States of America for the southern district of New York, held in the month of November, A. D. 1861, Nathaniel Gordon was indicted and convicted for being engaged in the slave-trade, and was by the said court sentenced to be put to death by hanging by the neck on Friday the 7th day of February, A. D. 1862;

And whereas a large number of respectable citizens have earnestly besought me to commute the said sentence of the said Nathaniel Gordon to a term of imprisonment for life, which application I have felt it to be my duty to refuse;

And whereas it has seemed to me probable that the unsuccessful application made for the commutation of his sentence may have prevented the said Nathaniel Gordon from making the necessary preparation for the awful change which awaits him:

Now, therefore, be it known that I, Abraham Lincoln, President of the United States of America, have granted and do hereby grant unto him, the said Nathaniel Gordon, a respite of the above-recited sentence until Friday, the 21st day of February, A. D., 1862, between the hours of twelve o'clock at noon and three o'clock in the afternoon of the said day, when the said sentence shall be executed.

In granting this respite it becomes my painful duty to admonish the prisoner that, relinquishing all expectation of pardon by human authority, he refer himself alone to the mercy of the common God and Father of all men.

Perhaps few acts of Lincoln's administration gave him more satisfaction than his Amnesty Proclamation, issued December 8, 1863, offering complete pardon to all participants in the Rebellion, with certain specified exceptions, on condition of their return to loyalty.   The leading paragraph in this proclamation reads:

I, Abraham Lincoln, President of the United States, do proclaim, declare, and make known to all persons who have, directly or by implication, participated in the existing rebellion, except as hereinafter excepted, that a full pardon is hereby granted to them and each of them, with restoration of all rights of property, except as to slaves, and in property cases where rights of third parties have intervened, and upon the condition that every such person shall take and subscribe an oath, and shall thenceforward keep and maintain said oath inviolate.

An interesting group of endorsements in Lincoln's handwriting was at one time in possession of the government with regard to certain doubtful cases of Confederates who had applied for permission to take the oath of allegiance under Lincoln's Amnesty Proclamation of December 8, 1863. These letters have now been dispersed, but it was my good fortune to see a considerable number of them after they had gone into private hands (by what process or what right I know not) and before they went to the four winds to purchasers of Lincoln's autograph. From this collection it appeared that in a good many cases in which the officers were in doubt, usually, I judge, on account of the previous record of the applicant, and a suspicion that he would not respect his oath, the question came up to Lincoln. I can not suppose that this would have been done if Lincoln had not himself asked that in these cases the matter should be brought to his attention before final refusal. There is, of course, no way of knowing how many of these men Lincoln finally permitted to remain in prison; all the endorsements in the collection which I inspected were, naturally, of successful applicants, and were preserved as authority of the officers for discharging these prisoners. It was evident, however, that, not always content with a reading of the documents, Lincoln personally interviewed some of these men. In general, the endorsements were brief, merely directing that the within named man be permitted to take the oath and be discharged, but a few of them bore special endorsements indicating something of the nature of the charge or the reason for the president's decision. One of these I copied, because it displayed at once Lincoln's mercy and humor, and the suggestion of a suspicion on his own part that he was influenced unduly by the applicant's ability to talk:

> This man, being so well vouched, and talking so much better than any other I have heard, let him take the oath of Dec. 8, and be discharged.
> July 1, 1864,   A. Lincoln.

The significance of this portfolio of letters is in its disclosure that Lincoln, having issued his proclamation offering amnesty to all who had been bearing arms against the government on condition of their taking the oath of loyalty, but stipulating that there must be evidence of good faith on the part of the applicant, did not leave the order to the administration of subordinates, but was deeply concerned for the exceptional men whom the subordinates doubted or deemed unworthy, and that he gave to many such men their freedom, now and then with a twinkle in his eye by reason of his suspicion that he was being imposed upon.

This Amnesty Proclamation was much misused during and after the World War in demands for the pardon of men convicted of treasonable utterance during that war. Lincoln, it was alleged, would have pardoned them long before. But this is by no means certain, nor is the Amnesty Proclamation pertinent as evidence in the case. It was just this kind of offender toward whom Lincoln seemed almost cruelly indifferent.

In no city except New York was there wide-spread and violent opposition to the draft. But there were in many places men in good standing who conducted an active propaganda to oppose enlistments and encourage desertion. Against these men Lincoln entertained an honest and determined indignation. When one of the agitators fell into the hands of the military authority for an overt act of which the government could take cognizance, Lincoln had no temptation to employ that executive clemency which in the judgment of his military advisers he so often abused. When he was called upon to condemn a private soldier for desertion, Lincoln invariably pitied the deserter, and again and again interfered, to prevent such men from being shot, while on the other hand, he poured out his burning indignation against the supposedly respectable men who conducted their campaigns for the encouragement of desertion and of opposition to the enforcement of the draft. To punish these active agitators he went the full length of his authority, not only as president, but as commander-in-chief of the army. Lincoln could be as stern as he was kind; as inflexible as he was sympathetic. A communication of his on the degree of guilt which he believed to attach to those men who sought to break down what we have learned to call the morale of the army, contains the following paragraph:

Must I shoot a simple-minded soldier boy who deserts, while I must not touch a hair of a wily agitator who induces him to desert? This is none the less injurious when effected by getting a father, or brother, or friend into a public meeting, and there working upon his feelings until he is persuaded to write the soldier boy that he is fighting in a bad cause, for a wicked administration of a contemptible government, too weak to arrest and punish him if he shall desert. I think that in such a case, to silence the agitator, and save the boy, is not only constitutional, but withal a great mercy.

On occasion Lincoln could be very stern, and could refuse with stubborn resolution an appeal for pardon when men were guilty of deliberate crime. The following letters illustrate this quality in his nature:

EXECUTIVE MANSION,
WASHINGTON, D. C., November 23, 1863.

E. P. Evans,
West Union, Adams County, Ohio.
Yours to Governor Chase in behalf of J——A. W—— is be-

fore me. Can there be a worse case than to desert, and with letters persuading others to desert? I cannot interpose without a better showing than you make. When did he desert? When did he write the letters?

A. Lincoln.

EXECUTIVE MANSION,
WASHINGTON, D. C., April 21, 1864.
MAJOR-GENERAL DIX,
New York.

Yesterday I was induced to telegraph the officer in military command at Fort Warren, Boston Harbor, Massachusetts, suspending the execution of C— C—, to be executed to-morrow for desertion. Just now, on reading your order in the case, I telegraphed the same order withdrawing the suspension, and leaving the case entirely with you. The man's friends are pressing me, but I refer them to you, intending to take no further action myself.

A. Lincoln.

WAR DEPARTMENT,
WASHINGTON CITY, April 25, 1864.
Major-General Meade,
Army of Potomac.

A Mr. Corby brought you a note from me at the foot of a petition, I believe, in the case of D——, to be executed to-day. The record has been examined here, and it shows too strong a case for a pardon or commutation, unless there is something in the poor man's favor outside of the record, which you on the ground may know, but I do not. My note to you only means that if you know of any such thing rendering a suspension of the execution proper, on your own judgment, you are at liberty to suspend it. Otherwise I do not interfere.

A. Lincoln.

Military sentences did not require the approval of the president. The military courts had power to enforce their own sentences. Cases came to the president on the appeal of relatives or friends. They added greatly to the burden of his labor. "Tomorrow is butchering day," he would say on Thursday, and he labored long over the petitions, and it was hard for him to deny appeals.

Lincoln was not easily moved in cases where the man con demned was a man of intelligence and influence. An interesting case was that of Louis A. Welton, a man justly sentenced to im prisonment in the summer of 1864, and who was able to secure the support of Senator Morgan, of New York, H. J. Raymond of the *New York Times,* and Thurlow Weed. The appeal came to Lincoln at a time when he could not afford to lose any of his political support; and there were not in the country three men for whose support just then he cared more than for these three. New York seemed at that time practically certain to vote against Lincoln, and these three men, and Horace Greeley, had mighty influence in New York. Lincoln did not want to lose any strength which he had in so important a state. But not even for the good will of these men would he pardon a man whom he be lieved to be justly accused unless they would assume the respon sibility. He required them to enter their request for the pardon on the very document in which he set forth his reasons for be lieving that it ought not to be granted. He would not argue the case nor invite them to argue it. If after they had read his re view of the case they still would request the pardon, and write the request upon his statement of the case as he understood it he would issue the pardon. This is a document of remarkable interest.*

EXECUTIVE MANSION,
WASHINGTON, August 31, 1864

Mr. Louis A. Welton came from the rebel lines into ours with a written contract to furnish large supplies to the rebels, was ar rested with the contract in his possession, and has been sen tenced to imprisonment for it. He, and his friends complain of this, on no substantial evidence whatever, but simply because his word, only given after his arrest, that he only took the contract

---

*So far as I am aware this has never been published. I am permitted to use it by Mr. Oliver R. Barrett, in whose collection it is.

s a means of escaping from the rebel lines, was not accepted
s a full defense—He perceives that if this had been true he
vould have destroyed the contract so soon as it had served his
ourpose in getting him across the lines; but not having done
his and being caught with the paper on him, he tells this other
ıbsurd story that he kept the paper in the belief that our gov-
rnment would join him in taking the profit of fulfilling the
ontract. This is my understanding of the case; and I can not
onceive of a case of a man found in possession of a contract to
urnish rebel supplies, who can not escape, if this be held a suffi-
ient—ground of escape—It is simply for the accused to escape
oy telling a very absurd and improbable story. Now, if Sena-
or Morgan, and Mr. Weed, and Mr. Raymond, will not argue
vith me that I *ought* to discharge this man, but will, in writing
on this sheet, simply request me to do it, I will do it solely in
leference to their wishes.

The following endorsements appear on this letter:

. . . .

We respectfully request the President to pardon the within
named Louis A. Welton, now at Fort Delaware.

Thurlow Weed

. . . .

I have read Mr. Welton's statement and if it is true, (and I
know no reason for distrusting it,) his pardon would be an act of
justice. I concur in Mr. Weed's request.

H. J. Raymond.

While Lincoln could be and often was very stubborn in dealing
with trying situations, he sometimes displayed great shrewdness
in evading a decision where he preferred not to assume respon-
ibility which did not fairly belong to him. One of his assistant
secretaries, William O. Stoddard, gives in detail the narrative of
an effort that was made on behalf of a guerrilla for whose pardon Lincoln received a long petition followed by the personal
appeal of an influential delegation. Lincoln knew the man was
guilty, for he had sent for the papers in the case and had satisfied himself not only that the man deserved to die, but that the

region where the crime had been committed was one which
needed the lesson. The sentence stood until the morning of the
execution.   Then a large and eminent delegation came to the
White House and brought to bear upon the president a very
considerable pressure. Lincoln, however, would take no action
without reviewing again the papers in the case. He instructed
Stoddard to look for the papers. Stoddard did so, and could not
find them. Lincoln suggested to the delegation to go to the
War Department. They went, but returned with the information that the papers were not at the War Department, they had
been sent to the White House at the president's own request and
had not been returned. Further search failed to disclose the
documents, and the delegation went away sorrowful. Hardly
had they left the White House when a telegram was handed to
the president. Lincoln thus remarked:

"What did you say? A telegram? You don't tell me! Has
that man been actually hung? It's a pity about his papers! It
seems to me—well, yes, I remember now. I know where—well
if I did; I guess I wouldn't. Not now. But if they are ever
called for again, and they won't be, they ought to be where they
can be found. Certainly, certainly. But it is just as well that
one murderer escaped being pardoned by Abraham Lincoln.
Narrow escape, too. The merest piece of luck in all the world."

CHAPTER XIX

RADICALS AND COPPERHEADS

LIKE all men conservative by nature but committed by conviction to a polity of progress, Abraham Lincoln won severe
criticism from two widely divergent groups. Politics proverbially makes strange bed-fellows. The administration of Lincoln produced a working coalition between some of the ultra
anti-slavery men in the North and others who represented diametrically opposite political convictions.

Mention has already been made of the political reaction of
1862, in which the northern states quite generally receded from
their whole-hearted allegiance to Lincoln, and sent to Congress a
largely increased Democratic minority. Note has also been taken
of the partial recovery, not in congressional representation, but
in popular confidence in the administration, as shown in the results of the elections of those few states that chose governors in
1863. This increase in confidence did not mean that the people
were less weary of the war, or that the men in the North who
opposed the war were less bitter in their opposition.

In various northern states, and especially in southern Ohio, Indiana and Illinois, were organized societies known as the
"Knights of the Golden Circle," "Sons of Liberty," "The Order
of the Star," and the "Order of American Knights." These
secret bodies enrolled large numbers of men, some of whom were
thoroughly disloyal to the Union, and others of whom professed
to be loyal to the government, but opposed to what they counted
the tyranny or the radical abolition policy of Abraham Lincoln.

Lincoln was not greatly disturbed by the so-called Copper-

271

head movement. He treated it, according to his secretaries Nicolay and Hay, with "good-humored contempt." "Nothing can make me believe," he said, "that one hundred thousand Indiana Democrats are disloyal."

In all probability he was right. Yet there were enough disloyal Indiana Democrats to make the Knights of the Golden Circle a formidable organization. Governor Morton, of Indiana, did not share Lincoln's complacent view, and Governor Richard Yates, of Illinois, was almost equally disturbed.

These Copperhead organizations had for their purpose the discouragement of enlistment and the encouragement of desertions the impeding in every practicable way of measures in the North for the putting down of the rebellion, and in general the giving of aid and comfort to the Confederate Army. Plans were made for the capture of the prisons in the North where Confederate soldiers were confined, for the destruction of arsenals and armories, and for other bold and terrible deeds. These larger and more heroic exploits did not get beyond threat and rumor; but there was secret and active propaganda, hostile to the government, that manifested itself in literally thousands of communities, and the personal abuse which was heaped upon Abraham Lincoln seems at this day all but incredible.

In a number of cities an opposing secret organization called the Union League was established. This society had its permanent monument in some northern cities in Union League Clubs.

A part of this hostility to Lincoln was not without apparent cause. Those reckon without knowledge of his character who assume that Lincoln was only a mild and irresolute man. He was by nature mild, and he was so cautious as to appear, and at times to have been, irresolute. But he was also a man of inflexible will. When he had definitely committed himself to a course, he could not only be consistently loyal to it, but very stubbornly earnest in his refusal to swerve.

Very early in the war Lincoln saw that some drastic measures would be necessary. Foes of the Union were everywhere, and especially in Washington. The District of Columbia lay adjacent to Virginia, which seceded, and within the bounds of Maryland, whose legislature in 1861 protested against the war as unconstitutional and unjust, and expressed a desire for the immediate recognition of the Confederate states. In the opening weeks of the Civil War, Washington was virtually in a state of siege. Lincoln knew that neither in Washington nor anywhere else in the North was there assurance of safety from the insidious work of those who were seeking the overthrow of the Union.

Further, Lincoln knew that if he waited until guilty men committed overt acts of treason before causing them to be arrested, the arrest would in many cases be impossible or would come too late to prevent the success of dangerous plots. He placed men in charge of Federal prisons who were capable of resisting very great pressure. Some of these wardens were charged to keep themselves inside the prison walls where they would be free from the possibility of reach by the civil courts. He appointed Ward Hill Lamon commissioner of the District of Columbia, and kept him in that position in spite of most emphatic demands for his removal. He knew that Lamon was a man of courage, and not overnice in his methods when drastic policies needed to be enforced.

In order the more fully to protect this policy, Lincoln suspended the writ of *habeas corpus*. The Old Capitol prison in Washington was kept moderately full of people against some of whom no formal charges were ever brought. These people and their friends, many of them very respectable people, made vociferous protest, and the president in general maintained a sphinx-like silence. He knew that the winning of the war made it necessary that some harsh things should be done.

Lincoln was himself so firm an advocate of adherence to the law and of loyalty to the Constitution as to be an object of perplexity and wonder to some even of his friends who observed him giving his adherence to policies that seemed so arbitrary and of such questionable legality. They reminded Lincoln how in times of peace he had said things strangely inconsistent with his present methods. Lincoln replied that when a man was sick he sometimes needed medicine, which would be very harmful to a well man, and that some things were necessary in times of war which a country could not tolerate in times of peace.

Lincoln's suspension of the writ of *habeas corpus* brought upon him not only the severe criticism of Congress and the press, but the official disapproval of the Supreme Court. Roger B. Taney still sat as chief justice of that dignified body. He was so old and in such frail health that Lincoln feared that he would die between the time of the election of 1860 and the inauguration in 1861. But Justice Taney lived so long that Lincoln grew to cherish unfeigned alarm concerning the fate of some of his war policies when they came up, as they were certain to come, for review before the Supreme Court at the end of the Civil War. He did not have to wait until the end of the war for his break with Mr. Justice Taney. On May 25, 1861, John Merryman, a citizen of Baltimore, was arrested charged with treason, and was committed to the custody of General George Cadwalader, then commanding Fort Henry. Chief Justice Taney, then resident in Baltimore in the house of his son-in-law, Mr. Campbell, issued, in chambers, a writ of *habeas corpus* calling upon General Cadwalader to produce the body of John Merryman before Justice Taney in the room of the circuit court of Baltimore.

It would appear from this distance that Justice Taney went somewhat widely out of his way to discover trouble for himself. The Supreme Court was not sitting, and the justice was not in the capital. But Judge Taney believed that the executive and military powers were overriding the functions of the legislative and judiciary powers of the government. So he issued the writ of *habeas corpus* directing the United States Marshal for the District of Maryland to produce in court the body of the imprisoned man.

The writ was returned served, and the officer to whom it was directed refused to produce the prisoner, giving as his reason that he was duly authorized by the president of the United States to suspend the writ of *habeas corpus* for the public safety. Justice Taney, receiving this report, excused the officer from further service in the matter, saying that while he had legal authority to call to his assistance an adequate *posse* to enforce the writ, it was clearly impossible for him to organize a posse of sufficient strength to overcome the resistance of the military authority of the United States. A day or two afterward the chief justice in a written opinion said:

As the case comes before me, therefore, I understand that the President not only claims the right to suspend the writ of *habeas corpus* at his discretion, but to delegate that discretionary power to a military officer, and to leave it to him to determine whether he will or will not obey judicial process that may be served upon him. No official notice has been given to the courts of justice, or to the public, by a proclamation or otherwise, that the President claimed this power, and had exercised it in the manner stated in the return. And I certainly listened to it with some surprise, for I had supposed it to be one of those points of constitutional law upon which there was no difference of opinion, and that it was admitted on all hands that the privilege of the writ could not be suspended except by Act of Congress.*

Lincoln made no attempt to argue this case with the chief justice of the United States. He knew that he was facing a desperate situation, and that he could not count upon the cooperation of the Supreme Court. Whether the plea of military necessity justified the position of Lincoln in this and other matters, need not here and now be discussed. Lincoln accepted what he believed to be the necessity of saving the Union, and he did not disguise the fact that the desperate emergency called for desperate remedies.

Memoir of Roger Brooke Taney, LL. D., by Samuel Tyler, LL. D., pp. 422-423.

Reference has already been made to the case of Clement G. Vallandigham. He had been a member of Congress since 1856, and was the rising leader of the Copperhead wing of the Democratic Party in 1863. General Burnside was in command of the Department of the Ohio. Vallandigham delivered a speech, about May 1, 1863, containing utterances alleged to have been treasonable. The address denounced the war as "wicked, cruel and unnecessary." He declared that war was being waged, not for the preservation of the Union, but "for the purpose of crushing out liberty and erecting a despotism." It stated that if the administration had so wished "the war could have been honorably terminated months ago." It declared that "war was for the freedom of the blacks and enslavement of the whites." General Burnside, himself a Democrat, a friend and admirer of McClellan, caused Vallandigham to be arrested. The evidence was conclusive, and Vallandigham was sentenced to be confined in Fort Warren in Boston Harbor. A writ of *habeas corpus* was issued, but its execution was denied. Bitter criticism fell upon the administration for this arrest. Lincoln set forth his view in the following statement:

Of how little value the constitutional provisions I have quoted will be rendered, if arrests shall never be made until defined crimes shall have been committed, may be illustrated by a few notable examples. General John C. Breckinridge, General Robert E. Lee, General Joseph E. Johnston, General John B. Magruder, General William B. Preston, General Simon B. Buckner, and Commodore Franklin Buchanan, now occupying the very highest places in the rebel war service, were all within the power of the government since the rebellion began, and were nearly as well-known to be traitors then as now. Unquestionably if we had seized and held them, the insurgent cause would be much weaker. But no one of them had then committed any crime defined in the law. Every one of them, if arrested, would have been discharged on *habeas corpus* were the writ allowed to operate. In view of these and similar cases, I think the time not unlikely to come, when I shall be blamed for having made too few arrests rather than too many. . . . Long experience has shown that armies cannot be maintained unless desertion shall be punished by the severe penalty of death. The case requires, and the law and the Constitution sanctions, this punishment. Must I shoot a simple-minded soldier-boy who deserts, while I must not touch a hair of a wily agitator who induces him to desert?

But though Lincoln defended the action of the government in the arrest of Vallandigham, he appears to have regretted that Burnside had taken this step. He refused to accept the resignation of Burnside growing out of the protest and criticism, saying that though all the Cabinet regretted the necessity of the arrest, some doubting the wisdom of it, all were in favor of sustaining Burnside in the matter.

Lincoln devised a method of relief which Burnside strongly opposed. Vallandigham was secretly conveyed to the Confederate lines under a flag of truce, and handed over to a Confederate picket.

This was a shrewd move on the part of Lincoln. The Confederate Government could hardly afford to accept Vallandigham as a Confederate and Vallandigham could not afford to be treated as one. On the other hand, the Confederate Government was unfeignedly grateful to him, though it did not know what to do with him. He was a white elephant on the hands of those who would gladly have regarded him as a friend. He protested that he was not a Confederate, but a loyal citizen of the United States and a prisoner of war of the Confederate Government. Certainly his whole value to the Confederacy was lost by his being placed within the Confederate lines. He could not be returned to the United States, for the United States would not take him. He was a man without a country, and his case led Edward Everett Hale to write his notable short story bearing that title.

The Confederate secretary of state protested against the sending of Vallandigham to the Confederate lines as an abuse of the flag of truce. He then issued orders that this "alien enemy" who was a "victim of unjust and arbitrary power," should be taken to the coast and given opportunity to make his way to some foreign country:

It is not the desire or purpose of this government to treat this victim of unjust and arbitrary power with other than lenity and consideration, but as an alien enemy he cannot be received to friendly hospitality or allowed a continued refuge in freedom in our midst. This is due alike to our safety and to him in his acknowledged position as an enemy. You have therefore been charged with the duty, not inappropriate to the commission you hold in relation to prisoners, etc., of meeting him in Lynchburg, and there assuming direction and control of his future movements. He must be regarded by you as under arrest, permitted. unless in your discretion you deem it necessary to revoke the privilege, to be at large on his parole not to attempt to escape nor hereafter to reveal to the prejudice of the Confederate States anything he may see or learn while therein. You will see that he is not molested or assailed or unduly intruded upon, and extend to him the attentions and kind treatment consistent with his relations as an alien enemy. After a reasonable delay with him at Lynchburg, to allow rest and recreation from the fatigues of his recent exposure and travel, you will proceed with him to Wilmington, N. C., and there deliver him to the charge of Major-General Whiting, commanding in that district, by whom he will be allowed at an early convenient opportunity to take shipping for any neutral port he may prefer, whether in Europe, the Islands, or on this Continent. More full instructions on this point will be given to General Whiting, and your duty will be discharged when you shall have conducted Mr. Vallandigham to Wilmington and placed him at the disposition of that commander.

On June 11, 1863, the Democratic Convention of Ohio nominated Vallandigham as governor of that state. He was defeated by a majority of almost a hundred thousand. Lincoln had accomplished what he sought, and had succeeded in discrediting without persecution the most violent of the outspoken enemies of the administration.

A few months later Vallandigham returned to the United States, and dared the president to arrest him. He made violent speeches, but the president ignored him. Vallandigham could thenceforth do the administration less damage out of jail than in.

For though Lincoln did not permit this violent Copperhead to be rearrested, he strictly maintained the righteousness of the arrest which had actually been made. He said in a letter to the Democratic State Convention of Ohio:

He who dissuades one man from volunteering, or induces one soldier to desert, weakens the Union cause as much as he who kills a Union soldier in battle. Yet this dissuasion or inducement may be so conducted as to be no defined crime of which any civil court would take cognizance.

Mr. Vallandigham avows his hostility to the war on the part of the Union; and his arrest was made because he was laboring, with some effect, to prevent the raising of troops, to encourage desertions from the army, and to leave the rebellion without an adequate military force to suppress it. He was not arrested because he was damaging the political prospects of the administration or the personal interests of the commanding general, but because he was damaging the army, upon the existence and vigor of which the life of the nation depends. He was warring upon the military, and this gave the military constitutional jurisdiction to lay hands upon him. If Mr. Vallandigham was not damaging the military power of the country, then his arrest was made on mistake of fact, which I would be glad to correct on reasonably satisfactory evidence.

If I be wrong on this question of constitutional power, my error lies in believing that certain proceedings are constitutional when, in cases of rebellion or invasion, the public safety requires them, which would not be constitutional when, in absence of rebellion or invasion, the public safety does not require them; in other words, that the Constitution is not in its application in all respects the same in cases of rebellion or invasion involving the public safety, as it is in times of profound peace and public security. The Constitution itself makes the distinction, and I can no more be persuaded that the government can constitutionally take no strong measures in time of rebellion, because it can be shown that the same could not be lawfully taken in time of peace, than I can be persuaded that a particular drug is not good medicine for a sick man because it can be shown to not be good food for a well one. Nor am I able to appreciate the danger apprehended by the meeting, that the American people will by means of military arrests during the rebellion lose the right of public discussion, the liberty of speech and the press, the law of evidence, trial by jury, and *habeus corpus* throughout the indefinite peaceful future which I trust lies before them, any more than I am able to believe that a man could contract so strong an appetite for emetics during temporary illness as to persist in feeding upon them during the remainder of his healthful life.

Already the political pot was brewing, and Lincoln was to hear of this and other cases in the campaign of 1864. Something of what was said to his discredit in that campaign we shall read in the next chapter. For the present we turn to opposition of a wholly different type which was rising against Lincoln, and which caused him almost as much embarrassment as the hostility of the Copperheads.

The opposition of the radicals to Mr. Lincoln was on the whole a higher grade than that of the Copperheads. It came from earnest and in good part from conscientious men, who were impatient with the president because he had not seemed to show more initiative and firmness in his advocacy of anti-slavery measures. He had indeed, issued the Proclamation of Emancipation, and was proposing that it be followed by a Constitutional Amendment prohibiting slavery throughout the United States; but he had done this avowedly as a war measure. He had declared that his paramount object was to save the Union, and that if he could have done this without freeing the slaves, he would have done so.

It is not surprising that Lincoln was severely criticized by the extreme abolitionists. Even if there had been no war, they would have felt justified in expecting from the first Republican president a more radical attitude in disapproval of slavery than they discovered in the early portion of Lincoln's administration; but when slavery brought forth its fruit in rebellion, and that which had been the curse of the Union became its destruction, they thought they had a right to expect that Lincoln would proceed with far more vigor than he did to carry out to its legitimate conclusion his and their hostility to slavery. Lincoln put a Democrat at the head of the army, and left John C. Frémont in comparative obscurity. Lincoln dismissed Cameron from his Cabinet, largely as was supposed because Cameron was more interested in abolition than Lincoln was. Lincoln nullified the orders of Hunter and of Frémont for the abolition of slavery in their respective military districts. The Emancipation Proclamation covered only that portion of the country that was in rebellion. Even after the Emancipation Proclamation, Lincoln permitted the officers of the army to return fugitive slaves to loyal citizens in the border states that had not seceded. It is little wonder that this displeased the rabid abolitionists. There was in Congress a group of men increasingly out of sympathy with Lincoln in these matters. Zachariah Chandler, of Michigan, Benjamin F. Wade, of Ohio, and Lyman Trumbull, of Illinois, were of this number. The unquestioned leader of the House of Representatives was the uncompromising Thaddeus Stevens. Had Lincoln lived he surely would have had trouble with Stevens. Thomas Dixon made no attempt to disguise him in the character which he calls "Stoneman" in his novel *The Clansman* and his photoplay *The Birth of a Nation*. But th characterization can not be acknowledged to be a just one.

The outstanding leaders, however, in the opposition to Lincoln in the campaign that was soon to occur, were a member of his own Cabinet and two generals in the Union Army, one of whom Lincoln had elevated to the foremost place of power, and the other of whom had been the first standard bearer of the Lincoln party as a candidate for the presidency.

By THE middle of Lincoln's first term, Republican leaders had quite generally come to an agreement that some other candidate would need to be nominated if that party were to win the election of 1864. On December 15, 1863, the *New York Herald* published an editorial headed "Grant as the people's candidate." To his lasting honor, General Grant turned a deaf ear to all suggestions that he should leave the leadership of the army and enter the field of politics against President Lincoln. Frémont, however, had no such scruples, and Chase conducted his own campaign from his chair in the president's Cabinet. Lincoln expressed in the hearing of John Hay his opinion of the various men who were opposing him. Chase's performance, he said, was in bad taste, but he had determined to pay no attention to it. He was a good secretary, and if he could be elected president he hoped the country would never have a worse one.

When viewed from this distance the operations of Secretary Chase on his own behalf while a member of Lincoln's Cabinet, appear so reprehensible we can hardly wonder that some authorities have regarded him as an absolute traitor to his chief. This view of the case is too severe. Chase never came to realize that the president was a greater man than himself. He was burdened with a hopeless inability to appreciate Mr. Lincoln's true greatness. He had no such limitation concerning his own ability. He had been an outstanding leader in the anti-slavery cause when Mr. Lincoln was an unknown man. He regarded Lincoln's first election as a political accident, and he intended to save the country from the misfortune of Lincoln's reelection, which, however, he did not regard as a possibility. He was entirely sincere in believing himself a much abler man than Lincoln. His most serious lack would seem to have been a sense of humor.

Chase put the conduct of his campaign into the hands of Senator Pomeroy, of Kansas. He could hardly have made a worse choice. Kansas itself was divided between its two senators, Pomeroy and Lane. Pomeroy issued a circular, and scattered it broadcast among the enemies of the administration. Many copies of it fell into the hands of Lincoln's friends who sent them to the White House with the expectation that Lincoln would immediately demand the resignation of Chase. Chase discovered the blunder involved in it, and wrote to Lincoln a letter denying all knowledge of it, and Lincoln acknowledged the letter in a courteous response in which he stated that copies of the circular had been sent him, but he had not read it and did not expect to do so.

The Pomeroy circular is of value at this date as showing how bitter, within Lincoln's own party, was the opposition to him. It said:

The movements recently made throughout the country to secure the renomination of President Lincoln render necessary counter-action on the part of those unconditional friends of the Union who differ from the policy of the Administration.

So long as no efforts were made to forestall the political action of the people, it was both wise and patriotic for all true friends of the Government to devote their influence to the suppression of the rebellion; but when it becomes evident that party and the machinery of official influence are being used to secure the perpetuation of the present Administration, those who conscientiously believe that the interests of the country and of freedom demand a change in favor of vigor and purity and nationality, have no choice but to appeal at once to the people before it is too late to secure a fair discussion of principles.

Those in behalf of whom this appeal is made have thoughtfully surveyed the political field, and have arrived at the following conclusion: *First,* that even were the reelection of Mr. Lincoln desirable, it is practically impossible against the Union of influences which will oppose him. *Second,* that should he be reelected, his manifest tendency towards compromises and temporary expedients of policy will become stronger during a second term than it has been in the first, and the cause of human liberty, and the dignity of the nation, suffer proportionately, while the war may continue to languish during his whole Administration, till the public debt shall become a burden too great to be borne. *Third,* that the patronage of the Government through the necessities of the war has been so rapidly increased, and to such an enormous extent, and so loosely placed, as to render the application of the one-term principle absolutely essential to the certain safety of our republican institutions. *Fourth,* that we find united in Hon. Salmon P. Chase more of the qualities needed in a President during the next four years than are combined in any other available candidate. His record is clear and unimpeachable, showing him to be a statesman of rare ability and an administrator of the highest order, while his private character furnishes the surest available guarantee of economy and purity in the management of public affairs. *Fifth,* that the discussion of the Presidential question, already commenced by the friends of Mr. Lincoln, has developed a popularity and strength in Mr. Chase unexpected even to his warmest admirers; and while we are aware that its strength is at present unorganized, and in no condition to manifest its real magnitude, we are satisfied that it only needs a systematic and faithful effort to develop it to an extent sufficient to overcome all opposing obstacles. For these reasons the friends of Mr. Chase have determined on measures which shall present his claims fairly and at once to the country. A central organization has been effected, which already has its connections in all the States, and the object of which is to enable his friends everywhere most effectually to promote his elevation to the Presidency. We wish the hearty coöperation of all those who are in favor of the speedy restoration of the Union on the basis of universal freedom, and who desire an administration of the Government during the first period of its new life which shall to the fullest extent develop the capacity of free institutions, enlarge the resources of the country, diminish the burdens of taxation, ele-

vate the standard of public and private morality, vindicate the
honor of the Republic before the world, and in all things make
our American nationality the fairest example for imitation which
human progress has ever achieved. If these objects meet your
approval, you can render efficient aid by exerting yourself at
once to organize your section of the country, and by corresponding with the chairman of the National Executive Committee
for the purpose either of receiving or imparting information.

Lincoln had no high opinion either of the loyalty or ability of
Frémont. He had stumped Illinois for Frémont in 1856, but
had seen that general display such an erratic temper in the early
years of the war that he came greatly to distrust him. John
Hay on May 21, 1864, wrote an entry in his diary that began
with a criticism of Burnside, and ended with a severer criticism
of Frémont:

Burnside is turning out much as I thought he would, perfectly
useless and incapable for campaigning. He quarrels with Grant
and Stanton, and makes a nuisance of himself. I said to the
President to-day that I thought Burnside was the only man in
the army to whom power was an injury. McClellan was too
timid and vacillating to assert; Grant was too sound and cool-
headed and unselfish; Frémont would be dangerous if he had
more ability and energy.

Lincoln seemed to Hay to assent to all the foregoing, and said
that Frémont was like Jim Jell's little brother. Jim used to say
that his brother was the biggest scoundrel that ever lived, but in
the infinite mercy of Providence, he was also the biggest fool.

General Frémont, however, was not easily disposed of. There
was a factional fight in Missouri urging his nomination. A
mass convention was held in Cleveland on May thirty-first. It
denounced Mr. Lincoln for his "imbecile and vacillating policy."
Wendell Phillips and other bitter opponents of slavery joined in
this movement, though William Lloyd Garrison and Oliver
Johnson stood loyally by Lincoln, and Owen Lovejoy remained throughout one of his warm supporters.

Lincoln never regarded the candidacy of Frémont with any great concern. Some one told him that Frémont supporters had assembled at Cleveland to place him in nomination, and that there were about four hundred of them. Lincoln's knowledge of the Bible stood him in good stead and he turned to the Bible, which his secretaries say "commonly lay on his desk," and read the verse I Samuel 22:2:

And every one that was in distress, and every one that was in debt, and every one that was discontented, gathered themselves unto him; and he became a captain over them; and there were with him about four hundred men.

For a time it appeared that the Fremont campaign might give Lincoln a considerable degree of trouble, but it soon became evident that his cause was hopeless. John G. Whittier and other prominent abolitionists were among those who advised Frémont to withdraw, which in due time he did.

A large section of the northern press was bitterly hostile to the president. On a Wednesday toward the end of May, 1864, the *New York World,* which was one of the president's severest critics, published an alleged proclamation signed by the president, appointing a day of fasting, humiliation and prayer for the success of the Union, and calling for a draft of four hundred thousand men. The effect of such a proclamation could only be to chill to the very heart the hopes of those who had been looking for a speedy ending of the war. The document was soon discovered to have been a forgery; most of the New York editors so pronounced it when it first came in and did not print it. But the *World,* whose editor was Manton Marble, and the *Journal of Commerce,* whose editor was William C. Prime, both published it. The editions containing this proclamation were promptly recalled, and other editions were sent out acknowledging that these papers had been deceived. Marble and Prime were arrested and their papers were suspended for a few days. The editors soon were able to show that they had been imposed on, and were permitted to resume publication, not, however, with any considerable degree of favor on the part of the authorities in Washington.

The truth was soon discovered. The author of the forgery was Joseph Howard, Jr., who had been city editor of the *Times*, and later Washington correspondent of the *Tribune*. He was a member of Plymouth Church and had reported many of the sermons of Henry Ward Beecher. He knew thoroughly the habits and customs of the newspaper offices in New York. He had suffered financial reverses, and he undertook this despicable plot in the assurance that it would cause a panic on Wall Street, from which there would be prompt recovery of prices when the truth was known. His relations with New York brokers were such that he hoped to make a fortune in a few hours. Fortunately for the country his plot did not succeed.

The Republican Convention of 1864 discarded its party name and called itself the Union Convention. It was held in Baltimore on June eighth. It met at the time when Grant was forcing Lee steadily back upon Richmond. There was only one candidate who under all the circumstances as they then were could possibly be nominated at that convention. The popular desire, based upon increasing military success, was overwhelmingly for Lincoln. It was a noisy and discordant convention, but one whose verdict was assured in advance. Abraham Lincoln was renominated.

The Democratic Party held its convention in Chicago, August twenty-ninth. It nominated as candidate for president, General George B. McClellan, and for vice-president, George H. Pendleton, of Ohio. The platform declared the war a failure. The Democratic Party has never since had any great pride in that declaration. McClellan himself, in his letter of acceptance, took pains to repudiate that plank. It was inevitable, however, that if he had been elected he would have been compelled by his party to seek an early peace. The fortunes of the Union and of freedom were bound up with the reelection of Lincoln.

It would be a disagreeable and profitless task to quote at any great length the literature of this period issued in opposition to Abraham Lincoln. It varied in quality and in tone. There was what might be called the "high-brow" literature of the period, issued by the Society for the Diffusion of Political Knowledge, an organization which dined stately at Delmonico's in New York City, and whose president was none other than Samuel F. B. Morse, the inventor of the telegraph. The pamphlets issued by this organization are in good literary form and made their appeal to the intellectual people of New York City and of the country. Governor Horatio Seymour, who was elected in the fall of 1862 and who was at best a passive resistant of the draft and other war measures, and who was believed to have presidential aspirations in 1864, was only one among the notable men in positions of large influence in a state of undisguised hostility to Abraham Lincoln and all his works.

At the other extreme of those opposed to Lincoln were the authors and publishers of ribald and libelous abuse, which sounds strange to those who have learned to hold in honor the name of Abraham Lincoln.

Lest we forget those days in which Lincoln numbered among his foes those who should have been of his own household, let us recall a few paragraphs from one of the most popular of the tracts of this time. A patriotic preacher, either in prayer or in discourse, had uttered the fervent ejaculation "God bless Abraham Lincoln!" To not a few Copperheads this seemed an utterly blasphemous prayer. It called forth in answer a pamphlet whose author had the grace to conceal his name, and whose title was that of the prayer "God bless Abraham Lincoln."

This pamphlet recited at considerable length and in detail the reasons why Abraham Lincoln deserved a very different fate at the hand even of the most merciful God. It ended with this perfervid peroration:

Let the merchants, when their ships lie rotting at the wharves,

and the bankers when the banks are closed and broken . . . cry
. . . "God bless Abraham Lincoln."

When the manufacturers find the loom idle and the shuttle
suspended in the sley and the male operators slain or disabled
and their wives and children houseless and starving—then let
them, as in duty bound, cry—"God bless Abraham Lincoln."

When the farmers find their fields laid waste, dwellings and
barns demolished, and all around desolation; no green spot to
refresh the sunken eyes, no flocks or herds in the distance low-
ing, rendering hill and dale joyous—let them not despair, but
with the eyes of faith, through the Higher Law, look to the
glorious future, when their farms will be the heritage of the re-
juvenated Ethiopians . . . and with pious resignation, repeat,
"God bless Abraham Lincoln."

Let the masters of the Church Militant from Rev. Henry
Ward Beecher and the sanctified and *Veracious* Dr. Tyng of
New York, to the meek and gentle Parson Brownlow and the
Reverend and Peaceful Jim Cartey of Nashville—let them, I
repeat, when they have preached the Gospel—driving Loyal
Hearers out of the churches, and the pews are empty, save when
filled as hospitals with the mutilated, wounded and brokendown
soldiers of this Righteous War; and when their eyes behold
nothing but wounds, bruises and putrefying sores, which they
helped to produce, oh: then let them lift their *spotless hands* to
the Lamb upon the throne, and exclaim, "God bless Abraham
Lincoln."

Let Harriet Beecher Stowe bring out the latest of her Uncle
Toms, drawn to be put upon the stage with all the effect artistic
skill can produce, in the center foreground should appear quivering limbs, once of the gentlest, rarest mold, now stained and
defiled with foulest pollution; showing also snow-white bosoms,
that ever throbbed in angelic purity to woman's soft emotions,
now blood-stained in the last heavings of unpitied, untold outrage, woe and wrong! Along the right and left side wings
should appear groups of fair and gentle creatures, with hair dis-
heveled, and eyes distended in hopeless despair, while the black
ourang-outangs are dragging them down to gratify their brutal
instincts . . . . When the curtain rises, let Harriet Beecher
Stowe enter with lofty brow to receive the plaudits gathered
upon Humanity's extended fold, and when advanced to the foot-
lights, let her give with dramatic effect, "God bless Abraham
Lincoln."

Finally, let Hell open its jaws, and, jubilant of the ranks of Abolitionism, belch forth flames and lightning, and, in derision of the Most High, *laugh out*—in thunders that will shake the earth and startle the Ear of Heaven—"God bless Abraham Lincoln!"

At the time of the nomination of Lincoln in the early part of June in 1864, there appeared not only no doubt of his being named upon the first ballot, but now of his triumphant reelection. Lincoln appeared to have unified his party and practically to have unified the sentiment of all the loyal states. Even his Cabinet acknowledged his supreme authority and responded heartily to his leadership. When the Baltimore Convention adjourned it had seemed a needless formality to telegraph the president concerning its result. Within a month, however, the party that nominated Lincoln was divided, and by the middle of the summer it appeared very doubtful whether Lincoln could be reelected. Early in his administration Lincoln had offended Henry Winter Davis, of Maryland, a cousin of his long-time friend, Judge David Davis, of Illinois. The rock upon which the supporters of his administration split was the status of the states in rebellion. Were they in the Union or out of it? Lincoln believed that the theory on which the Federal Government was fighting the rebellion was that no state could take itself out of the Union; and that the seceded states were to be recognized just as rapidly as they could organize governments loyal to the government of the United States. This theory, however, did not please the extreme leaders of the Republican Party. They desired, in the language of Andrew Johnson, "to make treason odious." As Congress was about to adjourn, at noon on July 4, 1864, a bill was passed which had been drawn by Mr. Davis, containing in its preamble the declaration that the seceded states were not in the Union, and calling for reconstruction on a basis which included the prohibition of slavery in the reconstructed states. Lincoln declined to sign this bill, and it failed to become a law for lack of Lincoln's signature. Instead Lincoln issued on July eighth a proclamation in which he stated his reasons for not approving the bill. He said:

Now, therefore, I, Abraham Lincoln, President of the United States, do proclaim, declare, and make known that while I am—as I was in December last, when by proclamation I propounded a plan of restoration—unprepared by a formal approval of this bill to be inflexibly committed to any single plan of restoration, and while I am also unprepared to declare that the free State constitutions and governments, already adopted and installed in Arkansas and Louisiana, shall be set aside and held for naught, thereby repelling and discouraging the loyal citizens who have set up the same as to further effort, or to declare a constitutional competency in Congress to abolish slavery in the States, but am at the same time sincerely hoping and expecting that a constitutional amendment abolishing slavery throughout the nation may be adopted, nevertheless, I am fully satisfied with the system for restoration contained in the bill as one very proper for the loyal people of any State choosing to adopt it; and that I am, and at all times shall be, prepared to give the executive aid and assistance to any such people, so soon as military resistance to the United States shall have been suppressed in any such State, and the people thereof shall have sufficiently returned to their obedience to the Constitution and the laws of the United States, in which cases military governors will be appointed, with directions to proceed according to the bill.

Not a few of the most vigorous members of the Republican Party were offended by this action. On August fifth, Senator Benjamin F. Wade* and Honorable Henry Winter Davis joined in a signed attack upon the president for what they called "a studied outrage on the legislative authority of the people." This, the most bitter attack made upon the president by members of his own party during his administration, contained the following paragraph:

---

*There is not space in a work such as this to do justice, and it has yet to be done, to Zachariah Chandler and Benjamin F. Wade. I can but feel that some recent biographies of Lincoln, in setting forth the opposition of these senators to Lincoln in some of his measures that appeared to them to invade the prerogatives of Congress, have done them injustice. Two inci-

Such are the fruits of this rash and fatal act of the President
—a blow at the friends of his Administration, at the rights of
humanity, and at the principles of republican government. The
President has greatly presumed on the forbearance which the
supporters of his Administration have so long practiced, in view
of the arduous conflict in which we are engaged, and the reckless ferocity of our political opponents. But he must understand
that our support is of a cause and not of a man; that the authority of Congress is paramount and must be respected; that the
whole body of the Union men of Congress will not submit to be
impeached by him of rash and unconstitutional legislation; and
if he wishes our support he must confine himself to his executive
duties—to obey and to execute, not make the laws—to suppress
by arms armed rebellion, and leave political reorganization to
Congress. If the supporters of the Government fail to insist on
this they become responsible for the usurpations which they fail
to rebuke, and are justly liable to the indignation of the people
whose rights and security, committed to their keeping, they sacrifice. Let them consider the remedy of these usurpations, and,
having found it, fearlessly execute it.

Wendell Phillips also strongly opposed President Lincoln's reelection, and made several warm speeches against Lincoln and
his policy.

When asked if he had read the Wade-Davis Manifesto or any
of Phillips' speeches, the president replied:

dents may be related concerning Wade. When he was a judge in Ohio, a
negro was introduced as a witness, and was objected to by opposing counsel.
There was a statute that forbade such testimony, but in the courts of Northern Ohio it was a dead letter and there were abundant precedents for its
non-observance. One lawyer argued the statute which was unmistakable,
and the other argued the precedents. "Let the witness be sworn," said Wade.
"No evidence has been introduced to show that this witness is a negro."

The other I give from memory as I heard it from a man who was present at a Fourth of July celebration at Jefferson, Ohio, while the war was in
progress. Wade was describing his last interview with Jefferson Davis, in
which Davis proposed that the southern states should be permitted to secede
peacefully, taking with them the forts, custom-houses, and other pieces of
property of the Federal Government located within them. Said Wade:

"When that old arch-traitor made that proposal to me, what answer do
you think I made to him? I said to him, 'I'll see you in hell first! With the
gate locked! And the key thrown away! And a strong northeast wind
blowing cinders into your damned old eyes!'"

Wade never used language quite as strong as this regarding Lincoln
but it was not very gentle.

"I have not seen them, nor do I care to see them. I have seen enough to satisfy me that I am a failure, not only in the opinion of the people in rebellion, but of many distinguished politicians of my own party. But time will show whether I am right or they are right, and I am content to abide its decision. I have enough to look after without giving much of my time to the consideration of the subject of who shall be my successor in office. The position is not an easy one; and the occupant, whoever he may be, for the next four years, will have little leisure to pluck a thorn or plant a rose in his own pathway."

It was urged that this opposition must be embarrassing to his administration, as well as damaging to the party. He replied: "Yes, that is true; but our friends, Wade, Davis, Phillips, and others are hard to please. I am not capable of doing so. I can not please them without wantonly violating not only my oath, but the most vital principles upon which our government was founded. As to those who, like Wade and the rest, see fit to depreciate my policy and cavil at my official acts, I shall not complain of them. I accord them the utmost freedom of speech and liberty of the press, but shall not change the policy I have adopted in the full belief that I am right. I feel on this subject as an Illinois farmer once expressed himself while eating cheese. He was interrupted in the midst of his repast by the entrance of his son, who exclaimed, 'Hold on, dad! there's skippers in that cheese you're eating!'

" 'Never mind, Tom,' said he, as he kept on munching his cheese, 'if they can stand it I can.' "

Lincoln could not always refrain from an apt repartee even when he knew it would give offense.

Ward H. Lamon told this story of President Lincoln, whom he found one day in a particularly gloomy frame of mind. Lamon said:

"The President remarked, as I came in, 'I fear I have made Senator Wade, of Ohio, my enemy for life.'

" 'How?' I asked.

" 'Well,' continued the president, 'Wade was here just now urging me to dismiss Grant, and, in response to something he said, I remarked, "Senator, that reminds me of a story." '

" 'What did Wade say?' I inquired of the president.

" 'He said, in a petulant way,' the president responded, ' "It is with you, sir, all story, story! You are the father of every military blunder that has been made during the war. This government is on the road to hell, sir, by reason of your obstinacy, and you are not a mile from there this minute." '

" 'What did you say then?'

" 'I good-naturedly said to him,' the president replied, ' "Senator, that is just about the distance from here to the capitol, is it not?" He was very angry, grabbed up his hat and cane, and went away.' "

At this time also, Horace Greeley, being assured that the time had come for a new effort on behalf of peace, entered into negotiations with certain commissioners of the Confederate Government, to that end. Lincoln had no faith in the undertaking, but gave to Greeley the following document written in the president's own hand:

EXECUTIVE MANSION,
Washington, July 18, 1864.

To whom it may concern: Any proposition which embraces the restoration of peace, the integrity of the whole Union, and the abandonment of slavery, and which comes by and with an authority that can control the armies now at war against the United States, will be received and considered by the Executive government of the United States, and will be met by liberal terms on other substantial and collateral points, and the bearer or bearers thereof shall have safe conduct both ways.

Abraham Lincoln.

Greeley proceeded to Niagara Falls, where he met the Confederate Commissioners, Clement C. Clay, Jacob Thompson, James P. Holcombe and George N. Sanders, offering them immunity from arrest if they would go to Washington carrying with them authority from the Confederate Government to negotiate for peace. Those commissioners, however, had no such credentials as could justify their accepting the invitation. Greeley found himself in a false position, and without stopping to ask whether he himself was not to blame for it, he blamed the president. In a letter which was not published until long afterward, Greeley made the president this hysterical proposal:

I fear that my chance for usefulness has passed. I know that nine-tenths of the whole American people, North and South, are anxious for peace—peace on almost any terms—and utterly sick of human slaughter and devastation. I know that, to the general eye, it now seems that the rebels are anxious to negotiate and that we refuse their advances. I know that if this impression be not removed we shall be beaten out of sight next November. I firmly believe that, were the election to take place to-morrow, the Democratic majority in this State and Pennsylvania would amount to 100,000, and that we should lose Connecticut also. Now if the rebellion can be crushed before November it will do to go on; if not, we are rushing to certain ruin.

What, then, can I do in Washington? Your trusted advisers nearly all think I ought to go to Fort Lafayette for what I have done already. Seward wanted me sent there for my brief conference with M. Mercier. The cry has steadily been, No truce! No armistice! No negotiation! No mediation! Nothing but surrender at discretion! I never heard of such fatuity before. There is nothing like it in history. It *must* result in disaster, or all experience is delusive.

Now I do not know that a tolerable peace could be had, but I believe it might have been last month; and, at all events, I know that an honest, sincere effort for it would have done us immense good. And I think no Government fighting a rebellion should ever close its ears to any proposition the rebels may make.

I beg you, implore you, to inaugurate or invite proposals for peace forthwith. And in case peace cannot now be made consent to an *armistice for one year,* each party to retain unmolested all it now holds, but the rebel ports to be opened. Meantime let a national convention be held, and there will surely be no more war at all events.

Missouri in those days was sadly divided. Two factions each

led by vigorous men, had long been at war in that state, and
Lincoln had in his Cabinet enough to remind him constantly of
the hostility of some of the Missouri politicians. It was not,
however, for the most part hostility to Lincoln. But he was so
situated as to take the buffetings of both factions on occasion.
The divided counsels of that state proved a bone of contention.

It was conditions such as these which confronted the president
in the summer and autumn of 1864.

When Lincoln was nominated in June of 1864, it seemed probable that the war would be ended within a few months, but that
summer wore away and the war did not end. Grant with an
army of 120,000 men started what had ruined many a brave
general before him, a campaign in Virginia. A terrific battle
was fought in the Wilderness, where Lee's 52,000 men, fighting on the defensive, were a full match for Grant's 120,000.
Then came the battle of Cold Harbor, with more loss of life.
In a month's campaign, Grant lost nearly 60,000 men. It is not
too much to say that the country was appalled by these losses.
Any previous general would have resigned the leadership of the
army in despair. Grant doggedly held on. His loss of 60,000
men had caused Lee a loss of 30,000. He was winning the war
in what was probably the shortest way, but the country was horrified by so much apparently fruitless bloodshed.

If the election had occurred while these battles were in progress, Lincoln would have been defeated. McClellan would
have been elected on his platform which declared the war to be
a failure. Lincoln himself on August twenty-third, if not earlier, reached definitely the opinion that he was to be defeated
and he handed to the Cabinet a sealed document which he asked
them to sign and witness. What it contained they did not know,
but the act was ominous.

There was, however, no longer any doubt what the armies
were fighting for. They were fighting to establish the truth
that this was one nation. Equally they were fighting to establish
the truth that this nation was a free nation.

Early in the war the soldiers had caught up a negro camp-meeting melody to which they fitted words of their own:

> John Brown's body lies a-mouldering in the grave,
>   But his soul goes marching on.
>   Glory, glory, hallelujah,
>   His soul goes marching on.

The song went into other stanzas declaring - among other things the intention to hang Jeff Davis to a sour apple tree; but these did not obscure the real spirit of the song. The armies caught the step; they were marching after the soul of Old John Brown.

Mrs. Julia Ward Howe caught the spirit of the melody, and wrote her *Battle Hymn of the Republic*:

> In the beauty of the lilies, Christ was born across the sea,
> With the glory in His bosom, that transfigures you and me;
> As He died to make men holy, let us die to make men free,
>   While God is marching on.

Freedom had become a watchword. George F. Root had written a rallying song to which men came, "Shouting the Battle Cry of Freedom." Lincoln had sought as his paramount object to save the Union. He now knew he was equally committed to the policy of making the whole Union free. The whole nation had come clearly to recognize this modification of the situation.

> All through the conflict up and down,
> Marched Uncle Tom and Old John Brown,
>   One face, one form, ideal;
> And which was false and which was true,
> The wisest sybil never knew,
>   Since both alike were real.

As to slavery and the border states, Lincoln now defined his attitude, tactfully but uncompromisingly, in a letter of April 4, 1864, addressed to A. G. Hodges, of Kentucky:

I am naturally anti-slavery. If slavery is not wrong, nothing is wrong. I cannot remember when I did not so think and feel, and yet I have never understood that the Presidency conferred upon me an unrestricted right to act officially upon this judgment and feeling. . . . When, early in the war, General Frémont attempted military emancipation, I forbade it, because I did not then think it an indispensable necessity. When still later, General Cameron, the Secretary of War, suggested the arming of the blacks, I objected, because I did not think it an indispensable necessity. When still later, General Hunter attempted military emancipation, I again forbade it, because I did not think the indispensable necessity had come. When in March, and May, and July, 1862, I made earnest and successive appeals to the border states to favor compensated emancipation, I believed the indispensable necessity for military emancipation and arming the blacks would come, unless averted by that measure. They declined the proposition, and I was, in my best judgment, driven to the alternative of either surrendering the Union, and with it, the Constitution, or of laying strong hands upon the colored element. I chose the latter. In choosing it, I hoped for greater gain than loss, but of this I was not entirely confident. More than a year of trial now shows no loss by it in our foreign relations, none in our white military force, no loss by it anyhow or anywhere. On the contrary, it shows a gain of quite an hundred and thirty thousand soldiers, seamen, and laborers. These are palpable facts, about which, as facts, there can be no caviling. We have the men; and we could not have them without the measure. . . .

I add a word which was not in the verbal conversation. In telling this tale, I attempt no compliment to my own sagacity. I claim not to have controlled events, but confess plainly that events have controlled me. Now, at the end of three years struggle, the nation's condition is not what either party or any man devised or expected. God alone can claim it. Whither it is tending seems plain. If God now wills the removal of a great wrong, and wills that we of the North, as well as you of the South, shall pay fairly for our complicity in that wrong, impartial history will find therein new cause to attest and revere the justice and goodness of God.

The president was gratified by the reception which the newsapers accorded this letter.   John Hay wrote on April 30, 1864:

The President came loafing in as it grew late, and talked
bout the reception which his Hodges letter had met with.   He
eemed rather gratified that the tribute was in the main inspired
y a kindly spirit in its criticism.   He thought of, and found,
nd gave me to decipher, Greeley's letter to him of 29 July,
861.*   This most remarkable letter still retains for me its
vonderful interest as the most insane specimen of pusillanimity
hat I have ever read.   When I finished reading, Nicolay said:
That would be nuts to the *Herald;* Bennett would willingly
ive $10,000 for that."   To which the President, tying red tape
round the package, answered, "I need $10,000 very much, but
e can't have it for many times that."

Lincoln made no campaign speeches either in 1860 or in 1864.
n his brief occasional utterances during the latter campaign,
e made no references to his own reelection or to the men who
vere opposing him.   He wrote no letters for publication, and
uthorized no interviews containing any direct reference to the
ontest between him and General McClellan.   He did, however,
rite out what he regarded as the platform upon which he was
eeking reelection.   He was invited to attend a union mass meet-
ng at Buffalo. He declined the invitation, but had some thought
hat it might be well to send a letter outlining his views on the
ampaign.   He finally decided that it would be more dignified
) maintain his silence, but the following fragment found among
is papers after he died, gives the platform upon which Lincoln
nderstood himself to be accepting his renomination:

Yours inviting me to attend a Union mass meeting at Buffalo
s received. Much is being said about peace, and no man desires
eace more ardently than I.   Still I am yet unprepared to give
p the Union for a peace which, so achieved, could not be of
1uch duration.   The preservation of our Union was *not* the sole
vowed object for which the war was commenced.   It was com-

*The text of this letter which followed the Battle of Bull Run, is quoted
the chapter relating to that battle.

menced for precisely the reverse object—*to destroy our Union.*
The insurgents commenced it by firing upon the *Star of the
West* and on Fort Sumter, and by other similar acts. It is true,
however, that the Administration accepted the war thus commenced for the sole avowed object of preserving our Union; and
it is not true that it has since been, or will be, prosecuted by this
Administration for any other object. In declaring this I only
declare what I can know, and do know, to be true, and what no
other man can know to be false.

In taking the various steps which have led to my present position in relation to the war, the public interest and my private
interest have been perfectly parallel, because in no other way
could I serve myself so well as by truly serving the Union. The
whole field has been open to me where to choose. No place
hunting necessity has been upon me urging me to seek a position of antagonism to some other man, irrespective of whether
such position might be favorable or unfavorable to the Union.

Of course, I may err in judgment; but my present position in
reference to the rebellion is the result of my best judgment, and
according to that best judgment, it is the only position upon
which any executive can or could save the Union. Any substantial departure from it insures the success of the rebellion. An armistice—a cessation of hostilities—is the end of the struggle,
and the insurgents would be in peaceable possession of all that
has been struggled for. Any different policy in regard to the
colored man deprives us of his help, and this is more than we
can bear. We cannot spare the hundred and forty or fifty
thousand now serving us as soldiers, seamen, and laborers. This
is not a question of sentiment or taste, but one of physical force,
which may be measured and estimated as horse-power and
steam-power are measured and estimated. Keep it, and you can
save the Union. Throw it away, and the Union goes with it.
Nor is it possible for any administration to retain the services of
these people with the express or implied understanding that upon
the first convenient occasion they are to be reenslaved. It cannot be, and it ought not to be.

This defined the issue as Lincoln held it in his own mind.
This was what the country accepted as the policy of Lincoln's
administration in its second term. This was the platform upon
which Abraham Lincoln was reelected. It was uncompromising

n its faith in an undivided Union which was also to be a free nation.

The question to what extent Lincoln permitted his power of patronage to be used in 1864 to carry the national election, is one whose answer depends somewhat upon the form of the question and definition of method. Campaign assessments were levied against officeholders according to the established custom of the time, and when Lincoln was informed of this fact he did not interfere. Perhaps he did not know of any other way in which the necessary expenses of a campaign could be secured than that which was then a recognized and established method. On the other hand, Mr. Arnold declares, and he was in position to know, that:

During the canvass made by the friends of the President for his nomination and election he never used his power or his patronage to insure success.

The following note, written in behalf of a friend in Illinois to an office-holder who was charged with using his power against his friend, will illustrate the views of the President:*

EXECUTIVE MANSION, Washington, July 4th, 1864.
To —— Esq.
Dear Sir: Complaint is made to me that you are using your official power to defeat Mr. —— ——'s nomination to Congress. I am well satisfied with Mr. ——, as a member of Congress, and I do not know that the man who might supplant him would be as satisfactory. But the correct principle I think is, that all our friends should have *absolute freedom* of choice among our friends. My wish therefore is, that you will do just as you think fit with your own suffrage in the case, and not constrain any of your subordinates to do other than he thinks fit with his. This is precisely the rule I inculcated and adhered to on my part, when a certain other nomination now recently made was being canvassed for.
                              Yours very truly,
                                        A. Lincoln.

*Quoted in Arnold: *Life of Lincoln,* p. 293.

Fortunately for the party that had nominated Abraham Lincoln, the situation of the Union Armies improved during the autumn months. From the depression of midsummer there grew an enthusiasm and a degree of confidence which made the election of Lincoln certain. Only three states, New Jersey, Delaware and Kentucky* gave their vote to McClellan. Lincoln had 212 of the 233 electoral votes. He had also a clear popular majority. In a total vote of 4,015,902, Lincoln's majority was 411,428.

The election, as Lincoln said, showed how strong and sound the nation was. It "demonstrated that a people's government can sustain a national election in the midst of a great Civil War."†

---

*Although Kentucky voted for McClellan, Lincoln had a strong vote there. It is interesting to know that his native county showed a larger vote for him in 1864 than in 1860, and that that county furnished a considerable number of Union soldiers.

The official vote of Hardin County for president in 1860 was: Breckenridge, 144; Bell, 1,029; Douglas, 912; Lincoln, 6. Of Larue County: Breckenridge, 32; Bell, 401; Douglas, 50; Lincoln, 3. (*Frankfort Tri-Weekly Yeoman*, Nov. 13, 1860.)

The official vote of Hardin County for president in 1864 was: Lincoln 83; McClellan, 1,010; Of Larue County: Lincoln, 17; McClellan, 700 (*Frankfort Commonwealth*, Nov. 22, 1864.)

On August 31, 1864, the nearest feasible date preceding the second draft Hardin's total quotas were 1,210, its total credits 797, and its resulting deficiency, 413. Larue's total quotas were 527, its total credits 495, and its resulting deficiency, 132. The net surplus for the fourth district, containing these counties, was 1,346, and the net surplus for the entire state was 7,065. (U. S. adjutant-general's office. Sen. doc. 142, 61st Cong., 1st sess., p. 13, 14. Thus, although Lincoln's native county furnished a large number of Confederate soldiers, its contribution to the Union Army was not small.

†An incident may illustrate the spirit in which some men cast their ballots for Lincoln in 1864. There was then living on a farm in the corner made by La Salle, Bureau and Lee Counties, Illinois, an aged farmer, whose house stood in La Salle County, just across the line from Lee, and whose vote had to be cast in Mendota. The day was cold and the road was rough and the conveyance was a heavy farm wagon without springs. He had not been out-of-doors for several days, and was wholly unfit to make the journey of five miles, but he made it. Arriving at Mendota, he found that the polling-place was in a hall, up-stairs. He sent up word that he was unable to ascend the stairs, and asked if the ballot-box might be brought down. This was deemed illegal, but willing friends offered to carry him up-stairs. He declined the proffered assistance, and, though he had not for months ascended the stairs in his own house, he painfully climbed the stairway on his knees. When he reached the top of the stairs, he did not rise. Again declining the assistance of those who offered to help him, he moved down the

On election night, November 8, 1864, John Hay wrote:

The house has been still and almost deserted today. Everybody in Washington, not at home voting,* seems ashamed of it, and stays away from the President. I was talking with him to-day. He said: "It is a little singular that I, who am not a vindictive man, should have always been before the people for election marked for their bitterness—always but once. When I came to Congress, it was a quiet time. But always beside that, the contests in which I have been present have been marked by great rancor!"

The returns received at the White House that night indicated the overwhelming defeat of two men who had been Lincoln's bitterest critics, one of them being Henry Winter Davis. Lincoln's secretaries and the others in small groups assembled at the White House, expressed deep satisfaction in the rebuke which Davis and his associates had received at the hands of their constituents. After a little Lincoln said:

You have more of the feeling of personal resentment than I. Perhaps I may have too little of it, but I never thought it paid. A man has not time to spend half his life in quarrelling. If any man ceases to attack me, I never hold the past against him. It

---

hall, still on his knees, and did not rise till he stood up to put his ballot in the box. He was too simple-minded a man to have done it for effect. The idea came to him as he was making his slow way up the stairs. He had a son in the army; he, himself had carried his regiment's flag in the War of 1812. He doubted if he could ever recover, and he did not recover, from the strain and exposure of that day. A few weeks later, a little lad not yet four years of age was lifted up and permitted to look at his face as it lay in his coffin, and he still remembers the dignity and honesty and strong character that showed in the features of the dead man. This is the story of the last ballot, and the last crossing of his own threshold, of Eleazer Barton, my grandfather.

*Some of the states arranged for the voting of soldiers in the field, and where such provision was not made, there was generous issue of furloughs to soldiers who wanted to go home to vote. In some regiments voting in the field, small account was made of the record of the family Bible. Jean F. Loba, who afterward became a distinguished clergyman and a Doctor of Divinity, was then a private, aged seventeen. His colonel called to him and asked him whether he had voted. "I am not of age," answered Loba. "Come up and vote," answered the colonel; "any man that is old enough to carry a gun in the Union Army is old enough to vote for Lincoln."

has seemed to me recently that Winter Davis was growing more sensible to his true interest and had ceased wasting his time by attacking me. I hope for his own good he has. He has been very malign against me but has injured only himself by it. His conduct has been very strange to me. I came here as his friend and wishing to continue so. I had heard nothing but good of him; he was the cousin of my intimate friend Judge Davis. But I had scarcely been elected when I heard of his attacking me on all possible occasions.

Lincoln took his reelection rather calmly. His most significant remark was that apparently the people thought "not well to swap horses while crossing the stream." On November 11, 1864, a Cabinet meeting was held. Again we rely on the contemporary record of John Hay's diary:

At the meeting of the Cabinet to-day, the President took out a paper from his desk and said: "Gentlemen, do you remember last summer I asked you to sign your names on the back of a paper of which I did not show you the inside? This is it. Now, Mr. Hay, see if you can get this open without tearing it?"

The outside of the paper bore the endorsement of William H. Seward, W. P. Fessenden, Edwin M. Stanton, Gideon Welles, Edw. Bates, M. Blair and J. P. Usher. The president had pasted it up in so singular a style that Hay had difficulty in getting it open, and it required some cutting to accomplish this result without mutilating either the contents within or the signatures upon the back. This was what the document contained:

"Executive Mansion,
Washington, Aug. 23, 1864.
This morning and for some days past, it seems exceedingly probable that this Administration will not be reelected. Then it will be my duty to so cooperate with the President elect, as to save the Union between the election and the inauguration; as he will have secured his election on such ground that he cannot possibly save it afterward.

A. Lincoln.

The president explained to the Cabinet his reasons for having asked them to sign their names as witnesses of this sealed paper: "You will remember that this was written at a time, six days before the Chicago nominating convention when as yet we had no adversary, and seemed to have no friends. I then solemnly resolved on the course of action indicated above. I resolved in case of the election of General McClellan, being certain that he would be the candidate, that I would see him and talk matters over with him. I would say, 'General, the election has demonstrated that you are stronger, have more influence with the American people than I. Now let us get together, you with your influence, and I with all the executive power of the government, and try to save the country. You raise as many troops as you possibly can for this final trial, and I will devote all my energy to assisting and pushing the war.'"

Stanton said: "And the general would answer you, 'Yes, yes,' and the next day when you saw him again and pressed these views upon him he would say 'Yes, yes,' and so on forever; and would have done nothing at all."

"At least," added Lincoln, "I should have done my duty, and have stood clear before my own conscience."

It may be questioned whether history contains any parallel for Lincoln's magnanimity in this incident. Only a man with the highest and finest nobility of soul could have done what, under those circumstances, Lincoln did regarding a man who had so disappointed and abused him, and on behalf of a country that seemed about to repudiate him.

In another act equally magnanimous Lincoln had already risen above all partisan relations with Governor Seymour, of New York. According to Thurlow Weed, shortly after Seymour's election as governor in the fall of 1862, Lincoln authorized Weed to go to Seymour and say to him that Seymour, as the Democratic governor of New York, could, if he desired, bring his whole party into line in an effort to save the Union; and that if he would do so, Lincoln would do everything in his power to pave

the way for Seymour to become president in 1864. Even i
Weed's memory of this incident led him somewhat to exaggerat
the affair, and Lincoln's offer to Seymour was somewhat les
definite and specific, still there can be no doubt that Lincol
held toward Seymour essentially the attitude which Weed de
scribes. In this matter we have Lincoln's own very gracious let
ter to Seymour, and Seymour's exceedingly distant and ver
guarded reply. Lincoln wrote to Seymour addressing him a
"the head of the greatest State in the nation," and asking for a
frank understanding with him as to their substantial agreemen
concerning their joint duty in "maintaining the nation's life an
integrity." Seymour declined to commit himself in this mat
ter, but said that he was confident that his opinions were share
by fully one-half of the population of the northern states, an
he said:

I intend to show to those charged with the administration o
public affairs a due deference and respect, and to yield them a
just and generous support in all measures they may adopt withir
the scope of their constitutional powers. For the preservatior
of this Union I am ready to make any sacrifice of interest, part
or prejudice.

The first of these two sentences was the really significan
one. Governor Seymour did very little if anything, to show hi
deep interest in the preservation of the Union, and he did ver
much to show that he was no friend of Lincoln.

The president's message to Congress in December, 1864, tool
occasion to comment upon the election in its relation to his owr
war policy, and he viewed it with frank satisfaction. Moreover
he reflected that the nation's losses, heavy as they had been, ha
not really weakened it to a point below its effective strength wher
the war began. He said:

While it is melancholy to reflect that the war had filled sc
many graves, and carried mourning to so many hearts, it is some
relief to know that compared with the surviving, the fallen have

been so few. While corps, and divisions, and brigades, and regiments have formed, and fought, and dwindled, and gone out of existence, a great majority of the men who composed them are still living. The same is true of the naval service. The election returns prove this. So many voters could not else be found. The States regularly holding elections, both now and four years ago . . . cast 3,982,011 votes now, against 3,870,222 cast then; showing an aggregate now of 3,982,011. To this is to be added 33,762 cast now in the new States of Kansas and Nevada, which States did not vote in 1860; thus swelling the aggregate to 4,015,773, and the net increase during the three years and a half of war, to 145,551. . . . To this again should be added the number of all soldiers in the field from Massachusetts, Rhode Island and New Jersey, Delaware, Indiana, Illinois, and California, who by the laws of those States could not vote away from their homes, and which number cannot be less than 90,000. Nor yet is this all. The number in organized Territories is triple now what it was four years ago, while thousands, white and black, join us as the national arms press back the insurgent lines. So much is shown, affirmatively and negatively by the election.

It is not material to inquire how the increase has been produced, or to show that it would have been greater but for the war, which is probably true. The important fact remains demonstrated that we have more men now than we had when the war began; that we are not exhausted, nor in process of exhaustion; that we are gaining strength, and may, if need be, maintain the contest indefinitely. This as to men. Material resources are now more complete and abundant than ever.

Lincoln took occasion in this same message to consider the importunity of those who were insisting that he should hold a conference with Jefferson Davis in an effort the more speedily to win the war. The election had given him new assurance that the nation was prepared to stand by and see the war through to a successful finish. This, he believed, was the plain duty of the nation. The victory at the polls was also virtually a victory upon the battle-field:

On careful consideration of all the evidence accessible, it seems to me that no attempt at negotiation with the insurgent leader could result in any good. He would accept nothing short of severance of the Union—precisely what we will not and cannot give. His declarations to this effect are explicit and oft repeated. He does not attempt to deceive us. He affords us no excuse to deceive ourselves. He cannot voluntarily re-accept the Union; we cannot voluntarily yield it. Between him and us the issue is distinct, simple, and inflexible. It is an issue which can only be tried by war, and decided by victory. If we yield, we are beaten; if the Southern people fail him, he is beaten. Either way it would be the victory and defeat following war.

CHAPTER XXI

THE SECOND INAUGURAL

LINCOLN entered upon his second administration with a number of changes certain in his group of intimate associates. Hannibal Hamlin, vice-president in his first administration, gave place to Andrew Johnson, of Tennessee. Mr. Hamlin would have welcomed a renomination and reelection. Lincoln carefully concealed from Hamlin his own preference in the matter. It appears to be quite certain, however, that Lincoln favored Johnson. The reason was not that Hamlin was either personally or politically repugnant to Lincoln; but that important changes had occurred since 1860. In that year a former Democratic vice-president from New England had been desirable; in 1864 it seemed to Lincoln more important that the vice-president should represent the loyal South. It can not be said that the country profited by changing Hamlin for Johnson.

There were changes in the Cabinet. Montgomery Blair was unpopular with a large faction of the Republican Party, and he wearied Lincoln with his own suspicion against other prominent men. A little more than a month before the election, Mr. Lincoln asked for Blair's resignation, which Blair promptly tendered in a spirit much to his credit.* Lincoln appointed as his successor Governor William Dennison, of Ohio.

Mr. Bates, the Attorney General, also found himself wearied with his administrative cares, and out of sympathy with the fac-

---

*Blair considered the request for his resignation "a peace-offering to General Frémont and his friends, dictated by Seward at the request of Thurlow Weed."

tions that had come to control the Republican interests of his own state. He resigned, his resignation to take effect the last of November, 1864. Lincoln accepted this resignation, and after an endeavor to secure as attorney general Judge Joseph Holt, of Kentucky, he appointed to the vacant position James Speed of the same state, a brother of his early friend, Joshua F. Speed.

Most important, however, of the changes in Lincoln's official family, was the resignation of Secretary Chase, which had already occurred, January 29, 1864. This event had been long in coming, and like all events long expected, its arrival was a shock.

After Lincoln's removal of General W. S. Rosecrans following his defeat at Chickamauga, September 19 and 20, 1863, Hay recorded in his diary:

I told the President Chase would try to make capital out of this Rosecrans business. He laughed and said, "I suppose he will, like the blue-bottle fly, lay his eggs in every rotten place he can find." He seems much amused at Chase's mad hunt after the presidency. He hopes the country will never do worse.

Only a great man could have borne this situation as Lincoln did, and he had his reward. Lincoln bore with Chase, utilized him, and by his courtesy and magnanimity, strengthened his own administration.

In 1864 when Chase's plan to secure the nomination had become public property, Chase offered to resign and Lincoln would not accept his resignation. He said:

It is a question which I will not allow myself to consider from any standpoint other than my judgment of the public service, and in that view I do not perceive occasion for change.

Some of Lincoln's intimate friends once called his attention to the fact that Chase, while a member of his Cabinet, was quietly working to secure a nomination for the presidency, although knowing that Lincoln was to be a candidate for reelection. Lincoln's friends insisted that a Cabinet officer ought to be made to give up his presidential aspirations or be removed from office. The situation reminded Lincoln of a story: "My brother and I," he said, "were once plowing corn, I driving the horse and he holding the plow. The horse was lazy, but on one occasion he rushed across the field so that I, with my long legs, could scarcely keep pace with him. On reaching the end of the furrow, I found an enormous chin-fly flying up and striking him under the chin and I knocked him off. My brother asked me what I did that for. I told him I didn't want the old horse bitten in that way. 'Why,' said my brother, 'that's all that made him go.' Now, if Mr. Chase has a presidential chin-fly biting him, I'm not going to knock him off, if it will only make his Department go."

The resignation of Chase at first threatened seriously to weaken Lincoln's cause with the financiers of the country. Money is notoriously timid. The financiers of the country believed in Chase and were apprehensive of change of policy under his successor. As John Hay moved around Washington, he overheard many comments which made him wish that the president who had been patient so long, could have been patient a little longer. He wrote in his diary:

If the President has made a mistake (as I think he has) in allowing Chase to shirk his part of duty, Chase's leaving at this time is little less than a crime.

Speaking to Whitelaw Reid, Chase said that he supposed that the root of the matter was a difference in temperament between Lincoln and himself. "The truth is that I have never been able to make a joke out of this war." There is good reason to believe that when Chase's resignation had actually been accepted, he regretted having sent it in. He had become so used to resigning and being urged to remain, he supposed the process could go on forever. But he did not long have occasion to regret his rashness. A providential event occurred which made a better place for Chase and displayed again the magnanimity of Lincoln.

From the beginning of his administration, Lincoln had looked forward to the time when he could have opportunity to fill the place of chief justice of the Supreme Court. The four years of his administration went by, and Chief Justice Taney clung to life as a withered oak-leaf clings through the winter and the early spring. Lincoln said:

No man ever prayed as I did that Taney might outlive James Buchanan's term, and now I am afraid I have overdone it.

There was indeed some occasion for Lincoln's fear that he had prayed too hard. If Taney had lived to have his successor appointed either by George B. McClellan or by Andrew Johnson, it might have gone ill with the Supreme Court.

On October 12, 1864, Chief Justice Roger Taney died. The announcement of his death came in the midst of rejoicing over Union victories and over the election returns from the October states, making the reelection of Lincoln more than ever certain. Lincoln's opportunity had come to appoint to the Supreme bench a man of his own choosing. It was by all odds the most important appointment he could ever hope to make. Lincoln thoughtfully considered the matter until December sixth, and then without communicating his intention to any one, not even to his appointee or to any member of the Cabinet, he wrote out with his own hand his nomination for the position of chief justice and sent it to the Senate. The Senate confirmed the appointment without an hour's delay. That night when Salmon P. Chase went to his home, his daughter Kate met him at the door, and saluted him as chief justice of the United States.

In three important particulars the Cabinet stood unchanged. Seward had become one of Lincoln's closest friends and sincerest admirers. Stanton, too, had long since ceased to refer to the president in terms of contempt. Both these men were ready and were destined to stand by Lincoln until the end. Seward almost shared his martyrdom, and Stanton was faithful unto death.

Gideon Welles, also, retained his position as secretary of the navy.

One incident may be given, especially as it relates to an interesting aspect which the draft assumed in the later months of the war. So continuous had been the calls for troops that many states and districts were far behind in their quotas. Continued remonstrance was made to Lincoln that the quota of some particular state or district was too large. It was a great relief when any state or military division filled its quota completely. In the later months of the war there were Indian uprisings in the West, and these caused the withdrawal of certain regiments from the front. It was suggested that there were many Confederate soldiers confined in northern prisons, who would be glad to enlist in the United States Army to fight against the Indians, if they were assured that they would not be sent South to fight against their own people. The Federal authorities had stopped the exchange of prisoners. One Confederate soldier shut safely away in a northern prison, was more than the equivalent to a Union soldier sent back from the South unfit for military service. The Confederate prisoners had become convinced that there was no hope of being exchanged.

A prominent man in Pennsylvania conceived a brilliant idea. His district was behind in its quota. If he might be permitted to go to the Federal prisons he could offer a small bounty which his district would very gladly pay, and recruit a regiment of soldiers to fight against the Indians. Presumably they would very gladly accept a hundred dollars bounty, and the current rates were as high as a thousand. He went to the president and set forth his theory. He said that even the thousand-dollar volunteer was likely to be a foreigner, and quite possibly a coward and a bounty jumper. Whereas, the Confederates were fighters and would gladly devote their unexpended military energy to the conquest of Indians. Lincoln thought the idea a good one, and went with the Pennsylvania official to Stanton. Stanton was not sure that these prisoners would make good soldiers, but was willing to give the experiment a trial. He was utterly opposed, however, to the idea that Pennsylvania should receive any credit on her quota for such enlistments. Why should Pennsylvania save her own manhood in this fashion, or be permitted to buy herself off at a saving of nine hundred dollars a soldier? These prisoners belonged to the United States, and if they were enlisted for service, no one state should have the credit for them.

Stanton was indubitably right in this contention. Pennsylvania deserved no credit at all for any such enlistment. But Lincoln had approved the idea with the promise of this credit to the state from which the suggestion had come. If Stanton's logic convinced him, as it seems it must have done, at least it did not change his resolution. Quietly but firmly Lincoln overrode Stanton, and Pennsylvania received credit for the first group of these enlistments. It will be of interest to note that the idea proved to be a good one. Major Rathbone, a personal friend of Lincoln, and the same who was with the president in the box at Ford's Theater on the night when the president was assassinated, was sent to the Federal prison at Rock Island, Illinois, where eighteen hundred Confederate prisoners were enlisted as soldiers. Their readiness to enlist caused the plan to be tried in other prisons and with like success.*

---

*The secretary of war furnishes this information: In the years 1864 and 1865 there were organized six Union regiments of volunteer infantry, the enlisted men of which were principally deserters and refugees from the Confederate Army and prisoners of war who had taken the oath of allegiance to the United States. A historical memorandum on the subject was printed in the *Congressional Record* of March 20, 1908, pages 3752-3754. Those regiments were called, respectively, the 1st, 2nd, 3rd, 4th, 5th and 6th United States Volunteer Infantry. They were organized respectively, as follows: 1st at Point Lookout, Maryland, March to June, 1864; 2nd at Point Lookout, Maryland, October, 1864; 3rd at Rock Island, Illinois, October, 1864; 4th at Point Lookout, Maryland, October 1864; 5th at Alton, Illinois, and Camp Douglas, Illinois, May, 1865; 6th at Columbus, Ohio, Camp Morton, Indiana and Camp Douglas, Illinois, April 1865.

It appears that the members of those regiments were enlisted without any special written stipulations relative to pay, bounty or pension or as to where they should serve, although it appears to have been the understanding that they enlisted without expectation of bounty or pension. These regiments were employed principally on the western plains, some of them in connection with Indian hostilities. Some of the men at least received bounty, and the members have been accorded a pensionable status.

Colonel H. S. Huidekoper in his pamphlet of *Personal Notes and Reminiscences,* says:

The eighteen hundred soldiers enlisted as above described, were formed into two regiments, which did excellent service till the end of the war. Not a man ever deserted, and all proved loyal to their new allegiance. From other prisons, other men were subsequently enlisted, making in all 5,738 reconstructed Rebels who served under the old flag before the close of the war.*

Thus Lincoln was ready for his second administration with a Cabinet considerably changed; but his secretaries of state, war and navy remained with him.

The story of Andrew Johnson does not belong to this volume. Yet it must be recorded that the auspices under which he assumed the office of vice-president were inauspicious from the beginning. It was widely if not generally believed by those who saw him inducted into office, that the vice-president was intoxicated at the time. Honorable John W. Forney thus recorded his experience:

I can never forget President Lincoln's face as he came into the Senate chamber while Johnson was delivering his incoherent harangue. Lincoln had been detained signing the bills that had just passed the old Congress, and could not witness the regular opening of the new Senate until the ceremonies had fairly commenced. He took his seat facing the brilliant and surprised audience and heard all that took place with unutterable sorrow. He then spoke his own short inaugural from the middle portico of the Capitol, and rode quickly home. Bitter maledictions were

---

*A story is related concerning a regiment of a thousand men who were enlisted at Alton, Illinois, and Camp Douglas, in Chicago. They left Chicago on two special trains. Each man had in his pocket two hundred dollars bounty in United States greenbacks, and none of them had any other money. During the period of their imprisonment the most of them had become habitual card players, if they had not previously been so. It is said that before they reached their destination a very few individuals had the lion's share of the money. Perhaps never before on earth was there so equitable an experiment in the results of starting men out in life on the basis of an equal division of property. The equal division appears not to have lasted very long.

immediately hurled against the new Vice President. I hastened to his defense to the best of my ability, believing the affair to have been an accident. Threats of impeachment were common in both parties, especially among the Democrats; and the crusade got so fierce at last, that I found myself included among those who had helped Mr. Johnson to his exposure. But no voice of anger was heard from Abraham Lincoln. When nearly all censured, and many threatened, Mr. Lincoln simply said, "It has been a severe lesson for Andy, but I do not think he will do it again."

So it came about that, soon after one o'clock on March 4, 1865, Abraham Lincoln stood for the second time upon a platform at the eastern portico of the capitol and took the oath of office as president of the United States. The morning was cold, stormy and cloudy, but at noon the rain ceased and the sun came forth. The procession from the White House was dignified and solemn. In the group that surrounded the platform, large numbers of wounded soldiers were conspicuous. Behind the president as he took his place upon the platform were the judges of the Supreme Court in their official robes, the diplomatic corps in their uniforms, and distinguished officers of the government both in military and civil life. Among these appeared the tall form of the president advancing to take the oath of office. Stephen A. Douglas was not there to hold his hat. Roger B. Taney was not there to administer the oath of office. Both these distinguished men were dead. Salmon P. Chase, the new chief justice of the Supreme Court of the United States, stepped forward with a Bible open at the fifth chapter of Isaiah, which the president reverently kissed, and which the chief justice later presented to Mrs. Lincoln.

The oath of office was administered by the man who had sought to supplant Lincoln, and to whom Lincoln had returned good for evil by placing him in this highest judicial position.

The second inaugural address measures the intellectual power and the moral purpose of Abraham Lincoln at high-water mark

Noble as was the Gettysburg Address, this rises to a still higher
level of nobility. Perhaps there is no state paper in the history
of the government of modern nations that breathes so distinctly
a religious tone. The first inaugural was conciliatory, patient
and persuasive; the second embodied a spirit as generous and
devout as it was wise and statesmanlike. It is the greatest of
the addresses of Abraham Lincoln, and registers his intellectual
and spiritual power at their highest altitude.

In a clear voice, which sometimes trembled with emotion, Lincoln read his second inaugural:

Fellow Countrymen:—At this second appearing to take the
oath of the Presidential office, there is less occasion for an extended address than there was at the first. Then, a statement
somewhat in detail of a course to be pursued, seemed very fitting
and proper. Now, at the expiration of four years, during which
public declarations have been constantly called forth on every
point and phase of the great contest which still absorbs the attention and engrosses the energies of the nation, little that is new
could be presented. The progress of our arms, upon which all
else chiefly depends, is as well known to the public as to myself,
and it is, I trust, reasonably satisfactory and encouraging to all.
With high hope for the future, no prediction in regard to it is
ventured.

On the occasion corresponding to this, four years ago, all
thoughts were anxiously directed to an impending civil war. All
dreaded it, all sought to avoid it. While the inaugural address
was being delivered from this place, devoted altogether to saving the Union without war, insurgent agents were in the city,
seeking to destroy it with war,—seeking to dissolve the Union,
and divide the effects by negotiation. Both parties deprecated
war, but one of them would make war rather than let the nation
survive, and the other would accept war rather than let it perish;
and the war came. One-eighth of the whole population were
colored slaves, not distributed generally over the Union, but
localized in the southern part of it. These slaves constituted a
peculiar and powerful interest. All knew that this interest was
somehow the cause of the war. To strengthen, perpetuate, and
extend this interest, was the object for which the insurgents

would rend the Union by war, while the government claimed no right to do more than to restrict the territorial enlargement of it.

Neither party expected for the war the magnitude or the duration which it has already attained. Neither anticipated that the cause of the conflict might cease with, or even before the conflict itself should cease. Each looked for an easier triumph, and a result less fundamental and astounding.

Both read the same Bible, and pray to the same God, and each invokes His aid against the other. It may seem strange that any men should dare to ask a just God's assistance in wringing their bread from the sweat of other men's faces. But let us judge not, that we be not judged. The prayer of both could not be answered. That of neither has been answered fully. The Almighty has his own purposes. "Woe unto the world because of offenses, for it must needs be that offenses come, but woe to that man by whom the offense cometh." If we shall suppose that American slavery is one of these offenses, which in the providence of God must needs come, but which, having continued through his appointed time, he now wills to remove, and that he gives to both North and South this terrible war as the woe due to those by whom the offense came, shall we discern there any departure from those divine attributes which the believers in a living God always ascribe to him? Fondly do we hope, fervently do we pray, that this mighty scourge of war may speedily pass away. Yet if God wills that it continue until all the wealth piled by the bondsman's two hundred and fifty years of unrequited toil shall be sunk, and until every drop of blood drawn with the lash shall be paid by another drawn by the sword, as was said three thousand years ago, so still it must be said, that "the judgments of the Lord are true and righteous altogether."

With malice towards none, with charity for all, with firmness in the right as God gives us to see the right, let us finish the work we are in, to bind up the nation's wounds, to care for him who shall have borne the battle, and for his widow and his orphans, to do all which may achieve and cherish a just and a lasting peace among ourselves and with all nations.

CHAPTER XXII

LIBERTY AND UNION

THE Proclamation of Emancipation was a war measure. According to the president's interpretation of his own constitutional prerogative, he had no authority to issue such a proclamation on other grounds than those of military necessity. The proclamation went into effect on January 1, 1863, and it became immediately effective in states that were then in rebellion against the government wherever the armies of the United States controlled the situation. The area within which the proclamation operated widened with each success of the Federal Army. Great numbers of slaves in territory still held by the Confederates escaped through the lines and sought shelter and protection from the Union Army. What to do with them was a question, nor had it been certain in the early days of the war by what legal right they could be held. General Butler had proclaimed them "contraband of war." This ingenious definition availed, and was employed with great freedom and elasticity until the Proclamation of Emancipation was issued. After that negroes escaping from bondage in the states in rebellion were free whenever they could get to where their freedom could be made effective. A hundred thousand negro soldiers were soon bearing arms and fighting for their own freedom; and that number before the end of the war was practically doubled.

As the end of the war grew visibly near, the question became a pressing one whether the Emancipation Proclamation, distinctly issued as a war measure, would hold after the war was over. Lincoln himself believed that, with the return of peace, the voters of each state would have to settle whether that state was to be free or slave.

Furthermore, the Proclamation of Emancipation was limited in its operation to those states actually in rebellion. The president had no authority to extend its operation into the border states where slavery existed but rebellion did not. Lincoln had from the very first dealt very tenderly with the border states. He had understood them better than any one else in Washington. He realized their value to the Union cause. It was hard enough for them to remain within the Union, even with the slavery question eliminated from their immediate consideration. Lincoln therefore was very desirous of relieving the border states from every needless divisive question.

But it became evident as the war drew near the close that slavery must by some means be prevented from reasserting itself in the territory that had belonged to the Confederacy; and it also became a question whether the government was to have two great free areas, one north and the other south, with slavery existing and protected within a thin buffer area between these two. Such a consideration was preposterous. Lincoln again took ground upon his declaration preceding his debates with Douglas that this nation could not permanently exist partly slave and partly free. The divided house must no longer remain divided.

Lincoln was a firm believer in the Constitution. He believed that in the time of war the Constitution gave to the president power which would be dangerous for a chief executive to possess in time of peace. He gave earnest thought to the question of the status of the freed slaves, when the president's war powers should cease. Three questions he propounded for himself as follows:

Firstly—Had the president of the United States, in the exercise of his war powers, a right, under the Constitution and by public law, to decree, on grounds of military necessity, the emancipation and perpetual enfranchisement of slaves in the insurgent states and parts of states?

Secondly—Did such proclamation work, by its own vigor, the immediate, the unconditional and the perpetual emancipation of all slaves in the districts affected by it?

Thirdly—Did such proclamation, working *proprio vigore,* not only effect the emancipation of all existing slaves in the insurgent territory, but, with regard to slaves so liberated, did it extinguish the status of slavery created by municipal law, insomuch that they would have remained forever free, in fact and law, provided the Constitution and the legal rights and relations of the states under it had remained, on the return of peace, what they were before the war?

Lincoln knew well the degree of legal uncertainty in the answer to each of these questions.

The Emancipation Proclamation was extra-constitutional. Not even on the plea of military necessity could the president amend the Constitution. Furthermore, it fell outside the jural relations of slavery under international law. The slaves were property when the war began, and that relation was implied in the proclamation itself. Under what terms and for what purposes might enemy property, confiscated in time of war, and as property, be changed in character from property to persons, and retain that character after the close of war? Were they confiscated as "enemy property" and for the purpose of weakening the enemy, or was the confiscation penal in character, as a punishment for treason? In either event, the confiscation should legally have been by legal process; and there had been no such process. Was the Emancipation Proclamation ever legal? Many of the ablest lawyers denied its legality even as a war measure; few doubted its illegality after peace was restored. Moreover, it was only slaves of enemies, escaping to the Union lines, and slaves in certain designated states in rebellion that were freed. No one knew better than Lincoln that his proclamation stood by virtue of bayonets of the army, not by affirmative decision of the courts.

At the opening of Congress on December 14, 1863, Honorable James M. Ashley, of Ohio, introduced a joint resolution submitting to the states a proposition to amend the Constitution by abolishing and prohibiting slavery. Other members of the House and Senate introduced resolutions slightly differing in form, but to the same purport. The real author of the amendment, as it was ultimately adopted, was Lyman Trumbull, Senator from Illinois. He was now chairman of the Judiciary Committee of the Senate, and was a legislator of great practical ability, a ready speaker and an able debater.

In support of his resolution Senator Trumbull said:

No superficial observer even of our history, North or South, or of any party, can doubt that slavery lies at the bottom of our present troubles. Our fathers who made the Constitution regarded it as an evil, and looked forward to its early extinction. They felt the inconsistency of their position, while proclaiming the equal rights of all to life, liberty, and happiness, they denied liberty, happiness, and life itself to a whole race, except in subordination to them. It was impossible in the nature of things, that a government based on such antagonistic principles could permanently and peacefully endure, nor did its founders expect it would. They looked forward to the not distant nor, as they supposed, uncertain period, when slavery should be abolished, and the government become in fact what they made it in name, one securing the blessings of liberty to all. The history of the last seventy years has proven that the founders of the republic were mistaken in their expectations; and slavery, so far from gradually disappearing as they had anticipated, had so strengthened itself, that in 1860, its advocates demanded the control of the nation in its interests, failing in which, they attempted its overthrow. . . .

I think, then, it is reasonable to suppose, that if this proposed amendment passes Congress, it will within a year receive the ratification of the requisite number of states to make it a part of the Constitution. That accomplished, and we are forever freed of this troublesome question. We accomplish then what the statesmen of this country have been struggling to accomplish for years. We take this question entirely away from the politics of the country. We relieve Congress of sectional strife, and what is better than all, we restore to a whole race that freedom which is theirs by the gift of God, but which we for generations have wickedly denied them.

Among the foremost advocates of the amendment was Henry Wilson. He had been a diligent student and an earnest advocate of universal freedom. He had in preparation a book on the anti-slavery legislation of the war congresses. This he afterward expanded into a large *Rise and Fall of the Slave Power in America*. He said:

The enforcement of this proclamation will give peace and order, freedom and unity, to a now distracted country; the failure to enforce it will bring with it discord and anarchy, a dissevered Union, and a broken nation. . . . But, sir, the crowning act in this series of acts for the restriction and extinction of slavery in America, is this proposed amendment to the Constitution, prohibiting the existence of slavery forevermore in the republic of the United States.

Both in its language and in the form of argument this paragraph so precisely follows the thought of Lincoln, I suspect that the president himself was the author of it.

The amendment passed the Senate on April 8, 1864, though not without vigorous opposition. In the House, the debate began on March 19, 1864, and was not ended until June fifteenth.

During this debate it is probable that no one in the House of Representatives stood closer to Lincoln than Honorable Isaac N. Arnold, of Illinois. His address before the House contained the following impassioned appeal:

Our aim is national unity without slavery. Not "the Union as it was, and the Constitution as it is," but a nation without slavery, the Constitution the Magna Charta which shall secure liberty to all. . . . The wandering stars must be brought back with their lustre brightened by the ordeal through which they have passed. . . . We can have no national harmony and union without freedom. The fearful error of uniting free and slave states, we shall never repeat. But if the grand idea can be realized of a free, homogeneous people, united in a great continental republic based on liberty for all, and retaining the great principles of Magna Charta, we shall see realized the noblest structure of government and national polity ever organized on earth. . . .

The Thirty-seventh Congress will live in history as the Congress which prohibited slavery in all the territories of the Union, and abolished it at the national capital. The President of the United States will be remembered as the author of the proclamation of emancipation, as the liberator of a race, the apostle of freedom, the great emancipator of his country. The Thirty-eighth Congress, if we pass this joint resolution, will live in history as that which consummated the great work of freeing a continent from the curse of human bondage. Never, since the day when John Adams plead for the Declaration of Independence, has so important a question been submitted to an American Congress, as that upon which you are now about to vote. The signing of the immortal Declaration is a familiar picture in every log cabin and home all over the land. Pass this resolution, and the vote which knocks off the fetters of a whole race, will make this scene immortal. Live a century, nay a thousand years, and no such opportunity to do a great deed for humanity, for liberty, for peace and for your country, will ever again present itself. Pass this joint resolution, and you will win a victory over wrong and injustice, lasting as eternity. The whole world will rise up to do you honor.

When the vote was reached on June 15, 1864, it stood ninety-three in favor and sixty-five opposed. This was less than two-thirds vote.

Lincoln was disappointed and much chagrined. He had held repeated conferences with the friends of the measure, and had himself dictated a form of test vote which he thought would pretty certainly indicate a final alignment. His test resolution passed the House by a substantial majority, but lacked the necessary two-thirds. Lincoln, therefore, was prepared for this defeat, but nevertheless, was saddened by it.

When the Republican Convention convened in Baltimore in June, 1864, Lincoln himself wrote the third article of the platform, and gave it to Senator Morgan, of New York, Chairman of the National Committee, with instructions to make it the keynote of the convention. That article read:

Resolved, That as slavery was the cause, and now constitutes the strength, of this rebellion, and as it must be, always and everywhere, hostile to the principles of republican government, justice and the national safety demand its utter and complete extirpation from the soil of the republic; and that while we uphold and maintain the acts and proclamations by which the government, in its own defense has aimed a death-blow at this gigantic evil, we are in favor, furthermore, of such an amendment to the Constitution, to be made by the people in conformity with its provisions, as shall terminate and forever prohibit the existence of slavery within the limits of the jurisdiction of the United States.

When Congress convened in 1864, after Lincoln's election, Lincoln reminded that body that the national vote by which he had been reelected had virtually reversed their action of the preceding year in refusing to submit to the states a constitutional amendment abolishing slavery. The Congress to whom he delivered this message was the same that had refused the necessary two-thirds vote in favor of the amendment. New members had been elected, but they would not take their seats until March 4, 1865.

Very courteously and tactfully he proposed to this session of Congress that it should not wait to have its action reversed by the new Congress which had already been elected. He said:

Although the present is the same Congress and nearly the same members, and without questioning the wisdom or patriotism of those who stood in opposition, I venture to recommend the reconstruction and passage of the measure at the present session. Of course the abstract question is not changed, but an intervening election shows, almost certainly, that the next Congress will pass the measure if this does not. Hence there is only a question of time as to when the proposed amendment will go to the States for their action. And as it is to so go, at all events, may we not agree that the sooner the better? It is not claimed that the election has imposed a duty on members to change their views or their votes any further than as an additional element to be considered, their judgment may be affected by it. It is the voice of the people now for the first time heard upon the question. In a great national crisis like ours, unanimity of action among those seeking a common end is very desirable—almost indispensable.

Under these conditions it would seem that the passage of the amendment must have been a foregone conclusion. The Senate, which already had acted favorably upon it, repeated its favorable action, but no one knew how the House would stand. Opposition there was very strong. The most notable speech upon the subject was delivered by Thaddeus Stevens. He was chairman of the Committee of Ways and Means, and the recognized leader of the House. He was aged and infirm. He seemed hardly equal to the making of a speech, but every one knew that if he spoke his words would be notable. As he clumped down the aisle to begin his address, his club-foot seemed to waken reverberations that went through the Capitol. Senators rushed in, and judges from the Supreme Court left the bench, and every available inch of space in the House was occupied as Stevens spoke. He said:

When, fifteen years ago, I was honored with a seat in this body, it was dangerous to talk against this institution, a danger which gentlemen now here will never be able to appreciate. Some of us, however, have experienced it; my friend from Illinois on my right [Mr. Washburne] has. And yet, sir, I did not hesitate, in the midst of bowie knives and revolvers, and howling demons upon the other side of the House, to stand here and denounce this infamous institution in language which possibly now, on looking at it, I might deem intemperate, but which I then deemed necessary to rouse the public attention, and cast odium upon the worst institution upon earth, one which is a disgrace to man, and would be an annoyance to the infernal spirits. . . .

Perhaps I ought not to occupy so much time, and I will only

say one word further.   So far as the appeals of the learned
gentleman [Mr. Pendleton] are concerned, his pathetic winding
up, I will be willing to take my chance when we all molder in
the dust.   He may have his epitaph written, if it be truly written,
"Here rests the ablest and most pertinacious defender of slavery
and opponent of liberty," and I will be satisfied if my epitaph
shall be written thus: "Here lies one who never rose to any emi-
nence, and who only courted the low ambition to have it said that
he had striven to ameliorate the condition of the poor, the lowly,
the downtrodden of every race and language and color."

   I shall be content, with such an eulogy on his lofty tomb, and
such an inscription on my humble grave, to trust our memories
to the judgment of other ages.

   We have suffered for slavery more than all the plagues of
Egypt.   More than the first born of every household has been
taken.   We still harden our hearts, and refuse to let the people
go.   The scourge still continues, nor do I expect it to cease
until we obey the behests of the Father of men.   We are about
to ascertain the national will by an amendment to the Constitution.   If the gentlemen opposite will yield to the voice of God
and humanity and vote for it, I verily believe the sword of the
destroying angel will be stayed, and this people be re-united.   If
we still harden our hearts, and blood must still flow, may the
ghosts of the slaughtered victims sit heavily upon the souls of
those who cause it.

   Although the Republicans had a substantial majority, and
every Republican vote was certain to be favorable to the passage of the amendment, it was necessary that there should be
some Democratic votes if the amendment passed the House.
There were no test votes.   The only roll-call which indicated the
probable success or failure of the amendment was that on the
main issue.   Schuyler Colfax was in the chair, and the House
and its assembed audience waited breathlessly for his reading of
the result of the vote.   It stood, ayes 119, noes 56.   The constitutional majority of two-thirds had voted in the affirmative, the
joint resolution had passed.

   The language of the Thirteenth Amendment was substantially
that of the Ordinance of 1787, under which slavery, or involun-

tary servitude, except for punishment of crime, was foreve
prohibited from the Northwest Territory out of which had been
carved the five states of Ohio, Indiana, Illinois, Michigan and
Wisconsin.

The Constitution may be amended only by a two-thirds vote
of both Houses of Congress, and a confirming vote of three
fourths of the states. Some of the states were certain to vote
against the amendment. Could a three-fourths vote of the states
be counted on? A new state had been admitted to the Union in
1863. Forty-eight of the western counties of Virginia, lying
principally west of the Alleghenies, contained a population overwhelmingly loyal. In the summer of 1861 these counties had
taken measures to form themselves into a separate state, and in
April, 1862, they adopted a state constitution.

Lincoln had not been enthusiastic over the admission of West
Virginia as a state. He did not feel sure that it was consistent
on the part of the government to be waging a war to disprove
the right of a state to secede from the nation, and at the same
time approve of the secession of a part of a state from the state
itself. Senator Browning, who took to Lincoln on December
15, 1862, the bill for the admission of West Virginia, recorded
in his Diary that Lincoln was "much distressed." Before deciding whether to approve or veto the bill, Lincoln presented
to his Cabinet a request that each member submit a written
opinion in answer to two questions: 1. Is the Act constitutional? 2. Is it expedient? There were at that time only six
members of the Cabinet, Caleb B. Smith having retired to a
judgeship in Indiana, and a new secretary of the interior not
having been appointed. Of the six remaining members, Seward,
Chase and Stanton answered both questions in the affirmative,
and the other three in the negative. Lincoln after mature consideration, said:

We can scarcely dispense with the aid of West Virginia in
this struggle; much less can we afford to have her against us in

Congress and in the field. Her brave and good men regard her
admission into the Union as a matter of life and death. They
have been true to the Union under very severe trials. We have
so acted as to justify their hopes, and we cannot fully retain
their confidence and cooperation if we seem to break faith with
them.

He signed the bill that made West Virginia a state. It was
another war measure. When the vote of states came on the
Thirteenth Amendment, Lincoln was glad enough of West Virginia and would have welcomed another state like her.

A careful count of the states showed that it was still somewhat
more than doubtful whether the amendment would be confirmed
by the necessary three-fourths. One more state was needed. In
October, 1864, the territory of Nevada was admitted as a state.
Nevada had an exceedingly small population, and was not entitled to become a state, either by the number of its inhabitants
or the prospects of its growth. Small as its population was,
that population diminished rather than increased. The admission of Nevada, however, was deemed a political necessity. If
the war should end leaving the Emancipation Proclamation
hanging like Mahomet's coffin between earth and heaven, a
situation of chaos was certain to ensue. Lincoln himself favored
all necessary elasticity of construction of constitutional prerogatives in order to secure the admission of Nevada.* Nevada was
admitted, and dutifully ratified the amendment. Lincoln said it
was better to admit Nevada than to have to raise another million
men.

The states made haste in their votes of ratification. On November 18, 1865, William H. Seward, Secretary of State, certified that the requisite three-fourths vote of ratification had been
duly certified and the Thirteenth Amendment had become a

---

*Charles A. Dana's *Reminiscences* tell in detail the lengths to which Lincoln went to secure the admission of this state.

part of the Constitution, abolishing slavery forever wherever the flag of the United States shall float.*

During the latter part of the war, Lincoln was much concerned with the question how to restore the seceded states to the Union. His attitude toward the secessionists, both as individuals and states, was distinctly conciliatory. Had Lincoln lived he would certainly have come into collision with those leaders of his own party who favored retributive measures.

But upon what basis were the seceded states to be restored to their place in the family of the Union? The war had been fought upon the theory that this nation was one, and the Union indissoluble. But was a state that had passed an ordinance of secession to be readmitted merely by conquest? Must there not be some overt act on the part of the state itself, rescinding its ordinance of secession, and indicating its desire to be considered a state belonging to the Federal Union?

Lincoln felt the constitutional difficulties of this problem, but he was deeply interested in the practical result of getting these states back into normal relations with their sister states and with the Federal Government. His practical solution of the problem is set forth in the following words:

We all agree, that the seceded States, so called, are out of their proper practical relation with the Union, and that the sole

---

*A few other states subsequently added their vote of ratification. On August 22, 1866, Secretary Seward furnished the following list of the states which up to that time had ratified the Amendment, together with the dates of their ratifying vote:

Illinois, February 1st, 1865; Rhode Island, February 2nd, 1865; Michigan, February 2d, 1865; Maryland, February 1st and 3d, 1865; New York February 2d and 3d, 1865; West Virginia, February 3d, 1865; Maine, February 7th, 1865; Kansas, February 7th, 1865; Massachusetts, February 8th 1865; Pennsylvania, February 8th, 1865; Virginia, February 9th, 1865; Ohio February 10th, 1865; Missouri, February 10th, 1865; Nevada, February 16th 1865; Indiana, February 16th, 1865; Louisiana, February 17th, 1865; Minnesota, February 8th and 23d, 1865; Wisconsin, March 1st, 1865; Vermont March 9th, 1865; Tennessee, April 5th and 7th, 1865; Arkansas, April 20th 1865; Connecticut, May 5th, 1865; New Hampshire, July 1st, 1865; South Carolina, November 13th, 1865; Alabama, December 2d, 1865; North Carolina, December 4th, 1865; Georgia, December 9th, 1865; Oregon, December 11th, 1865; California, December 20th, 1865; Florida, December 28th, 1865 New Jersey, January 23d, 1866; Iowa, January 24th, 1866.

object of the government, civil and military, in regard to those States is to again get them into the proper practical relation. I believe that it is not only possible, but in fact easier, to do this without deciding or even considering whether these States have ever been out of the Union, than with it. Finding themselves safely at home, it would be utterly immaterial whether they had ever been abroad. Let us all join in doing the acts necessary to restoring the proper practical relations between these States and the Union, and each forever after innocently indulge his own opinion whether in doing the acts he brought the States from without into the Union, or only gave them proper assistance, they never having been out of it.

CHAPTER XXIII

THE last hope of the Confederates received a severe shock when Lincoln was reelected. The party which had declared the war a failure, and the candidate whose whole military career had been a disappointment to his friends, went down to overwhelming defeat. Still the struggle was not ended without some futile attempt at peace without victory.

Alexander H. Stephens, Vice President of the Confederacy, had been a Whig, and had known Lincoln during Lincoln's one term in Congress, 1847-1848. He had long desired a personal interview with Lincoln. In June, 1863, when Lee was beginning his invasion of the North, Mr. Stephens set forth from Richmond for Fortress Monroe, and notified the admiral in Hampton Roads that he was the bearer of a communication in writing from Jefferson Davis, and asked leave to proceed to Washington for a personal conference with President Lincoln. The request was received at the very time when Lee was meeting his crushing defeat at Gettysburg. Lincoln declined the request, and Stephens did not proceed to Washington.

These measures and others fostered by Fernando Wood or by Horace Greeley, Lincoln had met successively at intervals during the war.

Near the end of December, 1864, Lincoln permitted Francis P. Blair, Sr., to go through the lines into the Confederacy. Blair was permitted to see Jefferson Davis, who expressed an earnest desire for peace "between the two countries." The result of this negotiation was that President Davis appointed three commissioners with authority to proceed to General Grant's headquarters to confer with Secretary Seward in regard to peace. Lincoln gave to Seward these three conditions upon which alone the United States Government would consider a cessation of hostilities.

1. The restoration of the national authority throughout all the States.

2. No receding by the executive of the United States on the slavery question from the position assumed thereon in the late annual message to Congress, and in preceding documents.

3. No cessation of hostilities short of an end of the war and the disbanding of all forces hostile to the government.

Seward departed for Grant's headquarters on January 21, 1865, and on the following day Mr. Lincoln himself left Washington to participate in the conference. Apparently he felt that in a matter of such moment no one but himself could speak for the administration.

The meeting between Lincoln and Seward on the one hand, and the three Confederate envoys on the other, was conducted on board the United States steamer *River Queen,* lying off Hampton Roads. The following account of the interview appeared in a Georgia paper, and is said to have emanated from the pen of Alexander H. Stephens. It preserves a characteristic anecdote of Lincoln and one which we can not afford to lose:

The three Southern gentlemen met Mr. Lincoln and Mr. Seward, and after some preliminary remarks, the subject of peace was opened. Mr. Stephens, well aware that one who asks much may get more than he who confesses to humble wishes at the outset, urged the claims of his section with that skill and address for which the Northern papers have given him credit. Mr. Lincoln, holding the vantage ground of conscious power, was, however, perfectly frank, and submitted his views almost in the form of an argument. . . . Davis had, on this occasion, as on that of Mr. Stephens's visit to Washington, made it a condition that no conference should be had, unless his rank as Commander or President should first be recognized. Mr. Lincoln declared that the only ground on which he could rest the justice of war—either with his own people, or with foreign powers—was that it was not a war for conquest, for that the states had never been separated from the Union. Consequently, he could not recognize another government inside of the one of which he alone was President; nor admit the separate independence of states that were yet a part of the Union. "That," said he, "would be doing what you have so long asked Europe to do in vain, and be resigning the only thing the armies of the Union have been fighting for."

Mr. Hunter made a long reply to this, insisting that the recognition of Davis's power to make a treaty was the first and indispensable step to peace, and referred to the correspondence between King Charles I. and his Parliament, as a trustworthy precedent of a constitutional ruler treating with rebels. Mr. Lincoln's face then wore that indescribable expression which generally preceded his hardest hits, and he remarked: "Upon questions of history I must refer you to Mr. Seward, for he is posted in such things, and I don't pretend to be right. My only distinct recollection of the matter is that Charles lost his head." That settled Mr. Hunter for a while.

Lincoln also gave an account of this conference, or at least of a story which he was reported to have told on that occasion. This is recorded by Henry J. Raymond, who asked Mr. Lincoln concerning the truth of the report. "Why, yes," replied Mr. Lincoln, manifesting some surprise, "but has it leaked out? I was in hopes nothing would be said about it, lest some over-sensitive people should imagine there was a degree of levity in the intercourse between us." He then went on to relate the circumstances which called it out.

"You see," said he, "we had reached and were discussing the slavery question. Mr. Hunter said, substantially, that the slaves, always accustomed to an overseer, and to work upon compulsion, suddenly freed, as they would be if the South should consent to peace on the basis of the 'Emancipation Proclamation,' would precipitate not only themselves, but the entire southern society,

ON BOARD THE RIVER QUEEN

Sherman describing his march to the sea to President Lincoln, General Grant and Admiral Porter

Painting by G. P. A. Healy

into irremediable ruin. No work would be done, nothing would be cultivated, and both blacks and whites would starve!"

Said the president: "I waited for Seward to answer that argument, but as he was silent, I at length said: 'Mr. Hunter, you ought to know a great deal better about this argument than I, for you have always lived under the slave system. I can only say, in reply to your statement of the case, that it reminds me of a man out in Illinois, by the name of Case, who undertook, a few years ago, to raise a very large herd of hogs. It was a great trouble to feed them, and how to get around this was a puzzle to him. At length he hit on the plan of planting an immense field of potatoes, and, when they were sufficiently grown, he turned the whole herd into the field, and let them have full swing, thus saving not only the labor of feeding the hogs, but also that of digging the potatoes. Charmed with his sagacity, he stood one day leaning against the fence, counting his hogs, when a neighbor came along. " ' "Well, well," said he, "Mr. Case, this is all very fine. Your hogs are doing very well just now, but you know out here in Illinois the frost comes early, and the ground freezes for a foot deep. Then what you going to do?"

" 'This was a view of the matter which Mr. Case had not taken into account. Butchering time for hogs was 'way on in December or January! He scratched his head, and at length stammered: "Well, it may come pretty hard on their snouts, but I don't see but that it will be root, hog, or die." ' "

It was this story which made the phrase "Root, hog, or die" so widely current at the close of the Civil War.

The Hampton Roads Conference failed entirely in its attempt to establish peace by any other means than a complete surrender of the Confederate Army, and the overthrow of the rebellion. It probably had its value in convincing the Confederate leaders that no compromise at that time was possible. Sherman had captured Savannah, and presented it to the Nation as a Christmas gift. Lincoln, who had never been quite sure of Sherman's wisdom of his march to the sea, acknowledged Sherman's success in a characteristic letter, and the armies settled down to their final struggle.   The letter of Lincoln is as follows:

Executive Mansion,
Washington, December 26, 1864.

My Dear General Sherman:

Many, many thanks for your Christmas gift, the capture of Savannah.

When you were about leaving Atlanta for the Atlantic coast, I was anxious, if not fearful; but feeling that you were the better judge, and remembering that "nothing risked, nothing gained," I did not interfere.   Now, the undertaking being a success, the honor is all yours; for I believe none of us went further than to acquiesce.

And taking the work of General Thomas into the count, as it should be taken, it is indeed a great success.   Not only does it afford the obvious and military advantages; but in showing to the world that your army could be divided, putting the stronger part to an important new service, and yet leaving enough to vanquish the old opposing force of the whole,—Hood's army,—it brings those who sat in darkness to see a great light.   But what next?

I suppose it will be safe if I leave General Grant and yourself to decide.

Please make my grateful acknowledgments to your whole army —officers and men.

Yours very truly,

A. Lincoln.

As the spring of 1865 opened, Lincoln left the White House for a little time, and for about ten days he and Mrs. Lincoln lived on the steamer *River Queen* at City Point near the head-quarters of General Grant. There General Sherman came from his headquarters at Goldsboro, North Carolina, and Lincoln conferred with the two generals as to the fighting that still needed to be done.   Lincoln desired that the end might come as speedily as possible, but with as little bloodshed as could possibly be.

On March thirty-first Grant began his forward movement. Lincoln remained at City Point and eagerly heard the news.   On

April first, Sheridan won a brilliant victory at Five Forks. On
April second, Petersburg and Richmond were evacuated by the
Confederates. On April fourth, Lincoln started up the river and
visited Richmond, where he spent two days. There he received
an ovation from the liberated slaves, and when he returned to
City Point he was cheered by a crowd of Confederate prisoners.
This gratified Lincoln even more than the rejoicing of the freed-
men. It assured him that those men would never again take up
arms against the national government.

Lincoln returned to Washington soon after his visit to Richmond. Almost immediately after reaching the city the good news
came for which so long he had waited. Lee sent a flag of truce
to Grant, asking for a suspension of hostilities pending a conference with reference to the surrender of Lee's army. The conference was held at Appomattox, Virginia, on Palm Sunday morning, April 9, 1865. The generous terms offered by General
Grant were promptly accepted; the army of General Lee was
surrendered; his soldiers were permitted to retain their horses
for use in the tilling of their farms, and the Civil War was virtually at an end.

CHAPTER XXIV

THE DEATH OF LINCOLN

THE surrender of General Lee led to immediate measures looking to the end of the war. The Confederacy still existed as a government upon paper, but its principal army had been captured, its president was a fugitive, and its capital was in the hands of the Union Army. There still were scattered military organizations in arms against the Federal Government, but they were feeble, ineffective and disheartened. It would require some weeks officially to terminate the rebellion, but practically the Confederacy went down with the evacuation of Richmond and the surrender of Lee's army. The draft was suspended. Edwin M. Stanton, his profanity to the contrary notwithstanding, was a religious man, and caused the new dome of the capitol to be surrounded by a transparency bearing these words:

> "THIS IS THE LORD'S DOING,
> AND IT IS MARVELOUS
> IN OUR EYES"

Friday was the regular day for the Cabinet meeting. General Grant had come to Washington and was invited to be present. Apparently not much business was done. There was general rejoicing over the end of the war, and a consideration of what would follow by way of reconstruction.

Gideon Welles recorded concerning this meeting, that the president warned his Cabinet that he would not participate in any vindictive measures against the South.

He hoped there would be no persecution, no bloody work, after the war was over. None need expect he would take any

338

part in hanging or killing these men, even the worst of them. "Frighten them out of the country, let down the bars, scare them off," said he, throwing up his hands as if scaring sheep. "Enough lives have been sacrificed. We must extinguish our resentment if we expect harmony and union." There was too much desire on the part of our very good friends to be masters, to interfere with and dictate to those states, to treat the people not as fellow-citizens; there was too little respect for their right. He didn't sympathize in those feelings.

Secretary Stanton recalling this Cabinet meeting in the light of the sad events of that night, recorded on Saturday:

He was more cheerful and happy than I had ever seen him, rejoiced at the near prospect of firm and durable peace at home and abroad; manifested in a marked degree the kindness and humanity of his disposition and the tender forgiving spirit that so eminently distinguished him.

President Lincoln was a close observer of his own dreams. He was subject to them, and could not let them go without wondering what they might portend. At this last Cabinet meeting he told of a dream he had the night before, and one which he was confident portended some important event, the nature of which he did not attempt to conjecture. Secretary Welles thus recalls the president's recital of his dream:

He said it was in my department, it related to the water, that he seemed to be in a singular and indescribable vessel, but always the same, and that he was moving with great rapidity toward a dark and indefinite shore; that he had had this singular dream preceding the firing on Sumter, the battles of Bull Run, Antietam, Gettysburg, Stone River, Vicksburg, Wilmington, etc. . . . Victory did not always follow his dream, but the event and results were important. He had no doubt that a battle had taken place, or was about being fought, "and Johnston will be beaten, for I had this strange dream again last night. It must relate to Sherman; my thoughts are in that direction, and *I know of no other very important event which is likely just now to occur.*"

Through all the years of his life in the White House Lincoln had been in receipt of letters threatening his assassination. He did not pay much attention to these. He was a brave man. He had abiding faith that he had been called to do a great work, and he believed that he would live to finish it. He had no great faith that any precaution of his would avert whatever destiny was in store for him. Moreover, he had in him a strain of innate superstition. Herndon is unquestionably right in saying that his tendency to fatalism was intensified by the Baptist preaching which he heard in his boyhood and youth. The backwoods Baptists of that day believed in predestination of a most intense and effective sort.

Lincoln had moved steadily forward through abundant and repeated warnings of assassination with as little apparent concern as Admiral Farragut had shown when his flagship, the *Hartford*, was steaming ahead through the torpedoes of Mobile Bay. Apparently it did not occur to him that the dream which conveyed some premonition of an impending event was a portent of personal evil to himself.

On the afternoon of that Friday Lincoln said good-by to Schuyler Colfax who was going west, and spent a little time with a cheerful group of friends, among them Richard Oglesby, of Illinois. He had so merry a time with them it was difficult for Mrs. Lincoln to get him away from them to dinner.

After dinner, George Ashmun, of Massachusetts, who had presided over the convention that nominated Lincoln in 1860, called, and Mr. Lincoln made an appointment to meet him with a friend on the following morning. The last bit of writing which Lincoln ever did was a card* bearing these words:

> April 14, 1865.
> Allow Mr. Ashmun
> & friend to come in
> at 9—A. M. tomor-
> row—
>   A. Lincoln

---

*The friend of Mr. Ashmun referred to on this card was Judge C. P. Daley, of New York.

Mrs. Lincoln had been disappointed in her effort to lionize General Grant on the occasion of his visit to the White House when he became commander-in-chief of the army. She arranged a theater party for that evening at which the general and his wife were to be her guests. Laura Keene was playing *Our American Cousin* at Ford's Theater. The manager of the theater did not fail to make it known in the afternoon papers that "the president and his lady" and "the hero of Appomattox" would attend the theater that night. The president's box was draped with flags. General and Mrs. Grant decided to leave for Burlington, New Jersey, that night. Mrs. Lincoln invited Major H. R. Rathbone and his financée, the daughter of Senator Ira Harris, to take the place of General and Mrs. Grant.

The president and his party reached the theater about nine o'clock. The president and his wife were greeted with applause as they entered their box from the rear, and took the places assigned. The interruption was brief, and the play proceeded.

The president sat down in a rocking chair which had been provided for him, and watched with interest the scene upon the boards. It was broad comedy, and Mr. Lincoln enjoyed it, all unconscious of the tragedy which soon was to supersede it.

That tragedy was not long delayed. John Wilkes Booth, the assassin, who knew the theater well, and had made his plans carefully, entered the box quietly and fired the fatal shot from a Derringer pistol. The audience at first did not realize that the pistol-shot was not a part of the performance. Major Rathbone was the first to understand what had occurred. He grappled with the assassin, who had already drawn a dagger, and who viciously stabbed the young officer. The blow was aimed at his heart but was warded off and received in the arm.

"*Sic Semper Tyrannis!*" exclaimed Booth.

Booth then vaulted from the box to the stage. An American flag, draped below the box, caught his spur and flung the murderer to the stage with a broken leg. Thus did the nation's flag become the mute avenger of its country's chief.

Booth rose to his feet and moved quickly to the stage exit. Although his leg was broken, he escaped to the alley behind the theater, where a horse awaited him, and he hurriedly left the city.

As soon as the spectators realized what had occurred, there was a rush of people to the box. Among them was Laura Keene, the actress, and others crowded in, bewildered. A surgeon was helped over the balustrade and into the box. The president was borne from the theater at first with no plan where to take him. Nearly opposite the theater was a lodging-house, occupied by the family of William Peterson. A young man named Clark who roomed there was standing upon the steps when men appeared in the street bearing the president. Into this young man's room on the ground floor and toward the rear of the house, they bore the unconscious form and laid it upon the bed. Eminent surgeons were summoned, and the members of the Cabinet were called. A night of unspeakable agony followed. The president never regained consciousness.

For a time Washington was in terror. It was not known at once how many of the officers of the government might have been stricken. It seemed as though conspiracy stalked everywhere, and murder lurked in every doorway. Those who lived in Washington can never forget the horror of the night when Lincoln was killed.

The same night of Lincoln's assassination an attempt was made to murder also the secretary of state, William H. Seward. He was almost fatally stabbed, and his son Frederick was very severely wounded.

General Grant had left the city for Burlington, New Jersey, a few hours before the time fixed for his assassination. Those who were to have assassinated the remaining members of the Cabinet either lost courage, or drank too heavily, or were prevented by other causes not known.

A defective door-bell on Stanton's house was probably the reason for his own escape from assassination on the same night.

There is good evidence that he was included in the general plan. At the hour fixed for the attack, an attempt was made to enter his house, but his door-bell was out of commission, and the supposed conspirator was frightened away by the approach of witnesses. Stanton was in his own home, in the back room playing with his children, when the attempt was made to enter his house. "The bell wire was broken a day or two before," he said, "and though we had endeavored to have it repaired, the bell hanger had put it off because of a pressure of orders."

Very soon after, a messenger arrived at Stanton's informing him that Secretary Seward and his son, the assistant secretary, had been stabbed. Stanton hastened thither, and saw the two men, both of whom seemed to be fatally wounded. While there, he learned that the president had been assassinated. He went at once to the headquarters of General C. C. Augur, which was next door to Seward's house, and left orders for him as military governor to hold his troops in readiness for any emergency. Then he and Secretary Welles hastened to the house where the dying president lay. The entire vicinity was filled with people who had gathered before the secretary arrived, but the crowd parted and made way for him.

All the remaining members of the Cabinet except Seward, were summoned, and all came. Andrew Johnson, Vice-President, was not there.*

---

*Doctor J. Franklin Jameson calls my attention to the fact that the *Washington Star* of Saturday, April 16, 1865, mentions the vice-president as being at the president's bedside at one time during the night after the assassination. Honorable James Tanner ("Corporal Tanner") who served as stenographer that night, in a letter to a friend, written on Sunday, the seventeenth, mentions Johnson as present. It is alleged that Mr. Johnson did, indeed, come in for a few minutes, but that his condition and conduct were such as to increase Mrs. Lincoln's grief, and that he withdrew, and was found in the morning in the condition which Stewart describes. This would harmonize all accounts. But it is not difficult to explain the account in the *Star* on the hypothesis that the reporter, himself on the outside of the house, and making up his report at second hand, heard or assumed, that Johnson was present with the Cabinet. Mr. Tanner subsequently came to believe, and still believes, that he was mistaken about Johnson's having been there. My own impression is that if he had actually been there, and especially if he had been there in a condition of intoxication, we should have more evidence on the subject. Out of twelve different contemporary pictures of the death of the

In that crisis it was Stanton who rose to the emergency. For the next few hours he was virtually president. He called his assistant, Charles A. Dana, who was a stenographer. He dictated orders and a brief account of the assassination, which is still, in some respects, the very best record we have of that event. That record reads thus:

This evening at 9:30 o'clock at Ford's Theater, the President, while sitting in his private box with Mrs. Lincoln, and Major Rathbone, was shot by an assassin who entered the box and approached behind the President. The person then leaped upon the stage, brandishing a large dagger or knife, and made his escape in the rear of the theater.

The pistol ball entered the back of the President's head, and penetrated nearly through it. The wound is mortal. The President has been insensible ever since it was inflicted, and is now dying.

About the same hour, an assassin, whether the same or not, entered Mr. Seward's apartment, and, under a pretense of having a prescription, was shown to the Secretary's sick chamber. The assassin immediately rushed to the bed and inflicted two or three stabs on the throat and two on the face. It is hoped that the wounds may not prove fatal. My apprehension is that they will prove fatal.

The nurse alarmed Mr. Frederick Seward, who, from an adjoining room, hastened to the door of his father's where he met the assassin, who inflicted upon him one or more dangerous wounds. The recovery of Frederick Seward is doubtful. It is not probable that the President will live through the night.

General Grant and his wife were advertised to be at the theater this evening, but he started to Burlington at 6 o'clock.

This evening at a cabinet meeting, at which General Grant was present, the subject of the state of the country and the prospect of a speedy peace was discussed. The President was very cheerful and hopeful, and spoke very kindly of General Lee and others of the Confederacy and of the establishment of the government in Virginia. All the members of the cabinet, except Mr. Seward, are waiting upon the President.

---

president, three show the vice-president present. Corporal Tanner died while this book was in press.

THE STAGE OF FORD'S THEATER

From rare photograph made immediately after the tragedy, the flag torn by Booth's spur still hanging before the president's box

I have seen Mr. Seward, but he and Frederick were both unconscious.

Stanton sent a notice to the vice-president that the president could not live; whether Johnson was in condition to read and understand it, is a disputed question. There were those at the time who declared that he did not need the information,—that he was involved; this charge appears utterly unfounded. There were others who declared, and the charge is not so easily disposed of, that Johnson was sleeping off the effects of a carouse. As it was said that he was intoxicated when he took the oath of office as vice-president, so it is declared that he was in the same condition when called upon to assume the duties of the presidency. It was a night of wild rumor and vague surmise, and perhaps also, of foul slander. Unfortunately, the vice-president did not appear at the Peterson house that night, and is not known to have been seen by any reliable person who can assure the world that he was in condition to appreciate the solemnity of the hour. Stanton notified Chief Justice Chase that the president could not live, and directed him to be ready to administer the oath of office to the vice-president. From time to time during the night Stanton issued bulletins, apprising the public of the president's condition. At about one-thirty in the morning, Stanton wrote a formal notification of the death of the president, addressed Andrew Johnson, leaving blank the hour of the president's death. This was followed by a paper signed by Stanton, McCulloch, Dennison, Welles, Speed and Usher, informing the vice-president that if he would make known his pleasure, such arrangements as he desired would be made. These documents, prepared five or six hours before the president's death, were held in reserve until morning.

There was no discussion as to who should assume authority in that hour. Stanton assumed it by divine right, and no one challenged his prerogative.

The entire military and police force of the District of Columbia was called out. All members of the Union League were notified by their secret call—two short sharp raps, thrice repeated—and these men held themselves ready for duty.

To the Cabinet assembled in the Peterson house in the room adjacent to that in which the president was dying, the explanation of the events of that night appeared evident. The assassination was believed to be the signal for a new uprising of the Confederacy. The Confederate Government, though represented by a fugitive president and a scattered and fleeing Congress, was believed to have struck a desperate blow for life in a deliberate attempt to wipe out the entire leadership of the Union Government. This attack, it was believed, was to have been followed by a new uprising of the paroled Rebel Armies. How many murders the morning would show to have been committed, or in how many and how widely separated places, no one dared to predict. All awaited in terror the relevations of that fateful night.

Stanton sent for Chief Justice David K. Carter of the District of Columbia, who arrived at once and began in an adjoining room to take testimony concerning the tragedy. This required further stenographic assistance, which, fortunately, was secured next door in the person of James Tanner. At the outset it was not known who had committed the murder, but very soon evidence was secured from those who had been present at the theater, including some of the employees who knew Booth, which disclosed the name of the assassin.

Stanton issued orders for the arrest of Booth. He sent a telegram to General Grant at Philadelphia, informing him that the president had been shot, and directing him to return to Washington. He directed the Assistant Adjutant General, Thomas M. Vincent, to take charge of the Petersen house, guarding the door and limiting the admittance. He telegraped the chief of police in New York to send his best detectives. He gave directions to the president of the Baltimore & Ohio Railroad Company to intercept General Grant at Philadelphia, and bring him to the capital at once, preceding his special train by a pilot locomotive.

Mrs. Lincoln had followed the prostrate form of her husband when it was borne across the street from the theater to the Petersen house. She was in a frenzy of grief. General Vincent wrote concerning her:

I cannot recall a more pitiful picture than that of poor Mrs. Lincoln, almost insane with sudden agony, moaning and sobbing out that terrible night. Mr. Stanton attempted to soothe her, but he was full of business, and knew, moreover, that in a few hours at the most she must be a widow. She entered the room where her husband lay motionless but once before the surgeon announced that death was fast descending, and then fainted and was practically helpless.

When, about half past one in the morning, Stanton came out of the death chamber bearing in his hand the notification he had written of the death of Lincoln, and gave it to General Vincent with directions to have a fair copy made for presentation to the vice-president, Mrs. Lincoln, whose eyes that night followed Stanton's every move, sprang forward with a terrible scream, "Is he dead? Oh, is he dead?" Stanton informed her that the president still lived, and did his best to speak some reassuring words, but his manner told beyond any power of deception what he regarded as the inevitable end of their vigil. The poor grief-stricken woman moaned out her sorrow that was beyond all human comfort.

Lincoln had believed that some tragic end awaited him, but he appears to have had no apprehension of this on his last day. On the last Sunday of his life, as he was returning from City Point upon the steamer, he read from Shakespeare. Senator Charles Sumner records that as he read a particular passage from *Macbeth,* his attention was arrested, and he repeated these lines:

> Duncan is in his grave;
> After life's fitful fever he sleeps well;
> Treason has done his worst; nor steel, nor poison,
> Malice domestic, foreign levy, nothing,
> Can touch him further.

These lines seemed so significant that after his assassination those who knew of Lincoln's use of them could not refrain from adding as their own expression of their application to Lincoln and the tragedy of his death, these additional lines from the same play:

>   This Duncan
> Hath borne his faculties so meek, hath been
> So clear in his great office, that his virtues
> Will plead like angels trumpet-tongued against
> The deep damnation of his taking-off.

The room where the president lay was small* and the ceiling was low. The group about the president's bed changed from time to time during the night. The various pictures that were made of the death-bed scene show more people than were present at any one moment, but most of those whom the pictures portray were in the room at some time during the night. Mrs. Lincoln was the only woman present. She came at intervals, and was led away and sat in the adjoining room pouring out the agony of her grief in uncontrollable sorrow. Lincoln's pastor, Reverend Phineas D. Gurley, came and offered prayer, and remained to the end. There was little change in the president's condition during the night. As morning dawned, his heavy breathing grew more quiet and the pulse grew weaker. Bulletins announced the nearer approach of death. At twenty-two minutes past seven o'clock on Saturday morning, April 15, 1865, Abraham Lincoln died. Those present at the time of his death included Mrs. Lincoln, Secretaries Stanton, Welles and Usher, Senator Charles Sumner, Robert T. Lincoln, the Reverend Doctor Phineas D. Gurley, John Hay, the physicians and a few other friends. The moment came when the breathing ceased, and the surgeons could feel no pulse. The president was dead. The silence that followed was broken by the prayer of Doctor Gurley and the memorable words of Stanton: "NOW, HE BELONGS TO THE AGES."

---

*The room has been enlarged by the removal of a partition.

CHAPTER XXV

THE GOVERNMENT STILL LIVES

"GOD reigns, and the Government at Washington still lives." So said James A. Garfield, when the tragic news of the assassination of Lincoln reached the horrified nation. The fact that the government could live through a long civil war and the assassination of its president as the war was ending, may justly be regarded as one of the strongest tests of the stability of American institutions.

As soon as it was evident that the president was dead, the company that had watched over him through the long night dispersed, some to rest and others to continue their official duties through a day as laborious as the night had been. There was a sense of relief when the several commanding generals were heard from, and it was found that none of these had been assassinated; and the morning brought hope of recovery of the secretary and assistant secretary of state, which hope was ultimately fulfilled. Warning telegrams were sent to leading officers in the army, reminding them of the danger that they also might be assassinated, and the members of the Cabinet also took precautions.

No coroner's inquest was held over the body of Abraham Lincoln. No official inquiry was ever made by any civil court, concerning the occasion of his death or the person or persons responsible for it.

Andrew Johnson, the Vice-President, was sworn into office on Saturday, April 15, 1865, immediately following the death of the president. There was no ceremony. The time and circumstances admitted of nothing but stern and swift action. There was, however, strong hope among those less patient and kindly than Lincoln had been, that the new president would prove a Joshua succeeding the dead Moses, at a time when more stern leadership was demanded than Lincoln would have brought.

The time has not yet come for complete justice to be done to the memory of Andrew Johnson. He did not fulfill the expectations of his friends and he narrowly escaped removal from his high office on impeachment. His was a difficult position; how much he deserved of the reproach which he received, some future historian will declare.

Of Andrew Johnson's inaugural as vice-president and Lincoln's second inaugural, on the fourth of March preceding, Gideon Welles wrote in his diary:

The inauguration took place to-day. There was great want of arrangement and completeness in the ceremonies. All was confusion and without order—a jumble. The vice-president elect made a rambling and strange harangue, which was listened to with pain and mortification by all his friends. My impressions were that he was under the influence of stimulants, yet I know not that he drinks. He has been sick and is feeble; perhaps may have taken some medicine, or stimulants, or his brain from sickness may have been over-active in these new responsibilities. Whatever the cause, it was all in very bad taste.

The delivery of the inaugural address, the administration of the oath, and the whole deportment of the president, were well done, and the retiring vice-president appeared to advantage when contrasted with his successor, who has humiliated his friends. Speed, who sat on my left, whispered to me that "All this is in very bad taste," and very soon he said, "The man is certainly deranged." I said to Stanton, who sat on my right, "Johnson is either drunk or crazy." Stanton replied, "There is evidently something wrong." Seward says it was his emotion on returning and revisiting the Senate; that he can appreciate Johnson's feelings, who was much overcome. I hope Seward is right, but don't entirely concur with him. There is, as Stanton says, something wrong. I hope it is sickness.*

*Diary of Gideon Welles, vol. ii, pp. 241-2.

Secretary Welles was not among those present at Johnson's taking of the oath of office as president, and it is not certain just how much he saw of Johnson that day, or whether he saw him at all. He tells of a Cabinet meeting, held at noon, and of Johnson's being invited to be present, and of his deporting himself admirably. But he later changed this entry, and changed it twice, and it is not certain just what his final impression was of Johnson's deportment that day:

I arranged with Speed, with whom I rode home, for a Cabinet meeting at twelve, meridian, at the room of the Secretary of the Treasury, in order that the Government should experience no detriment, and that prompt and necessary action might be taken to assist the new Chief Magistrate in preserving and promoting the public tranquility. We accordingly met at noon. Mr. Speed reported that the President had taken the oath, which was administered by the Chief Justice, and had expressed a desire that the affairs of the Government should proceed without interruption. Some discussion took place as to the propriety of an inaugural address, but the general impression was that it would be inexpedient. I was most decidedly of that opinion. President Johnson, who was invited to be present, deported himself admirably, and on the subject of an inaugural said that his acts would best disclose his policy. In all essentials it would, he said, be the same as that of the late President.*

Gideon Welles remained in the Cabinet, and became a strong partisan of Johnson. After the inauguration of Grant, Welles wrote in his *Diary,* March 17, 1869:

I this evening parted with President Johnson and his family, who leave in the morning for Tennessee. No better persons have ever occupied the Executive Mansion, and I part with them, socially and personally, with sincere regret. Of measures he was a good judge, but not always of men.

Just what he would have said in 1869 about Johnson's inaugu-

Diary of Gideon Welles, vol. ii, p. 289.

ration either as vice-president or as president we may not know, but his diary was still in his own possession, and he left his record of the vice-presidential inaugural as it had previously stood, and what he finally intended to leave of record concerning Johnson's induction into the presidency must be judged from his hesitation and erasures.

The account of the inaugural of President Johnson given in his *Life,* by John Savage, says that the ceremony took place in the private parlor of the vice-president, in the Kirkwood, and names those present as Chief Justice Chase, Secretary McCulloch, Attorney General Speed, Francis P. Blair, Sr., Montgomery Blair, Senators Foot, of Vermont, Yates, of Illinois, Ramsey, of Minnesota, Stewart, of Nevada, Hale, of New Hampshire, and General Farnsworth, of Illinois, twelve persons, including President Johnson. Only two members of the Cabinet appear to have been present.

Apparently, therefore, Andrew Johnson, who had not been present at any time during the period between the assassination and death of Lincoln, was notified by two members of the Cabinet and the chief justice of the Supreme Court, and these and eight other men, including Senator Stewart were by the largest possible count the only ones present when the oath of office was administered. We have as yet no adequate and impartial Life of Andrew Johnson. The present author will not trench upon the ground which belongs to some future biographer by attempting to decide whether Andrew Johnson was drunk or sober on the occasion of either of his inaugurals.

While rumors which the country heard of Johnson's condition at the time of his inauguration brought sorrow and shame to many, there were others, and a far larger number, who felt that, with all his faults, Johnson was the safer man to have at the helm to deal with the rebellious South. Honorable George W. Julian says:

I spent most of the afternoon in a political caucus, held for the purpose of considering the necessity for a new Cabinet and a line

THE HOUSE WHERE LINCOLN DIED

of policy less conciliatory than that of Mr. Lincoln; and while everybody was shocked at his murder, the feeling was nearly universal that the accession of Johnson would prove a godsend to the country.*

By the murder of Lincoln, the South lost its best and most generous friend.

John Wilkes Booth was recognized by habitual theater-goers present at the assassination, and a pursuit was immediately instituted. He immediately fled from Washington, his broken leg giving him great pain and impeding his progress. He was compelled to stop and have his leg set, and then proceeded upon his hopeless attempt at escape.

He was surrounded in a barn where he had taken refuge, and resisting arrest was shot against orders by Boston Corbett, a fanatical member of the military detachment that pursued him.†

No doubt existed at the time and no reasonable doubt exists now, that the assassination of Lincoln was the result of a conspiracy. At the time it was believed that high officials of the Confederate Government, including Jefferson Davis, had guilty knowledge of the plot. This charge was not sustained by the evidence. A number of persons were arrested as those who were believed to have participated in the conspiracy. These were tried before a military commission composed of nine officers,‡ with Judge Joseph Holt as advocate general, Judge John A. Bingham, as special advocate general, Henry L. Burnett as special assistant, and General John F. Hartranft as provost marshal. The trial began in the old arsenal in Washington on May tenth, the day of the capture of Jefferson Davis, and continued until June thirtieth. Lewis Payne, D. C. Herold, George B. Atzerot and

---

*Political Recollections, p. 255.

†I am aware of the various accounts of Booth's alleged escape and his suicide many years after the war, and have seen and inspected the embalmed body that is alleged to have been his; but these stories are unfounded.

‡The Commission was composed of Generals David Hunter, Lew Wallace, August V. Kautz, A. P. Hour, R. S. Foster, J. A. Elkin, T. N. Harris, Colonels C. H. Thompkins and D. R. Clendenin.

Mrs. Mary E. Surratt were sentenced to be hanged. Edward
Spangler, Michael O'Laughlin, Doctor Samuel T. Mudd and
Samuel Arnold were imprisoned. All the prisoners except
O'Laughlin, who died in the military prison on the Dry Tortugas,
an island off the coast of Florida, were pardoned by Andrew
Johnson. The first to whom a pardon was issued was Doctor
Mudd, who was held to be an accessory after the fact, as he set
Booth's leg, and thereby assisted in his escape. Sympathy
for him seemed to be justified by his character and his professional sense of duty. The greatest interest, however, was in
the case of Mrs. Surratt. Her house in Washington had been a
meeting-place of the conspirators, and had long been a harbor for
enemies of the republic. Evidence was introduced to show that
she had actual knowledge of the plot to murder Lincoln. Strenuous effort was made on her behalf, but she was condemned to
die, and appeals addressed both to Stanton and to Johnson did
not avail to secure her release. She was hanged with Payne, Herold and Atzerot on Friday, July seventh.

Mrs. Surratt's son, John H. Surratt, escaped, made his way to
Rome, and under an assumed name joined the Papal Zouaves in
the town of Velletri, in Italy, forty miles from Rome. There
he was identified by another American serving in the same
company. The American consul was informed, and Surratt was
arrested, but escaped and made his way to Egypt. Again he was
arrested, and brought back to the United States. Unlike his ac-
complices, who were tried by a military commission, he was
indicted by the grand jury of the County of Washington, District
of Columbia, and tried before a civil court, charged with "the
murder of one Abraham Lincoln," and under other counts of
the indictment, with "conspiracy to murder Abraham Lincoln."
Surratt escaped punishment, and lived for many years in Baltimore. After he had been set at liberty, he delivered a lecture
at Rockville, Maryland, in which he stated that he had been
engaged in the secret service of the Confederate Government
almost constantly from the time he left college in the summer of

861, and was very active in it. He admitted his conspiracy with
Booth to capture President Lincoln and carry him to Richmond,
but claimed that he had no knowledge of Booth's plan to assassinate the president nor any share in the murder. Whether this
was true or not, there was rather general satisfaction in the fact
that he was not hanged as his mother had been. In one sense, he
secured freedom by his mother's execution. That both were
conspirators against the government there was no doubt.
Whether the mother and son participated in the plot for the
assassination is a question on which there is violent difference of
opinion.

CHAPTER XXVI

THE FUNERAL OF LINCOLN

ABRAHAM LINCOLN was shot not far from ten o'clock on Good Friday night, April 14, 1865. He died next morning at twenty-two minutes after seven. The morning papers in every American city announced the shooting, but the first editions were all issued before the president's death. By seven-thirty the editors in the larger cities knew that the president was dead, and by eight o'clock extra editions were on the streets informing the people that the end had come. In cities and villages more remote and towns that had no daily papers or no facilities for extra editions, the news spread more slowly.*

Lincoln died on the morning before Easter Sunday. Easter was not so universally celebrated then as now, but that was an unusual Easter. On Palm Sunday, Robert E. Lee had met

---

*In the little town in Illinois where I was born, my father was on a ladder before noon, nailing up black cotton cloth on the front of his little drug store, and my aunt was mildly protesting that he was using an extravagant quantity of muslin, and telling how much it cost a yard at that time of high prices, and I, not yet four years old, was handing him the hammer, and taking in with a child's understanding the significance of the event. My father was a job printer, as well as being physician, druggist, postmaster, notary public and superintendent of the Sunday-school. That afternoon he set up and printed a placard *OUR NATION MOURNS*. It was printed in red and blue, bordered with black, and was posted about town and displayed that night in a public meeting convened in the church. Father was somewhat disappointed that people who posted up his placard, freely given to the public, did not note that he had used the national color and black, necessitating three impressions. I think he had never attempted anything quite so ambitious in the way of color work before; but nothing was too good for that day. Indeed, nothing that he could do for others was ever too good. This is my one contemporary recollection of Abraham Lincoln; I remember the morning of his death, the mighty sorrow, the fierce indignation against a "copperhead" who was alleged to have said he was glad of it, the threats that were freely made and never executed against him, and the three-color printing.

Ulysses S. Grant at Appomattox, and Lee had surrendered his army. The end of the war had really come. Officially, it had to continue a little while longer, but that was the end, and the nation knew it. All over the country the ministers spent that week preparing Easter sermons unlike any that they had ever preached before. Most of those sermons were finished, or practically so, before Friday night.

On Saturday morning those sermons were worthless.

The ministers who had prepared them never preached them.

About eight o'clock on Saturday morning, the ministers who lived in the cities knew that they must prepare new sermons for the next morning. From that hour until noon, the ministers all over the country were receiving the same information. At least ten thousand new sermons must have been prepared that Saturday afternoon and night.

What kind of sermons were they?

A very considerable number of the sermons preached on Sunday morning, April 16, 1865, were requested for printing by the congregations to whom they were addressed, and were issued in pamphlet form. Not less than three hundred of those sermons and the sermons on the days immediately following have been discovered and duly listed in the Lincoln bibliographies.

Few people care to read these addresses, but they are of remarkable interest, and worthy of rather more than a casual examination.

All over the country, this, or something like this, occurred. The minister rose on Saturday morning with the comfortable feeling that he had only to add a few finishing touches to his Easter sermon, and it would be complete. Before he had eaten his breakfast a neighbor hastened in to tell that the president had been shot. The minister went forth to the telegraph office, or wherever the news came, and waited for the bulletins as they came over the wires, none of them bringing any hope. After the arrival of the news that the president was dead, there was a period of uncertainty, broken by the suggestion that a mass meet-

ing be called for that evening. Usually it was thought better
to omit the mass meeting, since the people would be coming together a few hours later on Sunday morning.

About noon the minister came home, tired, sorrowing, bewil
dered and tried to eat a little luncheon. After luncheon he said
to his wife, "My Easter sermon will not do. And what can I say
to-morrow? What theme can I select, what text can I choose
what words of wisdom or comfort can I find, for a time like
this?"

He felt helpless, and yet knew that the people would come to
hear him the next morning expecting from him some strong, true
helpful, uplifting word.

Ordinarily, the minister was not a great man, and did not
pretend to be one. He was just an ordinary preacher, as wise
and as good as the average, and no wiser and no better. Can we
imagine what went on in the thought of several thousand such
men as they entered their little studies on Saturday afternoon
and took down the Bible, and found that the letters blurred and
that wet spots appeared on the page? These were not statesmen
or theologians, for the most part, but just ordinary ministers of
Christ, suddenly confronted with a task too great for any man
How did they face that duty? Apparently, they faced it worthily
and in many instances notably so.

There are sermons preached in hospitals and at least one deliv
ered in a state prison, and there are sermons enough that are commonplace and mediocre that were preached in pulpits notable and
others obscure. But on the whole the sermons of that day were
good, strong, helpful discourses, and it is much to the credit o:
the congregations that heard them that so many of them were
printed. It is also much to the credit of the ministers of tha
day, most of them unknown, who threw aside their prepared
Easter discourses, and preached sermons that comforted and
helped their people in time of national calamity. A careful review
of these old discourses increases one's respect for the American
pulpit.

Henry Ward Beecher was not in his own pulpit on the Sunday immediately following Lincoln's assassination. He had gone south to deliver an oration at the raising of a flag over Fort Sumter. A week later he had returned. The closing words of his sermon on that day constitute one of the most eloquent of all perorations in the history of modern funeral oratory:

And now the martyr is moving in triumphal march, mightier than when alive. The nation rises up at every stage of his coming. Cities and towns are his pall-bearers, and the cannon beats the hours with solemn progression. Dead, DEAD, DEAD, he yet speaketh! Is Washington dead? Is Hampden dead? Is David dead? Is any man that was ever fit to live dead? Disenthralled of flesh, and risen in the unobstructed sphere where passion never comes, he begins his illimitable work. His life is now grafted upon the infinite, and will be fruitful as no earthly life can be. Pass on, thou that hast overcome! Your sorrows, oh people, are his peace! Your bells, and bands, and muffled drums, sound triumph in his ear. Wail and weep here; God makes it echo joy and triumph there. Pass on!

Four years ago, oh, Illinois, we took from your midst an untried man, and from among your people. We return him to you a mighty conqueror. Not thine any more, but the nation's; not ours, but the world's. Give him place, oh, ye prairies! In the midst of this great continent his dust shall rest, a sacred treasure to myriads who shall pilgrim to that shrine to kindle anew their zeal and patriotism. Ye winds that move over the mighty places of the West, chant his requiem! Ye people, behold a martyr whose blood, as so many articulate words, pleads for fidelity, for law, for liberty!

On Monday, April 17, 1865, a meeting of the members of Congress then present in Washington was held to arrange a suitable funeral for Abraham Lincoln. It was recalled that when the capitol was built, a vault had been prepared under it for the body of Washington; but the state of Virginia and the Washington family insisted upon his burial at Mount Vernon. Certain of members of Congress attending this meeting proposed that the body of Lincoln should be interred in this vault. The governor and senators of Illinois, however, insisted that Lincoln's body should be conveyed back to his own state.

It is affirmed, and generally believed, that it was Mrs. Lincoln who declared that the body of her husband must be returned to Springfield. This is an error. Mrs. Lincoln's first decision was emphatic, and was against a return of the body to Illinois, and especially to Springfield. Browning's *Diary* for April fifteenth and seventeenth is explicit on this point. Mrs. Lincoln had come to think of Springfield in terms of exasperating small-town gossip, and of the eagerness of its citizens to secure office. If the body went back to Illinois, it, she thought, should be buried in Chicago. The tomb of Stephen A. Douglas was there, in a public park named for him, and with an imposing statue above it. She did not like the proposal to hide her husband away in so inconspicuous a place as Springfield. Not until the morning of April twentieth did Mrs. Lincoln consent even to consider Springfield as a place of burial, and even then she refused the suggestion that she should return and make her home there.

In Springfield, a committee was organized to secure a suitable site for the tomb, and a contract was made to purchase the admirable site where now the state capitol stands. This property belonged to a family named Mather. Work was begun at once on a temporary vault, and such progress was made by the working of day-and-night shifts that the tomb was complete, save for the ornamental facing, in time for the funeral. But on the morning of the fourth of May, the very day of the interment, Mrs. Lincoln positively refused to permit her husband's body to rest for a single night in land that had been owned by the Mathers, and a change, regarded in Springfield as temporary, was made to the public receiving vault of Oak Ridge Cemetery, a comparatively new and beautiful burial-ground well out of the city. Six weeks later she wrote a letter to the committee "demanding that the remains should be buried on a lot at Oak Ridge Cemetery, that the monument should be erected thereon, and that the title to the same should be conveyed by deed to herself and her heirs." The *State Journal* of June sixteenth, states that:

After a full discussion of the question, and in the fear that, if Mrs. Lincoln's demands were not complied with, her threats to take the body back to Washington would be carried out, the Association finally, by a vote of eight to seven, resolved to accede to her terms.

The editor said that it was at least a satisfaction that the question which had caused so much discussion was now settled, and added consolingly, "We assure them [the people of Springfield] that Oak Ridge is a most beautiful spot."

One may read the records of these events with severe censure for a wilful woman who acted most disagreeably, or with profound compassion for a grief-stricken widow, mentally unbalanced, and facing the necessity of tragic decisions.

An official committee was appointed in Washington to conduct the remains of the president to Springfield. It consisted of one member of Congress from each state and territory of the Union, and the entire congressional delegation from Illinois.

By request of Mrs. Lincoln a second and smaller coffin accompanied that of the president. This contained the body of little Willie, who had died in the White House in the first few months of the family's occupancy of that home. His little body traveled with the body of his father, and the two were buried together. Subsequently, the body of little Eddie was deposited in the same vault with that of Willie. On the death of Tad, some years later, he also, was buried in the vault with his father. Last of all, after her death, July 16, 1882, Mrs. Lincoln was laid to rest beside her husband.

The funeral of Lincoln took place on Wednesday, April nineteenth. The services were held in the East Room of the White House. The Reverend Doctor Hall of the Church of the Epiphany read the burial service. Bishop Simpson of the Methodist Church offered prayer. Reverend Doctor P. D. Gurley, of whose church, the New York Avenue Presbyterian, Lincoln and his family had been regular attendants, delivered an impressive funeral address, characterized by dignity, courage, self-restraint

31

and comfort.   A single paragraph may be quoted from thi
address:

I speak what I know, and testify what I have often heard hin
say, when I affirm that the Divine goodness and mercy were th
props on which he leaned.   Never shall I forget the emphatic an
deep emotion with which he said, in this very room, to a com
pany of clergymen and others, who called to pay him their re
spects, in the darkest hours of our civil conflict: "Gentlemen, m
hope of success in this struggle rests on that immutable founda
tion, the justness and goodness of God; and when events are ver
threatening, I still hope, that in some way, all will be well in th
end, because our cause is just, and God will be on our side."   Sucl
was his sublime and holy faith, and it was an anchor to his sou
It made him firm and strong; it emboldened him in the pathwa
of duty, however rugged and perilous it might be; it made hir
valiant for the right, for the cause of God and humanity, and i
held him in steady patience to a policy of administration whic
he thought both God and humanity required him to adopt.

At two o'clock in the afternoon, amid the tolling of bells an
booming of cannon, the body of Lincoln was borne from th
White House to the rotunda of the capitol.   There it remaine
until the evening of the next day.   People passed by thousand
to look upon his face.

As soon as it was announced that Lincoln was to be buried i
Illinois, every city and town along the route pleaded that th
train might halt there and give to the people an opportunity o
manifesting their affection and reverence for Lincoln.   It wa
finally arranged that his body should return by a route essentiall
the same as that over which Lincoln had journeyed to Washing
ton in 1861.

At eight o'clock on Friday morning, April twenty-first, th
funeral train left Washington.   At Baltimore, where four year
previously, as was then believed, a plot existed for his assassina
tion, the train made a halt, the body was removed to the dome o
the exchange where it lay for several hours, viewed by larg
numbers of people.

That night, amid wind and rain, the train reached Harrisburg, and the body was borne through the muddy streets to the state capitol. On the following day, Saturday, the body lay in state until noon, whence it was carried again to the train, reaching Philadelphia that evening. All day Sunday the body of the president lay in state in Independence Hall. Here, on Washington's birthday in 1861, he had raised a flag above the belfry that first rang out the glad news of freedom, and said he would rather be assassinated on the spot than swerve from the principles embodied in the Declaration of Independence. At four o'clock in the morning of Monday, April twenty-fourth, the train left Philadelphia, arriving about ten o'clock in New York City. There it remained until late in the afternoon of Tuesday. Among those who came to visit it in the city hall, was General Scott, pale and feeble, who sorrowfully saluted his dead commander.

That night the train moved along the bank of the Hudson and about midnight arrived in Albany, where the body lay in the state capitol until the afternoon of the following day.

At Syracuse thirty thousand people came out at midnight in a storm, and at Rochester the same solemnities greeted the body of Lincoln as it passed through that city.

Buffalo was reached on the morning of Thursday the twenty-seventh, and Cleveland on Friday the twenty-eighth; and the train arrived in Columbus on the morning of Saturday the twenty-ninth. In Cleveland the exercises were held in the public square in an imposing tabernacle erected for the occasion.

The second Sunday was spent in Indianapolis, which city was left at midnight, and the body arrived in Chicago on Monday morning, May first.

The demonstrations in New York City had been most elaborate, but those in Chicago took on a far more personal character. In no city had there been lack of sincere sorrow and reverent affection. But in Chicago hundreds of people looked upon his face who had known him well in life. There the mourning lost its official character in the deep personal affection of those who had known and continued to love him.

At eight o'clock in the evening of Tuesday, May second, the train left Chicago, and on the following morning reached Springfield. All the preceding day the roads leading to that city had been bringing in loads of visitors. By the time the funeral train arrived it seemed as if there was hardly standing room for the population and those who had come to be present on that sad occasion. Among those who returned with his remains were three of the men who had gone out with him on his journey to Washington, Colonel Ward H. Lamon, Judge David Davis and Major-General David Hunter. Among his pall-bearers were old-time neighbors, including his sometime partner, Honorable Stephen T. Logan, and Honorable S. H. Treat, the judge in whose court he had so often appeared.

All that day and on the following morning the body of Lincoln lay in state in the old state-house. At ten o'clock, on Thursday, May fourth, the coffin was closed and conveyed to the hearse, and the funeral procession formed at the north gate of the court-house square, and moved to Oak Ridge Cemetery one and a half miles distant.

Prayer was offered by the Reverend Albert Hale, and the scripture was read by the Reverend N. W. Minor, local pastors. Then was read the greatest of all Lincoln's state papers, his second inaugural.

The funeral oration was delivered by Bishop Simpson of the Methodist Church, a worthy tribute to a great man.

The closing prayer was offered by the Reverend Doctor Gurley, Lincoln's pastor, and so closed that memorable day. Never in the history of America has there been another funeral like that.

As the body of Lincoln returned to the soil of his own state, Edna Dean Proctor, then a young woman, wrote a noble poem, a copy of which in her own handwriting hangs in the tomb of Lincoln, and from which a few lines may be quoted:

> Now must the storied Potomac
>   Honors forever divide;
> Now to the Sangamon fameless
>   Give of its century's pride;

THE LINCOLN FUNERAL CAR

Sangamon, stream of the prairies,
  Placidly westward that flows,
Far in whose city of silence
  Calm he has sought his repose.

Not for thy sheaves nor savannas
  Crown we thee, proud Illinois!
Here in his grave is thy grandeur,
  Born of his sorrow thy joy.
Only the tomb by Mount Zion
  Hewn for the Lord do we hold
Dearer than his in thy prairies,
  Girdled with harvests of gold.

No description can adequately convey the impression which Lincoln's homeward journey made upon the nation and the world. There was so much to remind one of his tour away from Springfield toward Washington. The two were so like, yet so sadly different. All attempts at description fail. Perhaps no writer has more truthfully caught the spirit of that journey than Walt Whitman. The lilacs were in bloom as the funeral train moved westward, and Whitman has forever associated their annual efflorescence with memories of the last journey of Abraham Lincoln:

When lilacs last in the door-yard bloom'd,
And the great star early drooped in the western sky in the night,
I mourned, and yet shall mourn with ever returning spring.
O ever-returning spring! trinity sure to me you bring;
Lilac blooming perennial, and drooping star in the west,
And thought of him I love.

Over the breast of the spring, the land amid cities,
Amid lanes, and through old woods (where lately the violets
    peeped from the ground, spotting the gray debris;)
Amid the grass in the fields each side of the lines—passing the
    endless grass;
Passing the yellow-speared wheat, every grain from its shroud in
    the dark-brown fields uprising;

Passing the apple-tree blows of white and pink in the orchards;
Carrying a corpse to where it shall rest in the grave,
Night and day journeys a coffin.

Coffin that passes through lanes and streets,
Through day and night, with the great cloud darkening the land,
With the pomp of the inlooped flags, with the cities draped in
      black,
With the show of the States themselves, as of crape-veiled
      women, standing,
With processions long and winding, and the flambeaus of the
      night,
With the countless torches lit—with the silent sea of faces, and
      the unbared heads,
With the waiting depot, the arriving coffin, and the somber faces,
With dirges through the night, with the thousand voices rising
      strong and solemn;
With all the mournful voices of the dirges, poured around the
      coffin,
The dim-lit churches and the shuddering organ—Where amid
      these you journey,
With the tolling, tolling bells' perpetual clang;
Here! coffin that slowly passes,
I give you my sprig of lilac!

CHAPTER XXVII

LINCOLN's sympathy with the common soldier grew out of his sympathy for the common people. He was sure that God loved the common people, because He made so many of them.

It is pertinent to ask, and the more so because so many have already attempted to answer the question, What was the attitude of Lincoln toward labor?

We may be sure it was an attitude of profound sympathy, held by a man who had been born to poverty; and who knew the story of labor as only those can know it who have eaten their bread in the sweat of their face.

A consideration of the attitude of Abraham Lincoln toward labor requires us to remember, first of all, that he lived and died before the present-day industrial system had come into existence. Several people who have wanted to quote him on labor have forgotten this, and have attributed to Lincoln statements which can not be found in his published works and which are the outgrowth of conditions which came into being after he was dead. For instance, a widely quoted statement concerning the threatened rise of great corporations is known to have originated with another man in 1873; but it is quoted as from the pen of Lincoln.

Another popular quotation is this:

I am glad that a system of labor prevails under which laborers can strike when they want to, where they are not obliged to work under all circumstances, and are not tied down to work whether you pay them for it or not. I like a system that lets a man quit

when he wants to, and wish it might prevail everywhere. I am
not ashamed to confess that twenty-five years ago I was a hired
laborer.

This quotation can not be called strictly accurate. It is a
garbled combination of two widely separated statements, each
of which is worthy of some study. ·

The last sentence is the more readily located. The statement
"Twenty-five years ago I was a hired laborer," was written, apparently, about a quarter-century after he ceased to work with
his hands for other men.

With this clue, we have not far to go. We find the document
on which this appears to be based. It is a fragment which he
prepared on July 1, 1854. Whether he delivered it as an address we do not know; but he probably did. It certainly served
as the basis of subsequent addresses. The fragment in full can
be found in any of the editions of his works:

Equality in society alike beats inequality, whether the latter
be of the British aristocratic sort, or of the domestic slavery
sort. We know Southern men declare that their slaves are better
off than hired laborers amongst us. How little they know
whereof they speak! There is no permanent class of hired laborers amongst us. Twenty-five years ago I was a hired laborer.
The hired laborer of yesterday labors on his own account to-day,
and will hire the labor of others to-morrow. Advancement—improvement in condition—is the order of things in a society of
equals. As labor is the common burden of our race, so the
effort of some to shift their share of the burden onto the shoulders of others is the great durable curse of the race. Originally
a curse for the transgression upon the whole race, when, as by
slavery, it is concentrated on a part only, it becomes the double-
refined curse of God upon his creatures.

Free labor has the inspiration of hope: pure slavery has no
hope. The power of hope upon human exertion and happiness is
wonderful. The slave-master himself has a conception of it, and
hence the system of tasks among slaves. The slave whom you
cannot drive with the lash to break seventy-five pounds of hemp
in a day, if you will task him with a hundred, and promise him

pay for all he does over, he will break you a hundred and fifty. You have substituted hope for the rod. And yet perhaps it does not occur to you that to the extent of your gain in the case, you have given up the slave system and adopted the free system of labor.

A study of this statement in the light of its context shows:

1. Lincoln was not contrasting capital and labor; and did not recognize the distinction between the capitalist and the laborer; he denied that America has, or then had, a permanent class of hired laborers. The hired laborer and the capitalist were to Lincoln the same man, in different steps of his career.

2. Lincoln was discussing, not the system of modern industry, but the system of negro slavery in its economic aspects and contrasting it with free labor.

3. He was not defending the right of the laborer to quit any more than he was defending or denying the right of the employer to quit hiring him; that right of either side was not challenged in Lincoln's day. The question of collective bargaining was not under discussion by Lincoln.

4. When Lincoln talked of the right of the working man to better his condition, as he did, he did not have in mind the strike as the working man's instrument, but was commending work and economy such that the working man might hope to rise out of the condition of a hired laborer into that of a man laboring for himself, and possibly employing others.

The other statement is less easy to locate. Lincoln lived so remote from a sphere of strikes, and his approach to the labor question was from so different an angle than that of the modern student of industrial conditions, it is not easy to think, at first, where he would have been likely to say such words as those attributed to him. He said them, or words much like them, in New Haven, Connecticut, on March 6, 1860, two months before his nomination for the presidency. He disclaimed much knowledge of strikes and of the industrial conditions out of which they grew, but replied to the argument that the strike which he found to be on in New England among the employees in the shoe factories of Lynn, Massachusetts, was the result of business conditions attributable to fear of a Republican victory. This charge Douglas and other Democrats had made, and Lincoln replied:

Another specimen of this bushwhacking—that "shoe-strike." Now be it understood that I do not pretend to know all about the matter. I am merely going to speculate a little about some of its phases, and at the outset I am glad to see that a system prevails in New England under which laborers can strike if they want to, where they are not obliged to work under all circumstances, and are not tied down and obliged to labor whether you pay them for it or not. I like the system that lets a man quit when he wants to, and wish it might prevail everywhere. One of the reasons I am opposed to slavery is just here. What is the true condition of the laborer? I take it that it is best for all to leave each man free to acquire property as fast as he can. Some will get wealthy. I don't believe in a law to prevent a man from getting rich; it would do more harm than good. So while we do not propose any war upon capital, we do wish to allow the humblest man an equal chance to get rich with everybody else. When one starts poor, as most do in the race of life, free society is such that he knows he can better his condition; he knows there is no fixed condition of labor for his whole life. I am not ashamed to confess that twenty-five years ago I was a hired laborer, mauling rails, at work on a flat-boat—just what might happen to any poor man's son. I want every man to have the chance—and I believe a black man is entitled to it—in which he can better his condition—when he may look forward and hope to be a hired laborer this year, and the next work for himself, and finally hire men to work for him. That is the true system.

When Lincoln expressed sympathy with the strike, confessing that he did not know about it, the first fact of notice is that his sympathies were immediately with the workmen. He suggested that they stop working in factories, and go out to the farms, and become independent. He believed that factory life was a life less free than life in the open, and he hoped that the workmen who found the conditions of labor hard in factories would move from

New England to Illinois. He said so in that same address. But his main point still was his contrast of free labor and slave labor, and he made the point, that the white free laborer could stop working for the man who did not pay him what his work was worth, and the black slave could not do so; and Lincoln wished that the condition in which a man might stop working if he was not paid might prevail everywhere, meaning specifically, in the states where there was slave labor.

There is one other reference in all of Lincoln's writings or speeches to a strike. It is in a note marked "Private" and sent to Secretary Stanton on December 21, 1863. He said:

Sending a note to the Secretary of the Navy, as I promised, he called over and said that the strikes in the shipyards had thrown the completion of vessels back so much that he thought General Gilmore's proposition entirely proper.

What General Gilmore's proposition was, the War Department does not know; but evidently some cherished plan of the Navy Department had to be abandoned or modified because at that critical period, when the effort to keep England and France from recognizing the Confederacy depended upon ships, supposedly loyal men working in the shipyards went on strike. It would be interesting to know whether Lincoln would have said that under those conditions he still wished men everywhere might feel free to strike. Perhaps he would have said it was their economic right to strike and their patriotic duty not to do so; but I will not attempt to put words into his mouth.

That the government had trouble with workmen in the navy yards, who insisted on higher rates of pay than those current in private establishments, and who threatened to strike, is known to be true, although a careful search of the records, reports, and histories of the various navy yards made by the Navy Department for this work fails to produce any mention of a strike which retarded the progress of construction of ships for the navy.

Referring to the laws of December 21, 1861, and of July 16, 1862, directing that "the hours of labor and the rate of wages of the employees in the navy yards shall conform, as nearly as is consistent with the public interest, with those of private establishments in the immediate vicinity of the respective yards, to be determined by the commandants of the navy yards, subject to the approval and revision of the secretary of the navy," the secretary in his report for the year 1865 says:

The operation of the rule thus sought to be established has been satisfactory neither to the men employed nor to the government, but, on the contrary, an unceasing source of disturbance and discontent. Committees have been appointed bi-monthly at each of the yards to ascertain the rates of wages paid to similar classes of workmen in private establishments, but it has been found difficult to obtain reliable data on this subject. Some parties decline to furnish the information sought, while others give imperfect statements. When, after inquiry and investigation, a scale is adopted, having in view the interests and rights of both the government and the laborers, there is dissatisfaction, especially if in the fluctuation of the currency, or of supply and demand, there has been a reduction, and the workmen, by visiting the different private establishments, are enabled to procure from some of them certificates that higher wages are paid in some instances than the rates adopted at the yard. These certificates do not state the number or proportion of men employed at these high rates, or whether these prices are paid to all of that class in such establishment. If, on inquiry, it is ascertained that only one or two men of unusual capability receive these high prices, and that those authorized by the government are fair average rates, the explanation fails to give satisfaction, for the evidence is produced that higher wages than those on the government scale are paid in private establishments in the vicinity. The impression that there is some unfairness is engendered, complaints and strikes follow or are threatened, vigilant officers who are faithful to the government become obnoxious, and discontent prevails. I would, therefore, recommend that the acts referred to be repealed.

Lincoln carefully wrought out one deliverance on labor, and one which satisfied him permanently; and it is good reading

)oth for the laborer and for the capitalist. In it he starts with
he same assumption, that the laborer is a potential capitalist, and
hat labor is itself the creator of capital; but he does not stop
here. He believed that in a country whose resources were as
arge as they were and are in America, the laborer, if wise, could
:eep himself independent of capital more easily than the capital-
st could make himself independent of labor. He noted the be-
;innings of a cleavage between labor and capital, and he found
iis sympathies on the side of labor. What he said on that sub-
ect he said to the nation and to the world. The paragraphs in
vhich he enunciated most completely his views on labor are in
)ne of his most carefully prepared papers, and one which be-
ore delivery he submitted to the reading of men in whose opin-
ons he had most confidence: for he did not feel that on that
)ccasion he could afford to say anything that would not bear the
nost careful scrutiny of the whole nation, North and South, and
)f other nations as well. Lincoln said:

Labor is prior to, and independent of, capital. Capital is only
he fruit of labor, and could never have existed if labor had not
irst existed. Labor is the superior of capital, and deserves much
he higher consideration. Capital has its rights, which are as
vorthy of protection as any other rights. Nor is it denied that
here is, and probably always will be, a relation between labor
ind capital producing mutual benefits. The error is in assuming
hat the whole labor of the community exists within that rela-
ion. A few men own capital, and that few avoid labor them-
elves, and with their capital, hire or buy another few to labor
or them. A large majority belong to neither class—neither
vork for others nor have others work for them. In most of the
Southern states, a large majority of the whole people, of all
:olors, are neither slaves nor masters; while in the Northern, a
arge majority are neither hirers nor hired.

This is from Lincoln's First Annual Address to Congress,
December 3, 1861. It is his most careful utterance on the sub-
ect. His sympathy as between labor and capital was with la-

bor; but he did not admit a natural antagonism, for he felt and
had his experience to prove, that a young man with character
and ambition and skill should not look forward to being, in
America, permanently in the class of those who are hired.

We find this same point of view in all of Lincoln's discussions
of labor. He began with a consideration of the difference between slave and free labor, and went on to a denial that to free
labor in America there was any necessary permanent relation of
subjection to capital. This he set forth· in his speech in Cincinnati, September 17, 1859, where his treatment of the theme
appears to have grown directly out of his discussions with
Douglas, in his debates with whom the matter had risen only
incidentally:

Some people assume that there is a necessary connection between capital and labor, and that connection has within it the
whole of the labor of the community. They assume that nobody
works unless capital excites them to work. . . . I say the whole
thing is a mistake. . . . That relation does not embrace more than
one-eighth of the labor of the country.

In another address he considered unnecessary transportation
as a waste of labor, and used his illustrations to encourage home
industries. In another he considered a depreciated currency as a
wrong to labor. In his Second Annual Message to Congress,
December 1, 1862, he considered the effect upon free white labor
of free negro labor, and declared that he believed that instead of
depreciating the value of free white labor, the freedom of the
slave would tend to increase it.

In his Third Annual Message, dated December 8, 1863, he
considered the labor shortage produced by the war, and advised
Congress to encourage immigration, for:

It is easy to see that, under the sharp discipline of civil war
the nation is beginning a new life.

In that same message he considered the possibility that the

new freedom of the slaves might involve some complications, on account of the resentment and fear of white labor in the states where there was a sudden competition of free black labor, but this he counted temporary, and to be charged to the evil of slavery, and not to any inherent hostility between labor and capital:

The proposed acquiescence of the national executive in any reasonable temporary State arrangement for the freed people is made with the view of possibly modifying the confusion and destitution which must at best attend all classes by a total revolution of labor throughout whole States.

On March 21, 1864, he received a committee from the Workingmen's Association of New York, and in reply to their address he quoted in full what he had said to Congress in 1861, and added:

The views then expressed remain unchanged, nor have I much to add. None are so deeply interested to resist the present rebellion as the working people. Let them beware of prejudice, working division and hostility among themselves. The most notable feature of a disturbance in your city last summer was the hanging of some working people by other working people. It should never be so. The strongest bond of human sympathy, outside the family relation, should be one uniting all working people, of all nations, and tongues and kindreds. Nor should this lead to a war upon property, or the owners of property. Property is the fruit of labor; property is desirable; is a positive good in the world. That some should be rich shows that others may become rich, and hence is just encouragement to industry and enterprise. Let not him who is houseless pull down the house of another, but let him work diligently and build one for himself, thus by example assuring that his own shall be safe from violence when built.

These were the most direct of all words ever uttered by Lincoln on the issue, then rising, of hostility between labor and capital, and they were his final words on this theme.

In his Fourth Annual Message to Congress, dated December

6, 1864, he spoke of the very high cost of labor, particularly as it affected the building of the transcontinental railways; but he did not go into the matter at length, merely congratulating the country that notwithstanding this added element of difficulty, the work was making progress.

One of the most striking of Lincoln's statements on labor was probably never published during his lifetime, but appears to have been used by him more than once in more or less formal addresses. It exists, like the 1854 document, in the form of notes. The notes on this topic were in a discussion of the tariff. They appear to have been made in 1847. The notes cover several pages, and seem to have been his own attempt to define to himself the underlying principles of tariff legislation. In the midst of the notes, I find this paragraph:

In the early days of our race the Almighty said to the first of our race, "In the sweat of the face shalt thou eat bread"; and since then, if we except the light and air from heaven, no good thing has been or can be enjoyed by us without having first cost labor. And inasmuch as most good things are produced by labor, it follows that all such things of right belong to those whose labor has produced them. But it has so happened, in all ages of the world, that some have labored, and others without labor enjoyed a large proportion of the fruits. This is wrong, and should not continue. To secure to each laborer the whole product of his labor, or as nearly as possible, is a worthy object of any good government.

He went on to a discussion of the means of eliminating unnecessary labor and idleness, and dwelt, as he did at other times, on the waste of useless transportation; and then returned to a consideration of the tariff. The foregoing paragraph is to be interpreted in the light of its context. It was the tariff question which Lincoln was just then considering, and the labor question came into it incidentally. Nevertheless, this is a striking paragraph, and shows how deep was his sympathy with the men who labor, and how clear his conviction that as labor produced wealth, the wealth produced belongs to the men who produce it.

One thing ought to be noted, which is that the laboring men of England recognized in Lincoln a friend of labor. The Civil War brought great hardships in the cotton mills of England, and England's temptation to recognize the Confederacy was strong. Henry Ward Beecher went to England and pleaded with the working men, who were at first very unwilling to hear him. His message was in effect what Lowell had said in his *Biglow Papers*:

> Laborin' man and laborin' woman
> Has one glory and one shame;
> Everything that's done inhuman
> Injures all on 'em the same.

The fight of the North for a free nation was stated strongly as a reason why England should suffer economic loss, if necessary, rather than support a moral wrong. It brought great joy to Lincoln when the cotton operatives of Lancashire, to the number of six thousand, at a meeting in Manchester, on New Year's Eve, in 1862, urged Lincoln to abolish slavery, and refused to petition Her Majesty's Government to recognize the cause of the South. On January 19, 1863, Lincoln replied to the Manchester working men in a letter which displayed sincere gratification.

In March, 1864, the Workingmen's Association of New York City made him an honorary member, following the lead of a convention of trade unionists who, assembled in Philadelphia as early as 1861, pledged Lincoln their support and urged the abolition of slavery. These evidences of the appreciation of working men, Lincoln, himself a working man, received with genuine interest and appreciation.

The main lines of Lincoln's views on labor appear to have been laid down in his notes in 1854, developed in his Cincinnati speech of September 17, 1859, and enlarged upon in an address not quite two weeks later before the Wisconsin State Agricultural

Society in Milwaukee. They are the same that he wrought into his First Annual Message to Congress, and to which he referred near the end of his life, in his letter to the New York working men as the views which he still held and to which he could add little.

These are the important authentic utterances of Lincoln on labor and are consistent throughout. As he defined his views they are virtually these:

Free labor is better, more righteous and more remunerative than slave labor. Labor is prior to capital and superior to it; but there is no inevitable antagonism between them, nor any unalterable division of men in America into permanent classes as capitalists or laborers. The laborer has a right to aspire to be a capitalist, and should act toward capital as he will wish laborers to act toward him when he becomes a capitalist. But man is not a commodity; the rights of labor, while giving it no privilege to destroy capital, are more sacred than the rights which inhere in capital: for capital is the fruit of labor.

As a laboring man, Lincoln was a friend of labor. As a man who had risen out of a condition of hard labor, he believed in ambition and aspiration for the laboring man. He believed in freedom because freedom is the mother of hope, and he wanted the privilege of hope preserved to all who perform honest labor.

CHAPTER XXVIII

LINCOLN THE ORATOR

Had Abraham Lincoln been everything else that he was and lacked his oratorical powers, he would never have been president of the United States.

Oratory is now in disrepute. It has practically disappeared from political campaigns. It is a lost art in the court room. It is little better than a stranger in both Houses of Congress. As for the Supreme Court, an orator might as well transport himself to the Gizeh Museum and attempt to be eloquent in addressing the mummified Pharaohs as the judges of that high tribunal. The pulpit is still the throne of eloquence, though there are influences at work that would drive it from this last place of vantage. Eloquence is the finest of the fine arts. The organs of speech are wholly other than the organs by which speech is received and interpreted; the lips and the ear are so constructed as not to suggest any possible relationship between them. Yet by a miracle in the presence of which all men must stand in wonder, sounds produced by one set of organs are capable of registering their effects upon the other in such manner that one man may speak and another may listen and the souls of the two be stirred by the same emotion. One man standing where a thousand others can hear him may see in their faces the effect of his words, and know that they are thinking his thoughts and are swayed by his passion and joining in his high resolves. He has no brush and palette; no mallet and chisel; no instrument of music, but he is privileged to do what the painter, the sculptor, the musician can never do, or do in part only.

It is said that when Lincoln was a boy he returned home from religious services and mimicked the preachers. The mirthful aspects of his performance appear to have impressed his cousin Dennis Hanks more deeply than any serious element which the preaching may have contained. It need not be inferred, however, that the boy's love of fun was the sole reason for these imitations. The mannerisms of the backwoods preacher could hardly have failed to excite his mirth; but beside his ridicule there was some real appreciation of the value of public discourse and aspiration to influence men through public speech.

His corn-field oratory was a ready invitation to the other boys to drop their hoes and listen, and was more appreciated by them than it was by Thomas Lincoln, whose corn needed hoeing.

During his boyhood Abraham now and then made his way to Rockport, the county-seat of Spencer County, Indiana, and there as also at Boonville, in the adjacent county of Warrick, he heard lawyers addressing juries. His court-room experience in this period, however, was limited, while regularly once a month there was preaching at the Little Pigeon church, and often more than one preacher spoke at the service.

By the time Abraham was of age, he had some local reputation as a public speaker; for, in the summer of 1830, John Hanks made the confident boast that Abraham could make a better political address than one which had just been delivered at Decatur; and Abraham, nothing loath, mounted a stump and made a speech. His experience in the debating society at New Salem gave him opportunity for the preparation of argumentative addresses, and his experience in the store brought him almost daily opportunity for discussion.

We do not know of any significant address delivered by Lincoln as a member of the Legislature; but we do know of his candidacy for reelection once in two years and of the growing appreciation which people showed of his power of speech. His campaign addresses of these years are not preserved, and we are quite sure that their destruction involves no serious loss. We have samples enough of Lincoln's early rhetoric and descriptions of his early stump-speaking to assure us that their value was chiefly in the preparation afforded for something better. He followed in those days the style which he supposed to be most cogent and effective. It was a stilted, artificial type of oratory, and Lincoln in time outgrew it.

We have many anecdotes concerning his court-room eloquence. His power with juries lay first in his power of fair and clear statements, his ability to strip a subject of its incidentals and to display it in its fundamental attributes. His homely good sense and man-to-man attitude commended him not only to the intelligence but the favorable judgment of juries. Of his fund of humor we shall have occasion to speak in a chapter by itself. It is to be noted, however, that Lincoln seldom told stories or cracked jokes in his more serious addresses. The proof of this is to be found in all the published editions of his speeches. A tradition is current in the county-seats where Lincoln was most frequently heard, to the effect that juries learned not to look for stories when Lincoln was entirely certain that the law and evidence were on his side. When Lincoln had a good clear case and could cite the evidence and the statutes, he found little occasion to tell stories.

Lincoln's temperance address delivered in Springfield on Washington's birthday in 1842, and his address on the *Perpetuation of our Political Institutions,* delivered before the Young Men's Lyceum on January 27, 1837, are sufficient indication of the character of his prepared discourses while he was yet a young lawyer in Springfield.

In these days a new member of Congress is not expected to obtain the floor during his first term, unless it be in a night session just before the adjournment of Congress when he may be permitted to rise and address the chairman *pro tem* and ask leave to extend his remarks in print in order that he may have some campaign literature to send to his constituents and assist toward his reelection. It was not so in Lincoln's day. Very soon after he got to Washington he was on the floor in an extended speech, arraigning President Polk for the war against Mexico. Before very long he was delivering a speech on internal improvements, and before summer he delivered a kind of stump speech in which he ridiculed General Cass, the Democratic candidate for president. Judged by our present-day standards, these speeches can not be considered great. But that is not the proper way to judge them. They were received at the time as adequate to the several occasions on which they were delivered and they told increasingly Abraham Lincoln's power as an orator.

It can do us no harm, and may be profitable, to read a portion of Lincoln's campaign speech in the presidential contest of 1840: The speech concludes with these swelling words:

Mr. Lamborn refers to the late elections in the States, and from their results confidently predicts every State in the Union will vote for Mr. Van Buren at the next Presidential election. Address that argument to cowards and knaves: with the free and the brave it will affect nothing. It may be true; if it must, let it. Many free countries have lost their liberty, and ours may lose hers; but if she shall, be it my proudest plume, not that I was the last to desert, but that I never deserted her. I know that the great volcano at Washington, aroused and directed by the evil spirit that reigns there, is belching forth the lava of political corruption in a current broad and deep, which is sweeping with frightful velocity over the whole length and breadth of the land, bidding fair to leave unscathed no green spot or living thing; while on its bosom are riding, like demons on the wave of Hell, the imps of the Evil Spirit, and fiendishly taunting all those who dare to resist its destroying course with the hopelessness of their efforts; and knowing this, I cannot deny that all may be swept away. Broken by it, I, too, may be; bow to it, I never will. The probability that we may fall in the struggle ought not to deter us from the support of a cause we believe to be just. It shall not deter me. If ever I feel the soul within me elevate and expand to those dimensions not wholly unworthy of its Almighty Architect, it is when I contemplate the cause of my

country, deserted by all the world beside, and I standing up boldly alone, hurling defiance at her victorious oppressors. Here,
without contemplating consequences, before Heaven, and in face
of the world, I swear eternal fealty to the just cause, as I deem
it, of the land of my life, my liberty, and my love. And who
that thinks with me will not fearlessly adopt that oath that I
take? Let none falter who thinks he is right, and we may succeed. But if after all we should fail, be it so. We still shall have
the proud consolation of saying to our consciences, and to the
departed shade of our country's freedom, that the cause approved
of our judgment, and adored of our hearts, in disaster, in chains,
in torture, in death, we never faltered in defending.

This lofty and artificial eloquence, in which the orator appears
as a kind of political Horatius guarding alone the bridge of his
country's honor, a sort of modern reincarnation of the lesser
Ajax defying the lightning, deserves the tribute of a passing
smile. But it deserves something more than that. It was a
carefully prepared address in the style then popular, and it was
part of the preparation of Lincoln for his life-work as an orator.
But it is a far cry from this sort of eloquence to the Gettysburg
Address and the second inaugural.

In Lincoln's earlier stump speeches he is described as indulging in the familiar oratorical tricks of the time and region. He
gesticulated with wide-reaching gestures. He stooped low, and
rose to his full height, raising his voice as he ascended, and
sometimes accentuating his stature by standing on tiptoe. All
this is to be charged up to experience in the career of Lincoln as
an orator. He outgrew all these tricks. He stood calmly in his
place, and if he moved, he moved with his thoughts, and the
movement was natural and not ungraceful. He gesticulated little,
and, that little being unstudied, was effective. His whole
progress was toward simplicity and effectiveness. His was a
very honest type of oratory, and it had weight with his hearers.

It may not be amiss to record one or two of Mr. Lincoln's
oddities of pronunciation. Reared as he had been in the backwoods, his forms of speech partook of the peculiarities of the

region in which he lived. In Lincoln's day, the sound of Italian *a* final, was rarely heard in America; even now, it is seldom heard correctly. An Italian speaks of his capital city as "Roma," giving full value to both vowels. But an American whose home town ends with that sound, is likely either to follow the final vowel with the sound of *r,* or corrupt it into a sound more nearly represented by the letters *uh.* In Lincoln's day, hardly any one said Americah; now and then some one said *Americur;* but Lincoln and most of his fellow-countrymen said *Amerikay.* Some philologist might find material for a treatise in the evolution of the pronunciation of the Italian *a* in England and the United States.

Lincoln pronounced the numeral *one* as if it were spelled *own;* but the word *only,* he pronounced *unly.* The word *idea* he pronounced in two syllables with accent on the first. Lincoln almost never made a pun, but one of his very few remembered puns* depends upon these pronunciations. At one time the three judges of the Supreme Court of Illinois were Walter B. Scales, John B. Carton and Sidney Breese, all of whom came to Illinois from Oneida County, New York. Lincoln had carried a case to the Supreme Court and had been beaten. Stephen T. Logan, who had once been Lincoln's partner, met him after the decision and in his habitual whining tone he inquired, "Well, Mr. Lincoln, how did you like the decision?" Lincoln answered, "It's all that can be expected from a Oneida (one-idea) court."

The mention of these solecisms must not, however, be understood as indicating that Lincoln's speech was slovenly, on the contrary it was surprisingly correct.

I call to mind the pronunciation of my own father, who went to Illinois in his boyhood and quickly exhausted the possibilities of the local schools. Except for the study of medicine in the office of an older physician, he was self-taught. He never studied grammar in school, and there were a very few words and

---

*The two puns here recorded, and one that appears in an earlier chapter, are among the few of record from Lincoln.

grammatical constructions where he made occasional mistakes. In the main, however, his pronunciation had a precision that would have shamed many a college graduate. His use of the unabridged dictionary was constant. He wrote a rapid and legible hand. He had a good literary style. He was able to converse with men who had had university training, and to hold his own in argument with them. It would easily be possible to recall a few little oddities of expression which he never outgrew. But these were not the tests of his education or his culture.

Judge Blodgett, of Chicago, remembered an occasion when Lincoln appeared before the Supreme Court of Illinois in a suit concerning a piece of property owned by Lincoln's client, on which there was a lien. Lincoln pronounced the word *lien* in one syllable, as if it were spelled *lean*. The judge was somewhat pedantic, and stopped Mr. Lincoln with the suggestion that the word should be pronounced li-en. "Very well, your Honor," said Mr. Lincoln, and corrected the pronunciation to fit that of the judge. Presently, however, he had occasion to use the word again and forgetting his recent instruction, he called it *lean*. "As you please, your Honor," said Lincoln, a little annoyed. "Not as I please," said the judge, "that is the pronunciation favored by Webster and by Worcester. It so obtains at Westminster Hall, and also at our own Supreme Court in Washington." Then again, Lincoln indulged in his rare use of a pun. "Certainly, your Honor, certainly," he said, "I only desire to say that if my client had known there was a *lion* on his farm I am sure he would not have stayed there long enough to bring this suit and I should have not had the pleasure of appearing before this honorable court."

Lincoln was not an easy speaker to report. At Gettysburg, he spoke with great deliberation, and with evident desire that his words should be accurately recorded. But when he spoke in extended discourse, his delivery was irregular, and resulted in widely varying reports of his addresses. A bitter controversy followed the Lincoln-Douglas debates on this point. The reports in the *Chicago Times* were rambling and illogical. Those in the *Press and Tribune* were clear and well expressed. The Republicans charged the *Times* with misrepresenting Lincoln; the Democrats charged the *Press and Tribune* with editing the speeches. Walter B. Stevens in his *Reporter's Lincoln* thus summarizes the results of his investigations:

His voice was clear, almost shrill. Every syllable was distinct. But his delivery was puzzling to stenographers. He would speak several words with great rapidity, come to the word or phrase he wished to emphasize, and let his voice linger and bear hard on that, and then he would rush to the end of his sentence like lightning. To impress the idea on the mind of his hearers was his aim; not to charm the ear with smooth, flowing words. It was very easy to understand Lincoln. He spoke with great clearness. But his delivery was very irregular. He would devote as much time to the word or two which he wished to emphasize as he did to half a dozen less important words following it.*

It is not necessary to refer again in detail to his eloquence in the court-room, further than to remind ourselves that in the years between his election to Congress and his election to the presidency, he became a much abler and more eloquent lawyer than before. He had ability not simply to sway the feelings of a jury, but to influence a bench of judges.

That which woke in Abraham Lincoln this full power of eloquence was the moral compulsion under which he returned to politics on the repeal of the Missouri Compromise. All of his clear and powerful analysis, his discriminating definitions, his cogent method of stating his own and his opponent's point of view, his facility in anecdote, his wit, his irony, his moral indignation, and his companionable sympathy, had been in training for this emergency. Abraham Lincoln as a man of eloquence had come to the kingdom for such a time as that. We can not wonder at the effect of his "lost speech" when we read the

*A *Reporter's Lincoln,* Missouri Historical Society, St. Louis, 1916, p. 53

'eoria speech, and know that the two must have been com-
ounded out of essentially the same ingredients.

Lincoln's speeches in his debates with Douglas can hardly be
alled eloquent. Their appeal is first to the intelligence rather
han to the emotions. But they are not lacking in any quality
vhich made them essential to their purpose. In them Lincoln
merged as a man capable of meeting on a common level one of
he foremost leaders in the United States Senate, the most prom-
nent of presidential candidates, and of holding his own in close-
y contested and sustained argument. These speeches met and
ustained two different tests. They were effective in their ap-
eal to the great crowds that heard them, and when printed and
irculated throughout the country they won the approval of vast
umbers of readers.

In a certain sense the Cooper Union address is the high-water
nark of Lincoln's oratory. When delivered it astonished the
eople of New York, and when printed it found for itself a per-
nanent place in political literature. It justified Abraham Lin-
oln's right to a foremost place among American orators.

As the Cooper Union speech was in some respects the greatest
f Lincoln's orations, so was it the last of his supremely great
oratorical achievements. The responsibilities of the position to
vhich he was soon elected afforded him little opportunity for
loquence. From the time of his election as president his speeches
nust be judged chiefly as literature.

Lincoln had been one of the readiest of stump speakers. Al-
hough his ordinary intellectual processes were slow, there was
hat in the atmosphere of the court-room or the political arena
hat remarkably quickened his perception and made him a master
f repartee. After his election to the presidency, however, his
abitual caution became accentuated. He learned that he must
ive account for every idle word. He would not respond even
o a serenade unless he had warning in advance and opportunity
o prepare his address in writing.

Although a ready debater, and rather quick with a repartee

or a pat illustration suggested by an opposing argument or passing incident, Lincoln was not a ready man in extempore address. His incidental speeches, delivered when he felt that he had nothing to say, were often disappointing. Thus R. E. Fenton wrote of him :*

Mr. Lincoln was not a successful impromptu speaker. He required a little time for thought and arrangement of the thing to be said. I give an instance in point. After the election to which I have referred, just before I resigned my seat in Congress to enter upon my official duties as Governor at Albany, New Yorkers and others in Washington thought to honor me with serenade. I was the guest of ex-Mayor Bowen. After the music and speaking usual upon such occasions, it was proposed to call on the President. I accompanied the committee in charge of the proceedings, followed by bands and a thousand people. It was full nine o'clock when we reached the Mansion. The President was taken by surprise, and said he "didn't know just what he could say to satisfy the crowd and himself." Going from the library room down the stairs to the portico front, he asked me to say a few words first, and give him if I could "a peg to hang on." It was just when General Sherman was *en route* from Atlanta to the sea, and we had no definite news as to his safety or whereabouts. After one or two sentences, rather commonplace, the President farther said he had no war news other than was known to all, and he supposed his ignorance in regard to General Sherman was the ignorance of all; that "we all knew where Sherman went in, but none of us knew where he would come out." This last remark was in the peculiarly quaint, happy manner of Mr. Lincoln, and created great applause. He immediately withdrew, saying he "had raised a good laugh and it was a good time for him to quit." In all he did not speak more than two minutes, and, as he afterward told me, because he had no time to think of much to say.

In reading Lincoln's formal addresses one sometimes misses the power of a stately peroration. In the Lincoln-Douglas debates his addresses would have gained in power if each one had

---

Reminiscences of Abraham Lincoln by Distinguished Men of His Time pp. 70-71.

sen to a final climax. We owe to the suggestion of Seward
he fact that the first inaugural has a climax with a ring of real
oquence, and the appeal of strong emotion. Lincoln was ad-
ressing his closing words to the people of the South. He
aid:

In your hands, my dissatisfied fellow-countrymen, and not in
ine, is the momentous issue of civil war. The government will
ot assail you. You can have no conflict without being your-
lves the aggressors. You have no oath registered in heaven
 destroy the government, while I have a most solemn one to
reserve, protect and defend it.

As Lincoln originally wrote the address this was the conclu-
on except for two additional sentences:

You can forbear the assault upon it; I cannot shrink from the
fense of it. With you and not with me is the solemn question
 "Shall it be peace or a sword?"

This seemed to Seward too blunt and abrupt and provocative
close, and he suggested two alternatives, one of which Lincoln
lected and with some modification, employed:

I am loath to close. We are not enemies but friends. We
ust not be enemies. Though passion may have strained, it
ust not break our bonds of affection. The mystic chords of
emory, stretching from every battlefield and patriot's grave to
ery living heart and hearthstone all over this broad land, will
vell the chorus of the Union when again touched, as surely
ey will be, by the better **angels of our nature.**

This peroration possessed the qualities of real eloquence.
Vhether it should be credited to Lincoln or Seward, or shared
etween them, we need not now discuss. Nor need we cite in
is place what has already been considered in its historic order,
incoln's second inaugural. That address belongs wholly to
incoln and it is eloquence of very high character.

CHAPTER XXIX

THE HUMOR OF ABRAHAM LINCOLN

BISHOP FOWLER in his noted lecture on Abraham Lincoln told his millions of interested hearers that Lincoln, before presenting to his Cabinet the Proclamation of Emancipation, read to them a chapter from the Bible. That is precisely what Lincoln would have done if he had been Bishop Fowler. What he actually did read was a chapter from Artemus Ward, concerning the virtue of the people of Utica, who would not permit that honest showman to exhibit his wax figures of the twelve apostles in that city because Judas was among them.

John Drinkwater in his noted play represents Abraham Lincoln as reading this chapter, but he prefaces the reading with a little lecture explaining that this is to relieve the tension under which they have been living. That is what Lincoln would have done if he had been John Drinkwater. But Lincoln made no explanation and felt no occasion for any.

Lord Charnwood in his excellent biography of Lincoln tells us that "It was precisely that sort of relief to which Lincoln's mind when overwrought could always turn"; and that "having thus composed himself for business" he produced the Emancipation Proclamation. That is the way Lincoln would have done it had he been Lord Charnwood. But we have no reason to suppose that Lincoln at that moment felt any special need of composing himself for the business of the occasion. Lincoln read to his Cabinet this chapter because he thought it funny. He had just received the book, and this story had occasioned a good laugh on his part. He wanted his Cabinet to laugh with him and more of them did laugh. All laughed, apparently, except Stanton and Chase. To Lincoln there was nothing inharmonious in this odd juxtaposition. To him the love of fun was so natural and the love of humanity so natural also, that he found nothing incongruous in the combination.

Lincoln's humor was an enormous relief to him from the over-strain of his presidential responsibility. But he did not turn from serious things to humor upon any schedule, or in accordance with any logical theory, as if the time had come to take a dose of medicine, and Artemus Ward or Petroleum V. Nasby had been the prescribed bottle. When anything funny came Lincoln's way, he stopped and enjoyed the fun and then went to work again. He could interrupt a solemn Cabinet meeting to answer the knock of Elijah Kellogg, of Illinois, and invite him to come in and tell the story of the stuttering justice. It was not because the Cabinet at that particular moment had reached the point where relief was a psychological necessity. It was simply because Elijah Kellogg was at the door, and Lincoln knew, for he had often heard, his story of the stuttering justice. Some good people have seemed to feel that they must show that Abraham Lincoln took his humor on a physician's prescription. He did nothing of the kind. When he lay awake at night reading Nasby and found something funny, he laughed because he enjoyed it; and if the enjoyment was more than usually great, he got out of bed and paraded around the White House in his shirt to discover if any one else was awake who could share the fun with him. He did not take up his humor as some men take up golf, for his health. It was good for his health, but he did it because he enjoyed it.

Many anecdotes are related in Illinois county-seats about the practical jokes which Lincoln is alleged to have played. For the most part, however, his humor survived in the form of stories. Several compilations of stories alleged to have been told by Lincoln are now in existence. Colonel Alexander K. McClure, of the *Philadelphia Times*, who knew Lincoln during

32

the war, compiled one of the fullest of these collections and one
that is perhaps as reliable as any. I own a copy of this book
which once was the property of Isaac N. Arnold. Upon its fly
leaf Mr. Arnold wrote that in his judgment about half of these
stories were probably stories that Lincoln had actually told. It
is quite certain that very many of the anecdotes attributed to
him are in no proper sense his.

The question has been hotly debated whether Lincoln ever
told immodest stories. The answer is that in the days when he
was riding the circuit, his taste in the matter of stories was on
a level with that of the other lawyers of the period. His growth
into an appreciation of higher and finer things was gradual
and was the more marked in that period of his spiritual evolu
tion which came with the war and Lincoln's heavy responsi
bilities.

It is almost hopeless to attempt to convey the essence of a
joke through the printed page alone. The aptness of Lincoln's
humor depended upon the circumstances, and also upon Lincoln's
own tone and manner. These we can not adequately reproduce.
A few of the better attested of Lincoln's stories are necessary to
a book like this, but only distantly can they suggest the meaning
which Lincoln and his associates found in them.

Early in January, 1861, Colonel Alexander K. McClure re
ceived a telegram from President-elect Lincoln, asking McClure
to visit him at Springfield. Colonel McClure described his dis
appointment at first sight of Lincoln in these words:

"I went directly from the depot to Lincoln's house and rang
the bell, which was answered by Lincoln himself opening the
door. I doubt whether I wholly concealed my disappointment at
meeting him.

"Tall, gaunt, ungainly, ill clad, with a homeliness of manner
that was unique in itself, I confess that my heart sank within
me as I remembered that this was the man chosen by a great na
tion to become its ruler in the gravest period of its history.

"I remember his dress as if it were but yesterday—snuff-col

Courtesy, George Grey Barnard

Statue by George Grey Barnard

ored and slouchy pantaloons, open black vest, held by a few brass buttons; straight or evening dress-coat, with tightly fitting sleeves to exaggerate his long, bony arms, and all supplemented by an awkwardness that was uncommon among men of intelligence.

"Such was the picture I met in the person of Abraham Lincoln. We sat down in his plainly furnished parlor, and were uninterrupted during the nearly four hours that I remained with him, and little by little, as his earnestness, sincerity and candor were developed in conversation, I forgot all the grotesque qualities which so confounded me when I first greeted him."

In Lincoln as in other strong men, there was marked individuality. Lincoln recognized this quality in other men, and he knew better than to expect great strength in any man without some counterbalancing weakness. As Lincoln was on his way to Washington to make his last desperate effort to secure appointment as land commissioner, he rode through Indiana on a stage. As they were approaching Indianapolis, Lincoln had as traveling companion an old Kentuckian who was returning from Missouri. Lincoln excited the old gentleman's surprise by refusing to accept either of tobacco or French brandy.

When they separated that afternoon, the Kentuckian to take another stage bound for Louisville, he shook hands warmly with Lincoln, and said, good-humoredly:

"See here, stranger, you're a clever but strange companion. I may never see you again, and I don't want to offend you, but I want to say this: My experience has taught me that a man who has no vices has very few virtues. Good day."

Few enough were the men who, having any little whim to gratify, considered the President too busy a man to serve their interests. To a curiosity-seeker who desired a permit to pass the lines to visit the field of Bull Run, after the first battle, Lincoln made the following reply: "A man in Cortlandt County raised a porker of such unusual size that strangers went out of their way to see it.

"One of them the other day met the old gentleman and inquired about the animal.

" 'Wall, yes,' the old fellow said, 'I've got such a critter, mi'ty big un; but I guess I'll have to charge you about a shillin' for lookin' at him.'

"The stranger looked at the old man for a minute or so, pulled out the desired coin, handed it to him and started to go off. 'Hold on,' said the other, 'don't you want to see the hog?'

" 'No,' said the stranger; 'I have seen as big a hog as I want to see!' "

An astonishing number of people wanted passes to the South. Some of these were mere curiosity-seekers. Some were people who professed to be able to exert influence that would assist in progress toward peace. Many were Confederate spies, who, on pretext of sickness in the family or other dire necessity, wanted liberty to pass through the Union into the Confederate lines. These requests were of course an embarrassment, but many such were made.

A man called upon the president one day and solicited a pass for Richmond.

"Well," said the president, "I would be very happy to oblige, if my passes were respected; but the fact is, sir, I have, within the past two years, given passes to two hundred and fifty thousand men to go to Richmond, and not one has got there yet."

The applicant quietly and respectfully withdrew.

Lincoln often surprised applicants for office by an apparently irrelevant story, and he sometimes cut the knot of a complicated tangle in a thoroughly characteristic and unexpected way.

A commissioner to the Hawaiian Islands was to be appointed, and eight applicants had filed their papers, when a delegation appeared at the White House on behalf of a ninth. Not only was their man qualified, so the delegation urged, but was also in bad health, and a residence in that balmy climate would be of great benefit to him.

The president was rather impatient that day, and before the members of the delegation had fairly started in, he suddenly closed the interview with this remark:

"Gentlemen, I am sorry to say that there are eight other applicants for that place, and they are all sicker'n your man."

Lincoln was constantly bothered by members of delegations of people who thought they knew all about running the war, but had no real knowledge of what was going on.

"How many men have the Confederates now in the field?" asked one of these bores one day.

"About one million two hundred thousand," replied the president

"Oh, my! Not so many as that, surely, Mr. Lincoln."

"They have fully twelve hundred thousand, no doubt of it. You see, all of our generals when they get whipped say the enemy outnumbers them from three or five to one, and I must believe them. We have four hundred thousand men in the field, and three times four makes twelve,—don't you see it? It is as plain to be seen as the nose on a man's face; and at the rate things are now going, with the great amount of speculation and the small crop of fighting, it will take a long time to overcome twelve hundred thousand rebels in arms."

Lincoln heartily disliked those boisterous people who were constantly deluging him with advice, and shouting at the tops of their voices whenever they appeared at the White House. "These noisy people create a great clamor," said he one day, in conversation with some personal friends, "and remind me, by the way, of a good story I heard out in Illinois while I was practising, or trying to practise, some law there. I will say, though, that I practised more law than I ever got paid for.

"A fellow who lived just out of town, on the bank of a large marsh, conceived a big idea in the money-making line. He took it to a prominent merchant, and began to develop his plans and specifications. 'There are at least ten million frogs in that marsh near me, an' I'll just arrest a couple of carloads of them and hand them over to you. You can send them to the big cities and make lots of money for both of us. Frogs' legs are great delicacies in the big towns, an' not very plentiful. It won't take me more'n two or three days to pick 'em. They make so much noise my family can't sleep, and by this deal I'll get rid of a nuisance and gather in some cash.'

"The merchant agreed to the proposition, promised the fellow he would pay him well for the two carloads. Two days passed, then three, and finally two weeks were gone before the fellow showed up again, carrying a small basket. He looked weary and 'done up,' and he wasn't talkative a bit. He threw the basket on the counter with the remark, 'There's your frogs.'

" 'You haven't two carloads in that basket, have you?' inquired the merchant.

" 'No,' was the reply, 'and there ain't no two carloads in all this blasted world.'

" 'I thought you said there were at least ten million of 'em in that marsh near you, according to the noise they made,' observed the merchant. 'Your people couldn't sleep because of 'em.'

" 'Well,' said the fellow, 'accordin' to the noise they made, there was, I thought, a hundred million of 'em, but when I had waded and swum that there marsh day and night fer two blessed weeks, I couldn't harvest but six. There's two or three left yet, an' the marsh is as noisy as it uster be. We haven't catched up on any of our lost sleep yet. Now, you can have these here six, an' I won't charge you a cent fer 'em.'

"You can see by this little yarn," remarked the president, "that these boisterous people make too much noise in proportion to their numbers."

Letters of advice to the president overloaded the patient messenger who regularly brought in the heavy bag containing White House mail. Most of these letters the president never saw. Once in a long time a letter came whose author knew that the thing which he proposed was absurd. One man from Tolona, Illinois, gave to the president a hearty laugh by his proposal to raise a regiment of cross-eyed men:

"I know enough cross-eyed men to fill up the regiment, and, by thunder, Mr. Lincoln, I am cross-eyed enough to be the colonel of it."

He proposed to arm his regiment with double-barreled guns, the barrels arranged to fire at different angles. He then would march his regiment along the river and clean up both banks at once.

Lincoln made no pretense of being a soldier, but he showed a good degree of military sagacity. When Hood's army had been scattered into fragments, after the battles of Franklin and Nashville, President Lincoln, elated by the defeat of what had so long been a menacing force on the borders of Tennessee, was reminded by its collapse of the fate of a savage dog belonging to one of his neighbors in the frontier settlements in which he lived in his youth. "The dog," he said, "was the terror of the neighborhood, and its owner, a churlish and quarrelsome fellow took pleasure in the brute's forcible attitude.

"Finally, all other means having failed to subdue the creature, a man loaded a lump of meat with a charge of powder, to which was attached a slow fuse; this was dropped where the dreaded dog would find it, and the animal gulped down the tempting bait.

"There was a dull rumbling, a muffled explosion, and fragments of the dog were seen flying in every direction. The grieved owner, picking up the shattered remains of his cruel favorite, said: 'He was a good dog, but as a dog, his days of usefulness are over.' Hood's army was a good army," said Lincoln, by way of comment, "and we were all afraid of it, but as an army, its usefulness is gone."

An officer, having had some trouble with General Sherman, and being very angry, presented himself before Mr. Lincoln, who was visiting the camp at City Point, and said, "Mr. President, I have a cause of grievance. This morning I went to General Sherman and he threatened to shoot me."

"Threatened to shoot you?" asked Mr. Lincoln. "Well, [in a stage whisper] if I were you I would keep away from him; if he threatens to shoot, I would not trust him, for I believe he would do it."

Lincoln showed great ingenuity in locating the incidents which he related. While he was on the circuit, he told stories of "a man I knew in Indiana," or "a woman who lived down in Egypt,"—that is, in southern Illinois. He was careful to place them far enough away to save the feelings of people near at hand, yet not too far to make them a part of his own experience. In this manner he worked over many old stories, and made them as good as new. In Washington, his stories were more frequently located in Illinois.

President Lincoln, in company with General Grant, was inspecting the Dutch Gap Canal at City Point.

"Grant, do you know what this reminds me of? Out in Springfield there was a blacksmith, who, not having much to do, took a piece of soft iron and attempted to weld it into an agricultural implement, but discovered that the iron would not hold out. Then he concluded it would make an ax, but having too little iron, attempted to make a claw-hammer. He decided after working a while that there was not enough iron left. Finally, becoming disgusted, he filled the forge full of coal and brought the iron to a white heat; then with his tongs he lifted it from the bed of coals, and thrusting it into a tub of water near by, exclaimed: 'Well, if I can't make anything else of you, I will make a fizzle, anyhow.'"

"I was afraid that was about what we had done with the Dutch Gap Canal," said General Grant.

When Governor Andrew Curtin of Pennsylvania, described

the terrible butchery at the battle of Fredericksburg, Mr. Lincoln was greatly distressed.

The governor regretted that his description had so sadly affected the president. He remarked: "I would give all I possess to know how to rescue you from this terrible war."

Lincoln's whole aspect suddenly changed, and he relieved his mind by telling a story.

"This reminds me, Governor," he said, "of an old farmer that I used to know, out in Illinois.

"He took it into his head to go into hog-raising. He sent out to Europe and imported the finest breed of hogs he could buy.

"The prize hog was put in a pen, and the farmer's two mischievous boys, James and John, were told to be sure not to let it out. But James, the worst of the two, let the brute out the next day. The hog went straight for the boys, and drove John up a tree, then the hog went for the seat of James' trousers, and the only way the boy could save himself was by holding on to the hog's tail.

"The hog would not give up his hunt, nor the boy his hold! After they had made a good many circles around the tree, the boy's courage began to give out, and he shouted to his brother, 'I say, John, come down, quick, and help me let go this hog!'

"Now, Governor, that is exactly my case. I wish some one would come and help me to let the hog go."

General Creswell called at the White House to see the president shortly before the latter's assassination. An old friend, serving in the Confederate ranks, had been captured by the Union troops and sent to prison. General Creswell had drawn an affidavit setting forth what he knew about the man, particularly mentioning extenuating circumstances.

Creswell found the president very happy. He was greeted with: "Creswell, old fellow, everything is bright this morning. The war is over. It has been a tough time, but we have lived it out,—or some of us have," and he dropped his voice a little

400 THE LIFE OF ABRAHAM LINCOLN

on the last clause of the sentence. "But it is over; we are going to have good times now, and a united country."

General Creswell told his story, read his affidavit, and said, "I know the man has acted like a fool, but he is my friend, and a good fellow; let him out; give him to me, and I will be responsible that he won't have anything more to do with the rebs."

"Creswell," replied Mr. Lincoln, "you make me think of a lot of young folks who once started out Maying. To reach their destination, they had to cross a shallow stream, and did so by means of an old flat-boat. When the time came to return, they found to their dismay that the old scow had disappeared. They were in sore trouble, and thought over all manner of devices for getting over the water, but without avail.

"After a time, one of the boys proposed that each fellow should pick up the girl he liked best and wade over with her. The masterly proposition was carried out, until all that were left upon the island was a little short chap and a great, long, gothic-built, elderly lady.

"Now, Creswell, you are trying to leave me in the same predicament. You fellows are all getting your own friends out of this scrape; and you will succeed in carrying off one after another, until nobody but Jeff Davis and myself will be left on the island, and then I won't know what to do. How should I feel? How should I look, lugging him over?

"I guess the way to avoid such an embarrasing situation is to let them all out at once."

Lincoln greatly enjoyed the effect of a little joke which he played now and then on people who thought he was about to confide to them some secret about military or naval movements. There was a certain naval expedition concerning which there was much anxiety, and more than one person called on Lincoln to learn its destination. "Can you keep a secret?" asked the president. "I'll tell you where it's gone; it's gone to sea!"

Colonel McClure had been in consultation with the president one day, about two weeks after Sherman's disappearance, and in this connection related this incident:

"I was leaving the room, and just as I reached the door the president turned around, and, with a merry twinkling of the eye, inquired, 'McClure, wouldn't you like to hear something from Sherman?'

"The inquiry electrified me at the instant, as it seemed to imply that Lincoln had some information on the subject. I immediately answered, 'Yes, most of all, I should like to hear from Sherman.'

"To this President Lincoln answered, with a hearty laugh: Well, I'll be hanged if I wouldn't, myself.'"

While humorous songs delighted the president, he also loved to listen to patriotic airs and ballads containing sentiment. He was fond of hearing *The Sword of Bunker Hill, Ben Bolt,* and *The Lament of the Irish Emigrant.* His preference of the verses in the latter was this:

> I'm lonely now, Mary,
>   For the poor make no new friends;
> But, oh, they love the better still
>   The few our Father sends!
> And you were all I had, Mary,
>   My blessing and my pride;
> There's nothing left to care for now,
>   Since my poor Mary died.

Lincoln was fond of the theater, and never, except in Washington, was he in a city where there was a theatrical performance every night. His official duties did not permit him to attend very often, and when he was able to go he enjoyed the play, whether comedy or tragedy. He had not sufficient experience to be a discriminating critic, and his tastes were elemental. He liked the jokes to be broad enough to be discoverable.

In Illinois, he was pleased when he could attend an entertainment of negro minstrels. The old-time minstrel show was a clean and wholesome frolic. Christy's Minstrels were nothing

less than an institution, and other shows took their key from
Christy. For this troupe Stephen C. Foster wrote most of hi
one hundred seventy-five songs, some of them exquisitely tende
others jolly and gay.

The old-time minstrel show had a group of performers seate
in a curve so that the interlocutor, who occupied the center chai
could talk with any performer, with the players of fiddles an
banjos and guitars on his right and left, and especially with th
two end-men, "Bones" and "Tambo," who were the chief con
versationalists. There were sentimental songs and noisy choruse
and merry dialogue and local jokes. There was the song abou
Jim-along-Josey:

> T'ree or fo' possum, five or six coon,
> Settin' on a pine-log singin' dis tune,
>   'Twas—
> Hey, come-along, Jim-along Josey,
> Hey come-along, Jim-along Joe.

There was one with a whirl and a jump:

> Twist around, turn around, jump just so!
> Every time you turn around you jump Jim Crow!

The phrase became so popular that when a person was startled
he was said to "jump Jim Crow" and the name has attached it
self to the railway car for colored people. But in the beginning
it was just a catchy melody with a whirl and a jump.

There was nothing subtle or delicate about this kind of humor
but it was mirth without malice, fun without filth. In the hearty
and boisterous laughter evoked by the dialogue and song and th
buck-and-wing dancing there was relief from care, and nothing
that left a bad taste in the mouth.

There has been some effort to learn whether Lincoln was i
St. Louis on a night when Thackeray gave a reading there and
if so, whether Lincoln attended. Mr. Weik probably secured the
correct information from a man who knew Lincoln, and wh
said, that if Lincoln was in town, and knew that Thackeray wa

to lecture in one hall, and Rumsey's minstrels were to give a burnt-cork show in another, it would have been useless to look for Abraham Lincoln at the lecture.

Probably Lincoln never heard the genuine Christy singers. While he was in Chicago in the spring of 1860, trying the "Sandbar case" he attended Rumsey and Newcomb's minstrels, and greatly enjoyed the evening. There, for the first time, he heard that "Ethiopian Walk-around," by D. D. Emmett, *Dixie*. Whitney says:

"It was then entirely new; and was the most extravagant minstrel performance I ever saw. Lincoln was perfectly 'taken' with it, and clapped his great hands, demanding an encore, louder than anyone. I never saw him so enthusiastic.*

Lincoln never ceased to enjoy *Dixie*. It was played at a White House serenade just after the surrender of Lee's army, and Lincoln made reference to it as having been captured from the Confederates, and being legitimately ours.

Lincoln enjoyed a story told concerning a son of President John Tyler, who went to the president of the Baltimore and Ohio railway and asked for a special train for the president, who had been invited to deliver an address in another city. The president of the railway was a Whig, and had no love for Tyler. "Our regular train is good enough," he answered curtly.

"But," said young Tyler, "you furnished a special train for the funeral of the late President Harrison."

To which the railway chief replied, "Tell President Tyler that under like conditions I shall be very glad to furnish a special train for him."

One of the humorists whom Lincoln greatly enjoyed was "Orpheus C. Kerr,"† or "Office Seeker" who wrote from intimate knowledge of Washington his then much enjoyed papers. To General Meigs Lincoln spoke of an incident which, he said, Or-

---

*Whitney's *Life on the Circuit with Lincoln*, p. 88.
†The real name of "Orpheus C. Kerr" was Robert H. Newell. He published one volume of sketches in 1862, and another in 1863. Both of those Lincoln read and enjoyed. A third volume was published later.

pheus C. Kerr would use to advantage, and he was surprised to know that Meigs had never heard of him. Lincoln said:

"Why, have you never read his papers? They are in two volumes. Any one who has not read them is a heathen." He added that he enjoyed those that made fun of members of his Cabinet, but he thought that those members liked better the ones that made fun of him. Lincoln said that he did not think those that made fun of him were really as funny as those that joked about his Cabinet. Some members of the Cabinet were present when Lincoln, himself joking, made these remarks. Lincoln said he especially enjoyed an allegorical poem by this author which represented McClellan as a monkey preparing to fight a serpent, but afraid to fight until he had more tail. So he repeatedly called on Jove for more tail, which Jupiter gave to him until the monkey was too much encumbered by his tail to move at all.

Henry J. Raymond, the editor of the *New York Times,* thus tells of Mr. Lincoln's fondness for the Nasby letters:

"It has been well said by a profound critic of Shakespeare, and it occurs to me as very appropriate in this connection, that 'the spirit which held the woe of Lear and the tragedy of *Hamlet* would have broken had it not also had the humor of the *Merry Wives of Windsor* and the merriment of the *Midsummer Night's Dream.'*

"This is as true of Mr. Lincoln as it was of Shakespeare. The capacity to tell and enjoy a good anecdote no doubt prolonged his life.

"The Saturday evening before he left Washington to go to the front, just previous to the capture of Richmond, I was with him from seven o'clock till nearly twelve. It had been one of his most trying days. The pressure of office-seekers was greater at this juncture than I ever knew it to be, and he was almost worn out.

"Among the callers that evening was a party composed of two senators, a representative, an ex-lieutenant-governor of a western state, and several private citizens. They had business of great importance, involving the necessity of the president's examination of voluminous documents. Pushing everything aside, he said to one of the party:

" 'Have you seen the Nasby papers?'

" 'No, I have not,' was the reply; 'who is Nasby?'

" 'There is a chap out in Ohio,' returned the president, 'who has been writing a series of letters in the newspapers over the signature of Petroleum V. Nasby. Some one sent me a pamphlet collection of them the other day. I am going to write to "Petroleum" to come down here, and I intend to tell him if he will communicate his talent to me, I will swap places with him!'

"Thereupon he arose, went to a drawer in his desk, and, taking out the 'Letters,' sat down and read one to the company, finding in their enjoyment of it the temporary excitement and relief which another man would have found in a glass of wine. The instant he had ceased, the book was thrown aside, his countenance relapsed into its habitual serious expression, and the business was entered upon with the utmost earnestness."

Concerning Lincoln's love for the Nasby letters written by David R. Locke of the *Toledo Blade,* there is abundant testimony. These letters with their atrocious spelling were mostly dated at "Confederit X Roads which is in the State of Kentucky." Their author, the Reverend Petroleum Vesuvius Nasby, was alleged to be pastor of a congregation in that place. His pastoral duties however, occupied small place in his correspondence. He was a seeker after political honors from the local postmastership to the presidency. Lincoln read these letters as they appeared from week to week. When the first group of them was issued in pamphlet form he read and reread the letters both for his own edification and the instruction of his friends. It is interesting to find him reading them to the dignified Senator Charles Sumner. So impressed was the Massachusetts Senator with Lincoln's love of this literature that the Senator himself consented to write the introduction to a collected edition of the Nasby letters issued in 1872. Senator Sumner's story of Lincoln's love for this literature constitutes the closing portion of this introduction:

I had occasion to see President Lincoln very late in the evening of March 17, 1865. The interview was in the familiar room known as his office, and was also used for cabinet meetings. I did not take leave of him until sometime after midnight, and then the business was not entirely finished. As I rose, he said, "Come to me when I open shop in the morning; I will have the order written, and you shall see it." "When do you open shop?" said I. "At nine o'clock," he replied. At the hour named I was in the same room I had so recently left. Very soon the President entered, stepping quickly with the promised order in his hands which he at once read to me. It was to disapprove and annul the judgment and sentence of a court-martial in a case that had excited much feeling. While I was making an abstract for telegraph to the anxious parties, he broke into a quotation from Nasby. Finding me less at home than himself with his favorite humorist, he said pleasantly, "I must initiate you." And then he repeated with enthusiasm the message he had sent to the author:

"For the genius to write these things, I would gladly give up my office."

Rising from his seat, he opened a desk behind, and, taking from it a pamphlet collection of the letters already published read with infinite zest, in which his melancholy features grew bright. It was a delight to see him surrender so completely to the fascination. Finding that I listened, he read for more than twenty minutes, and was still proceeding, when it occurred to him that there must be many at the door waiting to see him on graver matters. Taking advantage of a pause, I rose, and, thanking him for the lesson of the morning, went away. Some thirty persons, including senators and representatives were in the ante-room as I passed out. Though with the president much during the intervening time before his death, this was the last business I transacted with him. A few days later he left Washington for City Point, in the James River, where he was at the surrender of Richmond. April 6, I joined him there. April 9, the party returned to Washington. On the evening of April 14, the bullet of an assassin took his life. In this simple story, Abraham Lincoln introduces Nasby.

Lincoln's love for the writings of Artemus Ward was very great. He loved the autobiographical sketches by the proprietor of the "highly moral show" with which Artemus professed to be touring the country, and of his various adventures when en route. His "wax figgers" afforded him opportunity to discuss various historic characters. When the crowd pulled the hay out of the fat man, the palpable fraud which Artemus had been perpetrating caused the president to roar with appreciation. The kangaroo, "that amusin' little cuss," could be counted on now and then for a flying adventure, and Artemus had a "boy-constrictor" that was useful on occasion. But Artemus did not confine his discussions to the show business. He professed to have visited Washington and the White House, where he roundly lectured the office seekers for bothering Old Abe when they ought to have been in better business. He drove them out by threatening to turn his "boy-constrictor" in among them. When, according to this facetious narrative, Lincoln in gratitude asked the advice of Artemus about the composition of his Cabinet, Artemus advised him to select its members wholly from showmen—"Showmen are all honest; for particulars see small bills."

Artemus also journeyed to Richmond, according to these narratives, and interviewed Jefferson Davis, whom he scolded soundly for attempting to break up the Union. He opined "that it would have been ten dollars in Jeff's pocket if he had never been born." Meat was so scarce in the hotels in Richmond that Artemus forbore to order steak or roast; horses, cats and dogs, he averred, were substituting for those luxuries in the Richmond hotels. So Artemus ordered hash; then he knew just what he was getting.

Artemus was a patriot; he was determined to put down the rebellion if in the effort he sacrificed all his wife's relations. He was troubled for a time in Washington, to discover what the initials M. C. stood for, at length he learned. They stood for the title "Miserable Cuss."

When Charles Farrar Browne began writing these letters for the *Cleveland Plain Dealer,* he probably had little intention of going into military or political matters. He may or may not have known that the name he chose for himself, Artemus Ward, was, except for a slight variation in spelling, the name of a Revolutionary general.

Much of the quality which caused his humor to be most appreciated in its day was due to current interest in matters concerning which taste has changed and memory of events grown dim. But a student of the period of the Civil War would have no difficulty in understanding Lincoln's appreciation of this war-time humor. Artemus Ward may not have gone the full length of his generous offer in sacrificing all of his wife's relations to the putting down of the rebellion. But his broad wholesome humor together with his understanding of military and political conditions and his intelligent sympathy with Lincoln in the burdens he was bearing certainly contributed effectively to that result. He did help put down the rebellion.

CHAPTER XXX

MRS. LINCOLN

THE tomb at Oak Ridge received the mortal remains of Abraham Lincoln, and left his widow in her almost solitary grief. How alone she was, and how worse than useless was some of the advice she had, is pitifully evidenced in a book that betrayed her confidence and proclaimed to the public her aberrations and follies.* Not yet has the world been just to her. I should like, if I can, to give a fair and truthful picture of that much abused woman.

If the light that beats upon a throne is such as to reveal every sad frailty of him who occupies it, the light that glances upon and within the White House is still more cruelly searching. Not without reason has the presidency been declared a man-killing job. The bullet has killed three of our presidents; but these are not our only presidential murders. It is no part of the prerogative of this book to compile a list of them.

But if we are unintentionally cruel to our presidents, what shall be said of the manner in which we treat their wives? Who among them has escaped idle curiosity and even spiteful slander, from staid Martha Washington and gay Dolly Madison down to the second Mrs. Woodrow Wilson and Mrs. Warren G. Harding?

No woman who has occupied the White House has been more vulnerable to attack than Mary Todd Lincoln; and no one of them, unless possibly the wife of President Andrew Jackson, suffered such merciless slander. The time has come when it

---

*Behind the Scenes, by Elizabeth Keckly.

should be possible to tell the truth and the whole truth concerning Mary Todd Lincoln.

Both by birth and breeding, Mary Todd Lincoln was a proud and ambitious woman. In her girlhood she was admired rather than loved; for though she had a generous nature, and on occasion could go to great lengths of devotion for those she liked, she had a quick wit and a sharp tongue.

She was affectionate, ardent, passionate, and to a hot temper she joined a stubborn will. She married Abraham Lincoln as deliberately as such a woman ever could do anything. She was a creature of impulse, but she had her choice. She selected Abraham Lincoln from among her many suitors for two reasons; he was likely to gratify her ambition, and she sincerely cared for him.

Their courtship was tempestuous. We ignore all disputable details; they quarreled; they were foredoomed to quarrel. After their marriage, they still quarreled. He annoyed her often, infuriated her sometimes, by his disregard of convention and his lack of appreciation of her feelings. He was thick-skinned and oblivious of minor discomforts; she was sensitive to a degree.

Usually he bore her outbursts of temper with good-natured imperturbability; it did Mary good to scold, and did not hurt him. If she continued to scold, he put on his hat and walked to the office or to a seat in the corner store, and returned serenely after the storm had blown over. But there were times (and this is a part of the story as yet untold), when even his thick skin wore through. Once in a long while his sluggish but vehement temper got the better of him; and when it did, he said and did things which afterward caused him bitter self-reproach.

Those do greatly err who say that Mary Todd married Abraham Lincoln out of spite or revenge, or that he married her solely out of ambition. The fact is, that, spite of all their quarrels, they cared for each other.

Lincoln was a man of great ambition. He wanted office, always wanted it; and when in office always wanted a higher office. Ambition was the main spring of his career. Mary Todd was quite as ambitious as her husband, and had quite as sound judgment as he with regard to the best way to realize their ambition. She knew practical ways of assisting him, and she employed those ways.

Those who represent the married life of the Lincolns as unbroken by disagreement and quarrel hold their opinions in the face, or in ignorance, of a large body of incontrovertible evidence. On the other hand, those who assume that Lincoln and his wife did nothing but quarrel, are even more in error. Congenial they certainly were not, and they made each other uncomfortable. She nagged him unmercifully, and made home a place where he could not be assured of comfort. That was well for him. He was a man too fond of ease to have been successful in political life if wedded to a woman who made an ideal home.

That Lincoln felt the lack of a quiet and happy home life is undeniable, but he felt it less than a more finely sensitive man would have done. To spend his week-ends in distant taverns, while other members of the bar packed their saddle-bags and went home, was less of a trial to Lincoln than it would have been to most of them. But in his own big, undemonstrative, imperturbable way, Lincoln loved his wife, and was enormously proud of her. No letters are preserved which he sent home while away in those early days, but his telegrams and despatches addressed to her in the absences of Mrs. Lincoln from Washington showed real solicitude and careful consideration. He was proud of her beauty, her wit. Like other big men who have little wives, he enjoyed "the long and short" of their matrimonial combination. Usually he spoke of her as "Mrs. Lincoln," but in his letters to Speed he called her by his pet name for her, "Mollie."

It has been charged that Mrs. Lincoln's political faith was very different from that of her husband. It is true that after the death of Mr. Lincoln, she wrote letters of complaint in which she spoke of "the Republicans" as though she were not of them; but this had reference to personal grievances and apparent neglect. So far as I am aware no such letters exist for the period in which Lincoln was living. Her letters to her family in the years before the war, when the Republican Party was forming, and Mr. Lincoln was casting in his lot with them, show no lack of interest in his movements, but on the contrary display an active and intelligent support of him in all his plans. Thus she wrote to her sister in Kentucky on November 23, 1856:

Your husband, like some of the rest of ours, has a great taste for politics and has taken much interest in the late contest, which has resulted much as I expected, not as I hoped. Although Mr. Lincoln is or was a Fremont man, you must not include him with so many of those who belong to that party, an abolitionist. In principle he is far from it. All he desires is that slavery shall not be extended, let it remain where it is. My weak woman's heart was too southern in feeling to sympathize with any one but Fillmore. I have always been a great admirer of his—he made so good a President, and is so good a man, and feels the necessity of keeping the foreigners within bounds. If some of you Kentuckians had to deal with the Wild Irish as we housekeepers are sometimes called upon to do, the South would certainly elect Fillmore next time. The Democrats have been defeated in our state in their governor; so there is a crumb of comfort for each and all. What day is so dark that there is no ray of sunshine to penetrate the gloom? Now sit down, and write one of your agreeable missives, and do not wait for a return of each from a staid matron, and, moreover, the mother of three noisy boys.

Thus did Mrs. Lincoln write to her sister, Mrs. Ben Hardin Helm, just after the defeat of Frémont, wishing that the next president, to be elected presumably by the South, might be Fillmore. The South did not elect the next president, and the next president was not Fillmore. But the notable thing about this letter, and it is not the only such letter, is that Mrs. Lincoln wrote to her sister, wife of a Democratic politician who later became a Confederate general, expressing her regret that the Democrats had won the national election, and, knowing that her sister would not share her feeling in this matter, taking to herself a compensating "crumb of comfort" in the defeat of the Democrats in Illinois. There was nothing spiteful or tantalizing or untactful in this letter; it was written in the best spirit of sisterly frankness; its candor is unmistakable, as is her loyalty to her husband's political principles.

At length the incredible thing occurred which Mary Todd Lincoln had always believed would happen, and she became the first lady of the land. It was a position for which she was not well fitted either by nature or by training, and the conditions of those times were such as to show her in her least favorable light. The truth was bad enough concerning her infirmities of temper and the strain which the new position put upon her, but not every one stopped at the truth.

More than once, as just after the battle of Bull Run, the family of the president was advised to leave Washington. Mrs. Lincoln was by nature a woman of great timidity; her courage was the courage of sheer will-power and moral conviction; but she refused to go; and her presence was an encouragement to her husband.

Lincoln did not know how to bear lightly his terrible load of responsibility. His wife contrived to invite old friends to meals at the White House, especially to breakfast. She laughed and joked with them as they talked of old days in Illinois. Mrs. Lincoln assumed a benevolent despotism over her husband, and compelled him to drive with her every afternoon. This afforded him a blessed relief, and one he would not have taken had her sway over him been less absolute.

Her attempts to lift the cloud of gloom that hung over the White House were not wholly successful. If she gave a reception, she was criticized for displaying joy at a time when the nation was suffering defeat upon the battle-field and sorrow in its homes; if she did not give a reception, she was criticized for not doing so. Her social errors were noted, exaggerated, and made the subject of unbecoming mirth.

In the White House she displayed much want of tact. Her blundering outspokenness and disregard of diplomatic consideration were known and proclaimed throughout Washington and the nation. Her dress, which was extravagant rather than beautiful, her foibles and follies and inexperiences, all were whispered in ridicule or shouted from the housetop in contempt.

Nor did the gossip stop with ridicule of her social errors. It was charged that she did not love her husband and was planning to elope with a Russian count. The hyenas of Washington, some of them in the pay of the Confederate Government, said things about her as false as they were foul. On the other hand, it was very generally charged that she was a Confederate spy; and the soldiers around the camp-fire joined her name in ribald song with that of Jefferson Davis.

Peace came at last, and there was mercifully granted to Abraham and Mary Lincoln a brief interval in which they were permitted to build castles in the air. Up to the time of the second election, they had always assumed that when they left the White House they would return to Springfield to live. Now there were opened before them longer vistas. They would see the second term of office through, and the wounds of the country healed; there would be a policy of forbearance and forgiveness and good will. The period of office which had begun under the cloud of war would end in the sunlight of peace. Then they would travel. They would go to California and see men digging out the gold that was to pay the national debt. They would take the boys and go to Europe. They would visit the Holy Land. They were no longer sure that they would return to Springfield; if their hearts pulled them back to their old home, well and good; but if otherwise, they would find a home where it might seem best. In the meantime there was Peace, and immediately before them was the work of rebuilding the desolate places and healing the wounds which strife had caused. And under the stars and stripes there was not a single slave.

Mrs. Lincoln's mind in the months that followed went over and over the events of their last drive together on the afternoon preceding his assassination. In no one conversation did she tell all that she remembered, but she related it many times and to all her friends. Mr. Arnold thus records the story of that drive as Mrs. Lincoln related it to him.

After the Cabinet meeting he went to drive with Mrs. Lincoln, expressing a wish that no one should accompany them, and evidently desiring to converse alone with her. "Mary," said he, "we have had a hard time of it since we came to Washington, but the war is over, and with God's blessing we may hope for four years of peace and happiness, and then we will go back to Illinois and pass the rest of our lives in quiet." He spoke of his old Springfield home, and recollections of his early days, his little brown cottage, the law office, the court room, the green bag for his briefs and law papers, his adventures when riding the circuit, came thronging back to him. The tension under which he had for so long been kept was removed, and he was like a boy out of school. "We have laid by," said he to his wife, "some money, and during this term we will try and save up more, but shall not have enough to support us. We will go back to Illinois, and I will open a law-office at Springfield or Chicago, and practice law, and at least do enough to help give us a livelihood." Such were the dreams, the day-dreams of Lincoln, the last day of his life. In imagination he was again in his prairie home, among his law books, and in the courts with his old friends. A picture of a prairie farm on the banks of the Sangamon or the Rock River rose before him, and once more the plough and the axe were to become as familiar to his hands as in the days of his youth.*

These were the castles which together they built in the air. So far as we know the story of these last days, no cloud came between Abraham and Mary Lincoln and their vision of hope. At evening time there was light.

---

*Arnold: *Life of Lincoln,* pp. 429-430.

Then came the assassin's bullet, and the dark.

The widow of Abraham Lincoln never recovered from the night of the tragedy at Ford's Theater. Her mind, none too well balanced at the best, became less and less stable. It is unfortunately true that her unreasonableness did not begin with her husband's assassination. Long before this she had manifested erratic tendencies. Readers of General Badeau's *Grant in Peace* will find abundant evidence of mental traits which must have been a severe trial to her husband. After every allowance has been made for prejudice and possible exaggeration, the picture which Badeau draws is a painfully convincing and unattractive one. One may hear from people who knew her, incidents showing that even in her young womanhood she was capable of outbursts of ungovernable rage. I have heard many of these, and some of them I believe; indeed, I do not care to deny any of them.*

Mary Lincoln returned to Illinois, and lived in Chicago for a time, at 372 West Washington Street between Elizabeth and Ann, in one of the marble front houses then in vogue. There she sat in the ashes of her hopes, and brooded and raved amid the unpaid bills of the New York merchants from whom she had foolishly bought more silks than she could ever hope to wear. There little Tad died, July 15, 1871. He had never been a very strong boy, and had an impediment in his speech; and his mother's heart had clung to him with especial tenderness.

In November, 1866, eighteen months after the death of her husband, Herndon shamed her widowhood by proclaiming that Lincoln loved Ann Rutledge and never loved his wife. This act of Herndon's was the less commendable because he had but recently written to her, and she had met him by appointment in the St. Nicholas Hotel in Springfield, on one of her surreptitious

*If any future biographer of Lincoln shall present other evidence, taken from an important document whose use is now forbidden for any purpose derogatory to the character of Mrs. Lincoln, I suppose myself to be familiar with that document; and while observing, as I am in honor bound to do, the conditions under which it is permitted to be read, I have taken its content fully into account in my estimate of Mary Lincoln.

isits to her husband's grave, and had talked with him at length
nd in kindness, telling him many incidents of value to him for
he purpose of his proposed book about her husband. That was
n September, 1866. The following month, Herndon made his
isit to John McNamar; and in November he delivered his lec-
ure on Ann Rutledge. Only about a dozen people came out to
ear him, and the reception accorded the lecture and the sever-
ty expressed in the discussion that followed were so unfavor-
ble that Herndon never delivered it again. But the widow of
he president of the United States was thus publicly proclaimed
o have been unloved by the father of her children; and the
ountry and world began to shed tears at the grave of Ann Rut-
edge. That young woman deserved the affectionate remem-
rance belonging to a virtuous prairie maiden; but what of the
wo men who told her story as a slur upon the widow of Abra-
am Lincoln?

Some years ago I was in Springfield at a time when the Gen-
ral Assembly of Illinois by vote took adjournment for a half-
ay and motored over to New Salem where there were speeches
nd a picnic dinner and the laying of a wreath upon the grave of
Ann Rutledge. That evening was spent in the home of a niece
f Mrs. Lincoln, a woman of culture and refinement who is no
onger living. She had read in the evening paper a full account
f the day's performance, and was hurt and indignant. She
aid:

"Mrs. Lincoln's nieces and her other relatives have no occa-
ion to deny that Mr. Lincoln had a youthful sweetheart; most
en have that experience. Nor do they deny that Ann Rutledge
as a worthy young woman; but no one in Springfield ever
eard of her until Herndon delivered his cruel lecture declaring
hat Lincoln never loved his wife. We who were with Mrs.
incoln in those days, and who know the incurable wound which
his stab gave to her already broken heart, must be pardoned if
e are less enthusiastic than the world at large appears to be
ver the object of Lincoln's youthful affection. It is hard for

us to forgive the neglect and slander which thereby undeservedly
came to Mary Todd Lincoln."

I have repeatedly served for a day or a week at a time as chaplain of one or the other House of the Illinois General Assembly
I have learned—if I did not already know—that the chaplain i
not permitted to address the House, but is expected to direct hi
words to Almighty God. I therefore have never felt entitled t
introduce a motion in the Legislature of the sovereign state o
Illinois. If at any future time it should become my privileg
thus to propose an item of business or to vote upon a pending
measure, I would interpose no objection to any plan to visit Nev
Salem or to pay deserved honor to the memory of Ann Rutledge
But I might venture to suggest that the General Assembly, on it
return from New Salem, turn aside from the main highway tha
leads to the comfort of the Springfield hotels, and pause for a
reverent moment at Oakwood Cemetery and drop a tear and lay
a wreath upon the grave of Mary Todd Lincoln.

At present there would appear no probability that I shall have
opportunity to make such a motion upon the floor of eithe
House of the Illinois General Assembly. I may, therefore, us
such privilege as is mine in addressing the readers of this book
and suggest that they do not permit their just and proper regard
for Ann Rutledge to add even though unintentionally to th
humiliation that has attached itself to the memory of Abraham
Lincoln's wedded wife.

As a part of the preparation for this work I went to the offic
of the court of Cook County and asked for the papers relating
to the trial of Mary Todd Lincoln for insanity. A preliminary
search failed to disclose the record. The index contained no clu
to such a case. The oldest clerks were called, and they knev
nothing about it and were disposed to be incredulous. The
found the record, more by special providence than otherwise, an
so far as the office knew, no one had ever found those paper
since they had been put away.

So far as the records show, and by reading between the lines

he sad thing was done as decently and with as much dignity as
ossible. The complaining witness was, of necessity, one who
tood very near to Mrs. Lincoln, her own son Robert T. Lin-
oln. The jury was composed of twelve as prominent men as
Chicago had at that time. It would appear that everything was
one that legally could be done to carry out what was deemed
ecessary, with as little publicity and with as much regard for
ropriety as possible. No docket number appears to have been
iven to the case, and the loose papers were conveniently lost or
islaid. But the court record is there, with the names of judge
nd jurors; and they are of such character as to forbid the sus-
icion that they acted hastily or through prejudice. There is
lso a transcript of the evidence, and it leaves no reasonable
oubt. Mary Lincoln was found insane, and a fit subject for
onfinement in one of the state hospitals for the insane in the
tate of Illinois. She was not taken to a state institution, but to
 private asylum at Batavia, Illinois, where, after a little more
han a year, she was declared cured. Another jury found her
restored to reason." The date of her first trial at which she
as pronounced insane was May 19, 1875; the second which re-
ulted in her release was on June 15, 1876 That she was indeed
nsane would seem past dispute; that she was restored to reason
 far less certain.

Mary Lincoln went abroad. During her exile, or at least a
art of it, her son did not know where she was. She returned to
America in October, 1880. The *New York Sun* told this story
f her arrival in the land where she had been hardly less than a
ueen:

When the *Amerique* reached New York a throng was assem-
led on the dock and a greater throng was in the street outside
he gates. During the tedious process of working the ship into
er dock, there was a great crush in that part of the vessel where
he gang-plank was to be swung. Among the passengers who
ere here gathered was an aged lady. She was dressed plainly.
Her face was furrowed and her hair was streaked with white.

This was the widow of Abraham Lincoln. She was almost un
noticed. She had come alone across the ocean, but a nephew
met her at quarantine. She had spent the last four years in the
south of France. When the gang-plank was swung aboard
Mme. Bernhardt and her companions, including Mme. Colum
bier of the troupe, were the first to descend. The fellow voy
agers of the actress pressed upon her to bid her adieu, and
cheer was raised which turned her head and provoked an as
tonished smile as she stepped upon the wharf. The gates wer
besieged, and there was some difficulty on bringing the car
riage, which was to convey the actress to the hotel. She tem
porarily waited in the freight-office at the entrance to the whar
Mrs. Lincoln, leaning upon the arm of her nephew, walke
toward the gate. A policeman touched the aged lady on th
shoulder, and bade her stand back. She retreated with he
nephew into the line of spectators, while Manager Abbey's car
riage was slowly brought in. Mme. Bernhardt was handed int
the carriage which made its way out through a mass of strug
gling longshoremen and idlers who pressed about it, and stare
in at the open windows. After it, went out the others who ha
been passengers on the *Amerique,* Mrs. Lincoln among the res

This is a story to bring tears to the eyes and rouse the soul t
righteous indignation. And there is good reason to believe tha
it is literally true.

Mrs. Lincoln returned to Springfield, and to the home of he
sister, Mrs. Edwards. It was the home in which she had firs
met Abraham Lincoln, and the home in which they were marrie

The days were mercifully shortened. She died of paralysi
on July 16, 1882. The attending physician made a post-morter
examination, and issued a statement that for years she had bee
the victim of a cerebral disease. This ought to have been
sufficient explanation of all that needed to be explained of he
violence of temper and her unfortunate words and doings.

This is the statement of her physician, Doctor Thomas W
Dresser:

In the late years of her life, certain mental peculiarities wer
developed which finally culminated in a slight apoplexy, produc

ing paralysis, of which she died. Among the peculiarities alluded to, one of the most singular was the habit she had during the last year or so of her life of immuring herself in a perfectly dark room, and, for light, using a small candle light, even when the sun was shining bright out of doors. No urging would induce her to go out into the fresh air. Another peculiarity was the accumulation of large quantities of silks and dress goods in trunks and by the cart-load, which she never used and which accumulated until it was really feared that the floor of the store room would give way. She was bright and sparkling in conversation, and her memory remained singularly good up to the very close of her life. Her face was animated and pleasing; and to me she was always an interesting woman; and while the whole world was finding fault with her temper and disposition, it was clear to me that the trouble was really a cerebral disease.

Mrs. Lincoln was a sadly abused woman. After all has been said that may truthfully be said about her unhappy disposition, three facts seem true beyond any reasonable question.

The first of these is that Abraham Lincoln loved his wife. There is no adequate evidence either that Lincoln loved Ann Rutledge so devoutly as to be incapable of loving another woman, or that the demonstrations of Mrs. Lincoln's vehement nature destroyed his affection for the mother of his children. While she was often a trial to him, and he as frequently a trial to her, he was proud of her, exhibited a tender solicitude for her comfort, and in many ways manifested a sincere affection for her.

The second truth is that Mary Lincoln loved her husband. If she had not loved him there was no need of her marrying him, for many men sought her hand when she was at liberty to choose among the most brilliant men of Springfield. While he offended her by his lack of polish and his ignorance of social usage, he still realized in large measure her ambitious dreams of what her husband might be, and the position to which his success would and did evidently elevate her.

The third truth is that Mrs. Lincoln was loyal to the nation. She was exposed to constant suspicion and was made the object

of cruel calumny. There is no shred of direct evidence of any
disloyal word or act upon her part. Most of her blood relations
were on the side of the Confederacy. Her brothers were Confederate officers. Her sisters were the wives of Confederate
soldiers. Her heart must have been torn in her divided personal
sympathies; but through it all there is one continuous line of
testimony unbroken by any credible record of any disloyal word
or treasonable act. She deserves very high commendation for a
loyalty which under very trying circumstances she unfalteringly
maintained.

CHAPTER XXXI

MR. LINCOLN

IN THE several places associated with the life-work of Lincoln there still remain small and diminishing groups of those who remember to have met him or to have heard him speak. In every such place visited by the author in the years in which this book has been in preparation, it has been his endeavor to search out these men and women and to hear from their own lips what they remember about Lincoln. Extensive correspondence has supplemented this method of inquiry, and I suppose myself to be personally acquainted with no inconsiderable fraction of the total number of men and women now living who knew Abraham Lincoln. A somewhat recent visit to Bloomington brought together, for conference with me, the entire group of men now living who remember to have heard Abraham Lincoln's lost speech. A large meeting held both morning and afternoon with a picnic dinner between, brought to the churchyard where Thomas and Sally Lincoln are buried, practically all the people who remember Lincoln's father and Lincoln's last visit to his father's grave. Anniversary celebrations of the Lincoln and Douglas debates have gathered to these seven cities the people who were present in each of them at these battles of the giants. Innumerable have been my visits to Springfield, in which city less than fifty people now living can be said to remember Abraham Lincoln. This, among other things, impressed me as I moved among the men who had really known Lincoln. They did not speak of him as "President Lincoln," nor as "Abraham Lincoln," much less did they use that offensive affectation of familiarity and call him

"Abe Lincoln." They had not learned the simple tribute which the world pays to its supremely great men, in dropping all titles and given names and referring to them simply as "Napoleon," "Gladstone," or "Washington"; they did not call him "Lincoln." In general they referred to him as "Mr. Lincoln."

There are titles enough by which we might call him. He held a commission in the army and might have been called Captain Lincoln. He received from a reputable college and later from a great university, the title of Doctor of Laws, and it would be legitimate to call him Doctor Lincoln. The free courtesy of the courts and the fact that occasionally he sat upon the bench, would have given to many a lesser man the title, Judge Lincoln. We may, and sometimes we must, speak of him as President Lincoln. But "the captains and the kings depart" and with them go captaincies and kingships. Ultimately, a man must stand and answer to his own name without titles and submit to an estimate of his naked personality as it presents itself to the judgment of posterity. Stripping away all titles, save only that which his neighbors in affectionate and dignified courtesy bestow upon him, let us endeavor in this closing chapter to discover what manner of man was Mr. Lincoln.

I. LINCOLN'S PERSONAL APPEARANCE

Few faces are more familiar than that of Abraham Lincoln. His countenance looks down on us from the walls of homes, schools, and public buildings. His full-length figure towers in bronze above several American towns, and a few of the cities of Europe. But how did he really look?

Certainly he was not in appearance an insignificant man. He has been described as ungainly and awkward, but no one ever described him as contemptible. There was that about him which led men everywhere to take notice of him. He could not conveniently be hid. Men might hate Lincoln, but they could not well ignore him. To this day, he may be held up to ridicule, and it is not difficult to find in him material that lends itself to misrepresentation, but he can not well be overlooked. There is, there always was, in Lincoln, something that called for comment and possibly for explanation.

We possess a very large body of material that enables us to judge of the personal appearance of Lincoln. He emerged into prominence as the daguerreotype was coming into common use. Many photographers desired to make pictures of him, and Lincoln was not averse to having his picture taken. More than a hundred authentic and original photographs exist, showing his appearance from early in his career in Springfield to a few days before his death.

We have also oil portraits in considerable number. Soon after Lincoln's election, artists flocked to Springfield. They set up their easels in the vacant Legislative Hall of the old Capitol, and Lincoln was accustomed to sit for perhaps an hour each morning as they worked, reading his mail as he posed for them. Most, if not all, of these portraits are preserved. Some of them have merit and all of them have historic interest.

Of portraits after he became president, we have one in some respects the most interesting of all, and surrounded by remarkable associations, that of Frank B. Carpenter, made for and preserved in his notable historical painting. The likeness is preserved in the detail portrait and in the painting of *The Signing of the Emancipation Proclamation*. The events which accompanied the making of this portrait are recorded in Carpenter's book, *Six Months in the White House*.

We are peculiarly fortunate in possessing the life-mask of Lincoln as well as the casts of his hands, the face made in Chicago by Leonard Volk, in the spring before Lincoln's nomination for the presidency, the hands made in Springfield by the same sculptor, within a week after Lincoln's nomination. Volk was not a great artist, and he valued these casts for the sake of a statue which he made and which possessed no considerable merit. But the casts were well made; and they preserve to all coming time not simply the bony structure of the hands and head, but the living lineaments of Abraham Lincoln. To this undoubtedly authentic record of his features and his hands must every sculptor and artist refer.

Down to the time of Mr. Lincoln's election to the presidency, he was clean-shaven. His decision to wear a beard caused widespread regret; for the beard added little that was decorative, and did not conceal the lower lip which was Lincoln's least attractive feature, while it hid a well modeled chin, and a jaw that was at once kind and firm.

People misjudged Lincoln who set him down as a clown or a simple rustic. A second and more careful look at him showed elements of dignity and nobility. Lincoln was great and capable of looking great. His portrait as we have become familiar with it is the portrait of a great man. Of him we could almost say, as the Duke of Wellington said after he had seen Webster:

"Sir, no man could be as great as Daniel Webster looked."

It is said that no man attains to distinction in public life who is not easily caricatured. The man who is really great must emphasize some great quality, or group of qualities, to the dangerous margin of exaggeration. Lincoln was easily caricatured; how gleefully the newspaper artists of the time availed themselves of his peculiarities, the files of illustrated journals both in America and in England testify.

Lincoln was a tall man. In any company his height made him conspicuous. This quality he accentuated by the long black coat and tall stiff hat which he habitually wore. He recognized the value of his own physical stature.

In his eleventh year that remarkable and rapid growth became noticeable. It was accompanied by a change in his manner and habit of thought. He passed from childhood into adolescence with unusual rapidity, and became shy and timid in the presence of women and even of men. It was almost the last thing he ever did rapidly. By the close of his seventeenth year he had reached a stature which he proudly announced as six feet four inches. He was loose jointed and sometimes sagged down to less than his proper height. Leonard Volk, the sculptor, measuring him without his boots, pronounced his height a little over six feet and one inch. The undertaker who prepared his coffin found that he could use the measurements suitable to a large man six feet in height. Lincoln could seldom meet a tall man without proposing that they measure heights by standing back to back. Very seldom did he meet a man as tall as himself.

Lincoln was thin, sinewy and raw-boned. He was narrow across the shoulders. His usual weight was about one hundred and eighty pounds. Physically he was a very powerful man. He could lift four hundred pounds with ease, and in one case was known to have lifted six hundred pounds.

Lincoln's arms and legs were abnormally long. When sitting on a chair he appeared no taller than other men. It was only when he stood that he rose above them. He stood with his feet parallel; his toes did not turn out. When he walked he did not rise upon his toes but lifted his whole foot at once and put it down all at one time, not landing first upon the heel. A stranger seeing his walk might easily have gotten the impression of cunning and shrewdness in his gait, but his was the walk of firmness and caution.

Gaunt and awkward as he was, there was a certain symmetry in his ungainliness. He was a homely man, but not ugly or repulsive. There was, indeed, a kind of Herculean majesty in his gigantic, powerful figure, dominated as it was by a well poised head that displayed kindly and kindling eyes. He possessed a bearing marked at once by self-confidence and vigor.

Dwarfs are notoriously ill-natured; they have a constant feeling that nature has cheated them out of certain inches of stature which they are compelled to make good by self-assertion. Their life is one long protest against the world's temptation to ignore them. Giants, on the other hand, are habitually genial. They do not need to fight for recognition. Lincoln had the mental security, the complacent good-nature, which are native in a tall man.

That eminent psychologist, Doctor G. Stanley Hall, in a letter to the author, said:

The longer I live, the more importance I attach to physical traits. Lincoln's height, long limbs, rough exterior and frequent feeling of awkwardness, must have made him realize very early that to succeed in life he must cultivate intrinsic mental or moral traits which it is so hard for a handsome man or woman to excel in. Hence he compensated by trying to develop intellectual distinction. The mere factor of height and physical strength gives a man, even in civilized life, a certain superiority of which he and others are conscious. If Lincoln had been a little man, he would have been a very different one.

II. THE MIND OF LINCOLN

The study of the human intellect has passed through certain well-marked periods in the last half-century. In Lincoln's day phrenology was as popular as psychology is now. Those who attempted to analyze individual character studied the shape of the brain, believing themselves to be able to locate the different "organs" within it, by which the mind disclosed its various aptitudes. Phrenology is now an exploded science. Our present-day methods in psychology may one day be as obsolete as phrenology now appears to be. Many students when Lincoln was living or soon after he was dead attempted to account for him by the contour of his brain. Such methods would require extensive modification in the light of our present-day knowledge.

The study of psychology as conducted in colleges forty years ago considered the human mind as comprising intellect, sensibility and will. These were called "faculties." Memory and conscience were also sometimes spoken of as if they had their seat in some distinct portion of the mind. Faithful study of the phenomena of consciousness resulted in discarding the theory of faculties. The human mind came to be considered as a unit, in which perception and emotion and volition worked together.

Still another day has dawned, however. It is now clearly perceived that there is an ancient and primitive part of the brain common to all vertebrates. In this part of the brain the emotions have their seat. It is now held that the cerebral hemispheres are virtually a new brain. This new brain is not needed for emotion; a cat whose cerebral hemispheres are removed will snarl and show erection of its hairs quite as naturally as does a cat on which no operation has been performed.

It has been discovered that the ductless glands have an extraordinary influence upon behavior. There must have been a mighty stimulant of the pituitary gland in Abraham Lincoln just as he was emerging into adolesence. It would be an interesting and perhaps not a wholly unprofitable exercise for some psychologist to trace Lincoln's development in the light of such knowledge as we now have obtained concerning the glandular influences that regulate personality.

This we now know, that in the study of criminal tendency, it makes a difference in the hopefulness of the outcome whether a wayward boy is intellectually a criminal, or emotionally a criminal. We shall not return to the old psychology with its division of the mind into faculties, neither shall we be able to consider the mind so completely a unit as we once were disposd to think. The human mind has been described as a more or less disorderly attic, having in it some things that we have placed there, and many heirlooms and cast-off articles which we discover when we least expect and sometimes least desire them.

Not to all his associates did Abraham Lincoln appear to have a mind of unusual character. There were those among his acquaintances, including some who called themselves his friends, who believed his mind to be of mediocre quality, and who held that whatever there was about it that was distinctive contained nothing of which Lincoln had any occasion to be proud. Not a few men who knew Lincoln believed that his most important characteristic, as it related to his success in life, was a kind of cleverness which they described as "low cunning." Lincoln was secretive, Lincoln was shrewd. Certain people who thought they knew him spoke of him with his shrewdness and his love of humor as "a low, cunning clown." Not thus easily can we classify his mentality.

Lincoln's mind was deliberate, patient, capable of sustained effort and concentration. He had ability to reason from cause to effect. He possessed a clear discernment of power of motive. He had an understanding of the minds of men. His mental processes were slow but accurate, and he was quick to respond to stimuli in conversation or discussion. For a man so slow in his mental processes he was surprisingly quick in repartee. He shrank from the necessity of important decisions, yet when impelled by a sense of need or duty, he made his decisions with precision and with amazing firmness and courage. When he was certain in his judgment, it was exceeding difficult to move him. He was capable of resisting strong pressure. When he did not know what to do, he did not do anything. But when he decided he was inflexible.

But for all Lincoln's power of judgment, and his ability to reason, he held, in common with all great men, large confidence in his intuitions.

Every one knew that Lincoln was gentle and tender-hearted. He could not bear to see oppression in any form. He could not endure the thought of the infliction of needless pain. He was so kindly, so considerate, so patient, few people knew how capable he was of righteous indignation. Yet Lincoln had a mighty temper. He seldom lost control of it, but when he exhibited any outbreak of passion, it was not a thing to be lightly faced. Now and then a political opponent provoked him to wrath. Neither he nor those who heard Lincoln's treatment of him could ever forget the scourging that Lincoln would administer. One still may hear how he turned upon George Forquer with a sally as sharp as the point of the new lightning rod which Forquer had erected above his home, to protect him from the righteous wrath of an offended God for changing his politics simultaneously with his receiving a political appointment. The "skinning of Thomas" is an extreme instance of Lincoln's severity that drove his antagonist to tears, and caused Lincoln himself to feel that he had gone too far. Seldom did Lincoln's temper break away from the leash of his control, but when it did Lincoln was anything but a vacillating and feeble antagonist.

If it were necessary, illustrations might be multiplied of Lincoln's capacity for mighty wrath. Like his father, Thomas Lincoln, he was slow to anger, but like all truly great men he could be indignant when it was necessary, and in general, his periods of anger were well chosen. He was angry when he had need to be angry. The fact that he could and did become genuinely indignant is evidence that Lincoln was the kind of man he ought to have been.

Lincoln declared that he did not claim to have controlled events, but that he had been controlled by them. He spoke in part truly, but that was not the whole truth. In a very large sense he did control events, and his control was that of a man who trusted his own intellectual judgments and was capable of compelling other men to accept them, and approve them.

Lincoln possessed a mind capable of indefinite growth. Essentially one with the people among whom he was born and with whom he spent the years of his boyhood and youth, he early displayed a capacity for development that carried him beyond the horizon and above the level of the life of his associates. This he accomplished without at any point breaking his association with them. His root remained in the soil of his associations; but he grew until the terminal bud of his ideal was far above his associations.

He learned by his disappointments. Peter the Great is said to have accepted his early defeats in battle with a kind of glee— "They are teaching me how to fight," he is reported to have said. Lincoln fulfilled in his own career the old Latin proverb that it is lawful to learn from the enemy. He was educated by his defeats. After he suffered humiliation at the hands of Stanton in the Reaper case, he returned from Cincinnati to Illinois "to study law." He had learned something from a cruel disappointment, and he did not fail to make use of what he had learned. He returned from his one term in Congress, and mastered Euclid. He disciplined himself through his disappointments. Also, he grew through his successes. They increased his self-confidence, without spoiling him with vanity. Thus disciplined by both failure and success, Lincoln grew mentally, and he was growing to the very end of his life. His mind was a growing, a retentive, a noble, a truly great mind.

A sure test of Lincoln's intellectual processes is afforded by his literary style. The free use of words is no assurance of the ability to think. But Lincoln's clear, clean-cut, accurate and transparent use of English is the indubitable evidence of a mind working with precision, with conviction and with authority. Only a mind strong and clear and logical and well disciplined could have expressed itself as Lincoln's did in pure, accurate and forceful language.

Abraham Lincoln possessed a great mind. Born in the midst of penury, and destitute not only of educational advantages but of incentive to study, he obtained by force of will and strength of mental power a mind disciplined and of commanding ability.

He had a logical mind. He wanted, as he said, to be able to bound his subject, north, south, east and west. He had a fondness for mechanics which he transferred to his mental processes; he insisted on knowing the connections of truths, their causes and effects. He would be content with nothing short of truth.

Where he inherited this power and aptitude has given rise to much discussion. From his mother, as he believed, he inherited his power of analysis, his intellectual alertness, his gift of logic. But this is only a partial answer.

In his earlier environment there was, as he said, "absolutely nothing" to stimulate within him the love of learning; yet the love of learning was strong within him. Much did he owe to solitude, and the power of reflection. Yet his was a nature strongly social; and much that was inherent in him could not

have been evoked except in association and competition with
other men.

It is not to be wondered at that such attempts as have been
made to trace Lincoln's powers through his converging lines of
ancestry have been so clumsy and futile.   The requisite material
has not been available, and what little has been at hand has not
been explored in a scientific spirit.   The only group of his relations that has been investigated with anything approaching thoroughness has been certain of the Hanks families, and the less
said about these investigations the better.   They have not furthered reliable knowledge, and in the main have perverted truth.
As already stated, the largest present group of blood relations of
Lincoln are the Sparrows, descendants, some of them through
several lines, from his grandmother, Lucy Hanks.   But these
add their evidence to the maternal and not the paternal side.   As
yet we have quite inadequate material for an explanation of
Abraham Lincoln by heredity.   From whom did Abraham Lincoln inherit his mind?

Thomas Lincoln, certainly, was no such intellectual giant as
his son; and who among the Hankses could have fathered or
mothered such a mind as that of Lincoln?

It has been confidently asserted that Abraham Lincoln did
not have in him one drop of Lincoln blood; and that he betrayed this fact in his personal appearance, bearing a marked
resemblance to the Hanks family, which was a family of tall
men.*   Did he also resemble the Lincolns?   Most biographers
have traced resemblance or difference on the paternal side no
farther than to his father.   The extent to which he resembled
Thomas Lincoln has already been commented upon.   Abraham
Lincoln appears to have inherited quite as much from his father,
Thomas Lincoln, as his son, Robert Todd Lincoln, inherited
from him.   That Lincoln resembled his mother's family, the
Hankses, is undisputed; but it is not at all certain that this re-

---

*For a complete, and as I believe a final discussion of this question, I
refer to my book *The Paternity of Abraham Lincoln.*

semblance was more pronounced than that which he bore to the Lincoln side. There was more opportunity of comparison between him and the Hankses than between him and the Lincolns. When Thomas Lincoln, about 1802, removed from Washington County to Hardin County, Kentucky, he left the Lincoln family permanently behind. Members of the Hanks family, on the other hand, lived near him in Kentucky, followed him to Indiana and accompanied him to Illinois, where John Hanks was already located. At no time until his removal to Washington was Abraham Lincoln very far removed from representatives of his mother's family; but in all his life he appears to have met scarcely any of his father's relatives. Evidence is not lacking, however, that he was a thorough Lincoln, even in those very particulars that have been most confidently enumerated as belonging to the Hankses.

A striking illustration of this fact is found in the diary of John Hay in the year 1867 after his return from Washington to Illinois, and before his appointment to diplomatic service. Of a railroad journey in that state he left the following contemporary record:

Rode to Carthage in the same seat with Robert Lincoln, a second cousin of the late President. He is forty-one years old, looks much older. The same eyes and hair the President had—the same tall stature and shambling gait less exaggerated; a rather rough farmer-looking man. Drinks hard, chews ravenously. He says the family is about run out. "We are not a very marrying set." He is dying of consumption, he said very coolly. There was something startling in the resemblance of the straight thicket of hair, and the grey, cavernous eyes framed in black brows and lashes. He was a pioneer of our country. Knew my father since long years. Brought a load of wheat to Gould & Miller in 1842 with ox team; got $90 in gold for it. Told me that in 1860 he had talked with "Abe" about assassination. Abe said, "I never injured anybody; No one is going to hurt me." He says he was invited by "Abe" to go to Washington at the time of the inauguration, but declined, thinking it dangerous—a naivete of statement I thought would have been impossible out of the west.*

Mr. Hay was not writing with any thought of putting on record a piece of evidence regarding the paternity of Lincoln. He was simply recording the spontaneous impression which one received who had known Abraham Lincoln intimately, on meeting one of Lincoln's near relatives.

It has been my privilege to extend my study of Lincoln's antecedents much farther than Mr. Hay found opportunity to do, and to give some especial attention to the family group in which he discovered this striking resemblance. The conclusion is ineluctable; Abraham Lincoln was in very marked degree a Lincoln, even more than he was a Hanks. This fact does not wholly account for him; no great man can be accounted for. Thomas Carlyle had his scornful word concerning biographers who "do what they call account for" men of heroic mold. But it establishes Lincoln's place in the Lincoln family. In his personal appearance, movements of body and habits of thought, Abraham Lincoln was thoroughly a Lincoln.

The largest group of his blood relations on the Lincoln side are the descendants of Mordecai Lincoln, President Abraham Lincoln's uncle. These came to Illinois about a year before Thomas Lincoln migrated to Indiana, and made their home in Hancock County. There Mordecai Lincoln died in the winter of the deep snow, 1830. I have visited his descendants and have obtained not only facts and traditions and family records, but a considerable quantity of manuscript that comes direct from the Lincolns of the first generation in Illinois. Among these papers are many letters, accounts and essays of the second Mordecai Lincoln, first cousin of Abraham Lincoln. His handwriting is strikingly like that of his cousin Abraham, and his mental traits are arrestingly similar. It is little wonder that John Hay was impressed by the startling resemblance of one of these cousins,

---

*William Roscoe Thayer: *Life of John Hay*, i, p. 279.

one degree more remote, to "the great, dead man." These Lincolns resembled Abraham Lincoln not only in stature, color of hair, eyes, gait and manner of speech, but, what is more striking, they possessed and recognized as a family trait the moods to which the president was all his life subject. They went from boisterous mirth to the depths of despair without any visible occasion. They had what they called "the Lincoln horrors." None of them ever went insane, but all of them, the men even more than the women, were subject to violent transitions from one mood to another.

Lincoln's superstition, his fatalism, his belief in dreams and signs and portents was more than a family inheritance; it belonged to his environment. But certain mental predispositions appear to have been particularly characteristic of his family. Lincoln believed that he would die a violent death. That fact may not be difficult to account for considering the dangers in which he lived, and the repeated warnings received by him that his life was in danger. A premonition of approaching death was not, however, an unknown thing in the Lincoln family. One of his cousins was so sure of the manner in which he was to die, that his wife did not wish him to go to the woods alone lest a tree should fall upon him.

Our knowledge of the Lincoln family is far too meager to justify sweeping generalizations. It is a subject that will bear much more painstaking study than any one has yet devoted to it. Such study as I have been able to make appears to make it certain that some of Lincoln's most important characteristics were not purely individualistic, but are to be accounted for by family inheritance.

One subject, of very great delicacy and involving no little difficulty, will have to be considered in any thorough attempt to account for the mentality of Lincoln, and that is the degree of normality of his sexual life. The present would appear to be a time in which the phenomena of sex is finding over-emphasis, not only in current fiction and poetry but in more serious branches of literature. From this overstrained condition we may hope for a wholesome reaction. Nevertheless, the facts of sex are not to be ignored.

There is agreement among competent authorities that Abraham Lincoln lived a chaste life both before and after his marriage to Mary Todd. No charge of sexual irregularity, worthy of a moment's attention, has ever been made against him. Before his marriage he was shy in his relations with women; after his marriage, although he spent long weeks away from home and did not habitually return to Springfield for week-ends while he was riding the circuit, there lies against him no charge of loose conduct.

His first child, Robert T. Lincoln, was born on the two hundred and seventieth day following the marriage of Abraham Lincoln and Mary Todd, a period which tells its own story of immediate conception. His other children were born at regular intervals of about three years. Although he was neither impotent nor sterile, Abraham Lincoln had a morbid dread of the responsibilities of matrimony. In the case of Mary Owens, a partial explanation is to be found in his poverty, and the depression growing out of uncertainty regarding his own financial future.

But this does not wholly account for that strange courtship. In the case of Mary Todd, a partial explanation is to be found in such knowledge as we have of her violent temper and Lincoln's realization of his own lack of social grace. Other men, however, have contemplated marriage when disparities quite as great stared them in the face, and have made their decision unvexed by any such mental perturbation as characterized Abraham Lincoln. He was nearly thirty-four years of age when he married, and he contemplated the step with a thoroughly morbid hesitation.

It is unnecessary to review in detail the story of his courtship. We discover in Lincoln a man of domestic tastes and of pure life, a man who was upright in his relations with women before his marriage, was true to his wife and the father of a family of children, yet whose attitude toward marriage was influenced by a large degree of abnormality.

Robert Lincoln, the president's second cousin, told John Hay that the Illinois Lincolns "were not a marrying set." This fact has frequently been mentioned and commented upon in letters to me from members of the Lincoln family. The Lincolns tend to marry late if at all, and not to remarry in case of the death of husband or wife. The Hanks family was quite evidently adequately sexed. The Lincoln family appears to have been under-sexed.

There is a vague rumor to the effect that Lincoln was at one time in an insane asylum. That story appears to have no foundation whatever in fact; neither have I found records of near relatives of his who were pronounced insane. Twice, however, and perhaps oftener, Lincoln exhibited unstable mental equilibrium. One of these occasions occurred after the death of Ann Rutledge. The current accounts of his alleged insanity at that time have been considerably exaggerated; nevertheless there is adequate evidence of marked mental disturbance superinduced by grief.

The other period is that which followed what he called, "the fatal first of January," 1841. Here also there has been exaggeration as has been shown in another chapter. But his letter to Stuart can have no other meaning than this, that Lincoln believed himself to be in danger of going permanently insane.

Lincoln, in common with other members of the Lincoln family, had periods of profound depression, alternating with others of boisterous hilarity. Not only did he make others laugh when he was gay; he laughed uproariously at his own jokes. But there were other times when his gloom "dripped from him as he walked." His mind was rocked between mighty emotions, from gleeful mirth to profound melancholy.

Superficial critics have their easy way of accounting for Lincoln's moods. The sentimental ones among them like to think that he received such a shock by reason of the death of Ann Rutledge, that he never was completely happy afterward. Those who enjoy putting the worst possible aspects upon his none too happy married life, have no difficulty in explaining his moods by reference to the hot temper and unreasonable and capricious will of Mary Todd. There is no occasion to deny whatever of influence may properly be attributed to these conditions of Lincoln's life. But these alone do not account for his alternate mirth and melancholy. Something of the explanation is to be found in these incidents, but something also in those elements of the man himself which grow out of his heredity and his own peculiar psychological development.

No man has any right entirely to outgrow his emotions. Abraham Lincoln never did so. Affection, sympathy, mirth, and even capacity for mighty wrath, belonged to him. But the man who would think clearly must sometimes be able to keep his intellectual processes in one compartment, and his emotions in another, separated by a nearly water-tight bulkhead. If he can not do this he will find his thinking water-logged, and his conclusions will flounder and sink. There comes a time when a man must learn to get light without heat. Abraham Lincoln acquired that ability. He was able to face an intellectual problem intellectually, and resolutely think it through. He was gifted with a kind of remorseless logic, which upon occasion made him master of an intellectual adjustment almost mechanical in the perfection of its workings.

His very ability to tell a story or crack a joke in a time when the emotional strain grew tense, was evidence of a high degree of normality of judgment. It enabled Lincoln to accomplish an adjustment between emotion and sound logic which tended enormously to a clarity of judgment. "I laugh because I must not cry; that's all, that's all," he said. That was as good a reason, perhaps, as he could give to any one else, but there was a deeper psychological reason than he could have understood. He laughed because for him it was a time when laughter was the most normal method possible of adjusting the balance between intellect and emotion, and preparing for sound and sensible judgment.

This fact about Lincoln's poise of intellect and emotion must not pass without emphasis. Lincoln was by nature a man of powerful emotions. More than once in his youth his mind approached a condition of instability. Anger, lust and a melancholy so deep that it blackened the whole sky, were all within the potentialities of his nature. He learned self-control. Capable of towering rage, he seldom lost his temper. Capable of mighty sexual passion, he lived a life of chastity. And as the years went by, he so far mastered his moods as to make him capable of concentrated and continuous thought.

We are living in a time when it is fashionable to talk of "complexes" and "inhibitions," and there is much tendency to make men the victims of circumstances and the helpless puppets of their own subconscious minds. Lincoln taught his conscious mind and deliberate will to rule his spirit and direct his energies. He became master of his own destiny by being the captain of his own soul.

An important lesson is here for men and women who suppose themselves to be the inevitable victims of their own environment and heredity. Powerful as are the dead hands which reach down through heredity and grip the lives of successive generations, life and the mastery thereof belong not to the dead but to the living. Men are not inevitably the victims of their own debilitated wills or disordered imaginations. It is possible by patient, resolute, persistent soul-culture, to rise measurably above constitutional and hereditary limitations. Tennyson declared

> That men may rise on stepping stones
> Of their dead selves to higher things.

Rather more difficult appears the problem in the light of present day psychology. A man must rise, if he rises at all, on stepping stones of his living self to higher things. St. Paul was not the only man who discovered the necessity of buffeting his own body and keeping it under, lest having preached to others, he should himself become a castaway. The problem of triumphant life is that and more. A man must buffet and conquer certain elements in his own mentality, enthroning not simply the mind above the body, but enthroning also within the mind those powers and faculties which constitute his noblest self.

The lesson of the Chambered Nautilus is still as good as when Holmes wrote his poem about it. The soul must build itself, and the human mind has built for itself, "more stately mansions" than those which the anatomy of the human brain makes manifest as the evolution of the primitive heritage of vertebrate life. But we are not able wholly to "leave our low-vaulted past." As we bear about in our bodies rudimentary organs analagous to those of lower animal life, yet use instead of them those that are distinctive of our humanity, so we bear about in our minds the vestiges of impulse and desire whose enthronement within us would be fatal to all nobility of soul.

This we know about Abraham Lincoln, that with much in his environment unfavorable to higher development, and with inherent tendency to lethargy, indolence, torpor and a brooding melancholy which if indulged would have been fatal to all resolute endeavor, he made himself master of his environment and master of his own mind. Wise was the man who, in the book of Proverbs, is placed highest among the conquerors, the man that ruleth his own spirit.

III. LINCOLN AS A BUSINESS MAN

This topic might be treated with extreme brevity. It might be affirmed that Lincoln was not a business man, and that there was, therefore, nothing to be said about him in that capacity. If proof were demanded, a considerable body of testimony would be found available. It would be remembered that Lincoln was declared by his friends to "have had no money sense." It will be recalled that his successive ventures as a merchant in New Salem all were doomed to financial ruin. It will not be forgotten that for many years he was in debt, and did not succeed in paying

the last of his indebtedness until his term in Congress in 1847-8.
It will not be forgotten that in his second term in the Legislature
of Illinois he was on the Finance Committee, and that he had his
full share of responsibility for plunging Illinois into that morass
of speculation and wild financiering which wrought ruin for the
state and for all who shared the unfounded hopes of that period.
It will surely be recited that in those days Lincoln aspired to be
"the DeWitt Clinton of Illinois," considering himself to possess
a financial acumen which he did not possess then or afterward.
All this can be said and has been said, and it would seem to prove
the unwisdom of attempting to talk about Abraham Lincoln as
a business man. But it is that subject which we are to consider.

First of all, Abraham Lincoln was honest. He had that first
requisite for business success. Business is done on the basis of
confidence, and confidence must be founded upon the belief that
men are honest. He paid his debts; he paid the debts incurred
by his partner. It took him years to do it, but he did it. While
still a young man he earned the name of "Honest Abe," and he
held it and deserved it as long as he lived. In this particular, at
least, Mr. Lincoln had the fundamental qualification for a successful business life. He possessed moral character, and he was
able to make men believe in him. Without this quality there can
be no permanently successful business.

Further, we should remember, Lincoln did not fail permanently.
We are told every now and again that nine-tenths of American
business men fail. The proportion probably is not anywhere
nearly so large as this. But if they fail, they do not, for the
most part, fail permanently. The man who fails as a farmer
succeeds as an inventor. The man who fails as a school-teacher
succeeds as an editor. The man who fails as a preacher succeeds
as a doctor. The man who fails as a lawyer succeeds as a vendor
of real estate. This is the characteristic of American life, not
that no one fails in America but that very few men stay failed.
They rise again, if they have energy, character and enthusiasm;
and after one or more failures, they succeed. Lincoln failed as

the keeper of a country store. The town failed. It "winked out." It was not possible that any one should permanently succeed there. The hopes upon which the future of the town were based were insecure. But when the firm of Lincoln and Berry failed, Lincoln studied surveying and law, and he found something that he could do successfully.

To be sure, he gained money slowly. Fees were small, and Lincoln's fees were smaller than those of some of his associates. Still, he gained wealth in modest measure. He paid up his debt. He bought and paid for a home. He did not hesitate to sue the Illinois Central Railway Company for a good round fee, and he collected it. He was not covetous, but he knew the value of money, and the money that he earned he collected and kept. When he left Springfield for Washington, he had money in the bank, no large sum, but still quite enough to keep him out of fear of poverty, and his practise was growing more remunerative year by year. His investments were conservative, and the money which he gained was not wasted in idle neglect or covetous speculation. Had he lived on as a lawyer, he would never have been rich; but he would have developed more and more of business ability within the sphere of his experience, and would have been accounted a successful man. Such we may properly account him.

Lincoln's office has often been described as a very untidy and disorderly place. Lincoln had no system or order in the arrangement of his office affairs. But he was able to draw his papers in good form, and write out his documents in a clear hand and with precision of statement. His bookkeeping was of the very simplest character, if, indeed, he can be said to have kept any books. When he collected a fee, he divided it in two equal parts, and marked one "Herndon's half" and left it on his table. That was simple, but it was methodical. And it was sufficient for their needs.

Finally, Lincoln died possessed of a modest fortune. It is true that after his death many articles were published stating that Mrs. Lincoln had been left in a condition of penury. Mrs. Lincoln herself, in her disordered mental condition, contributed something to this impression. As late as December, 1922, letters of hers which had not previously been published appeared in the newspapers, telling of her poverty after the death of her husband. The truth is that at the time of his death, Lincoln was worth more than one hundred and ten thousand dollars, most of it invested in good government bonds. While he was not rich, even as wealth was then estimated among men in high official life, he left Mrs. Lincoln an assured income of about five thousand dollars a year, and Congress added to this a modest pension.

Thus, judged even from the standpoint of success in accumulating wealth, Lincoln can not be counted a failure as a business man. Judged by the principles which underlay this measure of success, his integrity, honesty and application to duty, Lincoln may be counted a success.

Nearly every man has to be a business man in some degree. Not every man has to be a merchant prince, but it is important that a man shall do well such business as he has to do. Judged by what was necessary to him in the conduct of the business that legitimately belonged to him, Abraham Lincoln was not a failure as a man of affairs. He may be considered something of a success; for he paid his honest debts and left his family sufficient provision for their requirements. That is success in business.

IV. THE CHARACTER OF LINCOLN

Some aspects of the character of Lincoln lie revealed upon its surface. His transparent sincerity, his rugged honesty, his exalted sense of honor, his kindness of heart, are written so plain that he who runs may read. Yet he who attempts to account for Abraham Lincoln by any simple canon of judgment will find himself baffled. Whatever consistency there was in Lincoln's life was made up of the union of antithetic elements. Of him might have been said as was said of Brutus:

> His life was gentle, and the elements
> So mixed in him that Nature might stand up
> And say to all the world, "This was a man."

All strong characters have to their credit some quality of obstinate and laudable inconsistency without which they could not be consistent with themselves. In them we discover that paradox which John Hay attributed to Jim Bludsoe, by reason of which the passengers of the flaming boat "put their faith in his cussedness, and knew that he'd keep his word." Tennyson recognized this strong moral paradox:

> His honor, rooted in dishonor stood,
> And faith, unfaithful, kept him falsely true.

What St. Paul and Augustine and Anthony found of the warfare within themselves is that which all great men have experienced. If the inconsistency be not in the sphere of ethics, still is it present in some mental maladjustment which provides at length its own equilibrium. The equipoise of mental traits that seem opposed and of moral principles in apparent conflict, constitute the centripetal and centrifugal forces of character. Few men have been so consistently inconsistent as Abraham Lincoln.

The character of Abraham Lincoln combined in marked degree humility and self-confidence. In some aspects of his life, his humility was very nearly complete. He felt his own limitations and acknowledged them with sincerity and sometimes with sorrow. On the other hand, he was strangely and profoundly conscious of his power. Seward and Chase and other men who knew the superiority of their training to his, and who heard him confess his own deficiencies, were amazed when he quietly ceased to defer to them and asserted his own judgment and conviction with a finality that brooked no further opposition. John Hay is right in saying that in this aspect of his character Lincoln was far from being a modest man, that this power of self-assertion in him was something which these men found almost intolerable, and were never able to forget.

Every truly great man recognizes his own limitations; Lincoln was painfully aware of them. But every great man is aware, also, of his power, and without that consciousness of power he could never become great. Lincoln had this consciousness of strength, and it combined with an enormous ambition. Not all his protestations of humility are to be taken at their full face value. Some of them were half ironical, and were used to disarm an opponent by a confession of inequality, an acknowledgement of his adversary's superior education or wealth or social position. They were sometimes as clever as were Mark Antony's declaration of his own lack of eloquence and unworthiness to speak at Cæsar's funeral, and his praise of Brutus and the other honorable men.

Lincoln was self-assertive to the point of arrogance. He made demands upon his friends which had no meaning except as he and they understood his position of superiority. The patient, humble Lincoln is known, or supposed to be known, to the world; but the men who really knew Lincoln knew a man so confident of his own powers, and so sure of his right to demand the loyalty and obedience of other men, that they never quite understood him. But they did his bidding.

Lincoln never worked well in a subordinate position. Dennis Hanks has told us how, in Lincoln's youth, if a stranger passed along the road and asked a question, it was Abraham who was ready with the first word, often to the displeasure of Abraham's father. Lincoln liked it little, when he entered Stuart's office, that he was expected to do the drudging work of the office while Stuart was out making political speeches; and when Lincoln became Judge Logan's junior partner, Lincoln was ambitious enough to aspire to the very office which Judge Logan wanted; in fact, Lincoln obtained it first, and his one term of Congress made it impossible for Logan to get there. When Lincoln worked to advantage, it was always in a position in which he could be the leader. He was never so constituted as to follow other men's lead. Writers who know only the imaginary Lincoln tell us much of his modesty; he was modest, in a sense. But the men who knew Lincoln did not think of him as modest. They thought of him as a man of towering ambition and inordinate self-assertion. It was this quality in Lincoln, a quality still for the most part unrecognized, and habitually denied, that combined with his modesty and made him capable of leadership.

Lincoln had a remarkable combination of caution and courage. His caution was nothing less than abnormal. His periods of indecision were marked by what seemed an almost hopeless inability to meet the situation. His hesitation when he was about to marry, as manifested in his relations with Mary Owens, and again with Mary Todd, are not the only instances of his great caution. He displayed that caution in the earlier periods of his anti-slavery convictions. Again and again it disappointed and even disgusted outspoken abolitionists that Abraham Lincoln did not seem to possess the courage of their convictions. On the other hand Lincoln had abundant courage both as to his own person and acts as to public policies and military movements.

It is not always understood to what extent Lincoln himself was compelled to direct the movements of the eastern army up to the very hour that Grant took hold of them. As a matter of fact he virtually compelled every move that the reluctant McClellan ever made, and he frequently devised plans more bold than his generals were willing to accept.

On September 11, 1863, John Hay wrote to his associate John G. Nicolay, who just then was away from Washington:

Some well-meaning newspapers advise the President to keep his fingers out of the military pie, and all that sort of thing. The truth is, if he did, the pie would be a sorry mess. The old man sits here and wields like a back-woods Jupiter, the bolts of war and the machinery of government with a hand equally steady and equally firm.

In John Hay's diary under date of April 28, 1864, he recorded:

The President told a queer story of Meigs. When McClellan lay at Harrison's Landing, Meigs came one night to the President and waked him up at the Soldiers' Home, to urge upon him the immediate flight of the army from that point—the men to get away on transports, and the *horses to be killed,* as they could not be saved. "Thus often," says the President, "I, who am not a specially brave man, have had to restore the sinking courage of these professional fighters in critical times."

Lincoln combined a certain coarseness and obtuseness to some of the niceties of convention with a remarkable delicacy and sensitiveness to some of life's finer obligations. This contradiction has been exploited with quite sufficient fullness by various writers on Lincoln, and need not here be enlarged upon. Alfred Tennyson had the same coarse streak in him, and so had Robert Browning. No English gentleman who called on Lincoln was ever more profoundly shocked, or with anything like so good reason, as was Henry W. Longfellow by the vulgarity of Alfred Tennyson. I have no occasion to reconcile that quality in any of these men with the undeniable high character of their thinking or the noble spirituality of the best that was in them. Still less do I find occasion to tell any lies about it. Lincoln was both coarse and delicate; sensitive and obtuse. I do not attempt to harmonize these contradictions. Abraham Lincoln was not a consistent man. After all, "consistency is the hob-goblin of little minds."

Lincoln was in some respects an excellent and in others a very poor judge of human nature. At times he had keen insight into men's motives, and at other times was strangely blind to them. Mr. Weik, in his recent volume* instances, and I think correctly, the case of Mark W. Delahay of Kansas. Delahay was a lawyer of no great ability, a distant relative of Lincoln on the Hanks side. He went to Kansas a Democrat, but changed his politics when the change became advantageous. Lincoln paid his fare to the Chicago Convention of 1860, and kept in telegraphic com-

The Real Lincoln, pp. 221-226.

munication with him from day to day.* Lincoln made him a Federal judge, a position which he was most unfit to fill, and from which he was subsequently removed in disgrace. By such men Lincoln was often imposed upon. In some respects Lincoln showed good judgment of men; in others his judgment of character was almost culpably weak. It is easy enough to say that Lincoln, in the goodness of his heart, assumed that other men were as guileless as himself; that explanation does not explain. Lincoln knew to his sorrow that many other men were not so honest and righteous as he. There is no easy explanation. Abraham Lincoln was not a man to be accounted for by rule of thumb. His consistency, if he was consistent, was not of that sort.

Lincoln combined strong animal passion with chastity and self-control. The world's work must be done by men of initiative, passion and power. Emasculated saintliness will never bring in the good time coming. But while the world's work requires men of virility, it requires also men who do not waste the energy which their power produces, or enfeeble themselves in sensual self-indulgence.

He held power in reserve. He created it and conserved it, and on occasion he used it; he never wasted it in futile rage or unreasonable vexation over minor discomforts or in the weakness of self-indulgence.

Lincoln rarely touched alcoholic liquor in any form, and he did not use tobacco. The reason he gave was that he did not care for them. It can hardly be said that he was a total abstainer on principle, but he was an earnest friend of the Washingtonian movement, and a believer in temperance. How he would have stood on the present-day question of prohibition, we may only conjecture. We know that he would have stood strongly for the enforcement of law. We also know that when, on January 23, 1853, Reverend James Smith preached a sermon in which he

---

*This fact I have from Addison G. Proctor, a delegate from Kansas, to whom Delahay showed the telegrams as he received them.

called on theLegislature then in session to enact a law forbidding the manufacture and sale of alcoholic liquor for use as a beverage, a strikingly advanced position at that date, Lincoln was one of those who, signing themselves "Friends of temperance," asked for the printing of the sermon.

It is claimed on what might seem good authority that Lincoln, in 1855, in company with another man of like view, made a tour of "more than six months" through a portion of Illinois and delivered temperance addresses. This story is vouched for by a man of such credibility that to deny the story may seem ungracious, but I do not believe it. The local newspapers, so far as examined, are silent as to these addresses, and Lincoln cared too much for the German vote to alienate it when he had no occasion for doing so. He knew he would need that vote in 1858. It is unpleasant to take direct issue with as many good men as I am compelled to contradict in this book. They were on the ground and I was not. But old men remember a great many things that never occurred, and too largely history is based on their imaginings.*

Lincoln was a man at times easily influenced. He liked to do

_____

*This declaration rests on the unsupported testimony of Reverend James B. Merwin, and is contained in a little volume entitled *Lincoln and Prohibition*, by my friend, Charles T. White. Mr. Merwin removed to Illinois in 1855, and became acquainted with Lincoln. He was a chaplain during a portion of the Civil War, his work being especially in hospitals. He affirmed that when he was in Washington during the war, he slept in a small room in the White House, and he claimed to have dined with Lincoln on the day of the latter's assassination, a claim which Robert T. Lincoln denies. Mr. Merwin had a watch which was presented to him in 1855. In it was an inscription alleged to have been composed by Abraham Lincoln. This was presented to Mr. Merwin in the rooms of the *Northwestern Christian Advocate* in Chicago, Abraham Lincoln, according to Mr. Merwin's memory, being one of the prominent participants. Mr. White naively states that he has looked up the incident in the files of the *Northwestern Christian Advocate*, and finds the incident recorded there, *except as to the presence of Lincoln.* My impression is that it would be safe to omit Lincoln from the rest of Mr. Merwin's recollections, except for two or three inconsequential matters. Mr. Merwin declared that in 1855, he and Abraham Lincoln stumped Illinois together for six months in the interests of a state law prohibiting the sale of liquor. It is not pleasant to brand such a statement as untrue, but I have no hesitation in doing so. If Lincoln, between his two campaigns for United States senator, had given six months to such lectures, the Illinois newspapers would have been full of it.

what he was asked to do. In many matters he was ready to accept the judgment of other men, and to modify his own judgment in view of what seemed to them to be desirable. But his pliability was counterbalanced by an element of dogged stubbornness. People who supposed that Lincoln was easily influenced, discovered that his will was a rock of adamant. Many men who had grown impatient with him because he was so slow to promulgate a policy of emancipation, really believed that some time between September, 1862, when the proclamation was issued, and January 1, 1863, when it went into effect, Lincoln would be prevailed upon by stronger wills than his own to modify, or even to rescind, that proclamation. Both they and those who opposed them in their desires, were amazed at the vigor with which Lincoln resisted every suggestion of this character. He would rather have been impeached and removed from office. He declared with the utmost vigor that if any president modified that proclamation, it would be another occupant of the White House and not himself. When it was suggested that the rebellion might end peacefully and on terms which involved the restoration of the emancipated slaves to their masters, Lincoln's indignation waxed hot at the thought of a proposal so dishonorable. Any such plan, he said, would involve stripping the uniform off the backs of black men who had been soldiers, and exposing those backs to the lash of the slave-driver.

Yet Lincoln knew that it was more than possible that just this might happen if the war should end and the seceded states be restored before the passage of the Thirteenth Amendment. Those men who had been unable to drive Lincoln to the issuing of the Emancipation Proclamation were astonished at the length he went in driving the nation toward the adoption of that amendment to the Constitution.

This insistence upon making slavery forever impossible in the United States Lincoln pushed without rancor though with tremendous determination. To the very end he would have been glad to equalize the economic burden north and south entailed by the freeing of the slave by some sort of compensated emancipation. It is not commonly known that as late as February 5, 1865, a short month before the second inaugural, Lincoln read to his Cabinet a short message which he proposed to transmit to Congress asking for an appropriation of $400,000,000, to be used at the discretion of the president, to be paid to the states then in rebellion, for emancipation, peace and the ratification of the Thirteenth Amendment. The Cabinet unanimously disapproved the project, and Lincoln did not further urge it. Lincoln did not need to buy the good will of the South by any such proposal; the South was hopelessly beaten; the end of the conflict was in sight. Had Lincoln been disposed, he might have taken the high ground, which his entire Cabinet took, that it was no time for any conciliatory measure. It is a fine tribute to his greatness of heart as well as to his sagacity and statesmanship that he wanted to go before Congress with a proposal to pay four hundred millions of dollars to the defeated South toward compensation for their liberated slaves and for the rehabilitation of that distressed region. The fact that Lincoln could advocate such a plan while remorselessly pushing his campaign for the Thirteenth Amendment speakes volumes for his wisdom and kindness.

The tests of greatness in politics are not immediate and undisputable. Lincoln was denounced in his own day in terms which were bitter, cruel and unjust. But he was able to hold men in working relationships and to accomplish his purposes and secure permanent results. In the best sense he was an opportunist. He combined vision with practical sagacity. He was subtle and at times stubborn. He was pliable and in time of need adamant. He was a man of strange and contradictory qualities.

Lincoln was unmethodical and disorderly in his office and unsystematic in his work of preparation for his cases. But he had a singular ability to discriminate in his mental processes between the essential and non-essential. This process he carried over into his moral judgments. He believed in a government dedicated to equality of rights before the law. We are much more likely to think ourselves the equal of Lincoln than to think humbler men our equals. Lincoln faced honestly the full implications of his convictions.

Lincoln took very little interest in local affairs. He did not greatly care who was mayor of Springfield unless the election of mayor had linked to it some measure which was likely to influence the district, state or national vote. He was not in any narrow sense a public-spirited citizen. He was not quick to see nor swift to contribute toward measures for purely local causes. Springfield was agitated several times over trials of runaway slaves. Lincoln, unless professionally employed as counsel, is not known to have offered his legal services or have made financial contribution in such cases. His mind moved in the political arena, and did not readily descend to the consideration of matters that were not related to his own ambitions or convictions. His mind lacked the power of generalized visualization, and the things which he did not see with his mind's eye fell on a brain rather obtuse and sluggish. But the things that he could visualize made a powerful appeal to his imagination and deeply stirred his sympathies.

He did not complain of dirty sheets and bad meals in the hotels when he was on the circuit, because they did not greatly annoy him. Largely his mind was on other things, and when he noticed small discomforts, he was not very sensitive to them. Some of the stings and smarts of his later official life were mercifully blunted by his convenient thick skin. But there were times when he suffered, and suffered most keenly. No one can tell just at what point he became sensitive or where he was oblivious of discomfort, for he was a man of strange contradictions.

Lincoln was a shrewd man, but a man unflinchingly honest. He knew how political situations were controlled, and he adapted himself to the political life of his generation. But he struggled on with poverty year after year. When he might have made his politics a basis for prosperity, he still remained poor and in debt. Interesting stories were told in New Salem concerning his truthfulness and honor. He made a mistake in the weighing of tea by using a lighter weight than he intended. He did not rest until he had carried the additional few ounces of tea to the woman to whom it belonged. He made a mistake in the change which he gave to a woman, and walked three miles to rectify his error. When the post-office at New Salem was given up, he owed the government a trifling balance and there was no officer present to whom he could pay it. Some months afterward when he had removed to Springfield, a post-office official called upon him for a settlement. Lincoln produced the money, of course, but the interesting thing about it was that he drew out an old blue sock and handed over the original copper cents and other fractional currency in which the amounts had been paid to him while he was postmaster at New Salem. While still in that little village he won the loving and appreciative title "Honest Abe." He deserved it then and continued to deserve it as long as he lived.

Lincoln was a man both just and generous. A man so loyal to a high standard of justice is not always considerate of those who fail to attain to his exalted station. Lincoln was as considerate in his judgment of other men as he was exacting in his own ethical standards.

Lincoln combined strong common sense with loyalty to conscience. He had an almost intuitive way of getting at the essential elements in any situation which he needed to appraise. As a lawyer he was noted for his habit of stripping a case of all its unnecessary and incidental features, and coming directly to the heart of the matter. His lucidity of expression was closely joined with his power of just estimation. Even in his advocacy of one side of the case, there was present a certain judicial quality. In the perplexing problems that came to him as president, the nation came to rely more and more upon these qualities of sound judgment and simple discernment of right. Disappointed as the people of the North were at the settlement of the Trent affair, and smarting as they did under a stinging sense of injustice, they accepted Lincoln's solution of the problem because they had come to believe in his discernment of the right. James Russell Lowell spoke for the nation when he represented Brother Jonathan as saying to John Bull:

> "We gave the critters back, John,
> 'Cause Abr'am thought 'twas right."

The country learned to trust his judgment concerning things that were right and wrong. He forced Douglas and the nation to deal with slavery as a moral question, and both Douglas and the nation came so to regard it.

Outstanding among Lincoln's high qualities was his magnanimity. In him was no petty malice, no spirit of revenge. He smarted under the sting of injustice, but he did not render evil for evil. Again and again he repaid with kindness those who had done him wrong.

Reference need not here be made to what has already been mentioned of his treatment of McClellan, Meade, Seward, Chase and Stanton. These outstanding examples of Lincoln's greatness, which caused him to rise above all personal resentment, must stand forever as high proofs of Lincoln's inherent nobility. They are examples of a magnanimity as meritorious as it is rare.

There are two essentials of leadership. The first is that he who leads a people shall be part and parcel of the life of those whom he leads. The other is that he shall have some quality which lifts him above and makes him superior to those whose leader he is. Many men possess one of these qualities, but very few possess them both. Abraham Lincoln combined them in preeminent degree. He was above the people but he was of the people. His life was bone of their bone and flesh of their flesh. Yet there was ever something in him that lifted him above other men. They felt it and he felt it. They did not approach him with rude familiarity, and call him by his first name. There was something in him that restrained them from such acts of unmitigated freedom. Lincoln was the embodiment of the life of the common people. He believed in them and thought God must love them because he made so many of them. On the other hand Lincoln embodied in himself those high qualities of superiority which men could not fail to recognize. Few men in all the world's history have held in such perfect equilibrium these two essential characteristics as did Abraham Lincoln.

Only those men professed to know Abraham Lincoln intimately who knew him very little if at all. Lincoln combined an engaging frankness with a nature phenomenally secretive. Those men who visited Lincoln and to whom he confided highly important information learned, in general, what all the world was certain to know a few hours later. The secrets that Lincoln wished kept, he did not tell.

If any man in Illinois knew Lincoln from the time he returned from Congress until his election to the presidency, that man was David Davis. He was judge in the Eighth Judicial District during nearly the whole period of Lincoln's later years at the bar, and Lincoln was the one lawyer who rode the whole circuit. He and Davis drove together in Lincoln's buggy, for Lincoln had little fondness for horseback riding and Davis was too heavy to ride a horse far. They ate and slept together. Lincoln repeatedly sat on the bench when Davis wished to be away for a day. Davis was Lincoln's campaign manager at the Chicago Convention. Lincoln elevated Davis to the Supreme Court. Davis was Mrs. Lincoln's attorney after her husband's death, knowing, as she could not help knowing, that there was no man whom her husband trusted more fully.

If any man knew Lincoln intimately in the four years of his presidency, it was Orville H. Browning. He and Lincoln had known each other in the Illinois Legislature. Browning was a trustee of Knox College, and was the man who introduced the motion, just after the Chicago Convention, that Knox confer its first honorary degree, the Doctorate of Laws, upon Abraham Lincoln, thus doing what Princeton did later. Browning succeeded Douglas in the Senate. He was a man of honor and of sincere religious principle. Lincoln held him in the highest possible esteem. He was often in the White House at meals. Even Isaac N. Arnold had to obtain from Browning his most important information as to the inside of the White House during Lincoln's administration.

On the day following Lincoln's death, these two men, Senator Browning and Judge David Davis, sat down together and confessed that they did not know Abraham Lincoln very well. Senator Browning recorded in his diary that in conversation with Judge Davis about Mr. Lincoln, Davis spoke of some of Lincoln's characteristics, saying he had neither strong friendships nor enmities. He declared that Lincoln had never written him, Davis, a letter, nor asked his opinion upon any subject since he was elected president.

No wonder his partner, Herndon, who also confessed that he was not well acquainted with Lincoln, denounced as liars the men who professed to have been taken into Lincoln's inmost confidence at first sight, and said that while Lincoln appeared to those who did not know him, to be a man who told his whole mind to any one who inquired of him, he was "the most secretive, shut-mouthed man that ever lived."

Having followed the trail of Lincoln for many years, and talked with innumerable men who knew him, I read with genuine admiration, if not with approval, the books by men to whom the mind and soul of Abraham Lincoln are not merely an open book, but a tablet so written that he who runs may read. Year by year, as these studies have gone forward, my admiration for Lincoln has grown; but I have less and less confidence in the popular interpretations of his life. His character was the synthesis of many contradictions.

The first biographer of Lincoln to visit Springfield and gather his material at first hand, was Josiah G. Holland. He wrote concerning Lincoln:

The writer has conversed with multitudes of men who claimed to know Mr. Lincoln intimately: yet there are not two of the whole number who agree in their estimate of him. The fact was that he rarely showed more than one aspect of himself to one man. He opened himself to men in different directions. To illustrate the effect of the peculiarity of Mr. Lincoln's intercourse with men it may be said that men who knew him through all his professional and political life offered opinions as diametrically opposite as these, viz: that he was a very ambitious man, and that he was without a particle of ambition; that he was one of the saddest men that ever lived, and that he was one of the jolliest men that ever lived; that he was very religious, but that he was not a Christian; that he was a Christian, but did not know it; that he was so far from being a religious man or a Christian that "the less said upon that subject the better"; that he was the most cunning man in America, and that he had not a particle of cunning in him; that he had the strongest personal attachments, and that he had no personal attachments at all—only a general good feeling toward everybody; that he was a man of indomitable will, and that he was a man almost without a will; that he was remarkable for his pure-mindedness, and that he was the foulest in his jests and stories of any man in the country; that he was a witty man, and that he was only the retailer of the wit of others; that his apparent candor and fairness were only apparent, and that they were as real as his head and hands; that he was a boor, and that he was in all respects a gentleman; that he was a leader of the people, and that he was always led by the people; that he was cool and impassive, and that he was susceptible of the strongest passions. It is only by tracing these separate streams of impression back to their fountain that we were able to arrive at anything like a competent comprehension of the man, or to learn why he came to be held in such various estimation. Men caught only separate aspects of his character—only the fragments that were called into exhibition by their own qualities.

Commenting on the foregoing Herndon said:

Doctor Holland had only found what Lincoln's friends had always experienced in their relations with him—that he was a man with many moods and many sides. He never revealed himself entirely to any one man, and therefore he will always to a certain extent remain enveloped in doubt. Even those who were with him through long years of hard study and under constantly varying circumstances can hardly say they knew him through and through.

V. LINCOLN'S RELIGION

Abraham Lincoln was a deeply religious man. He who would establish a contrary opinion must assume a burden of proof from which only confirmed prejudice or judicial incompetence could fail to shrink. To assure ourselves that he was religious is not difficult, but it is not easy to classify him among religionists or to define in terms of accepted creeds the precise tenets of his religious faith. His religion was part and parcel of his life, and his life was a life of growth.* In order to know something of the forms in which Lincoln's religious life expresses itself, it is important first to know what form of such life was known to him and available for his selection.

The religious background of the early life of Abraham Lincoln, was that offered by the organization and preaching of the Baptist churches in the backwoods districts of Kentucky and southern Indiana. It was a militant and dogmatic Calvinism. While those churches were democratic in their government, their conception of the administration of the universe was arbitrary and despotic. The sovereignty of God as it was preached in those churches practically eliminated the freedom of the human will. Lincoln probably never listened in his boyhood to a Baptist minister who believed the earth round. Profoundly affected in his thinking by the system or theology which he heard in his youth, he revolted against its interpretation of God and of human life. When he came to New Salem and read the works of Voltaire and of Paine, he was much influenced by them, and had some inclination toward skepticism.

---

*I have considered the question of the development of Lincoln's spiritual life in a volume entitled *The Soul of Abraham Lincoln*. To that volume reference is made for a full discussion of Lincoln's religion in the different periods of his life. This chapter attempts nothing more than a concise summary of the conclusions of that volume.

Two books which he read while living in Springfield impressed him deeply. One was Chambers' *Vestiges of Creation*. This gave to him a conception of the orderly working of a righteous God in creation and in human life. He came to believe in what he called "Miracles under Law." The other book was entitled *The Christian's Defense*. It was an imposing work on the evidences of Christianity, the outgrowth of a protracted debate, one of whose participants was the Reverend James Smith, pastor of the First Presbyterian Church in Springfield. In 1850 the Lincolns became affiliated with this church. Mrs. Lincoln united with the church in full communion, and Lincoln became a pew holder and habitual attendant.

Two markedly different strains in the mind of Lincoln contributed to the formation of his religious thinking. One was a powerful tendency toward rationalism. He desired and needed a consistent theory underlying all his thinking. The other was an equally strong strain of mysticism. His rationalism did not halt at the threshold of the supernatural. His was a mind that easily accepted forces whose origin and purpose were beyond human knowledge. Not only did he accept the supernatural, but he accentuated it to the point of superstition. Lincoln's superstition, however, was not the main current of his thinking; it was a kind of spiritual undertone. He never was wholly free from it, but the strong tides of his moral nature had currents, and reached elevations of their own.

A mighty factor in the formation of Lincoln's religious views, was his clear and unconquerable sense of justice. Believing as he did in the sovereignty of God, and holding it in terms of a Calvinism that would have out-Calvined Calvin, he believed also in a Divine justice and a Divine mercy which he never fully reconciled with his thoughts of God's sovereignty, but which produced in him a profound conviction that the Judge of all the earth would do right. He believed in future punishment, and thought that ministers preached that too little rather than too much; but he did not believe in the eternity of that punishment.

He believed that a righteous and all-powerful God would find it possible somehow to eliminate suffering and sin from His universe.

Holding these convictions and influenced by these ideas, Lincoln sought with great earnestness to work in his own mind a consistent theory of the purpose of God in the great Civil War. In the latter part of the year 1862, in the effort to clarify his own thinking, he wrote these words on a slip of paper which was not published until his secretaries Nicolay and Hay wrote their biography:

The will of God prevails. In great contests each party claims to act in accordance with the will of God. Both may be, and one must be, wrong. God cannot be for and against the same thing at the same time. In the present Civil War it is quite possible that God's purpose is something different from the purpose of either party; and yet the human instrumentalities, working just as they do, are of the best adaptation to effect his purpose. I am almost ready to say that this is probably true; that God wills this contest, and wills that it shall not end yet. By his mere great power on the minds of the now contestants, he could have either saved or destroyed the Union without a human contest. Yet the contest began. And, having begun, He could give the final victory to either side any day. Yet the contest proceeds.

As the war wore on it grew more clear to him that the purpose of God in America's great war involved the removal of slavery, with the inevitable punishment of the whole nation, North and South, for its share in that iniquity. Thus in his second inaugural, he said:

The Almighty has his own purposes, "Woe unto the world because of offenses! for it must needs be that offenses come; but woe to that man by whom the offense cometh." If we shall suppose that American slavery is one of those offenses which, in the providence of God, must needs come, but which, having continued through his appointed time, he now wills to remove, and that he gives to both North and South this terrible war, as the woe due to those by whom the offense came, shall we discern therein any departure from those divine attributes which the believers in a living God always ascribe to him? Fondly do we hope—fervently do we pray—that this mighty scourge of war may speedily pass away. Yet, if God wills that it continue until all the wealth piled by the bondsman's two hundred and fifty years of unrequited toil shall be sunk, and until every drop of blood drawn with the lash shall be paid by another drawn with the sword, as was said three thousand years ago, so still it must be said, "The judgments of the Lord are true and righteous altogether."

The quality of Lincoln's religious life is nobly illustrated in the threefold record of the Cabinet meeting in which he presented the Proclamation of Emancipation. He did not present that proclamation for any discussion of its main point. He had already settled that. He had made a solemn covenant with God and he fulfilled that covenant.

Lincoln did not speak easily or lightly of those things which were deepest in his life. He knew that his Cabinet was not united in its support of a policy of abolition. But his own statement of his reasons for the Emancipation Proclamation silenced every word of opposition. His Cabinet could not do other than accept it. Lincoln had promised his God that he would do it. His Cabinet knew better than to oppose him in that hour. He kept the promise which he had made to his God.

Abraham Lincoln never attempted to put his own convictions into the form of a creed. It is doubtful if he could have assented to any of the great orthodox creeds in the form and with the meaning which certain of the churches attach to them. In another and more extended study of Lincoln's religious life, I have endeavored to compile practically all of his religious affirmations that were embodied in signed documents or formal addresses. I did not think it wise to include any that depended upon the recollection of other people. In one chapter of the book already referred to, I made a selection from these utterances of Lincoln with something of their context, and then proceeded to extract from these more extended quotations some briefer sentences and clauses which might go toward the composition of something approaching a creed. No liberties were taken with Lincoln's words, except to change the number of some of the pronouns from plural to singular, or to make other verbal modifications necessary to the unifying of the statements, and to prefix the words "I believe." Any reader who would prefer to make a compilation of his own, will find in the volume already alluded to, material for his own work.

I do not here repeat the full and extended quotations, the quarry from which the several articles of this creed are taken, for these are available in the book already referred to; but copy here from that volume, the creed itself.

THE CREED OF ABRAHAM LINCOLN—IN HIS OWN WORDS

I believe in God, the Almighty Ruler of Nations, our great and good and merciful Maker, our Father in Heaven, who notes the fall of a sparrow, and numbers the hairs of our heads.

I believe in His eternal truth and justice.

I recognize the sublime truth announced in the Holy Scriptures and proven by all history that those nations only are blest whose God is the Lord.

I believe that it is the duty of nations as well as of men to own their dependence upon the overruling power of God, and to invoke the influence of His Holy Spirit; to confess their sins and transgressions in humble sorrow, yet with assured hope that genuine repentance will lead to mercy and pardon.

I believe that it is meet and right to recognize and confess the presence of the Almighty Father equally in our triumphs and in those sorrows which we may justly fear are a punishment inflicted upon us for our presumptuous sins to the needful end of our reformation.

I believe that the Bible is the best gift which God has ever given to men. All the good from the Saviour of the world is communicated to us through this book.

I believe the will of God prevails. Without Him all human reliance is vain. Without the assistance of that Divine Being I can not succeed. With that assistance I can not fail.

Being a humble instrument in the hands of our Heavenly Father, I desire that all my works and acts may be according to His will; and that it may be so, I give thanks to the Almighty, and seek His aid.

I have a solemn oath registered in Heaven to finish the work I am in, in full view of my responsibility to my God, with malice toward none; with charity for all; with firmness in the right as God gives me to see the right. Commending those who love me to His care, as I hope in their prayers they will commend me, I look through the help of God to a joyous meeting with many loved ones gone before.

VI. ABRAHAM LINCOLN, AMERICAN

Our country is large. It was perilously large in the beginning. It is a fair question whether the thirteen colonies could long have been held together but for the discovery of the uses of steam. From the time it became a nation, it was threatened with disruption; Washington sadly said, "We are one nation to-day, and thirteen to-morrow." Washington was himself the strongest of all those personal forces that bound the colonies together at the beginning, and as the nation has grown to vaster greatness, his name and personality have proved adequate to fit the American ideal. Still more potent in giving personality to a nation's best interpretation of its own life is the character of Abraham Lincoln.

Lincoln's life epitomizes American history. He was born in a cabin as primitive as that of the first settlers in the colonial period. He lived through the successive periods of American development as expressed in the backwoods settlement, the frontier town, the new state capital, and the seat of national power.

From the cabin on Nolin to the White House in Washington he expressed and embodied the life of the nation.

Lincoln was born in the South, but we do not think of him as a southerner. He directed the armies of the North, but we do not think of him as a northerner. He fought the war without hate, and he never cherished sectional jealousy or bigotry. The South had no truer friend; the spirit of unified nationalism had no finer or worthier exponent.

America makes high profession of faith when she claims Abraham Lincoln as the norm and exponent of her national life. The manhood of a nation that claims Lincoln should be clean, upright, honest, patriotic, sympathetic, magnanimous, noble. Can America make this claim for her manhood? It is her clear duty and her high privilege to aspire that this shall be true. She has a right to tell to her youth the story of Lincoln, and to teach her young manhood to emulate his simple virtues. She has a right to hang his portrait on the walls of her legislative halls and her courts of justice. She has a right to name him in her intercourse with other nations. She has a right to define her own principles in terms of his integrity and transparent righteousness. America that produced Abraham Lincoln can beget other sons in his likeness and train them up in his spirit. It will be a proud day for our country when other nations think of him, and believe that Americans are like him and that America is filled with his spirit. His name unifies America.

VII.   ABRAHAM LINCOLN, WORLD CITIZEN

A nation divided against itself, into ignorant and educated, righteous and unrighteous, can not stand. We must educate and elevate all our people and make the rule of the people something else than the rule of the mob. A world divided against itself can not stand. It can not endure half armed and half unarmed, half peaceable and half militaristic. It can not endure with one half cherishing hatred and contempt and suspicion against the other half. The world must learn a basis of self-government in righteousness. The world is just beginning to believe this; and that is one reason why the name of Abraham Lincoln is being honored in meetings for international good will, not in America only, but throughout the earth.

Democracy in America is more than a form of government; it is a confession of faith in the moral character of the universe. It is a philosophy of life, and the expression of a hope for the future of the human race. This is why, spite of all the unpleasant and self-assertive forms in which Americans have flouted their noisy patriotism in the face of other peoples, the world has an ever growing affection and respect for the character of Abraham Lincoln. England claims him by right of his descent, and the free nations of the world claim him by reason of the kinship they discover in his spirit. There is little danger that his fame will grow less; it is as certain as anything future can well be that it will grow from more to more until it is loved and honored the whole world around.

The personality of Abraham Lincoln grows dim with the flight of years. The last man who saw and knew him will soon be dead. A halo about his personality refracts the light of calm judgment. Already he is in good part a mythical character. To him are attributed many utterances which have no place in his writings or speeches. Concerning him are current past any hope of eradication incidents which never occurred or in which he had no part. Poetry and song and the myth-making tendency of the human mind are all at work, and have been at work for half a century. But only a mighty man could thus have been idealized. If the outline of his personality grows dim in the mists of the decades, his figure bulks big and regal. We measure his stature by the shadow which he casts; it is nothing less than colossal. And the crest of his character is the dignity of his moral grandeur.

Men whom the world counts great have been conveniently grouped into three classes—those who are born great, those who attain to greatness, and those who have greatness thrust upon them. The first two groups may in reality be one—those who, born with inherent qualities of greatness, attain to its realization and recognition by their own innate power, and its fortunate adaptation to opportunity. When a truly great man becomes the advocate of a great cause, and meets a great situation adequately, worthily and triumphantly, the patient ages rise from their somnolence and rejoice.

Those men who have greatness thrust upon them live not long in the rarified atmosphere to which they are suddenly elevated. They must die soon or they outlive their fame. Some of them, fortunately caught by death in the brief hour of their publicity, are impulsively enrolled among the notable men of their generation; but even so, they lengthen but little the period in which they are accounted notable. Die they soon or die they late, their fame fades, and they pass in due time to their own place in oblivion.

But they who, being great, match their quality against the challenging front of opportunity, achieve a distinction which grows toward immortality. Like snow-capped mountains hidden at close view by their own foot-hills, and emerging to appear at first only as slightly higher elevations in the range, they tower more loftily as the years recede, dwarfing all lesser hills of their contemporaries, until they stand in solitary grandeur. While the plain is yet dark, they greet with radiant crest the dawn of succeeding generations. Of these, greatest of all men of his generation was Abraham Lincoln.

THE END

APPENDIX

Perhaps the only man now living who was in the Peterson house on the night of Lincoln's assassination is Honorable James Tanner, to whom reference is made in the text of this volume. His account, written on Sunday, April 17, 1865, has recently been printed in the *American Historical Review* from which I quote. The foot-notes are by Professor J. Franklin Jameson.*

THE following letter, now in the possession of Mr. Hadley H. Walch, of Grand Rapids, Michigan, son of the man to whom it was addressed, was brought to the attention of the *Review* by Professor C. H. Van Tyne. The writer, Honorable James Tanner, now residing in Washington, where since 1904 he has been register of wills for the District of Columbia, kindly consents to its publication. Born in 1844, Mr. Tanner enlisted early in the Civil War in the 87th New York Volunteers, and lost both legs at the second battle of Bull Run.

In 1864 [he writes] I attended Ames's Business College, Syracuse, New York, for the purpose of studying shorthand. Hadley F. Walch, of Grand Rapids, Michigan, was a fellow student of shorthand and we kept up a desultory acquaintance for some years. That winter of '64 I came to Washington to take a clerkship in the War Department. Walch continued his study and perfected himself in shorthand and was for many years, I think, reporter in the courts at Grand Rapids, Michigan.†

Mr. Tanner remembers writing the letter to Walch. On the same day or the day preceding he wrote to his mother a long let-

---

*Vol. XXIX, April 1924, pp. 514.17.
†Mr. Walch occupied that position from 1869 till his death in 1920.

ter of similar purport. From that letter, which afterward came into his possession, a paragraph is quoted in an account by him of President Lincoln's death, in the *New York Sun* of April 16, 1905; this quotation is repeated in David M. DeWitt's *The Assassination of Abraham Lincoln,* p. 270.

> Ordnance Office, War Department,
> WASHINGTON, April 17, 1865.

Friend Walch :

Your very welcome letter was duly received by me and now I will steal a few minutes from my duties in the office to answer it.

Of course, you must know as much as I do about the terrible events which have happened in this city during the past few days. I have nothing else to write about so I will give you a few ideas about that, perhaps, which you have not yet got from the papers.

Last Friday night a friend invited me to attend the theatre with him, which I did. I would have preferred the play at Ford's Theatre, where the President was shot, but my friend chose the play at Grover's, which was "Aladdin, or the Wonderful Lamp."* While sitting there witnessing the play about ten o'clock or rather a little after, the entrance door was thrown open and a man exclaimed, "President Lincoln is assassinated in his private box at Ford's!" Instantly all was excitement and a terrible rush commenced and someone cried out, "Sit down, it is a ruse of the pickpockets." The audience generally agreed to this, for the most of them sat down, and the play went on; soon, however, a gentleman came out from behind the scenes and informed us that the sad news was too true. We instantly dispersed.

On going out in the street we were horrified to learn that Mr. Seward had been attacked and severely injured while in bed at his house. Myself and friend went up to Willard's,† which is a short distance above Grover's, to learn what we could, but could learn nothing there. The people were terribly excited. Ford's Theatre is on Tenth St. between E and F. Grover's is on the Avenue near Fourteenth St. and just below Willard's; it is about four blocks up from Ford's. My boarding house is right opposite Ford's Theatre. We then got on the cars and went down to Tenth St. and up Tenth St. to Ford's and to my boarding house. There was an immense throng there, very quiet yet very much

---

*Grover's, or the New National Theatre, still called by the latter name.
†Willard's Hotel.

excited; the street was crowded and I only got across on account of my boarding there. The President had been carried into the adjoining house* to where I board; I went up to my room on the second floor and out on the balcony which nearly overhangs the door of Mr. Peterson's house. Members of the cabinet, the chief justice, Generals Halleck, Meiggs, Augur and others were going in and out, all looking anxious and sorrow-stricken. By leaning over the railing I could learn from time to time of His Excellency's condition, and soon learned that there was no hope of him. Soon they commenced taking testimony in the room adjoining where he lay, before Chief Justice Carter,† and General Halleck‡ called for a reporter: no one was on hand, but one of the head clerks in our office, who boarded there,** knew I could write shorthand and he told the General so, and he bade him call me, so he came to the door and asked me to come down and report the testimony. I went down and the General passed me in, as the house was strictly guarded, of course. I went into a room between the rear room and the front room.†† Mrs. Lincoln was in the front room weeping as though her heart would break. In the back room lay His Excellency breathing hard, and with every breath a groan. In the room where I was, were Generals Halleck, Meiggs, Augur and others, all of the cabinet excepting Mr. Seward, Chief Justice Chase and Chief Justice Carter of the District of Columbia, Andrew Johnson‡‡ and many other distinguished men. A solemn silence pervaded the whole throng; it was a terrible moment. Never in my life was I surrounded by half so impressive circumstances. Opposite me at the table where I sat

*The Petersen house at 453, (now 516) Tenth Street, still standing, in which the present occupant, Mr. O. H. Oldroyd, has for many years preserved his Lincoln Memorial Collection.

†David K. Carter, chief justice of the supreme court of the District of Columbia.

‡Mr. Tanner tells the editor that the name of Halleck was written by inadvertence; it was Major-General C. C. Augur, then commanding the department of Washington.

**It was Albert Daggett, afterward of some prominence as the contractor for post-cards.

††The house was two rooms deep, but with an L. The President had been laid on a bed in the L room on the first floor, here designated as the rear room. There is a diagram of the house in Nicolay and Hay's *Abraham Lincoln*, X. 300, and a diagram and a picture in Oldroyd, *Assassination of Abraham Lincoln*, pp. 36, 30.

‡‡Mr. Tanner thinks that this was an error, that Johnson was not present; but there is evidence that the Vice-President came in for a brief period.

writing sat Secretary Stanton writing dispatches to General Dix and others, and giving orders for the guarding of Ford's and the surrounding country. At the left of me was Judge Carter propounding the questions to the witnesses whose answers I was jotting down in Standard Phonography. I was so excited when I commenced that I am afraid that it did not much resemble Standard Phonography or any other kind, but I could read it readily afterward, so what was the difference? In fifteen minutes I had testimony enough down to hang Wilkes Booth, the assassin, higher than ever Haman hung.* I was writing shorthand for about an hour and a half, when I commenced transcribing it. I thought I had been writing about two hours when I looked at the clock and it marked half past four A. M. I commenced writing about 12 M. I could not believe that it was so late, but my watch corroborated it. The surrounding circumstances had so engrossed my attention that I had not noticed the flight of time. In the front room Mrs. Lincoln was uttering the most heartbroken exclamations all the night long. As she passed through the hall back to the parlor after she had taken leave of the President for the last time, as she went by my door I heard her moan, "O, my God, and have I given my husband to die," and I tell you I never heard so much agony in so few words. The President was still alive, but sinking fast. He had been utterly unconscious from the time the shot struck him and remained so until he breathed his last. At 6:45 Saturday morning I finished my notes and passed into the back room where the President lay; it was very evident that he could not last long. There was no crowd in the room, which was very small, but I approached quite near the bed on which so much greatness lay, fast losing its hold on this world. The head of the bed was toward the door; at the head stood Capt. Robert Lincoln weeping on the shoulder of Senator Sumner. General Halleck stood just behind Robert Lincoln and I stood just to the left of General Halleck and between him and General

---

*Mr. Tanner writes, "Various witnesses were brought in who had either been in Ford's Theatre or up in the vicinity of Mr. Seward's residence. Among them were Harry Hawk, who had been Asa Trenchard that night in the play, *Our American Cousin,* Mr. Alfred Cloughly, Colonel G. V. Rutherford, and others. . . . Through all the testimony given by those who had been in Ford's Theatre that night there was an undertone of horror which held the witnesses back from positively identifying the assassin as Booth. Said Harry Hawk, 'To the best of my belief, it was Mr. John Wilkes Booth, but I will not be positive,' and so it went through the testimony of others but the sum total left no doubt as to the identity of the assassin."

Meiggs.* Secretary Stanton was there trying every way to be calm and yet he was very much moved. The utmost silence prevailed, broken only by the sound of strong men's sobs. It was a solemn time, I assure you. The President breathed heavily until a few minutes before he breathed his last, then his breath came easily and he passed off very quietly.

As soon as he was dead Rev. Dr. Gurley, who has been the President's pastor since his sojourn in this city,† offered up a very impressive prayer. I grasped for my pencil which was in my pocket, as I wished to secure his words, but I was very much disappointed to find that my pencil had been broken in my pocket. I could have taken it very easily as he spoke very favorably for reporting. The friends dispersed, Mrs. Lincoln and family going to the White House, which she had left the night before to attend the theatre with him who never returned to it except in his coffin.

Secretary Stanton told me to take charge of the testimony I had taken, so I went up to my room and took a copy of it, as I wished to keep both my notes and the original copy which I had made while there in the house. They will ever be cherished monuments to me of the awful night and the circumstances with which I found myself so unexpectedly surrounded and which will not soon be forgotten.‡

Saturday night I took the copy I had made to the Secretary's house, but as he was asleep I did not see him, so I left them with my card. I tell you, I would not regret the time and money I have spent on Phonography if it never brought me more than it did that night, for that brought me the privilege of standing by the deathbed of the most remarkable man of modern times and one who will live in the annals of his country as long as she continues to have a history.

Frank Leslie's Illustrated** will have a good picture of the building there made celebrated by this sad event on that evening. I saw the sketch made by the artist of the theatre, and it was very

---

*See the diagram in Nicolay and Hay.

†Rev. Dr. Phineas D. Gurley, of the New York Avenue Presbyterian Church.

‡They were subsequently bound in a volume, and presented by Mr. Tanner to the Union League Club of Philadelphia, of whose Lincoln Memorial Collection they now form a part.

**Leslie's Illustrated Weekly for April 29, has drawings, by Albert Berghaus, of the scene in the President's box at Ford's Theatre, and of the scene in the room where he died; the issue for May 20, of the exterior of the theatre and of the Petersen house, showing also the house next door, and its balcony.

correct, indeed. He also sketched the inside of the room where the President died, also the outside of the building, as well as the adjoining buildings on both sides. You will see the house I board in has a balcony along the front of the two rooms on the second floor; I occupy both of those rooms.

You can imagine the feeling here by judging of the feeling in your own place, only it is the more horrifying from the fact that the President lived in our midst and was universally beloved by the People.

This morning there was published in the Chronicle the statement of one of the witnesses whom I reported, Mr. James B. Ferguson.* You will doubtless see it in your papers as it is most important. I have an idea, which is gaining ground here, and that is that the assassin had assistance in the theatre, and that the President was invited there for the express purpose of assassinating him. The theatre is very strictly guarded now night and day.

Very truly your friend,

James Tanner.

I inquired of Mr. Tanner how far this contemporary account, whose vividness carries its own evidence of its essential truthfulness, accorded with his mature recollections, as he checked them up with the memories of other men, especially with reference to the presence of Andrew Johnson, at Lincoln's deathbed. By way of reply he gave me in manuscript what he had used once or more as an address, in part following the content of his letter, but making one or two corrections, the most important of them being with reference to Andrew Johnson. I am permitted to use this interesting document:

II.   THE PASSING OF ABRAHAM LINCOLN

By James Tanner

Among all the characters who loomed large in the public mind from 1861 to 1865, one came to stand apart and alone in

---

*Washington Morning Chronicle. Testimony of Ferguson, who kept a restaurant adjoining the theatre, is also in Benn Pitman's edition of the *Trial of the Conspirators*, pp. 76-77.

supremacy, finally recognized almost unanimously the world over as without a peer. It took the perspective of many years to enable us to get a correct view of the greatness of his character, his transcendent intellectual endowment, the utter unselfishness of his purpose, his absolute devotion to the interests of the nation which had called him to its leadership and the great agony endured by his loving gentle heart as he staggered under his awful burden, an agony never equaled since the Savior of mankind passed the night in the Garden of Gethsemane.

Our people have shown in a thousand ways and particularly in his recent centennial that every atom relating to the life of Abraham Lincoln is of intense and continuous interest to them and because of this and because of the fact that I was a spectator of the final scene of the supreme tragedy of that time on the morning of April 15, 1865, I pen these lines.

At that time I was an employe of the Ordnance Bureau of the War Department and had some ability as a shorthand writer. The latter fact brought me within touch of the events of that awful night. I had gone with a friend to witness the performance that evening at Grover's Theater, where now stands the New National. Soon after ten o'clock a man rushed in from the lobby and cried out, "President Lincoln has been shot in Ford's Theater." There was great confusion at once, most of the audience rising to their feet. Some one cried out, "It's a ruse of the pickpockets; look out!" Almost everybody resumed his seat, but almost immediately one of the cast stepped out on the stage and said, "The sad news is too true; the audience will disperse."

My friend and myself crossed to Willard's Hotel and there were told that Secretary Seward had been killed. Men's faces blanched as they at once asked, "What news of Stanton? Have they got him too?" The wildest rumors soon filled the air.

I had rooms at the time in the house adjoining the Peterson house, into which the president had been carried. Hastening down to Tenth Street, I found an almost solid mass of humanity blocking the street and the crowd constantly enlarging. A silence that was appalling prevailed.   Interest centered on all who entered or emerged from the Peterson House and all of the latter were closely questioned as to the stricken president's condition. From the first the answers were unvarying—that there was no hope.

A military guard had been placed in front of the house and those adjoining but upon telling the commanding officer that I lived there, I passed up to my apartment, which comprised the second story front of the house.   There was a balcony in front and I found my rooms and the balcony thronged by the other occupants of the house.   Horror was in every heart and dismay on every countenance.   We had just about a week of tumultuous joy over the downfall of Richmond and the collapse of the Confederacy and now in an instant all this was changed to the deepest woe by the foul shot of the cowardly assassin.

It was nearly midnight when Major General Augur came out on the stoop of the Peterson House and asked if there was any one in the crowd who could write shorthand.   There was no response from the street but one of my friends on the balcony told the general there was a young man inside who could serve him, whereupon the general told him to ask me to come down as they needed me.   So it was that I came into close touch with the scenes and events surrounding the final hours of Abraham Lincoln's life.

Entering the house I accompanied General Augur down the hallway to the rear parlor.   When we passed the door of the front parlor the moans and sobs of Mrs. Lincoln struck painfully upon our ears.   Entering the rear parlor, I found Secretary Stanton, Judge David K. Carter, Chief Justice of the Supreme Court of the District of Columbia, Honorable B. A. Hill and many others.

I took my seat on one side of a small library table opposite Mr. Stanton, with Judge Carter at the end.   Various witnesses were brought in who had either been in Ford's Theater or up in the vicinity of Mr. Seward's residence.   Among them were Harry Hawk, who had been Asa Trenchard that night in the play, *Our American Cousin,* Mr. Alfred Cloughly, Colonel G. V. Rutherford and others. As I took down the statements they made we were distracted by the distress of Mrs. Lincoln, for though the folding doors between the two parlors were closed, her frantic sorrow was distressingly audible to us.

She was accompanied by Miss Harris, of New York, who, with her fiancé, Major Rathbone, had gone to the theater with the President and Mrs. Lincoln. Booth in his rush through the box after firing the fatal shot had lunged at Major Rathbone with his dagger and wounded him in the arm slightly. In the naturally intense excitement over the president's condition, it is probable that Major Rathbone himself did not realize that he was wounded until after he had been in the Peterson House some time, when he fainted from loss of blood, was attended to, his wound dressed, and he taken to his apartments. He and Miss Harris subsequently married.

Through all the testimony given by those who had been in Ford's Theater that night, there was an undertone of horror which held the witnesses back from positively identifying the assassin as Booth. Said Harry Hawk, "To the best of my belief, it was Mr. John Wilkes Booth, but I will not be positive," and so it went through the testimony of others but the sum total left no doubt as to the identity of the assassin.

Our task was interrupted very many times during the night, sometimes by reports or despatches for Secretary Stanton but more often by him for the purpose of issuing orders calculated to enmesh Booth in his flight. "Guard the Potomac from the city down," was his repeated direction. "He will try to get South." Many despatches were sent from that table before morning, some to General Dix at New York, others to Chicago, Philadelphia, etc.

Several times Mr. Stanton left us a few moments and passed back to the room in the ell at the end of the hall where the president lay. The doors were open and sometimes there would be a few seconds of absolute silence when we could hear plainly the stertorous breathing of the dying man. I think it was on his return from his third trip of this kind when, as he again took his seat opposite me, I looked earnestly at him, desiring yet hesitating to ask if there was any chance of life. He understood and I saw a choke in his throat as he slowly forced the answer to my unspoken question—"There is no hope." He had impressed me through those awful hours as being a man of steel but I knew then that he was dangerously near a convulsive breakdown.

During the night there came in, I think, about every man then of prominence in our national life who was in the capital at the time and who had heard of the tragedy. A few whom I distinctly recall were Secretaries Welles, Usher and McCullough, Attorney General Speed and Postmaster General Dennison, Assistant Secretaries Field and Otto, Governor Oglesby, Senators Sumner and Stewart, and Generals Meigs and Augur. I have seen many asserted pictures of the deathbed scene and most of them have Vice-President Andrew Johnson seated in a chair near the foot of the bed on the left side. Mr. Johnson was not in the house at all but in his rooms in the Kirkwood House and knew nothing of the events of that night till he was aroused in the morning by Senator Stewart and others and told that he was President of the United States.

With the completion of the taking of the testimony I at once began to transcribe my shorthand notes into longhand. Twice while so engaged, Miss Harris supported Mrs. Lincoln down the hallway to her husband's bedside. The door leading into the hallway from the room wherein I sat was open and I had a plain view of them as they slowly passed. Mrs. Lincoln was not at the bedside when her husband breathed his last. Indeed, I think it was nearly, if not quite, two hours before the end, when she paid her last visit to the death chamber and when she passed our door on her return, she cried out, "Oh! my God, and have I given my husband to die!"

I have witnessed and experienced much physical agony on

battle-field and in hospital but of it all, nothing sunk deeper in my memory than that moan of a breaking heart.

I finished transcribing my notes at six forty-five in the morning and passed back into the room where the president lay. There were gathered all those whose names I have mentioned and many others—about twenty or twenty-five in all, I should judge. The bed had been pulled out from the corner and owing to the stature of Mr. Lincoln, he lay diagonally on his back. He had been utterly unconscious from the instant the bullet plowed into his brain. His stertorous breathing subsided a couple of minutes after seven o'clock. From then to the end only the gentle rise and fall of his bosom gave indication that life remained.

The surgeon general was near the head of the bed, sometimes sitting on the edge thereof, his finger on the pulse of the dying man. Occasionally he put his ear down to catch the lessening beats of his heart. Mr. Lincoln's pastor, The Reverend Doctor Gurley, stood a little to the left of the bed. Mr. Stanton sat in a chair near the foot on the left, where the pictures place Andrew Johnson. I stood quite near the head of the bed and from that position had full view of Mr. Stanton across the president's body. At my right Robert Lincoln sobbed on the shoulder of Charles Sumner.

Stanton's gaze was fixed intently on the countenance of his dying chief. He had, as I said, been a man of steel throughout the night but as I looked at his face across the corner of the bed and saw the twitching of the muscles I knew that it was only by a powerful effort that he restrained himself.

The first indication that the dreaded end had come was at twenty-two minutes past seven when the surgeon general gently crossed the pulseless hands of Lincoln across the motionless breast and rose to his feet.

Reverend Doctor Gurley stepped forward and lifting his hands began, "Our Father and our God"—I snatched pencil and note-book from my pocket but my haste defeated my purpose. My pencil point (I had but one) caught in my coat and broke, and the world lost the prayer—a prayer which was only interrupted by the sobs of Stanton as he buried his face in the bedclothes. As "Thy will be done, Amen," in subdued and tremulous tones floated through that little chamber, Mr. Stanton raised his head, the tears streaming down his cheeks. A more agonized expression I never saw on a human countenance as he sobbed out the words, "He belongs to the ages now."

Mr. Stanton directed Major Thomas M. Vincent of the staff to take charge of the body, called a meeting of the Cabinet in the room where we had passed most of the night and the assemblage dispersed.

Going to my apartment, I sat down at once to make a second longhand copy for Mr. Stanton of the testimony I had taken, it occurring to me that I wished to retain the one I had written out that night. I had been thus engaged but a brief time when hearing some commotion on the street, I stepped to the window and saw a coffin containing the body of the dead president being placed in a hearse which passed up Tenth Street to F and thus to the White House, escorted by a lieutenant and ten privates. As they passed with measured tread and arms reversed, my hand involuntarily went to my head in salute as they started on their long, long journey back to the prairies and the hearts he knew and loved so well, the mortal remains of the greatest American of all time, bar none.

(Signed)   James Tanner.

III.   THE DIARY OF JOHN WILKES BOOTH

Interest in matters relating to John Wilkes Booth has been increased in recent years by a book written by Finis L. Bates, of Memphis, entitled *The Escape and Suicide of John Wilkes Booth.* Mr. Bates knew, in 1872, a man who called himself John St. Helen, then living at Granberry, Texas. This man he firmly believed to have been Booth. On January 13, 1903, a man committed suicide at Enid, Oklahoma, whose name as known in that locality was David E. George. This man, by a chain of evidence which need not here be repeated, was believed by some to have been Booth. Mr. Bates went to Enid and became convinced that George was the man he had known in 1872 as St. Helen, and he secured additional evidence which caused him to believe that this was Booth. Reverend Clarence True Wilson has delivered a lecture setting forth this claim, and it has been accepted by the Oklahoma State Historical Society. Ray Stannard Baker, in *McClure's* for May, 1897, gives in detail the story of the death and burial of Booth. William G. Shepherd in *Harper's Magazine* for November, 1924, investigates and denies the Bates claim. There can be no doubt of Mr. Bates' good faith, and his evidence was worked up with real ability. He died on Thanksgiving Day, 1923.

The Library of Harvard College has the record book of the Baltimore cemetery in which the stubs show a receipt for the body of Booth. This shows unquestionably what Booth's relatives believed, or at the very least what they wished the public to think they believed. Mr. H. H. Kohlsatt recently published in the *Saturday Evening Post* the letters of the Booth family to Andrew Johnson and President Grant asking for the body, which eventually they obtained and buried in Baltimore.

The War Department has, and keeps with great care, the *Diary* of John Wilkes Booth, recovered from his body as he was shot in the Garrett corn-crib. It is a small volume, bound in red leather, lined with silk. I have copied its story of the assassination and of the events that followed. In one or two places I am unable to decipher the words. It is apparent that Booth expected to be hailed as a hero and was horrified that he was regarded as a common criminal.

It was written at two different times. The entry dated April fourteenth may be presumed to have been penned in the house of Doctor Mudd, where Booth rested for a few hours while his leg was set, and the other, dated April twenty-first, four days before his discovery.

April 14. Friday the Ides. Until to-day nothing was ever thought of sacrificing to our country's wrongs. For six months we had worked to capture. But, our cause being almost lost, something decisive and great must be done. But its failure was owing to others who did not strike for their country with a heart. I struck boldly, and not as the papers say. I walked with a firm step through a thousand of his friends, was stopped, but pushed on. A Colonel was at his side. I shouted *sic semper* before I fired. In jumping, broke my leg. I passed all his pickets, rode sixty miles that night with the bone of my leg tearing the flesh at every jump. I can never repent it. Though we hated to our country owed all her troubles to him, and God simply made me the instrument of his punishment. The country is not what I have loved. I care not what becomes of me. I have no desire to outlive my country. This night before the deed I wrote a long article and left it for the *National Intelligencer* in which I fully set forth our reasons for our proceedings. We of the south.

Friday 21. After being hunted like a dog through swamps, woods, and last night being chased by gunboats till I was forced to return, wet, cold and starving, with every man's hand against me, I am here in despair, and why?

For doing what Brutus was honored for—who made Tell a Hero. And yet I have stricken down a greater tyrant than they ever knew. I am looked upon as a common cut-throat. My action was purer than either of theirs. One hoped to be great himself, the other had not only his country's but his own wrongs to avenge. I hoped for no gain. I knew no private wrongs. I struck for my country, and for that alone. A country ground down under this tyranny, and prayed for this . . . . yet now behold the cold hand they . . . . to me. God cannot pardon me if I have done wrong. Yet I cannot see any wrong except in serving a degenerate people.

The little, the very little I left behind to clear my name, the Govmt will not permit to be printed. So ends all. For my country I have given all that makes life sweet and Holy, brought misery upon my family, and am sure there is no pardon in the Heavens for me, since Man condemns me so . . . . of what has been done . . . . I did myself and it fills me with horror.

God! try and forgive me and bless my mother. To-night I will once more try the river with the intention to cross, though I have a greater desire and almost a mind to return to Washington, and in a measure clear my name which I feel I could do. I do not repent the blow I struck. I may before my God, but not to man. I think I have done well, though I am abandoned, with the curse of Cain upon me, when, if the world knew my heart, that one blow would have made me great, though I did not desire greatness.

To-night I try to escape the bloodhounds once more. Who, who can read his fate? God's will be done . . . . too great a soul to die like a criminal.

May He, may He spare me that, and let me die bravely! I bless the entire world. Have never hated or wronged any one. This was not wrong unless God deems it so, and it's with Him to damn or bless me. And . . . . this brave boy Herold with me . . . . often prayes (yes, before and since) with a true and sincere heart. Was it a crime in him?

If so, why can he pray the same? I do not wish to shed a drop of blood, but I must "fight the course." 'Tis all that's left me.

There is little need to comment on these records, or to emphasize the contrast between the frame of mind the writer was in at the time when he made the first of them and that which succeeded in the distressing week that followed.

His attempt to escape did not succeed. The pursuing avengers hemmed him in closer and yet more closely. Late on the afternoon of April twenty-fifth, a cavalry squad located him in a barn in Virginia, and ordered him to surrender. On his refusal, they fired the barn. Booth still refused to come out, but asked that Herold be permitted to surrender, and he was taken prisoner. As the flames lighted up the interior of the building, Booth was seen with a carbine, and was shot, against orders, by a half-insane soldier, Boston Corbett. The bullet lodged in the base of Booth's brain, and he was paralyzed below that point, but fully conscious until his death. The wound he received was similar to that he inflicted upon the president, with this difference, that Lincoln knew no moment of suffering, and Booth must have suffered exquisite pain from the moment he was wounded until his death on the following morning.

IV. HOW EDWIN BOOTH SAVED ROBERT LINCOLN'S LIFE

Edwin Booth was playing in Boston when his brother murdered President Lincoln. He did not complete his engagement, and the theater was closed for an indefinite period. Some newspapers made a commendable effort to dissociate his name from that of his brother by affirming that he had always been a friend of the Union. The *New York Times,* on Sunday, April 16, 1865, the day following the death of Lincoln, in an editorial on the murder, related the following incident, which proves, on investigation, to have been substantially correct. It is certainly a coincidence worth recording that only a few weeks before the assassination, the brother of Lincoln's murderer saved the life of Lincoln's son:

Quite recently his brother Edwin ejected him (John Wilkes Booth) from his house in New York, simply because his expressions were unbearable to a man of loyalty and intelligence. And here it is only thoughtful and just to say that the Union cause has no stronger or more generous supporter than Mr. Edwin Booth. From the commencement he has been earnestly and actively solicitous for the triumph of our arms and the welfare of our soldiers. An incident—a trifle in itself—may be recalled at this moment when the profound monotony of grief overwhelms us. Not a month since, Mr. Edwin Booth was proceeding to Washington. At Trenton there was a general scramble to reach the cars, which had started, leaving many behind in the refreshment saloons. Mr. Edwin Booth was preceded by a gentleman whose foot slipped as he was stepping on the platform, and who would have fallen at once beneath the wheels had not Mr. Edwin Booth's arm sustained him. The gentleman remarked that he had had a narrow escape of his life and was thankful to his preserver. It was Robert Lincoln, the son of the great, good man who now lies dead before our blistered eyes, and whose name we cannot mention without choking.

In some way this incident came to the knowledge of Lieut-General Grant, who at once wrote a civil letter to Mr. Edwin Booth and said that if he could serve him at any time he would be glad to do so. Mr. Booth replied, playfully, that when he

(Grant) was in Richmond, he (Booth) would like to play for him there. It was a trifle, but it is well to remember trifles when a man so stricken and overwhelmed as is Mr. Edwin Booth is spoken of.

V.   THE GETTYSBURG ADDRESS

It is surprising that so short an address should exist in so many varying yet apparently authoritative forms. It will be found of value to have for comparison the most interesting and significant of the drafts and press reports.   Doctor Charles Moore, head of the Manuscripts Division of the Library of Congress, has compiled a typewritten text of seven different versions from original documents.   These have been collated with meticulous care.   I am using these by his courtesy and am adding certain others which for particular reasons are of special value in this work.

As here arranged, Numbers One and Two, which are known as the First and Second Library of Congress drafts, are bound in a single cover.   The first is a rough and the second a fair copy of the same version of the address.   These manuscripts were given to the Library of Congress by the children of John Hay. Apparently both were written before the address was delivered. The first page of Number One is written on a sheet of Executive Mansion paper, in ink.   The second page is written in pencil on a sheet of foolscap, and a few words at the bottom of the first page are changed in pencil.   According to Nicolay's account *(Century Magazine,* February, 1894,) these changes were made by Lincoln after he arrived in Gettysburg.   If so, the second Library of Congress draft must also have been written in Gettysburg, after the first draft was corrected and before delivery.   It contains certain phrases that are not in the first draft, but *are* in the reports of the address as delivered and in subsequent copies made by Lincoln. It seems probable that this second Library of Congress draft was the final revision before delivering the address, and was the copy that Lincoln held in his hand while speaking, although he apparently referred to it so little that some of those present thought he

35

spoke extemporaneously. The words "under God," in the last sentence of the address as reported, and in all subsequent copies made by Lincoln, are not in either of the Library of Congress drafts.

Number One

First Library of Congress draft

Four score and seven years ago our fathers brought forth, upon this continent, a new nation, conceived in liberty, and dedicated to the proposition that "all men are created equal."

Now we are engaged in a great civil war, testing whether that nation, or any nation so conceived, and so dedicated, can long endure. We are met on a great battle-field of that war. We have come to dedicate a portion of it, as a final resting place for those who died here, that the nation might live. This we may, in all propriety do.

But, in a larger sense, we can not dedicate—we can not consecrate—we can not hallow, this ground. The brave men, living and dead, who struggled here, have hallowed it, far above our poor power to add or detract. The world will little note, nor long remember what we say here; while it can never forget what they did here. It is rather for us, the living, we here be dedicated to the great task remaining before us—that, from these honored dead we take increased devotion to that cause for which they here gave the last full measure of devotion—that we here highly resolve these dead shall not have died in vain; that the nation, shall have a new birth of freedom, and that government of the people by the people for the people, shall not perish from the earth.

Number Two

Second Library of Congress draft

Four score and seven years ago our fathers brought forth, upon this continent, a new nation, conceived in Liberty, and dedicated to the proposition that all men are created equal.

Now we are engaged in a great civil war, testing whether that nation, or any nation, so conceived, and so dedicated, can long endure. We are met here on a great battle-field of that war. We have come to dedicate a portion of it as a final resting place for those who here gave their lives that that nation might live. It is altogether fitting and proper that we should do this.

But in a larger sense we can not dedicate—we can not consecrate—we can not hallow this ground. The brave men, living and dead, who struggled here, have consecrated it far above our poor power to add or detract. The world will little note, nor long remember, what we say here, but can never forget what they did here. It is for us, the living, rather to be dedicated here to the unfinished work which they have, thus far, so nobly carried on. It is rather for us to be here dedicated to the great task remaining before us—that from these honored dead we take increased devotion to that cause for which they here gave the last full measure of devotion—that we here highly resolve that these dead shall not have died in vain; that this nation shall have a new birth of freedom; and that this government of the people, by the people, for the people, shall not perish from the earth.

Number Three

The Associated Press Report

Different newspapers using the Associated Press report made mistakes in transcription. That report is given in the text, and is the basis of all reports that showed "Applause." The *New York Tribune* was one of several papers having special correspondents present, and used the Associated Press report, probably in a special dispatch from Gettysburg. It is one of the most careful of the special reports.

(Special Correspondence New York Tribune, November 21, 1863.)

Four score and seven years ago our fathers brought forth upon this continent a new Nation, conceived in Liberty, and dedicated to the proposition that all men are created equal. [Applause].

Now we are engaged in a great civil war, testing whether that Nation or any Nation so conceived and so dedicated can long endure. We are met on a great battle-field of that war. We are met to dedicate a portion of it as the final resting-place of those who here gave their lives that that nation might live. It is altogether fitting and proper that we should do this.

But in a larger sense we can not dedicate, we cannot consecrate, we cannot hallow this ground.   The brave men living and
dead who struggled here have consecrated it far above our power
to add or detract.   [Applause].   The world will little note nor
long remember what we say here, but it can never forget what
they did here.   [Applause].   It is for us, the living, rather to be
dedicated here to the unfinished work that they have thus far so
nobly carried on.   [Applause].   It is rather for us to be here dedicated to the great task remaining before us, that from these honored dead we take increased devotion to that cause for which
they here gave the last full measure of devotion; that we here
highly resolve that the dead shall not have died in vain [Ap-
plause] ; that the nation shall, under God, have a new birth of
freedom; and that governments of the people, by the people and
for the people, shall not perish from the earth.   [Long-continued
applause.]

Number Four—Charles Hale's Report

The Fourth is the report taken down by Charles Hale, and
incorporated in the Report of the Massachusetts Commissioners
to Governor John A. Andrew, and by him included in Massachusetts Legislative Documents (Senate, 1864, No. 1, p. lxii) presented to the Legislature.   Mr. Hale affirmed that Lincoln spoke
very deliberately and that Hale took down every word precisely
as Lincoln uttered it.   This, presumably, gives us precisely the
words which President Lincoln actually spoke at Gettysburg:

As reported by the Massachusetts Commissioners.   [In Massachusetts Legislative Docs. Senate. 1864].

Four score and seven years ago, our fathers brought forth
upon this continent a new nation, conceived in liberty and dedicated to the proposition that all men are created equal.

Now we are engaged in a great civil war, testing whether
that nation—or any nation, so conceived and so dedicated—can
long endure.   We are met on a great battle-field of that war.   We
are met to dedicate a portion of it as the final resting-place of
those who have given their lives that that nation might live.   It
is altogether fitting and proper that we should do this.

But, in a larger sense, we can not dedicate, we can not consecrate, we can not hallow, this ground.   The brave men, living

and dead, who struggled here, have consecrated it, far above our power to add or to detract. The world will very little note nor long remember what we say here; but it can never forget what they did here. It is for us, the living, rather, *to be dedicated,* here, to the unfinished work that they have thus far so nobly carried on. It is rather for us to be here dedicated to the great task remaining before us; that from these honored dead we take increased devotion to that cause for which they here gave the' last full measure of devotion; that we here highly resolve that these dead shall not have died in vain; that the nation shall, under God, have a new birth of freedom, and that government of the people, by the people, for the people, shall not perish from the earth.

Number Five

The Philadelphia Inquirer's Report

Of the reports that attempted some degree of independence of the manuscript of the reporter for the Associated Press, some are of considerable interest, two of them markedly so. The first of these is the report that appeared in the *Philadelphia Inquirer* of November 20, 1863. The Philadelphia papers appear to have been the only ones that reported Lincoln as speaking of "our *poor* power." Neither the Massachusetts nor the Associated Press report contains the adjective. It was in the manuscript which Lincoln held and in his later revisions, but he appears inadvertently to have omitted the word. The *Gettysburg Compiler* used this report in its account of the ceremonies, November twenty-third; so this is the version which the Gettysburg people had before them as that which they had heard from the lips of Lincoln.

Four score and seven years ago our fathers brought forth upon this continent a new nation, conceived in liberty and dedicated to the proposition that all men are created equal. Now we are engaged in a great civil war, testing the question whether this nation or any nation so conceived, so dedicated, can long endure. We are met on the great battle-field of that war. We are met to dedicate it, on a portion of the field set apart as the final resting place of those who gave their lives for the nation's life, but the nation must live, and it is altogether fitting and proper that we should do this.

In a larger sense we cannot dedicate, we cannot consecrate, we cannot hallow this ground in reality. The number of men, living and dead, who struggled here have consecrated it far above our poor attempts to add to its consecration. The world will little know and nothing remember of what we see here, but we cannot forget what these brave men did here.

We owe this offering to our dead. We imbibe increased devotion to that cause for which they here gave the last full measure of devotion; we here might resolve that they shall not have died in vain; that the nation shall, under God, have a new birth of freedom, and that the Government of the people, for the people, and for all people, shall not perish from earth.

Number Six

The Cincinnati Gazette's Report

A number of papers, among them the *Cincinnati Daily Gazette* for November twenty-first, gave to their readers this very faulty version of the Gettysburg Address:

Four score and seven years ago our fathers established upon this Continent a Government subscribed in liberty and dedicated to the fundamental principle that all mankind are created free and equal by a good God. And now we are engaged in a great contest deciding the question whether this nation or any nation so conserved, so dedicated, can long remain. We are met on a great battle-field of the war. We are met here to dedicate a portion of that field as the final resting place of those who have given their lives that it might live. It is altogether fitting and proper that we should do this.

But in a large sense we cannot dedicate, we cannot consecrate we cannot hallow this ground. The brave men, the living and the dead, who struggled here, have consecrated it far above our power to add to or detract from the work. Let us long remember what we say here, but not forget what they did here.

It is for us, the living, to be dedicated here to the unfinished work that they have thus far so nobly carried forward. It is for us here to be dedicated to the great task remaining before us, for us to renew our devotion to that cause for which they gave the full measure of their devotion. Here let us resolve that what they have done shall not have been done in vain; that the nation shall, under God, have a new birth offered; that the Government of the people, founded by the people, shall not perish.

Number Seven

The Baltimore Copy

The first two versions here given, and the three that are to follow, are all in existence, and in Lincoln's handwriting. Any one of them may be considered correct. The last three represent not only the careful preparation before the delivery of the address, but the thoughtful revision which Lincoln gave to it afterward in the light of his comparison of his manuscript with the press reports. These three copies vary in very small and immaterial details, but they illustrate the evolution of Lincoln's final text. The copy which we number seven was made by Lincoln for the Sanitary Commission Fair in New York in 1864, and is now (1925) owned by Senator Henry W. Keyes, of New Hampshire.

Four score and seven years ago our fathers brought forth upon this continent, a new nation, conceived in Liberty, and dedicated to the proposition that all men are created equal.

Now we are engaged in a great civil war testing whether that nation, or any nation so conceived and so dedicated, can long endure. We are met on a great battle-field of that war. We have come to dedicate a portion of that field, as a final resting place for those who here gave their lives, that that nation might live. It is altogether fitting and proper that we should do this.

But, in a larger sense, we can not dedicate—we can not consecrate—we can not hallow—this ground. The brave men, living and dead, who struggled here, have consecrated it, far above our poor power to add or detract. The world will little note, nor long remember, what we say here, but it can never forget what they did here. It is for us, the living, rather, to be dedicated here to the unfinished work which they who fought here, have, thus far, so nobly advanced. It is rather for us to be here dedicated to the great task remaining before us—that from these honored dead we take increased devotion to that cause for which they here gave the last full measure of devotion—that we here highly resolve that these dead shall not have died in vain—that this nation, under God, shall have a new birth of freedom—and that, government of the people, by the people, for the people, shall not perish from the earth.

Number Eight

The Bancroft Copy

Lincoln, having made a copy to accompany the Everett oration and to be used at the Sanitary Fair in New York, was invited to write another copy to be used with facsimiles of the writings of many authors in a volume to be sold at the Soldiers' and Sailors' Fair in Baltimore. His first copy made for this purpose was not available because it was written on both sides of the sheet. He therefore wrote another and a final copy, permitting this one to be retained by Honorable George Bancroft, in whose family it now (1925) remains.

Four score and seven years ago our fathers brought forth, on this continent, a new nation, conceived in Liberty, and dedicated to the proposition that all men are created equal.

Now we are engaged in a great civil war, testing whether that nation, or any nation so conceived, and so dedicated, can long endure. We are met on a great battle-field of that war. We have come to dedicate a portion of that field, as a final resting-place for those who here gave their lives, that that nation might live. It is altogether fitting and proper that we should do this.

But, in a larger sense, we can not dedicate—we can not consecrate—we can not hallow—this ground. The brave men, living and dead, who struggled here, have consecrated it far above our poor power to add or detract. The world will little note, nor long remember what we say here, but it can never forget what they did here. It is for us the living, rather, to be dedicated here to the unfinished work which they who fought here have thus far so nobly advanced. It is rather for us to be here dedicated to the great task remaining before us—that from these honored dead we take increased devotion to that cause for which they here gave the last full measure of devotion—that we here highly resolve that these dead shall not have died in vain—that this nation, under God, shall have a new birth of freedom—and that government of the people, by the people, for the people, shall not perish from the earth.

Number Nine

The Standard Version

The final copy made for the Baltimore Fair is known as the Standard Version, and is that found in facsimile in the volume *Autograph Leaves of our Country's Authors*. The original is owned (1925) by Professor William J. A. Bliss, Baltimore.

Four score and seven years ago our fathers brought forth on this continent, a new nation, conceived in Liberty, and dedicated to the proposition that all men are created equal.

Now we are engaged in a great civil war, testing whether that nation, or any nation so conceived and so dedicated, can long endure. We are met on a great battle-field of that war. We have come to dedicate a portion of that field, as a final resting place for those who here gave their lives that that nation might live. It is altogether fitting and proper that we should do this.

But, in a larger sense, we can not dedicate—we can not consecrate—we can not hallow—this ground. The brave men, living and dead, who struggled here, have consecrated it, far above our poor power to add or detract. The world will little note, nor long remember what we say here, but it can never forget what they did here. It is for us the living, rather, to be dedicated here to the unfinished work which they who fought here have thus far so nobly advanced. It is rather for us to be here dedicated to the great task remaining before us—that from these honored dead we take increased devotion to that cause for which they gave the last full measure of devotion—that we here highly resolve that these dead shall not have died in vain—that this nation, under God, shall have a new birth of freedom—and that government of the people, by the people, for the people, shall not perish from the earth.

INDEX